THE PAPERS OF

Andrew Jackson

•

HAROLD D. MOSER,
EDITOR-IN-CHIEF

THE PAPERS OF

VOLUME VI, 1825–1828

HAROLD D. MOSER

J. CLINT CLIFFT

EDITORS

WYATT C. WELLS, ASSISTANT EDITOR

•

THE UNIVERSITY OF TENNESSEE PRESS
KNOXVILLE

Library of Congress Cataloging in Publication Data
(Revised for vol. 6)

Jackson, Andrew, 1767–1845.
The papers of Andrew Jackson.
Vol. 2 edited by Harold D. Moser and Sharon Macpherson.
Vol. 6 edited by Harold D. Moser and J. Clint Clifft.
Includes bibliographical references and indexes.
Contents: v.1. 1770–1803. —v. 2. 1804–1813—[etc.]
—v. 6. 1825–1828.
1. Jackson, Andrew, 1767–1845.
2. United States—Politics and government—1829-1837—Sources.
3. Presidents—United States—Correspondence.
I. Smith, Sam B., 1929–   .
II. Owsley, Harriet Fason Chappell.
III. Moser, Harold D.
IV. Title.
E302J35   973.5'6'092   79-15078
ISBN 0-87049-219-5 (v. 1: cl.: alk. paper)
ISBN 0-87049-441-4 (v. 2: cl.: alk. paper)
ISBN 0-87049-650-6 (v. 3: cl.: alk. paper)
ISBN 0-87049-778-2 (v. 4: cl.: alk. paper)
ISBN 0-87049-897-5 (v. 5: cl.: alk. paper)
ISBN 1-57233-174-7 (v. 6: cl.: alk. paper)

Advisory Board

Publication of
The Papers of Andrew Jackson
was assisted by grants from
THE LADIES' HERMITAGE ASSOCIATION
THE UNIVERSITY OF TENNESSEE
THE NATIONAL HISTORICAL PUBLICATIONS
AND RECORDS COMMISSION
THE TENNESSEE HISTORICAL COMMISSION
and
THE PROGRAM FOR EDITIONS OF THE
NATIONAL ENDOWMENT FOR THE HUMANITIES,
AN INDEPENDENT FEDERAL AGENCY

For Carolyn Irene,
Andrew Paul, Anna Elizabeth,
my Beth, and Keri Lynn

Contents

For the page number on which each document of The Papers begins,
see the Calendar.

Illustrations

Frontispiece: *Andrew Jackson,* oil on canvas by Aaron H. Corwine, 1825. Courtesy of Sam and Robbie Vickers Florida Collection, Jacksonville.

Following page 336.

Andrew Jackson, stipple engraving by James Barton Longacre, after Ralph E. W. Earl, 1828. Courtesy of the Print Collection, Miriam and Ira D. Wallach Division of Arts, Prints and Photographs. The New York Public Library: Astor, Lenox and Tilden Foundation, New York.

The Old House of Representatives, 1822, oil on canvas by Samuel F.B. Morse. Courtesy of the Collection of the Corcoran Gallery of Art, Washington, D.C., Purchase, Gallery Fund, 11.14.

John Quincy Adams, oil on canvas by Chester Harding, 1827–28. Courtesy of the Redwood Library and Athenæum, Newport, Rhode Island.

John Caldwell Calhoun, oil on wood by John Trumbull, 1827. Courtesy of the Yale University Art Gallery, Trumbull Collection.

Andrew Jackson, silhouette on paper by William James Hubard, 1828. Courtesy of the Tennessee State Museum Collection, Nashville.

Rachel Jackson, silhouette on paper by William James Hubard, 1828. Courtesy of the Tennessee State Museum Collection, Nashville.

Shadrach Penn, stipple engraving. Courtesy of The Filson Club Historical Society, Louisville, Kentucky.

Duff Green, marble bust by Hiram Powers. Courtesy of the Ackland Art Museum, The University of North Carolina at Chapel Hill.

Joseph Gales, oil on canvas by Charles Bird King. Courtesy of the Redwood Library and Athenæum, Newport, Rhode Island.

Charles Hammond, engraving by E. D. Marchant. Courtesy of the Cincinnati Historical Society, Cincinnati, Ohio.

Henry Clay, oil on canvas by Matthew Harris Jouett, c1826. Courtesy of Transylvania University Library, Lexington, Kentucky.

John McLean, oil on canvas by Thomas Sully, 1831. Courtesy of The Pennsylvania Academy of the Fine Arts, Philadelphia.

Samuel Lewis Southard, oil on canvas by Charles Bird King, 1828. Courtesy of the Redwood Library and Athenæum, Newport, Rhode Island.

James Barbour, oil on canvas by Chester Harding. Courtesy of The Virginia Historical Society, Richmond.

James Buchanan, engraving by John Sartain. Frontispiece from George Ticknor Curtis, *Life of James Buchanan* (New York, 1883), Volume 1.

Joseph Desha, oil on canvas by unknown artist. Courtesy of the Kentucky Historical Society, Frankfort.

DeWitt Clinton, oil on canvas by Samuel F. B. Morse. Courtesy of The Metropolitan Museum of Art, Rogers Fund, 1909 (09.18), New York.

George McDuffie, oil on canvas by Charles Bird King, c1828. Courtesy of the Redwood Library and Athenæum, Newport, Rhode Island.

Symptoms of a Locked Jaw, engraving by David Claypoole Johnston, August 1827. Courtesy of the Tennessee State Library and Archives, Nashville.

Richard III, engraving by David Claypoole Johnston, 1828. Courtesy of the Tennessee State Library and Archives, Nashville.

Andrew Jackson, stipple engraving by Orramel H. Throop, 1828. Courtesy of The Baltimore Museum of Art: Gift of Aaron Strauss and Lilly Strauss Foundation, Inc., BMA 1958.1284.5, Baltimore, Maryland.

Rachel Jackson, engraving by Joseph How. Courtesy of The Hermitage, Home of Andrew Jackson, Hermitage, Tennessee.

John Patton Erwin, engraving from Ira P. Jones, *The City of Nashville, Illustrated* (Nashville?, 1890).

James Shelby, oil on canvas by unknown artist. Courtesy of The Filson Club Historical Society, Louisville, Kentucky.

Leslie Combs, stipple engraving by J. Ourdan, frontispiece in *Narrative of the Life of General Leslie Combs* (New York, 1852). Courtesy of the Margaret I. King Library, University of Kentucky, Lexington, Kentucky.

Truth's Advocate and Monthly Anti-Jackson Expositor (Cincinnati, March 1828), title page. Courtesy of Special Collections, Hodges Library, The University of Tennessee, Knoxville.

Andrew Jackson, detail of sulphide portrait in base of tumbler made by Bakewell, Page & Bakewell, 1825, Pittsburgh, Pennsylvania. Courtesy of The Corning Museum of Glass, Corning, New York.

Andrew Jackson, oil on canvas by Ralph E. W. Earl, c.1826. Courtesy of The Hermitage, Home of Andrew Jackson, Hermitage, Tennessee.

Introduction

ANDREW JACKSON, 1825–1828

"[If] I knew nothing about myself, but what I see in [the] administration papers, I would conclude I w*[as a]* mere devil incarnate." Andrew Jackson's assessment, made in May 1828, accurately summed up how John Quincy Adams's supporters had portrayed him. His comment embodied an element of humor, but behind it lay anger and frustration. Jackson was exasperated that his opponents had explored almost every aspect of his public and personal life and had resorted to innuendo, hyperbole, misstatements, and even outright lies to characterize him as unfit for the presidency, and yet he had to restrain his natural instinct to defend his honor through the accepted methods of the day.

By May 1828, Jackson was livid and anxious to assail his antagonists, to set straight the record of his public service, to clear the aspersions on his character, and to protect his hard-earned honor. But rather than succumb to the taunts of his opponents, a ploy intended to goad him into a reckless response, Jackson heeded the advice of his friends and, at least publically, maintained a stoic silence. "My philosophy is almost worn out," Jackson declared in August, "but all my enemies expect is, to urge me to some rash action, this the cannot do until the election is over, if my hands are not tied by the event, there will be a final settlement."

The presidential campaign of 1828 was a long and hard contest, and it is the main focus of this sixth of sixteen proposed volumes of the papers of the man who became the seventh president of the United States and a symbol of an era. The election of John Quincy Adams in 1825 through an alleged "corrupt bargain" between Adams and Henry Clay had defied the will of the people, who had given the popular vote to Jackson. In light of the precedent of the succession of secretaries of state to the presidency, many contemporary observers contended that this arrangement endangered the republic and threatened to establish a corrupt dynasty, an aristocracy of power built upon bargains and dubious political alliances dedicated to its perpetuation in office. Simply put, Adams and Clay had betrayed the will of the people for office and power and would engage in the lowest sort of electioneering to keep it.

Thus, Jackson's cause and the defense of his honor had become intertwined with the cause of the people and the cause of democracy. For Jackson, and for many of his supporters, the campaign had become a crusade. "Truth is mighty & will prevail" was Jackson's constant refrain during the years 1825–1828. His supporters echoed this battle cry as they fought to insure his victory in 1828. To them, the moral fabric of the republic was threadbare, and the existence of the democracy endangered. The federal government at Washington seemed to have lost sight of the nation's principles and heritage and had, according to the Jacksonians, become a government of officeholders for officeholders.

As the documents in this volume show, the Jacksonians claimed to wear the mantle of democracy and sought to represent the people and to portray their opponents as corrupt, self-seeking politicians. To sustain their view, the Jacksonians had ample evidence, which they effectively used in the campaign: the "corrupt bargain" stood out first and foremost, but there was also the use of patronage, at times in defiance of the will of the people as in the case of the appointment of the Nashville postmaster in 1826, the franking and forging of documents, the use of newspapers such as the *Cincinnati Gazette* and the Washington *National Journal* to slander Jackson, and the circuit-riding campaign tactics of Adams's cabinet. Cabinet officers such as Secretary of State Clay, Secretary of the Navy Samuel L. Southard, and Secretary of War James Barbour had in one way or another questioned Jackson's reputation and character in public forums. Indeed, the cabinet, led by Clay, not Adams, seemed to be Jackson's opponent in the campaign.

Neither Adams nor his cabinet had any doubts about who their opponent was—it was Andrew Jackson. In early 1825, Clay had labeled Jackson, the "people's choice" in the 1824 election, a mere "military chieftain" in the first of many attacks on the westerner from Tennessee. In the campaign, the Adams-Clay Republicans had a heyday exploring Jackson's qualifications for the highest office in the country. They subjected his public and private life to the closest scrutiny. They attributed comments to Jackson that he flatly denied, as in the case of "Mr. H." They manipulated public documents to portray him in an unfavorable light, as in the case of Secretary of War Barbour's release of war department documents. They examined his past political career and charged that he lacked the dedication and temperament to remain in any public office for a full term.

Adams supporters even questioned Jackson's military ability, focusing particularly on his policies and actions in the War of 1812, on his 1818 invasion of Florida, and on his tenure as governor of the territory. Secretary of the Navy Southard even dared to suggest that then Secretary of War James Monroe was actually responsible for the 1815 victory at New Orleans, the cornerstone of Jackson's fame.

It was, however, the examination and discussion of Jackson's personal life that most galled Jackson and his friends and political supporters. The allegations of his collusion in the schemes of Aaron Burr, his quarrels with

John Sevier and others, his killing of Charles Dickinson in a duel, and charges of slave trading, all paled in comparison to the discussion of the Jacksons' marriage and of his parentage.

No aspect of the campaign so hurt and angered Jackson as the aspersions upon Rachel Jackson, his wife of almost forty years. Pro-Adams newspapers compared her to "a dirty black wench" and had called his mother a prostitute. Under these assaults, Jackson anticipated that truth would prevail and expressed the hope in early 1828 that "providence . . . will prolong my days, untill I can both speak and act, when an awful retribution upon the heads of the leaders, & exciters, will come." All of these charges and the efforts of Jackson and his supporters to counter them are covered in considerable detail in this volume.

The barrage of charges, accusations, and innuendo was so great that Jackson's advisors felt forced to set up committees to deal with the relentless attack before Jackson did. In Nashville, Washington, D.C., Philadelphia, Cincinnati, and other important cities throughout the nation, political leaders and ordinary citizens, motivated by the intensity of the campaign, organized corresponding committees, bought and published newspapers, and wrote and distributed pamphlets to defend Jackson and attack the administration. Jackson maintained the public stance that he did not seek and would not campaign for office, but would serve the republic if called upon by the voice of the people. With few exceptions, such as his clash with Southard and his skirmishes with Clay, Jackson followed the recommendations of his advisers and did not write for public consumption.

But as this volume illustrates, Jackson was much more deeply involved with the work of the various committees, and particularly with the Nashville "character-cleaning up board," as his opponents called it, than has previously been thought. In many instances, he took the lead in the collecting, assembling, and distributing of information for the numerous committees. The committees answered the specific charges against Jackson and relied on him, in most instances, for advice, information, and documentation to rebut the accusations. Frequently, he became irritated that they responded too slowly and Jackson prodded them to action by threatening to publish items himself, and on a few occasions he did just that.

Electioneering for the presidency in 1828 involved much more than committees, pamphlets, and newspaper skirmishes. In many states, elections for state legislatures and congressional seats turned on the presidential question. This volume offers considerable insight into those contests in the states, particularly in Tennessee and Kentucky. The documents also shed light on the efforts in many state legislatures, and in Congress, to promote electoral reform. The time span covered in this volume encompasses the drama of the presidential contest in Congress as committee after committee rummaged through the archives of the executive departments to illuminate the past for partisan purposes. The Jacksonians in Congress denounced the supposed abuses of the Adams administration; Adams-Clay supporters focused on the alleged military blunders and other transgressions of Jackson.

The volume, however, is not all political, all campaigning. The letters and documents presented reveal much about Jackson, the man and his personal life, and about the social mores and cultural life of the times. His immediate family, Rachel, Andrew Jackson, Jr., and his ward Andrew Jackson Hutchings; his extended family of the Donelsons and the Coffees; and his friends, the Calls, and Duvals, all figure prominently in the daily life of the Hermitage and in the documents of this volume. The Hermitage witnessed a procession of visitors in this period, some friendly, like the Marquis de Lafayette; some of questionable motives, such as Carter Beverley; and some enemies, like Leslie Combs. Friends and strangers alike were welcomed.

Jackson was also a farmer: cotton was his money crop and slaves were his labor force. The documents selected offer extensive insight into the management of his plantation, his use and treatment of slaves, his dealings with overseers and cotton factors, and his efforts to make a living and keep his expenses in check. Of particular importance in illuminating the harshness of slavery are those documents dealing with the 1827 killing of Gilbert, a slave at the Hermitage, which opened Jackson up to charges of abuse and neglect by his opponents.

The four years covered in this volume were some of the most trying in Jackson's life. It was, however, the death of his wife Rachel, his lifelong love, in December 1828, that hurt Jackson most. In his mind, the incessant slanders of the campaign had contributed to Rachel's death and, in his personal correspondence, he swore vengeance upon those he held responsible—there would be an "awful retribution." The loss was indeed great for him personally, but Jackson found solace and vindication in his victory. The cause of truth had indeed prevailed; the voice of the people had been heard and it had registered against the corrupt would-be dynasty of officeholders. Liberty, not power, had triumphed. Much of the philosophy and future policies that were to characterize the Jackson administration were forged from 1825 to 1828 and are covered in the documents of this volume. Reform was at hand, and retribution would surely follow.

ACKNOWLEDGMENTS

This volume of The Papers of Andrew Jackson, like the five preceeding, is the product of a major collaborative effort involving thousands of institutions and individuals. The list is too long to mention each separately, but to all of those who responded to our requests for documents, we are grateful, and especially to those furnishing manuscript copies for this volume.

Several institutions deserve special mention, mainly for the magnitude of their contributions. Chief among these are the Library of Congress, the

National Archives, the Tennessee State Library and Archives, the John C. Hodges Library, University of Tennessee, and the Alabama Department of Archives and History. At the Library of Congress, John McDonough, Manuscript Historian, assisted the project at every turn: he has made the Library's Jackson collection readily available, he has answered innumerable research questions, and he continues to share with us his extensive knowledge. At the National Archives, the research staff of the National Historical Publications and Records Commission, and particularly Timothy Connelly, Michael Meier, and Dane Hartgrove have been indefatigable in unearthing documents and answering difficult questions. Our demands at Hodges Library, University of Tennessee, have been incessant, but Bill Eigelsbach, Nick Wyman, and Aaron Purcell in Special Collections have always gone out of their way to service our requests and to make their collections available. The staff of the Tennessee State Library and Archives—and especially Marylin Bell-Hughes and Fran Schell—has been equally cooperative and helpful. At the Alabama Department of Archives and History, Rickie Louise Brunner, Public Services Division, has helped us above and beyond the call of duty, saving us endless hours and considerable cost in locating materials.

We are also deeply obligated to several individuals who have assisted us far beyond any normal expectations: to Bill Cook in Lebanon, to George E. Webb, Jr., in Rogersville, and to Marsha Mullin, Curator at the Hermitage. Each of them has kept us informed of documents recently appearing on the market and provided us with materials that we otherwise might have missed. To each of them we offer our sincere thanks. Our indebtedness to Sharon Macpherson is great: from retirement she came to the project to assist with illustrations and wound up assisting us with the final revision of the volume. As always, Dorothy Brooks, administrative assistant with the Jackson project, was there when we needed her and able to retrieve materials for us that otherwise might have been irretrievably lost. Until her retirement, she kept the office running while the editors looked at Jackson.

Our sponsors have seen to it that the work continue, and our indebtedness to them is great and our appreciation sincere: to Jim Vaughan, past Executive Director of the Hermitage, and to Patricia Leach, current Director, to the Board and members of the Ladies' Hermitage Association, for their financial and moral support; to the staff of the National Historical Publications and Records Commission and that of the National Endowment for the Humanities for their support of the editing of this and previous volumes; to the Tennessee Historical Commission, Herbert L. Harper, Executive Director; and finally, to our fiscal agent, the University of Tennessee-Knoxville. At the University, we are fortunate to receive the encouragement and support of Eli Fly, interim president, Clifton Woods, past interim provost and Loren Crabtree, his successor; but we are particularly appreciative of the Office of the Dean, College of Arts and Sciences—Dean Lorayne W. Lester, Administrative Assistant Lou E. Cox, and Executive Assistant Ann Robinson-Craig and her associates Jennifer Barnett and Nancy M. Fox—for their patience, understanding, and guidance in the day-to-day administration of the project. Without the assistance of all of these, this volume would be considerably less than it is. To each, we offer our thanks.

And finally, to my family—Carolyn, Andrew, Beth, and Keri—I want to say thanks for sustaining me while I grappled with the problems of Jackson's life, often at the expense of depriving them of my time and attention.

Editorial Policies

PLAN OF WORK

The goal of the Papers of Andrew Jackson is to bring together the literary remains of Andrew Jackson and make them accessible to both the general reader and the serious scholar. An international search of almost 6,000 repositories, contacts with hundreds of private collectors, and an examination of newspapers, magazines, journals, and monographs has yielded a collection of some 100,000 documents. To make this material available, complementary letterpress and microfilm series will be published.

The microfilm publication, thirty-nine reels issued in 1987, is a supplement to the Library of Congress Andrew Jackson Papers and the National Archives microfilm series. It includes *all* Jackson documents found in the project's search to that date and *not* included in those two publications. The entire body of Jackson papers in the three publications—the Supplement, the Library of Congress Presidents' Papers Series, and the National Archives records—can be accessed through *The Papers of Andrew Jackson: A Guide and Index to the Microfilm Editions* (Scholarly Resources, Inc., 1987). Microfilm supplements will make available newly located documents when sufficient numbers accumulate.

The letterpress series will be a selective edition of sixteen volumes, accompanied by a cumulative index. With its annotations, it will stand alone as a unit, but it will also facilitate access to the much larger body of material available on the microfilms. Each volume will include a calendar in which all unselected documents, except the most routine, will be described by their writer or recipient, subject matter, provenance, and location on the film collections. The letterpress series will thus serve as an indispensable guide to the entire body of papers.

EDITORIAL METHOD

In the interest of stylistic continuity in the letterpress series, the present editors have adopted generally the editorial practices established in the previous five volumes.

The editors have broadly defined "papers" as outgoing and incoming correspondence, financial records, deeds, records of litigation, speeches and essays, memoranda, and military orders. In addition the editors have included in the Calendar all of Rachel Jackson's correspondence, whether or not with Jackson, and a small number of particularly significant third-party items essential to the understanding of an otherwise obscure event in Jackson's life. All documents are listed in the Calendar following *The Papers*, with page numbers indicated for those selected, and writer or recipient, provenance, and subject matter described for the others.

Documents in this volume are arranged in chronological sequence. The only exception is with enclosures, which generally appear immediately following the document they accompanied. All letters are reproduced in full, except when the only surviving text is incomplete. If several copies of a document are available, the editors have relied upon the recipient's copy (whether AL, ALS, or LS) for the text. Where that is missing, they have selected the most authoritative manuscript available. Generally, printed copies have been used only in the absence of manuscript versions, or when the manuscript has been mutilated or is a badly garbled copy. In several instances, variant manuscript copies of documents have been found containing additional text. If short, it has been incorporated into the document, with attention called to the source of that portion in footnotes. When lengthy or when some portion of the document may still be missing, the text source has been identified in an unnumbered provenance note immediately following that portion. Texts are taken from the first cited source.

The prime consideration in preparing the documents for publication has been fidelity to the original text. With the few exceptions noted below, the editors have made an effort to reproduce the papers exactly as written with all their peculiarities of spelling, capitalization, and punctuation. To aid readability dashes after commas, semicolons, colons, or periods have been omitted. Abbreviations, including the commonly used ampersand and contractions, have been allowed to stand as written, with expansion in square brackets only when necessary for the understanding of the contemporary reader. Apostrophes below the line have been raised to their modern position above the line, and superscripts have been dropped to the line, retaining punctuation as in the original. Addressees' names, often written at the end of a document, have been omitted, as have words inadvertently repeated in the text. Dates written at the end of a document have been transferred to the beginning; interlineations and marginalia have been incorporated into the text as indicated by the writer.

Occasionally bracketed matter has been introduced into the text to clarify otherwise questionable or unrecognizable words, to supply characters in mutilated documents, to indicate with ellipses a missing portion of a document (italicized in these last two instances), and to insert the full name(s) of persons upon their first appearance. Dates and names furnished by the editors for undated, misdated, unsigned, and unaddressed documents are also enclosed in brackets, with a question mark if conjectural. Significant cancellations have been incorporated in angle brackets.

Immediately following each document is an unnumbered note giving the provenance of that item and, if appropriate, identifying the writer or recipient. Significant postmarks, address instructions, endorsements, and dockets have also been included here. The symbols used in this note appear in the List of Abbreviations. The document's location on microfilms is also noted in parentheses, with reel number alone referring to the Jackson Papers on the Library of Congress Presidents' Papers Series; with reel and frame number separated by a dash, to the Jackson Papers Series (Scholarly Resources, Inc., 1987); and M or T followed by a dash and reel number, to the National Archives publications, which are conveniently listed in the Repository Symbols of this volume.

Introductory notes and footnotes are used to supply context and continuity and to identify persons, places, and events, usually at their first appearance in the text. Persons in the *Dictionary of American Biography* and the *Biographical Directory of the United States Congress, 1774–1989,* have been identified only briefly, and symbols at their names in the index have been used to direct the reader to additional biographical information in those publications.

DOCUMENT SYMBOLS

AD   Autograph Document
ADS   Autograph Document Signed
AL   Autograph Letter
ALS   Autograph Letter Signed
AN   Autograph Note
ANS   Autograph Note Signed
DS   Document Signed
LC   Letterbook copy
LS   Letter Signed

REPOSITORY SYMBOLS

A-Ar   Alabama Department of Archives and History,
                  Montgomery
CtY   Yale University, New Haven, Conn.
CU-BANC   Bancroft Library, University of California, Berkeley
DLC   Library of Congress, Washington, D.C.
DNA   National Archives, Washington, D.C.
                  RG 15, Records of the Veterans Administration
                  RG 28, M601, Letters Sent by the Postmaster General,
                  1789–1836

RG 45, Naval Records Collection of the Office of Naval Records and Library

RG 45, M124, Letters Received by the Secretary of the Navy: Miscellaneous Letters, 1801–84

RG 45, M209, Miscellaneous Letters Sent by the Secretary of the Navy, 1789–1886

RG 46, Records of the United States Senate

RG 59, M439, Letters of Application and Recommendation during the Administration of James Monroe, 1817–25

RG 59, M639, Letters of Application and Recommendation During the Administration of Andrew Jackson, 1829–37

RG 75, M21, Letters Sent by the Office of Indian Affairs, 1824–81

RG 77, Records of the Office of the Chief of Engineers

RG 94, Records of the Adjutant General's Office

RG 94, M91, Records Relating to the U.S. Military Academy, 1812–67

RG 94, M688, United States Military Academy Cadet Application Papers, 1805–66

RG 98, Records of the United States Army Commands, 1784–1821

RG 107, M6, Letters Sent by the Secretary of War Relating to Military Affairs, 1800–89

RG 107, M22, Register of Letters Received by the Office of the Secretary of War, Main Series, 1800–70

RG 107, M220, Reports to Congress from the Secretary of War, 1803–70

RG 107, M221, Letters Received by the Secretary of War, Registered Series, 1801–70

RG 107, M222, Letters Received by the Secretary of War, Unregistered Series, 1789–1861

RG 217, Records of the United States General Accounting Office

F	Florida State Library, Tallahassee
FHi	Florida Historical Society, Tampa
FrN	Université de Nantes, Nantes, France
FWpR	Rollins College, Winter Park, Fla.
IaU	University of Iowa, Iowa City
ICHi	Chicago Historical Society, Chicago, Ill.
ICN	Newberry Library, Chicago, Ill.
InHi	Indiana Historical Society, Indianapolis
InU-Li	Lilly Library, Indiana University, Bloomington
KyHi	Kentucky Historical Society, Frankfort

KyLoF	Filson Club, Louisville, Ky.
LNHiC	The Historic New Orleans Collection, New Orleans, La.
LNT	Tulane University, New Orleans, La.
LU	Louisiana State University, Baton Rouge
MB	Boston Public Library, Boston, Mass.
MdHi	Maryland Historical Society, Baltimore
MH-H	Houghton Library, Harvard University, Cambridge, Mass.
MnHi	Minnesota Historical Society, St. Paul
Ms-Ar	Mississippi Department of Archives and History, Jackson
N	New York State Library, Albany
NaII	Albany Institute of History and Art, Albany, N.Y.
NcD	Duke University, Durham, N.C.
NcGM	Greensboro Historical Museum, Greensboro, N.C.
NcSal	Rowan Public Library, Salisbury, N.C.
NcU	University of North Carolina, Chapel Hill
NHi	New-York Historical Society, New York City
NIC	Cornell University, Ithaca, N.Y.
NjMoHP	Morristown National Historical Park, Morristown, N.J.
NjP	Princeton University, Princeton, N.J.
NN	New York Public Library, New York City
NNC	Columbia University, New York, N.Y.
NNMu	New York Municipal Archives, New York City
NNPM	Pierpont Morgan Library, New York, N.Y.
NSyU	Syracuse University, Syracuse, N.Y.
OClWHi	Western Reserve Historical Society, Cleveland, Ohio
OHi	Ohio Historical Society, Columbus
OkTG	Thomas Gilcrease Institute of American History and Art, Tulsa, Okla.
PCarlD	Dickinson College, Carlisle, Pa.
PHC	Haverford College, Haverford, Pa.
PHi	Historical Society of Pennsylvania, Philadelphia
PMA	Allegheny College, Meadville, Pa.
ScCleU	Clemson University, Clemson, S.C.
T	Tennessee State Library and Archives, Nashville
TFWi	Williamson County Archives, Williamson County Court, Franklin, Tenn.
THer	Ladies' Hermitage Association, Hermitage, Tenn.
THi	Tennessee Historical Society, Nashville
TMM	University of Memphis, Memphis, Tenn.
TNDa	Davidson County Archives, Davidson County Court, Nashville, Tenn.
TNJ	Jean and Alexander Heard Library, Vanderbilt University, Nashville, Tenn.
TU	University of Tennessee, Knoxville

Tx	Texas State Library and Historical Commission, Austin
TxHSJM	San Jacinto Museum of History Association, Deer Park, Texas
TxU	University of Texas, Austin
ViHi	Virginia Historical Society, Richmond
ViMtvL	Mount Vernon Ladies' Association of the Union, Mount Vernon, Va.
ViRVal	Valentine Museum, Richmond, Va.
ViU	University of Virginia, Charlottesville
ViW	College of William and Mary, Williamsburg, Va.
WHi	State Historical Society of Wisconsin, Madison

SHORT TITLES

Annals of Congress The Debates and Proceedings in the Congress of the United States . . . 42 vols. Washington, D.C., 1834–56.

ASP American State Papers: Documents Legislative and Executive, of the Congress of the United States . . . 38 vols. Washington, D.C., 1832–61.

Bassett John Spencer Bassett, ed., *Correspondence of Andrew Jackson.* 7 vols. Washington, D.C., 1926–35.

Burke Pauline Wilcox Burke, *Emily Donelson of Tennessee.* 2 vols. Richmond, Va., 1941.

Calhoun Papers W. Edwin Hemphill and Clyde N. Wilson, eds., *The Papers of John C. Calhoun.* 25 vols. to date. Columbia, S.C., 1959–.

Clay Papers James F. Hopkins et al., eds. *The Papers of Henry Clay.* 11 vols. Lexington, Ky., 1959–92.

Gayarré Charles Gayarré, *A Sketch of General Jackson, by Himself.* New Orleans, 1857.

Heiskell Samuel G. Heiskell, *Andrew Jackson and Early Tennessee History.* 2 vols. Nashville, Tenn., 1918 (1st Edition); 3 vols. Nashville, Tenn., 1921 (2nd Edition).

House Journal U.S. Congress, House of Representatives, *Journal of the House of Representatives.*

HRDoc U.S. Congress, House of Representatives, *House Documents.*

HRRep U.S. Congress, House of Representatives, *House Reports.*

Jackson Harold D. Moser et al., eds. *The Papers of Andrew Jackson.* 6 vols. to date. Knoxville, Tenn., 1980–.

mAJs	Microfilm of The Papers of Andrew Jackson, Supplement (forthcoming).
Memoirs of John Quincy Adams	Charles Francis Adams, ed., *Memoirs of John Quincy Adams, Comprising Portions of His Diary from 1795 to 1848.* 12 vols. Philadelphia, 1874–77.
NYPLB	*Bulletin of the New York Public Library.*
Parton	James Parton, *Life of Andrew Jackson.* 3 vols. New York, 1860.
Polk Correspondence	Herbert Weaver, Paul H. Bergeron, and Wayne Cutler, eds., *Correspondence of James K. Polk.* 9 vols. to date. Nashville and Knoxville, Tenn., 1969–.
Register of Debates	U.S. Congress, *Register of Debates in Congress.* 14 vols. Washington, D.C., 1825–37.
RegKyHi	*Register of the Kentucky Historical Society.*
Richardson, *Messages and Papers of the Presidents*	James D. Richardson, ed. *A Compilation of the Messages and Papers of the Presidents, 1789–1897.* 10 vols. Washington, D.C., 1896–99.
SDoc	U.S. Congress, Senate, *Senate Documents.*
Senate Journal	U.S. Congress, Senate, *Senate Journal.*
THQ	*Tennessee Historical Quarterly.*
U.S. Statutes at Large	*Statutes at Large of the United States of America, 1789–1873.* 17 vols. Boston: 1850–73.
Webster Papers: Correspondence	Charles M. Wiltse, Harold D. Moser et al., eds. *The Papers of Daniel Webster: Correspondence Series.* 7 vols. Hanover, N.H., 1974–89.
Works of James Buchanan	John Bassett Moore, ed., *The Works of James Buchanan, Comprising His Speeches, State Papers, and Private Correspondence.* 12 vols., Philadelphia, 1908–11.
Writings of James Monroe	Stanislaus Murray Hamilton, ed. *The Writings of James Monroe, Including a Collection of His Public and Private Papers and Correspondence Now for the First Time Printed.* 7 vols. New York, 1898–1903.
Writings of Sam Houston	Amelia W. Williams and Eugene C. Barker, eds., *The Writings of Sam Houston, 1813–1863.* 8 vols. Austin, Texas, 1934–75.

Chronology

1825

Jan 1	Attended dinner honoring the Marquis de Lafayette at Williamson's Hotel in Washington
Jan 3	Robert Owen, a British social reformer, purchased land in Indiana for his utopian community, New Harmony
Jan 4	Dined at Joel R. Poinsett's with John Quincy Adams, Lafayette, and others
Jan 5	Voted for ratification of convention with Russia regarding the Northwest; treaty ratified
Jan 8	Accompanied by Rachel Jackson, attended ball in his honor hosted by Jacob Jennings Brown
Jan 9	Charles Pendleton Tutt warned that opponents were planning a public discussion of Rachel Jackson's divorce
Jan 12	Attended dinner hosted by Martin Van Buren, Louis McLane, and Stephen Van Rensselaer
Jan 13	Voted for ratification of convention with the Bey of Tunis; treaty ratified
	Voted for ratification of treaties with Iowa Indians; with Sauk and Fox Indians
	John C. Wright from Ohio proposed to the House that a committee be appointed to recommend procedures for electing the president should the electoral college fail; laid on the table
Jan 15	*Augusta Chronicle and Georgia Advertiser* reported rumors from non-Washington sources that "corrupt bargaining" was likely involved in quest for presidency
Jan 18	Voted yea on passage of engrossed bill to abolish imprisonment for debt; measure failed
Jan 19	Rumors accuse Jackson of disparaging Kentuckians' courage at the Battle of New Orleans
Jan 21	*Charleston Mercury and Morning Advertiser* reported combinations forming in Washington to defeat Jackson

Jan 24	Henry Clay announced that he would support Adams for president
Jan 25/28	George Kremer of Pennsylvania addressed letter to the editor of the Philadelphia *Columbian Observer* claiming that Clay supported Adams as part of a "corrupt bargain"
Jan 26	In a letter to Francis T. Brooke of Richmond, Clay declared his intention to support Adams for president and his unwillingness to see a "military chieftain" in the post
Jan 26	Voted yea on bill to authorize the president to order survey of road from Missouri to "New Mexico" (present Texas); bill ordered printed
Jan 27	*Washington Gazette* reported Clay definitely committed to Adams
	In message to Congress, President James Monroe declared the removal of the Indian tribes from the states and territories to unoccupied western lands a matter "of very high importance to our Union" and urged enabling legislation
Feb 3	Clay addressed the House of Representatives suggesting that Kremer's allegations might require investigation; John Forsyth's motion to refer the address to a select committee postponed
Feb 4	House of Representatives agreed to Forsyth's motion to appoint committee to investigate Kremer's allegations of a "corrupt bargain"
Feb 6	House of Representatives appointed a committee to propose procedures for electing the president; Wright, Philip P. Barbour (Va.), Edward Livingston (La.), Louis McLane (Del.), Daniel Webster (Mass.), Dudley Marvin (N.Y.), and Samuel D. Ingham (Pa.) appointed
Feb 8	House of Representatives adopted eight rules proposed by the select committee for governing procedure of electing the president; agreed to convene in joint session with the Senate on the following day to open the ballots of the electors
	Kremer reported to Jackson James Buchanan's efforts early in January to strike a deal for Clay's support
Feb 9	John Quincy Adams elected president by the House of Representatives, over Andrew Jackson and William Harris Crawford; John C. Calhoun elected vice-president (Jackson received 13 votes for vice-president)
Feb 11	Called on William H. Crawford, accompanied by Samuel Swartwout
	Adams asked Clay to serve as his secretary of state

	Joseph Gales and William Winston Seaton of the *National Intelligencer* chosen printers for House of Representatives
Feb 12	Treaty of Indian Springs ratified, ceding Creek lands in Georgia; soon repudiated by disgruntled Creeks, and signer William McIntosh later murdered
Feb 15	Voted nay on indefinite postponement of bill to amend the federal judiciary to add three circuit judges in the West; measure failed
Feb 17	Voted nay on amendment to judiciary bill to prohibit Supreme Court judges from presiding over new circuits; measure defeated
	Voted nay on amendment to reduce number of new circuits to two; measure passed
Feb 18	Spoke in favor of bill to extend relief benefits of Seminole War veterans to two companies of Mounted Rangers
	Voted yea on offer of $5,000 for Rembrandt Peale's equestrian painting of George Washington, Lafayette, and others; measure returned to committee
	Washington Gazette published Kremer's letter to his constituents accusing Clay of corrupt bargain
Feb 20	Clay accepted Adams's offer of secretary of state post
Feb 21	Voted yea on amendment to the annual appropriations bill providing $80,000 for two forts in North Carolina; measure passed
	Again spoke in favor of the Mounted Rangers' relief bill; measure passed
Feb 22	Voted yea on engrossment of bill to allow persons in Missouri and Arkansas territories to institute proceedings to validate their claims under French or Spanish grants; measure passed
Feb 22–26	American artisans' and manufacturers' exhibition held in Capitol rotunda
Feb 23	Voted yea on bill to purchase Rembrandt Peale painting; measure passed
Feb 24	Voted yea to third reading of bill to extend Cumberland Road to Zanesville, Ohio; measure passed
	Voted yea to third reading of bill authorizing federal government's subscription of 1,500 shares of Delaware and Chesapeake Canal stock; measure passed
Feb 25	*Nashville Gazette* announced Jackson's 1828 presidential candidacy
Feb 26	Pamphlet *Kremer & Clay* published by Kremer, one day after the *National Intelligencer* had refused to publish his letter

March 1	Voted nay to tabling of bill to occupy mouth of the Oregon [Columbia] River; tabling approved
March 3	Eighteenth Congress adjourned
March 4	Adams and Calhoun sworn in as president and vice president
	New York National Advocate published Jackson's Feb 22 letter to Samuel Swartwout, replying to Clay's "military chieftain" argument
March 4–9	Special session of the Senate met to receive communications from Adams
March 7	Voted nay to seating of James Lanman as Connecticut senator; voted nay on confirmation of Clay as secretary of state
March 8	Voted for removal of injunction of secrecy from proceedings on the confirmation of Clay
March 10	Left Washington for Tennessee
March 11	Arrived in Baltimore: feted with dinner and ball; on 12th, with dinner and visit to theater
March 13	Departed Baltimore
March 15	Celebrated birthday at public dinner in Elkton, Maryland
March 15	*Richmond Enquirer* republished a Kanawha County, Virginia, newspaper report of alleged Jackson conversation with "Mr. H"
March 23	Writing from Wheeling, Virginia, Jackson labeled alleged conversation with "Mr. H" a canard
March 24	Mexican state Texas-Coahuila declared its borders open to American settlers
March 26	Clay published his *Address To the People of the Congressional District Composed of the Counties of Fayette, Woodford, and Clarke in Kentucky,* justifying his support of Adams and acceptance of the state department post
March 27	Arrived at Cincinnati for four-day stay: attended Sunday services at First Presbyterian church, a militia review, a Masonic lodge meeting, a public dinner; sat for portraitist Aaron Corwine; departed the evening of March 30, leaving Rachel Jackson and the Donelsons in Cincinnati
March 31	Arrived at Louisville, Kentucky: attended the circus, a ball, Sunday services at Episcopal church, a dinner, and the theatre
April 7	Trustees of Cumberland College voted to seek endowments for two professorships named in honor of Jackson and Lafayette
April 9	*Nashville Whig* denied first publication of "Mr H" letter as claimed by some newspapers

April 13	Arrived at the Hermitage
April 16	Honored at Nashville public dinner
April 28	Lafayette arrived in Nashville for visit
May 5	Entertained Lafayette at the Hermitage
May 30	Appointed by Presbyterian General Assembly chairman of commission to select site for a western theological seminary
July 4	Attended Independence Day celebration at Franklin, Tennessee
Aug 30	Attended public dinner at Florence, Alabama
Sept 1	Attended public dinner at Tuscumbia, Alabama
Sept 14	Reelected a vice-president of the Nashville Bible Society Left Nashville for visits in West Tennessee
Sept 17	Steam locomotive in England pulled thirty-eight cars at speeds varying between twelve and sixteen miles per hour, surpassing speed of a running horse over distance
Sept 19	Honored at public dinner in Jackson, Tennessee
Sept 27	Attended public dinner in Paris, Tennessee
Oct 4	Attended commencement ceremony of Cumberland College
Oct 6–7	Nominated for president by Tennessee General Assembly meeting in Murfreesboro
Oct 14	Appeared before Tennessee General Assembly; submitted resignation from the United States Senate
Oct 26	Erie Canal officially opened
Nov 2–3	Mexico and Columbia invited the United States to attend a congress of independent American states in Panama
Dec 5	Nineteenth Congress, First Session, convened
Dec 9	George McDuffie of South Carolina introduced in the House a resolution to amend the Constitution by providing for election by districts in presidential elections
Dec 13	Czar Alexander I of Russia died; succeeded by Nicholas I
Dec 26	Adams recommended that the Senate approve delegates to the Panama Congress
1825	Samuel Putnam Waldo published his *Civil and Military History of Andrew Jackson*

1826

Jan 3	Hugh Lawson White introduced in the Senate a resolution to amend the Constitution's provision for presidential election
Jan 9	Attended ball at the Nashville Masonic Hall commemorating the Battle of New Orleans

Jan 24	Creek Indians signed Treaty of Washington, voiding Treaty of Indian Springs and agreeing to a smaller land cession
Feb 6	*United States' Telegraph* began publication in Washington as anti-administration paper
	James Fenimore Cooper's *Last of the Mohicans* published in Philadelphia
Feb 15–16	House of Representatives debated constitutional amendments introduced earlier in the month by George McDuffie regarding presidential elections
March 14	Senate approved Adams's nominees for delegates to the Panama Congress
cMarch 20	John P. Erwin appointed Nashville postmaster; appointment protested by the Tennessee congressional delegation
March 22	Sold 1825 cotton crop in New Orleans
March 27	Elected trustee of Cumberland College, Nashville; continued on roster until his death
April 1	In address to the United States House of Representatives, Robert P. Henry of Kentucky attacked Jackson for alleged insult of Kentucky troops' courage at Battle of New Orleans
	House tabled further consideration of specific proposals to amend Constitution re presidential election
April 8	Clay and John Randolph dueled in Virginia; neither wounded
April 13	Attended meeting of Board of Trustees, Cumberland College
cApril 15	Made trip to Florence, Alabama, to check on Andrew Jackson Hutchings's farm; returned April 30
April 26	United States signed treaty of amity, commerce, and navigation with Denmark
May 13	Attended meeting of Board of Trustees, Cumberland College
May 22	Nineteenth Congress, First Session, adjourned
May 27	Attended meeting of Board of Trustees, Cumberland College
June 1	Charles Cutler Torrey published his engraving of Ralph E. W. Earl's military portrait of Jackson
June 20	In the *Liberty Hall and Cincinnati Gazette*, Charles Hammond complained of newspapers bought to promote Jackson's presidential candidacy
June 22	Panama Congress convened without delegation from the United States in attendance

June 27	Prospectus of Boston *North American Democrat,* a new Jackson paper, appeared
	Duff Green ordered the printing of copies of the prospectus of the *United States' Telegraph* to distribute in Cincinnati and Louisville
cJuly 1	At a dinner party near Fredericksburg, Virginia, Samuel L. Southard reported that then secretary of war James Monroe, not Jackson, deserved credit for the victory at New Orleans
July 4	John Adams and Thomas Jefferson died
	Attended Independence Day celebrations in Pulaski, Tennessee
July 6	Honored with public dinner at Fayetteville, Tennessee
July 8	Attended public dinner in Shelbyville, Tennessee; honored by local Masons
July 10	Jonathan Roberts, former United States senator from Pennsylvania, wrote to Philadelphia Jackson Committee, branding Jackson a military despot and giving Monroe primary credit for the New Orleans victory
July 20	Hosted dinner at the Hermitage for Eaton
July 25	Chaired Nashville meeting to arrange a ceremony memorializing Jefferson and Adams
Aug 2	Philadelphia Jackson Committee replied to Roberts's military characterization of Jackson
Aug 3	Attended memorial service for Adams and Jefferson in Nashville
cAug 9	Duff Green, traveling through the western states to raise money for the *United States' Telegraph,* spent several days in Nashville
Aug 30	Eaton replied to Roberts's charges re responsibility for victory at Battle of New Orleans; response appeared as a serial publication in *Philadelphia American Sentinel,* beginning September 26, and was shortly issued as a campaign pamphlet
Sept 9	*Christian Advocate* began publication in New York
cSept 13	Abduction of William Morgan in Canandaigua, New York, allegedly to halt his planned publication of the secrets of freemasonry
Sept 27–Oct 5	Attended examinations, commencement, and meeting of trustees of Cumberland College
Sept 28	Samuel Houston and William White dueled in Kentucky over dispute growing out of Houston's effort to block the appointment of Erwin as postmaster of Nashville
Oct 2	Attended annual meeting of Masonic Grand Lodge of the State of Tennessee in Nashville

Oct 15	In a letter to Worden Pope, John Adair gave Jackson's conduct at New Orleans high praise, in essence refusing to revive the dispute of 1817 over the alleged insult of Kentucky troops
Oct 16	*Kentucky Reporter* published editorial defending Adams's purchase of billiard table for the White House James Buchanan replied to Duff Green's inquiry about his meeting with Jackson before the House election of Adams; denied that he carried an offer from Clay to make a deal
Oct 23	Jackson denounced Southard and other cabinet members who were traveling about attacking his reputation
Oct 24	Administration congressional candidate in East Tennessee, Thomas D. Arnold, allegedly solicited a statement from Jackson regarding internal improvements and domestic manufacture
Oct 25	Attended performance of *Town and Country* at the Nashville theater
Nov	Jackson papers, *Missouri Herald* and Natchez *Mississippi Statesman,* began publication
Nov 4	Tennessee General Assembly re-elected Eaton to the United States Senate
Nov 14	Hammond's *Cincinnati Gazette* declared that the Jacksons' marriage involved a matter of "character" that he intended to treat at length; referred to Rachel Jackson as "the woman he and others call Mrs. Jackson"; denied rumors that his visit to Clay in Lexington, Kentucky, was to acquire evidence on the Jackson's marriage
Nov 22	Henry Lee published prospectus for a biography of Jackson in the *United States' Telegraph*
Nov 24	Biographical sketch of Jackson by Alfred Balch (under pseudonym "T") published in *Richmond Enquirer;* later appeared as a pamphlet and circulated in states along the east coast
cNov 26	Left Nashville on trip to Alabama; returned December 6
Dec 2	Sarah Michie Smith provided document relating to Rachel Jackson's marriage to and divorce from Lewis Robards
Dec 4	Nineteenth Congress, Second Session, convened
Dec 10	Mary Bowen provided affidavit on the Jacksons' marriage
Dec 21	Elizabeth Craighead provided affidavit on the Jacksons' marriage
	At Jackson's request, Eaton asked Clay to confirm the rumor that he had given Hammond documents about

	Rachel Jackson's first marriage and subsequent divorce during his visit to Clay in the summer
Dec 23	From Washington, Clay wrote Hammond about Eaton's "call" on December 21, which prompted Hammond to write Eaton eleven days later
cDec 25	Van Buren and Calhoun met in Virginia and agreed jointly to promote Jackson's candidacy
Dec 30	Attended trustees' meeting of the University of Nashville, formerly Cumberland College

1827

Jan 2	House of Representatives appointed committee to investigate allegations against John C. Calhoun regarding Rip Raps Shoal contracts
Jan 3	Hammond wrote Eaton denying that he received documents from Clay; informed Eaton that he received the materials from Edward Day
	Massachusetts Journal, an Adams-Daniel Webster paper, commenced publication in Boston
Jan 5	Through Houston, Jackson demanded Southard's source for the statement that Jackson was bound for home when Monroe ordered him to New Orleans to defend the city
Jan 7	Eaton requested Overton to begin work on a narrative of the controversial marriage events and to hold it for publication if needed
Jan 9	Attended meeting of University of Nashville Board of Trustees
Jan 19	Philadelphia Jackson Committee passed resolution urging formation of similar committees in the various states and in the District of Columbia
Feb 3	Jackson Central Committee formed in Washington, D.C., with John Van Ness chairing
Feb 9	Southard assured Jackson that his comments in Fredericksburg praising Monroe's role in Battle of New Orleans victory were not intended to depreciate Jackson's fame
Feb 12	*Thomas D. Arnold to The Freemen of the Counties of Cocke, Sevier, Blount, Jefferson, Grainger, Claiborne, and Knox* published, discussing Jackson's character—his dueling, his cock-fighting, and his stealing another man's wife

· *The Papers of Andrew Jackson* ·

Feb 13	House committee exonerated Calhoun in Rip Raps Shoal investigation
Feb 24	*Nashville Republican* characterized Arnold's publication as "too scurrilous and contemptible" for comment
Feb 26	*Nashville Republican* accused the *National Crisis and Cincinnati Emporium,* published by S. J. Browne, of issuing an "infamous libel on Gen Jackson"
Feb 28	Woolens bill defeated in Senate by vote of Vice President Calhoun
Feb	Aristides, pseudonym for Samuel Swartwout, published *Concise Narrative of General Jackson's First Invasion of Florida and of His Immortal Defence of New-Orleans* in New York City
March 3	Nineteenth Congress, Second Session, adjourned
March 8	Carter Beverley reported from the Hermitage that Jackson had revealed to him the efforts of Clay's forces to bargain for Jackson's support in the House presidential election of 1825
March 9	Louisiana legislature approved resolution inviting Jackson to the 1828 celebration of the Battle of New Orleans
cMarch 10	William B. Lewis learned from a source in Cincinnati that a public discussion of the Jacksons' marriage was about to begin
March 13	Attended public dinner at Gallatin, Tennessee
March 16	Richmond *Whig* noted the publication of Arnold's pamphlet, quoted extracts from it, and briefly discussed the circumstances of the Jacksons' marriage
March 17	Nashville Jackson Committee organized with John Overton chairing
March 19	In public speeches, two Kentucky congressmen attacked Jackson for execution of the six militiamen
March 23	Hammond's *Cincinnati Gazette* accused Jackson of convincing "the wife of Lewis Roberts of Mercer county, Kentucky, to desert her husband, and live with himself, in the character of a wife"
March 26	*National Journal,* leading administration newspaper in Washington, reprinted the Richmond *Whig* article on the Jacksons' marriage
March 27	Adams ordered American ports closed to British ships sailing from Western Hemisphere
March	Van Buren began a two-month tour of Georgia, South Carolina, North Carolina, and Virginia in an effort to bring former Crawford supporters and disaffected Clayites into the Jackson camp

March	*American Quarterly Review* began publication in Philadelphia
April 1	Lewis prepared his own summary of the marriage controversy to send Thomas Cadwallader of Philadelphia, who had recently visited Nashville
April 5	Beverley's letter of March 8, disclosing Jackson's discussion of the Clay forces' efforts to bargain the presidential election in 1825, printed in the Fayetteville (N.C.) *Carolina Observer*
April 7	In response to Hammond's publication of March 23, *Nashville Republican* printed an account of the separation and divorce of Rachel and Lewis Robards and of Rachel's marriage to Jackson
April 14	Frankfort *Commentator,* in a parody illustration, compared Rachel Jackson to "a dirty black wench"
April 16	Steamboat *Philadelphia* completed its run from New Orleans to Cincinnati in nine days and three hours, surpassing the earlier record by sixteen hours
April 18	Frankfort *Argus* responded to the *Commentator*'s attack on the Jacksons' marriage with affidavits regarding the Robards' marriage and divorce
April 21	*Nashville Republican* reported that administration newspapers were reprinting Arnold's publication
April 25	Nashville Jackson Committee issued its report on Jackson's military accounts and the execution of the six militiamen
April 27	*Richmond Enquirer* endorsed Jackson for president
May	Henry Lee and his wife arrived in Nashville; spent "some days" at the Hermitage; took lodgings nearby and remained until late June 1828
May 12	Van Buren ended his southern tour in Washington
May 15	Beverley asked Jackson for confirmation of their March 8 conversation
May 17	James Fenimore Cooper's *The Prairie* published in Philadelphia
May 24	Arnold published another pamphlet supporting his campaign for Congress, in which he included copious detail of "Gen Jackson's intrigue with Mrs Roberts"
June 2	Lexington *Kentucky Reporter* published anti-Jackson remarks attributed to Jefferson
June 5	Jackson confirmed to Carter Beverley the conversation they held on March 8 Nashville Committee published reply on marriage issue with supporting documents; later appeared as pamphlet Purchased pet parrot, "Poll," for Rachel Jackson

	by David Claypoole Johnston, announced in the Washington *National Journal*
Aug 17	William H. Crawford authorized Van Buren to make his support for Jackson "known," but declined to make a public endorsement
	Nashville Republican responded to charges against Jackson as a "Negro Trader" and an unprincipled duelist
Aug 28	Hermitage overseer Isaac Walton killed Jackson's slave Gilbert
Sept	In the *Virginia Advocate*, Thomas Jefferson Randolph reported that Thomas Jefferson, some months after John Quincy Adams's inauguration, had remarked that Jackson was the last best hope to preserve the Constitution's limits on federal power
Sept 5	Frankfort *Argus of Western America* exposed executed militiaman John Harris's February 1815 letter to his wife as a forgery
Sept 18	*Nashville Republican* published statements of Eaton, John Branch, and Jacob C. Isacks attempting to reconcile Jackson's and Buchanan's recollections of the "corrupt bargain" conversation
Sept 27	Tennessee General Assembly re-elected Hugh Lawson White to the United States Senate
	United States and Great Britain agreed to arbitration of the disputed boundary between Maine and New Brunswick
Oct 1	Attended inauguration of Governor Samuel Houston and public dinner honoring Hugh Lawson White
Oct 3	Attended graduation ceremonies of University of Nashville
Oct 11	"Wythe" commenced publication of anti-Jackson series on the "military chieftain" theme in the Washington *National Intelligencer*
Oct 13	Attended meeting of University of Nashville trustees
Oct 15	John Adair of Kentucky praised Jackson's role in the defense of New Orleans
Oct 30	Left the Hermitage for Florence, Alabama; returned November 6
[cNov 1]	Administration presses took up issue of Jackson's violent behavior by citing his alleged threat to cut off the ears of Senator John W. Eppes during the congressional review of his military actions in Florida, 1819
Nov 7	Frankfort *Argus of Western America* began publishing a serialized biographical sketch of Jackson; appeared weekly until February 13, 1828

Dec 3   Twentieth Congress, First Session, convened with Jacksonian majority; Andrew Stevenson of Virginia chosen Speaker of the House

New York Common Council awarded Jackson a gold medal commemorating the opening of Erie Canal; presented to him in New Orleans during Jackson's 1828 visit

Dec 4   Duff Green, Jacksonian editor of the *United States' Telegraph,* chosen printer for the Senate

Dec 13   *National Intelligencer* published letter from William Martin of Tennessee, one of Jackson's officers in the Creek War, announcing his support for Adams and opposition to Jackson because of Jackson's treatment of troops on the "term of enlistment" question

Dec 18   In letter to his nephew in Virginia, Nathaniel W. Williams accused Jackson of complicity in the 1806 Burr affair

Dec 21   First installment of Henry Lee's articles defending Jackson on accusations of a violent and authoritarian disposition published in *Nashville Republican* over pen name "Jefferson"

Dec 23   Richard Keith Call denied the story that Jackson threatened to "cut off the ears" of John W. Eppes

Dec 27   Departed Nashville for New Orleans aboard the *Pocahontas* with a large body of family, friends, and supporters

1827   First section of John J. Audubon's *Birds of America* published in London

1828

Jan   *The Southern Agriculturist* commenced publication in Charleston, South Carolina

Jan 4   *Pocahontas* landed at Natchez, Mississippi, with the Jackson party

Jan 8   Jackson party arrived in New Orleans for a six-day celebration of the Battle of New Orleans

Jan 8–13   Nathaniel W. Williams's letter implicating Jackson in the Burr conspiracy circulated at the Virginia anti-Jackson convention in Richmond

Jan 11   Congressman John Sloane of Ohio introduced resolutions calling on the secretary of war to lay before the House all the documents in his office relating to the execution of the six militiamen

Jan 12   Left New Orleans for the plantation of Samuel McCutchon

Jan 14	Jackson party left the McCutchon plantation to return to Tennessee
Jan 16	Sloane's resolutions adopted by House
	Louisville *Public Advertiser* published Clay's *Address . . . to the Public, Containing Certain Testimony in Refutation of the Charges Against Him, Made by Gen Andrew Jackson, Touching on the Last Presidential Election*
Jan 20	Honored at Vicksburg, Mississippi, by state legislators
cJan 24	At Smithland, Kentucky, Jackson allegedly saw Clay's *Address . . . to the Public,* lost his temper, and cursed Clay; incident reported in administration papers as example of Jackson's violent disposition
Jan 26	Arrived at Nashville aboard *Pocahontas*
Jan 30	"A Tennesseean," pseudonym for Dr. James L. Armstrong, commenced a series of eight anti-Jackson articles in the Lexington *Kentucky Reporter*
Jan 31–cFeb 5	Kentucky legislature investigated Clay's role in convincing the state's congressmen to vote for Adams in 1825 in violation of the legislature's instructions to vote for Jackson
Jan	Cincinnati *Truth's Advocate or Monthly Anti-Jackson Expositor* commenced publication with a twenty-page article, "View of Gen. Jackson's Domestic Relations in Reference to His Fitness for the Presidency"
Feb 7	Sloane introduced resolution calling on the secretary of war to furnish the House of Representatives copies of all the correspondence between the war department and Jackson from the beginning of the Creek War to March 1, 1815
Feb 11	Report of the House Committee on Military Affairs exonerated Jackson in the execution of the six militiamen
	DeWitt Clinton died
Feb 19	*Boston Medical and Surgical Journal,* forerunner of the *New England Journal of Medicine,* founded
Feb 21	*Cherokee Phoenix* began publication in New Echota, Georgia
	Washington *National Journal* published Jackson's alleged "midnight assassin" note to Peter Force et al.
Feb 28	Stated his views on internal improvements and the tariff in a letter to Indiana Governor James B. Ray
Late Feb–early March	John Binns published the "Coffin Handbill," focusing on Jackson's many alleged executions
March 1	*United States' Telegraph Extra,* supporting Jackson, commenced publication in Washington

	First issue of pro-administration *We the People* appeared in Washington
March 3	Jackson and William B. Lewis began distributing copies of Lee's "Jefferson" pamphlet to committees in Kentucky, Ohio, Indiana, Illinois, Mississippi, Louisiana, Pennsylvania, Virginia, Maryland, New Jersey, New York, and New Hampshire
March 4	Pro-administration congressmen introduced resolution to compensate widows of the six militiamen, who had been "unjustly" executed
March 7	*Nashville Republican* published second installment of Lee's "Jefferson" letters
March 15	Honored at birthday dinner in Murfreesboro, Tennessee
March 22	Moses Dawson began publication in Cincinnati of *The Friend of Reform and Corruption's Adversary,* specifically to answer anti-Jackson charges in *Truth's Advocate*
March 25	*Nashville Republican* published letter of Dr. Jesse Miller, a passenger aboard the *Pocahontas,* denying that Jackson reacted violently upon reading Clay's *Address* at Smithland
	United States' Telegraph accused Andrew Erwin of writing "Tennesseean" essays for the Lexington *Kentucky Reporter*
March 26	Attended meeting of University of Nashville trustees and examination of students
March 27	In report on Indian affairs, James Barbour published Jackson's private letter to George W. Campbell of October 15, 1812, condemning and threatening Silas Dinsmoor, Choctaw agent
March 28	*United States' Telegraph Extra* published Nashville Committee's report on the Jacksons' marriage
March	*View of General Jackson's Domestic Relations . . . ,* a pamphlet on the Jacksons' marriage, printed and widely circulated by the Adams coalition
April 8	Informed John Coffee that "upwards of 15,000 copies" of *View of General Jackson's Domestic Relations* had been franked by congressmen
April 11	James K. Polk wrote Dabney S. Carr in defense of Jackson, published as "Six Militia Men," in the *Baltimore Republican*
April 21	Noah Webster's *American Dictionary of the English Language* published
April 26	Russia declared war on Ottoman Empire in support of Greek independence

May 6	Denied that he wrote or sent "midnight assassin" note to Peter Force et al., editors of the Washington *National Journal*
	Western Cherokee chiefs signed treaty exchanging land in Arkansas for territory farther west
May 10	Jackson Central Committee in Washington responded to Clay's *Address* . . .
May 12	Sat for portrait by Orramel Hinckley Throop at Hermitage
May 14	*Kentucky Reporter* published Armstrong's article accusing Jackson of complicity in the Burr conspiracy
May 15	House of Representatives Select Committee on Retrenchment issued report discussing the Adams administration's expenditures (for electioneering purposes) from contingent funds
May 16	Jacksonians responded to Armstrong's claim of Jackson's dishonesty in the Allison land claims dispute with Andrew Erwin
May 19	"Tariff of Abominations" became law
May 21	*Kentucky Reporter* published letter by John Harris blaming Jackson for the execution of his father, one of the militiamen
	In *Kentucky Reporter,* Andrew Erwin accused Jackson of trafficking in "human flesh"
May 26	Twentieth Congress, First Session, adjourned
May	James B. Longacre published 500 copies of his engraving of Ralph E. W. Earl's 1826 portrait of Jackson
May	First U.S. "labor party" organized in Philadelphia
June	Asher Durand published his engraving of John Vanderlyn's military portrait of Jackson, completed for the Corporation of the City of New York in 1820
June 1	Lyncoya died
June 7	Attended meeting of University of Nashville trustees
June 11	Armstrong's "Catalogue of Genl Jackson's Juvenile Indiscretions" published in the Lexington *Kentucky Reporter;* shortly circulated as a pamphlet
June 19	Sent William B. Lewis materials to prepare defense on the Dickinson duel and on his altercations with Nathaniel McNairy, John Sevier, and Jesse and Thomas Hart Benton
June 20	*National Banner and Nashville Whig* published Andrew Erwin's account of Jackson as a slave trader
June 21	Washington *National Intelligencer* published first of nine anti-Jackson editorials: "The Acts of Gen Andrew

Jackson as a Legislator"; final installment appeared on September 23

June 27   In the *Nashville Republican,* William B. Lewis published defense of Jackson and his actions in the Dickinson duel

cJune 30   Henry Lee left Nashville

June   Clay published *Supplement to the Address . . . to the Public* on the corrupt bargain and other matters

July 1   *Nashville Republican* took note of Clay's *Supplement* and published explanation of Jackson's vote against endorsing George Washington's address to Congress, 1796

July 2   Attended public dinner in Lebanon, Tennessee

July 4   Attended public celebration in Carthage, Tennessee
Nashville Republican countered Erwin's charge of slave trading
Eaton inscribed to Jackson a copy of his recently published *The Life of Major General Andrew Jackson,* a revision of the 1816 biography
Adams headed groundbreaking ceremony for Chesapeake and Ohio Canal near Washington
Nashville Republican labelled Andrew Erwin an "ingrate" and repeated the story of Mrs. Erwin's tearful appeal to Jackson to forgive the $10,000 settlement imposed by the compromise in the suit concerning the Allison lands

July 5   Attended public dinner in Hartsville, Tennessee

July 11   In *National Banner and Nashville Whig,* Erwin discussed his lawsuit with Jackson over the Allison lands and denied that his wife had approached Jackson regarding the settlement
Nashville Republican continued to discredit Andrew Erwin for his accusation that Jackson was a slave trader

July 14   Boyd McNairy, in the *National Banner and Nashville Whig,* denied any role in the disclosure of Jackson's bank book but insisted that Jackson had been involved in slave trading

July 16   Began vacation at Hagan (Tyree's) Springs
Shelby family, in the *Kentucky Reporter,* disclosed Jackson's allegedly "rash, hot-headed temper" at the Chickasaw negotiations in 1818
Kentucky Reporter published William P. Anderson's article giving full text of the Francis May letters of 1817 regarding the Dickinson duel; also published

	Anderson's accusation of Jackson's collaboration with Robert Hays to defraud creditors
July 25	*Nashville Republican* discussed the Issac Shelby-Chickasaw treaty issue
July 26	*National Intelligencer* and *United States' Telegraph* published Nathaniel Williams's charges re Jackson and Burr and Jackson's response of February 23
July 28	Proposed making a public response to "all the slanders that have been propagated against me"; dissuaded by advisers
July	"Working Men's Party" organized in Philadelphia "Monumental Inscriptions," a re-working of the Coffin handbill, published
July–Aug	Kentuckian George Brown (d. 1829) traveled through Ohio, exhibiting a certificate of William Rogers, Clark County, Ohio, testifying that Jackson's mother was a British camp follower and his father a mulatto slave
Late July–Aug	Jackson collected testimony regarding his parents' respectability
Aug 1	In *Richmond Enquirer,* "Brutus" responded to Nathaniel W. Williams's charges re Jackson and Burr
Aug 2	*National Banner and Nashville Whig* published Andrew Erwin's open letter re Jackson's slave trading, with supporting testimony; widely circulated as a pamphlet, *Genl. Jackson's Negro Speculations*
Aug 4	Antimasonic convention met in Utica, New York, to nominate candidates for state offices
Aug 5	Under pseudonym, "A Volunteer," Jackson denounced William Martin's view of the "terms of service" question from the Creek War
Aug 8	*Nashville Republican* denounced Erwin's accusations of Jackson's slave trading
Aug 12	Boyd McNairy published Andrew Jackson-William P. Anderson letters allegedly supporting Nathaniel W. Williams's charges re Jackson and Burr
Aug 25	Engraving of Jackson portrait by Throop published in Baltimore
Aug 29	*Nashville Republican* offered definitive reply to the William P. Anderson charges
Aug 30	*Anti-Jackson Bulletin and Messenger of Truth* began publication in Lexington, Kentucky
Sept 12	Nashville Committee published in the *Nashville Republican* its refutation of charges that Jackson conspired with Burr

Dec 18	Rachel Jackson taken suddenly ill
	South Carolina legislature adopted resolutions calling the May 19 tariff unconstitutional, oppressive, and unjust
Dec 19	John C. Calhoun's state rights doctrine, the "South Carolina Exposition," introduced as committee report in the South Carolina House of Representatives
Dec 22	Rachel Jackson died
Dec 23	Public ball scheduled in Nashville to honor Jackson cancelled
Dec 24	Rachel Jackson buried in the Hermitage garden
Dec 30	Jackson gave power of attorney to John Coffee to superintend all business of Andrew Jackson Hutchings
	Georgia legislature protested tariff

The Papers, 1825–1828

1825

When the votes were in following the election in 1824, no one of the four candidates had been elected president. Andrew Jackson, then serving his second stint in the United States Senate from Tennessee, had garnered a plurality of the popular votes. But where it counted, in the electoral college, Jackson's ninety-nine votes were too few, not the majority prescribed by the constitution. Secretary of State John Quincy Adams (1767–1848; Harvard 1787) had eighty-four; Secretary of the Treasury William Harris Crawford (1772–1834) had forty-one; and Kentucky's Henry Clay (1777–1852) had thirty-seven, not enough to remain as a contender in the election that would be decided by the House of Representatives, where he was speaker.

Upon their arrival in Washington on December 7, 1824, the Jackson party settled in at Gadsby's Hotel on Pennsylvania Avenue, and Jackson immediately took his seat in the Senate chamber. Already, maneuverings and negotiations were underway to influence the outcome of the election, but the "people's choice," Andrew Jackson, claimed to remain aloof of the bargaining.

Whether at home or away from the Hermitage, Andrew Jackson generally left close supervision of his "Negro family" to overseers, few of whom lasted longer than two years. The document below is the only surviving inventory of slaves in Jackson's hand, and it is little more than a quick count by households for the assessment of taxes.

Memorandum of Slaves and Land in Davidson County, Tennessee

[January 1, 1825]

Old Hanna & her family squire wife & child, Bet, husband & child, & George in all[1] 8
Blacksmith Aron wife & 3 children[2] 5
Charles wife & child[3] 3
Tom wife & 9 children[4] 11
Ben wife & 4 children[5] 6

old Sampson wife, & 9 children (grace's 2)[6] 11
Dunwody, Ned, Guilbert & Tom[7] 4
Polydore wife & 2 children[8] 4
Sally & her 4 children[9] 5
Titus Candis & child John Fulton[10] 4
Aron wife & 2 children[11] 4
Big Sampson wife & child[12] 3
Arguila wife & 4 children[13] 6
Jame wife & 4 children[14] 6
                                                80
7 over 50—not taxable[15] 7
                                                73
41. over 12. & under 50 Taxable 41
32 under 12 years of age 32
forty one blax poles first day of Janry 1825
640 acres of land Do Do Do County of Davidson whereon he lives.

Andrew Jackson

ADS, DLC (33). Published in Bassett, 3:271–72. On the reverse of this document is a similar census of slaves, noting only taxables and exempts over fifty and endorsed "Black polls in 1825 AJ." The two documents have nearly the same information with certain variations. In the second, the total number of slaves is 83 with 35 under 12 years of age. A taxable slave, Easter, is present on the second list as part of a household with Gilbert and Argyle and his wife. The household of Peter with his two taxable sons, Jack and Jacob, absent from the first list, is on the second, as is Old Penny. Other differences are noted below.

1. AJ bought Hannah (c1770–1846+) and her daughter Betty (1793–1863+) in Sumner County in 1794. Hannah and Betty were in succession the Jackson family cooks. Betty's husband was Ned (c1800–55+), bought in Virginia in 1820. Her son was Alfred (c1813–1901). Squire (c1799–1870+) and Gincy (c1801–70+) were husband and wife. George (c1807–65) became AJ's personal servant.

2. AJ had purchased Aron (c1785–1878) in 1791 in Sumner County, and Hannah (c1801–95), about 1808. Hannah was personal servant to Rachel Jackson. By the mid-1820's she was head of the household servants.

3. Charles (c1795–1855+), in New Orleans with AJ in 1814, was AJ's military servant, 1817–19. He was the family carriage driver for many years and helped Dunwoody train the thoroughbreds. His wife was Charlotte (c1800–55+), whom AJ wrote that he bought at Charles's request to be his wife.

4. Tom (c1790–1846+) and his wife Molly (c1800–49) were field slaves.

5. Ben (c1794–1861+) was a caretaker of the plough horses and later a ginner. His wife Creasy (c1800–61+) was at one time a weaver.

6. Sampson (c1770–1833), probably bought from the Samuel Donelson estate in 1804, was the gardener at the time of his death. AJ purchased his wife Prissy (c1770–1861+) in 1805. Four of their children were taxable: Grace (c1809–55+), Littleton (c1810–49), Orange (c1812–55+), and Essex (c1813–49). Grace's children were Sylva and Franky.

7. Dunwoody (c1770–c1845) was the trainer of the racing stock. His name in the bill of sale was Dinwiddie (the Virginia county of his original owner), but AJ, his family, and racing friends all called him Dunwoody. Old Ned (c1770–1829) was possibly one of the servants with AJ in New Orleans in 1815. Gilbert (c1794–1827) was purchased in Virginia about 1820. He ran away from both AJ's Alabama farm and from the Hermitage, and in

1827, he was killed by the overseer. Tom, also Big Tom and Tom Franklin (c1794–1849), bought in 1820 in Portsmouth, Virginia, was also a runaway slave in 1820–21.

8. Polydore (c1789–1861+) was purchased in 1822 from Catalina Mir Satorios, widow of a Charleston, South Carolina, merchant. He had been in AJ's household since 1818, when AJ seized him as a runaway. His wife was Sally (c1804–61+), probably the slave AJ bought in Washington in 1819. For Polydore's early history, see *Jackson,* 5:41, 173–74.

9. Sally (c1800–32+), also known as Indian Sally and Alabama Sally, had one taxable son, John (c1813–29+).

10. Titus (c1789–1833) was purchased in 1820 in Portsmouth, Virginia. AJ purchased his wife Candis (c1805–61+), already living at the Hermitage in 1825, with her daughter, from James R. Donelson in 1829. AJ purchased John Fulton (c1811–66+) in Florence, Alabama, in 1823; and in 1825, Jackson gave him to Andrew Jackson Donelson as a wedding gift. Fulton served as a courier for both AJ and Donelson.

11. Aron (c1793–1829+) was purchased from Elizabeth R. Donelson in 1823. His unnamed wife was listed as tax-exempt in the second 1825 taxables document, over 50 years old. In an 1829 inventory, Aron is listed as the husband of Mary, both 40 years old.

12. Sampson, also "Big Sampson" (c1788–1833), his wife Pleasant (c1781–1847), and their son George (c1810–30) were bought as a family in 1814 in Mobile.

13. Argyle (c1797–1855+) was purchased in 1820 in Portsmouth, Virginia, for AJ's farm in Alabama. No information has been found about the origins of his wife Creasy (c1800–55+).

14. Jame, also James and Jim (c1795–1829) was at the Hermitage as early as 1813; he was AJ's military servant, 1815–17, and was frequently used as a messenger by both Rachel and Andrew Jackson. His wife was Hannah (c1800–55+), also known as "Ingen Hannah."

15. The seven slaves who were tax exempt by virtue of age over fifty were Old Hannah, Dunwoody, Old Ned, Old Sampson and his wife Priss, Aron's wife, and Old Penny (c1776–1855+; purchased in 1816), absent from this list but named on the 1825 taxables list.

To John Coffee

Senate Chamber
Janry 5th. 1825

Dear Genl

your letter of the 8th. ult[1] is Just recd —It contains the first information from you since you left us at the Hermitage, and we are happy to learn that you & family[2] reached home in health, and that you still enjoy that blessing.

We sincerely regret to hear of the continued indisposition of Eliza—our prayers for the restoration of her health we beg you to present to her.[3]

I am glad to learn that you cotton & that of Andrew J[ackson] Hutchings will be in the markett early, as the prospects of a good price is flattering.[4]

I was apprised of the remonstrance of some of your citizens praying for a posponement of the land sales being forwarded before the receipt of your letter, but from a conversation I had with the commissioner of the land office, that posponement will not take place; I shall see the president on this subject and advise you of the result.[5]

The stiffness of J. ought to be a source of but little regret, only as it may interrupt the harmony & socibility of the female part of the families—as to him, you can do without his society—[6]

The political contest you will have discovered is over with the Electoral colleges, and has resulted, in bringing before the House of Representatives, myself, Mr Adams, and Mr Crawford—how it may be decided by that body I know not, an[d] I am determined, to continue my cour[se] & not interfere in any way, if I am placed there, it shall be without any solicitation or interference on my part—my choice would be on the Hermitage enjoying the blessings of solitude & private happiness with my friends. I named in my last to you that I had some doubts whether my funds here would meet my expence; but from the shortness of little Andrews crop, it will not be more than sufficient to meet the purchase of the forfeighted lands, therefore will endeavour to do with the surpluss of my own crop—I would if the crop had been as productive as I expected asked you to have spared me $500 but fearfull that it will be wanted I now decline asking for it, least an injury might accrue to my little ward.[7] We are all well, they young Ladies Mrs. Call, & Donelson, at parties when they choose; & Mrs. Jackson at the church[8]—and myself harrassed with business, & letters on business, but still my health has improved. Please write me as soon [as yo]u hear from orleans the price of cotton [the]re, that I may form an estimate of the probable amount of the proceeds of my own crop. Mrs. J. Mrs Call, & Mrs Donelson with their Husbands unite with me in respects to your lady & family & Capt [John] Donelson & Elisa, and believe me your friend.

[Andrew Jackson]

P.S. My dear sir let us hear from you as[9]

AL (signature removed), THi (10-1032). Published in Bassett, 3:272–73 (extract). Coffee (1772–1833), AJ's comrade-in-arms during the Creek and New Orleans campaigns, at this time farmed a plantation, Coxes Creek, north of Florence, Alabama, and served as federal surveyor for the northern district of the state.

1. Not found.

2. Coffee and his family, his wife Mary Donelson (1793–1871), AJ's niece, and their six children—Mary Donelson (1812–39), John Donelson (1815–37), Elizabeth Graves (1817–38), Andrew Jackson (1819–91), Alexander Donelson (1821–1901), and Rachel Jackson (1823–92)—had visited the Jacksons in October 1824.

3. Eliza Eleanor Butler (1791–1850), daughter of AJ's close friend Edward (1762–1803), had married John Donelson (1787–1840), AJ's nephew, in 1823. At this time they lived near the Coffees in Alabama. Eliza had been in ill health since the birth of her daughter Mary in the fall of 1824.

4. AJ served as guardian for his grandnephew Hutchings (1811–41), the son of John Hutchings (c1776–1817) and Mary Smith (d. 1813). Both AJ and Coffee were executors of the Hutchings's estate, with Coffee, living near the young Hutchings's Lauderdale County, Alabama, property, generally supervising the day-to-day operations of the farm. Coffee consigned the sale of his cotton to Maunsel White (1783–1863) of New Orleans, a company which AJ also selected as his agent in 1826. He consigned the sale of Hutchings's cotton to the young man's uncle, John Robertson Bedford (1782–1827), formerly a physician and now a businessman in the Florence, Alabama, area and in Louisiana.

5. AJ was likely referring to the October 23, 1824, Madison County resolutions forwarded to James Monroe calling for the postponement of the sale of relinquished Alabama lands scheduled for March 1825 (Huntsville *Alabama Republican,* October 29, 1824). Upon learning of the petition, sometime before December 29, 1824, AJ conferred with his long-time acquaintance George Graham (1772–1830; Columbia 1790), formerly in the war department and now commissioner of the general land office, and learned that the prospective sales had not been canceled. By January 6, however, when AJ visited Monroe to discuss the matter, Monroe had proclaimed the postponement of the sales of the lands (Washington *National Intelligencer,* December 31, 1824).

6. AJ was alluding to the strained relations between him and his long-time friend and business associate James Jackson (1782–1840), now a resident of Florence, Alabama. The differences between the two grew out of complex issues involving a business misunderstanding, the marriage of Richard Keith Call and Mary Letitia Kirkman at the Hermitage in 1824, and political views and opinions (*Jackson,* 5:432–33).

7. In accordance with the relief act of 1821 (3 *U.S. Statutes at Large,* 612–14), AJ had relinquished the SW¼ and SE¼ S15T3R12 of Hutchings's Lauderdale County plantation. He did not repurchase the land for Hutchings until 1830. On December 27, 1824, AJ had asked Coffee for a loan (*Jackson,* 5:457–59).

8. AJ's wife Rachel (1767–1828), his nephew and secretary Andrew Jackson Donelson (1799–1871; Military Academy 1820), and Donelson's wife, also AJ's niece, Emily Tennessee Donelson (1807–36), and several servants had made up the Jackson party headed to Washington in November 1824. At Gadsby's, the Jackson party shared accommodations with John Henry Eaton (1790–1856; University of North Carolina), and with Richard Keith Call (1791–1862), AJ's former aide-de-camp and at this time congressional delegate from Florida Territory, and Call's wife, Mary (c1801–1836).

9. AJ failed to complete the postscript.

To John Coffee

City of Washington
Janry. 6th. 1825

Dear Genl

On yesterday I wrote you from the senate chamber,[1] stating to you, from the information of Mr Graham, Commissioner of the land office, that the sales of the forfeighted lands would not be posponed, and I would see the President on the subject & give you the result of the interview. You can judge of my astonishment, when I called today & found that some days ago, the order for posponement had Issued—and that the land would not be sold under a Twelve Month—Things are as unstable here as our climate. However you see, that the speculators has obtained one year more to increase their funds to the great injury of the prosperity of your state—I will thank you on the receipt of this to inform me what period of the present year would be most advantageous for the sales of the forfeighted lands—or whether as a posponement has taken place, another crop would or would not [be] advantageous to the general mass of your citizens, and the erangement shall be made accordingly—should you be of opinion that it should be posponed untill after christmas next—you may remit me five hundred dollars, which will be ordered with the Interest to be paid you by Colo.

Ant[h]ony Winston out of his first bond then due, should you remit, please to send it so that it will reach me by the first of March[2]—should I not be detained here officially—I shall endeavour to leave here by the 5th. of March.

How the presidential question may be decided I know not—information of today, gives some reasons to believe that a coalition is about to be formed—which may be called the trio, the interest of Crawford, Clay & Adams combined, for the purpose of defeating my election—be this as it may, I shall continue my course, of independence of intrigue & management—and if elected it shall be without any interference of mine—If not elected by this independent course, I shall retire upon magnanimous ground, and I assure you I shall not envy the man who places himself in the chair of state by intrigue of his friends[3]—Present us all affectionately to Polly & the children, & Ma[r]y Eastin,[4] and receive for yourself our kind salutations—your friend

Andrew Jackson

ALS, THi (10-1042). Published in Bassett, 3:273 (extract).
1. See above.
2. Coffee forwarded AJ $500 on January 29, which AJ, in accordance with his pledge, repaid in April with funds received from Winston, Jr. (1782–1839), formerly of Davidson County and an Alabama legislator at the time, who had purchased AJ's Big Spring plantation in Franklin (now Colbert) County, Alabama, partly on credit in 1822.
3. The exact nature of AJ's "information" regarding deals to carry the presidential election has not been established; the source of information may have involved James Buchanan (1791–1868; Dickinson College 1809), who, according to AJ and revelations made during the Carter Beverley affair in mid-1827, visited AJ about this time and relayed the offer of Clay's forces to support him for the presidency should AJ pledge the post of secretary of state to Clay.
4. Mary Ann Eastin (1810–47), daughter of William (1784–1829) and Rachel Donelson Eastin (1791–1822), was Coffee's niece and AJ's grandniece.

From John Holmes Overton

Monroe, Jany. 7th 1825.
Dear Genl.

From the long and constant friendship you have always shcwn to our family, I trust I may be excused this, in addition to what I once observed to you in relation to the destination of my Brother James.

In pursuance to your views of the preparation required in order to a successfull and honorable prosecution of the Studies at West Point, I have entered him at Cumberland College.[1]

My instructions to Doctor [James] Overton[2] under whose charge I have placed him, are to confine his attention to Mathematics and the Sciences—His progress I hope will equal the most sanguine expectations of his friends. Your kindness in proffering me your influence in procuring him a warrant, I shall rely upon. Knowing that in consequence of the great number of applications, a rejection of some must follow, I must beg of you the favour to loose no time in proferring his name.[3] James G. Overton Born Feb 7. 1809. This with the many and warm attentions you have always shewn us I shall never forget.

In the vote of our state I was much disappointed—My Brother writes me, that yours and the Clay ticket were so clearly ballanced, that 7 or 8 members favourable to Adams had it in their power completely to have given Mr. C. the ascendency—Their intrigues and propositions called for the adoption of the course pursued. I hope the people will now see that their rights are improperly withheld, and in bad hands too.[4]

I shall yet have the pleasure, I hope and trust, of congratulating you, notwithstanding every obstacle, upon your elevation to the chief magistracy of the union. Your triumph over all—all by the people; of which I think there is no doubt, will certainly be regarded by their immediate representatives.

I should feell highly honored and gratified by a letter from you when at leisure. My best respects to Mrs J—& accept the sincere esteem and regard of yr. fr[iend]—

J. H. Overton

ALS, DNA-RG 94 (M688-38). Overton (1797–1883), a Louisiana lawyer, legislator, and later judge, was the son of General Thomas Overton (1753–1824), AJ's second in the 1806 duel with Charles Dickinson.

1. Following his brief period of study at Cumberland College, later the University of Nashville, James G. Overton (1809–28) received an appointment to West Point.

2. James Overton (1785–1865), the son of Waller (1757–1827) and a cousin of John H. and James G., lived in Nashville.

3. In support of James G.'s appointment, AJ forwarded John H.'s letter to Secretary of War John C. Calhoun.

4. Louisiana's electors, chosen by the legislature, gave three votes for AJ, two for Adams. John Holmes's half-brother was Walter Hampden Overton (1788–1845), who had served under AJ during the New Orleans campaign of 1814–15, and at this time represented Rapides Parish in the Louisiana House.

To James Mease

Washington City
January 8h. 1825.

Dear Sir,

Your favor of the 3d instant, by our young friend Mr [Edward Augustus] Rutledge, has just been handed to me, for which and the beautiful medal, accompanying it, I cannot thank you enough.[1]

The two events which the medal designs to commemorate, are justly

regarded as important epochs in the life of Genl [George] Washington—
they will be remembered long as Liberty and virtue have a place in the
world. Both the surrender of his sword to Congress at the termination of
the Revolutionary War, and his relinquishment of the Presidency, are im-
perishable monuments of self-conquest, from which future generations
will learn how vain is the fame of the Warrior or the renown of the statesman, when built upon the ruin and subjection of a country, contrasted
with that which establishes its freedom and Independence; the fame of a
Cesar and Bonaparte, with that of a Washington—[2]

I am grateful Sir, that with this tribute of veneration for our illustrious
Washington, you have been pleased to associate your approbation of my
Public services—

With my best wishes for your prosperity believe me Sir, your obliged
& obt sert.

Andrew Jackson

LS in Andrew J. Donelson's hand, PHi (10-1046). Mease (1771–1846; Pennsylvania 1787)
was a Philadelphia physician, scientist, and author.

1. See Mease to AJ, January 3. Rutledge (1802–26), of Nashville, grandson of Edward
Rutledge, a signer of the Declaration of Independence, had been employed by AJ as a trans-
lator in Florida in 1821.

2. Mease had probably sent AJ one of the John Reich medals portraying a bust of Washington (1732–99) in civil dress on the obverse and a pedestal with the U.S. shield on the reverse.
The reverse legend read "Commiss. Resigned: Presidency Relinq." Like Washington, Julius Caesar (102?–44 B.C.) and Napoleon Bonaparte (1769–1821) were noted republican generals, but
Caesar became dictator of Rome, destroying the Roman Republic, and Bonaparte became em-
peror of France, ending the republican experiment that followed the French Revolution.

To *Chandler Price*

Washington City
Janry. 9th. 1825

Dear Sir

your confidential letter of the 5th instant has been recd, and its contents duly noted.[1]

your favored friend will be provided for, (if my influence can prevail) if
the corps is enlarged as the President intimates it should be—But without
this change the Sec of war upon the principles which regulate the appointment and rank of Engineers, will not be enabled to effect his transfer.

There are strong reasons for enlarging the corps, either by a new modi-
fication of the Topographical, or Engineer *proper* part of it; and should
this take place, so far as I can serve Mr [Constant Mathieu] Eakin he
shall be gratified.[2] He supported an excellent charecter at West Point—
and was part of his time there, acting professor of Engineering, from
which circumstance there can be no doubt of his qualifications.

I am gratified to know that you think him worthy of the hand of your daughter.[3]

With regard to the Presidency, My Dear Sir, you must excuse my inability to inform you—I know nothing of the movement of parties, or of the combinations, which are alledged to be in secret caucus. It is true rumours of the kind exist—But it has been my only wish that the dignity and welfare of the nation should be represented on this question, which is certainly the most serious & important one, that can come before the american people. I have always looked upon the office of chief magistrate, as too responsible to be approached with confidence by any one, and certainly too sacred to have an incumbent, who owes his success to any influence, but that which flows from the affections and will of a majority of the people. on these principles, if another be the choice of Congress, I shall cheerfully acquiesce: and upon the same principle should I be elected, I would suppose—and with confidence calculate, that all around the standard of the law would unite, and aid me in the discharge of the arduous duties. An election upon different principles, I would regard as a degradation, and forfeiture of Patriotism & virtue, and if the prominant gentleman you have called to my attention, is seeking a coalition with others, in disregard of this doctrine, I can only say I lament it for the honor of my country. and for myself I would feel ever degraded, was I placed in the office by such corrupt means.[4] With great respect & Esteem, believe me to be your friend

Andrew Jackson

ALS, PHC (10-1051). Price (c1766–1827), a Philadelphia merchant, had been a leading supporter of AJ's presidential candidacy in Pennsylvania.

1. Not found.

2. In his annual message of December 7, 1824, Monroe had recommended enlarging the Army Corps of Engineers to meet requirements for the survey of roads and canals, but Congress failed to enact legislation on the matter (see *Register of Debates*, 18th Cong., 2nd sess., Appendix, p. 5). Price had recommended Eakin (c1794–1869; Military Academy 1817), a lieutenant in the Second Artillery, for a post in the Corps.

3. Price's daughter Elizabeth (b. c1808) married Eakin in 1828.

4. It is not known who the "prominant gentleman" was or whom the alleged "coalition" supported for the presidency.

As Jackson's popular support increased in Pennsylvania in the campaign of 1824, his candidacy finally achieved credibility and with that, his background closer scrutiny. His military career, the foundation of his enormous popularity, had already been probed and evaluated. Now his opponents began to investigate his character hoping to stifle his presidential bid.

In late December 1823, rumors regarding improprieties in the marriage of the Jacksons surfaced in Pennsylvania, and they were shortly repeated in Ohio and in Washington. In sum, the tale was that Jackson had driven off Rachel's husband Lewis Robards (1758–1814) and had lived with her several years before she and Robards were divorced. The anti-Jacksonians threatened to go into print with the account, as Jackson had heard and discussed in the letter below, but the threat was not carried out until 1826, when they moved the marriage issue from innuendo to explicit controversy (Eleanor P. C. Lewis to Elizabeth B. Gibson, February 2, 1824, in Patricia Brady, ed., George Washington's Beautiful Nelly: The Letters of Eleanor Parke Custis Lewis to Elizabeth Bordley Gibson, 1794–1851 *[Columbia, S.C., 1991], pp. 144–46).*

To Charles Pendleton Tutt

City W.
Janry 9th. 1825.

Dr. sir

your letter of the 4th & 6th. is Just recd.[1] I thank you for the information communicated I never had a doubt of the honour of some of my political enemies, but that they would attempt to disturb the repose of an innocent female in her declining years is a species of wickedness that I did not suppose would be attempted—

One thing I can assure you whenever my enemies shall think it worth while to investigate my or the charecter of Mrs. J I fear not the result, I as well know how to defend my & her charecter as I have done the rights of my country, whenever it can be traced to a source worthy of notice—I am aware of the plan of my enemies, to endeavour to exite & provoke me—This cannot be done, untill calm reflection, convinces my Judgt that Justice requires attonement of the invaders of Female Charecter

A. Jackson

ALS draft, DLC (33). Published in Bassett, 3:273–74. Tutt (1780–1832) was a Loudoun County, Virginia, planter.
   1. Not found.

From Charles Pendleton Tutt

Locust Hill near Leesburg
Jany. 9th 1825

Dear Sir

I wrote to you on the 6th Inst.[1] in consequence of information communicated to me by a most respectable Gentn. a friend of yours, who particularly advised me to do so, to guard you against the base attempt of your enemies, it was with great reluctance I did so, and nothing but a sense of duty could have induced me to do any thing that would have caused you a moments uneasiness, since then I have seen the Gentn. from Alexa. who made the communication to our mutual friend, and I happy to state to you that it is true such papers are in the hands of an individual in Alexa. for such objects but he is himself uncertain as to the truth of them and is besides afraid to communicate or even to speak about them[2]—so that it does not appear that there will be the vilianous attempt to injure you that I apprehended, at least I hope and believe there will not. it would be well however for your friends to keep a sharp look out, without their even intimating the least knowledge of the circumstance—I do not know when I was more irritated than when the circumstance was communicated to me. the very great regard and most exalted opinion I have ever entertained for Mrs. Jackson contributed to increase my disgust at the base attempt.

I hope in the course of a few weeks to have the pleasure of introducing to you & Mrs. Jackson my two oldest daughters[3]—they are very impatient to visit Washington, and are quite as anxious about your success as I am myself. be pleased to remember me most kindly to Mrs. Jackson and believe me to be with great respect Yr. friend & most obt. Servt

Chas. Pen. Tutt

ALS, DLC (33). Published in Bassett, 3:274 (extract). Locust Hill was Tutt's Virginia plantation.
1. Letter not found.
2. The papers probably related to the investigation into the Jacksons' marriage.
3. Ann Mason Tutt (1807–73) and Eliza Pendleton Tutt.

To John Overton

City of Washington
Janry 10th. 1825

Dear Sir

your letter of the 22nd ult came duly to hand,[1] and I have delayed answering, untill I supposed it would meet you at Nashville on your return from Memphis. I thank you for the information relating to my farm, it is the first I have recd since I left it, altho I instructed [Benjamin P.] Parsons[2] to write me often, I have not recd a line from him—I am sure you are right in exposing to sale the [John Hamlin] *Camp place,* to meet the debts against your deceased brothers estate;[3] altho, I think ten dollars pr acre very low—still, if no more can be obtained, better at that price than to have, under execution, to meet a greater sacrafice—nothing so injurious as debt hanging over a dead mans estate—therefore I think you are right in preparing to meet it promptly—was I free from my political enthralment, I would endeavour to buy it—but this I am not, and when I get clear it is uncertain how my pecuniary means may, be—as my expence here is great.

I have requested Genl Call to attend to your request, by waiting on Mr [Stephen] Pleasonton & enquire whether he has answered Mr [Henry]

Crabbs letter respecting the security of Capt [Richard Ivy] Ea[s]ter but recollecting the old adage, that when you want business well done to attend to it yourself—I happened to meet with Mr Pleasonton and named the subject—he replied that it was his intention that the securities should be exonerated; and to that effect he would write Mr Crabb—when you receive this, if you apply to Mr Crabb, he will inform you, as I suppose, that he has recd the letter from Mr Pleasonton & the securities are to be exonerated.[4]

On the subject of the *Presidential election* I can only say, that you will find that I have not, nor will I, depart from that calm deliberate rule I have prescribed to myself—I will not, have not, in the least interfered—I would feel myself degraded to be placed into that office but by the free unsolicited voice of the people—Intrigue may stalk around me, but it cannot move me from my purpose—nor slander irritate me for the *present*—I hope you know, when I mature my course, I am unmoveable.

The Tugg of war, as you say, is to come, and on yesterday I was advised by a friend, if I do succeed, it will be in opposition to all the aristocratical influence here—meaning as I understand him, a coalition of all the influencial interests of the Cabinet—with the exception of Mr [John Caldwell] Calhoun, who is suspected by some, but not by me[5]—but the combination, if one exists, must develope itself in the end to the people, and I envy not the man who may climb into the Presidential chair in any other way, but by the free suffrage of the people; to me it would be gratefull to return to the Hermitage in March next—*The great whore of babylon being prostrated, by the fall of the caucus,*[6] the liberty of our country is safe, & will be perpetuated, and I have the proud consolation to believe, that my name aided in its downfall; and if another is preferred, I have this consolation, that by the voice of a majority of the people, my pretensions have been preferred—hence then my friend, I have no cause but that of rejoicing; should another be preferred by Congress, as it will affo[rd m]e honourable retirement to the pe[aceful] walks of private life—there is nothing [that] can draw me from that composure, and [ele]vation of charecter, that I have prescribed the rule of my conduct.

Mrs. J. presents to you and Mrs. O.[7] & family her best respects—receive & present mine to your lady & family—your friend.

Andrew Jackson

ALS, THi (10-1062). Published in *THQ*, 6(1947):169–71. John Overton (1766–1833), AJ's longtime friend, was a Davidson County lawyer and former judge of the Tennessee Supreme Court. In 1827 he was named chairman of the Jackson Nashville Committee.
    1. Not found.
    2. Person, who had served with John Coffee's mounted gunmen during the 1814–15 Gulf campaign, was overseer at the Hermitage, 1823–26.
    3. On October 9, 1824, Overton had advertised for sale his brother Thomas's planta-

tion on the Cumberland River about a mile and a half from the Hermitage, a farm Thomas had bought from Camp (1783–1829), a physician and state legislator, in 1817 (*Nashville Republican,* October 9, 1824).

4. Overton had apparently asked AJ to check with Pleasonton (d. 1855), auditor in the treasury department, about the query from Crabb (1793–1827), United States attorney for the Western District of Tennessee, concerning the deficit accounts of Easter (d. 1825), a former AJ aide and clerk in Overton's law office, for whom he and AJ served as sureties. As AJ predicted, the treasury department released their bonds on June 20 (see papers in the case, *U.S. v. John Overton and Andrew Jackson,* May 27, 1824).

5. Calhoun (1782–1850; Yale 1804), Monroe's secretary of war, had withdrawn from the presidential race in February 1824, becoming instead the victorious vice-presidential candidate. AJ's friend has not been identified.

6. AJ was comparing William H. Crawford, the caucus nominee, to "the great whore that sitteth upon many waters" of Revelation, chapter 17.

7. Mary McConnell White (1782–1862), whom Overton had married in 1820, was the sister of Hugh L. White and widow of Francis May,

To William Berkeley Lewis

City of Washington Janry 11th. 1825

Dear Major

your letter of the 20th. ult has been recd.[1] & its contents duly noted. The course, you know, which I have chaulked out for myself prevents me from a personal knowledge of any intrigues, or combination, if they exist; and the only source of information I have is through my friends, who will not be let into others secretes. It was stated to me yesterday, that if I was elected, it would be against the whole Cabinet influence, combined with that of the speaker. If this is true, and success should be mine it is the greater triumph of principle over intrigue and management. Whether there is any truth in this rumor I know not, and if there is, I would suppose that Mr Calhoun is not in the combination—Let things terminate as it may nothing will induce me to depart from that course I have adopted— If I go into the office it shall be by the unsolicited will of the people, & I shall not envy the man who gets there in any other way.

We are in tollerable health—present us to your family affectionately & believe me to be your friend

Andrew Jackson

ALS, NNPM (10-1069). Lewis (1784–1866), a longtime friend who had actively promoted AJ's presidential candidacy in 1823–24, became a member of the Nashville Committee in the 1828 campaign and later a member of the "Kitchen Cabinet." In 1829 AJ appointed him second auditor of the treasury.

1. Not found.

Account with the Franklin House Hotel, Washington

Genl. Jackson & Lady, 4 Horses & 3 Servts.
To John Gadsby, Jr   Dr.
Jany. 1825
17th.   To 1 Weeks Board &c $30.00
                        To   Do.   Do.   3 Servants   15.00
                        To   Do.   Do.   Livery of 4 Horses   16.00
                        To   Do.   Club   11.71
                                                                      $72.71

Genl Jackson $94.25
Mr Donelson   30.29
Extra dinner   53.00
                         $177.54

Received payment
Janry 1825 Club
11th.   To 8 Bot Porter 2.00 Pint Whiskey 50 $2.50
             To 3 Bot. Wine   7.50
             To 2 Extra Dinners in Private Parlour   2.50
14   To 3 Bot. Wager Wine   9.00
             To 2 Bot. Claret 3.00 Segars 25   3.25
             To Pint Brandy 50 Pint Whiskey 50   1.00
             To Bot. Champaigne   3.00
             To 3 Extra Dinners to P. Parlour   3.75
             To 1 Extra Supper   1.50
15   To 3 Bot. Porter 75 Extra Supper.50   1.25
16   To 2 Bot. Porter 50   .50
17   to 1 Do. 25— Segars 12   .37
                                                                     $35.12
                                    Club   11.71
Recd. Payt. For Jno. Gadsby, Jr P. Brady

ADS, DLC (10-1067). The Franklin House Hotel, located at the northeast corner of Pennsylvania Avenue and 21st Street and at which the Jacksons resided during the Second Session of the Eighteenth Congress, had formerly been owned and operated by William O'Neale, father of Margaret (Peggy) Timberlake, later Eaton's wife. In 1823, when O'Neale was in severe financial straits, Eaton bought the property, and sold it to John Gadsby about a year later.

To William Berkeley Lewis

Janry 21rst 1825
Senate Chamber

Dear Sir

I had the pleasure of receiving your letter of the 5th. instant with its inclosure,[1] it came to hand yesterday; The same information contained in the inclosure, was recd by Major Eaton; and as you have made no request that the inclosure should be returned I have burned it—There are many rumors of combinations, union of interests, &c &c in circulation here—whether well or ill founded, I cannot say—

If these rumors are true if I am elected it must be in opposition to the whole influence of the Cabinet officers—and if this be true, if preferred by the people & those governed by their voices, the more honourable to me & to the nation—and if another should be preferred, on any other ground than the will of the people I envy them not—and will with great pleasure retire to my Hermitage, & by so doing will maintain those principles, which I have allways acted upon I therefore at present can give you no information with regard to the result of the election of President, one thing you will believe, that I will have no agency in unions, combinations or intrigue to get there.

I thank you for the information regarding my little ward A. J. Hutchings and have to say that I wish him under the charge of some good man who will controll him—The Revd. Mr. [Allan Ditchfield] Campble was to have placed him, if possible, under the charge of Mr. [Philip] Lindsley and in his family if possible.[2] If Mr Campbell cannot get him with Mr Lindsley—I wish him placed with some person who will controll him—I pray you to attend to this, and have placed under the charge of some good man—I am compelled to close this letter. Present Mrs. J. to the Ladies and accept our best wishes adieu

Andrew Jackson

ALS, NN (10-1078). Published in *NYPLB,* 4(1900):196–97.

1. Not found.

2. Hutchings was in school in Nashville. Campbell (1791–1861; Pennsylvania) was pastor of the First Presbyterian Church in Nashville. Lindsley (1786–1855; Princeton 1804) was president of Cumberland College, having assumed that post in January.

To John Coffee

Washington City
Janry 23rd. 1825

Dear Genl

Having a respite from company this evening owing to a snow storm gives me a little leisure to convert to contemplation & friendship, I therefore employ the leisure thus afforded to write you. It is surely pleasant after a continued bustle for weeks that a calm should present itself. It would be still more pleasant, if the rational mind could pass these scenes in review and approve them—This is not my case, for altho there is party after party Mrs. J. & myself do not attend them—except the 8th. and Mrs. Monroes drawing room we have not parti[ci]pated[1]—These were anough—it was easily to discover that there was nothing but shew—nothing of pure principles of friendship in these crowds—hypocrisy and hollow heartedness predominates in this great city—from this picture, I would make many exceptions—but when applied to the great mass of this mixed assemblage it is true. How often does my thoughts lead me back to the Hermitage there in private life surrounded with a few friends, would be a paradise, compared to the best situation here; and if once more there it would take a writ of habeas corpus to remove me into public life again—situated as I am, patience & fortitude must be exercised, and the will of providence cheerfully submitted to. you see I am still in the habit of ascribing the lott of man to the will of an allruling providence—and should I be brought into the Presidential chair it must be by his influence counteracting the intrigue of men, and the union of interests here—If rumour is to be creditted I have all the influence of the Executive Cabinet—except Calhoun, and by many (not by me) he is suspected—with this influence combined with Mr Clay, providence alone can counteract—still my friends are confident of success—The people having placed me on high grounds, I have no feelings on the occasion—and pursue my independent course from which I have not, nor will I depart, no influence has, or will be used by me; if I am selected, it will be without promise, without being committed to any one—attempts have been made through friends, which was repulsed at the threshold[2]—from these hints you can draw a picture how things are said to be managed here.

The ladies are all in good health & spirits—but Emily, who has a cold which is common here. but will be able to vissit the theatre tomorrow evening if the weather will permit[3]—Mrs. J spend her time on sundays at church, on thursdays at prayer meetings the ballance of the week in receiving and paying vissits & so much for our time.

In my last I brought to your view, the want of funds, and requested you to forward me five hundred dollars—If you can do this out of A. J. Hutchings funds it will oblige me, and I will be able to have it refunded out of my crop as soon as it is sold at markett[4] —I have to day received a letter from Persons,[5] stating he has delivered 51 one Bales averaging upwards of 500 lb each & the ballance he will soon have ready—he has posponed ginning part of mine to ginn Capt. J[ohn] Donelsons for Mr [John Christmas] McLamore, Mr [Josiah] Nichols having directions to pay his account and some other little debts out of the first sales[6] —I may not be able before the 1rst of March to get a remittance from him—Therefore have made the request of you. five hundred will clear me of the city if permitted to leave it the 4th. of March next—if not I can easily return you the amount—I wish you therefore to send me $500.

I would be glad to hear from you—we all join in good wishes to you & your family, & to Capt J.[7] & Eliza—your friend

Andrew Jackson

ALS, THi (10-1081). Published in Bassett, 3:274–75 (extract).
1. The Jacksons attended the reception of Elizabeth Kortright Monroe (c1763–1830), the president's wife, on January 1, and a ball in AJ's honor hosted by General Jacob J. Brown (1775–1828), on January 8.
2. AJ may have been alluding to an offer allegedly made through James Buchanan, subsequently the central issue in the correspondence with Carter Beverley, below.
3. January 24 marked the opening night of *Virginius; Or the Liberation of Rome,* plus a farce, *The Village Lawyer,* with the celebrated Thomas Abshire Cooper (1776–1849) in the title role.
4. See above, AJ to Coffee, January 6.
5. Not found.
6. John Donelson (1755–1830), AJ's brother-in-law, owned a plantation near the Hermitage. McLemore (1790–1864) was Donelson's son-in-law. Nichol (1772–1833) was a Nashville merchant and banker.
7. Captain Jack was the familiar name applied to John Donelson (1787–1840).

The name Henry Clay lay at the center of rumors of intrigue and bargaining in Washington in early 1825. The House speaker was no longer in the running for the presidency himself, but he had carried Kentucky, Ohio, and Missouri in the recent contest and presumably had sufficient influence with their delegations to determine the outcome of the vote in the House.

In Kentucky, the legislature sought to implement the popular mandate with resolutions "requesting" its congressional delegation to vote for Jackson, who had come in second in the presidential contest in the state. As a proponent of the measure warned, summarizing one rumor concerning the bargaining for office: "He did not wish the vote of Kentucky to be bartered away, or that Mr. Clay should be Secretary of state to the exclusion of Jackson as president" (Frankfort Argus of Western America, *January 5;* Acts Passed at the First Session of the Thirty-Third General Assembly for the Commonwealth of Kentucky . . . *[Frankfort, 1825], p. 279).*

But negotiations and deals had already gone too far in Washington to change things. On January 9, five days before news of Kentucky's resolutions reached Washington, Clay disclosed to John Quincy Adams that he

was his choice for the succession to Monroe and, on January 24, Clay publicly confirmed that decision, with the result that all the western states that Clay had carried voted for Adams. Adams then named Clay his secretary of state.

For Jackson these acts were in defiance of the popular vote and of legislative instructions. They constituted a "corrupt bargain," one of the key issues in the 1828 presidential campaign.

To William Berkeley Lewis

(private)

Senate Chamber
Janry 24th. 1825

Dear Major

I wrote you in great haste the other day in which I gave you the rumors that were in circulation of intrigue, union, and corruption, about the Pl. election[1]— I am told it has this morning developed itself, & that Mr Clay has come out in the open support of Mr Adams—This, for one, I am pleased with—It shews the want of principle in all concerned—and how easy certain men can abandon principle, unite with political enemies for self agrandisement. I have said I was pleased with this developement; it will give the people a full view of our political weathercocks here, and how little confidence ought to be reposed in the professions of some great political characters. one thing I know, intrigue cannot deprive me of—that is, the high ground the people have placed me on, and the pleasure with which I can return to my Hermitage, carrying with me, my independence & my poli[ti]cal principles, pure & uncontaminated by bargain & sale, or combinations of any kind.

I write under debate &, for the present, bid you farewell—yours

Andrew Jackson

ALS, NN (10-1084). Published in *NYPLB*, 4(1900):197.
   1. See above, AJ to Lewis, January 11.

Rachel Jackson to Mary Purnell Donelson

january the 27—1825

Dear Sister Mary

I received your letter[1] & I have intended writing you from time to time, but knowing Andrew & Emmiley have written. in fact there is not an hour, But some one is Calling to see us & Mrs Call & Emily Do not see them unless they are Dressed but they see me as I am—We are all well Except bad Colds (Mr Jackson has not been very well sinc He Left home) his mind has kept him Down he Longs for retirement at His own fire side I knew from the first how wrong it was, but my advise was nothing—I leave the Event to the Almighty whome I know will Do all things well I feel more Enjoyment than I Expected, I have the privilege of going to Church twice every sunday, prayer meeting twice a week—& if it was not for Mrs [Elizabeth Courts Love] Watson[2] Dear Woman I should [have] no one to go with me, while I am at meeting they are at the theatre and parties & &. The Church I mostly attend is the Presbyterian, the parson (an Excellent man) he puts me in mind of Mr [William] Hume but more warm in preaching.[3] The pious here are not like those at home, they are too much Divided with the world. that is not according to Scripture. you may Depend I have taken a strong ground, I have resisted all those invitations Except the 8th january. We get two and three invitations of a day some times—I think some of our friends might write to us now & then while in this terrible place. Its Enough to ruin any Mans fortune. Every week our board is nearly one Hundred. Mr Jackson set out with two thousand Dollars, all spent & gone, he pays the bord every week,[4] how much better at home would we be, His health is not good, but a Continual uneasy mind keeps him unwell, but I saw from the first it was wrong for him to fatigue Himself with Such an important office, Even if He obtains it, in the End it will profit Him [n]othing. Mr Monroe is going out poor & much Dissattisfyed[5] —We are in the hands of God to do with me what seems best, the Judge of all the Earth will do right—This is a very imperfect letter I think I have I have been interrupted twenty times. Please to remember me to all my friends. Brother Johney has not written Mr J. one line nor William.[6] May the blessing of almighty God rest on you all is my prayer, th[r]ough Christ our Lord whome you serve & whose you are unto perfection and sanctification and believe me your friend and Sister

Rachel Jackson

I rote Sister Betsey and Rachel [Hays] Butlar a letter sometime ago[7] remember their absent friend to Mrs Winston.[8] O how often I think on our neglected Church I have so often prayed for it to bring fourth much fruit. next Sunday week the sacrament will be administered in parson Bakers Church which is the one I attend. We had two fine Sermons yesterday. The text in the afternoon was "remember lots wife" the morning was "how did our Hearts burn within us by the way"[9]

I have received two letters from my Dear Andrew.[10] I pray to god almighty to permit us to meet againe. I feel requited by his love

ALS with revisions in an unknown hand, Mrs. John L. Merritt (mAJs); Copy, DLC (10-1086). Published in Pauline Wilcox Burke, *Emily Donelson of Tennessee* (2 vols.; Richmond, Va., 1941), 1:130–31 (extract). Donelson (1763–1848), wife of John Donelson (1755–1830), was Rachel Jackson's sister-in-law.

    1. Not found.

    2. Watson (c1778–1853), a resident of Washington and longtime acquaintance of the Jacksons, was the widow of James Watson and the sister of Charles J. Love, who had settled near the Hermitage about 1820.

3. The Jacksons attended the Second Presbyterian Church in Washington (now the New York Avenue Presbyterian Church), whose pastor was Daniel Baker (1791–1857; Princeton 1815). Hume (1770–1833), a Nashville Presbyterian minister, had dedicated the Hermitage church in 1824.

4. See above, Account with the Franklin House Hotel, January 11, for an example of the Jacksons' boarding costs.

5. Monroe was still seeking reimbursement from the government of some $50,000 in expenses and interest arising out of his missions to France, 1794–96, and to France, Spain, and England, 1803–1807 (Monroe to AJ, July 3).

6. John Donelson (1755–1830) and his son, William (1795–1864), a Jackson nephew.

7. Letter not found. Betsy was probably Elizabeth Rucker Donelson (1782–1828), widow of Severn Donelson (c1759–1818). Butler (1786–1852), a Jackson niece, was the wife of Robert Butler (1786–1860), AJ's former adjutant general and since May 1824 surveyor of public lands for Florida Territory.

8. Probably Keziah Jones Winston (1760–1826), wife of Captain Anthony Winston (1750–1827), a Jackson neighbor.

9. The sermon texts came from Luke 17:32 and 24:32.

10. Letters not found. Andrew Jackson, Jr. (1808–65), a son of Severn and Elizabeth R. Donelson adopted by the Jacksons, was in Nashville in school.

To William Berkeley Lewis

City of Washington
Janry 29th. 1825

Dear Major

Your letter (6) dated the 13th instant[1] is this moment recd. in answer to mine of the 27th. ult.[2] I thank you kindly for your ideas with respect to my little friend & ward Hutchings, and have wrote Mr Campbell respecting him, and expect from his letter to me, that he will take him to his house to board him.[3] I rejoice to be informed that Doctor Lindsley has taken charge of the college, I hope it will prosper under his guidance & superintendance. Mr. Campbell speaks well of the conduct & demeanor of my son, I know him to be of a very amiable disposition, & capacity, if he will only have proper application, I thank you for the interest you have taken in his welfare & will feel under obligations to you for a continuation of your attention to his conduct.

I have noted the postcript of your letter—The commissioners appointed to select a proper site for a Foundery and Arsenal has reported, but not having seen it, I cannot inform you what it contains—I am told they have recommended a place near Pittsburgh on a stream called Beaver, the Report is in the hands of the printer, and I suppose will in the hands of the members on Monday next.[4] I will forward you a copy.

you will see from the public Journals the stand Mr Clay has taken for Mr Adams—This was such an unexpected course, that self-agrandizement, and corruption, by many are attached to his motives—be what it may, nothing can save him from the condemnation of all highminded and honorable men—

many of his warm admirers, I have heard, condemn him—he is greatly fallen, never to rise again in the estimation of the ame[ri]can nation.[5]

Intrigue, corruption, and sale of public office is the rumor of the day— How humiliating to the american charecter that its high functionaries should so conduct themselves, as to become liable to the imputation of bargain & sale of the constitutional rights of the people. My friends stand firm on the principle that the people have a right to Govern—their will, they will obey; and succeed, or not, they will maintain principle. upon this alone, I would accept the office, and to be brought into it in any other way I should feel myself degraded and could not receve it.

Some weeks since there was a *book* in pamphlet form circulated *secretely* th[r]ough the members of Congress by Mr Adams friends, that might have come from Nashville; From its low abuse, and fulgarity of stile this was inferred.[6] It hurt those who attempted to use it more than myself, and if it was the child of Jessee [Benton], & [Alfred] Balch, *it was still born*—great exertions were made before a copy could be procured, which is preserved for a proper moment.[7]

Say to Miss Mary Ann, that her aunt J. has recd her letter, and thanks her for it, will write her when leisure will permit—Present Mrs. J & myself affectionately to her, your sister, and Miss Mary Claibourne not forgetting our friend Mr [Thomas] Crutcher,[8] & receive for yourself our kind salutations Genl Call & Lady, Mr D & Lady are all well, & desire to be presented to you & your family—your friend in haste

Andrew Jackson

P. S Since I have sat down to write this I have been interrupted twenty times & oblige now to close it hastily—A.J.

ALS, NN (10-1090). Published in *NYPLB,* 4(1900):197–98.
1. Not found. The insertion of the parenthetical numeral 6 may possibly refer to the number of letters Lewis had written AJ since the Jacksons left for Washington.
2. See AJ to Lewis, December 27, 1824 (*Jackson,* 5:459).
3. Letters not found.
4. The commissioners were William McRee (1787–1833; Military Academy 1805), surveyor of public lands for Illinois, Missouri, and Arkansas Territory and a former colonel of engineers; Roswell Lee (c1777–1833), a former infantry lieutenant colonel who was superintendent of the Springfield, Massachusetts, armory; and George Talcott (1786–1862), a brevet major of artillery who later served as army chief of ordnance. They analyzed the costs and advantages of a number of locations for a national armory, including Shoal and Cypress creeks in Alabama and the Harpeth River in Tennessee, two sites in which Jackson and perhaps Lewis as well had been long interested. Their report, *HRDoc 55,* 18th Cong., 2nd sess., Serial 115, generally favored the Big Beaver site near Brighton, Pennsylvania.
5. Clay's January 24 announcement that he would support Adams provoked a severe editorial attack in the *Washington Gazette* of January 27.
6. *A Review of Gen. Jackson's Letters to Mr. Monroe, Dedicated, with Great Respect, to the Members of the House of Representatives of the United States* [n.p, January 1, 1825?]. The anonymous tract cited and criticized AJ's letters of 1816–17 advising Monroe on the makeup of his cabinet. The anonymous author concluded that AJ was unfit for the presidency—he was

"the notorious violator . . . of every law of God and man" and "illiterate and barbarous" with a "manner of expression" that exemplified "vulgarity and rudeness." For the letters discussed, see *Jackson,* 4:68–71, 73–75, 80–82, 102–103.

7. Thomas H. Benton's brother Jesse (d. 1843), who had shot AJ in an 1813 fracas in Nashville, had published an anti-Jackson tract, *An Address to the People of the United States, on the Presidential Election,* in September 1824. AJ's association of Balch (1785–1853; Princeton 1805), a Nashville lawyer and admirer of Martin Van Buren, with Benton, probably resulted from Balch's support of William H. Crawford in the campaign of 1824. Balch shortly reconciled with AJ and served on the Jackson Nashville Committee in the 1828 campaign.

8. Mary Ann Lewis (c1814–66) was William B.'s daughter; Elizabeth Berkeley Lewis (c1795–1877), his sister; and Mary E. T. Claiborne (c1805–52), his niece. Crutcher (1759–1844) was co-executor, along with AJ and Balch, of the estate of William T. Lewis, Balch's and William B.'s father-in-law.

On January 24, Clay announced that he intended to support Adams's election. The next day, "a Member of the House of Representatives, from Pennsylvania," a Jacksonian later identified as George Kremer (1775–1854), wrote a scathing attack on him. He pronounced Clay's act "one of the most disgraceful transactions that ever covered with infamy the Republican Ranks . . . a bargain as can only be equalled by the Famous Burr Conspiracy of 1801." Clay's decision reflected his willingness to support "those who would pay best," or, in other words, those who would assure Clay the state department post. Clay's supporters, Kremer added, had approached the Jacksonians on the matter, only to be scorned, whereupon Clay announced his support for Adams (Philadelphia Columbian Observer, January 28).

Clay exploded when he read the charges. In the January 31 National Intelligencer he branded the Observer's pseudonymous correspondent as "a base and infamous calumniator, a dastard and a liar," and, by implication, threatened a duel if the writer dared "unveil himself." Three days later, on February 3, the congressman from Pennsylvania, referred Clay to the Observer's editor for his identity. At the same time, Kremer declared himself "ready to prove . . . the accuracy of the statements . . . contained in that letter."

On the same day, Clay requested the House to investigate the charges; and on February 4, the House authorized a committee to look into the matter. The report, delivered just before the presidential vote on February 9, proved anticlimactic. When Kremer refused to testify, denying the House's jurisdiction to investigate statements made outside the House and declining to appear as Clay's accuser "upon charges not my own," the committee concluded that it lacked the specific knowledge to investigate further. As Kremer informed the committee, his charges of a corrupt bargain were to be adjudicated not by Congress but by the American people (Register of Debates, 18th Cong., 2nd sess., pp. 440–44, 463–86, 522–25).

To William Berkeley Lewis

Senate Chamber
Febry 7th. 1825

Dr. Major

The Public Journals will have informed you of the letter to the Editor of the Columbian Observed from a member of Congress[1]—the *card* of *Mr. Clay,* and the reply by *another Card,* and the proceedings of the house of Representatives thereon, who have raised a committee, and referred the *ver[b]a* dictum of Mr. Clay to that committee. This is thought here by many a *very novel* proceeding without any parlimentary precedent to warrent it[2]—What the committee may do, I cannot conjecture—But you may prepare to hear a debate, (if a report is made) of great excitement, not very creditable to our country—

It is believed by some, that this course was taken to inveigle Mr Kreamer into an apology—but if I am a Judge of humane nature they have mistook the man—he would suffer Martyrdom before he would decend to such humiliation—I am told he has ample proof of the application of Mr Clay friends to support his statement in his letter. if this is true, the committee will not oppen the case for this proof—should it refuse, there will be no course left Mr K. but to protest vs the proceedings and appeal to the nation

How the Election of President may result is *impossible* to tell. The rumor of Barter of office, intrigue & corruption still afloat, which I hope for the honor of our country there is no truth in. I am in haste your friend

Andrew Jackson

ALS, NN (10-1098). Published in Bassett, 3:275–76.

1. Stephen Simpson (1789–1854) edited the Philadelphia *Columbian Observer,* a pro-Jackson sheet.

2. Because Clay requested an investigation orally, rather than in writing, some members questioned whether the House could act on the matter.

John Henry Eaton to John Overton

Washington 7th. Feby 1825

My dear Sir

In 2 days our troubles begin, if in fact they have not already begun: what may & will be the issue a higher intelligence than mine can alone decide. Things left to move on fair and open principle would leave little or no doubt on the subject; but when intrigue with all its windings & various bearings, is brought to operate on one who practices no deceit, no bargaining, yet keeps the noiseless tenor of his way, apart from every thing like motive, it is indeed difficult to conceive how he can maintain his ground & prospects, when every thing the reverse of his virtues is brought to bear against him. Jackson you well know will not intrigue or trade for any thing in the shape of office, & I love the man, the more that he will not; and this, if he had an honorable & high minded corpse to deal with would be very well; but then when you are informed, what the fact is, that the veriest combination that we have yet seen, is in progress, it is indeed marvelous to conceive how & by what means a man assuming a lofty independent ground can be, or will be maintained; yet do I assure you, that amidst all the embarassments produced by our honesty we yet hope effectually to sustain him; tho how far those hopes be well founded you can infer when you shall perceive the whole ground, & the entire intrigue against us—Congress have been engaged for two days on the subject of making a reference of the dispute which has lately arisen between Mr. Clay & Mr Kremer, the nature of the corruption charged you will learn from the late publications in the papers. Kremer has charged him with going over to Adams, from considerations of self & motive. What has Congress to do with this: nothing I would say: private disputes, are for private adjustment, certainly not for the interference of Congress; their duties are of a different cast of character: besides Mr. Clay proclaimed publickly that if the author would unveil himself, he would demand personal satisfaction (see his card) behold tho when Kremer came forth an appeal is made to the house and the original high ground taken by Clay abandoned

Excitement here is considerable, & is fast spreading every where The bare suspicion of any existing combination to deprive the people of their choice, commenced the excitement; which has been added to by Kremers repeated assertions that he will establish it to the satisfaction of unprejudiced minds and on *quid pro pro* [*quo*] consideration. If so what will the nation say; & what will they not have a right to say concerning such an outrage upon their rights. The committee was yesterday appointed consisting of [Philip Pendleton] Barbour [John] Forsyth [Romulus Mitchell] Saunders [William] McLean (Crawford men) [Daniel] Webster & J[ohn] W. Taylor (Adams) & [Christopher] Rankin a Jackson man.[1] Kremer I understand will, not withstanding prossecute the enquiry Tomorrow he intends addressing a note to the committee demanding to know if they mean to prossecute the enquiry fully and fairly, that if so he will appear forthwith before them with his proofs; if not he will not appear but submit his facts to the American people in his own way

Early in the session, & up to a very recent period no doubt was entertained or spoken of as to any western state with the exception of Ohio: in all calculations made it seemed to be admitted & agreed that 8 of the Western States would be with us Mr [Daniel Pope] Cook of Illinois was open that he could vote in no other way: some Kentucky members now adverse to J. had uniformly declared him their choice next to Clay. Louisiana was not questioned: and [John] Scott had been heard to say that the wishes & wants of his Constituents had been too strongly expressed for him to misconceive or not to regard them:[2] and thus things remained until after this long juggle which Kremer declares he can prove, when Mr. Clay (all along silent) came out for Adams, intending as the current report said to carry with him those 5 States. It was strange & wonderful to all. The wish of the people to the west was at war with such a course. Adams & Jackson before them, there could be no contest; and besides this it was well known that Mr. Clay had imputed to Adams a disposition at Ghent to sacrafice the interest of the west:[3] none therefore could calculate on such a course, and all heard with astonishment the rumor as it spread. But tis even so; Clay is against us, and we are assured and believe it that Kent Ohio & Illinois will go with him—Lousa & Missouri we think will not. From exertions making & to be made we calculate that N. York may remain divided & give no vote even to the end. For Mr. Adams then there will be in N. E. 6 votes. in the west 3.=9. N. York divided is—10 Jackson in the west. 6. Jersey Pensyl Maryland (certainly after the 1st. ballot) & So. Ca—10 While Mr. Crawford will have Dela. Virga. No Ca. & Ga—4[4] Thus the ballot will probably stand for some time until Crawfords folks give way when 3 of his votes going over to Jackson & Delaware to Adams will make the vote A 11 J. 13. If however they obtain as they think they will Loua & Missi the result will be reversed, unless NY still keeps divided Mean time we entertain a hope that Kentucky may change her ground; for there we have 5 fast friends I'm told—Adams 7:[5] one vote over, & the state will be divided & her vote lost. In Lousa. [Edward] Livingston is firm for J. [William Leigh] Brent for A of [Henry Hosford] Gurley some maintain that he will follow the fortunes of his friend Clay;[6] others that he will certainly vote for Jackson: thus you see that all things even at this advanced period of the contest are quite uncertain[7]

I entertain tho a belief from very many slight circumstances & considerations that the design of the matter is to elect yet Crawford. Jackson & Adams friends thus placed in hostility, & Crawford's states standing firm the idea I think is entertained, & will after a while be attempted, to persuade the So & west that J can not succeed, & that by uniting on Crawford will be the only means of defeating Adams; but in this they will fail Jacksons friends will stand immovable & firm, let things end as they may: that is the motto they take; & unless the combination & arrangement has gone to the extent of electing Mr. Adams at once, (contrary to any belief I have on the subject) I think in the end the west will break and come right. News of the confederacy will have reached the interior & every day will be wafting to us the wishes of the people expressed to their representatives. We owe all of our confusion to Clay, had he regarded the wishes of the people, or even stood silent (voting as he pleased) and such surely was the course for one who had himself been a candidate, all things I am persuaded would have moved on harmoniously & well

The old man goes quietly on, undisturbed & unmoved by the agitation around; even enemies speak highly of his course—with great regard

J. H Eaton

My respects to Mrs. Overton if you please

ALS, THi (mAJs).
1. Barbour (1783–1841; William and Mary 1799) was representative from Virginia; Forsyth (1780–1841; Princeton 1799), from Georgia; Saunders (1791–1867), from North Carolina; McLean (1794–1839), from Ohio; Webster, (1782–1852; Dartmouth 1801), from Massachusetts; Taylor (1784–1854; Union 1803), from New York; and Rankin (1788–1826), from Mississippi.
2. Cook (1794–1827) of Illinois and Scott (1785–1861; Princeton 1805) of Missouri cast their states' votes for Adams.
3. Some observers held that Clay had instigated Jonathan Russell's attack on Adams's conduct at the Treaty of Ghent. Russell had asserted that Adams was willing to sacrifice navigation of the Mississippi River to secure New England fisheries. Drawn into the fray, Clay, on November 15, 1822, declined to support Russell's charges or Adams's rebuttal, but noted "some errors" in Adams's pamphlet (*National Intelligencer,* December 17, 1822). The *Washington Gazette* reprinted Clay's letter in its January 27 editorial criticizing Clay's support for Adams.
4. Eaton's estimate of votes for Crawford proved correct.
5. Only four Kentucky representatives voted for Jackson: John Telemachus Johnson (1788–1856), Thomas Patrick Moore (1797–1853), Charles Anderson Wickliffe (1788–1869), and Robert Pryor Henry (1788–1826; Transylvania).
6. Livingston (1764–1836; Princeton 1781) voted for Jackson, but Brent (1784–1848) and Gurley (1788–1833) both voted for Adams.
7. In the final vote for president, Adams carried New York and Maryland in addition to the six New England and five western states.

To John Overton

Washington City
February 10th 1825

Dear Friend
The Election is over, and Mr Adams prevailed on the first Ballot; Mr Clay had influence anough to Barter the votes of Kenty Missouri, Elinoi, Louisiana, which drew after it Ohio, These with Maryland giving way decided the vote—Thus you see here, the voice of the people of the west have been disregarded, and demagogues barter them as sheep in the shambles, for their own views, and personal agrandisement. Mrs. J. has not been well for some days, is now better—we will be on our return home in March, and hope [to] reach the Hermitage in april.
Mrs. J. Joins me in respects to you & Mrs. Overton & believe me yr friend,

Andrew Jackson

ALS, THi (10-1102). Published in *THQ,* 6(1947):171.

The letter below, in response to an invitation from Jackson supporters who were in Washington for the presidential election, became political fodder in the 1828 campaign. Administration presses quoted it to show that Jackson had no notion of a corrupt bargain in early 1825; and Jacksonians, to illustrate his noble sentiments on the election.

To Samuel Swartwout et al.

10*th February*, 1825.

GENTLEMEN:

I have received your polite invitation,[1] in behalf of yourselves and a number of citizens "in this city, from different states in the Union," to partake of a public entertainment tomorrow. For your politeness, pray accept my thanks. I cannot decline, and ought not; yet I cannot refrain from suggesting to you and my friends the propriety, perhaps necessity, of forbearing to confer upon me, at this moment, any such prominent mark of your regard. You cannot, I am persuaded, mistake my meaning. A decision of a matter, about which much public feeling and concern has been manifest, very lately has taken place. Any evidence of kindness and regard, such as you propose, might, by many, be viewed as conveying with it exception, murmuring, and feelings of complaint; which I sincerely hope belong not to any of my friends. I would, therefore, beg leave to suggest to you, that, on reflection, you may deem it proper to forbear any course to which, possibly, exception might be taken.

Please to accept my thanks, and tender them to the gentlemen respectively.

ANDREW JACKSON.

Printed, Washington *National Intelligencer*, Feb 12 (mAJs), *Niles' Register*, Feb 19 (10-1104), and other newspapers. Swartwout (1783–1856), from New York, had been acquainted with AJ since the Aaron Burr trial in 1807; in 1829, Jackson appointed him collector of the port of New York.
1. See Samuel Swartwout et al. to AJ, February 10.

To William Berkeley Lewis

City of Washington
Fbry 14th. 1825

Dear Major

I am informed this day by Colo. R[ichard] M[entor] Johnston of the Senate[1] that Mr Clay has been offerred the office of Sec of State, and that he will accept it Mr Clay told Colo. J the above—so you see the *Judas* of the West has closed the contract and will receive the thirty pieces of silver—his end will be the same. was there ever witnessed such a bare faced corruption in any country before—The *Senate,* (if this Nomination is sent to it) will do its duty—No imputation will be left at its door.[2] we will soon be with you, farewell.

Andrew Jackson

ALS, NHi (10-1110); Photocopy of ALS and Copy, DLC (72, 10-1113); Facsimile of ALS, Parton 3:72 (10-1112). Published in Bassett, 3:276.

1. Johnson (1780–1850), later vice-president under Martin Van Buren, was from Kentucky.

2. On March 5, Adams sent Clay's nomination as secretary of state to the Senate, and the Senate confirmed two days later, with AJ one of fourteen senators opposing.

From John Pemberton

Philada. Feby—15—1825

Dear General,

I have not language to express to you, the deep sorrow, and mortification I feel in the result of the late Election, by the Representatives of the People (falsely so styled) in their choice of a President of the US. The *west,* surely will not, through their partiality for an Individual, protect those men they have sent to do their *Will.* nor let them go unpunished, for the open insult offered them, and deep injury they have received by their going in known opposition to the Peoples choice! It is ardently to be wished that those Members of Congress, who have voted against the undisputed will of their constituent, may have the finger of scorn, pointed at them wherever they go—so that fear, may hereafter make them do their duty, when Integrity will not—

Louisianeans! Degraded—Ungrateful Men!! to vote against you! you!! who under God, they are indebted to for the possession of their soil! The Protector of the Chastity of their wives, and daughters!! You—who saved them from the brutal lusts of a mercenary soldiery!!! the heart sickens at the thought—and almost makes me believe that gratitude is too noble a virtue to dwell among us.

The Pride of Kentucky (Henry Clay.) like Lucifer has fallen! and still hopes to involve you in the vortex of his ruin! He never can forgive you, for the noble services you have done your Country! nor for being in the way of his towering ambition! You will pardon my telling you we all feel an honest pride, in your dignified conduct, during the late contest for the Presidency; and your subsequent magnanimity has extorted praise, even from those, who would have sacrificed you, to promote their unhallowed ends! So powerful is the upright man, that the most depraved have to make obeisance to him—

I hope you will not think of returning home until you visit us?[1] We want your presence to cheer us up after the cruel blow we have had—that the welcome you will receive, will be in sincerity of heart, I am sure you have no doubt—

When you can spare a moment, it will gratify me to have a line from you, and I hope you will let me know, when we shall have the pleasure of seeing you.

Wishing you as much happiness, as I do for myself I am Dr General most sincerely your friend

John Pemberton

ALS, DLC (33). Pemberton (1783–1847), a Philadelphia merchant, had probably met AJ during Jackson's 1819 visit to the town. In 1829, Jackson appointed him naval officer for Philadelphia.

1. AJ planned to return to Tennessee by way of Baltimore and Philadelphia, but Rachel Jackson's ill health forced a change in his plans.

To Martha A. Mitchell and Sally Anne Arbuckle

Washington City
February 16th. 1825—

Ladies,

I have the honor to acknowledge the receipt of your letter of the 15 instant[1] inclosing the constitution of the Dorcas Society over which you preside. Your exertions in the cause of religion and humanity are highly praiseworthy and, I hope, may meet with proper encouragement and success.

I, with cheerfulness, send you my mite. It is small; but when it is considered that every section of our country has to support its own poor, as well as to meet the various applications for charity, I trust it will be received as an evidence of my willingness to support all charitable institutions as far as my funds will authorise me. Your's very respectfully

Andrew Jackson

LS in Andrew J. Donelson's hand, FrN (10-1118), and address leaf, NN (10-1119). Addressed to the "care of the Revd Danl Baker." Arbuckle (d. 1838), the wife of Washington postal clerk Thomas Arbuckle, and Mitchell headed the Washington Dorcas Society, a women's charitable organization named after the woman "of good works and alms-deeds" healed by the apostle Peter (Acts 9:36–42).

1. Not found.

To *Squire Grant*

(Private)   City of Washington, Febry 18th. 18*[25]*
Dear Sir
   On yesterday your friendly *[letter]* of the 20th. ult was recd.[1] It would aff*[ord Mrs.]* J. & myself much pleasure to meet with you, & if we can make it convenient will see you on our return.[2]
   The Public Journals will have advised you of the result of the Presidential election—Mr. Clay (*like Judas of old*) it is said *sold himself & his influence* to Mr Adams, and carried a majority of the Kentuckians with him, for which (it was predicted) he was to receive the appointment of Sec of State—This office has been offerred to him, and it is said he has agreed to accept it—
   If the citizens of Kentuckey submit to be thus bartered for office for a Demagogue, they may bid farewell to their freedom—our Goverment rests upon virtue, its *[pilla]*rs you see are becoming rotten, and unless repaired by *[the]* virtue of the people, the fair fabric of *[libe]*rty must tumble.
   Mrs. J. Joins me in respects to you & your family and believe me to be yr mo obdt. servt.

Andrew Jackson

ALS, WHi (10-1122). Published in Bassett, 3:276 (extract). Grant (1764–1833), a Campbell County, Kentucky, surveyor and planter, had been one of Jackson's business associates and legal clients in the 1790s. During the 1824 presidential campaign, he ran as a Jackson elector.
   1. Not found.
   2. The Jacksons did travel through Campbell County, Kentucky, on their return from Washington, but it is not known if they visited the Grants.

From *Samuel Swartwout*

New York 18th feb 1825

My dear Sir,
   The very singular reason which Mr. Clay has thought proper to give to Judge [Francis Taliaferro] Brooke of Virginia, in his letter of the 28th. Ult. for the choice he had determined to make amongst the Presidential candidates, has excited more surprize than apprehension in the public mind—[1]
   Upon what grounds of anology Mr. Clay can sustain his objections is not perceived—If we are to Judge of his meaning by his words, he has certainly placed himself in a dilemma, and his character for learning must be

considered in equal danger with his reputation for integrity—To apprehend disaster to our institutions from the same causes which occasioned the overthrow of the ancient Republics, is to suppose the govts. the same and the people of this country as ignorant, oppressed and corrupted as they were—Their overthrow it is well known (as far as history may be credited) was occasioned by the ignorance & slavish oppression of the people and the corruption & profligacy of their rulers. But this is not yet the case with us thank God! Our people are free, are educated, inteligent & happy. The Govt is founded in knoledge & virtue and derives its stability from the representative principle—These did not belong to the Ancients & hence the difference between us & them—Ours is a government of trusts & responsibilities, of equal rights & obligations—And, as all power is derived directly from the people, who are the sovereigns of this country, they will never surrender their liberties, (being free inteligent & virtuous) nor be alarmed for their security by the cries of the Demagogue—

I have been induced to make these remarks from the perusal of Mr. Clays letter published in one of Our journals—The deep solicitude which he seems to feel for the welfare of his country is very interesting & truly remarkable—It appears that he "interogated his conscience as to what he ought to do & that that faithful guide told him how to vote"—It is really a pity that the same scrupulous conscience had not admonished him of his obligations to the constitution, whilst he was plotting the most deadly blow to the liberties of his country that it has ever recd. in the daring & open infraction of the Representative duty—

It is supposed by many that you intend to notice this production—I know not if you do, but if you should, your friends feel persuaded that the same mild, & dignified language will characterize it, which has so conspicuously marked your other productions during the Presidential con troversy—Your dignified deportment & magnanimous submission to the recent outrage, have confirmed the opinions your friends had conceived of your character and drawn from your enemies expressions of admiration & confidence, which nothing but the most exemplary conduct could have elicited—

I have said that many suppose that you intend to notice this production, and many imagine that you design to pass it over in silence—and, I must confess that there is a decided majority of those who entertain the latter opinion—It is really gratifying to your friends to witness the deep feeling that pervades the country upon the subject of the recent usurpation & your conduct under it—Society is filled with conjecture & anxiety—one person wonders whether you intend to hold Mr. Clay personally responsible, & another conjectures you will not whilst all commend the silence with which you have hitherto treated the reports of your enemies—Intrigue & corruption have deprived the people of their President; but neither has been able to deprive the man of the people of his dignity or of the fast hold he has in the affections of 10 millions of freemen—Your gallantry & services to your country, won the hearts of your friends, whilst your temperance & forbearance have subdued your enemies—Your silence & neglect of Henry Clay will mortify him more than volumes of reproaches—His card astonished all parties[2] and he only waits an opportunity of being associated, in controversy, with men of high character to imbezzel himself into decent society again—Every man, excepting his coadjuters and followers, considers him as irrevocably lost—And nothing, I think, would have so great a tendency to reconcile society to his name again & to weaken the moral odium of his disregard of the Representative obligation, as a spirited controversy with a dignified adversary—He has fallen so low that he can never rise again except from personal contact with one greatly above him.

I hope my dear sir that you will consider these sentiments as proceeding from a heart deeply alive to your present situation—I feel the importance of every act you do, however minute, upon the present welfare, perhaps the future destiny of our country—The eyes of the whole union are upon you—The deepest solicitude pervades all ranks of people. Jackson, greater in adversity than in prosperity, is the only man who can rally the Nation & restore the Govt to its primitive purity—The calm, erect & dignified deportment of the truly great, will achieve a thousand times more, than the best told tale or the sharpest satire—

Will you, my dear Sir, pardon me for this long letter and believe that it is penned in the same spirit of affection & attachment with which I shall always remain your obt Sevt.

Saml Swartwout—

ALS copy, TNJ (10-1125). Published in *Proceedings of the American Antiquarian Society,* 31(1921):80–83. Endorsed by Swartwout: "This letter was written to indevour to prevent Genl. Jackson from noticing Mr. Clay's remarks made to Judge Brook. It was not deemed necessary to publish it at the time, altho it may be thought adviseable at some future day to show the immediate cause of the Genls. celebrated reply to it." Contrary to his stated motive, Swartwout immediately published AJ's response (see AJ to Swartwout, February 22, below). Sometime later, after Clay published his address to the voters of his congressional district in late March, Swartwout added the following: "P.S. Mr. Clay in his address to his constituents amongst his other defences charged an understanding and concert between Genl Jackson & myself, on this subject—I therefore state most solemnly that I never conversed with him on the subject while at Washington or elsewhere and that no communication ever took place between us, at any time or place, excepting the above or within."

1. In his letter to Brooke (1763–1851), judge of the Virginia Supreme Court, Clay wrote: "As a friend of liberty and to the permanence of our institutions, I cannot consent, in this early stage of their existence, by contributing to the election of a military chieftain, to give the strongest guarranty that this Republic will march in the fatal road which has conducted every other Republic to ruin" (*Richmond Enquirer,* February 8).

2. A reference to Clay's note regarding Kremer in the *National Intelligencer* of January 31.

Account with the Franklin House Hotel, Washington

Genl. Jackson

To John Gadsby, Jr. Dr.
18th. Feb— 1825.

To 2 Bowls Apple toddy	$4.00
To 2 Do. Punch	4.00
To 8 Bot. Wine	20.00
To 2 pints Brandy	1.00
To 2 Do. Whiskey	1.00
To 3 Bot. Cider	0.75
To 4 Bot. Champaigne	12.00
To 2 Bot. W. Wine	6.00
To 23 Dinners etc etc	<u>46.00</u>
Amt. brot. forwd	$94.75

Deduct for 3 Bot. Wine 7.50
Do. pt. Brandy 0.50   8.50
Do. pt. Whiskey 0.50

—————
$86.25

Recd. payt. for J. Gadsby Jr

Peter Brady

ADS, DLC (33). Published in Bassett, 3:277.

To John Coffee

City of Washington Febry 19th. 1825

Dear Genl

This morning I recd your letter of the 29th. ult.[1] Inclosing me five hundred dollars in united state notes for which I return you my sincere thanks—This being out of the funds of my little ward, you will please enter it, so that it will bear Interest untill I return—I will have it in my power the moment I reach Nashville to return it, as I have recd. from Mr Josiah Nichol information of my Cotton safe arival at Orleans, and that he will forward a bill on Mr Jones of Baltimore for $1000—[2]

My situation here was one of great expence, I had anticipated this and brought on with me $2300, This with my pay, I did suppose would be sufficient; In this I was mistaken, and my fear that Doctor [John Robertson] Bedford would not remit to Mr Josiah Nichol in time to reach me by the rise of Congress I addressed you, and am now in a situation to get home with oeconomy without want.[3]

Mr Donelson has wrote you at my request to day, and to his letter I refer you, for the result of the Presidential election.[4] I weep for the liberty of my country when I see at this early day of its "successfull experiment," that corruption has been imputed to many members of the House of Representatives, and the rights of the people have been bartered for promises of office, Mr Clay their chief has recd. by way of the fulfilment of the rumored contract with him a tender of the office of sec of state, and it is said he has agreed to accept it. How far the Senate will support his nomination & consumate this corruption a few days will determine—There are many of them I am Sure will never do an act to cover themselves with the imputation of favouring such corruption.

Mrs. J. has been & is still unwell,[5] so soon as congress adjourns we will set out for home by the way of Baltimore and Philadelphia—In the mean time we tender to you & family & friends our kindest salutations—your friend

Andrew Jackson

P.S. Clay is dispised here by all good men; Human nature even when depraved will profit by the Treason, and despise the Treator—he is called the Judas of the west, & will receive his 30 peces of silver

ALS, THi (10-1129). Published in Bassett, 3:277–78 (extract).
  1. Not found.
  2. Probably Talbot Jones (c1771–1834), a merchant.
  3. AJ's compensation as senator for the Second and Special Sessions of the Eighteenth Congress was $1,344.
  4. See Andrew J. Donelson to Coffee, February 19 (DLC).
  5. Rachel Jackson was afflicted with a cold and had been bled twice, according to Donelson.

To William Berkeley Lewis

City of Washington Fbry 20th. 1825

Dear Major

you have seen from the public Journals that the rumors of union, & barter for office, between Mr Clays friends & Mr Adams, have been verified by the result of the Presidential election. The information now is, that the contract, so far as Mr Clay is concerned, is fulfilled, by the offer of Mr Adams to Mr Clay of the appointment of Sec of State, which it is said Mr Clay has agreed to accept. I have, as you know, allways thought Mr Adams to be an honest, virtuous man, and had he spurned from him those men who have abandoned those principles they have allways advocated, (that the people have a right to govern) and that their will should be allways obayed by their constituents; I should still have viewed him an honest man; and that the rumors of bargain and sale was unknown to him

But when we see the predictions verified on the result of the Presidential election—when we behold two men political enemies, and as differrent in political sentiments as any men can be, so suddenly unite, there must be some unseen cause to produce this political phenomona—This cause is developed by applying the rumors before the election, to the result of that election, and to the tendering of, and the acceptance of the office of Sec of State by Mr Clay. These are facts that will confirm every unbiased mind, that there must have been, & were a secrete understanding between Mr Adams & Mr Clay of and concerning these scenes of corruption, that has occasioned Mr Clay to abandon the will, and wishes of the people of the west, and to form the coalition so extraordiary as the one he has done.

You know my inmost feelings upon the subject of the presidential election—I can reiterate with truth, that if it had not been for the means used, I would be happy at the result, as it gives me the liberty, when I choose, to retire once more to my peacefull dwelling. But when I reflect that the result has been brought about by the offer to Mr Clay of the Sec of States office and his influence with other members I look forward & shudder for the liberty of my country—If at this early period of the experiment of our Republic, men are found base & corrupt enough to barter the rights of the people for proferred office, what may we not expect from the spread of this corruption hereafter—May we not expect to see not only profer of office, but direct bribery, by an ambitious demagogue, who is guided by no principle but that of self agrandisement. From Mr Clays late conduct, my opinion of him, long ago expressed, is but realised—from his conduct on the Seminole question, I then pronoun[c]ed him a political Gambler[1]—and from his late conduct in the abandonment of all those republican principles which he allways professed, & by which he had obtained the support of the people, and forming such an aliance so unexpectedly, with a man he had denounced before the nation, and all this for the office of Sec of State realises the fact of his P gambling. would it be too much to infer that his ambition might induce him to reach the Executive chair by open & direct bribery, as well as the barter of office—These are my reflections, and I cannot from the scenes lately, & now acting here, refrain from shuddering for the liberty of my country. There is no other correctiv of these abuses, but the suffrages of the people; if they apply calmly, & Judiciously, this corrective, they may preserve & perpetuate the liberty of our happy country—If they do not, in less than 25 years, we will become the slaves, not of a "military chieftain," but of such ambitious demagogues as Henry Clay. It is then necessary that the people should look to it now, as corruption is in the bud, before it extends itself farther amonghst the representatives in congress. Mrs. J. has been unwell for some weeks but is now mending, and I hope will be able to travel as soon as the Senate rises, which I cannot leave untill it does, as I have a hope, there is a redeeming spirit in the virtue of the Senate, which may prevent the consumation of this corruption, of barter for office

We will be with you I hope shortly in the mean time present us affectionately to your family & receive for yourself our best wishes adieu

Andrew Jackson

(Private)

P.S. On the result of the election, a number of my friends requested that I should not answer that I would, or would not, suffer my name again to be run as president[2]—nor to say whether I would resign or not my seat in the senate—It is said that Mr Adams has agreed with Clay to give him all the support he can, to keep up his name in the west. I have, *now,* no doubt, but I have had opposed to me all the influence of the Cabinet, except Calhoune—would it not be well that the papers of Nashville & the whole State should speak out, with moderate but firm disapprobation of this corruption—to give a proper tone to the people & to draw their attention to the subject—When I see you I have much to say—There is more corruption here than I anticipated; and, as you know I thought there was anough of it.

A.J.

ALS, NN (10-1134). Published in Parton, 3:73–75.
1. Clay had strongly criticized AJ's conduct of the Seminole campaign before the House of Representatives on January 20, 1819. For AJ's response then to Clay's remarks, see *Jackson,* 4:268–70.
2. On February 25, the day after the arrival of the news of Adams's election, the *Nashville Gazette* proclaimed AJ's candidacy for the presidency in 1828, but AJ himself continued to hold to the maxim that the presidency should be neither sought nor declined.

To George Wilson

City of Washington, Febry 20th. 1825.

Dear Sir

The public journals will have given you the result of the presidential election, and how it was brought about by the Union of Clay and his friends with Mr. Adams—The predictions in part have been fulfilled, Mr. Clay, it is said, has been offerred the office of Sec of State, and it is also said he has agreed to accept it. This to my mind is the most open daring corruption that has ever shown itself under our government, and if not checked by the peopl[e], will lead to open direct bribery in less than twenty years—for what is this barter of office for votes but bribery—Mr Clay is prostrate here in the minds of all honest & honourable men— What will be his fate in Kentucky I cannot say, but Mr. [George Minos] Bibb who is here, says this act will prostrate him in Kentucky.[1]

I recd your letter[2] and disposed of it as you had directed, I regret I had not it in my power to serve you, it will give me pleasure when an occasion occurs. I can do nothing with your claim, had Mr. Dinker sent on his deposition I have no doubt but I could have got the account settled; I could have obtained a refferrence to the atto. Genl. Had your statement or memorial been deposed to, I could have obtained a reference and the atto. Genls opinion; as it is, I will bring on your letter & memorial, and you can have them aranged, and transmitted in the recess, and have the opinion of the atto. genl on it.[3]

Mrs. J. has been unwell for about 3 weeks She is recovering, and I hope will be able to travel so soon as the Senate can rise. I cannot leave it untill it rises, for in the Virtue of the Senate I have great hopes will prevent the consummation of those corrupt bargains for office.

Mrs. J. Joins me in respects to you, your amiable daughter & family, & believe me sincerely your friend

Andrew Jackson

ALS, THi (10-1139). Published in Heiskell, 1:608–609. Wilson (1778–1848) was editor of the *Nashville Gazette,* a Jackson paper.
1. Bibb (1776–1859; Princeton 1792), a lawyer, former judge and United States senator, was at this time a leader of the "new court" faction in Kentucky.
2. Not found.
3. Neither Dinker, possibly Drucker, nor the nature of Wilson's account has been identified.

From Robert Pryor Henry et al.

House of Representatives
February 22th 1825

Sir,
In a late number of the Argus of Western America, you are reported to have said, at Lexington on your way to this city, in November last[1] upon the authority of Mr. William T. Willis that "forty thousand muskets would be required, to rectify the politics of Kentucky."[2] The undersigned, having supported your election, in the House of Representatives; and believing you incapable of making the remark imputed to you, deem it their duty to afford you an opportunity of contradicting the report, if untrue, for the satisfaction of all, who, at any stage of the Presidential contest, took an interest in your success.

With sentiments of respect, we are Sir, your most obedient serts.

Robt. P. Henry
T. P. Moore
J T Johnson
C A Wickliffe

ALS in Henry's hand, also signed by others, DLC (33). Published in Lexington *Kentucky Gazette*, March 10, and other newspapers.
   1. The *Argus* of February 9 attributed the comments to November 16 or 17, 1824.
   2. Willis (c1796–1847), a lawyer, represented Green County in the 1824 Kentucky legislature.

To Robert Pryor Henry et.al.

22. Feby 1825

Your letter of to day[1] is recvd, and has been read with something of surprise. I did not use the expression which you quote, "that forty thousand muskets would be required to rectify the politicks of Kentucky," nor any expression like it. my stay at Lexington was a short one, and during the time I have no recollection of speaking at all about the local affairs of your State; it is a subject about which I should not feel myself at all at liberty to interfere. As to Mr. Wm. T. Willis I have no recollection of him, nor do I believe I ever had an acquaintance with him: it is scarcely possible, that sharing as I did the politeness & hospitality of the citizens of Lexington I should venture to insult them by so unkind a remark I did not: it bears no resemblance to me; for if so then indeed might I be considered a "military chieftain" as has been charged—

A Jackson

Copy in John H. Eaton's hand, DLC (33). Published in Lexington *Kentucky Gazette*, March 10, and other newspapers.
   1. See above.

To Samuel Swartwout

Washington City Fbry 22nd 1825

My Dear Sir

I was quite concerned that you left the city so suddenly, as that I was denied the pleasure of seeing & shaking you by the hand. you took with you however my best wishes for your safe arival home. I beg you to present to Mrs. S.[1] my & Mrs. Jackson's affectionate regard.

yesterday I recd your communication adverting to the reasons and defence presented by Mr Clay to Judge Brooke why duty & reflection imposed upon him the necessity of standing in opposition to me, because of my being as he is pleased to style me, "a Military Chieftain."[2] I had before seen the letter; first when it appeared, I did entertain the opinion, that perhaps some notice of it might be necessary, for the reason that the expression seemed to carry with it more the appearance of personality than any thing else; and could the opinion be at all entertained, that it could meet the object, which doubtless was intended, to prejudice me in the estimation of my countrymen, I might yet consider some notice of it necessary: such a belief however I cannot entertain, without insulting the generous testimonial, with which by ninety nine electors of the people I have been honoured.

I am well aware that this term "Military Chieftain" has for some time past been a cant phrase with Mr Clay & certain of his retainers; but the vote with which by the people I have been honored, is anough to satisfy me, that the prejudice by them, sought to be produced availed but little. This is sufficient for me. I entertain a deep and heartfelt gratitude to my country, for the confidence & regard she has manifested towards me, leaving to prejudiced minds whatever they can make of the epithet "Military Chieftain."

It is for an ingenuity stronger than mine to conceive what idea was intended to be convayed by the term. It is very true, that early in life, even in the days of my boyhood, I contributed my mite to shake off the yoke of tyranny, and to build up the fabrick of free goverment; and when lately our country was involved in war, bearing then the commission of Major Genl of Militia in Tennessee, I made an appeal to the patriotism of the western citizens, when 3000 of them went with me to the field, to support her Eagles.[3] If this can constitute me a "Military Chieftain" I am one. Aided by the patriotism of the western people, and an indulgent providence, it was my good fortune to protect our frontier border from the savages, & successfully to defend an important & vulnerable point of our Union. Our lives were risked, privations endured—sacrafices made, &, if Mr Clay pleases, martial law declared, not with any view of personal agrandisement, but for the preservation of all and every thing that was valuable, the honor safety & glory of our country. Does this constitute a Military Chieftain? and are all our brave men in war, who go forth to defend their rights, & the rights of their country to be termed Military chieftains, and therefore denounced? if so, the tendency of such a doctrine may be, to arrest the ardor of usefull and brave men, in future times of need & peril: with me it shall make no differrence; for my country at war, I would aid assist & defend her rights, let the consequence to myself be what they might. I have as you very well know, by some of the designing politicians of this country, been charged with taking bold & high handed measures; but as they were not designed for any benefit to myself I should under similar circumstances not refrain from a course equally bold: that man who in times of difficulty & danger shall halt at any course, necessary to maintain the rights and priviledges and independence of the country, is unsuited to authority; and if these opinions & sentiments shall entitle me to the name & character of a Military Chieftain I am content so to be considered, satisfied too for Mr. Clay if he chooses, to represent to the citizens of the west, that as the reason why in his opinion I meritted not his & their confidence.

Mr Clay never yet has risked himself for his country—sacraficed his repose, or made an effort to repel an invading foe; of course his "conscience" assured him that it was altogether wrong in any other man to lead his countrymen to battle & victory. He who fights, and fights successfully must according to his standard be held up as a Military chieftain: even Washington could he again appear among us might be so considered, because he dared to be a virtuous and successfull soldier, an honest statesman & a correct man. It is only when overtaken by disaster & defeat, that any man is to be considered a safe politician & correct statesman.

Defeat might to be sure have brought with it one benefit, it might have enabled me to escape the notice and animadversions of Mr Clay but considering that by an opposite result, my country has been somewhat benefitted, I rather prefer it, even with the opprobrium & censure which he seems disposed to extend. To him thank god I am in no wise responsible, there is a purer tribunal to which in preferrence I would refer myself—to the Judgment of an enlightened patriotic & uncorrupted people—to that tribunal I would rather appeal whence is derived whatever reputation either he or I are possessed of. By a refferrence there, it will be ascertained that I did not solicit the office of president, it was the frank & flattering call of the freemen of this country, not mine, which placed my name before the nation; when they failed in their colleges to make a choice, no one beheld me seeking thro art or management to entice any Representative in Congress from a conscientious responsibility to his own, or the wishes of his constituents. No midnight taper burnt by me; no secret conclaves were held, or cabals entered into, to pursuade any to a violation of pledges given, or of instructions received. By me no plans were concerted to impair the pure principles of our Republican institutions, or to prostrate that fundamental one which maintains the supremacy of the peoples will; on the contrary, having never in any manner either before the people or Congress in the slightest manner interfered with the question, my conscience stands void of offence, & will go quietly with me, heedless of the insinuations of any, who thro management may seek an influence, not sanctioned by merit.

Demagogues I am persuaded have in times past, done more injury to the cause of freedom & the rights of man, than ever did a Military Chieftain; and in our country, at least in times of peace, should be much more feared. I have seen something of this in my march thro life, and have seen some men too, making the boldest professions, who were more influenced by selfish views & considerations, than ever they were by any workings of an honest conscience.

I became a soldier for the good of my country: dificulties met me at every step; I thank god that it was my good fortune to surmount them

The war over & peace restored I sought to retire again to my farm, & to private life, where but for the call made by my country to the Senate I should contentedly have remained. I never yet have been a hanger on upon office & power, or was willing to hold any post, longer than I could be usefull to my country, not myself, and I trust I never shall. If this makes me so, I am a "Military Chieftain."

I had intended vissiting Philadelphia and hoped probably I again might have seen you in person but the health of Mrs. Jackson may prevent me—should I not have the pleasure of seeing you rest assured of my sincere friendship & esteem. I am very respectfully yr mo. obdt. servt.

Andrew Jackson

ALS, TNJ (10-1148). Published in the *New York National Advocate,* March 4, and in other newspapers, and in Bassett, 3:278–80.
1. Alice Ann Swartwout, née Cooper (1789–1874).
2. See above, Swartwout to AJ, February 18.
3. AJ was referring to his service as general in the Tennessee militia and in the U.S. Army.

To William Berkeley Lewis

Washington City Febry 27th. 1825

Dr. Major
The enclosed paper will shew how things are going on here.[1] [Joseph] Gales & [William Winston] Seaton before their election by the house, had pledged themselves, as I am informed by two members, that their colums should be open to all[2]—from the stand taken, after Mr Kreamers defence was in type, I have no doubt but in effect, gag laws & sedition laws, will be practically enforced[3]—I am told Mr Kreamers expose is strong, & will carry conviction every where of the corruption of Clay & others

I enclose you the paper that you may have it replublished in such papers in Nashville as you may deem best.[4]

I will leave here in a few days Mrs J has been quite unwell but is recovering with good wishes to you & family adieu

Andrew Jackson

ALS, NNPM (10-1187).
1. The enclosure was almost certainly an editorial, "The Liberty of the Press," from the *Washington Gazette,* February 26, accusing the *National Intelligencer* of partiality in refusing to publish Kremer's address to his constituents on the "corrupt bargain" charges against Clay.
2. Gales (1786–1860) and Seaton (1785–1866), editors of the *Intelligencer,* had been elected printers to the House of Representatives on February 21.
3. Kremer had submitted his letter to the *Intelligencer,* presumably understanding that it would be published; but the paper's editors withdrew it, explaining, after it was set in type, that it was inappropriate for their columns. On February 28, the *Intelligencer* again refused to publish it, and, at that time, the pro-Jackson *Gazette* printed the address.
4. On March 19, the *Nashville Republican* republished the "Liberty" essay.

On February 12, the mixed-blood Creek chief William McIntosh (c1775–1825) and about fifty lesser chiefs and warriors signed the Treaty of Indian Springs. By that accord, they ceded their remaining lands in Georgia to the United States. Within the nation, there was considerable opposition to the cession. Creek agent John Crowell (1780–1846) had warned Washington that the signers were mostly of low rank and represented only a fraction of the Creek towns, but the Senate ratified the treaty with little debate and President Adams signed it on March 7.

Shortly after ratification, some Creeks protested the treaty, but plans for an early survey of the cession moved smoothly in Georgia until the early morning of April 30, when nearly 200 Creek warriors, acting in accordance with a tribal law that threatened death to any chief who signed away Creek lands without the approval of the nation, killed McIntosh and set fire to his house. The remainder of McIntosh's party appealed for protection to Georgia governor George Michael Troup (1708–1856; Princeton 1797), who in turn asked Washington to intervene. On May 18, the secretary of war ordered General Gaines to Georgia to quell the uprising and dispatched Major Timothy Patrick Andrews (1794–1868), an army paymaster, to investigate Troup's charges that Crowell had incited the Creeks to oppose the treaty.

National attention, initially drawn to the incident by the fame of McIntosh and by alarmist concerns about possible Indian hostilities against whites in Georgia, increased as Gaines and Andrews, accepting Crowell's assessment, came into conflict with Troup, with Gaines and Troup engaging in a bitter public exchange regarding the authority of the national and state governments. In mid-June, newspapers such as the National Journal and National Intelligencer reported on the controversy between Georgia and the administration. At that time, the Washington Gazette published the "Talk of an aged Indian Chief, of the Creek Nation, to the Hero of New Orleans," below, which protested further white appropriation of Creek lands. No other publication of the document has been found nor have any further references to the alleged appeal to Jackson.

From a Creek Chief

[cFebruary–June]

Brother! I take you by the hand—your hand is strong. It slew many red men. I rejoiced in their fall: they were enemies, and the enemies of my people. They displeased the Great Spirit, and he permitted you to destroy them. The stranger who came over the big water fell by the strength of thy arm: they were scattered over the plain like the dead leaves of the forest, by a blast of wind. Their bones whiten on the shore of the great rolling river.

Brother! The red people were very numerous. They covered this land, like the trees of the forest, from the big waters of the east to the great sea, where rests the setting sun. The white people came—they drove them from forest to forest, from river to river—the bones of our fathers strewed the path of their wandering.

Brother! You are now strong; we are weak: we melt away like the snow of Spring before the rising sun. Whither must we go now? Must we leave the home of our fathers, and go to a strange land, beyond the great river of the West? That land is dark and desolate—we shall have no pleasure in it. Pleasant are the fields of our youth. We love the woods where our fathers led us to the chase. Their bones lie by the running stream, where we played in the days of our childhood. When we are gone, strangers will dig them up.

Brother! The Great Spirit made us all. You have land enough. Leave us, then, the fields of our youth, and the woods where our fathers led us to the chase. Permit us to remain in peace under the shade of our own trees. Let us watch over the graves of our fathers, by the streams of our childhood.

May the Great Spirit move the heart of our Father the President, that he may open his ear to the voice of his children; for they are sorrowful.

Printed, *Washington Gazette*, June 23, 1825 (mAJs).

To John Coffee

Washington City
March 2nd 1825

My dear Genl

I have just recd your letter of the 9th ult.[1] with the order on Mr George Graham inclosed for one $1000. having sufficient funds to take me home without this, I have burnt the order without presenting it.

For this further mark of your kindness, & liberality, please receive my thanks; under all circumstances I have experienced your friendship, and in none more than the present, and none more highly appreciated.

I will send you to day Mr Kreamers address to his constituents,[2] developing the corruption here, and in a course of reasoning combined with facts, clearly shewing Clays intrigue & corruption, in bringing Mr Adams into office, his recompence the office of Sec. of State, which has been offered and accepted by Mr Clay—whether there is as much virtue & independence in the senate to arrest these corrupt proceedings a few days will determine.

We shall leave here in a few days for home taking Baltimore in our way—the road direct to Frederick Town being impassible. Mrs. J has been very unwell, but is recovering & I hope will be able to travel so soon as I am able to leave here; which I am determined not to do, untill I see the cabinett presented to the senate, & acted on. Mr Clay is prostrate in the opinion of all honourable & honest men, how his constituents, and the whole people of Kentucky may feel, on this occasion, I cannot say, but it is thought here that they will discard him forever from their confidence.

Mrs. J. Joins me in kind salutations to you all, in which Mr & Mrs. D. unites. Believe me your friend

Andrew Jackson

ALS, DLC (10-1201).
    1. Not found.
    2. AJ probably sent Coffee a copy of the February 28 issue of the *Washington Gazette*, which printed Kremer's address.

To highlight the growth of domestic industry, American artisans and manufacturers from nine states and the District of Columbia held an exhibition in the rotunda of the Capitol from February 22 through February 26. The exhibitors also formed a committee to sponsor a second exhibition in November. Peter H. Schenck (1779–1852) was the New York representative on the committee, and he and his co-proprietor of the Glenham Woolen Factory in Dutchess County, Abraham Henry Schenck (1775–1831), a former congressman, used the occasion to present Jackson with a suit of clothing from their factory. Hector Craig (1775–1842), a member of the House Committee on Manufactures and one of two New York congressmen who had supported Jackson in the balloting for president, made the presentation. In his letter of thanks, below, Jackson used the occasion to present his views on industrial development.

To Hector Craig

Washington March 2nd. 1825

Sir

I cannot accept the very flatering present of Messhrs. P. H. and A. H. Schenck presented thro you, without soliciting that you will tender to them my very gratefull acknowledgements for there politeness & for the kind feelings which in there behalf you are pleased to express.[1]

To me it is a matter of proud pleasure to witness the march of our country to the perfection of those arts without which she can never attain complete Independence. During the last war the malancholy spectacle was afforded of our utter inability, by virtue of our own resources, to clothe either our soldiers or our ships: our dependence was upon our enemies, for a supply of articles essential to the maintainance of our rights & our liberty. I trust those times will never again recur; and looking to the active zeal with which under the guidance of patriotic citizens, our domestic enterprise is progressing I am sure that in any future conflicts, the means of waging successfully our defence, will be found to exist amonghst ourselves: There is nothing I more cordially desire; nothing that this country next to the perpetuation of her liberties, should more sincerely wish for. our resources fairly brought into operation, with the brave yeomanry, our country every where affords, we need not fear for the perpetuation of our liberties & Independence.

Permit me if you please to reciprocate the friendly wishes you have expressed for my future health & happiness. With great respect & regard I am sir yr mo. obdt. Servt.

Andrew Jackson

ALS, IaU (10-1206); ALS draft, DLC (33). Published in Washington *National Intelligencer,* March 3, and other newspapers.
1. See Craig to AJ, March 2.

To Samuel Swartwout

Washington City March 6th. 1825

Dr. Sir

Your kind favor of the 27th ult[1] came to hand in due time but for the want of opportunity it has not been in my power to thank you for it untill now.

yesterday Mr Adams was inagurated amidst a vast assemblage of citizens, having been escorted to the capitol with a pomp and ceremony of guns & drums not very consistant, in my humble opinion, with the charecter of the occasion. Twenty four years ago when Mr [Thomas] Jefferson was inducted into office no such machinery was called in to give solemnity to the occasion—he rode his own horse and hitched him himself to the enclosure.[2] But it seems that times are changed—I hope it is not so with the principles that are to Characterise the adminstration of Justice and constitutional law. These in my fervent prayers for the prosperity and good of our country will remain unaltered, based upon the sovereignity of the people and adorned with no forms or ceremonies save those which their happiness and freedom shall command.

I have not recd as yet your *New York* paper, in which as I inferred from your letter my remarks upon the term military chieftain are before this published.[3] To this I have nothing to say. Mr Clay has used no delicacy towards me, and as I have never written any thing whether private or public which my heart and Judgement did not sanction, I am not afraid of the publication of these remarks or any other which I have made.

Mrs. Jackson still continues unwell, but I hope her health will allow us to take up our march to the Hermitage Tuesday or Wednesday next. we shall go by Baltimore in order to avoid the bad road between this and Frederic.

We both Join in kindest wishes to yourself & amiable Lady & child.[4] May you all be as happy as I wish you. your friend Sincerely.

Andrew Jackson

ALS, Clermont State Historic Site, (mAJs); Copy in Andrew J. Donelson's hand, dated March 5, DLC (33). Published in Bassett, 3:280–81 (from copy).
1. Not found.
2. Adams's inauguration was on March 4; Jefferson (1743–1826; William and Mary 1762).
3. Swartwout had apparently informed AJ that his letter of February 22 would be published in the *New York National Advocate*. It appeared on March 4.
4. Mary Colden Swartwout (1820–64).

From George Kremer

Washington March 8th 1825

Dear Genl

Agreeably to your request, I communicate to you the substance of a conversation which I had early in January last with the Hon James Buchanan—He inquired of me when I had seen Genl Jackson, I replied not for some time he then said there was a great intrigue going on and that he thought it right to let me know it & that if he was known as I was to be the intimate friend of Genl Jackson he would inform the Genl of it & that he thought I ought to acquaint Genl Jackson, That the friends of Adams were making overtures to the friends of Clay to this effect, That if they the friends of Clay aided to elect Adams Clay should [be] Secretary of State & that he thought we were in great danger unless we would consent to fight them with their own wepons, That the friends of Adams were urging as an argument to induce the friends of Clay to accede to the proposition that if Genl Jackson should be elected, Adams would be continued Secretary of State & repeated that he thought I ought at least to get myself authorized to say that if Genl Jackson was elected President Mr Adams should not be continued Secretary of State I told him that I could not do so That we must carry Genl Jackson on the ground of principle & that his friends could not make any promises or give any pledges that I did not beleve that General Jackson ever had disclosed his mind to any man as to who he would appoint should he be elected, nor did I beleve he would untill it became his duty. He then said I was unacquainted with the intrigues of these men, I then told I could not believe it possible that such an intrigue could prevail—he said I might rest assured it was going on, That he knew the fact & repeated that it was necessary for the friends of Jackson to fight them with their own weppons at least so far as to say whether Adams should remain Secretary of State or not. I will not be certain that I have used Mr Buchanans own words I am however certain that I have in Substance stated our conversation correctly With great respect I remain your friend fellow Citizen

G. Kremer

P S Mr. Buchanan stated that him & Mr Clay had become great friends this winter, this he said as I thought to enforce on my mind the authority from whence he had derived the information[1]

ALS, DLC (33). Published in Bassett, 3:281–82.
    1. When Buchanan's overtures were mentioned in connection with the Carter Beverley correspondence published in 1827, Buchanan recalled conversations of this nature with John H. Eaton and AJ himself, but denied that he had acted as an emissary for Henry Clay. In 1934, Richard R. Stenberg (*Pennsylvania Magazine of History and Biography*, 58, January: 61) claimed that the postscript to Kremer's letter had "every appearance of being a forgery added by Jackson himself." The postscript, however, is not in AJ's hand; the handwriting appears clearly to be Kremer's.

From Isaac Lewis Baker

St Martinsville Loua. 21 March 1825.
Dear General,
    Your letter of the 10th. of february from Washington City[1] came duly to hand by the last mail. Steam Boats & Expresses had however several days previous brought us some Details of the unrighteous result of the Presidential Election. Success was not requisite to your fame and the will of a great majority of your countrymen had been so emphatically pronounced that you have the high gra[t]ification of knowing you hold the first place in their hearts. To say I was not greatly mortified at the success of such a scandalous intrigue would be a gross sin against candor & truth—Yet since I have been advised of the honest indignation which the scene has produced from the Hudson to the Balize and that you will [be] before the people again I feel greatly consoled by the belief the people will now act in such a manner as to prevent any such shameful barter for the future and you will live to shew to Clay & Co. that virtue & service can, must & shall triumph over slang whanging & base Intrigue. We have not yet heard who is to compose the Yankee Cabinet but if Clay goes into it he & Mr Adams will do well to perform all the good or Evil in the next four years which they ever intend doing as they will at the end of that period return to the dull pursuits of private life—
    Brent and Gurley are viewed as they ought to be. I scarcely think Brent

will ever return to Louisiana. He is overwhelmed with debt and is accused of perjury, swindling & Extortion under such fair prospects of establishing the charges that I think he will keep away—I wrote to you formerly that he was for sale to the highest bidder & the result has proved I was not mistaken. If he ever intends to offer for Congress again he has committed a gross blunder in voting against you as your friends in his district were his warmest supporters. They all abandon him now—and tho he is one of the ablest & most unprincipled men in the way of Electioneering I do not think he can ever recover from this shock. He no doubt calculates on being paid for his recreant vote with some fat office—but I think that Mr. Adams to foil public Indignation will be apt to yankee his congressmen out of their expected rewards. If he does not he must sink with them—

I have lately had several letters from men of Influence in Gurley's District. The population is almost entirely American—they view his treason to his constituents as they ought & he is down forever—[2]

Tell Mr. Donelson that before the rect of his letter the resolution was taken to lay the conduct of certain persons before the people in its proper colours—Ridicule is a powerful engine—& I send you the first shaft leveled at Brent by the mail—It is in Doggrel Rhyme and will take among all classes[3]—The newspapers shall not be idle.

The last legislature of this state restored to the people the usurped right of choosing their Electors for President and Vice president—Henry Johnson and all the miserable fry of office hunters cannot on another occasion sell the vote of the State or any part of it in the electoral College—[4]

I desire greatly to go to Tennessee in June—but cannot yet say if I can do so. My practise is getting very good and between it and a large planting establishment I have not time to a[ttend] to any thing else. Mr. [Donelson] Caffery[5] will make the trip early in the Summer & if he will attend to my business I rather think I will be obliged to stay at home.

We have had a very mild winter. The heavy money Embarrassments which so long & so cruelly oppressed this State are rapidly disappearing—I want much to get my personal affairs in good trim this year as I feel strongly inclined to take the field in 1826 as a candidate for Congress—[6]

Mr. Crutcher has not written to me for four months—Please desire him to do so the next time you meet him.

Mr. [Ralph Eleazar Whitesides] Earl[7] promised me your portrait four years ago but has never sent it. Please mention the subject to him. I paid him 20$ of the price when I asked him for it—My brother[8] Joins me in many kind wishes to Mrs. Jackson Mr. Donelson & Lady—& desires to be remembered to you

I remain Dear General with the highest Respect & warmest Regard your obliged friend & obt Servant.

Isaac L. Baker.

ALS, DLC (33). Baker (1792–1830), a son-in-law of William Terrell Lewis and a former AJ aide-de-camp, was a Louisiana planter and lawyer.

1. Not found.

2. Contrary to Baker's predictions, both William L. Brent and Henry H. Gurley were reelected to Congress in 1826.

3. Baker was referring to his *Defence of Col. William Lovetruth Bluster in a Letter to William Wagtail, Esquire, Done into Verse by Mr. Aminidab Sledgehammer, Poet Laureate of Catahoula* (New Orleans, 1825). A year later Baker issued another attack on Brent, *A Further Defence of Colonel William Lovetruth Bluster, in a Letter to Major Joseph Antick . . .* (New Orleans, 1826).

4. The state legislature had chosen Louisiana's five electors in 1824—three for AJ and two for Adams—but by an act of February 2, 1825, the legislature provided that future electors would be selected by popular vote (*Acts . . . First Session of the Seventh Legislature of the State of Louisiana . . .* [New Orleans, 1825], pp. 64–70). Johnson (1783–1864) was governor of Louisiana.

5. Caffery (1786–1835), AJ's nephew, had a plantation near Franklin, Louisiana.

6. Baker did not run against Brent in the 1826 election.

7. Earl (1788–1838), who married AJ's niece Jane Caffery (c1801–19) in 1818, painted more than thirty portraits of AJ during his career. The result of his commission from Baker is unknown.

8. Joshua Baker (1799–1885; Military Academy 1819), later governor of Louisiana, had been Andrew J. Donelson's roommate at West Point.

Beginning in mid-March a number of newspapers carried a report of an alleged conversation between Jackson and an "officer formerly in the southern army," identified only as "H." According to H., he met with Jackson at Washington, Pennsylvania, in November 1824, while Jackson was en route to the capital, and their talk had naturally turned to Jackson's probable elevation to the presidency. Jackson expressed some surprise at his success, stating that he had "thought the unanimous voice of the nation would be heard in ridicule of my pretensions" as no "serious effort" was likely to put a "military man" in charge of "a government purely republican, in which the Military should be subservient to the Civil power." He went on to express doubts about the stability of republics, noting that "unobtrusive merit" was unlikely to receive public honors, while "the mass of the people . . . always ripe, for novelty and innovation" was easily captivated by "a mere name—a Hero" (Richmond Enquirer, March 15).

For Jackson's enemies this revelation of his private opinions was almost too good to be true. If true, not only had the general demonstrated a disdain for the people who supported him, he had also agreed with his opponents' concerns about a military chieftain as chief executive. In addition, as reported by H., Jackson revealed in the conversation that, contrary to public proclamations of obeying the people's call, he had "directed my adherents in the Tennessee legislature to pass the resolutions" nominating him for president in order to frustrate the ambitions of another western aspirant whom he considered an enemy. Despite the skepticism with which H.'s letter was published, Jackson had to respond publicly, as he did below. Once he denied the conversation, the matter of H.'s letter rather quickly disappeared from the newspapers.

The identity of H. is not known, nor is the newspaper which first published the account. The Enquirer *attributed it to the* Nashville Whig, *but the* Whig *flatly denied the report (April 2), and no Mr. H. ever came forward to avow authorship.*

To John Henry Eaton

Wheeling, Va., March 23, 1825.

Dr. Sir,

I have this moment received your letter of the 17th inst., enclosing a conversation with Mr. "H," and which is now travelling about a Sinbad story.[1] This officer of the southern army may be ascertained, when I reach Nashville; and *when he is,* it is quite probable, he will be found to be some tool who has sold his signature.

I am very certain that at Washington, Pa., in November last, I saw no individual, a former officer with me; and I am also equally certain, that I have never in my life uttered any such sentiments as are ascribed to me in that letter. They are a fabrication from beginning to end. Neither General Call, nor Mr. Donelson, who were with me, recollects any such individual.[2] They well remember, that I arrived at Washington, Pa., in the evening, much indisposed, and departed early the next morning.

Washington, (Penn.,) seems to be a fatal place: it will be recollected by you that sundry reports grew out of my meeting there last year Gov. [Ninian] Edwards;[3] while as I came back Mr. "H" was there. You may be assured, however, that the inhabitants of that place have nothing to do with these tales: they cherish no hypocrites; nor do they countenance those miserable attempts against my character.[4] The citizens there have treated me with the utmost attention and kind feeling. Your friend,

ANDREW JACKSON.

Printed extract, *Washington Gazette,* March 29 (mAJs; 10-1227); published in other newspapers.

1. Not found. Eaton probably sent the account from a newspaper published outside Washington, since the first account in Washington papers appeared on March 18, the day after he wrote AJ.

2. Call confirmed AJ's denial in the *Richmond Enquirer* of April 8; Donelson's comment, however, has not been found.

3. When AJ arrived at Washington, Pennsylvania, on May 27, 1824, en route to Nashville, he met Edwards (1775–1833; Dickinson 1792), who was on his way to Washington, D.C., to give testimony regarding the "A.B." letters and the charges against William H. Crawford. According to the Washington, Pennsylvania, *Reporter,* May 31, 1824, AJ advised Edwards to continue on to the capital to defend his character. Jesse Benton later called that meeting to public attention, combining it with Edwards's visit to Tennessee in 1823 to imply an alliance between AJ and Edwards (*Richmond Enquirer,* August 31, 1824).

4. In the Washington, Pennsylvania, *Reporter,* April 18, local citizens supported AJ's recollection.

To Edward George Washington Butler

Wheeling March 25th. 1825

Dear Edward

yours of the 18th instant[1] has just been handed me, as I was preparing to go on board the Steam Boat—and I have but one moment to write

The letter you allude to, which has made its appearance in the Whig, is one of the vilest fabrications ever published—No such character as the supposed writer was met by me on my Journey to Washington P. as is recollected either by Genl Call or Capt Donelson, who is now with me, or by myself; and from my arrival at Washington P. I was surrounded with a crowd until I retired at eleven oclock, and no private conversation was had with any one by me, nor was I in a private room until I retired to bed; and we left there at sunrise the next morning—Mr. [Peter] Force well knew it was a fabrication,[2] but being now wielded by Mr Clay, he will delight in publishing such fabrications—So soon as I reach Nashville the name of this old acquaintance & brother soldier of mine must be yielded to me—My own opinion is that it was either fabricated by J[ohn] P[atton] Irwin, part editor of the Whig, and whose brother married Clay's daughter,[3] or by Clay in Washington, & sent for publication in the Whig—be this as it may, you can at all times & on all occasions pronounce a base fabrication from beginning to end—The Boat summons me on board— Mrs. J's health is improving—I have had a sudden & severe attack here, am getting over it—Tender to Mrs. & Miss Lewis,[4] our affectionate regards & believe me your friend

Andrew Jackson

P.S. present us kindly to Genl & Mrs. [Edmund Pendleton] Gains.[5] adieu AJ

If my friend Major Eaton is in the City you can show him this scroll & present my best respects to him.

ALS, DLC (10-1228). Butler (1800–88; Military Academy 1820), son of Edward and aide-de-camp to Edmund P. Gaines, was at this time in Washington.
1. Not found.
2. Force (1790–1868) was publisher of the pro-Adams Washington *National Journal,* which reported the alleged conversation between AJ and "H" on March 18.
3. The two Erwins were sons of Andrew of Bedford County, Tennessee. John P. (1795–1857), a Nashville lawyer and merchant, had joined the *Whig* in October 1823 and remained an editor until Adams appointed him postmaster in 1826. His brother James (1796–1851) had married Anne Brown Clay, Henry Clay's daughter, in 1823.
4. Eleanor Parke Custis Lewis (1779–1852) and her daughter, Frances Parke Lewis (1799–1875), descendants of Martha Washington. Frances was Butler's fiancé.

5. Gaines (1777–1849) was commander of the Eastern Division of the army. His wife was Barbara Grainger (c1792–1836), a daughter of former Tennessee senator William Blount.

From John Blair

Jonesborough March 30th. 1825

Dear General

I have returned in safety to my family & have again engaged in the labours of my profession: I find from mixing with the people, and converseing with your friends, an utter aversion to your leaveing the senate, for the four years to come: on this subject I had so little conversation with you that I was left somewhat in doubt as to your ultimate course. I now believe it would not do for you to decline on many accounts—and one particularly that your friends so far as I have seen them from all quarters protest against it—on this subject I would at your leisure be glad to hear the inclination of your mind: I have resolved (if the people are as willing as myself) to see Mr Adamses four years out I have as yet no oposition but am threatened by both [John] Rhea & [John] Tipton, and in all probability will have their oposition.[1]

Our mutual friend Capn John Phagan late of the 39th Regt. who was with you at the Horsesho, is now over from N Carolina, and with me at present—he desires to be rememberd to you, & that I should say since he left the army, that he has been unfortunate, & if an opportunity offers would be glad of getting into an Indian agency or some other appointment, which would be calculated to bread his children[2] —I knew not how the appointments stand so as to inform him whether or not there be any vacancies, but presumed you would know, haveing seen to what extent the executive had made his appointments—I feel for the honest soldier who stood for his country in the day of peril, & particularly for him who done it with so great a share of credit, as did my friend Phagan—should you know of any office or appointment being subject to disposal, I feel satisfied he deserves it—& requests your aid in his behalf—he resides in the upper district of N Carolina, which was represented by Docr [Robert Brank] Vance[3] I might also add he is one of the fraternity, for whom, friendly feelings must be excited. give my kind respects to Mrs Jackson & believe me to be your friend & mo obt servt

John Blair

ALS, DLC (33). A lawyer, Blair (1790–1863; Washington College 1809) represented Tennessee in the U. S. House of Representatives, 1823–35.

1. Rhea (1753–1832), a former congressman, did not contest the August election for representative of Tennessee's First Congressional District. Blair won with nearly 52 percent of the vote, defeating Tipton (1769–1831), a former state legislator whom Blair had also out-polled in 1823.

2. In January 1826, Adams appointed Phagan (c1786–1858) subagent for the Florida Indians and, in 1830, AJ made him agent.

3. Vance (1793–1827), of Asheville, served one term in Congress.

From Samuel Swartwout

New York 2nd. April 1825

My dear Sir,

It freequently happens to us in this life that we are benefited greatly by the chances & accidents of it, though the most unhappy consequences might be apprehended from them at the time. It is owing to one of these crooked circumstances that I am indebted for the pleasing inteligence of your being so far advanced on your way home, in health I hope & Mrs. Jackson also, as Wheeling on the 23rd of March—I presume I am to thank Mr. H. your very oblidging accuser for this pleasure, and if you will allow me, I must say that I do feel oblidged to him in a double sense, first for having enabled me to know that you had progressed, safely & happily, thus far on your journey; and secondly as it afforded an opportunity for virtue & honor to triump over forgery & baseness—You must percive that I alude to your letter to Major Eaton of that date[1]—My dear & honored friend, the assurances which you have given in that letter were not necessary to prove that the letter was a fabrication—Your friends *know* you, and your enemies *too*. If the wretches who thus attempt to injure you, did but know that every shaft that is aimed at your breast must recoil to wound themselves, they would forbear—But knavery & folly are synonimous, altho the authors of mischief may be blessed with talents—Truth will prevail and where it is left free to combat falshood & error will triumph in despite of the influence of *Station* or *patronage*—

The prompt refutation of the base slander of that writer who signed himself H. has induced many persons to apprehend, who are really & truly your decided friends that you might consider it necessary to say something in reply to the flumery letter of Mr. Clay to his constituents recently manufactured at Washington[2]—Altho He has introduced your name into his letter & treated you rather unceremoniously, I hope it may not be deemed necessary by you to make any reply to him, for here the whole publication is considered fatal to him—He could not have received more decided injury from his worst enemy than he has inflicted upon himself by this publication—What he has stated of me, I shall not notice—My friends advise me to take not the least heed of it[3]—Mr. Adams friends are mortified to death that he has made such a fist of it—Clay expects & hopes that you & others will undertake a defence, as in that event he can keep up a newspaper war that will enable him to continue explanations & statements to his own benefit. For every respectable adversary he can get by provocations and statements in the newspapers will add to his own respectability. To show how extremely low the creature is in decent society, I need barely mention a fact which occurred at our South-American dinner last week—The company was mixed, but most respectable, when I say mixed I mean as to politicks, no particular party having joined in the cellebration Mr. Clay's hea[l]th was proposed, as the champion of south American independance, and to the mortification of the gentleman who gave it & of Mr. Clay, out of 100 persons not 5, drank it! I never witnessed such a thing before—when however I gave your name, the company rose in a body & drank it standing with 6 cheers—I send you the papers which contain the account of it.[4]

From these facts it clearly appears that Mr Clay is *sunk in society*—He is not entitled to your notice—He does not merit the respect of a reply to any thing that he may say or do—

In making these remarks & in urging your silence, I feel my dear Sir, that I am taking a liberty with one whom I more venerate & respect than any other being on earth. Your services, your talents, the rank you hold in this country, in the World! places you at such an eminent height above me that I fear no explanations of respect, regard & solicitude will excuse me to you—But yet my heart tells me that you will not condemn entirely a feeling which has its source in no selfish or sinister principles, but in love for you & in hopes for my country—The deep wounds recently inflicted upon our glorious country & Constitution, are only to be healed through the exemplary greatness of such men as yourself—You have, by your dignity and forbearance under all these outrages, won the people to your love—They look forward to the period when they can have an opportunity of testifying their admiration of your conduct, their confidence in your talents & their security in your integrity—No one thing has occurred to change the favourable impressions made upon them before you left Washington—They behold in your deportment, the same dignity, and forbearance—and I hope to God that no supposed necessity on your part to vindicate yourself from the aspersions of such a man as Henry Clay may be entertained by you, for the public know you both too well to require it—Who ever before heard of a secretary of State, upon his entering on the duties of his office, commencing by a publication of 8 columns in a news paper to prove that he was not the greatest scoundrel in the Country?[5] The very fact that he himself deemed it necessary, is sufficient to condemn him—No. Henry Clay is down—damned—and nothing would tend to ellevate him so much as to get you to notice what he says—Your letter in explanation of his "military chieftain" epithet was admirable.[6] That vindication was necessary, was full, complete—But I hope to God that neither epithets nor falshoods when under the signature of Henry Clay, may ever again meet with even a notice from your pen—

When you shall find yourself sufficiently over the fatigue of your journey, I will ask for the favour of a line from you—we are very anxious to hear how Mrs. Jackson stood the journey home & how her health is—

Mrs. Swartwout joins me in affectionate regards to her, and for yourself my dear friend believe me ever most faithfully & affectionately your friend & sevt

Saml Swartwout

P.S. I avail myself of the room afforded by this envelope which I consider necessary, the paper being stronger than the letter paper, to repeat that it is pretty well ascertained that every occasion will be seized upon to *draw* you out, as it is impudently termed, Mr. Clay considering his chances in the *game* greater in proportion to his success in finesse. What a set of scoundrels to dare to use such language towards you—Let them do it, the people appreciate their motives & will take care that no artifice or villiany of the Kind succeed—They, the people, in the next great national *game* will hold the honors I hope and will win too in despite of knaves bullets & braggers—

In order to get Govr. [DeWitt] Clinton out of the way, Mr. Adams has actually renewed his request that he would go to England[7] & as an additional inducement has signified his determination to add a mission to Spain by way of double douceur—I understand he will decline this too—Should this be the case, Judge [Jonas] Platt of the State of N. York is to be sent to France.[8] What new expedient besides is to be adopted to gain more new friends, I know not—all sorts of things will however be resorted to to fortify & streng[t]hen the frail tottering fabrick—

Please to remember me with kindest regard to Genl Call & his lady & Major & Mrs. Donalson—once more adieu & may God preserve you for our country's Glory & happiness S. S—

ALS, DLC (33).
1. See above, AJ to Eaton, March 23.
2. *Address to the People of the Congressional District Composed of the Counties of Fayette, Woodford, and Clarke, in Kentucky* (Washington, 1825).
3. In his letter, Clay suggested that something was odd concerning the "circumstances" of AJ's letter of February 22 to Swartwout (above), as Swartwout had remained in Washington long enough to give "full opportunity" for "a personal interview" on the subjects raised in that communication. Specifically, Clay accused Swartwout of complicity with AJ in the publication of the letter, timing its publication to influence the Senate vote on Clay's confirmation as secretary of state. Swartwout did reply to Clay's remarks in the *New York American*, April 6.
4. The dinner was at the City Hotel in New York on March 21.
5. Clay's *Address* first appeared in the Washington *National Journal*, March 28.
6. See above, AJ to Swartwout, February 22.
7. Adams first offered Clinton (1769–1828; Columbia 1786) the English mission on February 18, which Clinton declined a week later (Washington *National Intelligencer*, March 21). With Clinton's rejection, Adams offered the post to Rufus King of New York.
8. The French post went not to Platt (1769–1834), formerly a congressman and judge of the New York Supreme Court, but to the incumbent, James Brown (1766–1835), former senator from Louisiana.

From Henry Baldwin

Pittsburgh 11 April 1825

Dear Sir

A few days after writing my letters and before I heard or could know when you were expected to be on your return home my business compelled me to go about fifty miles to an iron establishment where my personal presence was indispensible on my return your two letters[1] were recived but too late for me to reach you at Wheeling or I would have left home immediately A number of your friends would have accompanied me to Washington [Pa.] and were prepared to set out at an hours warning we were excessively mortified and disappointed at not being able to pay you our respects to me it was peculiarly so—for my wish to see you was more from personal than any other feeling. At this time it was not my wish that you should come here but on your return to Washington [D.C.] shall hope to see you among us to witness the general expression of respect and attachment which is felt & will be expressed in a manner which will gratify every friend of yours and give no color for any remarks or misconstruction My professional business has been & is very extensive & laborious in addition to this burthen I have been obliged to take on myself the personal direction of the large iron works at this place which employ 80 workmen and the superintendance of a furnace 50 miles from this at which there are about the same number employed—this puts my time entirely out of my control and will explain to you the reason why even the risk of not meeting you could not detain me at home Be assured it was only owing to circumstances over which I had no discretion that I left home my return was much longer delayed than was expected but could not be avoided—I well know that you would put down the circumstance of my not meeting you to any account other than the want of a desire to do it but it was due to you to give the reasons—

As there are now no reasons for my obtaining proximity to you I shall on the first good opportunity write you fully on both the past & the future— freely & without reserve but not by the mail—It was my intention to have relinquished politicks in the event of your election unless it would have been useful to have returned to my former station—now I shall again enter into the contest not as a candidate or an officer but as one of the people having in view the same object—the same purpose—& the same policy which have hitherto guided all my conduct—the time has not yet arived for action there is an effervescence in the public mind which must subside a good deal before it is prudent to attempt to control its action but now is the time for organization—for examining the maps charts & statisticks preparatory to a campaign—My first desire is my only one—under all circumstances death alone excepted on this subject we in Penna. have no negociation no terms to ask or give independent of all other reasons the welfare of the country the safety of its institutions point to one and the only one who can secure & perpetuate them—With a steady eye to this one object we shall soon be ready to make an appeal to the good sense of the county and once begun the performance will be worthy of the great & good cause which will draw out our exertions Mr Clays appeal has produced no effect in restoring him to public confidence[2]—he can never rise—far from supporting he is a drag on Mr Adams— If the selection of a Cabinet had been left to his worst enemy there could not have been one formed less able to give strength to his administration Every thing indeed seems to combine in favor of the overthrow of the coalition which has defeated the voice of the people & the choice of the states—the letter to Judge Brooke has roused more indignant feelings than I have ever heard expressed[3] it would have been pity if it had not been written I shall send to Mrs Jackson a piece of glass which it was my intention to have presented to her at Washington it is a handsome specimen of the perfection of the arts and is exclusively of domestic materials—as completely American as the likeness it contains[4] I sent one to Governor Clinton in his letter received to day he says it is equal to the best specimen of Paris manufacture

The Baltimore American falsely asserts that we have made tumblers with the likeness of Mr Adams in them it is not true[5]—the only likenesses which have been perpetuated in Pittsburgh glass are Washington—and Lafayette—If the Pittsburgh Mercury reaches your place you will see a paragraph on that subject—[6]

I am happy to hear of your improvement in health let me intreat you to make it not only your constant but chief care remember that your are now public property your friends and your country have a right to ask that much of you   they will do the rest—yours with esteem

Henry Baldwin

ALS, DLC (35). Baldwin (1784–1844; Yale 1797), a lawyer and former congressman, was an ironmaster in Butler County, Pennsylvania. In 1830 AJ appointed him to the U.S. Supreme Court.

1. Not found.

2. Clay's *Address* to his Kentucky constituents.

3. Clay's letter to Francis T. Brooke, January 28, had been published in the *Richmond Enquirer*, February 8.

4. The "piece of glass" was a tumbler containing a likeness of Jackson in the base (see illustration).

5. Baltimore *American & Commercial Daily Advertiser*, March 18.

6. The *Pittsburgh Mercury* not only denied that the Pittsburgh firm of Bakewell, Page, and Bakewell had produced tumblers carrying the image of Adams, but insisted that there was no particular reason for manufacturers to perpetuate his image (as reported in the *Cincinnati Advertiser*, June 15). Marie Joseph Paul Yves Roch Gilbert du Motier, the Marquis de Lafayette (1757–1834), was on an American tour honoring his services in the Revolution.

From James Hervey Witherspoon

Waxhaws, Cane Creek Apl. 16th. 1825

Dr Sir,

Your letter of the 18th August[1] now past was duly received, for which I beg you to accept my warmest thanks. You will I trust excuse me for not answering your kind letter at an earlier period. The only reason for my delay was founded on the strong hope of the pleasure of a personal interview with you, at which time, I would have duly acknowledged your letter, and gave you all the information that was in my power relative to your desire of Mrs. [Agnes] Barton pointing to the Grave of your Mother—[2]

I have examined Mrs Barton on that subject (she lives in one mile of me), she states that if it was in her power to point to the spot she would fondly do so. As well as she remembers, & from all the information on the subject, your Mother was burried in the Suburb's of Charleston, about one mile from what was then called the Governors Gate, which is in and about the forks of the Meeting, & Kingstreet Road's. Mrs Barton states that your Mother was buried by her Husband, & two men of the name of Hood's[3] from the Waxhaws,[4] one of them is now dead, the other is living on Beaver Creek Mrs B. is of the Opinion that after so long a time of nearly fifty years, she would have no Knowledge of the particular Spot, but she is of the Opinion that Mr Hood can point to the place, for he has frequently in Conversation with Mrs B. told her, that he often has noticed the little House where they all lived in passing to Charleston with his waggon, and spoke of your Mother &c. I would have long ere this have called on Mr Hood, who lives about 12 or 15 miles from me, for information, but defered it untill you would come out, when you would have seen him yourself; but the first good opportunity, I will see him—It is almost unnecessary to say to you, how much I was disappointed, "together with the Citizens of Lancaster Dist.,["] with a few remaining Relations & friends, at your not Visiting us this Spring—As we have been deprived of the pleasure of a Visit from you, will you yet, my dear General, favor the place of your *Nativity,* the place that gave you *birth,* the place of your *boyhood,* and early habits, with a Visit. So. Ca. hails you as one of her sons, and would take a delight in paying *Honors* to a man who have rendered such eminent services to our Country—We have just paid Honors to Gen. Lay Fayettee, and would take as much pleasure in paying Honors to Gen. Jackson[5]—There is a number of old men in our Dist still alive that knew you when you was a boy, I will here beg leave to name a few of them. "My Father in law" Isaac Donnom, Masseys, Whites, McIlwain Hoey, &c &c. All the old Stock of the Crawfords, & the Fosters are dead. Of Major Robert Crawfords family that are alive only four children, one son John Crawford who lives at the *old place,* and Mary who married Doctor [Samuel C.] Dunlap (now a widow) lives four miles from her Brother John's—You have

Second Cousins, Messrs. Lathems, & Faulkners. Your only Cousin Sarah Lathem whose maiden name was Lessley, died about a year past, leaving several Children—[6]

Your friends in the So. was truly mortified at the late events at Washington. Mr Adams is elected President. he is the Choice of Congress, but not of the *People*. which have been clearly shewn by the Electoral Colleges. I am proud that our members have all *[done]* their duty to their Constituents, by represe*[nting]* their views & wishes on that occasion. Other members have not done so, I hope they will give an account of their Stewardship to the People who sent them—I have paid great attention to the public prints since the 9th of Febry. Mr Clay may as well attempt to turn the wind, as to Convince the *public* of his motives, he has had the hardihood, to brunt public opinion and seek as a refuge, Secretary of State. You Gen. have retired from the Contest justly loaded with Honors, and Mr Clay to *dishonor,* and all his *Art* can not, affect you in the Hearts of your Countrymen, for with the *People* you stand as firm as a Rock, and may God Continue his choicest blessing upon you, and give you grace to withstand all the evil ones—As the above subject is a delicate one, & perhaps not agreeable, I now dismiss it—You will I hope receive this as I intend it, from the best of motives, proceeding from a friend—Your little name sake Andw Jackson Witherspoon (my son) is a hearty little fellow now 9 months old can nearly stand.[7] The rest of my family are all well. My Father in law Isaac Donnom sends his best love to you and says that he wishes to see you before he dies, he is very well & hearty, and a few years older than yourself about 61 years old I hope to hear from you before a great while, whenever you can spare time, With my best wishes for your Prosperity, I conclude with sincere regard & Esteem

James II. Witherspoon

ALS, DLC (33). Published in Bassett, 3:282–83 (extract). Witherspoon (1784–1842), a Lancaster County planter, served as lieutenant governor of South Carolina, 1826–28.

1. See AJ to Witherspoon, August [18], 1824, (*Jackson*, 5:437–39).

2. Barton (c1757–1846), variously identified as a relative or an acquaintance, reputedly assisted her husband William, a carpenter, in the burial of Elizabeth Hutchinson Jackson (d. 1781) on their property near Charleston. No evidence has been found to suggest that AJ ever located the burial site.

3. Not further identified.

4. The Waxhaw District embraced the portions of Lancaster County, South Carolina, and Mecklenburg (now Union) County, North Carolina.

5. From March 6 to 17, Lafayette was in South Carolina, where he attended receptions in his honor at Cheraw, Camden, Columbia, and Charleston.

6. Donnom (1764–1830) had married Sarah Crawford (1764–1805), a daughter of Robert Crawford (1728–1801) and niece of AJ's aunt Jenny (Jane, Janet) Hutchinson Crawford. Robert's son John (1778–1831), and daughter Mary (1767–1845), who had married Samuel C. Dunlap (1765–1810), were Donnom's in-laws. Sarah Leslie Latham (c1760–c1824) was a daughter of AJ's aunt, Sarah Hutchinson Leslie, and her husband Samuel (b. c1735). Another Leslie daughter, Mary (b. c1772) had married James Faulkner.

7. Andrew J. Witherspoon (1824–91; South Carolina 1844) was later a Presbyterian minister in Alabama and at New Orleans.

The Senate adjourned on March 9 and the Jacksons left Washington the next day. Jackson had declined numerous invitations, citing Rachel's poor health, but still the journey home to Tennessee was slowed as the citizens of Baltimore, Cincinnati, Louisville and several other places honored him. He was already a nominee for the presidency in 1828, the Nashville Gazette having announced his candidacy on February 25, the day after news of Adams's election arrived. The Jacksons reached at the Hermitage on April 13, and on the 16th, friends and supporters welcomed Jackson with a public dinner at the Nashville Inn. About four miles from town, two companies of cavalry met him, joined a mile and a half out by the Nashville Guards and the Lafayette Rifle Corps. The cavalcade entered Nashville to an artillery salute, and, at the court house, John Overton formally welcomed him, praising his military accomplishments, private virtues, and conduct in Washington during the recent campaign. In his response, below, Jackson reemphasized that he did not seek the presidency but would serve if elected, a theme that permeated his public and private utterances for the next four years as it had the previous three.

To John Overton and the Citizens of Nashville

[April 16, 1825]

Sir:

I have not language strong enough to express my thanks to you, and those of my fellow-citizens in whose behalf you have addressed me,[1] for the very flattering manner with which you have presented another token of their unabated regard for my public, as well as private character.

A few years after the Revolutionary war had closed, but before the blessings it had diffused along the Atlantic borders were extended to this remote section of the Union, I came among you. We clung together until every difficulty and danger were surmounted, and after our territory was secured against the ruthless and savage attacks of Indian Hordes, we grew strong, and claimed the privileges of a free and independent state. Many of those whom we remember as benefactors, at that period, now sleep with their fathers. Others have sprung up, who, both in civil and in military life, have rendered important services; particularly in the last war, when rallying under the eagles of their country, in defence of our common rights, they, by their patriotism and undaunted spirit, contributed to raise their country's glory to an eminence from which it can survey, with pity the boasted *invincibility* of tyrants.

When I see sir, interspersed through this assembly, many who have borne a part in those scenes—an assembly, I may say, composed entirely of men who have been associated with me either as participators, or witnesses, of whatever agency, public, or private, it has pleased Providence I should have in them, what language can convey the feelings, inspired by this additional evidence of their kindness and regard, which is now presented to me through you! The approbation of those who have been witnesses of my conduct, thro' all the varying scenes of life, is to me, next to an approving conscience, the sweetest reward this world can bestow.

It is true sir, that without any agency whatever on my part, I was brought forward by the Legislature of Tennessee as a candidate for the Presidency. This, the members of that body well know; and particularly, the Hon. Felix Grundy, who, as I have since been informed, was the member who drafted the Resolutions that were introduced and adopted on the occasion.[2] When thus brought before the people, the canvass was conducted without any interference of mine: nor did I, when the election devolved upon the House of Representatives, attempt, in any manner, to influence its decision. The Presidential chair I have always viewed as a situation too responsible to be sought after, by any individual, however great his talents, or eminent his services. It is one which the immortal Washington approached with awful forebodings, conscious that the destiny of a free people—of unborn millions, were committed to his charge; that without the smiles of Providence, and the confiding, and indulgent support of the people themselves, his exertions would be unequal to the task. With such authority to support the maxim which I have endeavoured to follow through life—"Neither to seek, nor decline public favour," I offer my past conduct as proof of my sincerity.

Printed, *Nashville Republican,* April 23 (mAJs), *Niles' Register,* May 21 (10-1238), and other newspapers.
1. See Overton to AJ, [April 16].
2. Grundy (1777–1840), formerly a congressman and later a senator, was at this time a member of the Tennessee House of Representatives.

From John Spencer Hitt

Bourbon County Ky—
April 22nd 1825

Honored and verry Dear General.

I received yours from Georgetown D. C. bearing date 5 March 1825[1] which I would not have missed for any consideration: I cannot keep the little pamphlet at home[2] it pleases hundreds of Mr. Clays former friends. I found the little book at our Aprile court there I took it up to Mr Clays mouthpiece for Publication with a determined resolution to withdraw my name from him as a subscriber to the Western Citizen But he then promised to publish Mr Kremers Letter to his constituents.[3] I will spare no pains to have that well circulated in Bourbon There I am of Opinion, it will aid and assist to throw difficulties in Mr Clay and his faithfull friend General [Thomas] Metcalfs path so as to leave them with their faithfull wives and children: As for Mr [David] Trimble he can easily share the same fate. as I have been informed by some of his constituents, many of his friends fear and Tremble on his Account. In my opinion they are fallen fallen to rise no more.[4] This is the opinion of hundreds of Gentlemen in this part of the country. I think that Mr Kremer is to become a popular man in this favored Land of Kentucky many men of information aids me in this belief. it has not been long since in a conversation one night at my house in company with several Gentlemen from Fayette County when talking about yourself and H. Clay one of those Gentlemen rising on his feet and raised his arm with his fist in a striking posture and swore he did wish Old Jackson would put a ball through Clays brains With this remark that he had been Mr Clays strong friend but he was done with him forever. General Metcalf did stand as high in his District with his constituents as any other representative in Congress but he is down and not to rise to that eminence where he has lately fallen from. So says numbers of his former and warm friends, But I do assure you I am sorry for his fall only it is pleasing to me that all Public men should smart for not doing that which their people wants them strictly to and going contrary to the known will of the majority of this nation. Mr Clays Letter to judge Brook of virginia informing him why he did stand so obstinately against you soon appeared in our paris paper but to little effect Yours to Mr S. Swartwout of New York did soon make its appearance in the same paper it does well please a number of Mr Clays former friends.[5] But now yours sincerely and I do hope will remain yours forever and his no more. Some days since Mr. Allen[6] was in conversation with me concerning your Letter as notice to Mr Clay to judge Brook he gave it as his opinion you did bring in a Military Chieftain to please him the best of any thing he ever read and sead he did vote for Mr Clay But he was sorry for it and did sincerely wish he could see you and Clay before the poeple of Kentucky single handed, for he did believe in his soul the General would beat him with ease. I should have written you as soon as I did think you had arrived at home. Only Mrs. Hitt some what flattered me with favoring me with giving birth to a fine son. Which we had long since had set a name for it, Which name was Andrew Jackson. But providence favored us with a daughter. Mrs Hitt and myself concludes we are not to give up our name entirely we call her Rachel Andrew Jackson[7] Mrs Hitt joins me in tendering our warmest love to you and Mrs Jackson: you will believe me your constant & undeviating friend

J. S. Hitt

P.S. Dear General if those illiterate lines can find favor with you: And you can take time to enclose me a few lines you will do me a grate Favor indeed. Adue. J. S. H.

ALS, DLC (33). Hitt (1781–1847), sometimes called Jackey, had probably met AJ in Washington briefly in January 1825 while there for the election in the House. He later was called to testify before the Kentucky legislature in the "corrupt bargain" investigation. In 1828 he served as Bourbon County delegate to the 1828 Kentucky state Jackson convention and as Kentucky delegate to the 1835 Democratic convention in Baltimore.

1. Not found.

2. Hitt was probably referring to *Kremer & Clay* . . . (Washington?, 1825), which contained Kremer's letter to his constituents and other documents relating to his "corrupt bargain" charges.

3. No imprint of the Kremer pamphlet from Joel Reid Lyle (1774–1849), editor of the Paris, Kentucky, *Western Citizen,* has been found.

4. Metcalfe (1780–1855) and Trimble (1782–1842; William and Mary 1799), both Kentucky congressmen, were reelected in August.

5. Henry Clay to Francis T. Brooke, January 28, and, above, AJ to Samuel Swartwout, February 22.

6. Possibly Tandy Allen (d. 1835), a Jackson elector in 1828.

7. Matilda Jacobs Ayres Hitt (1791–1859) and their daughter, Rachel (1825–1899).

To John Coffee

Hermitage april 24th. 1825

Dear Genl

We reached home on the 13th. instant all in ordinary health—have been amidst the bustle ever since—all is now hurry in preparation to receive our nations guest, who is expected on tuesday next.[1]

We were detained on our return by the indisposition of Emily—she came home much mended, but I learn this morning, she is again confined with a return of her complaint—but it being a complaint originating from a slight cold, as I believe, a few days will, I hope, restore her to usual health—she is a very delicate constitution, & takes too much medicine to maintain good health.

I learn from Major [Anthony] Latepee[2] who is just from Florence that you & your family are in good health—and that Mrs. Eliza Donelson is on her feet again. The papers will give you the political news, to them I refer you—The poor Devil H. Clay, has come out with an adress to his constituents, in a begging cringing tone, to clear himself from the corrupt intrigue & management to procure for himself the office of sec of state—but he steers entirely clear of denying this charge—The various papers are commenting upon it—and will bring to his recollection before they are done the adage, "O that my enemy would write a Book"[3]—how little common sense this man displays in his course, a man who dwells, as he does, in a glass house, ought never to cast stones—silence would have been to him *wisdom.*

My Cotton has been sold badly, the second Lott—at 13¹/₂ when other lotts from Nashville by other houses sold much higher, This I do not understand, and unless explained I must change my commission merchant. The last lott I have not heard from, Mr Josiah Nichol changed the houses, and I expect this Lott will sell for at least 20 to 25 cents if there is fair play. Cotton sells in Nashville for 22½ cents specie, of course the orleans markett must be better.[4]

So soon as I receive remittance from my last cotton will return the $500 to the Estate of Little Hutchings—I name this, that if it can be done any thing with, untill the land sales, it may be thus invested.

It would afford me great pleasure to be with you a short time, I may ride out this summer & see you—I will thank you for information how Mr [Malachi] Nicholson is progressing with the farm, & the p[ros]pects of a crop—and how the Cotton fro[m the] farm sold, & whether Doctor Bedford [has] furnished a good Ginn—[5]

We are burnt up here with the drougth, our cotton not up, nor can it vegetate before it rains. Mrs. J. unites with me in affectionate regard to you, your Lady & family, & to the Capt & Elisa. yours respectfully

Andrew Jackson

See P.S. other side—
P.S. Since closing the within I have just recollected, that the note to Bennett Smith becomes due the first of June next[6]—would it not be well to take up this note by the mony in my hands; your advice on this subject is requested A. J

ALS, THi (10-1242). Published in Bassett, 3:283 (extract).
    1. Lafayette did not arrive in Nashville until May 4.
    2. Latapie (c1787–1835) was a Nashville merchant.
    3. AJ was quoting Job 31:35.
    4. AJ's "last lott" of cotton, sold on April 28 by the New Orleans brokers Banks, Miller, & Kincaid, realized 30 cents per pound on most bales.
    5. Nicholson (d. 1825), formerly from North Carolina, was the overseer for Andrew J. Hutchings's Alabama farm. AJ was probably inquiring about the Carver gin that Bedford had purchased for the Hutchings plantation in 1824.
    6. Smith (c1764–c1848), Andrew J. Hutchings's grandfather, was a Rutherford County, Tennessee, planter and lawyer. The promissory note for $400 arose out of the final June 1 settlement of *Bennett Smith* v. *John Hutchings's Executors*.

Account for Postage, Nashville Post Office

To The Post Officc Nashville   Dr
May 4th To Postage on Washington City Gazette to Jany 1 1826 $145½

To Ditto	on Florence [Alabama] Gazette	to Do . . .	48¾
To Ditto	on [Baltimore] American Farmer	to Do . . .	48¾
To Ditto	on Louisville Publk Advertiser	to Do . . .	97½
To Ditto	on [Washington] National Journal	to Do . . .	145½
To Ditto	on [Philadelphia] National chronicle (Daily)	to Do . . .	291
To Ditto	on [Baltimore] Niles Register	to Do . . .	48¾
To Ditto	on [Columbia, Tennessee] Columbian	to Do . . .	30½

To Ditto	on [New Orleans] Louisiana Gazette	to Do . . .	145$\frac{1}{2}$
To Ditto	on [Lexington] Kentucky—Gazette	to Do . . .	48$\frac{3}{4}$
To Ditto	on Baltimore morning Chronc (Daily)	to Do . . .	2.91
To Ditto	on Jackson [Tennessee] Gazette	to Do . . .	30$\frac{1}{2}$
To Ditto	on Knoxville Enquirer	to Do . . .	30$\frac{1}{2}$
To Ditto	on [Pittsburgh] Alegheny Democrat	to Do . . .	48$\frac{3}{4}$
To Ditto	on Mobile Commercial Register	to Do . . .	97$\frac{1}{2}$
To Ditto	on [Cincinnati] National Republican	to Do . . .	97$\frac{1}{2}$
To Ditto	on Knoxville Register	to Do . . .	30$\frac{1}{2}$
Aug 15. To Ditto on [Tallahassee] Florida Intelligencer		to Do . . .	20$\frac{1}{2}$

1697

On The above papers there is an allowance made from the first Monday in Oct to the date of the Genls resignation as U S Senator[1]
To Postage on letters & packages from May 4 to Nov 3rd 1825   2193
                                               $38.90
Received payment in full of the above for R[obert] B[rownlee] Currey

B[enjamin] F[ranklin] Currey

ADS, DLC (33). Published in Bassett, 3:284. The Curreys were respectively postmaster and assistant. B. F. (d. 1830) was the nephew of R. B. (1774–1848).
   1. AJ submitted his resignation to the Tennessee General Assembly on October 12.

To Richard Keith Call

Hermitage May 7th. 1825

Dear Call

I have had the pleasure to receive your kind letters, the first from Board the Steam Boat at Natchez, the other, Orleans 15th. ult.[1]

Mrs. J & myself feeling the most lively interest in your, & Marys welfare, will always be gratified in hearing from you & hope you will continue to write us often; Mrs. J as soon as she has leisure (for she has had none yet) will write Mary.

When this reaches you, we hope you will be seated at home, in the enjoyment of good health, and all the happiness we wish you—should the summer prove unhealthy—let me conjure you to send Mary to the Hermitage, where as long as it is possessed by its present incumbents, she will find a home, & where you know you will be always welcome—say to Mary, a ring is making, when finished; I will send it to her by the first safe convayence.[2]

I am happy you were present in N Orleans on the reception of Lafayette, he expressed to me great pleasure in meeting you and Mary there.

The description you have given of the reception of Mr. Brent in Orleans at the dinner, was such as I had a right to expect from the kind feelings of the Louisianians always expressed toward me—But be assured, that Brent was sent there by Clay as a pioneer to make smooth his political path with the Louisianians for the <corrupt> course he pursued in the Presidential election—Brents reception may be therefore considered, as a fair indication of the feelings of the citizens of Orleans toward Mr Clay—Having shewn your letter to a mutual friend, he requested permission to publish an extract from it—witholding your name—this was granted, which I hope you will not disapprove;[3] it would not have been permitted, had it not have been to counteract the various publications in the washington City Journal announcing the entire approbation of Louisiana & all the western states in the election of Mr Adams, & the appointment of Clay Sec of State.

Since my arival home I have been attacked with a renewal of the complaint I had when I left you—which has been increased by the fatigues I have encountered since I came home—first the renewed attention of the citizens to me—and then to Lafayette—I am now in dry dock for repairs—The Genl left us yesterday morning at day light well pleased with his reception, & carrying with him the benedictions of every patriot—for details I refer you to the Nashville papers.[4]

It appears that the letter of my *Dear friend H.* never was published in the *Nashville Whig* its first appearence in a paper [was] in a paper published in <Conoway> the western part of Virginia from the *Nashvill Whig*—when this Editor is applied to, it appears he published from some paper as from the Nashville Whig—but does not know what paper[5]—This will not do—it proves that the prime mover of this wicked forgery must not be known—It must come out—

Mrs. J has regained her health, & Joins me & the little Andrews in kind salutations & good wishes for you & Mary to whom present us affectionately yr friend

Andrew Jackson

P.S. Genl [Samuel] Houston has reached me on his return this morning—it is *said* he is to be opposed by Mr Grundy[6]—Genl [George W.] Gibbs in Houstons absence has been saying some severe things of him, This may lead to unpleasant events[7]—Sam is now on the spott, and the electioneering campaign will commence—give my compliments to Major [Samuel Ragland] Overton, Major [Cary] Nicholas,[8] and all my friends—if R. I. Easter is with you present me affectionately to him A. J.

ALS, DLC (10-1260).
1. Only an extract of the letter from New Orleans, April 15, has been found. The Calls were en route to Florida, having traveled with the Jackson entourage from Washington to Tennessee.

2. AJ forwarded the ring on June 24.

3. On May 14, Abram Poindexter Maury (1801–48), editor of the *Nashville Republican,* published an extract of Call's letter of April 15, reporting that William L. Brent had fled a public dinner in New Orleans after the first two toasts praised Jackson and Edward Livingston.

4. AJ greeted Lafayette at his arrival on the morning of May 4 and presided over a public dinner in his honor. In the afternoon on May 5, he hosted Lafayette at the Hermitage for dinner. Both the *Nashville Republican* and the *Nashville Whig,* May 7, published detailed accounts of the visit.

5. Both John P. Erwin, editor of the *Nashville Whig,* and Mason Campbell (b. c1798), editor of the Charleston (Kanawha County) *Western Courier,* denied first publication of the letter (*Nashville Whig,* April 2, and *Richmond Enquirer,* April 19 and 22).

6. Grundy did not run against Houston (1793–1863), who easily won reelection to Congress in August.

7. On March 6, in Murfreesboro, Gibbs (1785–1870), a Nashville lawyer, reportedly questioned Houston's veracity and character in public.

8. Overton (d. 1827), a nephew of John Overton, was a commissioner of Florida land claims. Nicholas (1786–1829), a nephew of the Virginia governor Wilson Cary Nicholas, was postmaster and editor of the Pensacola *Floridian.*

To John Coffee

Hermitage May 8th. 1825

Dear Genl

I recd by due course of mail your letter of the 23rd ult.[1] but from affliction, and the bustle of preparation for the reception of Genl Lafayette I could not answer untill now I hope the letter intended to be handed you by Colo. [Edward] Ward,[2] but when he declined, was forwarded by him has reached you.

Mrs. J & myself sincerely thanks you for your kind greeting for our safe arival at the Hermitage—Mrs. Donelson health is perfectly restored—it was nothing serious, but new maried people generally make a great deal out of small attacks, when the Doctor magnifies it, to increase his fee—They matrons said her complaint was not serious—She is in good health & attended the Lafayette ball & was much complimented on her fine appearence.

It would have afforded me much pleasure to have seen you here at the reception of Lafayette—it would have been highly gratifying to him as he often said he had a great desire to see you, and all those who shared in the defence of Orleans. on the subject of the congressional candidates I think you have observed well, "never give a tried politician for one doubtfull"—your old member as far as I have been informed has acted well—It was a great pity that Judge [William] Kelly was left out, I think, as you know, well of Doctor [Henry H.] Chambers, but Kelly was one of the firmest men in the Senate.[3] When I regain my health I will write you more fully and if I can will Vissit you this summer, if you do not come in—I have noted your letter on the subject of mony matters and little A. J. Hutchings cotton &c&c—I never will (untill the Doctor explains to me why my second shipment did not bring as much as the first, and as much as other houses obtained the same day) trust one other bale to his care.

Mrs. J. & myself reciprocates to you Mrs Coffee & the family, the kind Sentiments you have expressed for our wellfare—Mrs J is in good health again your friend

Andrew Jackson

P S. Mr McLamore is mending & I hope to get him up to my house to day with Mrs J. who is at Nashville—he must abandon business and attend to his health or he is gone—

ALS, THi (10-1264). Extract published in Burke, 1:141.
    1. See Coffee to AJ, April 23.
    2. Ward (d. 1837) was AJ's neighbor.
    3. In December 1824 the Alabama legislature had chosen Chambers (1790–1826; William and Mary 1808) to replace Kelly (1786–1834) in the U. S. Senate.

To Samuel Swartwout

Hermitage near Nashville T.
May 16th. 1825

My Dear Sir
    your friendly letters of the 2nd & 5 ult[1] reached me by due course of mail, and would have been replied to when recd had my health permitted.

Owing to the fatigue I underwent on my Journey home, brought on me a severe affliction that confined me for many days: The arival of Genl Lafayette aroused me from my bed to hail him welcome, which retarded my recovery, and has prevented me untill now from replying to your letters.

I had seen Mr Clays laboured address to his constituents before your letters reached me, I viewed it (as it is generally viewed here) the dying struggle of a political gambler who having abandoned his political principles, & the expressed wishes of his constituents, sacraficed at the alter of self agrandisement; and then forsooth, whiningly asks forgiveness for his corruption—because, all this was done with the sole view of bringing himself into the office of Se[c]ratary of State—from whence, by *"the safe precedents established,"* he would of course step into the Presidential chair[2]—I must confess there is more candeur in this *precious confession* than good common sense—your view of the subject is certainly correct and the course pointed out; I had determined to adopt, before your friendly letters had reached me—still Mr Clay had left himself in his address, so open to a severe scourging that it has been with dificulty I could withold my pen. I too could have unfolded some *"voluntary information*

given," that would have been usefull to a full understanding of the corrupt course of Mr Clays friends & himself—The information given, first
to Major Eaton, then to Mr Kreamer, by a Representative from Pensylvania,
that they might communicate it to me, and which, on their refusal to be
the organ, he personally communicated to me, would be an important
link in the portrait of the corrupt scenes at Washington, of which Mr
Clay has become the most conspicuous charecter.[3] I think with you that
he has fallen below any thing but contempt, he never can rise again except by noticing him in such a manner, that he & his friends, can cry out
persecution—Therefore for the present I have determined to be silent—If
a time should arise when I conceive it proper for me to speak, I will endeavour to speak to the point, and with that energy and freedom, that the
subject may require, regardless of consequences—when you will find that
this *braggadocio will cower.*

I have with pleasure perused the letter of my Revolutionary friend Mr
Little;[4] he breaths the sentiments of the patriot of 76, who fought, & suffered privations to obtain the blessings we now enjoy, and who wishes to
perpetuate the pure principles of our Republican institutions to our latest
posterity—I have no doubt but he is an honest man, who, in my estimation, is "the noblest work of god,"[5]—should you see him, present me respectfully to him.

Mrs. Jackson health is perfectly restored; as soon as we got on the
mountains, the healthfull breeses operated as a specific, and she mended
by the hour—she is now in good health, and Joins me in the kindest salutations to Mrs. Swartwout and yourself. I shall be happy to hear from
you often—accept assurances of my sincere friendship & esteem.

Andrew Jackson

P.S. My general health is good, my affliction arose from fatigue & riding
on horseback, which occasioned an inflamation in the rectum, which communicated to the bladder, & affected the prostrate glands—rest has removed all pain.

ALS, TNJ (10-1268). Published in *Proceedings of the American Antiquarian Society,*
31(1921):87–88.
    1. Only the letter of April 2 (above) has been found.
    2. In his *Address,* Clay wrote of a "fearful precedent" of "military idolatry" in the event
of AJ's election, whereas Adams's involved "no dangerous example" but "only conformity
to the safe precedents which had been established in the instances of Mr. Jefferson, Mr.
Madison, and Mr. Monroe" (pp. 18–19).
    3. Implying the agency of Eaton and Kremer in generating the "corrupt bargain" charge,
Clay wrote that he "was voluntarily informed" that the two had been "closeted for some
time" together the night before Kremer published his famous note claiming authorship of
the charge (p. 7). Both Eaton and Kremer denied the accusation in 1828. James Buchanan
was not named as the Pennsylvania representative conveying the offer from the Clay forces
until 1827 during the Carter Beverley discussions.

4. Not identified.
5. Jackson was quoting from Alexander Pope's *Essay on Man.*

Rachel Jackson to Katherine Duane Morgan

Hermitage May 18th. 1825

My Dear Madam,

Your very kind letter of the 12th ulto[1] was recd in due time; but the variety of dear little interests renewed with my Home and not at all diminished by the scenes at Washington City, form an apology for thanking you at so late a period as this, which I trust will be accepted by you; if indeed I can offer any thing as thanks for the delight your letter afforded both Mr J and myself.

Were I, like you, in the possession of that power by which the heart engraves its features upon the letters that guide the distant friend to its feelings I might attempt the expression of those pleasures which the Humble and peaceful Hermitage present to me; and I might offer them as a feeble testimony of my gratitude for the kindnesses you paid us while within the reach of your hospitality, and subsequently for the favorable recollection with which you are pleased to associate my name with that of my dear Husband—Here, however, as I feel not less assured of my own inadequacy than of the safety with which I may rely upon your indulgence, I must be silent, and leave to yourself the picture of the rural scenery now surrounding us, in contrast with the substitute you have so eloquently described—I mean the duties which would have fallen to me had the Presidential election terminated differently—I need only assure you that referred to my own wishes that question would no longer disturb Mr Adams, so far as the General is concerned. To me the *Presidential charms* by the side of a *happy retirement from Public life* are as the tale of the candle and the substantial fire, the first of which it is said is soon blown out by the wind but the latter is only increased by it.

Our journey onward was retarded by the sickness of Mrs Donelson who is now however entirely restored. With this exception our time was delightfully occupied on the road, with the various objects presented by a country thro which I had never passed before. It would take more space than is allotted for a letter to give you the details of the journey. One remark however I will not omit in justice to the citizens with whom we had the pleasure of an acquaintance, that is, that from Baltimore to our farm we were honored by the most friendly and hospitable attentions, for which I shall ever feel grateful, and I assure you at your pleasant town, instead of being reminded of the privations at Fort Strother, my Husband was penetrated with the warmest feelings of gratitude for the generous testimonials of confidence and esteem which were exhibited by all your citizens, for both his public and private character—[2]

I thank you for the anticipated honours which you pay to my Prophecy. Mr Js mother was called Elizabeth—she encountered many hardships while on this earth, but is now at rest I trust with the spirits of the good and just—It is probable that from this cause my Husband obtained the fortitude which has enabled him to triumph with so much success over the many obstacles which have diversified his life. May their history benefit your little Jackson,[3] and contribute to perfect your own hopes of him, with which permit me to mingle mine.

Tender to Mr Morgan, with Mr Jackson's, the assurances of my best wishes for your mutual prosperity and happiness, as a token of which and my esteem for you receive a lock of my hair, enclosed. yours Respectfully

Rachel Jackson

N. B. Mr [&] Mrs Donelson also unite with us in a tender of their thanks for your attentions while at Washington. They have not forgotten the supply of medicines and cakes which were recd from you, and of which they often speak in terms of the warmest gratitude. R J

LS by proxy (Andrew J. Donelson), OClWHi (10-1271). Morgan (c1787–1855) was the daughter of Philadelphia editor William Duane and sister of William J. Duane, who served briefly as treasury secretary under AJ. Morgan's husband Thomas (1784–1855), a lawyer and former state legislator, edited the pro-Jackson *Democratic Eagle* in Washington, Pennsylvania.
1. Not found.
2. On March 21, the Jacksons had attended a public dinner at Briceland's Hotel in Washington, Pennsylvania. Fort Strother, on the Coosa River, had housed AJ's troops in the winter of 1813–14, when a shortage of supplies threatened the campaign against the Creek Indians.
3. Not further identified.

To John Coffee

Hermitage May 19th. 1825

Dear Genl

I have Just recd. advice of the sale of my last parcel of Cotton at Orleans; Mr Parsons says it was inferior to the two first Lotts sent down, which was sold at 13.3/4–13.1/2—This last sold for 30 cents—except one bale which sold for 25—my cotton on the day it was sold brought 2 & 3 cents more than any cotton sold, This shews that it was well handled. Cotton is still rising and where it is to stop is probmatical—The great rise is owing, to the great demand in urope & the great competition between France & England, our Domestic manufactories consume better than one third of all the raw material raised in the U. States, this withdrawn from the uropean markett, lessens the stock on hand there, and produced the great demand & the present high price of the article: I have no doubt but cotton *[wi]*ll open next year at 20 cents—The great demand for cotton fabricks in South america, in Spain & many parts of Urope will keep up the price of the raw material—added to this cause the increased home consumption of the raw material, will keep up the price of cotton; so much for the Tariff—I suppose my Irish friends, will not now, as they are getting such high prices for their cotton, think that the Tariff is so great an evil to the Southern planters[1]—our cotton is small here, the dry spring has made it very backward—but we have good stands—and hope for tolerable crops if our summer & fall should prove favourable. I am anxious to hear how your crops are, and the health of your country, and particularly that of your family & Capt Donelson—I see Capt [Samuel] Savage has advertised his land for sale; ¿is he going to leave your neighbourhood[2]—¿how does Nicholson get on, and what is his prospects of a crop—Should my health permit I will endeavour to see you in the course of this summer. I have, as I wrote you determined to pay the debt to Major B. Smith, $400—being the amount of the compromise of the suit him vs the Executors of J. Hutchings, I have thus informed him & made deposit in bank of that amount

would it not be well for the Citizens *[of]* Alabama, to send on a remonstrance to *[the]* president u states, to bring the forfeighted land in markett, say in december next, having a reservation to the occupants of their crops; This would give time to those who might not buy, to look out for places to seat themselves on—I have but little doubt but a remonstrance of This kind would induce the President to bring the land into markett.[3]

you recollect the promise made by James Jackson, to come in and settle the amount of his part of my Judgtment vs the heirs of David Allison used to secure the title to the Duck river land, & to bring with him, the Coopy of the record, I had obtained, which he took & requested to keep untill he came in—he failed to come in before I went on to the city as he had promised[4]—I h*[ad]* thought I would write him on the subje*[ct]* & bring to his mind the subject, & his promise & failure to comply with it—I confess I have such a contempt for the man, I hate to have any thing to do with him—still I cannot think of letting him get off from paying this mony—give me your opinion—will [Hugh] McVay out pole him—[5]

Mrs. J. Joins me in best wishes to you your lady & family, to whom she requests to be kindly presented—your friend

Andrew Jackson

P.S. Since closing the above letter, I thought I would adress James a note, which I enclose[6]—wish you to read and if you think proper, have handed to him A. J.

ALS, THi (10-1275). Published in Bassett, 3:285 (extract).
1. AJ's "Irish friends" included James Jackson and probably James's sister Sarah Jack-

son Hanna (c1769–1843). In part, James had made AJ's vote for the 1824 tariff the occasion for publicly breaking with him.

2. Savage (d. 1837) was AJ's friend and political ally, then living in Lauderdale County, Alabama.

3. On December 10, Adams proclaimed a sale of the relinquished lands for May and June 1826, but that sale was subsequently suspended and remained so until AJ's proclamation of December 3, 1829, setting sale for June 1830.

4. Following Allison's bankruptcy and death in Philadelphia in 1798, the United States marshal in 1802 auctioned 85,000 acres of Allison land along the Duck River in Middle Tennessee to satisfy a creditor. When it was later revealed that the sale was illegal, AJ, who had obtained 10,000 acres as the creditor's agent, set out to clear his title to that land. He used the debts owed him by Allison to obtain a judgment on December 17, 1810, against the Allison heirs and then went to Georgia, where, on August 3, 1812, he secured from the heirs a deed of release to the entire 85,000 acre tract. Meanwhile, Andrew Erwin of Bedford County had purchased a large portion of the Duck River property. By 1814, AJ and his partners James Jackson and Jenkin Whiteside had entered into a protracted lawsuit with Erwin over title to the land. Following settlement of the case in 1824, AJ and James Jackson became embroiled in disagreements about the division of the costs and proceeds of the case.

5. McVay (1788–1851), the incumbent Lauderdale County senator seeking reelection to the Alabama legislature, was beaten by James Jackson.

6. Not found.

To Richard Keith Call

Hermitage May 26th. 1825

Dear Call

your letter of the 28th. ult. came duly to hand. Mrs. J. has had the pleasure of receiving Marys kind letter.[1] It was a source of much gratification to us, to learn that you were recd at Neworleans & Pensacola with so much good feelings by the citizens of both places[2]—They are a kind gratefull people, and to you they owe much. We once thought to have had Marys letter (or an extract from it) published in the Nashville Journals, but on reflection we concluded it was better to have the reception you met with made known in a different way—the citizens of Nashville are well acquainted with it—but your Motherinlaw, displays on all occasions, that inexorable, & savage disposition towards you, that has heretofore so much charectarised her, but the old Gentleman, as I am advised, when he hears you named is in the habit of enquiring after his dear Mary.[3] I name this to you, as a further confirmation of the real feelings of the old Gentleman, to you & Mary, when his mind was left free from the influence of his wife. We are happy to hear from Marys own pen that she is in fine health, & delighted with the climate & Town of Pensacola; the mind has great influence on the health of individuals, and the agreable society of the amiable Mrs. [Sarah Minge Walker] Walton,[4] will add much to Marys contentment, & happiness, whilst you are necessarily absent from her, and altho she has approached that Southern climate at an advanced season, we hope that she may enjoy uninterrupted good health.

Mrs. Jackson will write to her soon, & give her the news of this section of Country—Genl Lafayette often named you & Mary, & detailed to us your reception in Orleans & the kind attention of the Citizens to you.

I have seen Judge [Joseph Lee] Smiths respects to you in the Newspapers—your reply can easily put him down—the affidavit of the attorney upon which the application to the Representative branch of Congress was made is sufficient for your Justification—I will be happy to see your reply.[5]

I have Just recd a letter from our friend [James] Gadsden from St Augustine—I am informed he is at Tallahassee—I would write him if I knew where to address him, I am happy to hear from you, that the prospect of his election is flattering[6]—I wish him success with all my heart—and when you see, or write him, present Mrs. J. & myself kindly to him.

I will be happy to hear from you & Mary often—Present Mrs. J & myself affectionately to her, with our prayers for her continued good health—and for yourself accept our best wishes for your prosperity, and happiness thro life—your friend

Andrew Jackson

P.S. present Mrs. J. & myself kindly to C[olo.] Walton & Lady, to Major Nicolas Capt [. . .] & all our friends in that Country. [Please] say to Gadsden, on the event of his electi[on I] would be happy that he would advise me of it, & take the Hermitage in his rout to the City—I will be happy in his company, should I go on this fall, & be pleased to have him in the same house with me. A.J.

ALS, NAll (10-1279).

1. Letters not found.

2. In New Orleans, Call had been included in the festivities honoring Lafayette, and upon his arrival in Pensacola, he had been honored with a dinner and ball (*Pensacola Gazette and West Florida Advertiser*, April 30).

3. Mary Call's parents were Thomas Kirkman (c1779–1826), a Nashville and Philadelphia merchant, and Ellen Jackson Kirkman (1774–1850), James Jackson's sister. They had opposed Mary's marriage to Richard Keith Call.

4. "Sally" Walton (1792–1861) was the wife of Florida territorial secretary George Walton (c1790–1863; Princeton 1812). Call was preparing to move his family to Tallahassee.

5. On April 30, Smith (1776–1846), federal judge for East Florida, printed details of his dispute with Call, alleging that Call's request for a congressional investigation into his professional conduct grew out of a "personal pique" based on information from Edgar Macon (c1803–29), district attorney for East Florida. On May 7, Call responded, reaffirming his accusations (*Pensacola Gazette and West Florida Advertiser*, April 30, May 7).

6. Possibly James Gadsden to AJ, March 31. In February, when Call announced that he would not seek reelection as territorial delegate to Congress, Gadsden (1788–1858; Yale 1806) declared for the post. Generally considered the candidate of Call's faction in territorial politics, he was unsuccessful in the May election.

From James Buchanan

Lancaster 29 May 1825

My dear General,

Although I have no news of any importance to communicate, yet both duty & inclination conspire to induce me to trouble you with a few lines. Whilst you must be gratefully remembered by every American citizen who feels an interest in the character of his country; you have imposed the greatest personal obligations upon me, by your uniform kindness & courtesy.

In Pennsylvania, amongst a vast majority of the people, there is but one sentiment concerning the late presidential election. Although they submit patiently, as is their duty, *to the legally constituted powers;* yet there is a fixed & determined resolution to change them, as soon as they have the constitutional authority. In my opinion your popularity in this state is now more firmly established than ever. Many persons who heretofore supported your election did it chiefly from a sense of gratitude, & because they thought it would be disgraceful to the people not to elevate that candidate to the Presidential chair who had been so great a benefactor to the country. The slanders which your enemies had so industriously circulated against your character had notwithstanding produced some effect. Although none of your friends here ever doubted either your ability or patriotism; yet some of them expressed fears concerning your temper. These have been all dissipated by the mildness, prudence and dignity of your conduct last winter, both before & after the presidential election. The majority in Pennsylvania is so immense in your favor that in the interior there is now little or no newspaper discussion upon the subject. I most sincerely & fervently trust & hope that the Almighty may preserve your health, until the period shall again arrive when the sovreign people shall have the power of electing another President.

There never was a weaker attempt made than that to conciliate the good opinion of Pennsylvania in favor of the administration by the appointment of Mr. [Richard] Rush. Although no appointment could have produced the effect which they desired; yet if the President had selected Mr. [John] Sergeant, he would have chosen a man who had been his early & consistent friend, & one whose character for talents & integrity stands high with all parties in this state.[1] Mr. Rush was a candidate for the office of elector on the Crawford ticket—I verily believe his appointment will not procure for the administration, out of the city of Philadelphia, twenty new friends throughout the State. In that city their additional strength is limited to John Binns & a few of his devoted followers.[2]

You will perhaps be introduced in Tennessee to a young gentleman whose name is Frazer.[3] He left Lancaster with the view of practising law there under the protection of Mr. [James B.?] Reynolds.[4] He is I believe a promising young man & his connexions are highly respectable. His father has requested me to write to you concerning him. Any attention therefore with which you may think proper to honor him will be acknowledged with gratitude by me.

We have no local news here. We all feel much disappointed that Gen La Fayette has determined to go from Pittsburg to Albany by the Lakes & not to pass through Pennsylvania. The citizens of Lancaster had made preparations to receive you last Spring & were disappointed.[5] They have been again disappointed by La Fayette. They were much mortified on both occasions.

The earth in this County is literally covered with plenty. I have never seen such crops.

When I parted from Mrs. Jackson I felt some apprehensions concerning the termination of her disease. I hope ere this she has been completely restored to health. Please to present her my kindest & best respects & believe me to be ever Your sincere friend—

James Buchanan

ALS, DLC (33); ALS draft and Copy, PHi (10-1287). Published in George T. Curtis, *Life of James Buchanan* (2 vols.; New York, 1883), 1:44–45 (from ALS draft).

1. Adams had appointed Rush (1780–1859; Princeton 1797) secretary of the treasury. Sergeant (1779–1852; Princeton 1795) was a former Pennsylvania congressman. In 1826 Adams appointed him commissioner to the Panama Congress.

2. Binns (1772–1860), editor of the Philadelphia *Democratic Press,* supported William H. Crawford in the 1824 presidential campaign but had since shifted his support to Adams.

3. Probably Abraham Carpenter Frazer (1806–28; Pennsylvania 1825) or another son of William Clark Frazer (1776–1838; Princeton 1797), a Lancaster, Pennsylvania, attorney whom AJ appointed to a judgeship in Wisconsin Territory in 1836.

4. Reynolds (1779–1851) was a Clarksville, Tennessee, lawyer and congressman.

5. Expecting AJ to return to Tennessee through eastern Pennsylvania, the Lancaster common and select councils had voted on March 1 to honor AJ on the evening of his arrival.

From Charles Pendleton Tutt

Locust Hill near Leesburg Via.
June 1st 1825

My Dear Sir

I returned home a few days since after an absence of two months from home, and as I offered, when last I had the pleasure of seeing you to communicate any matters that might be interesting to you, I now have taken up my pen to comply therewith although I may not be able to communicate any thing that may be deemed of much importance, it nevertheless gives me pleasure to make the communication together with such speculations of my own as I may have to offer. first then as to the state of parties in New York, every thing appears quite tranquil after the tremendous political hurricane last fall, the friends of Mr. Clinton are satisfied that his administration of the Government has and will continue to increase his popularity,[1] his enemies are however only taking a little repose with their arms in their hands ready to renew the conflict, and so unsteady and uncertain popular favor is in that great state, that it is morrally impossible to say what may be the result of the next contest. in the mean time some of Mr. Clintons friends are particularly desirous to place him in the view of the public as our next President, repeated applications were made by them to me to learn how Mr. Clinton would stand in the South, and as I am partial to Mr. Clinton I i[n]variably told them that it would depend entirely upon the course Mr. Clinton took in the next Presidential contest, what would be the support he might expect from the South, that if he Mr. Clinton would not suffer himself to be named as a Candidate for the next Presidency, and would openly avow his preference of you, and after your election would become one of your Cabinet, that then I should have no hesitation in saying that the South would support him as your successor, and that if he was brought forward in opposition to you that it would ensure his Political death.

It gives me much pleasure to be able to state to you that I found in New York and elsewhere not only your old friends staunch, but that you have acquired a great accession of strength from the mild and dignified course pursued by you last Winter. I am concerned however to be compelled to state to you, that some of your friends there of high standing regretted exceedingly the publication of your letter to Majr. Swartout,[2] not on the grounds that they did not entirely approve of the subject matter or the content of that letter, but they said that the political standing of Majr. Swartout did not justify such a confidential communication on your part, that your communications of a political character should be made to men of the very first standing. they declared they were the friends of Majr. Swartout, but that it was perceptable to them that your confidential communication to him had done you some injury—you may judge how much pain this communication gives me when I assure you that I am the personal friend of Majr. Swartout, and that I am satisfied his great zeal and industry in your behalf was of considerable service to you, but I conceived it to be my duty and no feelings of regard or interest will ever I trust induce me to swerve from a rigid performance of that duty.

I contemplate spending the months of July and August in the state and city of New York with a part of my Family and if any thing should occur that would be interesting to you I will communicate it to you.

I have felt great anxiety to hear of Mrs. Jacksons restoration to health, be pleased my Dear Sir to remember me most kindly to her. and with best wishes for your health and happiness I am with very Sincere Esteem & respect Yr. Obt. Servt.

Chas. Penn. Tutt

P.S. I have heard nothing since I last had the pleasure of seeing you, of the Naval Agency in Florida[3] and I presume I never shall, as I am confident Mr. Adams is perfectly aware of the opinion I have always expressed of his union with Mr. Clay, but whatever may be the fate of the application I shall ever remember with gratitude the trouble you have taken to serve me. Tutt

ALS, DLC (33).
    1. Capitalizing on public anger over his removal as canal commissioner in April 1824, DeWitt Clinton, candidate of the People's Party in New York, had won election as governor in November.
    2. See above, AJ to Samuel Swartwout, February 22.
    3. During Monroe's presidency, AJ had recommended Tutt for the post at Pensacola, but he did not receive the appointment until 1829, from AJ.

From John Coffee

Coxes Creek, 2nd. June 1825

Dear Genl.

I received yours of the 19th. Ulto.[1] some time since, and would have written you sooner, but I was desireous of seeing Nickersons Crop before I wrote, and also to get some report from the sale of little Andrews last Cotton, in both of which I have succeeded—two days since I recd. advices and remittance from Doctr. Bedford & his new firm,[2] announcing the sale of the ten Bales of Cotton on the 18th. April at 18 cents—amounting to $645. united states bills, which sum he sent me by the Capt. of a steam boat, out of which I shall pay the account due to [John] Simpsons for last year about $230 dollars,[3] and the balance to Nickerson for his wages, having paid him heretofore $100. the amount recd. from [Lewis] Garner[4]—[William] Griffin has not paid a cent as yet, though he promises fair, I shall not let one other Court pass without sueing him if he does not pay[5]—I observe you say that you will pay the $400. to Bennett Smith, which I am glad you have done as that will finally close that business—as Major [David] Hubbard is going in and speaks of going to see you I have sent you the $300. paid by Anthony Winston as you may want it,[6] & the small balance that will remain to Andrew you can settle at any time it may be wanted—Bedfords reputation as an agent is sunk in this part of the Country. I do not know of one good sale that he has made the last season, he is done here—Our Cotton Crops are not promising in this Country generally, many have bad stands, & we have been more wet than usual untill a few days past, much cool weather and hail my Crop is what I call a bad stand, from frost, hail, and wet weather, it died out untill it is entirely too thin, but I hope what stands will be very good Cotton, on last saturday I went to see Nickersons Crop it is the best I have seen but one crop, he has it in good order for the season, and promises to be a fine

crop, his corn crop is very good, the family healthy, and all things is going on well; Nickerson was long confined with sickness during the latter
part of the winter & Spring, but he is now quite in hea[l]th—Major [Wil-
liam C.] Ward with Mr. [Lewis Buckner] Allen has the best stand of Cotton I have seen in this Country this season, and it is in fine condition, if
you see the Major please say so to him[7]—Capt. Savage did offer his farm
for sale, but his intention was to purchase near Florence to be convenent
to school his children, & I dont think he has full faith in the health of his
place, but he has no prospects of selling—Our Country is kept in a constant ferment with the Candidates on the electioneering business, a hard
race is to be run between McVay and Jackson, but tis thought by those
who have more information than I have that McVay will beat him far,
but great, very great, exertions are making by James & his satarlites to
procure his election. Old McVay tells the people that he has run against
all kind of nags but an imported one, that he thinks he can beat him too—
if Major Hubbard should call on you, I refer you to him for the news of
the day here—I certainly think you ought to call on James Jackson for his
proportion of the Allison Judgment, I gave the letter you enclosed to me,
to my Clerk [Ferdinand] Sannoner[8] to hand to him, he called to see him
and left the letter with young McCulloch for him,[9] no doubt he recd. it—
we meet and speak on business only, which is as near as I ever wish to be
connected with him in future—On the subject of memorialiseing the President on the subject of selling the public lands immediately I have some
doubts of the propriety at this time, the price of Cotton is now higher
than it was ever before known, and as such I fear the land will be raised
in a similar proportion shd. it come into market at the same time, but of
this I am not certain, we will reflect on this subject more before we act,
how much is it to be regretted that Mr. Monroe stoped the sale, he will
have injured this section of Country more by that one precipitate act, than
he could repair in an age to come—Our Country is generally healthy as
yet, my family have had good health except our little daughter Rachel,
who has had a bowel complaint about two weeks, with symptoms of
worms, and cutting her eye teeth, we have administered to her, and she is
getting better, hope in a few days she will be well—

Mrs. Eliza Donelson is mending fast she has been to see us several times
lately, & in 2 or 3 weeks will go to Tennessee—Polley and our little children unite with me in tendering to you and Mrs. Jackson our respects &
best wishes—Dr. Genl. yrs.

Jno. Coffee

Enclosed with the money is H[utchens] Burtons receipt for the rent of
field by your overseer [Stephen] Sharrock[10]—this rect. with the money
over pays the note I hold of Col Winstons a few dollars

ALS, DLC (33).
1. See above.
2. Bedford, Breedlove & Robeson.
3. Simpson (1790–1865), a Florence merchant and planter, had furnished supplies for Hutchings's farm.
4. Garner, Coffee's neighbor, owed AJ $320 for a stud horse.
5. Griffin (c1780–c1839), who later settled in Fayette County, Tennessee, owed AJ for a slave, George. No record of a suit against him has been found, and his debt remained uncollected until early January 1832.
6. Hubbard (1792–1874) was a lawyer in Florence at this time; Winston owed AJ for the Big Spring plantation.
7. Ward (d. 1827) was formerly from Nashville; Allen (1784–c1835), from Montgomery County, Tennessee.
8. Letter not found. Sannoner (1793–1859), an engineer from Italy employed by Coffee as a deputy surveyor in 1817, laid out the town of Florence and has been credited with naming it.
9. McCulloch, otherwise unidentified, was perhaps a relative of Sarah Moore McCulloch, James Jackson's wife.
10. Receipt not found. Sharrock had been employed as overseer of AJ's Big Spring plantation around January 1822 and was dismissed in March of that year. Burton (1789–1838), of Tuscumbia, claimed rent for a field cultivated on the school land near Big Spring.

To John Coffee

Hermitage June 6th. 1825

Dear Genl.

Inclosed you will receive a copy of the record Bennett Smith vs. the Executors of John Hutchings deceased (Madison County Alabama) shewing that the Executors are released from the effects of that Judgt & costs of suit—Inclosed in said copy you will find a note given by me as guardian of Andrew J. Hutchings to Bennett Smith with his receipt thereon for $400. You will please enter this sum to my Credit with the Estate of A. J. Hutchings, and preserve the vouchers on file with other vouchers in your possession—you will observe that the sum paid by me was in current notes—U. States notes when this note was taken up, was Eight percent advance—I sold for this advance, to make the $400 in current notes—you will credit my account, in part, for, the U. States notes you sent me to the city—say for $370—which is equal at 8 prct ad to $400 current notes.[1]

I will if possible come out and see you and the family in the course of this summer;[2] Major Eaton & Major Lewis say they will go—with me.

I have not heard of late the prospect of your crops, it has been very cold for some days past—on the night of the 3rd. cold anough for frost but none was to be found in the morning, we are very dry in our neighbourhood, my cotton is as good as I could expect from the season, and a tolerable stand, If the season should be favourable I will make a good crop, altho it is still dying, & will continue to die untill the cold weather ceases.

I have confidence in good prices for our cotton next fall & winter—it is still rising in urope—My last lot (altho the worst) of ten Bales, sold for thirty cents—This is the highest that had been sold, at our last advices.

I am anxious to hear from you—¿how is your family & friends, ¿how your crops, and how are your elections going on—will the Irish succeed &c &c &c &c—

How I regret by my vote upon the Tariff to have done Mrs. Hanna so great an i[n]jury as to raise the cotton markett, so that she has got thirty cents for her cotton, if she held on to it, & did not sell too soon; I am afraid she will never forgive me for this vote that has thus sacraficed the great interest of the cotton planters.

Major Eaton has returned & is in good health & spirits—all friends well—Mrs. J Joins me in affectionate regard to you & your family, Capt Jack & Eliza & to Mr Easton Mr William Donelson will give you news of the place,[3] your friend

Andrew Jackson

ALS, THi (10-1303).
1. See Release in *Bennett Smith* v. *Executors of John Hutchings,* June 1. AJ paid the $400 toward the $500 he had borrowed to defray expenses at Washington. AJ had paid Smith with notes of Tennessee banks, while Coffee had sent Bank of the United States notes to Washington.
2. AJ visited the Florence area in late August and early September.
3. AJ sent his letter by Donelson.

From Joseph Desha

Frankfort, June 8th 1825.
Dear Genl.

When I parted with Govr. [William] Carrol a short time since at Lexington, he informed me, that you had been considerably indisposed but was on the recovery.[1] I flatter myself, that you have recovered your usual health. It was mentioned here a few days ago, that you intended to visit the Harodsburg Springs[2] for the benefit of your health. If you should visit the springs this summer, we should be glad to see you at Frankfort, if you could make it convenient. You have some friends here who would be glad to see you.

On saturday last a dinner was given at this place to Mr. H Clay, something upwards of sixty attended and partook of the dinner. It was given in honor of Mr Clay and evidently in approval of his conduct in relation to the Presidential election. A number of us, and some specially invited, could not take dinner on such terms, and refused to attend. Some considered it an Adams dinner. The Federal party, or as some call them, the court party, will principally be Adamites, and will sustain those who by managment placed him in the Presidential Chair. A great portion of the republicans or the party of the people, as it is called, feel indignant at the management practised. They feel like important rights had been bartered away, but although there is much low murmuring, little is openly said. It is thought advisable to be silent till after our august election, after which I think it probable, there may be a considerable explosion. Kentucky, you know, is composed of warm materials, we must have something periodically to produce a fermentation in the body politic. The management in the late Presidential election will be the tub to be thrown out to the whale for the next season. The party of the people in this state are warm advocates for the right of instruction both implied and possitive, and consider, that the man who knows his masters will and fails, or refuses to obey it, deserves to be beaten with many stripes.[3]

Give my best respects to your lady. Accept my wishes for your welfare, and believe me to be Respectfully your Obedt. Servt.

Jos. Desha.

ALS, DLC (33). Published in Bassett, 3:286 (extract). Desha (1768–1842) was governor of Kentucky, 1824–28.
  1. Carroll (1788–1844) had accompanied Lafayette from Nashville to Lexington, where, on May 18, the citizens hosted a dinner for Carroll.
  2. A spa in Mercer County, Kentucky.
  3. Desha was referring to Clay's refusal to obey the resolutions of the legislature calling for Kentucky's representatives to support Jackson in the House vote for president in January.

To Richard Keith Call

Hermitage, June 24th. 1825

Dear Call

Colo. Butler has reached us in good health and handed me your letter of the lrst. Instant.[1]

I rejoice to learn that you are highly pleased with Talleshassee & the adjoining country, and that you have been so fortunate to obtain a Tract of good land to seat yourself & family upon adjoining the Town—I sincerely hope Mary may be equally pleased, and that you & her may enjoy good health, long life, & great prosperity in that country, in this wish your friend Mrs. J. cordially unites with me.

I sincerely lament that Gadsden has been unsuccessful, and what is equally coroding to my feelings, is that his defeat is to be asscribed to those professing friendship to me. Those who Colo Butler has named, there is only one in whom I have reposed confidence in his honesty & sincerity and that is Major Overton—he is sometimes credulous & may, by dissimulating designing men, be imposed on—but I believe, if he thought the man without principle, capable of intrigue, he would at once abandon him—Colo. R. M. Johnston has frequently named to me, that Colo [Joseph M.] White was a very high minded honourable man & much my friend—In this I never confided—I was informed of his connections in Kentucky, and I was sure if influenced by them, he was not really, if ostensibly, my friend:[2] Judge [Henry Marie] Brakenridge I knew had no stability of Charecter,[3] in those men I never confide—But you know one of my rules never to break my shins over benches that does not stand in my way,[4] and I viewed the Judge when appointed into office a bad selection, and who for the want of stability of Charecter would not give satisfaction to the Public. The two Judges (Smith & Brakenridge) will have before long to be reappointed, that part of your population who are dissatisfied with their administration of Justice ought to be prepared to remonstate against their reappointment, *If I am in the Senate,* you may rest assured I will attend to such a memorial.[5]

The present administration will wield all their influence to protect themselves, & continue their power, and the secratary of state will wield his influence over Colo White to convert him to his views: Colo. Johnston will endeavour to wield him to his, but the "Treasury pap," will always succeed with corrupt men, and you may calculate him with Clay and the influence of the administration wielded to support White & prostrate his political opponents you may prepare for this, and act accordingly—

I hope & trust the wisdom & intelligence of the people will rise in the majesty of its strength & prostrate corruption in our country, and all its disciples every where.

We are once more enjoying ourselves with our friends at the Hermitage Colo A[rthur] P[eronneau] Hayne & Lady with us[6]—Nothing disturbs our peace of mind but the idea of leaving it next fall for the city—This is unpleasant—My friends say I must not resign, my feeling & wishes say I must—what do you say, give me your thoughts freely; *My name is used by the nation*—on that subject I am bound to be silent—but I cannot believe it is necessary that I should bear the fatigue of these long journeys so injurious [to] my health.

Present Mrs. J. & myself kindly to Mary—say to her I have got a ring made for her set with my hair which I will send by the first opportunity, which I hope she will wear for my sake the little Andrews beg to be presented to you both—with our prayers for your happiness your friend

Andrew Jackson

ALS, Joseph S. Stern, Jr. (10-1315).
1. Not found.
2. Previously a member of the legislative council and a federal commissioner on Florida land claims, White (1781–1839), a leader of the anti-Call faction, had been elected the territory's congressional delegate, defeating James Gadsden and Joseph M. Hernandez. White was a son-in-law of former Kentucky governor John Adair.
3. Brackenridge (1786–1871), interpreter and private secretary for AJ during the Florida governorship, was at this time United States judge for West Florida.

4. A Scottish proverb dating at least from the seventeenth century.
5. Adams reappointed Brackenridge and Smith in 1828, but Jackson replaced both in 1832.
6. Hayne (1790–1867) had served under Jackson as acting adjutant general during the Gulf campaign, as Southern Division inspector general after the war, and as commander of the Tennessee Volunteers in the Seminole campaign. His wife was Elizabeth Laura Alston.

The two drafts below to Joseph Desha, one in Jackson's and the other in Andrew Jackson Donelson's hand, suggests how Jackson managed a portion of his correspondence during the 1828 presidential campaign: he would sketch a rough outline of what he wanted to write and hand it to one or another of his assistants for more polished composition. Before the letter or document was mailed, Jackson generally revised his assistant's draft. In this instance, the letter that Desha received has not been found.

To Joseph Desha

(rough draft to Govr Jos. Desha)   [June 24, 1825]
Dear Sir

I have the pleasure to acknowledge the receipt of your letter of the 8th. instant,[1] for the kind solicitude you have expressed for the restoration of my health, please accept a tender of my thanks—While Genl Lafayette was in this country & up to the time Gov. Carroll set out to accompany him to your State, I was severely afflicted, but my health is in a great degree restored; I had intended to have spent a few weeks at the Harrodsburgh Springs for the benefit of my health, and still do if I can with convenience accomplish it—Should I, I will with pleasure Vissit my friends at Frankfort and will apprise you of the period.

I have noted the information you have detailed with regard to the dinners, & the objects of them, given to Mr Clay. [. . .]

Mr Clay is araigned at the Barr of the peo[ple] and the good sense of Republican Kentuckey will pronounce Justly in his case.

I can assure you I have too much confidence in the virtue of the people to believe, that they can be induced by attachment to designing Demagogues to abandon those principles on which rests all our rights as freemen, and support men who have by their acts, and agency, have established a precedent, which if acted upon, must lead to the destruction of our Republican institution, & for the principle that a minority of demagogues must rule regardless of the will of the people.

<Should the people quietly rest under the late precedent>

Mrs. Jackson Joins me in reciprocating our good wishes to you & your Lady & believe respectfully yr mo. obdt. Servant

AL draft fragment, DLC (33).
   1. See above.

To Joseph Desha

Mr. Clay & the most of his present political associates became popular in Kentucky by advocating the doctrines of the Republicans, whose fundamental principle, certainly rests upon the right of the majority to govern, or in other words that government being instituted for the happiness and prosperity of the people, all legitimate power must be delegated by them and is necessarily subordinate to them: hence the obligation of the Representative to obey, as no circumstances can ever transfer to him the supremacy which is alone inherent in the people. How far Mr Clay & his party have incurred the penalty of this obligation is not a question for me to decide. It behooves them, charged as they are by so respectable a body as the Legislature of Kentucky, with a violation of the principles which advanced them into office, to shew that the charges are unsupported, and that neither the voice of the Legislature nor the various manifestations which were presented during the canvass, were fair expressions of the Public will. It is thus that Mr Clay stands arrayed at the bar of Kentucky, where I am sure her good Republican sense will render a just verdict—

I can assure you I have too much confidence in the virtue of the people, to believe that an attachment to designing demagouges can wean them from those principles which secure all our rights as freemen. They cannot support those whose agency is the establishment of an influence which must terminate in the destruction of the Republican maxims, and fix the contrary principle that a minority of Demogouges must rule regardless of the will of the majority.

Draft fragment in Andrew J. Donelson's hand, DLC (33).

To James Jackson

Nashville June 30th. 1825

Sir

yours of the 28th. of May[1] was handed on the 28th. instant, informing me that you had instructed Mr James Erwin merchant of Nashville, to pay your part, of our Joint note to Mr John Nichol[2]—upon its receipt, I went to Mr Nichol; & settled my part of the principle & interest of our Joint note had a credit for the same endorsed upon the note, & sent him to Mr Erwin to receive your part, agreable to your letter which I shew to him, and had no doubt but he would receive your part from Mr Erwin, and that our Joint note could be cancelled—you can Judge of my surprise when he returned & informed me that Mr Erwin said he had recd. no such instructions, that he had received a letter from you enclosing a note for collection &c &c &—and it appears notwithstanding your solicitude for winding up our business that your part of this Joint note remains unpaid & our Joint note uncancelled—you will direct therefore that this mony be paid, so that our Joint note may be destroyed[3]—It appears we view the record differrenly—I view the first item, the sum you bid for the Duck river land when sold, and the amount you are answerable for agreable to your proportion as pr agreement[4]—the 2nd. dated 1816 as the amount bid by Mr [John] Childress for the 5000 acres originally attached[5]—however this matters not, you know, being the buyer, that part of my Judgt was used to secure the land, & you can easily obtain the amount from the return of the execution under which you made the purchase, as you have often told me the sheriff was ready to make the titles—your proportion you will therefore please to remit me—or say you will not pay me your proportion agreable to your written agreement—it being the only consideration for all my debt—all my trouble & expence; I had a hope, under all circumstances, there would have been no hesitation on your part.

you are pleased to say in your letter now before me that "you advised me last fall, of an error in your favour in the settlement of costs the receipt of which has not been acknowledged." In reply I regret to be constrained to say, that when you thus write you were well aware, that there was no such error—and that such a suggestion, to save your feelings, could only be treated by me, with silent contempt.

you, who settled the whole business yourself, & in whose hand writing is the whole statement by which the costs was settled between the parties concerned—you, who never paid one cent to me for the interest you obtained, and who with Mr [Patrick Henry] Darby has recd. under my claim sixteen thousand two hundred dollars[6] *and myself not one cent*—you, who with the directions of Mr Darby settled up your & his part of the costs, & left the record open for execution against me, when you held in your hands upwards of two thousand dollars of mony loaned, & who had used my name in bank for your convenience as often, & as long, as it was a convenience to you—you, who took so little trouble about the suit, that in my absence it was delayed, neglected, & often on the point of dismissal for the want of prosecution, under all circumstances of the case, to talk about an error of costs in your favour, when you have only paid an equal portion of the costs with myself, when I had all the vexation, and the fatigue & expence of two trips to Georgia not taken into view on settlement, was well calculated to inspire in me, indignation, & illicit from me, that silent contempt, that such conduct & sugestions by you under all circumstances meritted; I had filed your letter of last fall with your statement of the costs,[7] as an evidence of your, truth, Justice, & liberality, where they would have decended to oblivion & forgetfullness had it not have been for your note before me; It was your statement in your letter of last fall concerned with other things which created in me, the desire expressed to close all our business—however I have no objections if it is your wish, in the presence of a few Gentlemen of standing; to have a reexamination of the whole business, and a full adjustment by them—In the mean time I wish you to have your part of our Joint note paid agreable to your letter of the 28th ult. & your proportion of the Judgt used in purchasing in the Duck river land, which will close this disagreable concern I am your most obdt. servt,

Andrew Jackson

P.S. on the subject of the Joint note to J. Nichol, & your determination as to your proportion of the part of the Judgt used, an answer is expected. A. J.

ALS copy, DLC (33).
1. Letter not found.
2. James Erwin (1788–1861), no relation to Andrew Erwin, was a partner in Kirkman & Erwin. John Nichol (1782–1853) was a brother of Josiah.
3. The debt was incurred on March 21, 1820, when Jenkin Whiteside (1772–1822; Pennsylvania 1792), a former congressman and a partner in the Duck River land venture, relinquished his interest in the 85,000 acres for a promissory note of $1,000 from AJ and James Jackson. Whiteside subsequently transferred the note to John Nichol. The note came due in March 1822, and a year later the two Jacksons redeemed it with a new note. On April 5, 1826, AJ paid off the note, but whether James Jackson contributed to the final payment is unknown.
4. The agreement of January 9, 1813, obligated James Jackson to pay one third of any judgment and one half of all court costs involving the lands purchased. In May 1816 James Jackson had purchased the lands in question at a forced sheriff's sale in Shelbyville for $1,282. When Whiteside left the partnership, presumably James Jackson and AJ agreed to split the costs equally.
5. On September 4, 1809, AJ obtained from a Maury County justice of the peace a writ of attachment to 5,000 acres located along Fountain Creek on the south side of Duck river for $5,000 against the David Allison estate. In December 1811, Childress purchased the land at auction (Maury County Deed Book C, p. 268). It is not known when the Jackson partners reacquired the land from Childress (d. 1819), a wealthy Nashville resident and marshal of the U.S. District Court for West Tennessee, 1803–19.
6. Darby (1783–1829), a journalist and lawyer in Nashville and Kentucky had acted for a time as AJ's and James Jackson's lawyer in the Allison lands case.
7. For a summary of the costs in *Jackson* v. *Andrew Erwin et al.,* see Memorandum, cJuly 1824. The trips to Georgia were to get a release of the claims of the Allison heirs to the lands.

To Charles Pendleton Tutt

[July 8, 1825]

My Dear Sir

I have received & read with great satisfaction your letter of the 1rst. ult.[1] and beg you to accept a tender of my thanks for the information it communicates; I have no doubt but the view you have taken of the political atmosphere, is correct, and Mr. Clinton will be solicited to come before the nation, the invitation to the west is preparatory to that event,[2] how far the south & west is prepared *at present* to support him, I am not advised, his talents are considered of the first order; and if he possesses political stability, & integrity, must become a usefull man to the nation, as he has been to the state of New york. There has been some who I have heard doubt upon this subject, and at present, might operate against him in the south & west—as to myself, I have always admired his talents, and have never had any evidence of his want of political stability or integrity.

I have always been in the habit of answering letters on political subjects when received from a respectable source; Major Swartwout had given evidence of great friendship for me, he adressed me on the subject, and I without hesitation, replied to his letter[3]—I believe him to be a man of great integrity & honor—and with me an honest man is the noblest work of god, it is with them I wish to associate, and with them to correspond whether in the humble walks of private life, or on the summit of wealth & influence—it is only with the honest there is safety—with them all is sincerity—with the others, all profession & hypocrisy—viewing therefore as I do Major Swartwout as an honest man and the substance of my letter to him approved I have nothing for regret in addressing it to him—particularly as I am insured by you who I know to be my friend, that you are the personal friend of Major Swartwout, which I am sure you would not be, if his private charecter did stand fair & unimpeached.

There will be a Naval Depo established at Pensacola—your claims by Colo. [Charles Fenton] Mercer & myself has been brought before the administration;[4] how far we have influence with the present administration is to be tested, as it has, as yet, gave us no evidence that we have any—none who we have recommended has as yet been appointed to of office; you may be assured that it will afford me much pleasure to have it in my power to serve you—and afford me great gratification to hear of your welfare & prosperity thro life

AL draft, DLC (33). Published in Bassett, 3:268 (extract). Date is derived from AJ's endorsement on Tutt to AJ, June 1.

1. See above.

2. The Ohio Board of Canal Commissioners had invited DeWitt Clinton to attend July 4 ceremonies for the commencement of work on the Ohio Canal.

3. See above, Samuel Swartwout to AJ, February 18, and AJ to Swartwout, February 22.

4. Mercer (1778–1858; Princeton 1797) was a Virginia congressman.

To John Coffee

Hermitage July 9th. 1825

Dear Genl

I have not heard from you since the return of our mutual friend Mr. Wm. Donelson when he reported, your family in good health, but your crop sufferring for want of rain My crop has suffered with the drougth but the rain falling last monday, and the crop being well cultivated, I have as promising a crop as I ever have seen; My cotton as a crop is as good as I have ever had, & if I had not sufferred for about two weeks for the want of rain, it would have been the best I have ever seen—I have had but one season since my crop was planted before last munday that wet my crop to the roots—I find good culture in a dry season will preserve the crop—my cotton has received eight plowings—I had blooms on the 20th of June, & my cotton is now more forward than it was last year on the 20th. of July, and my corn crop is promising.

I have recd from Mr James Jackson an answer to my note[1]—all *evasion* as to *[settl]*ing his part of the Judgt—*used*—he wrote me *[h]*e had instructed Mr Erwin to pay his part of our Joint note given to Mr [Jenkin] Whiteside—transferred to Mr John Nichol Executor, on the receipt, I went & settled mine, and sent Mr Jno Nichol to Mr Erwin to receive Mr James Jackson part, that the note might be cancelled—Mr Nichol informed me that Mr Erwin had told him he had received no such instructions, that Mr Jackson had sent him a note for collection, the proceeds of which was to be applied to our Joint note—I have wrote Mr Jackson a letter that will bring from him a declaration on the subject of the Judgt[2]—and a direct order to Mr Erwin to pay James part of our joint note—They are collectively the most equivocating set in mony matters I ever have had any thing to do with—& I am sure I will get clear of them shortly, and nothing could induce me to have any thing to do with them again.

How goes on your elections ¿will McVay succeed ¿how does my friend Capt Savage do, & who does he support—the Tariff having operated beneficially to our country as admitted by all—and particularly to the cotton growers, it being the means of increasing the price of the raw material; how does, J*[ames Jackson]* as a politician get o*[ver]* his great opposition to it—It must convince the good people of your county, that his political knowledge is unsound—*[. . .]* the *[. . .]*

Colo. Butler has returned in good health and has made a valuable purchase in Florida, and I have no doubt he will do well; If his family will enjoy health in that climate, he will be able to make himself independent there. Genl Call has made a purchase of a section of land adjoining the Town of Talisshassee, it cost him about $2800, and I have no doubt but in ten years it will command fifty doll*[ars]* pr acre—I have no doubt but Call wi*[ll]* succeed well—he writes me, & Mary writes Mrs. J. that he, & she, are delighted with the country—Mary is in good *sailing trim,* good balast, & all canvass spread—she is a remarkable fine woman of great oeconomy & industry—[3]

I will endeavour to vissit you in the course of this summer—till when accept for yourself & present to your lady & family Mrs. J. & my best wishes your friend

Andrew Jackson

ALS fragment, THi (10-1351). Published in Bassett, 3:287–88 (extract).
1. Not found.
2. See above, AJ to James Jackson, June 30.
3. Mary Call was preparing for the delivery of her daughter, Mary Ellinore (Ellen, 1825–1905), born in September.

Within a week after the presidential election, several members of Congress, led by John H. Eaton, began to raise funds for the support of an opposition newspaper in Washington, one free from the influence of Adams and his cabinet. Eaton's focus was on the ten-year-old Washington Gazette, *which had supported Crawford in the 1824 campaign. With the money raised, Jonathan Elliot (1784–1846), its editor, assumed a pro-Jackson stance, and continued to edit the paper for another year. In 1826, he sold it to the Jacksonians, who, after raising additional funds for its support from Tennessee, Pennsylvania, and South Carolina congressmen, selected Duff Green (1791–1875) as full-time editor of the* United States' Telegraph, *the* Gazette's *successor. The establishment of this press in Washington was but the first in a number of newspapers bought or supported by the Jacksonians during the four years leading to the election of 1828.*

To John Coffee

Hermitage July 23rd. 1825

Dear Genl

I have been requested by several Gentlemen who wishes to promote the circulation of the Washington City Gazzette to enclose you the address of the Editor & his subscription paper, and request your patronage & that of your friends to that paper. This is believed now to be the only paper in the City of Washington free from Executive influence & the only paper that has any claim to independence, I therefore enclose it to you knowing you will if you think it merits your patronage extend it.

I have recd lately several pressing invitations to vissit the Herrodburgh Springs—Governor Desha and Govr [William Pope] Duval of Florida who is now in K. have both written me on this subject.[1] I feel great delicacy in complying with their request—My political creed is neither to seek or decline office, and it might be considered a departure from this my Republican creed even to vissit the springs—however I have wrote Major Eaton on this subject[2] & would be glad of your opinion as soon after the receipt of this letter as your convenience will permit—

I was invited to a dinner to be given to the Kentucky delegation at paris K. Those four who voted for me on the presidential question on the 16 instant[3] I was expected to have been on my way to chilicothe as one of the commissioners appointed to fix the site for the Western Theological Seminary—The notification of this appointment did not reach me untill it was too late for me to reach the appointment[4]—Govr. Desha writes me he & Mr Bibb was there by invitation it was called the Jackson dinner, and four thousand people attended,[5] This is to be followed up by other dinners to counteract the impression abroad of Mr Clays having pursued the wishes of his constituents in his course on the Presidential question and I am told by Stockly who has Just returned from Lexington[6] that such will be the overwhelming majority against Clay—that it will silence his few corrupt supporters & prostrate him in his own state. Should the dinners to the four Representatives continue thus to be so numerously attended it will open the eyes of the nation fully to the corrupt combination at Washington—and when I thus view it, I think it perhaps my duty to go to the springs & if Invited to attend any dinners that I may be invited to, by a respectable assemblage but this requires deliberation.

My cotton crop is more promising than any I have ever seen—I[t] was dry but a fine rain has Just fell that will make my corn, and benefit my cotton.

All friends here enjoy health, I have not heard from Mr McLamore for some time, I feel about him much anxiety—but the nothern Journey was absolutely necessary to his existence, and I hope he will benefit by it.[7]

Mrs J. Joins me in respects to you Polly & the sweet little children & Capt Jack & Elisa and believe me your friend

Andrew Jackson

ALS, THi (10-1361). Published in Bassett, 3:288 (extract).

1. See Desha to AJ, June 8, and Duval to AJ, July 5. Duval (1784–1854) was a former Kentucky congressman.

2. Letter not found.

3. For the invitation, see Alexander S. Morrow to AJ, July 1; for AJ's response, see AJ to Morrow, July 22.

4. See Ezra Stiles Ely to AJ, June 4. The commission had been scheduled to meet on July 3.

5. Desha's letter has not been found. The *National Intelligencer* of August 31 carried a long account of the dinner at Paris, Kentucky, on July 16.

6. AJ's nephew Stockly Donelson (1805–88), son of John (1755–1830), had just graduated from Transylvania University.

7. On March 23, John C. McLemore fell ill with a fever and he remained bedridden for more than a month. Following his doctor's advice, he was at this time on a tour of the North and East.

To Edward George Washington Butler

Hermitage, July 25th. 1825

Dear Edward,

Your letter of the 17th. ult. from Indian Spring[1] has just been recd. Your narative of the Journey from charleston to Savanah shews that you experienced some peril; you tell me of being taken from the wreck of a Steam Boat, but how wrecked, you leave to conjecture;[2] I rejoice however that you & Genl. Gaines safely arived at Savanah & were kindly greeted by its inhabitants.

From your letter I perceive your Southern Tour has aforded you some amusement & much information—The scenes in Georgia give you a view of human nature when under the influence of party excitement, and selfish political views—The world had formed an exalted opinion of Governor Troup's talents, but I believe his late communications have shorn him of his character of high talents in public estimation, and of decorous deportment[3]—His whole conduct of late has afforded evidence of derangement from some cause, he certainly never could have obtained the high standing for talents that he had, without possessing some merit, which his late communications appear to be entirely destitute of. No body did believe that the Indians had any intention of committing hostilities on the whites—The whole excitement was produced by designing Whitemen to draw the public attention from the means used in obtaining this fictitious Treaty, signed by one or two chiefs & the rest self created, for the purpose of multiplying signers to the instrument—I am sure that, with the evidence now before the nation, the Senate would not have ratified this Treaty—What may be the course that will be taken will much depend on the information communicated to Congress by the President, procured through his special agent, sent to the nation for the purpose of investigation—When it was ratified, I was not in the Senate, being confined to my room by the then, severe indisposition of Mrs. J.—Had I been present, seeing none of the old chiefs names to it but McIntosh, I should have moved its posponement, & called for information from the President.[4]

your friends here are all well, Colo. Butler has Just returned from Florida, in high health & good spirits—I have heard from Elisa; her health is much improved; she still is much afflicted, but is expected in shortly, on a vissit to her friends. Her daughter[5] grows finely & enjoys good health.

I answered your letter on the subject of your intended union with the amiable Miss L. convaying our heartfelt approbation to the same—you have not acknowledged the receipt of that letter which leaves some doubt of your having recd. it[6]—present Mrs. J. & my respects to Mr & Mrs Lewis and the amiable Miss Lewis.

Mrs. J. Mr A. J. Donelson & his lady & the two Andrews Join in respects to you—present Mrs. J & my kind salutations to Genl Gaines & his lady—& believe me your friend—

Andrew Jackson

ALS, MnHi (10-1366); Extracts, LNT and LNHiC (10-1369). Published in Bassett, 3:288–89 (from Gayarré, p. 11).

1. Not found.

2. Stationed at St. Augustine, Butler and Gaines received orders on May 30 to repair to Georgia. They traveled via Charleston, which they departed on June 9. The boat wreck occurred on the Savannah River.

3. AJ was referring to Troup's messages of May 23, June 6, and June 7 to the Georgia legislature. In them, Troup complained of Creek agent John Crowell's interference with the Indian Springs treaty, protested federal postponement of the cession survey, and denounced federal intrusion on state rights.

4. The Senate ratified the treaty on March 3. For an appeal to AJ to intercede in the Creeks' behalf, see above, Creek Chief to AJ, [cFebruary–June].

5. Mary I. Donelson (1824–43).

6. Letters not found. Butler and Frances Parke Lewis , daughter of Lawrence (1767–1839) and Eleanor Parke Custis Lewis, married in April 1826.

To William Pope Duval

Hermitage July 25th. 1825

Dr Sir,

Your letter of the 5th instant[1] reached me yesterday. It is true when we parted I intended to visit the Harrodsburgh springs, being at that time a good deal afflicted; and I have since been seriously afflicted; tho my general health is now good, and the local cause in a great measure removed. Whether I can make it convenient to visit the springs, a few days will determine—should I, you shall be advised of my setting out and the probable day on which I will reach them, where it will give me great pleasure to meet you. Indeed to have the pleasure of seeing you there is an inducement for me to visit the springs.[2]

I have no doubt, as you remark, that every exertion has been made by Mr Clay's friends to get up dinners for him, that his course on the Presidential question might appear abroad as not only consistent with the will and wishes of his own immediate constituents, but also with those of the whole state, the resolutions of the Legislature of Kentucky to the contrary, notwithstanding. And unless the people of Kentucky do, by some public expression contradict this impression, it will be justly inferred that the Legislature mistook the will of the people and not Mr Clay. This is the object, and if it does not comport with the opinion of the majority of the good citizens of Kentucky, it would be but justice to themselves as well as to the nation—to counteract it, for I am sure it is intended to have an effect at a distance more than in the state. Mr Clay, no doubt, has discernment enough to see that the parade made, and dinners given, were not the spontaneous offering of confidence and good feeling, but a political mockery to bouy him up for the moment, and to trumpet him abroad. He must have felt, as every eye saw, his corruption, and the abandonment of those republican principles which gave him the confidence of the people for the pitiful consideration of the office of Secy of state. He must have felt his humbled situation to have kissed the hand and bowed the neck to Mr Adams, whom, as you informed me, he denounced in the presence of many of the citizens of Kentucky and in yours, as an apostate, as one of the most dangerous men in the Republic, and the last man in America who ought to be brought into the Presidency. After such denunciations, to have supported him, and received the office from him, is evidence of such humility and want of magnanimity that every one of his constituents must have seen, and himself most sensibly felt it. Who but such a man could have attended a dinner at Cincinnati under the public expression of disapprobation by a majority of the citizens of that place?[3] My feelings and views of propriety say none.

Col Butler has returned in good health and spirits to his family; and is preparing to remove in the fall with his family. I have no doubt, he will be happy to have you & Mrs Duval with him on the journey to Florida, provided he can arrange his affairs so as to set out at the time it will be convenient for you to leave here for Talahassee. Mrs J and myself will be happy to see you & Mrs Duval at the Hermitage.[4] She joins me in best wishes to you both. Accept assurrances of my regard and esteem, and believe me your's &c

Andrew Jackson

LS in Andrew J. Donelson's hand, THer (10-1373).

1. See Duval to AJ, July 5.

2. The previous winter Duval had accompanied the Jacksons from Washington as far as Kentucky on their return to Tennessee. On August 6, AJ finally declined the invitation to visit the Harrodsburg Springs.

3. The Cincinnati dinner for Clay was on July 13. In response to the invitation, another committee of Cincinnati citizens adopted a measure denying that the invitation represented the public will (*Cincinnati Advertiser,* July 13).

4. In 1804, Duval had married Nancy Hynes (1784–1841), a cousin of Andrew Hynes (1785–1841), AJ's former aide-de-camp. On October 12, the Duvals visited the Hermitage on their return to Florida.

To John Coffee

Hermitage August 2nd. 1825

Dear Genl

I am this moment in the receipt of your letter of the 28th. ult. in answer to mine of the 23rd.[1] I sincerely thank you for your candid advice on the subject requested—but all things considered, and being induced to believe that many wish to involve me in the politics of Kentucky for their own views, and there being a great heat at present on their local politics I have thought it for the present most prudent not to vissit the springs. It would be a feast to Clay & his friends was I to go there and the assemblage of people not greater, or the attention paid not more *[than that]* paid to him— I therefore conclude it is *[best to follow to th]e* end the course I have hereto*[fore pursued. So f]*or the present I have declined *[accepting the invi]*tation.[2] I have to go to the western District, & I must go & see you & your little family[3]—This will afford a sufficient apology to my real friends in Kentucky for not vissitting them this season, and the next will be free from the present objections.

I hope Mr [Gabriel] Moor & McVay may succeed in their elections[4]— the political enemy in your state is not dead but sleepeth, the abandonment of Judge Kelly is plain evidence of this fact—and they wish to get clear of Moor because he cannot be wielded to their views—the answer of McVay to his friends[5] is a good hit & shews him to be an adept at electioneering whilst he answers the questions he brings to the view of the people, that imported men are fond of foreign notions not congenial with the prosperity of our own country, this will & ought to have its effect.

We are now experiencing a severe drought, & the rust has made its appearence in our crops—they look fine but a few days continued drought and it may change our hopes, the squares are beginning to fall off—but my motto is that the lords will be done.

I will like to hear the result of your elections—Mr. McLamore is Just heard from at Pittsburgh his health greatly improved, all friends here are well—Mrs. J. Joins me in respects to you & family & believe me respectfully your *[friend*

Andrew Jackson]

AL signature removed, THi (10-1399). Published in Bassett, 3:289 (extract).

1. See above. Letter of July 28 not found.
2. See AJ to William Pope Duval, August 6.
3. AJ's trip to Tennessee's Western District was to honor an invitation of May 30 from the citizens of Madison County, Tennessee.
4. Moore (c1785–c1845; North Carolina 1810) won reelection to Congress; McVay lost the election to the Alabama senate to James Jackson.
5. Not found.

To Samuel Houston

Hermitage August 11th. 1825

Dear Sir

your letter of the 8th. instant[1] was handed me to day, and I am pleased to be informed that you are fully advised of "all the circumstances that surround you," being fearfull you were not, gave rise to the wish communicated thro Doctor [Martin W. B.?] Armstrong to you, of seeing you before you *set out for Kentucky*;[2] Colo. Butler for the same reasons, had a great desire to have seen you—but advised as you are, enables you *to Judge for yourself the course proper to pursue.*

It is true, I am the *friend* of Major Eaton, I am no less your *friend*; and it is well known I never abandon my friend without *good cause*—I know Major Eaton was your friend, & had a wish so to continue, but if I really know him, & I think I do, he will court no mans friendship[3]—as you & myself have fully conversed this matter over, I shall for the present add no more, barely bringing to your view the old adage "O that mine enemy would write a Book," and requesting you my young friend to profit by it.

The ballance of your letter I really cannot comprehend; I am fearful your fancy was riding on imagination & fiction, "your enemies on the house top &c &c &c" and the "declarations of Major Wm. B. Lewis & others &c &c &c" I cannot comprehend, I wish you had been more explicit—*it requires explanation before I can understand it*—will await your explanation—There is one thing I can assure you I fear not eve *"droppers,"* nothing falls from my lips injurious to my friends—I take principle for my guide, Justice the end in view, and I have no fears from secretes being revealed, always secure in the rectitude of my conduct with regard to my friends.

Mrs. J. Joins with me in best wishes for you—present us respectfully to Mrs. [John] Catron[4] & they ladies of your party—I am respectfully yr friend—

A. J.

ALS, DLC (33). Published in Bassett, 3:290.

1. See Houston to AJ, August 8.

2. Houston was traveling to the Harrodsburg Springs for a five-week visit. Armstrong (d. c1827), originally from North Carolina, had a medical practice at the Fountain of Health near the Hermitage.

3. To resolve the dispute between Houston and George W. Gibbs regarding comments against Houston's character, Eaton, a fellow Mason, had introduced resolutions before the Cumberland Lodge of Nashville. Houston held that the resolutions were unfair to him, and in October he asked the Grand Lodge of Tennessee to consider the issue (John Frizzell, comp., *Proceedings of the M. W. Grand Lodge, F. & A. M., of the State of Tennessee, from Its Organization, 1813–1847* [Nashville, 1873], 1:155–58, 161–64, 166–68).

4. Matilda Catron (c1802–c1872), daughter of John Childress.

To James Jackson

August 30th 1825

Sir

That our business may be finally closed, I again for the last time address you on the subject of that part of my Judgt of Allison heirs used to secure the title to the land on Duck river, which by the articles of agreement between us & Mr Whitesides on that subject (& which is in your possession) you are bound to pay me one third[1]—I now inclose an extract of the record shewing the sales of that land,

Amount of sales of the 15 tracts of 5000 acres each[2] $1282.

—your proportion one third—   427.33 $^{1}/_{3}$

Interest on this Sum from 18th May 1816 To the 18th of august 1825 nine years & three months at 6 pr cent—   236.98

due A. Jackson $664.31 $^{1}/_{3}$

you will examine the calculation & see that it is correct & remit me the amount, return me the inclosed record, if you remit me the amount that I may endorse on it receipt to you for the amount—and if you should not send me the amount due, that I may have it to use as evidence of the amount of my Judgt. used to secure the title to the land agreable to the articles of agreement between us.[3] I shall leave Genl Coffees for home on Saturday morning next.[4] I am yr obdt. Servt.

AL draft, DLC (33).
1. See *Jackson* v. *John Allison et al.,* December 17, 1810.
2. AJ was referring to the sheriff's sale of the Allison lands at Shelbyville (see above, AJ to James Jackson, June 30).
3. See Agreement of AJ, James Jackson, and Jenkin Whiteside, January 9, 1813.
4. AJ was visiting the Coffee family near Florence, Alabama. No further record regarding the Jacksons' settlement of their financial dispute has been found.

From James Gadsden

Charleston So C.
15 Sept 1825

My Dear General

I thank you for your prompt answer to my enquiry with regard to the Creek expedition into Florida[1] under Col [William] Miller[2]—It is in substance what I had anticipated—

On the subject of your remaining in the Senate of the U.S. your own judgement will be your best monitor—Whatever your enemies may say on the subject should be without influence; they will clamour and condemn act as you may—Their opposition is from interest and therefore will be directed by the objects they have in view—I know the immence sacrifice you make individually—Are they necessary? Does the public good with a view to the future imperiously demand this of you? are questions which must necessarily control your decision in the case; and on which I do not feel as well prepared as others, to give a correct opinion— That there is a strong feeling in the community as to the manner of Mr Adams' election; That Mr Clays agency in the affair has met with the unqualified disapprobation of all but his partisans; and that your character, under political defeat, has rather risen in estimation, is not to be doubted—All circumstances therefore seem thus far to demonstrate a determination, without anything like previous concert, in a large body of American citizens at the proper time to express their constitutional disapprobation of proceedings so alarming in the infancy of our government— In this event their attention will, as before, be directed to you, and your political creed will not permit you to deny the use of your name—Will your remaining in the Senate assist their views? and if so ought you with that *sole object* to do so? identifying yourself unavoidably, with a party which will be necessarily formed in opposition to the administration? are questions on which I entertain very great doubts, as at least not according with that pure & elevated course which you have pursued & which has so deservedly endeared you to the People—To be the head of a Party and merely to be supported by a party are very distinct—The latter cannot be avoided & the former I know you would resist; and individually I should regret seeing you, however remotely, identified in any systematic opposition to the present administration—I know what would be your course on the subject but both administration & anti administration men would unite in giving you to the opposition & the necessity of acting at times in the senate & the case on which you have already, with great propriety, expressed your opinion would all conspire to produce such an impression in the community—Opposition to the administration & the mode of the late election are very distinct and should be kept so—Mr Adams should be supported so far as his measures are approved, and the good of the country requires no embarrassment to an administration from causes which can only be rectified at their proper time—But approbation of his administration, should not necessarily sanction the mode of his Election; particularly as there are strong symptoms that the compact does not end with him—Mr Adams' reelection is to be repaid by Eastern support of Mr Clay as successor—Thus entailing upon our government, inheritance by compact, if not by primogeniture—All these portentous forebodings in the political horizon have awakened the vigilance of the People & at the proper time they will act if the purity of Elections & the stability of their institutions are still dear to them—They will then select you whether at the *Hermitage* or in the *Senate* and I am not certain that your remaining in the latter station will in any degree give strength to the great cause—It might subserve the views of party; if you could permit your name to be identified with it—but the great cause that of the right of the People to select their own Agents will remain the same—These are however the candid & hasty opinions of a friend whose removal from the active scenes of political life for the last two years has not afforded him opportunities of tracing the history of operations through a series of connected facts from which to deduce the most correct conclusions—

I have written to [William Savin] Fulton more than 3 months since on the subject of my Florence interest[3]—empowering him to divide the lots agreeably to your wish & to sell my share stock &c Could you or Gen Coffee assist him To commence a farm I have been compelled to contract debts—I left the Army as poor as I went into it—My friends have been kind but to meet my obligations & preserve my independence I wish to gather together all the means at my command—If $250. could be got for my stock it would assist me greatly—My kind regards to Mrs Jackson, the Andrews & friends generaly your friend

Gadsden

Will you write me addressed to Tallahassee via Early Court house (Geo) as to your final decision of the subject of returning to Washington

ALS, DLC (33).
   1. AJ's reply (not found) to Gadsden's inquiry of July 7 apparently denied having authorized the expedition.
   2. In the summer of 1821, Billy Miller, a mixed-blood Creek chief of Coweta and Thlecatchea (Broken Arrow) and a veteran of the Negro Fort expedition and the Seminole campaign, had gone into Florida to capture runaway slaves. At this time, Creeks and whites were disputing ownership of the slaves.
   3. In 1818, Gadsden, with AJ and James C. Bronaugh, had jointly purchased nine lots in Florence, stock offered by the first Cypress Land Company. Following Bronaugh's death in 1823, AJ and Gadsden had bought out Bronaugh's interest, AJ taking five lots and Gadsden four. Fulton (1795–1844), AJ's private secretary during the 1818 Seminole campaign, was at this time a judge in Florence. In 1829, AJ appointed him secretary of Arkansas Territory, and in 1835, governor.

On September 13, the Jacksons left the Hermitage, accompanied by John Overton and John H. Eaton, to attend a celebration in Jackson's honor in Madison County, Tennessee, and for the Jacksons to visit Donelson relatives in the area. While there, Jackson also accepted an invitation to Paris, Tennessee, delaying their return to the Hermitage until October 7.

To William R. Hess and the Masons of
Lodge 45, Jackson, Tennessee

[September 19, 1825]

Sir:

It had escaped my recollection, though I am flattered to learn it, that the dispensation under which you were installed, was during the period I had the honor to preside over the Grand Lodge of this state.[1] My pleasure is increased from a knowledge, derived by my visit here to day, that you have not neglected to patronize, and fully to practise upon, the great objects held out in your charter. Masonry brings into active operation, the important principles by which man in his pilgrimage below should be guided, and governed; properly practised upon, it renders him better, and teaches that essential dependence, without which every pursuit is but a gilded phantom.

I tender you my thanks for your flattering notice of those public events in which, heretofore, it has been my lot to be an actor, and for the friendly welcome you have kindly extended towards me.[2] I beseech you to go on, extend and improve the great principles of benevolence and charity, which are inculcated by your order, that you may so shine amongst men that you may prove a lamp to their path, and a light to their understanding;[3] thereby dispelling many of those prejudices, which, from a want of correct information; mankind, in different ages, and at different times, have entertained towards the institutions of Masonry.

Printed, *Jackson Gazette*, September 24 (10-1425). Hess, a Haywood County lawyer, was Worshipful Master of the Jackson, Tennessee, Lodge, chartered in 1823.
1. AJ was Grand Master of the Masonic Grand Lodge of the State of Tennessee from October 1822 until October 1824.
2. See Hess to AJ, [September 19].
3. AJ was paraphrasing Psalm 119:105.

To William Stoddert and the
Citizens of Jackson, Tennessee

[September 19, 1825]

Sir—

I reciprocate the kind sentiments which, on behalf of my fellow citizens, you have been pleased to express towards me.[1]

If, in my march through life, it has been my good fortune to be an actor in scenes which eventuated beneficially, my greatest satisfaction is in knowing that at this day they are considered as they were intended, for the benefit and advancement of our common country. The last spot on the globe where liberty has found a resting place, will not, I hope, want defenders, and sincere ones, whenever an assault may come. The world cannot remain at peace. Human nature is restless, and man, as he ever has been, is ambitious. Because our government is formed upon new principles, we must not trust alone to that, but mark with care and caution the secret and silent inroads which intrigue, ambition, and cunning, from time to time may originate. In selecting at any time, an agent to discharge those important functions, which, under our form of government, must necessarily be confided to him who represent[s] us, let *mind* be one great consideration; but, above all, let it be ascertained, that virtue and purity, have, with him, taken up their abode, dwelling with him and he with them. By this means, and only this, can our government go down unimpaired to posterity. Mere form and ceremony in the guidance of our affairs, can avail but little; we must be vigilent and careful to adhere to those great principles, which characterize and mark the government we possess.

It is true, sir, I was an agent in furthering the wishes of the general government, and was fortunate enough to conclude the treaty of 1818, which gave to our state the fertile and hospitable country which you occupy. The execution of this important trust had been assigned to me, in connexion with an estimable man, Gov'r [Isaac] SHELBY, of Kentucky.[2] We spared no pains, and left no exertion, proper to be used, untried to effect the purpose of our mission. We did effect it; and to me an increased satisfaction is derived from the evidences now offered, that the haunts of savage man have been exchanged "for the cultivated farm, the lively hum of population, the arts, the comforts, and the happiness of man."[3] You are yet young in years, but press on; practise industry and economy, and soon you will claim in the state that condition to which the fertility of your soil, and your already refined population, abundantly entitle you.

Be pleased to accept, and tender to the citizens you represent, my respectful acknowledgements for their polite attention.

Printed, *Jackson Gazette,* September 24 (10-1432). The second paragraph of the address was widely reprinted. Stoddert (c1796–1839) was a Jackson, Tennessee, lawyer.

1. See Stoddert to AJ, [September 19].

2. AJ and Shelby (1750–1826) had concluded the Chickasaw treaty negotiations on October 19, 1818, by which the tribe ceded its lands in western Tennessee and Kentucky.

3. AJ was quoting from Stoddert's welcoming remarks.

To Henry Lee

Hermitage Octr 7th. 1825

My Dear Sir,

Your letter of the 11th ulto[1] reached Nashville whilst I was absent from home on a visit of business, and to see some of Mrs J's relations in the

Western district of this state: so that I have not until now had the pleasure of its receipt, nor the opportunity to thank you for it.

I much regret the attack made upon you in the Nashville Republican which you have detailed in your letter before me. Altho, the editor of that paper, Mr Murray, was friendly to my election as President, and is esteemed as a private friend, still I assure you I have never been in his printing office in my life, nor on any occasion have I suggested, or attempted to regulate, the course pursued by him as public printer.[2] In that capacity like ourselves, he is amenable to the tribunal of the public, where he ought to be adjudged upon his own merits. It is to be lamented that of late this tribunal is a mask from which too much slander and abuse are directed against the character, public and private, of almost all those who are brought before it. Such however seems to be the morals of the times, to which source I assure you, I at once attributed the aspersions to which you called my attention, and not to any change of principle inferrable from the acceptance of the appointment now held by you. Since the receipt of your letter I have made some enquiry of a friend on the subject, and find that Mr Murray had received the letter referred to in his publication, and witheld it from the public until the one made its appearance in the Richmond enquirer with comments, when he gave the one he had recd a place in his paper.[3]

I am pleased to read your sentiments with regard to the support due to the administration so far as its measures may redound to the prosperity of our common country. Mr Adams is the Constitutional President and as such I would myself be the last man in the Commonwealth to oppose him upon any other ground than that of principle. How he reached the office is an enquiry for the succeeding canvass, when the principles of the constitution, apart from his ministerial acts, or at least without necessary opposition to them, will sanction the investigation. As to his character also, it is hardly necessary for me to observe, that I had esteemed him as a virtuous, able and honest man; and when rumour was stamping the sudden union of his and the friends of Mr Clay with intrigue, barter and bargain I did not, nay, I could not believe that Mr Adams participated in a management deserving such epithets. Accordingly when the election was terminated, I manifested publicly a continuation of the same high opinion of his virtue, and of course my disbelief of his having had knowledge of the pledges which many men of high standing boldly asserted to be the price of his election. But when these strange rumours became facts, when the predicted stipulation was promptly fulfilled, and Mr Clay was Secretary of State, the inferrence was irresistible—I could not doubt the facts. It was well known that during the canvass Mr Clay had denounced him as an apostate, as one of the most dangerous men in the union, and the last man in it that ought to be brought into the executive chair. This denunciation was made publicly as I was informed by Govr Duval, and taken into view with the publication relative to the treaty of Ghent,[4] when the nomination was made to the Senate, I do not think the human mind can resist the conviction that the whole prediction was true, and that Mr Adams by the redemption of the pledge stood at once before the American people as a participant in the disgraceful traffic of Congressional votes for executive office. From that moment I withdrew all intercourse with him, not however to oppose his administration when I think it useful to the country, Here feeble as my aid may be it will always be freely given. But I withdrew in accordance with another p[r]inciple not at all in conflict with such a course. It is that which regulating the morals of society, to superior office would invite *virtue unsuspected,* and in the private relations of life forbids an association with those whom we believe corrupt or capable of cherishing vice when it ministers to selfish aggrandisement.

Still Sir, I am too charitable to believe that the acceptance of an Office under Mr Adams is either evidence of a change of principle, or of corruption, and I entertertain the same opinion of you now, and of your adherence to political honesty that I ever did. Every freeman has a right to his opinion of both men and things, and it is his bounden duty to exercise it fearlessly and candidly. This liberty of opinion is the best boon of freemen, and he that makes it the agent of the greatest good establishes the most unquestionable claims upon the gratitude and love of his country. I am very respectfully yr mo ob Servt

signed—Andrew Jackson

LS copy in Andrew J. Donelson's hand, DLC (33). Published in Bassett, 3:291–92 (extract). Lee (1787–1837; William and Mary 1808), a son of "Light-Horse Harry" Lee, had been appointed to a minor clerkship in the post office department earlier in 1825. In 1827 he moved to Tennessee to work on a biography of AJ, but spent most of his literary effort as a propagandist in the presidential campaign. AJ later rewarded his services with an appointment as consul at Algiers, but the Senate refused confirmation.

1. See Lee to AJ, September 11.

2. On September 9, the *Washington Gazette* had reprinted an anonymous letter from Abram P. Maury's *Nashville Republican* of August 20, which intimated that Lee's post office appointment was a reward for his abandonment of the Jackson cause.

3. On August 5, the *Richmond Enquirer* had published a letter of the same import from Staunton, Virginia, which Maury also printed along with the one he had received.

4. Duval had informed AJ of Clay's comments when he stopped by the Hermitage earlier in 1825. For a discussion of Henry Clay's publication regarding the Treaty of Ghent, see above, John H. Eaton to John Overton, February 7.

On October 6, William E. Kennedy, senator from Lincoln and Giles counties, introduced before the Tennessee legislature a resolution "that General Andrew Jackson of this state be recommended to the freemen of the United States as a fellow citizen, who . . . merits to be elevated to the office of chief Magistrate of this union, at the next Presidential election." The motion passed unanimously in the Tennessee Senate, and with but one nay in the House, that from Lewis Reneau of Sevier County. For Jackson, who had considered resigning from the United States Senate, the resolution was decisive, as he informed John Coffee, below. On October 12, he wrote his resignation letter and set out for Murfreesboro to deliver it in person.

When he arrived at the capital, a legislative committee invited him to a joint session of the General Assembly on October 14 to receive "an address, expressive of . . . the great satisfaction they feel in relation to the course he pursued during the pendency of the late Presidential election." At noon on that day, legislators conducted him into the House chamber where, before a packed gallery, Robert C. Foster, speaker of the Senate, and William Brady, speaker of the House, welcomed him, whereupon Jackson handed them his letter of resignation (Journal of the Senate At the First Session of the Sixteenth General Assembly of the State of Tennessee, pp. 85–89).

Most Jacksonians approved Jackson's course, but Adams newspapers questioned his commitment to public service: his decision was one that put personal considerations of comfort and reputation above duty to country. He should have remained in the Senate, they contended, to fight for the constitutional amendment he endorsed in his resignation letter.

To John Coffee

Nashville Octbr. 12th. 1825

Dr. Genl

yours of the 6th. is Just recd.[1] I regret the death of Mr Nickerson sincerely,[2] it is a great loss to his helpless family as well as I feel it must be to my little ward. I thank you for your note to Capt Jack Donelson and hope it has been in his power to attend to it—

I would come out immediately, but I am compelled to go to Murfresborough & am now on my way, and whilst there have come to the determination to resign my senatorial appointment. a happy opportunity has presented itself, and I think propriety as well as the political principles I have always acted upon requires this course—The Legislature have again by resolutions brought my name before the nation for the Presidency—The amendment to the constitution to give the people a direct vote in the choice of the executive will be agitated, & every vote I might give on this question would & might be asscribed to selfish views &c &c &c this & other reason have induced this determination which I trust will be satisfactory [to my] friends, & my enemies I feel no solicitude about.[3] I would be happy If Capt Donelson could spare the time (if he cannot William [White] Crawford can)[4] to take an inventory of the negroes and stock—for really I do not know how many negroes has been born since Mr Nicholson has had the management there, and the Hoggs ought to be counted, & the horned cattle, or the negroes may destroy many of them—I will be out as early as I can employ an overseer should you inform me you have not been able.

I am happy to hear you have regained your health, and your sweet little ones, I hope you & your family will long enjoy that blessing.

On the subject of the *suit,* Mr Nicho*[lson's]* testimony was all important; but I still think, the Testimony of James Jackson, Mr [James] Hood & Mr [Thomas] Childress will defeat them—Mrs. [Penelope Winborne] Nicholson knows the well caved in & has heard [Samuel] Bell say that he would not do any more to it[5]—and she can testify that it was entirely filled up & Mr Nicholson waited a long time for Bell to proceed, dug a well near the house 90 feet and failed getting water—and after finding that Bell would not proceed, cleared out the well Bell had dug and proceed upwards of sixty feet before he got water, which cost more than two-hundred & fifty dollars labour. Bell was to get a sufficient supply of water to be adjudged of by Messhrs. Childress & Hood, & if he did not, it was positively understood he was to get nothing, it was, *no water no pay,* and James Jackson well knows this; I had paid for several wells, and had publickly said I would never employ another for the child upon any other terms, & if James will be candid, he can testify to this fact—I feel a great abhorrence to the attempt to fleece the orphant & wish you to have the suit *[t]*aken up by appeal if it goes against me, so that I may be at the trial.

I shall write you by Major [Thomas Jefferson] Green[6] a relation of yours & McLamores fro*[m]* NoCarolina who will be with you some *[time]* next week & send you powers of atto. from Mrs. [Catherine Donelson] Hutchings & Mrs [Jane Donelson] Hays to Locate their share of the grant seperately &c &c—[7]

your friends are all well, Mr & Mrs Martin has just reached Capt Donelson—[8]

Mrs. J. unites with me in prayers for your health & that of your family—your friend

Andrew Jackson

ALS, THi (11-0013). Published in Bassett, 3:292–93 (extract). Endorsed by John H. Eaton: "please get what subscribers you can, & forward in 2 or 3 weeks to me at Franklin the subscription paper to the Washington City Gazette."

1. Letter not found.

2. The date and cause of Nicholson's death have not been established.

3. For several years, efforts had been underway to reform the electoral system, and the House election of Adams in early 1825 had given new impetus to proposals. Already the Tennessee legislature had under consideration resolutions introduced by Robert C. Foster for amending the constitution to provide for a uniform system of electing the president and vice president. Foster's resolutions called upon Tennessee's governor to forward the resolutions to all the states in the union.

4. Crawford, a son of AJ's cousin James Crawford, Jr., had managed Andrew J. Hutchings's Lauderdale County plantation in 1818–19.

5. The dispute with Bell, who has not been further identified, stemmed from the agreement of September 20, 1820, with AJ for digging a well on the Hutchings's property. The record of Bell's suit, defended by David Hubbard, has not been found. Hood (1780–1839)

and Childress (d. 1844), formerly from Nashville, were at this time residents of Florence, Alabama. Penelope W. Nicholson (b. c1793), Malachi's widow, originally from North Carolina, continued to live in Lauderdale County following her husband's death.

6. See AJ to Coffee, October 12. Green (1802–63), from Warren County, had been active in supporting AJ's presidential candidacy. He later served in the North Carolina, Florida, Texas, and California legislatures.

7. By the act of May 24, 1824, Congress had granted the heirs of John Donelson (c1718–86) the right to claim 5,000 acres of public land in Alabama or Mississippi (6 *U.S. Statutes at Large* 313). Hutchings (c1752–1834), widow of Thomas (1750–1804), and Hays (1766–1834), widow of Robert (1758–1819), were AJ's sisters-in-law.

8. Probably James Glasgow Martin (1791–1849) and his wife Catherine Donelson Martin (1799–1836), daughter of AJ's neighbor Captain John Donelson (1755–1830).

To Robert Coleman Foster and William Brady

[October 12, 1826]

To the Honorable, the Speakers of the Senate and House of Representatives of the State of Tennessee.

Two years ago by the unsolicited suffrage of the Legislature, I was prefered to the situation, at present occupied by me, of Senator in Congress. Pursuing the principle by which I had ever been governed, "neither to seek after, nor decline office," the appointment confered was accepted.[1] Aware of the practice which had long prevailed, of selecting, from each extreme of the state, a person for the high and responsible situation of Senator, I felt regret at being brought forward to disturb a system, which had so long obtained; yet in as much as the Legislature, without any knowledge or understanding, on my part, had called me to the situation, it was impossible to withhold my consent; and accordingly, the appointment was, tho' reluctantly, accepted—not however, without its being professed by my friends, that a longer term of service than one Congress would neither be required or expected. That service has been performed. I was still pondering, and in doubt whether exceptions to my resignation might not be taken, and if it might not be proper for me to execute the full term which you had assigned me, when my mind was brought to a conclusion by some late proceedings of your own, and a determination formed to surrender immediately back into your hands the responsible trust you had heretofore confided.

One inducement to my determination is, that travelling to the City of Washington twice a year imposes no inconsiderable fatigue; and altho' this is a minor consideration, and one which would have been met with cheerfulness, if business involving the interest of our happy country had required the exertion; yet I am aware of nothing of great national importance which is likely to come before Congress, excepting a subject that you have lately had before your body—the amending the constitution of the United States, in relation to the choice of a chief magistrate.[2] Upon this matter, I greatly doubted, whether it might not be my duty again to appear in the Senate, and extend my feeble aid towards producing an alteration in which great interest with the people of the United States exists; and on which the security of our republican system may depend. But having been advised of a resolution of your Honorable body, presenting again my name to the American people for the office of chief magistrate of this union, I could no longer hesitate on the course I should persue; doubt yielded to certainty, and I determined forthwith to ask your indulgence, to be excused from any further service in the councils of the nation.

Thus situated, my name presented to the free men of the United States for the first office known to the Constitution, I could not with any thing of approbation on my part, consent, either to urge, or incourage an alteration, which might wear the appearance of being induced by selfish considerations—by a desire to advance my own views. I feel a thorough and safe conviction, that imputation would be ill founded, and that nothing could prompt me to any active course, on that subject, which my judgement did not approve; yet as from late events it might be infered, that the prospects of your recommendation could be rendered probable only by the people having the choice given to them direct, abundent room would be afforded to ascribe any exertions of mine to causes appertaining exclusively to myself. Imputations thus made would be extremely irksome to any person of virtuous and independent feelings: they would certainly prove so to me; and hence the determination to retire from a situation where strong suspicions might at least attach, and with great seeming propriety. I hasten therefore to tender this, my resignation, into the hands of those who confered it, that in the exercise of their Constitutional rights they may confide it to some one deserving their confidence & approbation.[3]

Being about to retire again to private life, it is probably the last time I shall have an opportunity of addressing you. Permit me then to suggest, some remarks upon the amendment which you have proposed to the Constitution of the U. States. Our political fabrick being regulated by checks and balances, where experience assures us, that those which have been resorted to, are inefficient; or that however well their boundaries have been defined, on the parchment of the Constitution, some new barrier to the encroachments of power, or corruption, in any of the departments of Goverment, is necessary, a corrective should be applied; and under such circumstances, it is the duty of the people to see, that one is provided. There is no truth more sacred in politicks, and none more conclusively stampted upon all the state Constitutions, as well as the Federal Constitution, than that, which requires the three great departments of power—the Legislative, Judicial & Executive, to be kept seperate & apart. But simple and manifest as this truth is, the difficulty of arriving it, in practice, with Constitutional restraints, still remains, and presents a question, whether the wisdom and virtue of the present generation, with a view to amendment, in this important matter, may not be usefully employed. Gratitude to the founders of our happy goverment cannot be lessened by honest efforts, on our part to improve, or rather to fortify the blessings which have been transmitted to us, with such additional guards as experience has proved to be necessary. Upon this principle, I venture fully to accord with you in the contemplated change proposed to the constitution; and indeed would go further. With a view to sustain more effectually in practice, the axiom which divides the three great classes of power into independent constitutional checks, I would impose a provision rendering any member of Congress ineligible to office, under the general goverment, during the term for which he was elected, and for two years thereafter, except in cases of Judicial office;[4] and these I would except, for the reason that vacancies in this department are not of frequent occurence; and because, no barrier should be interposed in selecting to the Bench, men of the first talents, and integrity. Their trusts, and duties being of the most responsible kind, the widest possible range should be permitted, that judicious and safe selections might be made. The politician may err, yet his error may be presently retrieved, and no considerable injury result; but with Judges, particularly in the last resort, error is fatal, because without a remedy.

The effect of such a constitutional provision is obvious. By it, Congress, in a considerable degree, would be freed from that connection with the Executive Department, which, at present, gives strong ground of apprehension and jealousy, on the part of the people. Members, instead of being liable to be withdrawn from legislating on the great interest of the Nation, thro' prospects of Executive patronage, would be more liberally confided in by their constituents; while their vigilence would be less interrupted by party feeling, and party excitement. Calculations from intrigue and management would fail; nor would their deliberations, or the investigation of subjects consume so much time. The morals of the Country would be improved; and virtue, uniting with the labours of the Representatives, and with the official ministers of the Law, would tend to perpetuate the Honor and Glory of the goverment.

But if this change in the Constitution should not be attained, and important appointments continue to devolve upon the Representatives in Congress, it requires no depth of thought to be convinced, that corruption will become the order of the day, and that under the garb of conscientious sacrafises to establish precedents for the public good, evils of serious importance, to the freedom and prosperity of the Republic, may arise. It is thro' this channel that the people may expect to be attacked in their Constitutional Sovereignty, and where tyranny may well be apprehended to spring up, in some favourable emergency. Against such inroads, every guard ought to be interposed, and none better occurs, than that of closing the suspected avenue, with some necessary constitutional restriction. We know human nature to be prone to evil: we are early taught to pray, that we may not be led into temptation; and hence the opinion, that by Constitutional provision all avenues to temptation, on the part of our political servants, s[hou]ld be closed.

My name having been before the nation for the office of chief magistrate, during the time I served as your Senator, placed me in a situation truly delicate; but delicate as it was, my friends do not, and enemies cannot, charge me with descending from the independent ground then occupied, or with degrading the trust reposed in me, by intriguing for the presidential chair. As your Honorable body, have, by a Resolution, thought proper, again to present my name to the American people, I must intreat to be excused from any further service in the Senate, and to suggest in conclusion, that it is due to myself to practice upon the maxims recommended to others; and hence feel constrained to retire from a situation, where temptations may exist, and suspicions arise, in relation to the exercise of an influence tending to my own aggrandizement.

Accept I pray you, for yourselves and tender to the Honorable Bodies over which you respectively preside, my sincere regard

Andrew Jackson

LS, T (11-0019); Copy in Benjamin F. Currey's hand, DLC (33); Draft in Andrew J. Donelson's hand, DLC (34, 58). Published in newspapers and in Bassett, 3:293–96 (from copy). The copy and several newspapers note the date and location of composition as "Hermitage Davidson County October 12 1825." The copy also carries an ANS by Benjamin F. Currey, one of Jackson's private secretaries at the time: "The latter part of the Genls letter is of great importance only as far as regards the practice of his own precepts; a departure from which would be food for his enemies." Foster (1769–1844) and Brady (d. 1835), were both lawyers, from Davidson and Rutherford counties, respectively.

1. Jackson was quoting loosely from his letter to H. W. Peterson, February 23, 1823 (*Jackson*, 5:252–54).
2. Foster's resolution calling for direct election of presidential electors nationwide.
3. On October 28, the Tennessee General Assembly elected Hugh Lawson White (1773–1840), from East Tennessee, to succeed AJ.
4. On November 23, Davidson County Representative George W. Gibbs introduced an amendment to Foster's resolution almost identical to AJ's recommendation above: "that no member of Congress shall be eligible to any office with in the gift or nomination of the President of the United States during the period for which he shall have been elected, and for two years thereafter." With an amendment to shorten the ban on post-term appointments to six months, both houses adopted the proposal and voted to submit it to Congress for consideration (*Journal . . . Senate, . . . First Session . . . Sixteenth General Assembly, . . . Tennessee*, pp. 367–73).

From Robert Coleman Foster

[October 14, 1825]

General Andrew Jackson,

The representatives of the people of the state of Tennessee, who now surround you, for themselves, and in behalf of their Constituents, greet your appearance in this Hall, with sentiments of the most profound regard

The homage we thus offer to your virtue, & your merit, eminates from the most lively effusions of that gratitude, which we in common, with millions of your Fellow Citizens, in every part of this Republic acknowledge, for the eminent services you have Achievd. the history of which, composes many of the brightest pages in the Annals of this Nation. In the will of providence it fell to your lot, to unsheath your sword on our southern borders, at a moment when gloom and dispair, had fastend. on our prospects and a conquering Army, of Chosen Veterans were about to pollute our soil, by their hostile tread, when the misgivings of others forboded the futility of all human opposition. Then sir, your Bold resolutions commencd. and your plans were laid. If Credulity should demand witnesses, to prove the splendor, and the glory, of the tryumphs of your Army, at your side sir, stands the Brave, the invincible Carroll, and other distinguishd Companions in Arms, and in this Assembly of the Representatives of the people, other living *Sponsors,* who having participated in those scenes, are ready to say, the half has not been told. To you sir, to them and the Brave Soldiers of your Banner; where ever they may be, we now tender, the renual of our eternal Obligations.

In the crowd that now presses around, and amongst those who now address you, behold sir, a mixd. multitude, of your intimate friends, and personal acquaintances, some of whom have shard. with you, in many of the trying and painful Vicissitudes of your eventful life, others who have heard the story of your renown, from afar, and not a few, who have associated with you, for near half a Century, these all unite with one accord and hail in your person, the able and virtuous defender, of their liberties and their Laws, and the scourge of their Enimyes.

But Sir, the Occasion that now brings us together, presents the first fit Opportunity and gladly we embrace it, of declairing to you, our unqullifyd. approbation of your conduct in the late Presidents Election. It is not for us now to impune the motives of those who, in the Congress of the United States, were instrumental in promoting the elevation of the distinguishd. individual who has been Constitutionally Calld. into office. That the great Body of the people had, however designated you as the object of their preference *none can doubt,* that in the elevation of an other, no matter how exalted his character, and his pretensions the express wishes of this Nation was unheeded, *none will deny.* Your personal Conduct through all the various scenes that accompanied the important Canvass, & its Issue, was markd. by that prompt and unyealding honesty which your fame and the exalted nature of the office demanded. The world then knew you only by the brilliancy of your Arms, and the native energy of your Actions. They are now convinced, that the Character of the *Military Chieftain* and the able Civilian may unite in the same individual, and that in the future elevation of him, whom we now address, the freedom, and rights, of this nation have nothing to dread. Sir the Legislature of Tennessee, have devolvd. on me, the pleasing the acceptable duty, of informing you, that they have again submitted your name to the Citizens of the United States, at their next Election for *Chief Magistrate,* in so doing, they most solemly declare, they have not been actuated by Local, or sectional feelings, nor are they willing, any should beleave, they feel a spirit of hostility to the present administration. It is enough to say, that on you, the wishes of the largest portion of the Republic had centerd. and that so far from abating the same feeling still pervades & increases. In the spirit then of those political truths that have guided your public and private life and which have always inducd. a willing submission to the call of your Country no matter how arduous the task, we now cherish the pleasing hope, that altho to you, the Sacrafice will be great, yet the service will be offerd. and our wishes recorded before the nation, by your Acquiescence.

May providence long preserve your invaluable life, and When the measure of your days shall have been filld. may your last moments be as serene, as your existance has been useful.

Foster

ADS, T (11-0035); Copy, DLC (33). Published in *Tennessee House Journal*, 16th General Assembly, 1st sess., pp. 143–45.

To the Tennessee General Assembly

[October 14, 1825]

Messhr[s]. Speakers, and Gentlemen of the two houses.

Silence, rather than any language I can adopt, might better speak to you my feelings, for your kind and friendly expressions towards me. Words are too feeble, to declare, how sensibly affected I am at meeting you on this occasion, and more particularly, in bearing in recolection, as I ever shall, the numerous evidences of kindness and affection, which from time to time, have by the Legislature of Tennessee been extended towards me. Before me are my acquaintances—neighbours—personal friends: Some of whom have known me, from early life, to the present moment; and many have gone with me thro those various vicisitudes of peril—trial, and danger, inseperable from war; and which they met with all that firmness which mingles in the soul of the soldier, when he goes forth the defender of his countries rights. It is to the zealous and correspondent services of those gallant men, aided by that power which controls the destiny of nations, that our country was enabled to rise above the dangers that met her in her march, and which has contributed to give me so flattering a place in the estimation and confidence of my fellow citizens. A General in command may devise plans, and industriously attempt their execution; but for success his dependence is on those, who go with him to battle. The approbation of such men is highly solacing; it brings to pleasurable recollection, days and dangers that have passed, and smooths the little march of life which yet hangs in advance. We must presently be gone; a few short years and the places we occupy shall "know us no more"; yet the remnant of our march will be sweet, & the recollections of our toils forgotten, if we can bear along the hope, that virtue in our country will be regarded; for then will independence & happiness be maintained, & her Republican institutions endure

The Legislature of Tennessee by a generous indulgence have placed me under many & various obligations. In early life when my merits and pretensions were perhaps better appreciated than they deserved, responsible trusts were conferred; and however feebly the duties assigned, may have been performed, a generous kindness on their part prevented every thing of complaint. At the onset of the late war, thro their patriotic liberality & a friendly confidence towards me, large & liberal appropriations were made by which the General Govt. was assisted, and I enabled to advance on the enemy, & preserve from desolation our exposed and defenceless borders; and now again Gentlemen am I cheered with the declarations freely offerred by you, that in my evening Pilgrimage thro life your friendly feelings are reiterated, and your confidence not impaired. To me 'tis happiness indeed; it is evidence of your friendly sentiments freely expressed, & by me so highly apreciated as to be borne while I live in grateful recollection.

Nor is it less a matter of pleasing reflection, that the course dictated by my own Judgtment as proper to be pursued on a late ocasion to which you have adverted, meets your approbation. It was impossible for me to have acted differently, because it would have been at war, with all the declarations I had made; and all the principles upon which thro life I had professed to act. To be sure the situation before me was a high & important one, yet it was hung around with fearful responsibility, too many & too variant to be undertaken but thro the sanction and approbation of the country freely given, without which no man could hope to administer its affairs with satisfaction to the public, and credit to himself. In Justice therefore to myself, & in regard to the great & permanant interests of the country, it was preferred by me to leave the matter where by the constitution it was placed, free from any attempted control, or interference of mine. Thro life I have not, for the remnant of it I certainly will not, become possessed of any situation or place, where to compromit any of the essentials recognised by the spirit and design of the constitution, or by the principles of our free Goverment shall constitute a condition.

For the very marked and respectful attentions, in your Legislative charecters, you have thought proper to extend, I beg you to accept my warm and heartfelt acknowledgements; and to receive my warmest supplications for your present & future prosperity & happiness.

A. J.

ADS, T (7-0388); Copy in Benjamin F. Currey's hand, DLC (33). Published in *Tennessee House Journal*, 16th General Assembly, 1st sess., pp. 147–50.

To John Coffee

Hermitage Octbr. 30th. 1825

Dear Genl

Your letter of the 23rd. instant[1] by Capt Donelsons boy was handed me today—I feel greatly obliged to you & Capt Donelson for your kind attention to A. J. Hutchgs business, and feel satisfied and indeed gratified in being informed that Mr [Jesse] Winburn has undertaken to finish the crop particularly as he does it for the benefit of Mr Dickersons family,[2] for whom I feel very much—I hope he will be attentive and carefull and have the crop well housed. I have not engaged an overseer, but one application well recommended, and he could not write—This was an insuperable objection—There is one in the neighbourhood of Franklin well recommended, who, I will endeavour to see as early as possible—and will be out as early as I can leave home—I should have been out before now, but my political situation hitherto, (since I heard of poor N. death) prevented me, and I have still some business with Major Eaton,[3] so soon as that is accomplished I will be out—in the mean time will endeavour to find out a fit charecter to oversee little Andrews place, but wish you to continue your inquiries & engage one that you may believe is honest, & industrious, and capable, if such present themselves. I shall not make a positive contract without notifying you first.

I am happy to hear that the political course my own Judgment pointed out, meets your approbation—It has met the uniform approbation of my friends here. The moment the Legislature of Tennessee again brought my name before the nation as a candidate for the presidency on the next canvass political consistancy at once pointed to the course I must adopt—The political maxims I had recommended to others became my duty to practice myself—in my declining years it would not do to depart from those political principles I had always advocated & professed to practice, a deviation from them, in my old age, would have done more injury to those republican principles I had always advocated than all the benefit I have been able to give to that cause through a long life; I viewed it a duty I owed to myself & to my country to resign—I did so—that my friends approve my course is a source of great gratification to me—my enemies would find fault I knew, but they would have had cause to rejoice, had I pursued a course that might have brought upon me the imputation of advocating measures for my own agrandisement.

I rejoice to learn that your health and that of your family is restored—I regret your cotton crop is so short, but If we enjoy health we ought to be thankfull—mine is turning out better than I expected.

I learn today that Judge Hugh L White has been elected as my successor by a unanimous vote—This is grateful to me & will give general satisfaction throughout the state. I view this as one of the greatest compliments the state could confer upon me—he stands well abroad as a man of high talents & great worth—to have been succeeded by any othe*[r]* charecter would have been paying me but a poor compliment—but in confidence, I expected this when I resigned—the Legislature has bestowed upon me the utmost liberality, I shall ever feel grateful for it—I shall vissit you soon—please present to your amiable family Mrs J. & my best respects & receive for yourself our prayers for your health & continued happiness—respectfully yr friend—

Andrew Jackson

ALS, THi (11-0051). Published in Bassett, 3:296 (extract).
1. Not found.
2. Winborne was a brother-in-law of the deceased overseer Malachi Nicholson. AJ mistakenly wrote Dickersons for Nicholson's.
3. The nature of AJ's business with Eaton is not known.

To John Telemachus Johnson

Hermitage Octbr. 30th. 1825.

My Dear Sir
    your kind letter of the 20th instant[1] has just reached me for which I thank you—You will have seen in the public Journals before this reaches you, that I have resigned my seat in the Senate of the U States—My reasons for this step you will see engrafted in my letter of resignation to which I refer you[2]—the reasons assigned were satisfactory to myself, I hope will be so to my *friends* as to my political enemies I care not—they would have desired to see me pursue a course at war with the maxims I had recommended to others, and differring from those political principles I had always acted upon—but the duty I owed to myself and country in the decline of life, is to shew by my acts that I have taken principle for my guide through life & in my old age I will not depart from them. You have Judged correctly of my *feelings*—I cannot depart from those principles upon which I have always acted, and upon which (as I believe) the durability of our happy goverment mainly depends. a departure in my old age from those political maxims I have recommended to others—I would do more injury to our republican principles, than all the aid I have been able to give them, thus far through life—you will easily infer from what I have said that I will not be at the city this fall and will not pass through Kentucky I need not say to you & your friends, that if I had went to the city (this fall) how much pleasure it would have afforded me to have passed through your state, vissited my friends—Joined you & your brothers & had you for my companions to the city of Washington[3]
    <If propriety admits,> I may next summer vissit the springs in Kentucky—on which event I will certainly do myself the pleasure to see you

& your brother <and perhaps vissit the canal on ohio>[4]—It appears as you have intimated *that great [learned] civilians* may use the Bayonetts "whether right or wrong," without bringing on them the imputation of *Military despotism*—*Gentle Souls,* a push of the Bayonett by their hands even to *prostrate* the *sovereign rights* of a *state* would be all right because it was not done by *a Military Chieftain*—The people must look to themselves, goverment was made for their prosperity & happiness not for designing Demagogues, whose <push with the Bayonett> intrigue & management is more dangerous to the liberties of our country than the arm of the "Military Chieftain," who has risqued his life to preserve & defend it.[5] Mrs J. Joins me in kind salutations to you & believe me to be respectfully yr friend

A. J

ALS draft, DLC (33).
    1. See Johnson to AJ, October 20.
    2. See above, AJ to Robert C. Foster and William Brady, [October 12]. AJ's letter had been widely published in contemporary newspapers.
    3. John T.'s brothers James (1774–1826) and Richard M. were Kentucky congressman and senator, respectively. John T. had not stood for reelection to Congress in 1824.
    4. AJ was probably referring to the Miami Canal, recently authorized by the Ohio legislature.
    5. AJ was alluding to the administration's refusal to allow Georgia to survey the lands ceded by the Treaty of Indian Springs. In his letter of October 20, Johnson had written: "had it fallen to your lot to forbid the surveys in Georgia with the penalty of Bayonetts, whether correct or not, a hundred papers with open mouths, would have bawled forth military despot." The phrase "Military Chieftain" was one that Clay had used to refer to AJ after the recent presidential campaign.

To *Valentine Giesey et al.*

Octbr 31rst. 1825

Gentlemen:

Your polite letter of the 10th instant in behalf of the volunteers of Brownsville,[1] wishing to know the probable time of my arrival at that place on my way to Washington this winter, and whether a military reception would be agreeable to me, is just received. I feel truly honored by this renewed testimonial of the confidence and respect of the volunteers of Brownville, and I shall thank you, Gentlemen, to accept and convey to them in return the homage of my sincere regard. It will have been discovered from the public journals, before this reaches you, that governed by those republican maxims which have been my guide thus far thro life, I have thought it my duty to resign my seat in the senate of the U states— After the proceedings of the Legislature of this state recommending me again to the notice of the nation, as a fit person for the Presidency, I felt that it was wrong to remain in a situation where I would be likely to incur the imputation of making my official station instrumental to the sinister purposes of self agrandizement—I am now too old to permit by any change of action a charge of this kind; and I set too a high value upon that fund of happiness which I have derived from such evidences of the good opinion of my Countrymen as that which you have just conveyed to me to think of exchanging it for the alloy of self—

Accept Gentlemen, for yourselves this assurance of my Respect and esteem and believe me to be &c &c

Andrew Jackson

Draft in Andrew J Donelson's hand, DLC (33). Published in *Liberty Hall and Cincinnati Gazette,* December 2. Giesey was a member of the Battalion of Volunteers in Fayette County, Pennsylvania. In 1824 and again in 1828, he served as a Jackson elector.
1. See Giesey et al. to AJ, October 10.

On May 30 the General Assembly of the Presbyterian Church in the United States of America, meeting in Philadelphia, voted to establish a theological seminary in the West and appointed a committee to select a site. It named Jackson chair of the committee, which also included Benjamin Mills (1779–1831) of Paris, Kentucky, a justice of the old Kentucky Court of Appeals; John Thompson (d. c1833?), a presiding judge of the Court of Common Pleas at Chillicothe, Ohio, 1810–24; Obadiah Jennings (1778–1832), at this time pastor at Washington, Pennsylvania, and later at Nashville; and Andrew Wylie (1789–1851; Jefferson 1810), president of Washington College (Pennsylvania) and later of Indiana University.

Jackson did not attend any of the meetings of the commissioners, neither that scheduled for Chillicothe on July 3 nor that for Washington, Pennsylvania, on November 23. His letter to the other commissioners, below, appears to have been his sole contribution to the deliberations. The seminary, which was initially located at Allegheny, Pennsylvania, ultimately became a part of the Pittsburgh-Xenia Theological Seminary.

To Benjamin Mills et al.

[October 1825]

Gentlemen

Circumstances have occured that made a strict adherence to some of my political maxims, that I should resign my seat in the Senate of the U States These reasons you will see assigned in my letter of resignation[1] which was satisfactory to myself & I trust to all who really practice upon the pure principles of our goverment—hence it will not be in my power to meet you at Washington Pa. at the time apointed in Novbr next. On the subject of Locating the Western Theological Seminary I do not possess sufficient information, to give an opinion with positiveness on the subject—The great object in selecting the site ought to be health and a point that would combine the States west of the Ohio in its support—for it is my opinion founded on some information communicated, that the states south of Kyt will not unite in a site farther north than Nashville T or at farthest Danville in Kyt—for the Present then I would give it as my opinion that the site ought to be established either in the vicinity of West union or Cincinati—These are the only two places that have made any offers to obtain it—These places are easy of access by the way of the Ohio, and on the score of health entirely unexceptionable. It is reported that the Citizens of West Union & its vicinity offer $7000 for the location of it there—The offer of the Citizens of Cincinati are inclosed[2] and if it should appear that their proposition are as valuable as that of West Union, then it is to be considered whether Cincinati being a commercial place will not afford some advantages in point of society, and still more in the case of access to it, and facilities of communicating with the Students friends & relations—as to the cheapness of living I am unadvised, but would suppose from the abundant supplies at both and the lowness of price in this particular there were no differrence—I would therefore give my vote for that place that would advance most aid to its establishment—If equal in this point I would decide in favour of Cincinati from its commercial advantages that will increase the number & respectability of its inhabitants and give a larger benefits to the student in his associations with its society should the states south & west of Kentucky not unite in aid of this establishment, it is sufficiently far north, to give room for an establishment in some healthy point in Tennessee or upper Alabama.

AL draft, DLC (33).
1. See above, AJ to Robert C. Foster and William Brady, [October 12].
2. The Cincinnati proposal offered land.

From Stephen Simpson

Philadelphia Nov. 3. 1825.

Dear Sir,

Although it is prohibited to the conductor of a newspaper, to Address a Candidate for the Presidency without subjecting him to evil imputations; yet I flatter myself that *a ci-divant* Editor may be free from that suspicion; but in case that should not remove all objection, I have still another justification for the present Letter, if one is needed—that I write on business. So much has been written in the public papers, as well as expressed in conversation, about the impropriety of a Candidate holding correspondence with any human being, that a foreigner would imagine we were too thoroughly corupt to permit the usual interchange of social civilities, without contamination. As this is a doctrine I most heartily despise, I can pay it no other regard than to say I condemn it; still, however, *delicacy* towards you, sir, restrains me from infringing on its precepts.

I must appeal to your indulgence for intruding with the enclosed account; the unpleasant duty of acting for the good of a general concern, having developed upon me the settlement of an unpropitious business.[1]

I had the pleasure to see Mr. McLemore the latter end of the Summer; as well as of Mr. Kremer, that honest sample of Pensya. german integrity. Mr. Kremer is still in town; & I can assure you, he can no better bear the sight of Mr. Adams now, then he could last Winter at Washington. We had occasion to go together to hear a public oration, where Mr. Adams was present;[2] but the atmosphere of the room was too warm for *him*; & I really beleive that he preferred, as he declared, *my company* to that of Mr. Adams—a matter of no common flattery.

With assurance of profound respect & unalterable attachment, I remain, Your friend & fellow citizen,

S. Simpson

My wife lately presented me with a Daughter.[3] Had it been a Son, I should had the pleasure of naming him after the *Second Saviour of his Country*

To Columbian Observer & Nl. Chronicle
Dr. 1822.

Augt. 3.	To Sub. to April 1. 1823 at $5 yer annum	$ 3.33
1823.		
April 1.	"Do to Nov. 2, 1825 —at $8."	20.70
		$24.03
Cr. 1825.		
Feb—By this Sum received by Mr [John] Conrad[4]		12.00
	Balance	$12.03

ALS, DLC (33). Published in Bassett, 3:297 (extract).
1. The Philadelphia *Columbian Observer*, a leading Jackson newspaper in the campaign of 1824, had ceased publication on November 2.
2. On October 24, Charles J. Ingersoll delivered an oration in Philadelphia celebrating the 142nd anniversary of William Penn's landing. Adams had been present for the speech.
3. The daughter of Mary Simpson (d. 1856) has not been further identified.
4. Conrad, from Philadelphia, was co-publishcr of the *Observer*. Their press had issued Eaton's *Letters of Wyoming* during the 1824 presidential campaign.

To Edward George Washington Butler

Hermitage, Novbr. 10th. 1825.

Dear Edward,

I had the pleasure to receive your several letters from Georgia & the creek nation,[1] which would have been earlier acknowledged had I been informed of your return to the city of Washington. I regret that my friend Genl. Gaines permitted himself to be drawn into a political newspaper controversy with Gov. T.[2] However Justifiable his conduct may be in this affair; Still, it will afford Troup's friends in Congress, a strong ground to assail the General as a military man—and it is to be tested how far the Executive will sustain him, should his own popularity be endangered in the least thereby—I still hope that the Executive will act justly by Genl Gaines, but he and myself have had sufficient experience to know, unless shielded by positive instructions, the executive will shield itself from responsibility if it can, and throw it upon its subordinate—I hope my fears for the Genl may be groundless—still, I cannot but feel for the safety of my friend, when I see an avenue through which he may be assailed, and his feelings corroded by Congress—present me to the General respectfully.

you will have seen from the public journals that I have resigned my seat in the senate of the U. States—Therefore will not have the pleasure of seeing you made happy by receiving the hand of the amiable Miss Lewis; Mrs. J. & myself send you and her our best wishes for your happiness—we anticipate the pleasure of seeing you both at the Hermitage—present us respectfully to Mr. & Mrs. Lewis.

your Sister Eliza is recovering, but has not vissited us this fall—she had a long and disagreable confinement—her daughter is a very fine, & sprightly child—she doats on it—I do not believe she is yet advised of Anthony's death[3]—altho' she must suspect it, from not hearing from him—but never names it—I hope she will perfectly recover, when I last saw her she was in fine spirits.

I shall be happy to hear from you from the city—give me the private, & political news. Present me to Colo. Robertson & my old friend Colo. [George] Gibson,[4] & all my military friends—& believe me your friend—

Andrew Jackson

ALS, MnHi (11-0056); Extract, LNT (11-0059). Published in Gayarré, p. 12 (extract).

1. Not found.

2. From July until September Gaines and Troup had engaged in an acerbic public exchange of letters regarding the implementation of the Treaty of Indian Springs.

3. Anthony Wayne Butler (1803–24; Yale 1823), Edward G. W. and Eliza's brother, had died in late 1824 en route from New Orleans to Connecticut to study law.

4. As quartermaster at New Orleans, Gibson (1783–1861) had supplied Jackson's troops during the 1818 Seminole campaign. He was at this time commissary general of subsistence in Washington. "Colo. Robertson" was probably William Robinson (1782–1857), a Fairfax County planter and relative of Butler's fiancée. He had been a delegate to the June 1824 Virginia Jackson convention.

To Richard Chester Langdon

Novbr 18th. 1825

Dear Sir

your letter without date postmarked Novbr 9[1] has just been recd. I have had the pleasure for a few months past, of receiving, and reading with much satisfaction the "Ariel" which you had the goodness to send me, for this token of your regard please accept my thanks.

It is true, I have resigned my seat in the senate of the u. states—pursuing those politica[l] principles which I at an early period adopted as my guide thro life, when my name was brought again before the nation by the Legislature of my state, as a candidate for the presidential chair on the next canvass, a duty I owed to those political maxims, which I had always practised upon and had recommended to others, made the course I adopted, a proper one—for be assured I never could recommend to others maxims, that I did not adopt in practice—My own Judgt has therefore approved the course and I trust all my friends who practice on the pure republican principles of our constitution and who wish to perpetuate our happy Govt will approve it also—Our political functionaries should be kept free from temptation—the checks & ballances of our constituted Govrt. must be kept seperate & distinct, or corruption & management will undermind the fair fabric & it must in time fall. Those who wish therefore to perpetuate our republican Goverment in its purity must foster these principles & watch over them with [entire?] vigilence.

I have fresh on my mind your letter alluded to,[2] I well recollect being introduced to your brother in Cincinati, and am happy to hear he is elected to the Legislature of ohio[3]—For your kind wishes expressed towards me in your letter, receive I pray you in return assurances of my great esteem & respect

A J

ALS draft, DLC (33). Langdon (1789–1845) made a career editing newspapers in Louisiana, Ohio, and Kentucky, and, at this time he was editor of the Natchez, Mississippi, *Ariel.* In 1829, he, while publishing a Xenia, Ohio, paper, he broke with Jackson over the administration's removal policy, whereby he became known as the "Xenia Apostate."

1. See Langdon to AJ, [November 9].
2. On hearing of Jackson's nomination as minister to Mexico in 1823, Langdon had asked to accompany him. His letter to Jackson at that time has not been found.
3. Langdon's brother Elam Potter Langdon (1794–1864), a deputy postmaster at Cincinnati, failed in his candidacy for Hamilton County representative.

To [Stephen] Simpson

H. Novbr 23rd. 1825

Dr. Sir

yours of the 3rd. instant[1] is Just recd. Whatever may be the opinion of the public on the subject of a Conductor of a newspaper addressing a candidate for the Presidency by letter, in the present instance no evil imputations could Justly arise—I never have obtruded my name upon the nation as a candidate—I have always been brought forward by the nomination of the people—the support given therefore through the colums of the paper conducted by you, must be ascribed to the principles of patriotism in support of the peoples will, and could not be ascribed to <a personal predilection for me, as we never had any personal acquaintance> any different cause for myself I pursue always the course my Judgt points, regardless of the imputations of the wicked, and will at all times be happy to receive any communication you may be pleased to make to me—but as in the present case, where business called, it required no appology—[2]

I enclose you the amount of the ballance of the account enclosed, & regret I have to send you three dollars in Tennessee paper, for the want of change—this paper is now at 3 percent discount—the acpt being $12.03— and I enclose you ten in u states notes & $3 in Tennessee will cover the account, & pay the postage on this letter—

I feel happy that you became acquainted with my friend Mr McLamore when he was on his eastern tour for his health—he is a gentleman of as much purity of principle, & independence of charecter, as any society can boast.

I am pleased to learn that the honest patriot Mr George Kreamer is with you, and that his stern integrity & virtue is truly appreciated by the good citizens of Pensylvania—so long as virtue & integrity is cherished, and predominates over corruption & intrigue; so long will the honest George Kreamer live in the hearts of the american people

I congratulate you on the birth of your fine daughter, may she grow & prosper, may she live to become an ornament to her sex and a blessing to her parents in their declining years—accept I pray you my sincere thanks for the honor you intended me had it been a son & receive assurance of my respect & Esteem—

A. J.

ALS draft, DLC (33). Published in Bassett, 3:297 (extract).

1. See above.

2. When Simpson's 1826 insolvency petition revealed a debt of $1,500 to John H. Eaton, Jackson's opponents alleged that the Philadelphia *Columbian Observer* and other similar Jackson presses were "hirelings" (Philadelphia *Democratic Press*, December 30, 1826, January 19, 27, 1827; *Register of Debates*, 19th Cong., 2nd sess., pp. 1343–44). On September 12,

1827, Eaton responded, acknowledging a loan to Simpson but denying that it had been made to secure endorsement of Jackson's candidacy *(Niles' Register,* October 6, 1827).

To John Coffee

Hermitage Decbr. 1rst. 1825

Dear Genl

When I last wrote you, it was my intention to have vissitted you about this time, but the indisposition of Mrs. J prevents me—and from present appearences will prevent me this winter—altho I have promised Colo Ward & Colo [Benjamin Brauch] Jones to go with them about christmas to divide the negroes belonging to the Estate of Doctor [William] Dixson deceased,[1] still the situation of Mrs Jackson I think will prevent me—She is much debilitated, her mind much affected, and spirits remarkable depressed, with want of appetite—and cannot sleep—I have had Doctor [Samuel] Hogg with her,[2] and have this day sent again for him—she has not slept any last night—but I still hope Doctor Hogg will be able shortly to restore her to health—

I hope the young man employed in the room of Mr Dickerson[3] deceased will answer—if he does, it will be a happy thing, as it will ensure the continued attention of Mrs. Dickerson to the negro children & the domestic affairs—while it on the other hand, will give her & the children a home.

I intend to vissit the place as soon as Mrs. Jacksons health will permit me; In the mean time, I hope it will be in your power to pay some attention to it—and that Capt Donelson may have it in his power to vissit it frequently.

I suppose there will be some corn to spare from little Hutchings farm—you will be the best Judge how much—and when to offer it for sale—the quantity that can be spared, can be best Judged of, after the crop is housed, & the Hoggs killed—as soon as the pork is fatted, direct that it be killed—This will save corn, as well as ensure the safety of the pork—for I anticipate an open winter after this month, with a great deal of rain; If in this I should be correct—some danger may be expected in saving pork after this month—I have killed half of mine—and on the change of this moon will slaughter the ballance—

Will you have the goodness to write Capt Jack Donelson by Stockly,[4] to give some attention to the place untill I can get out.

So soon as the crop is up—it will be well to instruct the young man to commence clearing the small peace of woodland that remains—to take the timber out of the plantation to repair the fences, and if a dry winter, to start his plows and break up and expose to the frost all his cotton land for the next year—will thank you to write me by Stockly and inform me how many work horses, will be necessary to have bought for that place, & I will have them procured—perhaps Mr Easton can furnish them.

I refer you to Stockly for the news of the place & the health of our friends—with best wishes to you, Polly, and the children I am your friend

Andrew Jackson

ALS, THi (11-0065). Published in Bassett, 3:297–98 (extract).

1. Dickson (1770–1816) a Nashville physician and former congressman, had designated Edward and William C. Ward and Benjamin B. Jones as his executors. By 1823 Jones (c1792–1830), a former army captain, had moved to Lawrence County, Alabama, where he served in the state legislature.

2. Hogg (1783–1842), of Lebanon, a surgeon in the Creek War and New Orleans campaigns and a Jackson elector in 1824, frequently treated Rachel.

3. AJ again mistakenly wrote Dickerson for Nicholson.

4. AJ sent his letter to Coffee by Stockly Donelson.

To Edward George Washington Butler

Hermitage. Dec. 8. 1855 [1825]

Dear Edward,

. . . I am happy to be informed by your letter,[1] that the President has refused to listen to the demand of the Gov. of Georgia for the arrest of Gen. Gaines—and I hope the treaty with the Indians for all the lands within the limits of Georgia will put to rest this disagreeable subject—the discussion of which would have involved some of the most delicate questions that could be brought before Congress, and is well calculated to disturb the harmony of our happy country, as well as the feelings of our friend General Gaines who would, no doubt, have been attacked by his enemies in Congress. *State rights and military despotism* are themes where eloquence can be employed, and the feelings of the *nation* aroused. I fondly hope that by the treaty you mention, both these themes will slumber for some other occasion . . .[2]

I am happy to find that you approve of my retiring from political life. My judgment said it was proper so to do. I have always thought it wrong to recommend maxims to others that I did not practice on myself. I am getting too old to abandon a course I have practised upon through a long life. My judgment approved and dictated the course I have taken. It is a great pleasure to me to find that it is approved by the virtuous and the good. I feel regardless of what my political enemies may say on the subject. They would rejoice if I was to do an act injurious to those republican maxims I have always advocated.

Extract, LNT (11-0069). Published in Gayarré, pp. 12–13 (extract).

1. Not found.

2. On August 31, Governor Troup had demanded that Adams order the arrest of

Gaines. In his letter, Butler had apparently mentioned that Gaines had persuaded the Creeks to send a delegation to Washington to negotiate a new treaty. Signed on January 24, 1826, the new treaty abrogated the Indian Springs accord but still ceded a portion of the Creek lands in Georgia.

To Samuel Swartwout

Hermitage near Nashville T.
Decbr. 15th. 1825

My Dear Sir

I have recd your letter of the 20th ult.[1] It is a source of much gratification to me to learn that the late course I have pursued meets the approbation of my friends—it was one that my Judgment pointed to as proper, & I could not hesitate in adopting it. I knew my enemies would attempt to censure this course & impute to me different motives than those by which I was governed, but I have always thought it right to pursue what the Judgment dictated, regardless of consequences—hitherto I have been guided by this rule and as yet, I have had no reason to regret, that I adopted it for my guide—having practised upon it so long I am sure I will not depart from it, hence arises the great consolation to me, that in my public course I have been fortunate anough to meet with the approbation of the virtuous & good, being the only portion of Society whose good opinion to me has been desirable.

The moment I was advised, that the Legislature of Tennessee had again brought my name before the nation as a candidate for the next presidential election, those political maxims which I had always inculcated, admonished me that my proper course was to resign my seat in the Senate of the U. States, & retire to private live, where I might be free from the imputations of intriguing for the office, or using official patronage to procure it—If ever I reach the presidential chair it will be with pure hands, and by the free Voice of the people, uninfluenced by me—This appears to me to be the only way the executive chair should be filled—it is the only way our republican Goverment can be perpetuated, and the fair fabric prevented from being undermined by corruption & thereby destroyed.

The good wishes you have been pleased to express for my long life & happiness, is Sincerely reciprocated—Mrs. J. Joins me in kind Salutations to you, & your amiable lady, with the assurance that it will afford us great pleasure to have the happiness to meet you any where—Mrs. J. is Just recovering from a severe illness, my own health is improving.

Accept assurance of my respect & Esteem & believe me to be yr. mo. obdt. Servt.

Andrew Jackson

ALS, Clermont State Historic Site, New York (mAJs); ALS copy, DLC (33).
    1. See Swartwout to AJ, November 20.

To Richard Mentor Johnson

[December 22, 1825]

My Dear Sir

yours of the 2nd instant[1] is just to hand, acknowledging the recpt of mine,[2] enclosing the claim of the good old veteran Mr [William] Taylor[3]— and I hope relief may be extended to him.

Permit me to assure you, that it would give me much pleasure to be with you—but I have always thought self gratification ought to yield to principle—the moment therefore, that I was advised that the Legislature of Tennessee had again brought my name before the nation, for the next presidential canvas the principles upon which I had always acted, pointed to the proper course I ought to adopt—I believed that the precedent I was about to establish if acted on by others might have a better effect to check the growing corruption of the times, than my best exertions otherwise could do—at least in future time it will have its effect; and my Dear Sir, I <never> could think of recommending maxims to others that I did not practice on myself—hence I resigned, to establish the only principle, that I believe will perpetuate our happy goverment that is, by keeping her agents free from temptation

I could not attend the meeting of commissioners appointed to fix upon a site for the Theological Seminary—I wrote the board—and gave it as my opinion, from the materials I had to form a Judgt. upon, that it ought to be located in Ohio—in West Union, or Cincinati whichever place would give it most[4]—I have not yet heard from the board.

Mrs. J. has had a very serious illness from which she is slowly recovering—this has confined me to my house for five weeks.

It will give me much pleasure to hear from you occasionally when a leisure moment occurs—present me to Mr Calhoun & your brother & colleage, and believe me your friend

A. J

ALS draft, DLC (33). The date has been supplied from Jackson's endorsement on Johnson's letter of December 2.
    1. See Johnson to AJ, December 2.
    2. Letter not found.
    3. Taylor (c1753–1830), a major of Virginia troops in the Revolution, and at this time a farmer, merchant, and tavern-keeper in Kentucky, had been denied a pension because he was considered wealthy.
    4. See above, AJ to Benjamin Mills et al., [October].

To John Coffee

Hermitage Decbr. 28th. 1825

Dear Genl

This moment yours of the 4th instant[1] has reached me—I have observed its contents and leave the contract with the blacksmith with regard to the negro boy entirely to your erangement. I am sure it is right to have a Blacksmith on the place, and belonging to it—and if one of the boys can be made a good one—on the terms proposed, and in the mean time produce $50 per anum it is the interest of the child that it should be done[2]—you have my approbation fully to this engagement—but I fear it is too good a one to be fully complied with by the Blacksmith—and in the article it will be well to bind him to good & humane treatment of the boy, & that he is not to remove him during the term from the plantation or place where his shop now is, if he does, a forfeiture of the agreement is to accrue & he answerable for hire of the boy—but I leave the agreement entirely to you with the above remarks—we cannot be too careful in wording contracts to keep clear of lawsuits, & without such a clause he might remove, & remove the boy with him, which might involve us in law.

I am happy Mrs. Nickerson is pleased & I hope all things will go on well—

I wish I had bought pork here & sold the corn—but it is too late—pork could have been got for $300—

Mrs. J. altho mended, is still in very bad health—if I could keep up her spirits I think she would soon get well. I shall write you shortly again I have not time at present to say more, as Mr Earl is waiting who is to hand this to the post office Nashville—accept the good wishes of Mrs. J. & myself for you your lady & family your friend

Andrew Jackson

ALS, InHi (11-0077).
1. Letter not found.
2. Coffee arranged with John David Gaisser (1776–1871) for Andrew J. Hutchings's slave Sam to serve as his apprentice from 1826 through 1828, for which Hutchings received $50 per year credit on his blacksmith bill.

1826

From John Fowler

Lexington 2. January 1826

Dear sir

Colo. [John] Peck[1] has called on me this morning for my commands (if I have any) to Nashville, and says he intends waiting on you whilst in your vicinity. Altho I have not time to go into detail will give you a hasty sketch of my views as to your prospect of obtaining the votes of this state at the next Presidential election.

I am fully satisfied that Mr. Clay has in a great measure lost his influence throughout this state except the Aristocrasy about this place and the dependencies on the United States Branch Banks, as far as their influence prevails they will sustain him. Should the Constitution of be so amended as to give the people the right of direct to vote for the President, I think you will obtain something like four fifths or at least three fourths of the votes of this State over any other candidate they may offer. during our late Session of the Legislature Mr. [John Jordan] Crittenden[2] offered resolutions approbating Mr. Clays course in supporting Adams in Congress at the late election for the Presidency. on motion the resolutions were laid on the table and never called up to act on them the friends to the measure having discovered that they would probably be rejected by a large majority of the representatives of the people.

As to our State political affairs we have two violent parties divided in support of the New and old Court.[3] It was very desireable that a compromise could be obtained at the late session of our Legislature and various propositions made but every effort has failed. and another campaign before the people at our next August election with all the misrepresentations that human Art can invent will go out to the prejudice of the New Court and its adherents.[4]

The Governors responce to the resolutions offered by Mr [Robert Jefferson] Breckinridge is in my estimation a great state paper and worthy the investigation of our ablest politicians throughout the United States.[5] I will enclose you a copy of this document as soon as I can procure one for your Consideration Its probable Colo Peck will take one with him.

please to accept assurances of high consideration respectfully yr. Obt servant

John Fowler

ALS, DLC (33). Fowler (1755–1840), from Kentucky, had been a colleague of AJ's in the Fifth Congress, 1797–98.

1. Peck (1770–1847), a Boston native, was at this time living in Lexington.

2. Crittenden (1786–1863; William and Mary 1806) was a member of the Kentucky House.

3. Fowler was referring to the Kentucky "relief war," a struggle between the state legislature and the judiciary over replevin and stay laws, which had resulted in the establishment of a "new court" to replace the old court of appeals when the old court declared the replevin and stay laws of 1820 unconstitutional. The 1825 legislature was divided on the issue, the House supporting the old court and the Senate, the new.

4. In the August 1826 elections the "old court" party regained control of the Senate and, in December, the legislature, overriding Governor Joseph Desha's veto, repealed the law that had abolished the "old court."

5. In response to Desha's message to the legislature on November 7, claiming that the Bank of the United States, the U.S. Supreme Court, and the old court of appeals had seized the property of Kentucky citizens and "set the legislative and executive powers of Kentucky at defiance," Breckenridge (1800–71; Union 1819), a member of the House from Fayette County, had introduced resolutions that challenged the governor to provide evidence for his claims. On December 17, Desha responded, citing *McCulloch* v. *Maryland, Wayman* v. *Southard, Bank of the United States* v. *January,* and *Bank of the United States* v. *Halstead,* the latter three decisions involving replevin issues that had been appealed to the Supreme Court from the Kentucky Circuit Court (Frankfort *Argus of Western America,* November 9, December 21, 28, 1825; *Journal of the House of Representatives of the Commonwealth of Kentucky . . . 1825 . . . ,* pp. 88–90).

From Arthur Peronneau Hayne

(*Private*)   West Bank Ala. 14th. Jany. 1826

Dear General,

I have had the pleasure to receive your two kind letters[1]—the first, I regret to tell you, did not reach Charleston, till the day, after my departure, from that place, & was forwarded—the last under date the 13th. ultimo, I have just received.

It was with sincere regret, that I learned from your letter, that our kind & excellent friend, Mrs. Jackson, has been quite ill—but rejoice to be informed, that at the date of your letter, she was better—& sincerely hope, ere this, she has been restored to health. I shall be anxious, till I again hear from you, & be informed of the perfect re-establishment of her health. The unfortunate situation of Capt Winston, I sincerely lament; for it must be looked upon by his amiable lady as a most severe affliction, & I do indeed, sympathize with her, on the melancholy occasion. I trust, a kind Providence, will yet restore him, to his reason.

I have the pleasure to inform you that I have at last succeeded in disposing of *West Bank* and 24 of my Negroes.[2] I sold for $20,000—payable in *ten equal annual instalments,* in such monies as may be receivable in debts due to the United States, with interest on the whole debt from date of sail, at the rate of 8 per cent, payable annually. The Purchaser, in order to secure the payment, of the debt, the Credit being a long one, has Mortgaged 15 other Negros, & another valuable Plantation, in addition to the property sold. The security I think ample. I fear, Land & Negros, are destined to sink in value.

It would have afforded Mrs. Hayne & myself peculiar pleasure, to have visited Mrs. Jackson & yourself, again this Summer, in compliance with your kind & friendly suggestion, & to have accompanied you to the Springs—but it is now near 3 years since we have seen our dear daughter[3]—& it is our wish to visit her this Summer, & have made arrangements for so doing.

I congratulate you, on the fine Crop, you have made—mine is a good one, but not quite equal to yours. With 16 very prime workers, I cultivated 100 acres in Cotton, & shall send to Market near 70 bales.[4] I have made 90,000 weight of seed Cotton—all of good quality; & I shd. here remark that I planted 25 acres in Low Grounds—which from Freshets & Caterpillar, produced but 500 weight of seed Cotton per acre—so the balance of my Crop yielded as much as yours.

I hear regularly from Judge [Thomas] Duncan,[5] & in his last letter, he begs me to assure you, of the high esteem, in which he holds, your private & public virtues; & of the indelible gratitude, which he will ever feel, towards you & Mrs. Jackson, for all of your kindness towards *my & his Sainted Frances.* He says, "On the subject of the Presidential election, pretending not to be a politician—but judging from a pretty general intercourse in this State (Penna.) Genl. Jackson has not lost any ground. If the Contest is to be between Adams & Jackson, I cannot see from what quarter, danger to the Genl. is to be apprehended. I do not see that an *Interloper* would have any chance of success—but he might distract." In Ala. you stand on a *firm foundation*—the *will* of the *people.*

Remember me to your Son—also to Mr. & Mrs. Donelson—If Mrs. H was present, she wd. join me, in affectionate remembrance, to Mrs. J. & yourself. Be pleased to present me respectfully to all of my friends in Tennessee. I remain Dr. Genl. yr faithful friend.

A. P. Hayne

ALS, DLC (33).
   1. Not found.
   2. West Bank was on the Alabama River, twelve miles south of Fort Jackson in Autauga County, Alabama. In December 1823 Hayne had advertised the property for sale.
   3. Frances, Hayne's daughter by his first wife, was living with her grandparents in Pennsylvania.
   4. In 1825 AJ had planted 130.72 acres in cotton, from which he netted 71 bales.

5. Duncan (1760–1827), a justice of the Pennsylvania Supreme Court, was the father of Hayne's first wife, Frances Duncan (c1797–1820).

To George Winchester

Hermitage 15th January 1826

Dear Sir,

Your letter of the 21st December ulto.[1] came to hand a few days since. The pamphlet published by Capt [Isaac] Phillips has been received, & I have read it with great attention.[2] It presents, as you observe, a very hard case; but so much time has elapsed since his removal that I fear Congress will not take it up without some reluctance. To reinstate him at this period might excite heart burning and collision among the officers of the navy, and this, you know, should it be the case, would be a difficulty with the members of Congress which it would not be easy for Capt Phillips to surmount.[3] One good, however, must result from the pamphlet—that is, it will remove every prejudice against the Capt. which his removal without trial may have created, & it may lead to an appropriation by congress in his behalf. The pamphlet is certainly well written; and the power of the executive to strike from the register a military officer, justly contested. For my own part, I never did believe that the executive, ex officio, possessed this power—I have thought that without an express law authorising it, the *[exe]*rcise of the power was an usurpation. There can be no *[ne]*cessity for the power, since the President is authorised to suspend by arrest, and order a courtmartial for trial: and when guilt is ascertained the *cashier* and dismissal follow of course.

You are pleased to make favorable mention of the considerations which detain me at home this winter. My determination to resign the office of Senator was not taken without much reflection. I knew that those who have assailed me heretofore, would hope to make this circumstance their passport to the confidence of the credulous and unwary, and I might add of the people generally, thro the influence of the administration, and that accordingly the store houses of calumny and detraction would be filled again—But I have too much faith in the virtue of our people to believe that they could be influenced by such vile acts, or even should they <succeed in prostrating me> be guiled, it will be a sufficient consolation to me to reflect that looking at the condition of our Govt. and the tendency of the executive branch of it to encroachment and corruption, I tendered my resignation as a precedent which would as I believed contribute more to the correction of these evils than any personal agency which I could use placed as I was by the Legislature of Tennessee in a situation where this agency would be ascribed to motives of self aggrandisement.

We have had the pleasure of seeing Mr & Mrs [David] Armour at our house and were much delighted with your niece.[4] She has promised Mrs J to visit us on her return from the Western district.

Mrs. J. has Just recovered from a severe illness which has confined her for six weeks, and begs me to present you her thanks for your kind recollection of her & to present you her best salutations—accept the assurance of my great respect, friendship & esteem. yr mo. obt. servt.

A. J.

LS draft in Andrew J. Donelson's hand, with last paragraph in AJ's hand, DLC (33). Winchester (1787–1840), nephew of James, was a Baltimore attorney and later president of the Baltimore and Susquehanna Railroad. In 1824 he had served as a Jackson elector for Maryland's third district.

1. See Winchester to AJ, December 21, 1825.
2. In his letter, Winchester forwarded Phillips's *Impartial Examination of the Case of Captain Isaac Phillips . . .* (Baltimore, 1825). Phillips, at this time a Baltimore merchant, had been dismissed from the U.S. navy after sailors from the *Baltimore*, under his command, had been seized by a British squadron off Havana in 1798.
3. On January 21 the House Naval Affairs Committee recommended against Phillips's memorial for restoration (*ASP, Naval Affairs*, 2:464–65). In 1829 AJ appointed him naval agent at Baltimore.
4. Armour (b. c1772), his wife, George Winchester's sister, Mary (1775–1856), and their daughter Janet (b. c1810).

To Jesse Bledsoe

[January 18, 1826]

Dear Sir,

I had the pleasure of seeing your friend Mr Peck upon his arrival in Nashville, and of receiving the flattering note of January 2d[1] of which he was the bearer from you. In reply allow me to reciprocate the compliments of the season, and express my hope that you are destined to outlive, yet, many years, in health and prosperity, notwithstanding the disappointment to which you allude.[2]

You say that *you are a stranger in Israel*. It was once prophesied that Zion would be built up with blood, and Jerusalem with iniquity; but then the judges thereof were to judge for reward, and the priests to take money for teaching.[3] This prophesy we are told has been fulfilled: and God forbid that the history of our Government shall ever realise the same awful words.

I regret to see the perturbed situation of your state,[4] but trust that harmony and quiet will soon be restored. No doubt the Governor's reply to the resolutions of the House will contribute much to this wished for result.[5] It is an able paper and is worthy the attentive examination of every enlightened politician, throughout the union.

Draft in Andrew J. Donelson's hand, DLC (33). Bledsoe (1776–1836; Transylvania University), former state legislator and U.S. senator from Kentucky, was at this time judge of the Lexington circuit court and professor of law at Transylvania.

1. See Bledsoe to AJ, January 2.

2. Bledsoe had written AJ that he had switched his allegiance from Clay because of Clay's actions in the election of 1825.

3. AJ was paraphrasing Micah 3:9–12: "Hear this, I pray you, ye heads of the house of Jacob, and princes of the house of Israel, that abhor judgment, and pervert all equity. They build up Zion with blood, and Jerusalem with iniquity. The heads thereof judge for reward, and the priests thereof teach for hire, and the prophets thereof divine for money: yet will they lean upon the LORD, and say, Is not the LORD among us? none evil can come upon us. Therefore shall Zion for your sake be plowed as a field, and Jerusalem shall become heaps, and the mountain of the house as the high places of the forest."

4. Kentucky's "relief war."

5. Desha's message of December 17 to the Kentucky legislature.

To Edward Livingston

Hermitage Janry 30th. 1826

Dr. Sir

I am requested by the late Govr. [Willie] Blount of Tennessee to write you on the subject of his claim now pending before congress[1]—I take the liberty to enclose you his own statement which will much better explain the nature & Justice of his claim, than I could possibly do[2]—his claim he alledges, rests upon the same principles that the claim of the late Govr. [Daniel D.] Tompkins of Newyork was founded; which was recognised by congress, and compensation allowed.[3] upon your examination of it, should you find that it is embraced in the principles that governed congress in extending relief to the late Govr. Tompkins, I trust you will give it your support.[4]

In the late war Govr. Blount exerted all his influence to raise the necessary funds for the active operations of the Tennessee militia, and I have no doubt incurred great responsibility, under the purests motives for the benefit of his country; to him therefore, ought to be meted, the same measure of Justice that has been extended to the late Govr Tompkins of Newyork.

You will confer an obligation on Mr Blount by consulting Colo. [James] Hamilton [Jr.] on the subject of his claim and shewing him the enclosed statement.[5]

Mrs. J. has had a severe illness, from which she is slowly recovering—she unites with me in a tender of kind salutations to you, your lady & daughter.[6]

accept I pray you assurances of my continued respect, friendship, & esteem

Andrew Jackson

(private)

P.S. I observe the 8th. of Janry has this year passed without notice in the City of Washington—not so elsewhere[7]—It might be dangerous *now* in Washington, to commemorate *military chieftains*—hereafter the defence of our Country will be left to the *splendour* of the *goverment,* not to the arms of military chieftains supported by the Yeomanry of the nation— may not this defence, be as feeble as [William] Hulls conquests by proclamation in the late war.[8]

ALS, NjP (mAJs).

1. Blount (1768–1835), governor from 1809 to 1815 and an 1824 Jackson elector, was seeking reimbursement for money advanced and losses sustained during the War of 1812.

2. AJ's enclosure was probably Blount's memorial of December 14, 1822 (*SDoc* 110, 20th Cong., 1st sess., Serial 166).

3. Tompkins (1774–1825; Columbia 1795) also served as Monroe's vice president.

4. On May 11, a House select committee passed a bill in Blount's favor, but the Senate failed to act and Congress did not authorize the compensation until 1836, a year after Blount's death (*HRRep* 121, 19th Cong., 1st sess., Serial 141; 6 *U.S. Statutes at Large* 280, 290, 319, 624).

5. Hamilton (1786–1857), from South Carolina, chaired the House Committee on Military Affairs.

6. Louise Moreau de Lassy Livingston (1786–1860) and their daughter Cora (1806–73).

7. Even though Lewis Carusi commemorated the anniversary with a ball at his assembly hall in Washington on January 9, the celebration received less coverage than the one at the Masonic Hall in Nashville.

8. Hull (1753–1825; Yale 1772), governor of Michigan Territory and commander of American troops on the northwestern frontier, had occupied the undefended Canadian village of Sandwich in July 1812 and proclaimed "eventual success," but failing to follow up on his initial advance, he surrendered his forces at Detroit on August 16.

To *Edward George Washington Butler*

Hermitage Febry 2nd. 1826

Dear Edward

I have Just recd your kind and affectionate letter of the 8th. of January last, with the estimable present from Mrs. Lewis enclosed. be pleased to present her with the enclosed acknowledgement of the precious relic.[1]

On the 8th. of January, a day, ever memorable in the history of my life, to receive the greeting of my friends is certainly most acceptable to me; and permit me to assure you My Dear Edward, that there is none more acceptable than yours; because *[I]* know the sincerity of your heart.

Mrs. J. Joins me Sincerely *[in]* reciprocating all the kind, & good wishes, of M*[rs.]* Lewis, Miss Frances, & little Miss Angela[2] and yo*[u]*rself, and we pray you to tender us to them all, affectionately. finding your Genl on the wing to the west, we count certainly on the promised vissit from you & our friend Miss. F.[3]

I have Just heard from your sister Elisa—she is regaining her health, & preparing to vissit some of the watering places, so soon as the spring opens, if she can prevail upon her Capt. to leave his cotton farm—should you be able to vissit us in the spring, you will probably meet your sister here.[4]

Mrs. J. Joins me in prayers for your welfare & happiness and that of the amiable Miss. F. who we expect to have the pleasure of seeing shortly at the Hermitage with you—your friend

Andrew Jackson

P.S. be pleased to put a suitable wafer in the letter enclosed to Mrs. E. P. L. & oblige A. J.

ALS, MnHi (11-0122).
    1. Neither the letter nor the acknowledgment has been found. Eleanor Parke Custis Lewis had sent AJ a lock of George Washington's hair.
    2. Mary Eliza Angela Lewis (1813–39) was Frances's sister.
    3. Gaines, whom Butler served as aide, was en route from the army's eastern headquarters to the western in Cincinnati, posts at which he and Brigadier General Winfield Scott alternated.
    4. John and Eliza Donelson visited the Jacksons in mid-June.

To John Coffee

Hermitage Febry 2d. 1826

Dr. Genl

I have recd. your letter by Mr Eastin[1] it was handed to me by John[2] last night—I expect to see Mr Eastin this evening—

John will leave here in the morning with the three horses, one of which I Bot. from Capt Donelson (a filly unbroke) she is of good blood, got by the Capts Pacolet out of his Truxton mare—and will make (with care) a good animal—she has never eaten a barrel of corn—and tho, I think her a good bargain, if I had seen her before I made the purchase I believe I should not have bot. her—she is one of Williams recommendations & after agreeing for her, I knew it would not do to say to the old Captain she was a bad bargain, for he had spoken highly of her—the two horses are well Bot the bay is one of the finest pulling animals I ever saw—the sorrel, said to work, he is only three years old, four this spring, a good riding horse, and well worth what he has costs—The bay horse cost $65, the Sorrel $80—The gray mare $50 in all $195 I suppose will cost $200 when they reach the farm—I have given John four dollars cash and three halters which I suppose will take him out—with provisions furnished him.[3]

I am happy to learn from your letter that cotton is rising at Orleans, I have determined to send mine to Colo. Maunsel White[4] I have never dispaired of getting a good price this spring—The mony failures in orleans has depressed the mony markett, but the embargo laid upon our cotton by the lowness of the waters, will end well for the farmers, our cotton reaching new orleans in small quantities, will prevent that glutt in the markett that was calculated by the speculators, and it is bought & shipped as fast as it reaches there—fifteen cents is a good price this will neat you 14 cents which will be an excellent sale—I shall be well contented If I get that for mine.[5]

I shall advise Mr Maunsel White that I intend sending my cotton to him by next mail. I have mine ready for shipment & have the promise of the William Penn now on her way from orleans, to freight it, her next trip[6]—it has the appearence of rain and it is now probable we will have a swell of waters shortly sufficient for our steams Boats to reach Nashville with safety. I see two Boats have lately been sunk in the Mississippi richly loaded with merchandize for the upper country the water is so low, that much damage may be expected from accidents to the steam Boats—I have made seventy one Bales of cotton—they are not all weighed & marked but I calculate they will weigh upwards of 33.000—This at fifteen cents will meet all my demands & wants—

Mrs. J. is recovering fast I hope she will shortly be restored to perfect health—she unites with me in respects to you & your amiable family—respectfully yr friend

Andrew Jackson

P.S. I write in haste, as I am much pressed with various letters that require answers—this is the twelfth today—most of which required much care—[7]

ALS, THi (11-0125).
1. Not found.
2. Probably John Fulton, whom AJ purchased in December 1822.
3. AJ was sending the three horses for use on Andrew Jackson Hutchings's farm.
4. White (1783–1863), who had captained a company of New Orleans volunteers in the Gulf campaign, was AJ's cotton factor from this year until AJ's death.
5. Most of AJ's cotton sold at twelve cents.
6. On February 26, AJ consigned his cotton to the *William Penn,* a steamboat operating out of Louisville.
7. Only three outgoing letters for February 2 have been found.

From Henry Banks

Frankfort Keny. Feby. 10. 1826

Dear Sir

I have recd. with much pleasure your letter of the 19th. of January,[1] and thank you for your condolence for my debility and complaints, and likewise for your good wishes for my recovery and the restoration of my former energy; and I also render thanks for your very favorable expressions of my patriotic devotion to those principles which I have avowed during the late

Presidential canvas.[2] They are the principles which I have always acknowledged and I sincerely hope will accompany me to the end of my life, and always be a part of myself

With respect to the preferance of the Candidate relating to the last Election, my opinions were positive and unchangeable, and so are yet, there does not now exist any thing in regard to my preferences which did not then exist, but there are some things which add new strength to my devotions. These are the usurpation and treacherous means used to produce the election; the setled and unalterable opinion which I entertain that no president should serve more than one term.[3] Such I understand are also your opinions, so that the causes of my preference are considerably stregthned by the full assurance of this fact, and if my health and restored energy should enable me to be of service that service shall be rendered.

With my acquaintances here the subject is sometimes discussed. To them I say "that General Jackson & myself have no personal claims on each other. I shall, as I now intend support him, but my first purpose is to pull down the tyranny, and overset the usurpation upon public libcrty lately made by Adams & Clay, by their expulsion from office & power, and whoso bids most fair to be the successful instrument him will I support and I prefer General Jackson for the reasons which formerly were avowed. But if any thing should prevent this my first wish then I will as a moral and political duty espouse the cause of him who shall be most likely to insure this purpose."

And now, my Dear Sir, let me in behalf of your Country & its future destinies make some devotion of your time by visits in this state & Ohio, and to Virginia having the success of this object in view. I know, with your candid and upright mind, that you will feel some compunctions of delicacy in this course, but I do not think that your character, popularity & correct principles are exclusively your own. They belong to posterity and to your Country. You are a fiduciary trustee and hold them for public Usefulness, and as a faithful Trustee you should employ such means as shall appear most likely to procure your own and thereby your countrys success

In regard to the political views contained in your letter both relating to this state and the United States, and also to the invitations of the president to give more power, where there is already too much, there is a perfect concurrence of opinion between us, and I rejoice that the avowal made by you is incorporated on the same sheet of paper which contains so many welcome things respecting myself.

I have shewn your letter to several leading characters of this place, all of them who belong to what is called the New Court party, who generally are your friends, are so much pleased with the opinion which you have given relating to Governor Desha's reply to the Legislature that many requests have been made to me to publish extracts from the letter. This I have declined because I do not apprehend that you had the publication in view, nor that you desired to identify yourself with them. You have many friends on the other side who might be displeased[4]

It is my Intention to publish another series of Philo Jackson as soon as the present Storm is over and I shall wish your approbation to make some extracts suitable to that purpose.[5]

next to the satisfaction which I shall enjoy in being useful to the general liberty and prosperity of our Country, I shall be gratified by communications from You, & now permit me to assure you of high esteem & great confidence

Henry Banks—

This Letter I expect will be handed by a young gentleman from Culpeper Co. in Virginia, named [William Banks] Slaughter he is my nephew, and being bred to the Law he is now on an excursion through the Western States to select a residence.[6] He can tell you how much more favorable to your election the Virginia People now are than at the last election, and can also inform you relating to Ohio—He is or has been one of Mr Adams adherents, tho much less so than formerly.

I shall be much obliged to you to give him a few introductory letters to your friends in the states below to which I hope he will do some credit. H. B.

ALS, DLC (33). Banks(1761–1836), formerly a Richmond, Virginia, merchant, at this time lived in Frankfort, Kentucky.

1. Not found.
2. In the campaign of 1824, Banks had written in support of AJ's candidacy in the *Louisville Public Advertiser* and he had published a series of seven "Philo-Jackson" pamphlets entitled *The Presidential Election . . .* (Louisville and Frankfort, 1823, 1824).
3. By 1831 some observers speculated that Banks would desert the Jackson camp because AJ was not committed to one term (Connersville, Indiana, *Political Clarion*, January 8, 1831).
4. For one of AJ's comments on Desha's message, see above, AJ to Jesse Bledsoe, [January 18].
5. No additional publications under that pseudonym have been found.
6. In 1826, Slaughter (1797–1879) settled in Bardstown, Kentucky. He later moved to Indiana and served as a state legislator. He eventually settled in Michigan Territory, accepting appointments from AJ as register at the Green Bay land office in 1834 and as secretary of the newly-created Wisconsin Territory in 1837.

From Maunsel White

New Orleans Feby 16th. 1826

Dear Sir

I have this day recd. your Letter of 3rd inst.[1] informing me that it was your Intention to send me your Crop of Cotton for sale, & that you would leave it to my own Judgment & discretion to do the best I could for you on its arrival, that you had confidence in me at the Lines below this City, & that, that Confidence still existed.[2] In calling to my recollection that circumstance you have awakened feelings which I can never forget nor need I tell you how they are Identified with the esteem and respect I have ever entertained for you.

I may err, but my Heart shall ever remain true to the Sentiments of Honor & Integrity; you yourself had an Opportunity of Judging me in the Field, & in the trying hour of adversity I have also been Judged by the Mercantile Community, & I defy my Enemies to say I have come out wanting. Such then are the guarantees I have to Offer you for the faithful discharge of the trust you repose in me, & if the Almighty does not change my Sentiments, which I most earnestly Pray he may not I hope I shall go down to my silent grave with a clear and good Conscience, doing all the good I can and as little harm as comes to the lot of us poor frail mortals.

I regret to inform you that Cotton is lower, than it is your Interest or mine to sell it at, but we all must bend to Circumstances & if we cannot Conquer, make the best retreat we can. The Character of your Crop will give me the advantage of a good position & I am determined not to be driven off the Field without making the Enemy pay for it.

Excellent Tennessee Cotton has been sold at 12 a 12^1/$_2$ cents, & before the bad news arrived 13 a 13^1/$_2$ was obtained for it. Some fine Alabamas were also sold since at 13^1/$_2$ & 13 cts. & good at 12^1/$_2$—Louisianas & Mississippies were sold yesterday & to day at from 12^1/$_2$ a 15^1/$_2$ cts. but mostly 14 cts. for good, one crop of the very finest mark went as high as 17 cents, but such sales are rare, & not to be quoted as a criterion—as much depends on the Caprice of the Buyer. Purchasers are of Opinion the article is still to be lower, but much on that subject depends on the advices expected from Europe, which in my Opinion cannot be much worse than they are & may be better.[3] When your Cotton is sold I shall pay particular Attention to remit you the proceeds in U States Bank notes, as you direct, & in meantime I shall purchase the articles you order, which shall have no influence on the sale of your Cotton & they shall be ready for the steam Boat William Penn, when she arrives—Permit me to present my best respects to Mrs. Jackson & accept my best wishes for hers & your Health & prosperity & Remain very Sincerely your mot Obt Sert

Maunsel White

ALS, DLC (33).
    1. Not found.
    2. In his letter, AJ had apparently praised White's service at the Battle of New Orleans.
    3. Reports of a "dull" cotton market in England reached New Orleans in late January and, after additional news of falling prices in Liverpool, prices at New Orleans began to drop. By February 14, long articles on "Commercial Distress" and "Financial Panic" reported numerous bankruptcies and a deepening depression in England. In late February, before much of the 1825 crop from the United States had arrived, the Liverpool market already reported a surplus and low prices continued in New Orleans during the remainder of the winter months (*Louisiana Advertiser*, January 17, 23, 25, 26, February 14, 25). In quoting commodities prices during this period, agents and newspapers used both "to" and "a" interchangeably.

Uncertain about the designs of Spain and of the Holy Alliance (an ar-rangement tying Russia, Prussia, and Austria together), the new republics of South America, led by Colombia and Mexico, proposed a meeting in Panama in October 1825 to discuss their common welfare. In April, as plans for the assembly inched forward, the sponsors invited participation of the United States and Washington accepted in late November.

The administration's decision did not, however, receive universal sup-port. Some feared that participation would compromise the nation's tra-ditional neutrality and might obligate the United States to defend the South American republics against Holy Alliance intervention. Others, such as Jackson in the letter below, questioned the president's authority to commit the United States without consent of the Senate. Some south-ern senators were concerned about the possibility of participation by the black republic of Haiti, fearing that the Panama Congress might adopt policies inimical to slavery.

After President Adams submitted his nominations for ministers to the conference on December 26, 1825, the Senate Foreign Relations Com-mittee reported unfavorably, attacking not the nominees but the mission itself. The ensuing Senate debate held up confirmation of delegates until March 14, and by the time appropriations were made and instructions issued, the United States appointees did not have time to reach Panama before the conference adjourned on July 15.

To John Branch

Hermitage near Nashville T.
March 3rd. 1826

My Dear Sir
    I have recd. your much esteemed favour of the 10th ult[1]—your kind expressions with regard to myself are duly appreciated—your uniform dis-interested & independant course in the Senate of the U. states & else-where, merits not only my confidence, but that of every virtuous patriot of our country—you possess it.
    The great body of the people rejoice to see the Senate pause & ponder well upon the Panama Mission—it is a subject of vast importance to our country—it might lead to serious & embarrassing consequences. To be represented at a congress of Independant confederated nations, is an event, which I presume, the framers of our constitution never thought of, whilst deliberating upon those Enumerated powers, which they conceived necessary & proper, to be given to our confederated goverment—the mo-ment our Representatives appear and take their seats at this Congress, we must be viewed by the Goverments of Europe, to be members of that Con-federation which compose it, and whether our representatives vote with the majority, or not, on measures that may be adopted, still these acts,

are our acts, in contemplation, and *may this not lead to War.* The ground taken by the President in his message, "that he had accepted the invitation, & ministers would be appointed, & commissioned, to represent us at Panama," gave much alarm to the republicans of the old school of 1798–9—But his friends explain, that he only meant to say, that he would do this, by, & with the advice & consent of the Senate—we await for the injunction of Secrecy to be taken from your procedings in the Senate, for a full explanation of his views of his constitutional powers[2]—It appears however, that he has assumed to himself the power of accepting the invitation, & giving a pledge that we would be represented there. Upon the most mature reflection on this Subject, I cannot bring myself to believe, that this is a case embraced in our constitution, *under the Treaty making power.* It would seem to me, that the consent of the people to the expediency of this measure, should have been first had, at least by their representatives in congress—before the invitation should have been accepted, & a pledge given that we would be represented there—Under the circumstances of this case, the course adopted by the leading members of the administration in the house of Representatives, is truly alarming, as well as, novel—that one coordinate branch of our goverment, should attempt to take up the subject whilst it was constitutionally before the other, and under discussion; with the avowal to *coerce it, into a complience with the Executive will*—is an attempt to destroy the constitutional checks of our goverment, and to reduce it to a despotism by making "the Senate a mere machine to register the *edicts* of the President," as has been well observed—when all these proceedings are laid before the people; when they see the whole ground, there will be such a burst of indignation, that must be felt by all the supporters of such measures.[3]

As you have anticipated, I am enjoying the true happiness of domestic quiett—your kind wishes add much to my gratification, and a casual letter from a friend in whom I have confidence enhances the pleasure of my retirement—altho, clear from the surrounding bustle of politics, when I see a course attempted by the agents of our goverment that may lead to its embarrassment, and perhaps to its destruction; I assure you, it disturbs my quiett. I have reflected calmly upon this Panama mission, and the proceedings in congress that it has lead to, and I can see no good that can result from it, but much evil—If information is wanted from Panama, why not obtain it in the usual mode, by an agent from our goverment—Why become a member of that confederated national congress before we are informed of its policy, & its plans—This is worse than folly. The moment we engage in confederations, or alliances with any nation, we may from that time date the down fall of our republic—

When I view the splendor & magnificence of the goverment, embraced in the recommendation of the late message, with the powers enumerated, which may be rightfully exercised by congress to lead to this magnificence together with the declaration that it would be criminal for the agents of our goverment to be palsied by the will of their constituents, I shudder for the consequence—if not checked by the voice of the people, it must end in consolidation, & then in despotism—Yet, I have great confidence in the intelligence, and virtue, of the great body of the american people; they never will abandon the constitutional ship; their voice will be raised, & must be heard—Instead of building lighthouses of the skies, establishing national universities, and making explorations round the globe; their language will be, pay the national debt—prepare for national independence, & defence[4]—then apportion the surpluss revenue amonghst the several states for the education of the poor—leaving the superintendence of education to the states respectively. This will be the safe course to perpetuate our happy goverment.

I sincerely congratulate you upon the birth of your fine son on the 8th. of January last:[5] this was once an auspicious day to our country. I hope it will be to this fine son—he must be a true patriot, & will become I trust, a bold and fearless defender of his countries rights—may he grow & prosper, become a comfort & blessing to his parents in their declining years, & an ornament, & example, to the society in which he may live; under your guidance, he will be taught his rights, and how to defend them, if invaded by foreign foes, or intestine Traitors—present him with my blessing.

Mrs. J begs me to reciprocate to you, in the kindest manner your good wishes—she has had a serious illness, her health is restored, have the goodness to present us to Major Eaton; and I pray you to accept for yourself the assurance of my great respect friendship and esteem.

Andrew Jackson

ALS, NcU (11-0150). Branch (1782–1863; North Carolina 1799), a North Carolina senator, served as AJ's secretary of the navy, 1829–31.

1. Letter not found.

2. Adams nominated John Sergeant and Richard C. Anderson, Jr., as delegates to the Panama Congress on December 26, 1825, but the nominations and debate on the mission were covered by the injunction of secrecy until March 21. AJ's quote was actually a loose paraphrase from Adams's first annual message of December 6, 1825 (*Register of Debates,* 19th Cong., 1st sess., Appendix, p. 3; *Journal of the Executive Proceedings of the Senate . . .* [3 vols.; Washington, 1829], 3:457–59).

3. Embarrassed by the Senate's dawdling on confirmation of delegates to the Panama Congress, administration supporters in the House of Representatives, led by Daniel Webster (1782–1852; Dartmouth 1801) from Massachusetts, moved in late January 1826 to "spur" the Senate to action by a resolution calling on the president for information about the proposed conference. David Trimble's speech of January 31 defending the resolution and the right of the House to "hasten or retard" action in the Senate led to opposition criticism of the attempt to coerce the Senate, but the resolution passed on February 3 (Henry Clay to Daniel Webster, [cJanuary 31], in Charles M. Wiltse and Harold D. Moser, eds., *The Papers of Daniel Webster, Correspondence, Volume 2, 1825–1829* [Hanover, N.H., 1976], pp. 82–83; *Register of Debates,* 19th Cong., 1st sess., pp. 1217–19, 1301). AJ's quotation was actually a paraphrase from Virginia Representative John Floyd's speech on February 3, calling on House colleagues to "recollect . . . [that] the Senators of the United States are not mere machines, and component parts of the Executive. They belong, also, to the States of this Union, and are responsible to them" (*Register of Debates,* 19th Cong., 1st sess., p. 1294).

4. AJ was referring to recommendations made by Adams in his annual message.
5. Elizabeth Fort Branch had actually given birth to a daughter, Susan, on January 8.

To Samuel Houston

Hermitage March 8th. 1826

Dear Genl

I have to thank you for several papers you have had the goodness to enclose to me—I have Just recd your favour of the 17th. ult.[1] ¿how my letter could have reached Florence; I am at a loss to conjecture, it was mailed at Nashville.

I was fearfull that there would be dificulty in obtaining a warrant for Junius [M. C.] Sanders—his father *[ha]*s been desirous to have one of his sons educated at *[the]* military academy[2]—he was unfortunate in his *[ambi]*tions with regard to his son Pascal [Washington Saunders], for whom *[a war]*rant was obtained, & very shortly after he entered, *[h]*is health gave way, his Phicians advised him to quit the academy,[3] & his father had to meet all the expence of his going to, & returning from there—he is poor, struggles hard to educate his children—and has taken pains to prepare Junius for the military academy—If therefore you can consistantly obtain a warrant for Junius, it will be gratefully remembered by Mr Sanders.

young Mr Overton obtained a warrant last year, was prevented by sickness in going on in due time—I wrote the Sec of War, and he was good anough to promise him a renewal of his warrant[4]—will you be good anough to see the Sec of War & ask him to send it on, young Mr Overton intends going on in May next—but I have said to him, he had better await information from the Sec of War.[5]

I have had the pleasure of reading Mr [George] McDuffie's speech (in the National Journal) on his Resolution to amend the constitution—it is a splendid display of cogent reasoning, combined with eloquence, that *[mus]*t realise the most sanguine expectation of his friends—and must carry conviction to the mind of even Mr Sec Clay, that the amendments proposed is necessary to be adopted, to perpetuate our happy goverment, by preventing its purity from being undermined by intrigue, management, & corruption[6]—I think it will require the best efforts of Mr Webster to answer it. This subject has interrested the whole american people; Mr McDuffie has opened it with great ability—and must draw forth all the talent on the other side—it is a fine field f*[or]* debate, and the result, of the first im*[portance]* to the american people.

I have noted your information w*[ith regard]* to Mr Clay—I would not be surprised if he did go crazzy—his ambition is great, he is constantly goaded by a wounded conscience—he sees himself on the verge of political prostration, & if the constitution is amended as proposed, he sees his political downfal certain, that all the patronage of the President cannot save him from the political death that hangs over him—he never had discretion, or much common sense—he cannot bear disappointment in his ambitious views, and I shoud not wonder, if he betakes himself to his bottle to bury in forgetfulness, the wicked course he has run, and to relieve him from the pricks of a wounded conscience.

The Senate has displayed great wisdom & energy in their calm deliberation of the Panama question—I wish I could pass the same encomium on the House of Representatives—the step taken by it, was premature—the subject was constitutionally before the Senate, and whilst under their deliberation & before it had come to a decision, that the house of Representatives should take it up, with the o[pen] a[vowal] of some of the leading members of the administration, that it was with a view to coerce the Senate into an acquiescence of the executive will, was to destroy the constitutional checks of the Goverment, and to make the Senate the mere machine to register the *Edicts* of the Executive, and reduce our goverment to a despotism—it is no wonder that their feelings were aroused, it was calculated to arouse deep indignation in every patriot[ic he]art—I was pleased with your course and sen[timen]ts on this occasion—and I am proud to [see h]ow well Colo Hamilton sustained himself [o]n that occasion—the Resolution was proper to be presented to the house, & laid upon the table untill you were called upon to act—then the information was necessary, & the call proper—what weakness, as well as wickedness, is displayed by the members who made the avowal that it was to *coerce* the Senate to act[7]—This must have proceeding from the indiscreet councils of Mr. Sec. Clay.

Every thing as regards yourself is moving on in this quarter smoothly— I was informed by Mr [Robert Johnstone] Chester[8] that your friend Colo [Newton] Cannon had vissited the western District this winter, to *meet* they *Engineers* but was *much disappointed, he did not meet them.*[9] We are all in bustle here—Cumberland river is now up, and every one is trying to get his produce to markett—the river is said to be now higher, than it has ever been—since Mrs. J. has recovered we have been confined at home by the weather, & now [hi]gh waters, so soon as the river subsides I will visit Nashville and give you the political news, that being the focus.

Mrs. J has Just recd. your much esteemed newyears gift—it was sent to her from Cincinati—she begs me to make to you a tender of her thanks, with her best wishes for your happiness & prosperity—have the goodness to present to Colo. [Nathan] Towson & Lady Mrs. J. my best respects with our best wishes for their happiness & the like to our friend Colo Gibson.[10] accept the assurances of my high re[spect] friendship & esteem.

Andrew Jack[son]

Photocopy of ALS, Tx (11-0159).
1. Letter not found.
2. In November 1825 AJ had recommended Junius Saunders (1809–29) for the Military

Academy, but he did not receive the appointment. William Saunders (c1776–1846), his father, operated the Fountain of Health spa near the Hermitage.

3. Pascal (b. 1805), also recommended by AJ, had been admitted to the Academy in 1823.

4. For AJ's efforts on behalf of James G. Overton, see AJ to James Barbour, August 6, and Barbour to AJ, September 3, 1825.

5. Barbour (1775–1842) forwarded Overton's warrant to AJ on April 18.

6. On December 9, 1825, South Carolina Representative McDuffie (1790–1851; South Carolina 1813) had introduced a resolution to provide for a uniform system of voting by districts in presidential elections in all states and to prevent the election from devolving upon Congress. The Washington *National Journal,* February 17 and 18, carried those remarks.

7. On December 16, 1825, only ten days after Adams sent to Congress his Panama proposal, James Hamilton, Jr., introduced a resolution in the House requesting information on the mission. The next day, he announced that he wished to postpone the inquiry. On January 30, 1826, however, in hopes of prodding Senate action, Thomas Metcalfe of Kentucky moved a similar resolution, but his was subsequently ruled out of order and Hamilton's earlier resolution became the focus of administration supporters. Hamilton, who opposed the mission, thus found himself in the odd position of opposing a resolution he authored, leaving Webster to complain that Hamilton too readily accepted the amendments of those opposed to the resolution. Nonetheless, those favoring the mission were able to shape the resolution's language and to pass it on February 3, with Hamilton and Houston opposing.

8. Chester (1793–1892) had married AJ's niece Elizabeth Hays (1805–41) in 1825.

9. In an effort to ensure that a portion of the contemplated national road from Washington to New Orleans pass through Tennessee, Cannon (1781–1841), appointed by the governor to confer with the engineers charged to recommend a route, had first met with the federal agents, William T. Poussin and Isaac R. Trimble, in East Tennessee in November 1825. Anticipating their return to Washington from New Orleans, Cannon had gone to West Tennessee in February to confer with them again. AJ's "your friend" was probably sarcastic; Cannon and Houston were both candidates in the 1827 gubernatorial race.

10. Towson (1784–1854), paymaster general of the army, and his wife Sophia (d. 1852), daughter of Boston educator Caleb Bingham.

From James Buchanan

Washington 8 March 1826

Dear General/

It is with the most sincere & lively pleasure I inform you that the convention which met at Harrisburg on the 4th. Instant; for the purpose of nominating a Governor, after they had unanimously recommended the re-election of Governor [John Andrew] Shulze,[1] adopted the following resolution by a vote of 98 to 7.

"Resolved that our confidence in the patriotism, talents & inflexible integrity of Gen: Andrew Jackson, is unimpaired; and that his conduct during the pendency of, & after, the late election of President of the United States is deserving the unqualified approbation of the American people."

Of the seven members who voted against this resolution, there were six, as we are informed by private letters, who declared themselves to be your friends; at the same time stating as a justification for their vote that the convention had been assembled for the purpose of nominating Governor & for that only, & they had no instructions from their constituents to proceed further. This was the fact: & the only reason why you were not formally, as you have been substantially nominated as our candidate at the next Presidential election. Jonathan Roberts your old friend was the only individual of the seven who was really opposed to you.[2]

I feel proud that my native State has thus early shewn herself to the world to be true to her principles & to be beyond the influence of Executive patronage. It had been industriously circulated here, that she was wavering & the friends of the administration had been or had pretended to be flattered into this belief. Their dreams will now vanish. The news from Harrisburg produced a strong sensation to day in the House, as it was wholly unexpected except by a few of us Pennsylvanians.

In addressing you this letter I cannot refrain from introducing the name of Molton C[ropper] Rogers late Secretary of State of Pennsylvania.[3] He has been from the beginning a uniform, a decided, a discreet & a most efficient friend of our cause. That the cause will triumph over the Union at the next election is not only my ardent wish; *but my firm belief.* Many of the former friends of Mr. Crawford are now decidedly your friends, & the remainder are almost universally opposed to the re-election of Mr. Adams & have shewn a strong disposition to harmonize with us.

The Senate have not yet disposed of the Panama mission. It is expected they will pass upon it finally during the present week. In my opinion from what I learn there will probably be a majority in its favor.[4]

Mr. M'Duffies proposed amendment to the constitution so far as it relates to districting the United States will not have a large vote in the House of Representatives. I do not think it has seventy friends in that body. There will I think be a majority—though perhaps not a constitutional one, in favor of taking the election from the House Leaving the balance of power among the several states to remain in its present condition. God send that we should be successful in this important measure.[5]

Col: Gibson requests me to give his *"undiminished love"* to you. Please to present my kindest & best respects to Mrs. Jackson & believe me to be your sincere & devoted friend.

James Buchanan

ALS, DLC (33); AL draft, PHi (11-0156). Published in Moore, *Works of James Buchanan,* 1:173–74.

1. Shulze (1775–1852), a former Calhounite who remained neutral during the 1828 presidential campaign, was reelected.

2. As senator from Pennsylvania in 1819–20, Roberts (1771–1854), AJ's "old friend," had been highly critical of the Seminole campaign, and at the 1824 Harrisburg convention, he had cast the only vote against AJ's presidential nomination. Later in 1826, the *Louisville Public Advertiser* (September 13) hinted that Roberts, perhaps in collusion with others, had stolen some of AJ's 1816–17 correspondence with James Monroe, all to cast doubts about AJ's qualifications for the presidency.

3. Rogers (c1785–1863; Princeton 1806) had resigned in January. In April he was appointed a justice of the Pennsylvania Supreme Court.

4. In mid-March the Senate confirmed Adams's nominations of ministers, but Congress did not appropriate funds for the mission until May.

5. In two votes on April 1, the House adopted, 138 to 52, McDuffie's proposal to amend the Constitution to prevent the presidential election from devolving on Congress, but opposed, 90 to 102, that for uniform voting by districts. The House referred the first resolution to a select committee, which failed to report any amendment (*Register of Debates*, 19th Cong., 1st sess., pp. 2004–2005, 2659).

From Samuel Delucenna Ingham

Washington 8th March 1826

My dear Sir

You will scarcely expect a letter from me, nor do I know what apology to make for intruding myself upon you in this way. I trust however you have not ceased in your retirement to take a lively interest in the transactions of the different branches of our Govt., (for as yet our movements at this Session are very much confined to the branches.) a prudent and wise administration of our public affairs is so necessary to give character to & inspire confidence in our system that every Patriot must feel great solicitude as to every new and important measure that shall be presented for our consideration—The proposed mission to Panama is of this character and while we should regret to see that or any other measure opposed for the sake of opposition, there is no less cause of regret that any measure should find advocates who support it merely for the sake of aiding the administration without reference to its intrinsic character, the latter disposition is quite as likely to exist as the former and it has more powerful motives to sustain it—The mission to Panama is a new measure in our annals. it involves very important considerations both as to general expediency and constitutional principles—Is it expedient to embarass our future operations and the freedom of action which belongs to independent nations either by implied or expressed complicated arrangements which we may not be able to get rid of except by a breach of faith or by obtaining the consent of several States which may have a common interest adverse to ours—What motives have we thus to entangle ourselves? will it promote our own safety or that of the S. American Republics? should the Holy Alliance be mad enough to attempt to exterminate Liberty from this continent, they will wage the war either here or in S. America:[1] *if here* we shall have to defend ourselves they can render us no essential aid, if *there* we can aid them better without specific engagements tending to embarass the freedom of our movements, than with them; What good then shall arise from this measure to us or them? without some obvious probable good, why shall we hazard the possibility of evil It is a trite maxim but nevertheless very true, "that it is much easier to avoid difficulties than to remedy them after they have overtaken us." It seems to me to be very applicable to this projected mission, I may however have misconceived its character & objects. but does the constitution authorise our Govt. to appoint *Representatives* to any congress of nations? if we can send to Panama may we not send to Verona?[2] the differences of *purpose* can make none as to the *power* of establishing such an office, and if the Power exists, where is its limit may we not unite in this establishment of congresses wherever three or more powers (no matter of what grade) shall think it expedient to make such a spectacle, to attract public attention from scrutinizing the deformities of their domestic organization, or for the purpose of extending the manna of Patronage to a more numerous list of favorites?

when I took my pen it was for the exclusive purpose of giving you some account of the proceedings of our state convention at Harrisburgh but I have been drawn off by the prevailing topic of the day which I have ventured upon, perhaps with too much freedom for a suitable deference for your unknown sentiments on this subject but I have long since abandoned all idea of speaking or writing in a disguise, and if my notions should be thought by you erroneous, you will receive them with a generous indulgence for honest errors—

Our convention met on the 4th. The Delegates from one District only were instructed to endeavor to procure the nomination of yourself for President: the instruction was accompanied with a *severe denunciation* of the present administration: after some consultation among the Delegates, it was thought inexpedient to introduce the measure in that shape. every prudent man considering, that violence generally tends to produce reaction a more moderate course was adopted and a resolution which I enclose was passed 98 to 7[3]—this circumstance acquires more strength when we consider that as the Presidential Election was not in contemplation when the Delegates were elected, the choice therefore as to that event was purely accidental, and by the vote of an assembly thus chosen we have the evidence that among the Republicans of our state public opinion is as 98 to 7 in favor of our Candidate—these facts will I trust satisfy you that Penna remains true to herself and steady to her friends whether in or out of Power—believe me dear Sir very sincerely your friend & humble Svt.

S D Ingham

ALS, DLC (33). Ingham (1779–1860), later treasury secretary under AJ, was at this time a Pennsylvania congressman.

1. The Holy Alliance, a document drawn up by the czar of Russia in September 1815, embodied the notion that Christian principles were to guide the signatories in dealing with their subjects and with each other. In the public mind, this alliance and the Quadruple Alliance of November 1815 were conflated. The latter tied the European powers together for the protection of their common interests, perhaps including, at least in the eyes of Americans, intervention in American affairs to protect and preserve European interests. The Panama Congress had been called in part to present a united front should the Quintuple Alliance, now including France, move to restore to Spain its former American colonies.

2. The Congress of Verona, meeting in October 1822, was the final international gathering under the auspices of the Quintuple Alliance. That meeting authorized France to intervene in Spain.

3. For the text of the Harrisburg Convention Jackson resolution, see above, James Buchanan to AJ, March 8. Ingham failed to note, however, as did Buchanan, that a motion to postpone indefinitely the resolution was defeated by a much narrower margin of 74 to 45.

To Richard Keith Call

Hermitage March 9th. 1826

Dr. Genl

I have the pleasure to acknowledge the receipt of your kind favour of the 26th. of Janry last[1]—it brings us the pleasing intelligence of the restoration of your health, and that your dear Mary & the sweet little daughter enjoy perfect health—this is truly gratifying to Mrs. J. & myself, as we have had great solicitude about your health, from the last letter of Mrs. Call.[2] May you, your Dear Mary & daughter long enjoy that blessing—This world is a blank to us without it.

Mrs. J. has had a severe illness, her health is measurably restored, and her spirits regained, altho her complection remains somewhat sallow— we kindly thank you, for your good wishes for our happiness, and with great sincerity reciprocate them.

Your reflections on the course & conduct of your mother in law, are certainly based upon those magnanimous feelings, which always accompanies the generous, liberal & noble heart, and which every good man must approve—I am sure with health, you must become entirely independent—still there is due to Mary a Justice, that the illiberality and cruelty of her relations, should not be permitted to dep[rive] her of. Your friends here, as far as they have the power, will endevour to prevent any Legislative act—that may be intended to affect the interest of Mary—and whilst I applaud your noble feelings on this subject, should circumstances arise from facts—that any unjustifiable course was about to be taken to deprive Mrs. Call of her rights—then it would become your duty to act promptly, regardless of your feelings or your pride—still for the present, your course is approved—wait for facts to be disclosed, that may make it necessary to act—I shall keep an eye to this business, and when informed of any facts, will communicate them promptly.

I am happy to say to you of late, as I am informed, the old lady has ceased to make you the object of her abuse; and I fondly hope, by a proper course of conduct toward you & Mary, she may in some measure attone for her past improprieties[3]—This will be a great gratification to all, & must be a blessing to her family.

I have no doubt but Mr Adams will endeavour to manage matters so as to secure if he can, his next election, this is natural to conclude from what we have already seen—he had given, as you must recollect, some evidences of a want of common sense in his note accepting of the Presidency[4]—this weakness had not before been ascribed to him—but his weakness thus displayed, induced many to believe, he was not the man of real wisdom, that had before been ascribed to him—part of his late Message to congress gave strong evidence of his want of discretion—his declaration that he had accepted of the invitation to be represented at the national congress of Panama, & "that he would appoint & Commission Ministers" to represent us there, was to my mind a strong & bold measure, devoid of due reflection, and well calculated to bring him into a conflict with the Senate & with congress[5]—this has turned out, as might have been expected, and will bring him under the severe castigation of every republican pen, in the union—it may lead to a break between him & his Sec of State; It is stated, he charges on Mr Sec Clay, that he is the father of this illegitimate Bantling, whether the Hon. Sec. may quietly father it, I have not heard—If the senate decides (which I think it must) that it is inexpedient for us to become a member of this Congress of Independent confederated nations by being represented there, I am sure Mr Sec Clay will go *quite mad* if he has to father the Bantlin—I am sure, the feelings of the american *nation* are not prepared for such a foolish, extravagant crusade as this proposed mission must lead to—The interest, as well as the feelings, of the american people are, a friendly intercourse with the Republics of the South, commercial treaties with them on the broad basis of reciprocity, but entangling alliances with none—This is our true policy.

There has been a new paper established at the city called the *United States Telegraph*; from its prospectus I would Judge, it is intended to sustain the amendment proposed to the constitution, and to oppose the principles by which Mr Adams got into the presidency; and to unite the republicans into one solid colum against Mr Adams second election—and as [Mordecai Manuel] Noah says, "unite upon one individual, in opposition to Mr Adams,"[6] if this is adopted Mr Adams cannot again be elected. Mr. Adams is really to be pitied—his own folly, with the weakness of his cabinet, and the indiscretion of Clay, must politically destroy him, this Panama mission, it is said is the child of Clay, and the late unfortunate movement in the House of Representatives, was by the advice of Mr Clay, with a view to coerce the Senate into the Executive measures, which has aroused the indignation of the Senate, and no doubt has made many enemies to the administration—if this is true, there must be a divorce between Mr A. & Mr. C.

you will have seen the resolutions laid before the Legislature of Kentucky by our mutual friend Mr. Crittenden—to say the least of it, this is very inconsist[ent] conduct in him—It may be usefull to me to have his letter if amongst your papers; I shall not use it, unless it should become necessary in self defence, therefore you will oblige me by sending it.[7]

It is very gratifying to me that Mary has recd the ring—still more so, that she appreciates it so highly, it being a token of my real friendship & esteem—she has always [a]ppeared to Mrs. J. & myself, more like a daughter, than [a]ny of our female friends, we will ever wear you & Mary in our affections; and at the Hermitage, you *[will always find a fa]*ther*['s]* dwelling so long as we live; and we look forward with pleasure to the time when we will again have the pleasure of seeing you once more at the Hermitage to introduce to us the young stranger—It will give Mrs. J. & myself pleasure to sitt to Mr Earl, & I will see him shortly on the subject.[8]

Present us kindly to Mary & kiss the little stranger for us, and accept for yourself & the whole family our kindest benedictions—your friend

Andrew Jackson

P.S. give our kind regard to Colo Butler Rachel & all the children, say to the Colo. I have wrote him lately[9] & will write him again shortly—present us to Gadsden, & Govr Duval & family & to Major Nicholas A. J.

ALS, DLC (33). Published in Bassett, 6:481–83, and in *American Historical Magazine*, 4(1899):101–104. Bracketed and italicized characters have been supplied from the *Magazine* publication.

    1. Letter not found.
    2. Not found.
    3. Ellen J. Kirkman had opposed the courtship and marriage of her daughter Mary to Call, and her husband Thomas had altered his will to exclude Call from any share of his estate.
    4. In his "want of common sense" phrase, Jackson probably had in mind Adams's comment of February 10, 1825, in which he wrote that could his refusal of the election allow the people to express with greater "unanimity the object of their preference," he would do so, but such a remedy was not prescribed in the Constitution (*Register of Debates,* 18th Cong., 2nd sess., pp. 546–47).
    5. AJ was paraphrasing Adams's first annual message.
    6. Noah (1785–1851), whom AJ later appointed surveyor and inspector for the port of New York, was at this time the editor of the *New York National Advocate.*
    7. Crittenden had introduced resolutions before the Kentucky legislature denouncing attacks on Clay for supporting Adams in the presidential election; and this, after he had written Call on January 8, 1825 (NcD): "I trust in God that we shall succeed after all in getting a Western President—And that Genl Jackson will beat the yankee." Soon after Crittenden introduced his resolves, Jackson newspapers attacked him for wavering. Whether Call forwarded a copy of the Crittenden letter to AJ is not known, but the letter continued to be an issue in the campaign of 1828 (Frankfort, Ky., *Argus of Western America,* August 22, 1827; and Lexington *Kentucky Reporter*, November 14, 1827).
    8. Earl painted and sent portraits of the Jacksons to the Calls in 1828. The Calls returned the portrait of AJ, which has not been identified, as unsatisfactory. For the Call portrait of Rachel Jackson, see *Jackson,* 1:93.
    9. Letter not found.

To Hugh Lawson White

Hermitage March 16th 1826

My Dear Sir

Your very interesting letter of the 19th ult[1] I have just received—your prompt attention to the claim of Capt Thos Shields receives my thanks—

he is an honorable & honest man as I have always thought—has rendered important services to his country & from misfortune is poor—I am sure he only wants a just & equitable settlement with his Govt. or I should not have asked your attention to his case[2]

I have read your remarks on the constitutional powers of the President & Senate with much satisfaction—the distinctions drew by you I view as altogether correct.[3]

When I first saw the message of the President to Congress and read from it that he had received & accepted of the invitation to be represented at the congress of Panama—that ministers would be appointed & commissioned to represent us there—I turned to the constitution to find from what number of that instrument such powers were derived & authorised him to give such a pledge without the advice & consent of the Senate & of Congress—I must confess that after all my research I was compelled to conclude that the framers of the constitution in all their deliberations on the powers necessary to be given to our confederated goverment, had never once thought of giving such powers to the Executive to appoint & commission ministers to represent us at such a congress—Nay sir, if we are to view the origin of that congress as arising out of the Treaty between the Republics of Mexico & Columbia—the objects as stated in the north american review[4]—Then, I would doubt whether the executive & Congress could find a constitutional power to authorise them to send representatives to that Congress of confederated independent nations—such a power I cannot find within the constitution—for surely the moment we are represented in that congress we become a member of the confederacy, stipulated in the Treaty between Columbia & Mexico which appear to me to be the basis of this congress—I therefore rejoice that the Senate has taken time seriously to deliberate upon this important subject that may be fraught with many evils & but few beneficial results, that cannot be better obtained in another way—*we the people* are anxiously awaiting the injunction of secrecy to be taken from your proceedings, when the whole ground can be seen—for I assure you altho we possess the most lively feelings for the liberty & prosperity of the Republics of the South the feelings of the people are entangling *alliances with no nation* this is our safe & true policy—whatever may be the opinion at Washington to the contrary.

The amendments proposed to the constitution are thought by the people to be necessary to keep our goverment pure & uncorrupted, and by that means make it perpetual—if congress does not adopt them I have no doubt but the people will take the subject up and pursue a course that will obtain the amendments proposed.[5]

The power of *internal* improvement by the general goverment within a state without its consent I never did believe was conferred by the Constitution—unless military roads to a fortress, & when made, only the common use—Congress being charged with the common defence of the country & for this purpose to build fortifications must have roads for their supply & reinforcement—I have thought that the states ought not to yield this power—the additional patronage it would give might prove dangerous—all internal improvements should be made by the states respectively, and so soon as our national debt is paid the surplus revenue apportioned amongst the states for internal improvement & educating the poor—important improvements altogether national ought to be carried into effect by the general goverment by & with the consent of the states—each state through which the improvement pass, binding themselves to keep the canal or road in repair

I am happy to learn that you & Colleague[6] harmonise so well—I know you will be pleased with him when you know him as well as I do—a better or safer man I never knew and his talents are not of the ordinary kind—may you & him for the benefit *[of]* the state & our common country long be colleagues *[toge]*ther—for I am sure when you really know ea*[ch othe]*r you will harmonise.

I have wrote you with the freedom of a friend that mutual confidence that once existed on my part have always continued and you[r] letters written for my eye will never be seen by any except a very confidential friend, & only then when it may be useful to our country.

There was no necessity for an apology for delay in writing me—I am fully aware of your situation, & altho it will always aford me much pleasure to receive a letter from you when leisure will permit—still I am aware that will occur but seldom—I have sensibly felt for your family affliction and offer you my heartfelt condolence on the mournful occasion[7]—your presence with your family would have afforded to them much comfort & consolation—still, as that could not be, a kind providence was their to comfort them—we must bend to circumstances & be reconciled to the will of providence, & with cheerfull heart be ready to say "the lords will be done["]—Present me to Major Eaton and accept the assurance of my continued respect and esteem & believe me your friend

Andrew Jackson

ALS, MB (11-0170).
  1. Not found.
  2. Letter not found. Shields (c1782–1827), navy purser in New Orleans from 1811 to 1819, had petitioned for settlement of his accounts for losses sustained. It is not known what action White had taken on the memorial, but the Senate failed to act on Shields's petition.
  3. In his letter of February 19, White had apparently outlined his views of the constitutional issues involved in sending a delegation to the Panama Congress, an argument he later used in his speech before the United States Senate (*Register of Debates*, 19th Cong., 1st sess., pp. 198–218).
  4. AJ was referring to the essay, "Alliance of the Southern Republics," in the *North American Review*, 22 (January 1826):162–76, which called attention to the October 3, 1823, treaty between Colombia and Mexico. The article noted that the United States might

benefit from sending a representative to observe the proceedings, but cautioned that it would be "manifestly premature and impolitic" for the United States to join the confederation.

5. In addition to McDuffie's proposition, discussed above, Congress had under consideration amendments prohibiting the appointment of members of Congress to offices during their elected terms and limiting presidents to two terms in office (*Register of Debates,* 19th Cong., 1st sess., pp. 16–20, 51–53, 114, Appendix, pp. 120–33).

6. John H. Eaton.

7. On January 18, Charles Andrew Carrick White (c1799–1826), Hugh's eldest son, had died in Knoxville.

To Samuel Houston

Hermitage March 20th. 1826

Dr Sir

I have recd your letter of the 22nd of February[1] to day with several papers und*[er]* your Frank for which I thank you—the amendments to the constitution under discussion afford ample range for debate—I have seen Mr [Henry Randolph] Storrs speech—he has thrown as you observe the Glove[2]—I will like to see his whole ground well examined and the veil of sop[h]istry taken from it—I will thank you for the papers that contain the debates on this question—I see the panama question is still debating under the mantle of Secrecy before the senate—the people are becoming solicitous for this mantle to be removed that they may see the whole ground—If without a treaty, or statute authorising the President to appoint ministers to represent us at such a congress as Panama, I would like to see where the power is derived from to authorise the appointment of ministers to represent us there—I think it is a da*[nge]*rous business and one which will lead u*[s]* into dificulties that may end in war *unprofitable war*—still I hope for the best—Mrs. J. desires me to present her to you respectfully your friend

Andrew Jackson

P S. please say to young Mr [Andrew Jackson] Watson that Mr McLamore is now at Orleans,[3] so soon as he returns will shew it to him & write him his reply—to the family present Mrs. J & myself—
P.S. I have recd. the Telegraph—its prospectus, breaths the republican creed—*let the tree be judged by its fruit*—so far as the acts of the Executive are based upon the Public weal, so far he will approve & support it—where acts have been, that militate against the principles of the constitution then he will oppose—If the Editor redeems this pledge to the Public he will meet with support[4]—This is the course of a true Patriot—I have also read the luminous report of the Committee of ways & means—it has placed the Sec of the T. in a dilemma from which I cannot see how he will relieve himself—has this mistake of six millions arose from the want of capacity, or from indolence[5]—A. J.

Photocopy of ALS, Tx (11-0175).

1. Not found.

2. On February 17, Storrs (1787–1837; Yale 1804), a representative from New York, had opposed McDuffie's amendment regarding presidential elections on the grounds that it was a "dangerous disturbance of the rights of the States" (*Register of Debates,* 19th Cong., 1st sess., pp. 1397–1417).

3. Watson, son of the Jacksons' friends, James and Elizabeth C. Love Watson, was a clerk in the first auditor's office. In 1831 AJ appointed him a naval purser, a position he retained until his disappearance in the Levant in 1860. McLemore was the Watsons' agent locating Tennessee land owned by the family.

4. On February 6, the *United States' Telegraph* commenced publication as successor to the *Washington Gazette,* under the editorship of John Sylva Meehan (1790–1863), whom AJ appointed in 1829 Librarian of Congress.

5. In his recommendation to Congress, Treasury Secretary Richard Rush had proposed borrowing $9,000,000 to pay the public debt, but the House Committee on Ways and Means had rejected the proposal, estimating the public debt for 1826 and 1827 as $6.6 million less than Rush's estimate (*SDoc* 6, 19th Cong., 1st sess., Serial 125; *Register of Debates,* 19th Cong., 1st sess., Appendix, pp. 105–116).

From Maunsel White

New Orleans March 22nd 1826

Dear Sir,

I sincerely regret that in making my debut in selling your Crop the Market should be so bad but upon the whole I cannot help thinking I have obtained for yours the very top of the market, and many Gentlemen from Tennessee who have cotton now here for sale consider that I have obtained for you such a price taking into view the quality & bad market as you will be well satisfied with; which I do sincerely hope may prove to be the case, Genl. [Jean Baptiste] Plauché was the Broker[1] who decided on the quality & his classification was indeed such as you merited from his hands there was 9 Bales rejected, the samples of which I send you by the present Occasion to shew you the necessity of your Overseers being more particular in picking & Cleaning your Cotton, with it I send you a few samples of General Coffees crop to shew your Overseer, & for him to take example by, in do which I beg you not to be offended with me as candour & your own Inderest demands I should do so. the best of your Crop was no way equal to Coffees & the only redeeming feature in yours was goodness of staple & Colour, for throout the whole Crop there was a great deal of Broken leaf, & very carelessly packed in the Bales & by some means or other the cotton on the outside under the Wrappers got wet & shewed an Incrustation of from one to two Inches deep which very much Injured the appearance, a little care, to prevent these objections would tend materially to improve your Cotton & give it a better appearance.

I now enclose you the Account Sales of your Seventy one Bales[2] Sixty two sold at 12 Cents lb. & nine at 10 Cents. Nt proceeds $3477 51/100— from which deduct the amount of your grocery Bill by the William Penn,

$498 ³³/₁₀₀ the Balance $2979 ¹⁸/₁₀₀ I have the pleasure of now enclosing you in United States notes, by Mr Anthony W[ayne] Johnson of Nashville,[3] $2975 in notes & he will pay you $4 ¹⁸/₁₀₀ in Silver—Colol. [Robert] Armstrong[4] wrote to me saying he did not want the money, & I therefore send you the whole amot. Col. Winstons Cotton is not sold, tis inferior he is here I understand & I shall as you direct, settle with him for it. I am D Sir very respectfully Yr Obt St

Maunsel White

LS, DLC (33). Published in Bassett, 3:298.
    1. Plauché (1785–1860), a major of New Orleans volunteers during the Gulf campaign and later a brigadier general of Louisiana militia, was a longtime friend of AJ's. He was a Jackson presidential elector in 1824, 1828, and 1832.
    2. See Account, March 21.
    3. Johnson (1797–c1888) was a merchant.
    4. Armstrong (1792–1854), who had served under AJ at New Orleans, was a Nashville merchant until appointed by AJ as postmaster in 1829.

In February Nashville's postmaster Robert Brownlee Currey announced his intention to resign. Tennessee's congressional delegation supported Currey's nephew and assistant Benjamin Franklin Currey for the post, but Adams appointed John Patton Erwin, editor of the Nashville Whig. *Erwin, the son of Andrew Erwin and brother-in-law of former senator John Williams, both among Jackson's enemies, also had ties to Henry Clay since Erwin's brother James was Clay's son-in-law.*

*Erwin's appointment created a whirlwind of opposition, particularly among Jackson's supporters. On March 20, on behalf of the entire Tennessee congressional delegation (save one), John H. Eaton and Samuel Houston wrote Postmaster General John McLean (1785–1861) asking him to present to Adams a protest to the appointment, which he did. But Adams refused to accept the protest or to budge on his appointment. Jacksonians described the action as a classic example of the administration's use of patronage for partisan purposes. According to their argument, the Erwin appointment, like the deal between Clay and Adams, was an affront to the popular will. Jacksonians also claimed that it was part of an effort by the administration to "spy" upon Jackson's correspondence (*United States' Telegraph, *March 22, 25, 29, 31, April 5).*

From John Henry Eaton

Washington City
29. March 1826

D Genl—

The papers will tell you all of Panama & how it has resulted in the Senate;[1] in support of the measure, you will be surprised to find the names of some gentlemen: but the fact & truth is, that in that phrase Patronage there is greater force & effect, than many conceive. When men want office, & place it is strange how they can be made to think well, of things which otherwise might not fare so favorably. A member of the Senate, representing an independent State, sharing the confidence of his Country so largely, to act upon the principle that the Executive can *do him a favor,* and place him on higher ground, is abominable If from any conviction of his merit, the President should think proper, to offer him any situation why well & good, but for him to alter his course, and seem to hang on frowns & smiles, ready to square & regulate his conduct, not as judgt dictates but as interest points, why then it looks alarming, & proves, that human nature even with our high minded Republicans, is a matter more talked of than practiced I hate any thing & every thing which goes to show, that we are not chaste pure & incorruptable, for by these alone can our institutions & principles of goverment be maintained & rendered secure—(Enough of this)

(*extract* of a *letter from J. HE* to a friend in this place)

Yesterday in the Senate we passed a bill about the Sale of the Lands in Alabama which I think will prove of great service; it passed the Senate so unitedly that I am satisfied it will become a law. It is this in substance: any person who retains any farm or settlement, is at liberty to enter before the Sales any land he may have relinquished not exceeding four quarter Sections at the following prices. If it cost orriginally 20 dollars or more he may enter it a[t] seven dollars—If 10, & under 20 at five dollars—If 10 & not less than 5. at three dollars and all other lands heretofore relinquished that cost less than five dollars may be entered at $1.25. This bill tho extends alone to persons who have made settlements, their heirs & assignees; & only to such relinquished lands, not exceeding four quarter sections, as lie contiguous to, & adjoining the reserved settlement. Our object was to protect the settler, & to enable him if he pleased to make his farm complete; that thereby he might be guarded from the encroachments of speculation. He is privileged to enter if he chooses to do so, or if he prefer, to risk himself at the sale, he can do so, in as much as none, but the orriginal relinquisher of title, his heirs or assignees, can claim the benefit of the law[2]

The conduct of the President in relation to the Po office has excited the indignant feelings of many besides the members from Tennessee: it is an example presented that affects every state & consequently the members here from every State. I hope & trust on your a/c the people of Nashville will act nothing rudely or violently in this business; they owe it to you not to do it. There is much in the act and the country will make much of it, to Mr. A & Clays injury & prejudice. The paper here will press *[the]* consideration of it, & others at a distance *[will]* catch the sound

Sappingtons papers I have not heard from, they are before Mr. [Peter] Hagner. If rejected they cannot be brought before Congress—there being no petition[3] My kind regard to Mrs. Jackson with great regard

Eaton

Let Maury or Wilson have this extract of my letter to publish in their papers, it may be acceptable to many.[4]

ALS, DLC (72).
1. On March 14, the Senate approved Adams's nominations of ministers to the Panama Congress.
2. The House Committee on Public Lands reported negatively on the bill with the result that it failed to pass.
3. The heirs of Nashville physician Roger B. Sappington (d. 1824) had entered a claim for his services in purchasing horses for the army in 1813–14 and 1818. Hagner (1772–1850), third auditor of the Treasury, decided against the claim (Hagner to Eaton, April 20, DLC-33).
4. The paragraph following Eaton's "extract of a letter . . ." appeared in Abram P. Maury's *Nashville Republican*, May 6. Maury noted that the extract "would have been published at an earlier day, but for the absence of the gentleman to whom it was addressed." In early May, Jackson had just returned from a trip to Florence, Alabama.

From Charles Pendleton Tutt

Locust Hill near Leesburg Via.
April 2nd 1826

My Dear Sir

I was much gratified on a late visit to Washington to hear of the good health of yourself and Mrs. Jackson from your friend Genl. Houston, he is in fine spirits as indeed were all your friends I met with there, and there appears to be little or no doubt but that Messrs Adams and Clay must of necessity surrender at discretion; I called to see Mr. Adams in relation to some recommendations left by you and my friend Mercer with Mr. Monroe shortly before the expiration of his term of service, I had upon the appointment being made to which they refered, written to Mr. Adams beging leave to withdraw them as I had no disposition to remain any longer an unsucessful applicant for office more particularly as it was generally understood that your friends were to meet with no consideration from the Executive, and it was a matter well known to them that I was guilty of that unpardonable sin of being your friend; well after great labor and difficulty they were found and I withdrew them from Mr. Adams's possession;[1] during my stay there I became convinced of one fact that there is more corruption in Washington at present than is to be found in any Government under the sun of the same age or not older. do you not recollect Mr. Wm. Lee 2nd auditor and a certain Doctr. [John Browne] Cutting both of whom I met frequently in your room last winter, they induced me to believe that they were warmly your friends and had your Election much at heart, and possibly may have produced the same impression on your mind, guess then at my surprise and astonishment when I was *credibly* informed that at that very moment they were doing, saying privately, and writing for the press many of those pieces that were published with a view to defeat you and Elevate Mr. Adams.[2]

I was in New York in Decr. every thing there promises well. Mr. Clinton is not sufficiently strong in his own state to enable him to become a candidate for the Presidency, that circumstance alone will ensure to you a majority of the votes in that state. as to Virginia, nothing could under any circumstances induce her to vote for Mr. Adams, indeed it is now well settled that as the contest will be between you and him, that you will get the vote of that state—the only paper in this county abuses Mr. Adams and supports your claims with a good deal of zeal and ability.[3]

My Dear Sir I should be much pleased to hear from you occasionally in relation to the health of yourself and Mrs. Jackson, and such remarks upon public measures as you may deem proper to communicate

Be pleased to present my most respectful compliments to Mrs. Jackson, and believe me to [be] most truly yr. friend & Servt

Chas. Penn. Tutt

ALS, DLC (33).

1. Tutt was referring to his application for naval agent at Pensacola.

2. Soon after becoming president in 1829, AJ dismissed Lee (1772–1840) and Cutting (c1755–1831), an army apothecary during the revolutionary war and war department clerk during John Quincy Adams's administration. Both were most likely writing for either the *National Journal* or the *National Intelligencer,* published in Washington.

3. Tutt was referring either to the Leesburg *Genius of Liberty* or to the Leesburg *Washingtonian.*

From John Hartwell Marable

Washington City
3rd April 1826

Dear sir,

It is an old saying that no man is so far from Trade as he who has nothing to trade upon—for a similar Reason I have not until this moment addressed you, even now nothing very important is within the perview of my Knowledge, on Saturday last Mr. McDuffie Genl. [Joseph] Vance and Mr. Trimble of Kentucky had some sparing in the House which grew out of Mr. McDuffie's argument in Favor of the amendments to the Constitution on Friday last, Vance in debate said if he suspected any one in the House for Corruption it would be the brawling blustering and vociferous Politician and declaimer and intimating and I think expressly referring to McDuffie, which I believe he Vance does not deny, Trimble also made several Inuendos which were not as the parliamentary Men say tangible; but tending evidently to be construed into Charges and imputations against McDuffie, Vance in the Course of his Talk said he was peculiarly situated that he had come from the very lowest order of society that at the Age of 22 years he could not connect the Letters of the Alphabet and that promoted as he was by the People of Ohio when an Imputation of Corruption was cast on them he must and would sustain their character at the hazard of his Life—Mr. Trimble made a Talk somewhat in the same way and said that he had not the Magnanimity to forget or forgive much less to vote for a Man who had if he had not slandered at least made wonderful Misrepresentations in Regard to the Kentucky Troops at the Battle of N. Orleans—McDuffie in reply said to Genl Vance he was happy to inform him he had not changed his destiny as regarded his grade in Society, that he had never recognized Vance or Trimble as gentlemen, but that he knew the great political Juggler, Poltroon and Puppy, the Secretary of State Clay, that he knew he had set on his Minions, that he knew they were the mere Poppets on the Tapis whilst the Master hand was behind working the Wires, that his Object was to give Mr. Clay his Compliments, but that if Mr. Vance or Trimble thought themselves agrieved he would for once forget that they were not Gentlemen and would attend to their Calls—The House was a perfect Scene of Confusion for half an hour, no one addressing the Chair, the Chairman crying out Order Order, Order, hurly burly, helter skelter, Negro states and yankies—the Matter is in statu quo it is now early in the morning when the House meets we may hear something *interesting* on the subject[1]—I heard Mr. [John] Randolph make a Phillippic last week in the Senate, yes says he Mr. R. with uplifted hands, I swear to my God and Country that I will war with this administration made up of the Union of Puritans and Blacklegs—speaking of the

Panama Mission he says I will prove to every Man living as plain as three times three makes nine and not ten, that the Mission was a Kentucky Cuccoos Egg laid in South America[2]—I send you some Speeches and documents consequently it is unnecessary to say any thing about wha*[t is]* going on in the H. Reps—I wish if in Conformity with *[your]* Opinion you would advise Houston to remain in Congress,[3] he is here bolde and energeti*[c,]* it is as much as his Friends can do to keep him from coming out as he says flat footed—S[amuel] P[rice] Carson of North Carolina[4] is the devoted Friend of our political Faith and is more than anxious to take a Chance in the Lottery as he calls it of Vance and Trimble; should be glad to hear from you, say my warmest Salutations to Mrs. Jackson, for yourself accept the renewed Pledge of my highest Regard

Jno H Marable

ALS, DLC (33). Published in Bassett, 3:299–300. Marable (1786–1844) was a Tennessee congressman.

1. Vance (1786–1852) was a congressman from Ohio. The debate on the constitutional amendment, beginning with McDuffie's argument on March 31 and continuing on April 1, included a lengthy discussion of Jackson's report of January 9, 1815, to then Secretary of War James Monroe on the role of Kentucky troops during the Battle of New Orleans (*Register of Debates,* 19th Cong., 1st sess., pp. 1960–2005).

2. Following the March 30 speech of Randolph (1773–1833), a Virginia senator (*Register of Debates,* 19th Cong., 1st sess., pp. 389–404), Clay challenged him to a duel, which took place on April 8 without injury to either party.

3. Houston had decided to run for governor of Tennessee rather than for reelection to Congress.

4. Carson (1798–1838) was serving his first of four terms in Congress. He did not engage in the debate.

To *James Buchanan*

Hermitage April 8th. 1826

Dear Sir

I received by due course of mail your friendly letter of the 8th. ult.[1] transmitting a resolution passed by the convention at Harrisburgh in which it is declared "that their confidence in me is unimpaired." This resolution adds another to the many obligations which I owe to the republicans of Pensylvania, and which shall be cherished as long as the feelings of gratitude and the sentiments of patriotism have a place in my heart—What greater consolation could be offered to my declining years than the reflection that my Public conduct, notwithstanding the dificulties thro which it has lead me, can still be honored with testimonials so distinguished as this from the enlightened and patriotic Pensylvanians; I desire no greater.

I have noted your remarks relative to Mr Molton C. Rogers—every information I have recd. concerning him, corroborates your account of him, and I have no doubt he fully merits the high character he sustains.

We have received the result of the Panama question in the Senate—from the whole view of the subject I have been compelled to believe that it is a hasty unadvised measure, calculated to involve us in dificulties, *perhaps war*, without receiving in return any real benefit. The Maxim that it is easier to avoid dificulties than to remove them when they have reached us, is too old not to be true: but perhaps this and many other good sayings are becoming inapplicable in the present stage of our public measures which seem to be so far removed from our revolution that even the language of Washington must be transposed in order to be reconciled to the councils of Wisdom! I hope I may be wrong—It is my sincere wish that this Panama movement may advance the happiness and glory of the country, but if it be not a commitment of our nutrality with Spain, and indirectly with other powers (as for example Brazil[)], I have misconstrued very much the Justice of the anathemas which have been pronounced upon the assembly at Verona as well as the true sense of the principles which form international law. Let the primary interests of Europe be what they may, or let our situation vary as far as you please from that which we occupied when the immortal Washington retired from the councils of his country, I cannot see for my part how it follows that the primary interests of the United States will be safer in the hands of others, than in her own; or in other words, that it can ever become necessary to form entangling alliances, or any connection with the Goverments of South America which may infringe upon that principle of equality among nations which is the basis of their independence, as well as all their international rules—The doctrine of Washington is as applicable to the present as to the then primary interests of Europe, so far as our own peace and happiness are concerned, and I have no hesitation in saying so far as the true interest of South america are concerned, maugre the discovery by Mr Adams that if Washington was now with us he would unite with him in sending this mission to Panama[2]—no one feels more for the cause of the South Americans than I do and if the proper time had arived, I trust that none would more willingly march to their defence—But there is a wide differrence between relieving them from a combination of leagued powers, and aiding them in forming a confederation which can do no good as far as I am apprised of its objects; and which we all know, let its objects be the best, will contain evil tendencies. Believe me to be with great respect, your most obdt. Servt.

Andrew Jackson

ALS, PHi (11-0184). Published in Bassett, 3:300–301 (extract) and Moore, *Works of James Buchanan,* 1:183–84.
    1. See above.
    2. AJ was reacting to Adams's March 15 message to the House of Representatives in which he argued that acceptance of the invitation to the Panama Congress was "directly deducible from, and conformable to" the policy recommended in George Washington's farewell address (*Register of Debates,* 19th Cong., 1st sess., Appendix, pp. 69–73).

To Samuel Houston

Hermitage April 15th. 1826

Dr. Genl

I wrote you some time since on the subject of Master James Overton,[1] who had obtained a warrant as a Cadet to enter the Military academy in June 1825, but owing to indisposition could not go on at the time—I wrote the secratary of war, who extended his time some months[2]—finding his health not perfectly restored, and his brother having died at the academy[3] I wrote to the sec. of war requesting an extension to June 1826—the sec received this letter at his seat in Virginia, and answered, that, so soon as he returned to the city he would forward a warrant for June 1826—This has never come to hand, and young Mr Overton does not know what to do—to set out with the sec letter which contains the promise above named, might be very precarious—will you on the receipt of this, call upon Mr Barbour—and bring to his recollection this circumstance and get him to forward a warrent for June 1826 as promised in his letter; or, if he does not intend it—to write me on this subject[4]—I would write direct to the sec, but from the result of the recommendation for Postmaster at Nashville I have determined to hold no correspondence with the Departments under the present Executive—but trust you will have the goodness to wait upon him on the receipt of this, & write me the result that I may communicate the same to Mr Overton who is now prepared to go on—it was the last & dying request of his father that he should receive a military education I have therefore exerted my influence in his behalf.

We have recd your & Major Eatons memorial to the President on the subject of the Postmaster at Nashville—you will see from the proceedings, that the people *will* sustain you[5]—This will be a lasting stain to the chief magistrate—whilst it will give you, & the major, as lasting a claim to the gratitude of the freemen of your congressional District. It displays a *littleness* that I did not suppose Mr Adams capable of, whatever I might have thought of Mr Clay—office is created for the benefit of the people, to be filled by honest men in whom they have confidence, and not for the exclusive benefit of patronage for the executive, & this, the good people will convince Mr Adams of, before he retires from his four years—

We have now the whole proceedings before the nation of this great *Spectakle* the Panama mission—I regret that we have humbled ourselves so far as to *beg an invitation* to this Congress—be it so—the people will now Judge of its expediency—and I have no doubt, will well sustain the minority in the Senate—it is *a useless & dangerous measure* without the promise of one solitary good, that could not have been obtained by a course that could not have jeopardised our peace. I have read the report

of the committee of foreign relations in your House—and [a] weaker production, from an enlightened committee I have never read—surely this is
not from the pen of Mr Forsythe—it must be from the genius of the late
sec. of the Navy Mr [Benjamin Williams] Crowningshield[6]—It will do no
credit abroad to the talents of your body, or yet to our enlightened nation. In haste respectfully yr friend

Andrew Jackson

Photocopy of ALS, Tx (11-0195).
1. See above, AJ to Houston, March 8.
2. See AJ to James Barbour, August 6, and Barbour to AJ, September 3, 1825.
3. William S. Overton (c1807–22), brother of James G., died the year of his admission
to West Point.
4. Barbour forwarded Overton's warrant on April 18.
5. On March 20, Eaton and Houston had, on behalf of the Tennessee congressional
delegation, protested the appointment of John P. Erwin as postmaster in Nashville. The
protest had been published in the *United States' Telegraph,* March 31, and reprinted in the
Nashville Republican on April 15. AJ's mention of "proceedings" may refer to a petition
(not found) that earlier circulated in Nashville in support of the appointment of Benjamin
Franklin Currey as postmaster.
6. On March 25 Massachusetts congressman Crowninshield (1772–1851) delivered the
majority report recommending appropriation of funds for the Panama mission. Forsyth, who
chaired the committee, reputedly opposed the recommendation (*HRRep* 132, 19th Cong.,
1st sess., Serial 142).

To *William Gibbes Hunt*

Copy   Hermitage May 3rd. 1826.
Dr. Sir
On my return home from alabama last evening the Nashville Whig was
handed, bearing direction in writing to me—in which it is made known
that it has been transferred to you, and all subscribers to that paper will
be continued as such, unless they otherwise make it known to you—
I have never viewed myself a subscriber to that paper since Mr Erwin
was interested in it,[1] altho it has been sent to me as many others are, &
have been, to which I have never been a subscriber, and viewing it sent to
me like many others gratis, I have paid the postage on it. I therefore think it
due to you that you should be advised thereof, that I may not be considered a subscriber to that paper. I am very respectfully yr mo. obdt. servt.

Andrew Jackson

ALS copy, DLC (33). Hunt (1791–1833; Harvard 1810), editor of the Nashville *National
Banner* in partnership with John S. Simpson, had just purchased the *Nashville Whig* from
James Erwin and united the two papers.

1. John P. Erwin joined the editorial department of the *Nashville Whig* in October 1823, becoming editor in January 1824 and retaining that position until April 1826, when, to qualify for the appointment of postmaster, he resigned.

To James Knox Polk

(Private)   Hermitage May 3rd. 1826
My Dear Sir

Having on my return from a vissit of business to Florence alabama, the pleasure of receiving your favour of the 3rd. ult.[1] for which receive my thanks—although at all times it afords me pleasure to hear from my friends in Congress, still I know their situation too well, to require any apology for not writing to me.

I have been leisurely viewing the passing scenes at Washington, and your speech on the amendment on the constitution I have read with much pleasure,[2] and I can assure you is well received by all your constituents, and gives you a strong claim to their future confidence—I agree with you, that the District System is the true meaning of the constitution, but as this cannot be obtained any uniform System ought to be adopted instead of leaving the election of President to Congress, we have seen anough to be convinced, that it will lead to the destruction of our happy Republican system if left to the house of Representatives—and every friend to the perpetuation of our happy system ought to meet upon this question with the true feelings of conciliation and compromise—and if we cannot obtain what we believe the best—let us for the welfare of our country and perpetuation of our happy goverment adopt what we may deem the next best—let it be uniform throughout the United States, and it will be beneficial compared to leaving it with the Representative branch. I have viewed with deep regret the warmth that I have seen displayed in the house of Representatives[3]—in that august body nothing but decorum ought to exist—every member is secured by the constitution the freedom of debate, and the conduct, and public charecters of all public men, are of right the Just subjects of investigation, and whilst the speaker confines himself to facts, he is within the pale of his constitutional duty—hence I am pleased to see the Tennessee delegation determined to support Mr. Mc.D. in his constitutional course—

I am happy to see that this dangerous project, the Panama mission, will be met fully in debate; to my mind, it is one of the most dangerous, and alarming Schemes that ever entered into the brain of visionary politicians—one, from which, many and multiplied evils, & dangers, may, & must result, without the promise of any real benefit that could not have been obtained in a differrent way without endangering our safety or our national faith, by persuing the policy of the father of our country; which he had acted on with Success, and had bequeathed as his last best gift to his prosperous country there was much safety—we are in peace with all the world, our commerce spread over the ocean, and great prosperity at home—to abandon a policy so wise in itself, and so beneficial an experiment to our country displays a weakness or wickedness not paralelled in the history of any country—it is a bold game of ambition, that puts at once to hazzard our peace, our happiness, and for what is known may lead to the destruction of our liberty at last, and all this without the least apparent cause for a departure from that wise policy recommended by Washington "peace with all nations entangling alliances with none"[4]— the South americas had our friendship, our sympathies, & good wishes, we have ministers with them to form commercial treaties, on the broad basis of reciprocity—in our nutral situation we could serve them more & better than any other way—the moment with them, we become beligerant, we raise up all Europe against them, & us, & thereby endanger the safety & independence of all—when alone & united, we put at Defience all invaders—and by the proposed Mission we lay a foundation of disagreable colision & dispute with these republics themselves—I can see in it nothing but great evils, & I hope the firmness of Congress will defeat this wild project—The eyes of the people are opened upon this subject, & it is unanimously disapproved here—the Documents has given them light and it is condemned.

I called at your fathers on the last day of april,[5] he had been very sick, was still weak but better, I hope he will be able soon to travel to the warm springs, the ballance of your family enjoy health—I had the pleasure of seeing your lady,[6] she enjoys good health, but as you may expect complaining of your absence—I write in haste for your own eye, I have not time to correct it, and you will excuse errors & this hasty scroll—I have Just got home, and have many letters to acknowledge—I [was] Glad to see the resolutions you have offerred,[7] they will bring every member to the true constitutional point—we will see the republicans of 98—and those who have sailed under false colours—these will prove the touchstone of political faith—I wish to see the yeas & nays, and on which side my friend Livingston records his vote[8]—see the Journals of former times how it may comport therewith—I am called by company and must close this hasty scroll, with my best wishes believe me yr f[r]iend

Andrew Jackson

ALS, DLC (11-0206). Published in *Polk Correspondence*, 1:41–43. Polk (1795–1845; North Carolina 1818) was a Tennessee representative.

1. See Polk to AJ, April 3.
2. In his speech of March 13, Polk had supported McDuffie's proposed amendment for election of the president through a uniform district system (*Register of Debates*, 19th Cong., 1st sess., pp. 1633–53).
3. AJ was probably referring to McDuffie's dispute with David Trimble and Joseph Vance, as described above in John H. Marable to AJ, April 3.
4. Jackson's quote embodied more the spirit of Washington's farewell address than the exact wording.

5. Samuel Polk (1772–1827), a Maury County farmer, surveyor, and land agent.
6. Sarah Polk, née Childress (1803–91).
7. On April 11, Polk offered a series of resolutions affirming the constitutional duty of the House of Representatives in making appropriations for foreign missions and recommending against funds for the Panama mission (*Register of Debates*, 19th Cong., 1st sess., p. 2166).
8. Livingston voted for the Panama appropriation.

From John Henry Eaton

May 5. 1826
W. City

Dr Genl

We are now within a short period of adjournment and shall thereafter hasten home, and leave an administration more delighted at our absence, than they were possibly at their own original promotion. Never have any people in power had such an up hill business of it, far as they have gone: there is scarcely a good and placid look that seems to pertain to the white House establishment, from Hal, (him I always place first being the creator) down to <Jamy Barber> James the man of war.[1] Good heavens! should Panama get us into a war, what a pleasant time the enemy will have under such a Commander in Chief of the Army & Navy, aided by such a martial Secty & backed by such a levee lounger as the general in Chief I really think that such a foe as the heroes of Bladensburg might capture such a force[2]

We have to day a long & able report from our Constitutional Committee on the subject of Executive patronage, with six bills introduced one as it regards the printing & printers—2d as regards Po. Masters, produced for the case at Nashville—3d. to restrain the power of dismissing from the Army & Navy but by court martial or request from both Houses of Congress. The others are minor points such as regards midshipmen & Cadets &c in a day or two it will be printed, when I will send you a Copy of the whole. The report is drawn by Col [Thomas Hart] Benton & is a very good production[3]

The administration vainly thought that patronage & power could sustain them and force the people to retain them. They are deceived, grossly deceived; & were the election to take place this year the concurrent voice here is that you would obtain every vote out of N England, certainly every one South of N York Should providence spare you, & you may so consider & believe, you will as assuredly have to spend your time here after 1829, as that J Q. is now here This administration, wretched & rotten, is already crumbling, yes broken down and nothing can keep it up. Hal walks alone, crest fallen, dejected and almost without associates, except some wretched cleavers to power, who are knuckling after some office, & seeking to obtain it at a sacrafice of all feeling, these flit about him; while the high minded stand off He has called upon none, who voted against him 17, so great is his rancor & spleen.[4] He & I as you would well suppose, have not even a passing acquaintance.

On arriving here, I considered well, & determined to go to the Presidents Accordingly I paid him the usual visit & was politely recvd—I determined too to go to a drawing room to see Mrs. A:[5] all this on the best reflection, lest he might, the world, impute a standing off on the part of your personal friends as the result of mortification. So go I did, & was received with much politenes; but I am now done, & have so declared—He has in the case of the Nashville Po Master treated the people & their *representatives,* not with disrespect but with contempt and therefore should be a king for life, no more shall his palace be troubled with my presence

I say he treated the whole delegation improperly, because the remonstrance as was stated in the communication made to Mr McLean, announced our procedure to be in behalf of *all,* & yet he spurned it as a paper, not proper for him to receive. You very well know I am not a hasty actor. The President I would offer nothing to, in the shape of indignity; & to be fully satisfied that nothing of this sort was done, being by the representation directed to draw up a remonstrance, with a suggestion that Houston & myself being at Nashville should alone sign it, I did so; and least any thing improper might be contained in it, we all aga*[in]* met, & the paper was read. Judge White in whose discretion & judgment great confidence was reposed was there; & having read it thro, I asked if there was in it an expression which could be construed into any thing of disrespect. Read over again was the reply, & again it was read & considered, when the answer of all was there is nothing in it at all indecorus, and without any alteration it was adopted & sent in; and came back as a paper not proper for him to receive.[6] Passion for the moment got ahead of his judgment, & yet the friends of this very passionate gentleman, who knows not how to get mad in the right place, were afraid of your ungovernable temper, & in favor of one who has more passion two to one, than even your enemies ever charged against you. He does not know even when, or how to get mad. He certainly knows very well indeed how to get into a passion, but then, he is quite ignorant of that sort of genteel ill temper which belongs to a gentleman

Clay & R duel is now an old subject. R. loses no opportunity to abuse him. He gives it to him & Adams in great style whenever he takes the floor. Yesterday he made a speech of 4 or 5 hours, whether the world will ever get his speeches is more than I know. Reporters will not offend their bread & butter.[7] He paid you yesterday a beautiful compliment, that too doubtless will never appear. After declaring, as he often does, that you are the only man in the nation who can be, & ought to be looked to, to rule the affairs of this Country, he spoke of the abuse you had recvd. from various sources heretofore, then said, that you would live and last with posterity when your detractors should have sunk to forgetfu[lne]ss, that like the great father of Rivers the Missippi your fame and splendid efforts for your Country would roll its mighty volume on thro time yet to come, while your slanderers like the muddy cediment which partially & for a while muddied the current of the Missippi would be born of[f] beyond & out of sight of your renowned battle ground sinking at the margin of the sea, & forming some wretched mound, for no other end or purpose than for some wretched *fisherman* to be wrecked on I [can] not quote him; it was something like this, tho a great deal better: You do not desire it, but your Country does & will desire you to take the helm of her affairs; & all that is necessary for you, is to be still & quiet, & let the buffetings gong as they may. The thing is fixed, nothing can stay it, even the friends of the Administration are some of them admitting it, and the drooping looks of Clay confirm the opinion. The only hope is to buy the people with their own money, but that we may yet before we adjourn partially & measurably stop under the Bills introduced to day. We never had a more federal band to rule us as Randolph says, it is more federal than federalism itself

You say that as regards my prospects of reelection things promise well. Upon this subject you know my feelings for heretofore I have as I always do, upon every subject spoken to you freely & fully. My feelings are not enlisted on the result as it regards myself. In reference to myself it would be better for me to stay at home & manage my own little pecuniary matters, least in old age, to which we must all at last arrive, like others I may be found a pauper & on the hands of some indulgent friend. But thank God, & to that I attribute a great portion of my quiet of mind, money never disturbed either my waking or sleeping visions. I have ever looked to its possession, with that view which [Robert] Burns has well described

> Not to be hidden in a ditch
> Nor for a train attendant
> But for the glorious privilege
> of *being Independent*—[8]

To this extent, & nothing beyond it, should every man become a worshipper at the shrine of Plutus.[9] While therefore no interest of mine could, or would at a moment like this, prompt me to retire I am nevertheless free to declare, that if the Legislature please so to order it, no pain will be inflicted either on my pride, or on my feelings; most cheerfully shall I yield, with thanks for kindnesses heretofore extended, greatly beyond even any fancied merit of my own, & certainly surpassing any calculations which even in moments of my most lively fancy I had ever dreamed of or expected. Weak tho as man is on the score of vanity I never attributed the success to any claims intrinsically my own, I owed it essentially to yourself, & materialy to another highly esteemed friend judge Overton, whose kindness I have too frequently received, not to be remembered ever. A strippling as I was in 1818, I had no claims, & hence the jealousy of some, & dislike of others; it was to friends who had weight that I owe all the little consequence I have in life, & I am amply compensated in the reflection that after a service of 8 years their friendship regard & confidence is still retained to me, & that I am returning to the place they found me in, with nothing on my part done, to forfeit their esteem. Let then, under these circumstances, whatever may happen, I shall be satisfied, & feel contented that another may be found better meriting the confidence of the State. My great desire is that at so perilous a time in our Republican history, & when a few corrupt aspirants are ready to sink the ship, if they can swim to shore with the Cargo, some care may be taken to send no one who may by possibility join in any way the piratical cruisers against the Liberties of the Country: this being done I am satisfied; for truly neither my heart, or my feelings are fixed upon office or place of any sort either in Congress or out of Congress

Genl Brady who left here yesterday, & to whom I extended while here what civility I could, conversed with me on this subject, & in this way. He said it had been stated of him, that from the patronage & favors extended to him lately by the Govr. he would not be right on *a certain matter*; but that it was altogether a mistake, it would have no influence with him.[10] I told him I had recvd letters stating that the Govr had like the President been exerting the patronage of his office, as was supposed with a view to particular objects; but that no correspondent of mine, had suggested aught that any effect would be thusly produced upon him. He answered they were right in their opinions!! I should indeed calculate that genl Brady was not thus to be won. If tho he shall, & may be he does, think that Carroll is better qualified, & can render greater services why then indeed he should support him; & if he thus believes I should desire him to do so most certainly

In your letter recvd. yesterday[11] you enquire after the warrant of Mr Overton, I have just recvd a note from Mr Barbour he says he has apprised genl Houston on this subject & that your wishes had been anticipated; that is I suppose the warrant has been forwarded

I am tiring you, therefore good by, & tender my regards to Mrs. Jackson thine truly

J. H Eaton

ALS, DLC (72).

1. Henry Clay and James Barbour.

2. Jacob Jennings Brown (1775–1828) was commanding general of the army. On August 24, 1814, British forces had routed American troops at the Battle of Bladensburg, opening the way for the capture and burning of Washington.

3. Benton (1782–1858) was senator from Missouri. The bill regarding executive patronage would have required Senate confirmation for certain postmasters appointed by the president; and the printing bill would have lodged appointment of government printers with Congress rather than with the Secretary of State.

4. Probably a reference to the vote in the Senate on the confirmation of Richard C. Anderson, Jr., as minister to the Panama Congress, which seventeen senators opposed.

5. Louisa Catherine Adams (1775–1852), née Johnson. Eaton called on the president on the morning of December 13, 1825, in company with Hugh Lawson White.

6. Eaton was referring to the Tennessee delegations' protest of the appointment of John P. Erwin as postmaster in Nashville.

7. For several days Jacksonians had charged that the administration presses in Washington, the *National Journal* and the *National Intelligencer,* suppressed publication of Randolph's speeches.

8. Eaton was "quoting" from "Epistle to a Young Friend" (1786) by Burns (1759–96).

9. Greek god of riches and wealth.

10. Ineligible to succeed himself as governor after his third consecutive term, William Carroll had been suggested as a candidate for Eaton's Senate seat. The patronage allusion was probably to Carroll's appointment of Brady as inspector general of the Tennessee militia in December 1825.

11. Not found.

From Henry Banks

Frankfort May 28. 1826

Dear Sir

I have been upon several occasions inclined to write to you, at some times and, indeed with very little intermission I have been restrained by a general debility and incapacity proceeding from an origin of about 16. months standing. The truth was I was on the 9th. day of last Feby. the day on which the congressional treason was perpatrated taken while at dinner with a difficulty in swallowing, proceeding as I then supposed from an affection of the stomach, since that time my speech, stomach, general system & qualifications for business have been more or less affected. sometimes to indicate dissolution, at other times to flatter me with renewed health—but while these feelings and excitements alternately flatter & frown I know that I every day not only grow older but rapidly approximate the gate from which no traveller ever returns.

Superadded to these afflictions I have been sorely annoyed with a pain on the left side near the back, from which, tho many remedies have been resorted to, I have found no relief or very little intermission of pain, until I resorted to the surgical operation of a lesion which now exists, since I have resorted to that remedy my general feelings & nervous strength has been something better, now I can ride on horse back some distance, heretofore I could with difficulty even with assistance get on horse back—

Besides all this I heard that the President had filled your post office with one of the government partizans, & that it would be unsafe through that channel to address a letter to you,[1] and while this last matter has been uppermost in my mind, pausing and hesitating whether I should write or not, I have the pleasure to become acquainted with one of your neighbors & friends, Colo Craig,[2] by whom I shall send this, letter to be put safely into your hands

Since my last I have taken some pains to asertain the state of Public sentiment in this state respecting your future election, and can assure you of a truth. that your popularity has greatly increased, I believe every where; there is no doubt that you will get a considerable majority in this Town and County, and I hear like tidings from Louisville & Lexington, and intelligence equally favorable from many other parts—I expect the present members of congress are equally divided, but while it appears there is no doubt of the reelection of your friends, there is much reason to suppose, that the usurpation will not be supported by more than 3. and even they will be opposed by popularity & zeal. It is within my knowledge that David Trimble will be opposed, and I believe with success. Metcalf & [James] Clarke I fear will hold their own, and if they are not opposed it will be because opposition will not bear a favorable aspect.[3]

The paper here called the Argus will either be for you or will be neuter, there are three partners, two of them are anti ministerial, the other feels some personal obligations to Mr. Clay and will not personally oppose him,[4] he is the most efficent man I have no doubt that he would sell his Interest on reasonable Terms, and there is as little that I would become the purchaser, if I was able to be useful, and it would [be] perfectly characteristic with my whole life, now to take hold of the plow if I could do so with effect.

I am now confident that my life is ebbing away and my attachment to it continues more vivid because I wish to see you the providential instrument of redeeming your country once more from the plots and contrivances of the internal liberticidal foe, as you once did with honor glory and effect from the phalanxes & Bayonets of your Countrys invaders— that a kind providence will enable me to salute my feelings with the knowledge that I have done something to secure the great purpose for which I believe you are destined is ever recollected and used in my more solicitous invocations to the great God of Heaven.

I will not pretend to say to you what I may think would be the more approved course to promote your own & your countrys success, but should it occur to you to make a visit and easy tour through this state, I think it would be advisable to postpone it until after the spirit of party shall hav[e] exhausted itself during the August [election?] when either the old court or new court will triumph. It may be now proper to say that many of the old court party are your opponents, and are willing to have it believed that you are a new Court man, your letter to me[5] has enabled me to silence some of them.

On the other hand the new Court party are very generally your friends, they say that your principles are those which they approve, and the Chief Justice says that he shall support you regardless of your preference of the courts.[6]

Should this letter afford you any information or amusement, equal to the trouble you will have in reading it, I shall be gratified therein, but be that as it may, my personal esteem for you, and my devotion to my country has required it of me as a duty, to embrace this safe oppy. of writing what truth has dictated and to assure you of my long standing & immutable regard

Henry Banks

I should be gratified in knowing that you had read the vindication of my Brother,[7] with attention, and regard for a patriot so young & effective as he was.

ALS, DLC (33).
1. Banks was referring to Adams's appointment of Erwin as postmaster.
2. Possibly William Craig of Williamson County, Tennessee.
3. As Banks predicted, Trimble was defeated, and Clark (1770–1839) and Metcalfe won reelection to the Twentieth Congress.
4. Amos Kendall (1789–1869), Robert Johnston, and Albert Gallatin Meriwether (d. 1848) published the Frankfort *Argus of Western America*. Following his graduation from Dartmouth College in 1811, Kendall had served as tutor in the Clay household.
5. Not found.
6. The "New Court" chief justice, William Taylor Barry (1784–1835; William and Mary 1803), ran unsuccessfully as the Jacksonian candidate for governor in Kentucky in 1828; AJ appointed him postmaster general in 1829.
7. Banks had sent Jackson a copy of his *Vindication of John Banks . . . Against Foul Calumnies . . . by Judge Johnson, of Charleston, South-Carolina, and Doctor Charles Caldwell, of Lexington, Kentucky . . .* (Frankfort, 1826), in which he had defended his brother John (c1758–84) against charges that he had been a lawless speculator in supplying Nathanael Greene's troops near Charleston during the Revolution.

To Felix Grundy

(private)   Hermitage May 30th 1826
Dr. Sir
When in Nashville on the 26th instant ruminating on the subject that would be before the Board of Trustees on the 27th.[1] I thought I would make an address to the citizens of Orleans on the subject of the endowment of the Lafayett & Jackson professorships in Cumberland College, on which I intended to have consulted you on saturday last, but your late arrival at the college prevented it—I had intended to have addressed the citizens of charleston &c &c &c also on this subject—but when I reached home, I concluded, I would forward this to my friends in Orleans, and if successfull there I would push it every where that I had any friends that I could address upon this subject on which I have, & still feel, great solicitude—

I now inclose a copy of the letter &c to my friends in New orleans for your inspection and advice[2] whether in your Judgt. the course I have adopted is a proper & prudent course—& whether it is best now, to address my friends elsewhere, or to await the result of the success at Orleans—and whether any, & if any, alteration in my address what, ought to be made—writing has become to me quite laborious—and if you are of opinion, that it is right to push my address to every quarter of this union now, you must aid me in having the address copied—for should I go further with it—I will send it to Mobile thro Alabama, Carolinas, Georgia, and as far east as Boston—but before I take another step, I shall await your advice on this matter—write me shortly—in haste yours respectfully

Andrew Jackson

P.S. altho I have been silent—I have not been idle—if this should not succeed, I will then try a lottery. A. J.

ALS, NcU (11-0223). Published in Bassett, 3:303–304. Jackson sent the letter to Grundy by Lyncoya.
    1. On March 27 AJ had been elected to the Cumberland College board of trustees.
    2. See below.

Enclosure: To Jean Baptiste Plauché et al.

(Coopy)   Nashville May 26th. 1826
Gentlemen
    I take the liberty to address you upon a subject on which I feel great interest, as it is one with which, I know the welfare and happiness of our country to be intimately connected—It relates to the blessings of education which, without doubt, constitute the chief support of the liberties which our forefathers have bequeathed to us.
    There is now in operation at Nashville a College which with a little more pecuniary aid, is likely to become one of the most flourishing institutions in the U. States. Situate in a healthful climate, in the great vally of the west, where the feelings, habits, & manners of the people, are purely republican; and where from its contiguity to the cumberland river the means of support are cheap and abundant, it will extend its advantages to the poor as well as the rich—can prepare for the service of their country the sons of the farmers and mechanics as well as those who by fortune are exempt from the necessities of labour. The President is an accomplished gentleman of the first acquirements: and the subordinate professors are gentlemen highly distinguished for literary & scientific attainments. But to place upon a lasting foundation the prosperity of this College, it is requisite to obtain funds for two more professorships which were created last year, and which the board of Trustees have thought proper (in honor of the good Lafayette, and the humble services of myself) to call by the names of Lafayette & Jackson.
    It is well known that the good Lafayette is destitute of the means to

make a permanant endowment of this nature, as is the case also with myself, otherwise these professorships would have been filled ere this—Situate as we are then, the only alternative is to appeal to the liberality of those who have the means to make donations and the disposition to yield them for the lasting benefit of an institution so well calculated to prepare the american youth for the councils of our common country.

Without doubt the Trustees had two motives in view in honoring Lafayette & myself (if I may be pardoned for speaking of myself in conjunction with that illustrious benefactor) with the names of these professorships—the one to compliment us with the perpetuity which it was hoped that the institution may experience—the other to operate upon the feelings of such as may derive an additional inducement from this circumstance to contribute to an endowment which, with the smiles of providence, will I trust redound to the credit of its patrons, and the general cause of knowledge.

The object of this letter then, Gentlemen, is, to ask you to present, or cause to be presented to the good citizens of Orleans the enclosed paper, or one of this purport, and to receive & remit such aid as each citizen may be disposed to give. It is not expected that any will give but a small sum—small donations will enable the more persons to aid in the establishment of these professorships, and to testify their respect for the cause of literature and science. I am respectfully your most obdt. servt.

Andrew Jackson

(Coopy of paper enclosed & referred to in the above letter)

Those citizens who are disposed to aid in the permanant endowment of the Lafayette & Jackson Professorships in the Cumberland College Nashville Tennessee, will subscribe their names hereunto which shall be enrolled in the archives of said college, presenting at the same time to the holder of this paper, such sum or sums as he or they may think proper to bestow, which donations shall remain and enure to the sole use & endowment of said professorships forever, the interest annually accruing only to be applicable to the salaries of said professors, but should there be an excess of interest, such surpluss to be applied by the Trustees to the rise & benefit of said college—

ALS copy, NcU (11-0219); Photocopy of ALS copy, DLC (33); AD of enclosure, NcD (mAJs). Published in Bassett, 3:302–303. Jackson's letter was widely republished in the next few years (minus the paragraph after the signature) as embodying "the essence of genuine Republicanism," an effort to diffuse "the blessings of education amongst all classes of the community, the *poor* as well as the *rich*" (Washington *United States' Telegraph*, October 3, 1826).

From John Caldwell Calhoun

Private   Washington
                                                         4th June 1826

My dear Sir,

I avail myself of the present safe conveyance to renew our correspondence, after so long a suspension.

Majr. Eaton will give you all of the particulars of the long and interesting session of Congress, which has just terminated. There has been much excitement, but for my part, I am neither surprised nor displeased at the depth of feeling displayed by the members on several occasions, as I believe, that it has been caused by a thorough and honest conviction, that the liberties of the country are in danger, and not by the sentiment of faction, nor disapointment, as has been attributed. In my opinion liberty never was in greater danger; and such, I believe, to be the impression of the coolest and most considerate of our citizens. An issue has been fairly made, as it seems to me, between *power* and *liberty*; and it must be determined in the next three years, whether the real governing principle in our political system be the power and patronage of the Executive, or the voice of the people. For it can scarcely be doubted, that a scheme has been formed to perpetuate power in the present hands, in spite of the free and unbiased sentiment of the country; or to express it more correctly, those now in power act on a scheme resting on the supposition, that such is the force of Executive influence, that they, who wield it, can mould the publick voice at pleasure by an artful management of the patronage of office. It must be obvious, if should prove to be the fact, that a radical change has already been effected in our system. If power can be acquired against the voice of the majority, and when so acquired, can be maintained and perpetuated by the influence, which it gives, our government may indeed retain the forms of freedom, but its spirit will be gone. Nor will it be long before the form will follow the spirit. Let the Presidency be transmitted by the exercise of a corrupt patronage from hand to hand, and we shall soon consider the form of electing by the people a mere farce; nor will it then be difficult to reconcile the people to the transmission of the Executive power by hereditary principle, in some imperial family.

I, however, hope for better things. I confide in the intelligence and virtue of the people, which have safely carried us through so many difficulties. Already, I see much to hope. The scheme appears to be well understood by many, and the publick indignation will swell just in proportion as it comes to be fully developed.

It will be no small addition to your future renown, that in this great struggle your name is found, as it always has been, on the side of liberty, and your country. Occupying the grounds that you do, there can be no triumph over you, which will not also be a triumph over liberty. That you may live to witness a successful termination of the struggle, and that you may be the instrument, under Providence, of confounding political machinations and of turning the attempts against the liberty of the country, into the means of perpetuating our freedom, is my sincere wish. As to myself, I am content, let what may happen, provided the cause triumphs. I know that much of the storm will fall on me; but so far from complaining, I deem it my glory to be selected as the object of attack in such a cause. If I had no higher object than personal advancement, my course would be easy. I would have nothing to do, but to float with the current of events. I feel, however, that such a course would be unworthy of the confidence, which the American people have reposed in me, and of the duty which any citizen owes his country. With sincere regards I am & &.

J. C. Calhoun

ALS, DLC (34). Published in Bassett, 3:304–305.

To Arthur Lee Campbell

Hermitage near Nashville. T.
June 12th. 1826.

Dr. Sir

your letter of 31st. ult.[1] is Just recd. I have read it with attention; your detail of public men and measures, with the general policy of your state, I have noted in my memory & disposed of your letter as you requested—I tender to you my thanks for this communication.

I deeply lament the cruel & untimely end of Colo [Solomon Portius] Sharp—I knew him in his boyhood & my acquaintance grew with his riper years—he was a man of talents & much worth, his untimely death, a great loss, not only to his family, but to his country. The only attonement for this cruel & unheard of murder is the blood of his slayer; it is therefore a gratification to learn that he is condemned to make an atonement on the gallows for this horid deed.[2]

My acquaintance with the amiable relict of Colo. Sharp[3] is too limited to take the liberty to address her—I therefore feel great hesitancy in writing her—Should a proper opportunity present itself hereafter when in accordance with propriety I can make to her a tender of my condolence on this mournful occasion I will with pleasure convay to her all the sympathy of my soul, with all the sincerity of my heart & feelings of friendship that I always cherished for her husband whilst living. It is needless for me to assure you that it would afford me pleasure to serve you, where I could do so with propriety.

On the subject of Mr P. H. Darby and the matters to which you allude, I have to observe that my absence from this state while those transactions took place, will convince you that I can have no knowledge of
them only from rumor[4]—the Revd. Hardy M[urfree] Cryer who lives near
gallatine Sumner County, is the son of the man whose name Mr Darby
was charged with forgeing, and as I am informed was a witness in behalf
of the commonwealth, whose deposition if taken will afford you a full
history of this transaction. The Revd. Mr Campbell of Nashville can give
you a full account of the other matter as he presided over the church at
the time Mr Darby was brought before it (being then a member) on a
charge of swearing falsly, or perjury—Mr Campbell testimony will give
you a detailed account of this matter, and I have no doubt will afford
much information of Mr Darby & his charecter here.[5] as to myself I never
did admire the principles of Mr Darby, and therefore never associated
with him more than as a professional man I was compelled, he having
been employed in a cause in which I had interest[6]—I felt happy when that
sociability ended with the compromise of the cause, since which, I have
not seen him—nor did my confidence increase with my acquaintance with
him, but having made it a rule thro life never to break my shins over *stools*
not in my way, I have never made inquiry into the various rumors &
charges against Mr Darby in this country—but by applying to those you
have named, and the Revds. Mr H. M. Cryer & Campbell, you can obtain the charecter & standing of Mr Darby here—there is one thing certain, his want of Judgt. & imprudence, will injure any cause which he
attempts to advocate. I am sir very respectfully yr mo obdt. servt.

Andrew Jackson

ALS, KyLoF (11-0248). Campbell (1780–1838), a veteran of the Creek War, was editor of
the *Louisville Gazette*.
    1. Not found.
    2. Sharp (1787–1825) was a former Kentucky congressman and state attorney general
identified with the "New Court" party. On November 7, 1825, Jereboam Orville Beauchamp
(1802–26) had murdered him. In his confession, Beauchamp asserted that he killed Sharp to
avenge the seduction in 1819 of Ann Cook (d. 1826), later Beauchamp's wife, but Sharp's
family and friends claimed that Sharp had been assassinated for political reasons. AJ's acquaintance with Sharp probably dated from his family's residence in Nashville in the 1790s.
    3. Eliza T. Sharp (1798–1844), née Scott.
    4. Campbell was seeking information on Darby's character, possibly to assist the Sharps
in their efforts to discredit Darby. Sharp's widow had already accused Darby of complicity
in the murder (Frankfort, Ky., *Argus of Western America*, March 22); and Sharp's brother,
Leander (c1788–1851) repeated the charge in his *Vindication of the Character of the Late
Col. Solomon P. Sharp, from the Calumnies Published . . . by Patrick Darby and Jereboam
O. Beauchamp* (Frankfort, 1827), asserting that Darby and possibly others of the "Old
Court" party had assisted, encouraged, or at least had foreknowledge of Beauchamp's in-
tentions.
    5. Cryer (1792–1846), a Sumner County minister and horse-breeder, was the son of
James Cryer (d. 1816), who represented Sumner County in the Tennessee House, 1807–09,
1815–16. Leander recounted both the accusation of forgery and Darby's resignation from

the Nashville Presbyterian Church in his pamphlet. Darby later accused AJ of involvement with the Sharps' charges (Frankfort *Commentator*, February 16, 1828).

   6. For a brief period, Darby had served as Jackson's attorney in *Jackson v. Erwin*.

To John Coffee

Hermitage June 19th 1826

Dr. Genl

   Capt. Jack & Elisa reached us on the 15th. instant, in improved health; a Sacrament being on hand which commenced the day after their arival we have had but little of their company—and I am informed by the Capt that he must be at Nashville to night on his return to Alabama—which gives me but a moment to write you—I have recd your letter of the 10th by Capt Donelson,[1] and have never seen in the papers where the bill introduced by Major Eaton in the Senate to give further time to the heirs of John Donelson & others have been passed into a law—I *fear it has not passed into a law*.[2]

   The amount of proceeds of A. J. Hutchings crop of Cotton for 1825 which you have recd I have noted[3]—it will be well to enter it on the Journal & file amou[n]t of sales with it.

   I am pleased to learn that Winburn is doing well, & has a good prospect of a crop, and that he has regained the mare that had ran away

   at the time I obtained a compromise between Judge Overton, and James Jackson & Darby,[4] I made a transfer of right to the lands within Tennessee, which I was invested with by virtue of the Deed made to me by the Heirs of David Allison[5] to James Jackson, P. H. Darby, and to yourself, reserving to Mr McLamore certain benefits & interest to lands that he was interested in by purchase &c &c all which will fully appear by refferring to the Deed[6]—I did this, as I was determined that my name should not be any more used in court, & if any benefit acrued under the Deed that you should be intitled to part of that interest—at the time this deed was made by me, I was advised by Mr Darby & others that there were two Tracts of land 640 acres each in Robertson and Montgomery, to which there was no adverse claim, that could be got, & Mr Darby was under promise to see into the title, & take possession of the land for the benefit of James Jackson yourself & him—since which I have made no enquiry into this matter, and I have no dout but these tracts could still be got, as they stand recorded in the name of David Allison, as I am informed by Mr Darby.

   We regret that it will be so long before we shall have the pleasure of seeing you & your family with us, but from what Elisa informs, we hope you will be fortunate, & we will have the pleasure of being introduced to a young stranger by Mrs. Coffee[7]—Mrs. J. Joins me in our best wishes for the health & happiness of you & your family, to whom we are to be kindly presented—yours

Andrew Jackson

ALS, THi (11-0253).
    1. See Coffee to AJ, June 10.
    2. The bill, extending the time for one year, had been approved May 15 (6 *U.S. Statutes at Large* 340).
    3. The net proceeds were $1,959.19 (Statement of account, April 11, 1828).
    4. AJ was referring to his 1822 settlement with John Overton regarding their conflicting claims to Allison lands. On the settlement, see *Jackson*, 5:122–24, 168–69, 312–14.
    5. Deed, David Allison's Tennessee lands, August 3, 1812.
    6. Coffee, having been told by James Jackson that AJ had conveyed certain Allison lands to them, had asked for information on the subject. The deed of conveyance to the four named has not been found.
    7. Mary Coffee gave birth to a daughter, Katherine (1826–81), on September 24.

To Eleanor Parke Custis Lewis

[cJune 1826]

Dr. Madam

    I have recd your letter of the 23rd ult.[1] and permit me to assure you that it gives Mrs. J & myself great pleasure to be informed that we will be honored by your vissit to the Hermitage next Summer—& we hope it may be convenient for your children to accompany you, as they will know, we will be happy to see them.

    The narative you have given me of the life & misfortunes of the Patriot Don Joachim M Carrasco[2] has aroused all my sympathise for him. I beg you to believe that every influence I have, will be employed with the Senators & others to procure him a situation where his education & talents may be usefully employed. I sincerely regret that my pecuniary funds at present will not permit me to remit him such sum as would relieve his present wants—the low price of Cotton, with my Current expences, which is to be met from the proceeds of my farm has left me at present without the command of mony—& I have, & mean to continue to live within my means—the situation of Jefferson has admonished me of the propriety of this course[3]—but I beg you to say to him, if he can reach the Hermitage, he shall have a room there with all the comforts that I possess. I am fearful from the enquiries I have made he will not meet with such encouragement in Nashville in a Spanish school as would meet my wishes or his wants but from his education he might turn his attention to the study of the law go to Louisiana and at the bar meet with Success[4]—this is what I have known some of the unfortunate French do, & are now in possession of independence

AL draft, DLC (33).
1. Not found.
2. Carrasco, a native of Madrid who ran a Spanish school in Alexandria, Virginia, was tutoring Lewis in Spanish. According to Lewis, Carrasco was a friend and aide to Rafael del Riego y Nuñez (1785–1823), a leader of the 1820 constitutional revolt against Ferdinand VII. Imprisoned in France, Carrasco had been released through Lafayette's influence (Patricia Brady, ed., *George Washington's Beautiful Nelly: The Letters of Eleanor Parke Custis Lewis to Elizabeth Bordley Gibson, 1794–1851* [Columbia, S.C., 1991], pp. 178–81).
3. Jefferson's financial difficulties had become so serious that the Virginia legislature had authorized him to dispose of his property by lottery, and Monticello was expected to be among the prizes (*Richmond Enquirer,* February 9, 21, March 24, April 4).
4. In the summer Carrasco decided to try his luck in Albany, New York.

Although Jackson declined all invitations outside Tennessee to avoid the appearance of seeking the presidency, he did accept them within the state. The speech below, given on his arrival in Fayetteville on July 5, was typical of those he delivered on his swing through the center of the state in the summer of 1826.

In spite of Jackson's public efforts to remain above the fray, Adams partisans sought to use Jackson's letters declining invitations for political mischief. For example, in the letter to Thomas Patrick Moore, July 31, below, they claimed that Jackson's remarks provided evidence of his political maneuvering, his hypocritical and demagogic attempt to arraign the administration on vague and unjust charges while pretending a high-toned indifference to politics. Moreover, before the campaign ended, they charged that Jackson's letter contained southern threats of disunion and rebellion (Liberty Hall and Cincinnati Gazette, *October 6, 31;* National Journal, *July 29, 1828).*

To William Pitt Martin and the
Citizens of Fayetteville, Tennessee

[July 5, 1826]
Your cordial welcome is grateful to my feelings.[1] It recalls to my recollection the urbanity and hospitality which were extended to me and my troops by the citizens of this town and county, in 1813, while encamped in its vicinity, on their march to protect our southern frontier from the ruthless savage. Sir, the orderly conduct of the brave men I had the happiness then to command, was honorable to them, to me, and to their country. Those high-minded men, whom patriotism alone had led to the tented field, to defend their country, and their country's right, *could not* trespass on, or infringe the rights and privileges of their fellow citizens of Fayetteville, and of Lincoln county. These were the wealth and sinew of your country—they were the citizen-soldiers, who appreciated, above all

earthly blessings, the liberties achieved by their fore-fathers, & had sworn to hand them down, unimpaired, to their children, or die in the attempt. With such an army your rights *could not* be infringed, nor your property molested. In the ranks of such men, order, discipline, and strict subordination were easily introduced and maintained. It was the prowess of those citizen-soldiers, that enabled me so promptly and effectually, to terminate a savage war—to meet and vanquish their more savage allies, the British, at New Orleans, which gave security to your borders, and peace to the nation. I, Sir, was only an humble instrument in the hands of a wise and superintending Providence, for the accomplishment of those important and beneficial objects.

My humble efforts in the service of my country, whether in the field or cabinet, I am fearful, are too highly appreciated by you. I can with candor, however, declare, that in every situation, to which I have been called by my fellow citizens, my best judgment has been exercised, and unceasing exertions been employed, to promote the best interests of my country. How far I have succeeded, is evidenced by your approbation.

You, Sir, have been pleased to pass in review my conduct in the late presidential contest.[2] I trust you will believe me candid, when I assure you that I have too long practiced the pure principles of Republicanism to abandon them at this late period of my life. I have always been taught to believe that ours is a Government based upon the will of the people, and established for their prosperity and happiness exclusively. In the adoption of our Constitution the people secured to themselves the right of choosing their own agents to administer the government agreeably to their own *will,* as expressed by the voice of a majority. Surely then, in the exercise of these important rights, they ought to be left to the dictates of their own unbiassed judgments. Acting, Sir, in accordance to these fundamental principles of our government, and having laid it down as a rule from which I have never departed, "neither to seek nor decline office, when freely offered by the people," I could not interfere in any manner whatever in that contest, while either before the people, or the people's representatives. Your approbation of my course is, therefore, truly gratifying; and particularly so, as my conduct on that occasion was dictated by my best judgment.

For the kind solicitude, you have expressed for my promotion in the estimation of my fellow-citizens, I tender you my sincere thanks.

Printed, Fayetteville *Village Messenger,* July 12 (mAJs; 11-0277); AD draft fragment, DLC (33; 11-0276). Martin (c1803–77), a Fayetteville lawyer and alderman, later moved to Columbia, Tennessee, where he became a circuit court judge.

1. See Martin to AJ, July 5.
2. Martin had stated that AJ could have had the presidency "on the same terms it is now occupied," alluding to Adams's and Clay's alleged bargaining, and commended him for not betraying the people's interest.

From Edward George Washington Butler

Cincinnati, Ohio,
July 14. 1826—

My Dear General,

Frances and myself had the pleasure to read your affectionate and kind letter some days ago,[1] and neither she or my own inclinations would have allowed delay in replying to it, had I not been incapacitated for so doing by a slight bilious attack, from which I am just recovering.

That the probability of your not visiting Harrodsburg diminishes the hope of our seeing you this summer, and, consequently, occasions us disappointment, is not to be denied; but *your* judgment and delicacy have dictated such a course, and it would be as selfish and unbecoming as fruitless in your friends to attempt to influence your determination. I know that there exists a desire to blend your, or rather the people's cause, with that of a faction in Kentucky; and I know, moreover, that there are miscreants who would gladly avail themselves of the circumstance, or of any movement you may make, to misrepresent your motives, and create a momentary delusion. The scorching and uninterrupted influence of a people's anger could not be endured by certain violators of their rights, were it not for the occasional darkness produced by their misrepresentations, in which they enjoy, like reprieved victims, the pleasures of free respiration.

Since I wrote to you last I have seen the *substitute* for the Treaty of the Indian Springs,[2] with sufficient evidence to convince me that, had not the Senate interposed its strong arm, a proceedure even more corrupt than that which gave birth to that ill fated and infamous Treaty, would have received the *concurrence,* if not the *sanction,* of our pure administration; and then, a scene like this would follow, and over it that Administration could exercise no control: The Creek nation—a brave, patient and injured people—rising in their majesty, and perceiving how basely their interests were betrayed, would have rushed, with the violence of a torrent, on their former favorite, and, I believe, still honest chiefs; and, driving them into the heart of the Cherokee Nation, (whose wily and unprincipled sons ([John] Ridge & [David] Van) had, for the consideration of forty thousand dollars, betrayed the confidence and sullied the proverbial honor & honesty of the Creek Delegation,) a scene of blood and carnage would have ensued, from which few would have escaped to tell of their former friendships, & of the policy and magnanimity of their *Great Father.*[3] We look for Genl. Gaines this evening, & I know not what he will say of the above transaction. He, like myself, was deeply interested in the fate of these poor Indians; and if ever an honest man labored for other's good, regardless of the consequences to himself, he did for theirs.

I *[se]*nd you, my dear general, the copy of gen'l. [Alexander] Hamilto*[n's]* order for Genl. Washington's funeral procession. I copied *[it]* from an official copy now in the hands of Lieut. Col. [John De Barth] Walbach, and doubt not that it be interesting to you.[4] Mrs. Gaines desired me to remember her most kindly to Mrs. J. & yourself, and to my sister & Mr. & Mrs. Donelson. As Frances is well & now playing on her Harp, which arrived from N. Orleans this morning, I will go & ask her commands, as neglect to do so, on this occasion, would subject me to outlawry.

Frances joins me in love to our sister, and in affectionate regards to Mrs. J. & yourself & Mr. & Mrs. Donelson, & desires me to say that she will write in a few days. Yours, Dear General, very sincerly

E. G. W. Butler

P.S. We heard last night from Woodlawn[5]—all were well and enquired after the inmates of the Hermitage.

ALS, DLC (72).
    1. See AJ to Edward G. W. and Frances P. L. Butler, June 22.
    2. The Treaty of Washington, signed with the Creeks on January 24, 1826.
    3. When the Creek delegation went to Washington to renegotiate the 1825 Treaty of Indian Springs, Ridge (1803–39) and Vann (1800–63), both Cherokees who had attended the Creek council and reputedly wrote the protest to the treaty, accompanied the Creeks. Although not stated in the treaty, they, along with Major Ridge, Ridge's father, were designated to receive $40,000 out of a total award of $217,600. Once the Senate learned of the allocation for the Cherokees, it insisted on amending the House appropriation to provide for the public payment of the award to the full Creek council (*Journal of the Executive Proceedings of the Senate of the United States* . . . [3 vols.; Washington, 1829], 3:538–39; *Register of Debates,* 19th Cong., 1st sess., pp. 766–81, 785, 2668–87; *ASP, Indian Affairs,* 2:665–67).
    4. Order of Hamilton, December 21, 1799, DLC (2). In 1799 Hamilton (1757–1804) was inspector general of the army with rank of major general. Walbach (1766–1857) was a career soldier who commenced service as an officer in 1799.
    5. Woodlawn was the Fairfax County, Virginia, plantation of Butler's in-laws, Lawrence and Eleanor P. C. Lewis.

To *William Berkeley Lewis*

July 15th. 1826—

Dr Major

I sent a memorandom yesterday to you by Capt A. J. Donelson,[1] by which you, him, & Mr Earl in part might be guided in inviting the guests to the Dinner to be given to Major Eaton Mr Maury & Lady & Major Baker—in which I omitted to name the Mr [Alexander] Porter, & Doctor Lindsley[2]—I pray you not to forget them & any others you may think proper. I have sent a note to Genl [Robert] Purday today[3]—I can dine fifty comfortably—if more we will have a plenty—

I wanted to have seen Major Eaton—I would not have a guest disagreable to him. yr friend

Andrew Jackson

ALS, NNPM (11-0320).
    1. See AJ to Lewis and Donelson, July 14.
    2. Maury had married Mary E. T. Claiborne, Lewis's niece, in January. Porter (d. 1833) was a Nashville merchant.
    3. Purdy (d. 1831), a longtime friend of Jackson, was federal marshal for West Tennessee. The note has not been found.

To John Haywood Lewis

Nashville July 18th 1826

Dr. Sir

I have recd a letter from Genl Call[1] requesting me to employ council with a view to contest the will of Mr Kirkman deceased, and has referred me to you & Mr Irby Jones for information as to the State of his mind before July 1820, and after that date[2]—The will was tendered for probate on yesterday bears date in July 1820—I wish you to write me on receipt of this giving me your & Mr Jones Knowledge of the time & circumstances that attended Mr Kirkman, at the time he had fits at Mr. Jones Tavern as is stated here in 1819, and the conversation you have had, if any, with Mrs Kirkman on the subject of the state of his mind—& whether from all the circumstances within your knowledge of the state of his mind, was it such as in contemplation of law, would enable him to make a will or could he be at that time considered, of sound mind, memory, & understanding—and whether it was not such as Mrs. Kirkman had complete controle over his mind.

I pray you answer this spedily as it is important to the Interest of Genl Call & Mary that this information should be had early—& Genl Call advised of it to be ready for trial next court please advise me of such other persons as was intimate with Mr Kirkman about that time & can give information as to the state of his mind. I am in haste respectfully yr friend

Andrew Jackson

ALS, NNC (11-0323). Lewis (c1794–c1858; Cumberland College 1813) was a Huntsville attorney and at this time president of the Huntsville Board of Trustees.
    1. Not found.
    2. At issue was the codicil to the will, which authorized Kirkman's executors, in the event of the marriage of his daughters, to withhold their portion of the estate from the control of their husbands (Will Book 9, p. 127, TNDa). Irby Jones owned the Huntsville Inn and Bell Tavern.

To John Caldwell Calhoun

[July 18, 1826]

Your kind letter of the 4th ult,[1] by our mutual friend Maj Eaton, was received on my way to Pulaski where I was specially invited by my friends of Giles County to spend the fiftieth anniversary of our independence. On my return, I embrace the earliest opportunity to thank you for it.

I have been an attentive observer of the interesting subjects brought into discussion in the last congress. The message of the President at the commencement of the session was well calculated to swell to indignation the dissatisfaction which the mode of his election had already created. Until I saw this message, judging Mr Adams to have a tolerable share of common sense, I took it for granted that the footsteps of his father would be carefully avoided, and that no questionable policy would be recommended; especially none that would revive the asperity which marked the struggle of 98 & 1800, and terminated in the prostration of the federal party.[2] By steering thus his political course, with a hypocritical veneration for the great principles of republicanism in the one hand, and an artful management of patronage in the other, the hope of success would then have rested upon the *credulity* and *apathy* of the people, precisely where the enemies of freedom in all ages have placed the foundation of their power. With the same end in view, or in other words that which seeks to make the influence of office superior to a just responsibility to the people, Mr Adam's first efforts have certainly taken from him those strong agents. The panama mission, and the doctrine of his party upon the question of amending the constitution have unmasked his designs; & I am happy to see that the Republicans so well sustained themselves in the just defence of the liberty of the country.

I was not surprised, Sir, to see the ministerial journals wantonly assailing you,[3] and bearing the shafts of the administration against McDuffie & Randolph & all those who had the independence to stand forth the champions of the constitution & the people. This will always be the case when the schemes of <the usurpers> an unholy coalition are unravelled. But, sir, the people are awake, and are virtuous; & it is a pleasing consolation to the patriot to know that their voice & strength is with the minority of the senate. you may still confide in the support of the people; they may be led away for a moment by designing demagogues, and the influence of men who in the pursuit of office will sacrifice the greatest good of the country to procure it, but their reason is soon enlightened by truth and rallying round their true interests, they will throw aside the instruments of corruption, and accept those of good and faithful service.

I trust that my name will always be found on the side of the people, and as their confidence in your talents and virtue has placed you in the second office of the government, that we shall march hand in hand in their cause. With an eye single to the preservation of our happy form of government, the missiles of slander will fall harmless at your feet—The approbation of the virtuous yeomanry of the country will constitute a shield which the administration cannot destroy—it will live when the abuse of its hireling presses shall be forgotten.

Draft in Andrew J. Donelson's hand, DLC (34). Published in Bassett, 3:307–308 (dated July 26). Dated by Calhoun's response of January 24, 1827, below.
  1. See above.
  2. The presidency of Adams's father, John (1735–1826; Harvard 1755), had been severely criticized for the Alien and Sedition acts of 1798, which, in part, accounted for the Federalist party's defeat in the election of 1800.
  3. In the Washington *National Journal,* May 1 and June 7, "Patrick Henry" had specifically complained that Calhoun's appointments of Senate committees and his failure to restrain John Randolph's invective demonstrated a partisan opposition to the president.

From Arthur Perroneau Hayne

Private.   Ballston Springs. State of New-York 20th. July 1826
My Dear General,
   Your kind letter from the Hermitage, with those inclosed,[1] I received safely while in Phila. in June, & for which be pleased to accept of my sincere thanks. I have not as yet had an opportunity of using any them, but with the exception of that to Mr. [James] Lloyd, will on my return to Phila. use them all.[2] Mrs. Hayne & myself have been made quite happy in hearing of the perfect restoration to health of Mrs. Jackson, & of your recovery from a severe cold. On our arrival at New-York, Mrs. Hayne was taken ill, but is now restored to her usual health.
   Coll. [William] Drayton[3] is here with his family, & from information derived from him, & what I have collected myself on the subject of politicks, I am induced to believe that Mr. Adams is becoming unpopular—& this is said to be the case even at the North & East. The federal party who supported him are dissatisfied with the policy he has pursued—they expected he would bring into the Administration some of the Leaders of that party; & being disappointed in that, they have become restive—so [Robert] *Walsh* says, the Editor of the National Gazette in Phila. & a most devoted friend of Mr. Adams.[4] Clinton it is supposed will remain quiet, so far as relates to himself touching the next Presidential election, in which case Mr. Adams & yourself are the only persons spoken of as Candidates for that station. I have not seen Mr. Clinton—but I have understood the Administration have made certain propositions to him, & have given him an invitation to fall into their ranks, & shd. he not accede

to their terms, they threaten to *Wield* against him the whole power & patronage of the Government for the purpose of destroying him.[5] In point of power & popularity he is now thought worthy of being Courted—for it is believed that he may be able to control the two great states of New York & Ohio—but it is distinctly understood that his influence can in no event extend further. It cannot be denied that Clinton would like to be a Candidate himself, & his friends some times say his name might by great exertions be forced into the house of R:—but they allow your strength to be five times as great as his; yet seem to think the election once in the House; & then if your friends would rally on C— he wd. beat Adams. Thus they wd. merge the greater fraction into the less which wd. be absurd. That a decided Majority should rally on a small minority, seems so absurd that we are at a loss to know how any of the friends of Mr. C— could for a moment wish to take that Ground. Some of C's friends say he is getting old, is 60, & has no time to Spare. Coll. Drayton thinks your chance is decidedly better at present than that of any other man. Virginia is changing fast—the Western part of the State was always disposed to support you—& in the Eastern section of the State a change is gradually taking place. For example—such men as Mr. [William Segar] Archer of the house of representatives, whom you will recollect as having once introduced certain resolutions into Congress in opposition to some of your Mily. conduct, he is now your warm friend.[6] This fact connected with others which I could mention proves that Virginia may be calculated upon as being friendly to your election. In North Carolina the administration have made a tender of the friendship & kind feelings, which they entertain for the Crawford party, & are pressing upon that party the necessity of a junction between them & the Adams party—but we have with us at Ballston intelligent men from that state, all of whom concur in the opinion that No. Ca. will support you. Georgia is safe—just as much so as South-Carolina. In my mind, Clinton will not be a Candidate, & will support you. I hope he will do so from principle, & I cannot but believe after all he said on a former occasion of your peculiar fitness for the Office, that he will pursue any other course of conduct, but such as will be honorable to himself, & beneficial to his Country. Adams & Clay are one, & therefore if they wished it they could not serve him. And therefore Clinton's only chance of ever being elevated to the Chief Magistracy of the Country is in the exhibition of great patience & in his throwing his influence on the side of virtue & principle, & which will be on the side of the people, & in favor of the people's Candidate.

It is with the most heartfelt sorrow, I inform you, of the unfortunate Death, of your young friend, Edward Rutledge. In a fit of *Insanity,* on Monday evening, he blew his brains out, with a Pistol, at the Saratoga Springs—his Father[7] & family were in the house at the time. He had the Varaoloid in Charleston last Winter, which disease produced unusual debility, & depression of Spirits, which notwithstanding all the exertions of the kindest friends continued to afflict him, & at last terminated in his destroying himself. Major Rutledge is at present at this place with all of his family. We know Mrs. J. & yourself will sympathise with the family of our lamented young friend.

Mrs. Hayne will very shortly write Mrs. Jackson & give her an account of Frances. She is a sweet little girl & in every respect very engaging. Remember us kindly & affectionately to Mrs. Jackson. To Mr. & Mrs. Donelson remember us—also to Andrew & all of our kind friends, and believe me dear General to be your faithful & affectionate friend.

A. P. Hayne

Please direct your letter to New York.

ALS matched fragments, DLC (34 and 59; mAJs). Published in Bassett, 3:306–307 (extract).
   1. Letters not found. On April 6, Hayne had requested letters of introduction to AJ's friends in New York, Philadelphia, Baltimore, and Washington.
   2. Lloyd (1769–1831; Harvard 1787), Massachusetts senator, 1822–26, had recently settled in Philadelphia.
   3. Drayton (1776–1846), a former Federalist whom AJ had recommended to Monroe for secretary of war, was at this time a South Carolina congressman.
   4. Walsh (1784–1859; St. Mary's Seminary 1806), was also a lawyer, writer, and teacher.
   5. Rumors of propositions to DeWitt Clinton were common at this time and had been for more than a year. On July 28, for example, the Philadelphia *Democratic Press* reported that New York Jackson forces had agreed not to oppose Clinton for governor in return for his support of AJ for president and, furthermore, that Samuel Houston had been authorized to offer Clinton any position in AJ's cabinet. Also, on June 1, 1825, Charles P. Tutt had informed Jackson of a proposal he had himself made to Clinton.
   6. Hayne was referring to the resolutions of March 5, 1822, introduced by Archer (1789–1855; William and Mary 1806), criticizing AJ's actions as Florida governor (*Annals of Congress,* 17th Cong., 1st sess., pp. 1195–96).
   7. Henry Middleton Rutledge (1775–1844) of Nashville.

To Richard Keith Call

Nashville, *July* [26], 1826.

Dear Call.

I am glad to learn that the difficulty between you & White is adjusted.[1]

You cannot have forgotten the advice I give to all my young friends, that is—to say, as they pass through life have *apparent confidence in all, real confidence* in none, until from actual experience it is found that the individual is worthy of it—from this rule I have never departed—but still in one or two instances only, have I misplaced confidence. Rest assured I am not easily taken in of late by politicians. I well know many of them stir with the currents, run with the hare, and cry with the hounds. When I have found men mere politicians, bending to the popular breeze and changing with it, for the self popularity, I have ever shunned them, believing that such were unworthy of my confidence—but *still* treat them with hospitality and politeness. I have been led here to make arrangements for paying the last respect due to the memory & manes of the sage of Monticello, the Father of Liberty, the patron of science, and the author of our declaration of Independence, who had the boldness by that instrument to declare to the despots of Europe in 1776, that we of right ought to be free, that all well organized governments are founded on the will of the people—established for their happiness and prosperity—This virtuous Patriot, Thos Jefferson is no more—he died on the 4th of July 10 minutes before one P.M. On yesterday when we met to make arrangements for this melancholy occasion the mail brought us the sad intelligence that another of the signers of the declaration of Independence was no more, that John Adams had departed this life also on the 4th of July at 6 o'clock P.M. Was well in the morning, heard the celebration, sickened at noon and died at 6 o'clock P.M. of the 4th inst.[2] What a wonderful coincidence that the author and two signers of the declaration of Independence, two of the Ex-Presidents, should on the same day expire, a half a Century after that, that gave birth to a nation of freemen, and that Thos. Jefferson should have died the very hour of the day that the declaration of Independence was presented to and read in the Congress of 1776. Is this an omen that Divinity approbated the whole course of Mr. Jefferson and sent an angel down to take him from the earthly Tabernacle on this national Jubilee, at the same moment he had presented it to Congress— and is the death of Mr. Adams a confirmation of the approbation of Divinity also, or is it an omen that his political example as President and adopted by his son, shall destroy this holy fabric created by the virtuous Jefferson. Your friend,

Andrew Jackson.

Printed, *The Collector,* March 1905, pp. 51–52 (11-0325); Extract, FHi (11-0327).
   1. The feud between Call and Joseph M. White resulted from name-calling in the canvass for congressional delegate in 1825. During the campaign, Call had written that his opponent "Col White has a few friends in Pensacola, the most of whom are as base and unprincipled as himself." When White won the electiton, he announced his readiness to give Call "satisfaction" (*Pensacola Gazette,* April 2, June 4, 1825). The two formally settled their differences in October without dueling.
   2. Jackson chaired the meeting in Nashville memorializing the lives of Adams and Jefferson (*Nashville Republican,* July 29).

To John Dabney Terrell

Hermitage July 29th 1826

Sir,

I have received by due course of mail yours of the 17th instant[1] and with pleasure take a leisure moment to reply to it—

The policy of concentrating our Southern tribes of Indians to a point west of the Mississippi, and thereby strengthening our Southern border with the white population which will occupy their lands, is one of much importance, and in the execution of which will be required some attention to the Indian character. In referrence to the proposed negotiation as a part of this policy, I think it will be useless to attempt to prepare the minds of the Chickasaws for the surrender of a part of their lands. From my knowledge of their character I have no doubt that an entire exchange will be effected with less difficulty than a partial one. And with them, as with all Indians, the best plan will be to come out with candor—tell them, situated where they now are, that they will always be exposed to encroachment from the white people who will be constantly harassing their father the President for the privilege of occupation & possession &c; and here the case of Georgia & the creeks & cherokees will furnish a striking example. Say to them, their Father, the President, will lay off a country of equal extent, transport them to it, and give besides a premium of money which will enable them to buy stock &c; that he will establish land marks for them never to be moved, and give them a fee simple title to the lands. You must be prepared to give assurrances of permanency of title, and dwell upon the idea that they will never be asked to surrender an acre more—It might not then be useless to bring to their view the hope of a union between the choctaws, creeks, & chickasaws, as a speedy means of making them a great, powerful, & happy people, &, when their children shall be educated, of enabling them to become a member of the United states, as Alabama & Mississippi are—

With these hints I shall only add that you should be careful to promise nothing to them, but what you will religiously perform, or they will say to you, you lye too much—nothing will defeat a negotiation with Indians so soon as the discovery of an attempt to deceive them. I am Sir, very Respectfully yr. obt svt

Andrew Jackson

LS in Andrew J. Donelson's hand, THi (11-0331). Published in Bassett, 3:308–309. Terrell (c1760–1850), formerly an Alabama legislator, had been appointed special commissioner to the Chickasaw Indians, preliminary to new treaty negotiations.
    1. Not found.

To John Coffee

Hermitage July 31rst. 1826

My Dear Genl

I recd your note from Fayettvill[1] and had the pleasure of hearing by Major [Benjamin] Clements that you were so far recovered as to be able to set out on Monday for home, where I hope you reached in safety & with restored health & found your family well, I have not heard from you since your arival at home[2]

I sent for the mares some time since yours with one of mine is still retained with the horse Mr [John] Shute is to inform me when they are done with the horse when I will have yours, with mine, brought up[3]

I have heard nothing from our old friends & neighbours Capt & Mrs Winston since they went out only that the old gentleman was dancing & playing cards—Mr [Joel] Walker Winston before they went out asked me if I would buy their place,[4] I told him I would give a fair price for it—I am ready to begin to clear & if I was to buy that place, I would save my timber to fence that, as it has none on it, and the only reason that I would buy is, to give me open land anough—& save my timber—should you see them I would be glad to be informed whether the old people intend returning to live here, if so, the place will not be for sale—if not I would like to know whether we could agree upon what I think a fair price, if I clear land enough on my own, I shall not want that, as the only inducement to buy would be, to save my timber & the trouble of clearing—that place is much worn, & very much out of repair, the present crop worth next to nothing.

Mrs J Joins me in best wishes for your & families health yr friend

Andrew Jackson

P.S. Elisa is much mended & all friends now well, Mrs McLamore & youngest child has been sick, but has recovered[5] A. J.

ALS, THi (11-0335).
1. Not found.
2. Coffee had joined AJ for the July 4 celebration at Pulaski and that of July 6 at Fayetteville, Tennessee. Clements (1776–1862), an early settler of Lincoln County, Tennessee, and a deputy surveyor under Coffee in Alabama and Robert Butler in Florida, served as vice-president of the Fayetteville dinner.
3. AJ had sent three mares and Coffee, one, to be bred at the stables of Shute (d. 1844), five miles south of Nashville.
4. The Winstons—Anthony (1750–1827) and his wife and son Joel W. (b. 1792)—had moved to Alabama. Jackson did not acquire the Winston property on Stoner's Creek in Davidson County until October 22, 1828.
5. Elizabeth Donelson McLemore (1796–1836) and Emily.

To [*Thomas Patrick Moore*]

Hermitage, July 31, 1826.

My dear Sir—

Your favor of the 21st instant is received,[1] reassuring me of the wish of many of my friends in Kentucky that I should visit the Harrodsburg Springs. I had spoken early in the spring of this visit, because those waters had been recommended as necessary to the restoration of Mrs. J's. health, and there was additional gratification derived from the hope that I would see many of my old friends in Kentucky, whose company at all times would be pleasing to me. But inasmuch as Mrs. J. is lately so far improved as *not* to render this trip necessary, it seems to me very questionable whether, without this necessity, I ought to yield to the other considerations, at this juncture. I know that so far as Kentucky is concerned, the unjust imputations which it is my wish to avoid, would never be raised; or rather, that a great proportion of her citizens would attribute to their proper origin, the objects of my visit; yet, when I reflect upon the management and intrigue which are operating abroad, the magnitude of the principles which they are endeavoring to supplant, and the many means which they can draw to their assistance from the patronage of the government, I feel it is not less due to myself and to principle, than to the American people, particularly so far as they have sanctioned my political creed, to steer clear of every conduct out of which the idea might arise that I was manœuvring for my own aggrandizement. If it be true, that the administration have gone into power contrary to the voice of the nation, and are now expecting, by means of this power, thus acquired, to mould the public will into an acquiescence with their authority, then is the issue fairly made out—shall the government or the people rule? And it becomes the man whom the people shall indicate as their rightful representative in this solemn issue, so to have acquitted himself, that while he displaces these enemies of liberty, there will be nothing in his own example to operate against the strength and durability of the government.

With this candid expression of my feelings on this subject, I hope you will recognize nothing inconsistent with the claims which my friends in Kentucky have upon me. Were I unconnected with the present contest, you may rest assured that wherever my presence or my labor would be useful in arresting the efforts of intrigue and management, I should not hesitate to repair to the post which my friends might indicate as the most exposed. It is a source of much regret to disappoint your wishes, and others our mutual friends in Kentucky; but as things are, unless Mrs. J's. health should render it necessary, I think you will coincide with me, that a visit to Kentucky would be improper at this period. I shall be happy to hear from you on the receipt of this. Hastily, your friend,

ANDREW JACKSON.

Printed, Frankfort *Argus of Western America,* September 27 (mAJs); Draft in Andrew J. Donelson's hand, DLC (34). Also published in other newspapers and in Bassett, 3:309–10 (from draft).
1. See Moore to AJ, July 21.

From Ebenezer Harlow Cummins

Baltimore August 10th. 1826

Dear sir

The election of representatives in the twentieth Congress, for the state of Maryland, will take place on the first monday in october next, at which your political friends will bear in mind its relation to the next election of president of the United States. Being among the candidates for this district,[1] and having espoused the cause to which your political friends are devoted, I have to make the following request.

In the canvass of 1824 for the presidency, a pamphlet was circulated largely in this state, charging you with the execution, during the late war, "of a preacher of the gospel," or, in another version, "of a methodist preacher"; which had a very prejudicial effect upon your polls.[2] In our state one of the largest and most respectable religious communions consists of methodists; and I have found among them individuals highly influential, and otherwise favorable to your political elevation, not a little adversely affected by what I know to be a most flagrant misrepresentation of the affair in question. I have thought it to be due to them, that some accurate and authentic account of it should be furnished; and have therefore resolved to make this appeal to you, hoping you will furnish me, with the least possible delay, a full narrative of the case in question, not only with your own signature, but also authenticated by such of your heroic comrades, acquainted with its circumstances[3]

To me no other proof is necessary, of the correctness of this and all other public and official acts of your life, other than your character as a man, and the history of your country since you became in its events an actor so conspicuous, honorable, and glorious; but there are such things as fastidiousness, and prejudice, which often take possession of the mind, and such results as convictions from the influence of false or colored testimony, that as often warp honest hearts and judgments, and alienate from us the most devoted friend. Instead, then, of disregarding these, it is no departure from dignity, to furnish, over and over again, the most particular and circumstantial evidence, to remove the doubts of those who love us, and leave those who hate us no excuse for their slanders of our best acts.

In the course of the impending canvass I wish to be able to put down the calumny of you, which the pamphlet before mentioned too extensively and successfully propagated.

The last letters I have had the pleasure of receiving from my most beloved father and your venerable preceptor, left him well in Georgia,[4] enjoying still the rosy health with which a kind providence has so long blest him. He remembers well when you, general [William Richardson] Davie,[5] and many others of your early compeers were his pupils, in that famous region of Carolina so devoted to the freedom of these states, and within a few miles of the spot where the first declaration of independence was formally and devotedly proclaimed. He was among the actors at the courthouse in Charlotte, Mecklinburgh county,[6] on that memorable occasion, as well as a participator in the subsequent robbery of the British army in the neighbourhood by a few hundred stout hearted whigs, who surprised [Charles] Cornwallis,[7] and to use his own language "cut out" twenty two of his baggage waggons, and made a great fare of their contents the next day in Charlotte. To this day the surviving heroes in that feat preserve the tropies of their daring; several of which remain in the mansion of my father near the village where you last saw him[8] With the greatest respect and veneration I am sir your Mo ob Sevt

E H. Cummins

ALS, DLC (34). Published in Bassett, 3:310–11 (extract). Cummins (c1780–1834) was the publisher of a short-lived *Evangelical Repository* (Philadelphia) and the author of several books, including *History of the Late War between the United States and Great Britain* (Baltimore, 1820) and *The Maryland Justice* (Baltimore, 1825).

1. Cummins, a Jackson candidate in Maryland's third congressional district, withdrew from the canvass before the October 2 election.

2. One of the pamphlets was likely Jesse Benton's *Address to People of the United States* . . . (Nashville, 1824) in which Benton wrote that among six militiamen executed in early 1815 for a mutiny at Fort Jackson was "one preacher of the gospel."

3. For AJ's response, see AJ to Cummins, September 4, below.

4. Francis Cummins (1752–1832), a Presbyterian minister and educator, reputedly taught AJ at one or the other of his several schools in North or South Carolina. At this time he resided in Greene County, Georgia.

5. Davie (1756–1820; Princeton 1776), raised in the Waxhaws, was a revolutionary officer, serving as commissary general for Nathanael Greene in 1781.

6. Cummins was referring to the Mecklenburg Declaration of Independence, a set of five resolves announcing independence from Great Britain, purportedly passed at Charlotte on May 20, 1775. Shortly after a Raleigh newspaper published the document in 1819, Francis Cummins gave a statement to Nathaniel Macon, November 16, 1819, testifying to his witness of the event (*The Declaration of Independence by the Citizens of Mecklenburg County* . . . [Raleigh, 1831], pp. 17–18).

7. Cornwallis (1738–1805) was the victorious British general at Camden in 1780.

8. AJ probably met with Francis Cummins when he was in Greensboro, Georgia, in 1820 to obtain a duplicate deed of release from the Allison heirs for use in the *Jackson* v. *Erwin* lawsuit.

Between the presidential elections of 1825 and 1828, the congressional canvasses in the states generally turned on support for the Adams administration or for Jackson, or, occasionally, some other candidate. Some of the more heated contests were in Pennsylvania, one of the earliest states to endorse Jackson for president in 1824 and among the first to second that endorsement at the Harrisburg convention in March of 1826.

As the congressional canvasses approached in 1826, the tempo of the presidential campaign increased. Jacksonians began to set up vigilance committees, supplementary to the newspapers they had already started or bought. In Philadelphia in May, they formed such a committee, endorsed the Harrisburg nomination, and issued a report extolling the virtues, intelligence, and valor of Jackson, and denouncing the Adams administration.

The Adams Republicans, failing to organize to the extent of the Jacksonians, responded to the Philadelphia Committee report through one of Jackson's longtime critics, Jonathan Roberts, former Pennsylvania senator. In his letter to the Philadelphia Jackson committee, Roberts intoned a litany of Jackson's military acts, questioned his qualifications for the presidency, and accused him of numerous acts of despotism. Roberts's account was a corollary to the "military chieftain" theme propounded by Clay in 1825, and it condemned Jackson's civil service, pointing out that Jackson had resigned or declined every office to which he had been elected or offered appointment.

In the letter below Jackson responded to a request for information from Eaton, who was preparing a defense of Jackson for the Philadelphia committee. The case discussed, one of many touched on by Roberts, involved the court martial of William King (d. 1826), a colonel of the 4th Infantry. One of the charges on which King had been convicted and suspended from the army was that of ordering deserters shot upon capture, of whom Neal Cameron (d. 1818) was one. Roberts had shouldered Jackson with responsibility for the act, since he was the commanding general, but Eaton argued, based on the information Jackson sent him, that the execution had occurred in Spanish Florida, territory beyond Jackson's jurisdiction, that Jackson had no knowledge of King's orders regarding deserters and, finally, that Jackson was in Nashville, four hundred miles away, when the incident occurred. Eaton's letter first appeared serially in the Philadelphia American Sentinel beginning on September 26, and shortly as a pamphlet, To Chandler Price, Chairman, Jacob Holgate and Henry Horn . . . (Philadelphia, 1826).

To John Henry Eaton

Sunday morning August 13th. 26

Dr Sir

I have just recd your note,[1] I have no printed copy of the Trial of Colo. King—send you the copy in manuscrip furnished by the Judge advocate, & all the original papers upon which his arrest was founded[2]—this arrest contrary to all *rule* was founded upon Capt [John Benjamin] Hogans report made to the war department *direct, and not to me as the rules required*—you will see my letter on the inside of the adjt. Genls to the Judge advocate on this subject—*look at it*—you will find Hogans report of the case of Cameron also[3]—I am sorry I have not time to arange them for you—you will have to get Major Lewis to look over & select such as you may think proper to use—I must here remark that I never heard of the case of Cameron—untill I heard of it in reading the charges forwarded from the War Department against Colo. King enclosing an order for his arrest & an order to detail a court for his trial[4]—The Colo arrest was founded, as you will see, on the report of Hogan made direct to the War Department & not thro me If you were here I could aid you—In haste your

A Jackson

ALS, DLC (34). Addressed to Eaton at "Major Lewis."

1. Not found.

2. See Trial of William King, Case File D31, Records of the Office of the Judge Advocate General, DNA-RG 153; *HRDoc* 119, 16th Cong., 1st sess., Serial 38. Stockley Donelson Hays (1788–1831), AJ's nephew, was judge advocate for the Southern Division, 1818–21.

3. Hogan (1787–1845), later appointed by Jackson as collector of customs at Mobile, was paymaster of the 4th Infantry. In his letter of December 29, 1819, Jackson had submitted the proceedings of the case to then Secretary of War Calhoun for a decision, in part because the order for King's arrest originated in Washington. Daniel Parker (1782–1846; Dartmouth 1801) served as adjutant and inspector general of the army from November 1814 to May 1822.

4. See general order for the court-martial of King, August 10, 1819. For AJ's contemporary opinion on King's conduct, before he learned of the orders to shoot deserters upon capture, see AJ to King, November 29, 1819, *Jackson,* 4:400–401.

To John Coffee

Hermitage August 20th. 1826

Dr Genl

This will be handed to you by Mr Eastin to whom I refer you for the news of this section of country, & for the information of the health of our friends.

Genl [Thomas] Hinds spent a short time with me, & promised to call & see you, I suppose from what he said, he will accept of the appointment as Commissioner to treat with the Indians, I have given him my opinion, you must get the whole Territory or none[1]—that If the Indians can be got to cede or exchange the whole of their country, I would not hesitate as to the price provided it can be had, for one third the vallue of the ceded country—allowing the other two thirds to indemnify the Goverment for the acre, for acre in exchange, and all expences in survaying & selling the land, if this should not meet the views of the President & Senate let them reject it—the chikesaw & choctaw country are of great importance to us in the defence of the lower country, a white population instead of the Indian, would strengthen our arm of defence much.

your mare is now here and thriving, & I think in foal, I hope you will be more fortunate with her hereafter—My wish in this respect, is much hightened, since I have broke her two year old filly, which promises to be amonghst the first runners in america, from the small trial, of ten days, that Dunwody has made with her—I was unfortunate to loose one of my Grays I got of you last evening; I believe there were one thousand worms sticking to his maw, & all remedies failed—he lived five days after he was first taken.

Mrs. Elisa Donaldson is mending very fast—& is looking for her Capt every day—say to the Capt he must come in shortly, or Elisa will apply for a divorce—say to him his little daughter is in good health—

Mrs J. Joins me in affectionate regards to you Polly & the children. I am respectfully your friend

Andrew Jackson

ALS, THi (11-0341). Published in Bassett, 3:310 (extract).
    1. In May Hinds (1780–1840), who had served under AJ as lieutenant colonel of Mississippi Territory troops in the New Orleans campaign, Coffee, and William Clark (1770–1838) had been appointed commissioners to negotiate treaties with the Choctaw and Chickasaw Indians. Meeting in November, they were unable to convince either tribe to sell or exchange any of their Mississippi lands (*ASP, Indian Affairs*, 2:708–27).

To John Coffee

Hermitage Septbr 2nd. 1826

Dear Genl
    I have Just recd. your letter of the 21rst ult. being at the Robertson Springs when it reached Nashville, will account for the delay in my reply.[1]
    I have read the instructions to the commissioners for holding a treaty with the chikisaw & choctaws with attention, and hasten to give you my opinion with regard to the restrictions therein contained.
    1rst The current expences of the treaty including compensation to the

commissioners is not to exceed Twenty thousand dollars the Sum appropriated. you are not restricted as to the price to be stipulated for any land you may obtain from the Indians, This as it ought to be, is left to the discretion of the commissioners—on the event of a Barter you are only restricted as to acre for acre, but as it must have been well understood that a barter could not be obtained without Boot, this is also left to your discretion—but the treaty having to be approved by the President & Senate the sums stipulated to be given must await This approval & an appropriation by congress—I would advise in all stipulations for *mony,* a stipulation for an annuity for a term of years *only.* The object of the Govt. is to obtain a cession of this Indian country for lands west of the Mississippi—it is the duty of the commissioners to obtain this cession on the best terms they can—leaving the President & Senate to ratify or reject as their Judgt. may dictate—It is well known that a Barter cannot be obtained without giving the Indians Boot, was I a commissioner before I would fail in the object I would give in Boot the excess in value of the acre of Indian land ceded, to the acre given by the U. States, taking into view the expence of survaying & selling the Public land—This section of country is of great importance to the prosperity & strength of the lower Mississippi, a dense white population would add much to its safety in a state of war, and it ought to be obtained, if it can, on any thing like reasonable terms.

I am happy to hear the health of your family is restored, I hope you may enjoy it throughout this season—We have some bilious attacks in our neighbourhood, my overseer lies very ill at present, all my other family are well.

I have recd a letter from a Mr James Garrett, as he says, former overseer for Mr Booker, informing me that Mr Winburn does not intend continuing another year, and wishing to be employed[2]—Mr Winburn has not intimated such a thing to me—will you advise me on this subject—and as to the charecter of Mr James Garrett as an overseer.

Mrs. J unites with me in good wishes to you, your lady & Sweet little family believe me your friend

Andrew Jackson

ALS, THi (11-0353). Published in Bassett, 3:312 (extract).

1. Letter not found. Robertson Springs was a noted spa on the headwaters of Sulphur Fork in Robertson County, about twenty-four miles from Nashville.

2. Letter not found. Garrett (b. 1792) was a resident of Lauderdale County, Alabama, having previously lived in Maury County, Tennessee. Booker may have been Peter Richardson Booker (c1783–1839), a Maury County planter. As a replacement for Jesse Winborne, AJ ultimately hired John W. Phillips.

To Ebenezer Harlow Cummins

Hermitage Septbr. 4th. 1826

Dr Sir

I have recd. your letter of the 10th ullt.[1] it reached me to day. I am aware of the great exertions that were made in 1824, by falshood and calumny, to prejudice me in the estimation of the public; & now that they can call to their aid the connivance of pamphlets and newspapers circulated by the panders of power, it is to be expected that I shall be assailed in every section of the Union. But truth is mighty & shall prevail—Intrigue & management incapable of blind folding the virtuous yeomanry of my country, will fail of their ends; nor can they impose any other task on me than that of defending myself against their imputations whenever the authors choose to unmask themselves—a task which I am always ready to perform. It was thus when a committee of congress undertook to defame me, that I stepped forward and exposed their falshoods, least the sanction of a report from so conspicuous a body might go down to posterity for truth.[2]

The case you allude to might as well be ascribed to the President of the United States as commander in chief of the land & naval force, as to me—but as you ask for a statement of the facts, I send them in a concise form. In the year 1814, Colo [Philip] Pipkin at the head of his Drafted Militia, was charged with the defence of Ft. Jackson in the heart of the creek nation, & within my Military District.[3] Whilst thus in command, part of his Regt. mutinied. at the head of this mutiny, was a Mr. [John] Harris, preacher, but as my memory now serves me, of the Baptist profession—He broke open the commissary stores, knocked out the heads of the flower barrels, taking what he wanted, and destroying what he pleased—proceeded then to the Bake house, and set it on fire and marched off in open defiance of the Colo, leaving the garrison without provisions, and so weakened by desertion, that it might have fallen a sacrafice to the Indians.[4] I was then at Mobile, informed of this mutiny and outrage by express, I ordered the mutineers & deserters to be pursued, apprehended & brought back for trial. The Ringleaders, Harris at their head, after some time, were apprehended, & brought to Mobile in irons, after I had left there for Neworleans, & had charged Genl [James] Winchester with the command of that Section of Country—They were tried by a courtmartial, & condemned to die; five were shot, and the ballance pardoned. The others who had deserted, before they reached home, became alarmed at their situation returned, before Harris & his party were arrested, joined me, & were forgiven—were with me when I marched to pensacola in 1814, followed me thence to Neworleans where they regained their former good charecter by their valorous & soldierly conduct and were honorably discharged—These proceedings are on file in the Department of War, where, those who wish for truth can be informed by applying to the record of the proceedings.[5]

It is for the public to Judge whether this professed ambassador of christ, did not well deserve death for the crimes of Robery & arson, & this outrageous mutiny which jeopardised not only the remainder of the garrison from its exposed situation, but the safety of our country—and whether this wolf in sheeps cloathing was not a fit subject for example. Harris when condemned to die wrote to me on this subject,[6] acknowledged the Justice of his condemnation, & stated, he had no hope of a pardon here, but that he had of forgiveness hereafter—which I trust he obtained thro the mediation of our blessed Saviour, and a sincere repentence for his crimes that brought on him this condemnation.

Let it be recollected that this mutiny occurred at a period when every nerve of our country was strained to protect it from the invasion of an overwhelming British force, whose agents were then engaged in stirring up the Creeks to the indiscriminate murder of our defenceless border citizens—These are the facts of this case for your information. I am sir very respectfully your most obdt. servt.

Andrew Jackson

ALS, ViHi (11-0357); AL draft (dated August 31), DLC (34); Draft in Andrew J. Donelson's hand, DLC (59; 11-0361). Published in 1827 and 1828 newspapers (extracts) and in Bassett, 3:310–12 (from AL draft).

1. See above.
2. AJ was referring to the Lacock report criticizing his conduct of the Seminole campaign and to his March 1819 "Strictures" on the report and his formal memorial to the Senate of February 23, 1820 (see *Jackson*, 4:275–76).
3. In September 1814 Pipkin (1770–1841), of Nashville, commanded the 1st Regiment of Tennessee militia, who were stationed at Fort Jackson, at the confluence of the Coosa and Tallapoosa rivers.
4. Harris (d. 1815) was from Franklin County, Tennessee. For AJ's contemporary discussion of the riots, see *Jackson*, 3:133–36, 140.
5. In his November 21, 1814, letter to Winchester (1752–1826) turning over command at Mobile, he advised of the pending court-martial and warned: "If great care is not used in detailing the court they will be acquitted—if so, you may expect mutiny to reign in every regt." See Courts-martial of John Strother et al., December 5, 1814.
6. Letter not found. On June 2, 1827, the anti-Jackson Philadelphia *Democratic Press* published a letter purportedly from Harris, dated January 15, 1815, but AJ branded it a forgery, claiming that news of the Battle of New Orleans, mentioned in the letter, had not reached Mobile by January 15 (see AJ to William Owens, July 26, 1827, below). In response to that publication, Jacksonians made public Jackson's letter above to Cummings.

From Anthony Butler

Monticello 4. Sept. 1826.

My dear General,

Your favour of the 8th. ulto.[1] has been received—The Newspapers informed me that you had been celebrating our Anniversary of freedom at a distance from your home, and I attributed the delay of your answer to that circumstance[2]—yet I feared perhaps the Post Office might be playing tricks with our Correspondence, and meant to write you by the present Mail whether your reply had reached me or not.

Our elections are over—I have been successful by an overwhelming majority[3]—still the man elected with me is a decided friend of [Thomas Buck] Reed's—he beat the gentleman who was run on my ticket by 14 Votes:[4] The result proves that it was a judicious course on my part to become a Candidate, for had I not done so, the whole Reed and Administration ticket might have been carried. Our adversaries selected for their ticket men of the greatest *personal popularity,* and it was so difficult to make the people understand the *true question* that our partial failure must be placed to that account—We are taking time by the forelock however and have now 7 memorials in different parts of the County procuring signatures *instructing* the Representatives of the County to vote agst. Major Reed[5]—In this we shall succeed to our wishes, as the people since the election is over, have been made to understand the points, upon which the Candidates divided better than we were capable of doing during the short period in which I was a Candidate. (but 3 week & 4 days.)—Cooper my Colleague promises to obey instructions so that all will work well.

I am glad you have seen Reed's Circular *in extenso*[6]—the man certainly never supposed it would travel beyond the limits of this State or his *prudence* would have prevented his so exposing himself: If Major Eaton has no copy of that Circular you should give him yours, that he may take it to Washington next Winter. My own copy I design sending to Colo. Benton, for I am determined that a brother soldier shall see the liberty taken with his political course by an Administration Agent. In the papers that publish an account of the dinner given Major Reed in Jefferson County—they make him in his speech *on that occasion* to say what amounts to an avowal that he is yet amongst those *who rank as your friends*—This is jesuitical on his part, but he knew that *in this state amongst the people at large* he dare not avow a contrary sentiment,[7] for I am proud to believe that Tennessee itself is scarcely more unanimous for you than the citizens of Mississippi. There are a few of Winthrop Sargeants old school federalists on the Mississippi River,[8] and the remains of the Old Spanish Aristocracy who are the other way, but we have no difficulty in keeping them in check; heretofore they opposed Maj. Reed violently in all his efforts at popularity now they are amongst the most clamorous of his supporters, but they can do nothing. Mr. [William] Haile our Representative to Congress, came out in his *handbill openly* declaring himself *a Jackson Candidate,* for this he was denounced in all the Newspapers on the River as *riding a Hobby,* and every effort made to put him down,[9] but the people very much approved the Hobby he was mounted upon and let him ride it into Congress with great ease. I shall write you as often as I have any thing worth writing about—and altho' I will be glad to hear from you as often as your leisure will permit, still I do not mean to tax you so heavily as to require a punctual answer to all of mine. Mrs. B.[10] begs a kind remembrance to Mrs. Jackson & yourself in which you must include very respectfully & faithfully yours

A: Butler

N.B. You may look out in the U.S. Telegraph for a squib or two before long.

ALS, DLC (34). Butler (1787–1849), a former South Carolina and Kentucky legislator whom Jackson had known at least since 1807, had moved to Mississippi in the mid-1820s. He supported Clay in the 1824 campaign but, after the election, switched allegiance to Jackson. In 1829, Jackson appointed him chargé d'affaires to Mexico.

1. Not found.
2. Butler was referring to AJ's attendance at celebrations in Pulaski, Fayetteville, and Winchester, Tennessee.
3. Butler had been running for a House seat in the Mississippi legislature from Lawrence County.
4. Joseph Cooper, an incumbent, along with Butler, were elected to represent Lawrence County. Reed (1787–1829), a state legislator, had been elected in January to fill the United States Senate vacancy on the resignation of David Holmes. Other candidates included James C. Bole and John Tomlinson, both defeated in the election.
5. Reed failed in his bid for reelection to the Senate in January 1827, losing to Powhatan Ellis (1790–1863), but won the seat again in 1829.
6. Reed's circular *To the People of the State of Mississippi,* May 22, 1826, detailed his reasons for failing to vote for Benton's amendment opposing the Panama mission—he had taken his Senate seat but three days before and was not informed on the issues.
7. In his speech at Fayette on July 18, Reed stated that, in the recent election, Adams had not been his first choice and he defied anyone "to designate aught, by word or deed" wherein he had opposed Jackson. At the same time, he defended the Adams administration. He later discussed his speech with Adams and "intimated that he was obliged to say that he preferred General Jackson for the Presidency, although that was not his real sentiment" (*Port-Gibson Correspondent, and Mississippi General Advertiser,* July 27; *Memoirs of John Quincy Adams,* 7:208).
8. Sargent (1753–1820; Harvard 1771) had been the first governor of Mississippi Territory.
9. Haile (1797–1837) was from Wilkinson County. Responses to his announcement as a Jackson candidate and Haile's defense of his course appeared in *Port-Gibson Correspondent, and Mississippi General Advertiser,* June 8, 15.
10. Ann Mary Butler, née Moore.

To Richard Keith Call

Hermitage Septbr 5th.—1826

Dear Genl

I have been vissitted by Colo. White your Delegate from Florida—in the course of his stay, I introduced the subject of your & his quarrel[1]—he spoke of it with regret, & in such a manner as induced me to believe, that there must be misconceptions, and busybodys at the bottom of it—I know not the state of your feelings, or how far this quarrel has gone between you—but as a friend I have barely to say to you, that from the propriety of his declarations to me, on this subject; should you conceive your situation such as to make it necessary that you should make a call upon him— let that call be such as will leave open a door for explanation; this I think is due to yourself, it is due to him, it is due to a magnanimous course; and I am sure you would not suspect me of recommending to you any other— The Colo. has said to me if called upon, if he cannot satisfactory explain, he will make honorable atonement—then surely he ought to be given an opportunity to explain before the door to the restoration of honorable friendship be closed—I have no doubt from what he states, that many things has been stated to you, of injurious expressions & conduct of his respecting you, which he declares is entirely groundless & false—hence then the propriety in you, in opening a door for fair & honorable explanation between you, before any harsh measures should be adopted—you have both families that cannot well do without you, hence the propriety, of not wantonly risquing your lives, if the dispute can be honorably adjusted without that risque or sacrafice—But you know what has been my course—If an injury is inflicted, if on a fair & honourable course, & investigation, satisfactory explanations are not made, and the injury repaired—then it is due to ones-self, it is due to his family that Justice should be done, & the slander & injury repelled at all hazzards & consequences; In this dispute then, let not the door be closed against Colo. White to honourable explanation, & I have but little doubt, your, & his dispute, will be honorably & amicably adjusted, which must be pleasing to all your real friends.

I wrote you on yesterday in answer to your letter of the 26th. of July[2]— and this letter is written at the request of several of your real friends, Genl Houston Mr. Curry & Colo. Bell who has a great desire that the misunderstanding between you & Colo. White should be accomodated on honourable terms without bloodshed.[3] I write by the same mail to Colo. Butler,[4] that carries this to you—I wish you to see him—Colo. White goes to Pensacola, and from thence will pass to Tallahassee and to St. Augustine to the city. Genl Houston is now engaged in unpleasant business with some of his enemies at Nashville, but I trust will come out with flying colours he has taken a course if he pursues, will put down his enemies—in a few days, the results will be known when I will communicate it to you.[5] with respects of Mrs. *[J]* and myself to Mary & the daughter, be assured of our friendship for you.

Andrew Jackson

ALS, Gilder Lehrman Collection, NNPM (mAJs); Printed in *The Collector,* November 1903, p. 3 (11-0365).

    1. For a brief discussion of the dispute, see above, AJ to Call, July [26], and AJ to Call, November 21, below.

    2. Letters not found.

    3. Probably Benjamin F. Currey and Montgomery Bell (1769–1855), Tennessee's most prominent iron manufacturer.

    4. Letter not found.

    5. Houston was engaged in a heated dispute with John P. Erwin and others over his opposition to Erwin's appointment as postmaster at Nashville. On September 5, the day that AJ was writing the letter above to Call, Erwin challenged Houston to a duel, but Houston declined, whereupon the incident provoked a duel with one of Erwin's friends, William White.

To John Rowan

Hermitage Septbr 5th 1826

Dear Sir,

    Your's of the 20th ulto[1] is just recd. It would afford me much pleasure to visit my friends in Kentucky could I do so in good faith to the principles which I think so essential to Republicanism & the cause of our country at this time. But every thing considered, I have come to the opinion that I cannot, and think that you will concur with me when it is recollected that in the present contest I can take no other ground than that upon which I have heretofore gone, and upon which the people have voluntarily offered me the most flattering tokens of their approbation & confidence. A movement thro' Kentucky however it might gratify my feelings by the company of yourself & other friends at the Greenville springs,[2] could be easily misrepresented abroad, and in the absence of all necessity for it now, would not fail to give rise to imputations extremely unpleasant to me, and possibly prejudicial to the great cause in which it seems by the current of events I am to bear a prominent part. Recollect that the *coalition* managers are on the alert in covering their own operations, while they meditate the destruction of those which spring from the people, their legitimate authority; and if they succeed, as in all cases where the government has aimed to be stronger than the people, the leading cause will be traced to the workings of a corrupt patronage, whose office it is to seize upon the questionable acts of those who are rallying round the public good, and so to misrepresent and distort them that the people shaken in their confidence, and divided in their action, shall lose both their advo-

cates and their cause. Thus the panders of power mocked the efforts of
the people in former times, because they were blinded by their arts, or
saw them too late to counteract them—their prominent friends and advocates, too, contributing to the calamities by attempting to fight them with
their own weapons, When it would take more than the strength of Her-
cules to grasp all the plans which these Protean monsters could devise—
Altho', as I hope, this state of things is far from our happy country, yet as
there is, in the mode of the last Presidential election, and in the subsequent policy of the Cabinet a manifest violation of some of our dearest
interests, I have thought these remarks not improper here; and, if they
answer no other purpose, that they will at least satisfy you that in declining the visit to Kentucky I am influenced by a high sense of public duty. I
am anxious since my friends have placed me again before my country for
the first office within its gift, that if it please Providence to make me the
instrument of reforming the abuses of which they complain, that I undertake the duties with clean hands, or rather that my example carry with it
nothing derogatory to the principles of Republican virtue. And to this end
I am unwilling that the coalition at Washington shall find me in a situation to which they can point, and say, *"see the man who neither seeks or
declines office taking an electionering tour. Why not ply our patronage—
if he be not seeking his own aggrandizement, why is he so busy with the
people abroad?["]*

Calumny and detraction will no doubt do their utmost against me, and
all those who take the side of their country, rather than that of the government right or wrong; but while we are true to the old landmarks and
by no unworthy manouvering shall forfeit the confidence of the people, it
is to be hoped that the late events by discovering the danger, point also to
the remedy, and will be instrumental to the erection of another *[bu]*lwark
for our liberties.

Mrs. J freely pardons you—and tenders you her kind salutations, & if
revisited by her last winters complaint will follow your prescriptions next
summer, when she will expect the pleasure of seeing you & your family
at the Springs I am Dr Sir very respectfully yr friend & Hble Sevt

A. Jackson

LS draft in Andrew J. Donelson's hand, with dateline and last paragraph in AJ's hand, DLC
(34). Rowan (1773–1843) was senator from Kentucky, 1825–31.
  1. See Rowan to AJ, August 20.
  2. A mineral spa located near Harrodsburg, Kentucky.

From Henry Lee

Buffalo. N.Y. 14th. Septr. 1826

dear Genl.

I have been in this neighbourhood some days—viewing or reviewing the falls of Niagara and examining the various Battle scenes on the Canada side; having it in contemplation to write a history of the last war.[1] On my way I visited and conversed with Govr. Clinton to whom I was recommended and by whom I was treated with much civility. His standing in the political world renders him an object of interest, and I proceed to give you the result of my observations. He is friendly *in his conversation* to your election and adverse to that of Adams; still more so to the succession of Clay In answer to questions from me he said "Adams has but little influence or popularity in this state." "Clay has few partisans & no prospects in this or the eastern states." "Jackson has some friends in N. York and in ohio I think he stands well." His expressions were altogether favourable to you, & decidedly hostile to Clay—but I am convinced from the whole tenour of his remarks that his object is to secure his own elevation at the next election if possible or the succeeding one at any rate. He would go as far as I could wish in reprobating the origin the doctrines, the practices, & the character of the incumbent administration, but he would never concur with me in the conclusion which I frequently presented for his adoption, that it was necessary for every conspicuous and enlightened patriot to support you as the only man who was now able to effect their overthrow. Here he was uniformly hesitating & evasive—saying "Jackson will beat any man in his own state & probably in Pena." As soon as I was satisfied that his mind was obstinately bent on this selfish object, I said according to my present sentiments Govr. Clinton, you may rely on my exertions to support you against Mr. Clay should he attempt to succeed Genl. Jackson. This remark obviously disconcerted him, & our conversation soon after glided into general subjects. Speaking candidly to you, I fear he is a man essentially little—nothing noble & disinterested in his composition. An occurrence happened while I was with him, which though trifling appears to me perfectly illustrative of his imbecility. While we were engaged in this political confabulation, & when it was rather interesting to him, a rap was heard at the door. He told the servant to "carry them back." The visitors (one of whom turned out to be a judge of the state, passed right by the door of the room in which we were & if they had have looked round might have seen us. Clinton stopped in the midst of a sentence as they passed, & shrank himself up into a corner of the room to prevent their seeing him. This I thought as little like a great man & as much like a little man as any thing I ever witnessed. It is impossible to conceive that Genl. Washington, or (if you will pardon me) Genl. Jackson ever exhibited such weakness.

I was surprised to find the conversation of Clinton, far below the style of a well educated gentleman. His manners are heavy & his language quite provincial. For example he told me Mr. Monroe & his Cabinet "had all tried *for* to crush him." The canal however is a lasting and a grand monument to his fame.[2] No traveller who sees it without seeing Clinton can help feeling gratitude and admiration for its Chief promoter. Travelling is cheaper in this state and more comfortable than I ever found it elsewhere you live in the best style all the way & are conveyed from N. York to this place a distance of 507 miles in 6 & ¹/₂ days for $13.62¹/₂. and you may come comfortably for 10 dollars. You ought to have a canal from the Tennessee to the Alabama.

Now I must touch on delicate ground. You must know that a vast portion of your country men desire your election, & that many enlightened & patriotic men deem it essential to the preservation of our free institutions & republican spirit. That I am an humble associate in the same fraternity and opinion you are not now to be told—and I have a right to believe that you are as ever devoted to the good of your country. I am therefore [sure] that you hold yourself bound to promote by every honest means the success of such measures as such of your fellow citizens as possess & deserve your confidence deem important to the maintenance of our liberty and our Constitution Among the steps conducive to this great end I am confident that many concur with me in believeing, that your presence in this and the eastern states would be probably the most efficient. I am not apprised that you have ever seen the falls of Niagara or the great inland seas which give this country the aspect of a new world. These great objects have a claim sanctioned by nature itself, to the admiration of all intelligent beings—and I am sure you could serve your friends your country & yourself by a visit next summer to this quarter. Mrs. Jackson would also be delighted with the novelty & grandeur of the scene. I am about returning to Washington where I should be highly gratified to hear from you Mr. [. . .] me [. . .] that [. . .] is friendly to [. . .] refuse "to whil[. . .] laud Clay"—Tha[t . . .] McCalla[3] [run? seen?] within [. . .] of the Clayites. In this state the people are waiting to be led—& all will depend on the course of Clinton. He will be undetermined until the 2 state conventions are over.[4] Yr. very sincere & respectful sevt.

H. Lee

ALS fragment, DLC (34). Published in Bassett, 3:312–13 (extract).

1. In 1827, Lee published a revised edition of his father's *Memoirs of the War in the Southern Department of the United States* (Washington), but no complete history of the War of 1812 has been found.

2. The Erie Canal, completed in 1825.

3. Not identified.

4. Nominated for governor at Utica on September 21, Clinton won reelection over his opponent, the Albany Regency nominee, William B. Rochester.

The votes of five western states influenced by Clay had been crucial to the election of Adams by the House of Representatives. Even apart from the explicit "corrupt bargain" charge, many of Jackson's supporters regarded the preference of western representatives for the easterner Adams as a betrayal of the West's native son, Jackson. Especially galling was the vote of Louisiana, for Jackson's public fame rested on his military defense of that state, and Jacksonians complained loudly and bitterly about the ingratitude of its representatives. In one such complaint, a circular letter of the Philadelphia Jackson committee charged that Louisiana, "abused by two of her representatives, turned upon her preserver, and against the will of her citizens, pierced him with the fang of unparalleled ingratitude." Jackson's long-time opponent Jonathan Roberts responded that Jackson had done no more than his duty at New Orleans and noted that "Mr. Monroe's extraordinary exertions, with Mr. Madison's co-operation, prepared the defensive force for that point and urged General Jackson to repair there" (Washington United States' Telegraph, July 1; Philadelphia Democratic Press, July 18).

Roberts's reply opened a new debate about Jackson's role at New Orleans. To refute the notion that primary credit for the 1815 victory belonged in Washington, Jackson began to gather evidence about the shortages of supplies that had handicapped his defense of New Orleans. Eaton's August 30 reply to Chandler Price et al. did not lay the matter to rest. Later reports of similar remarks by navy secretary Samuel L. Southard at an early July dinner in Fredericksburg, Virginia, drew an angry response on the matter from Jackson himself (see AJ to Samuel Houston, October 23; AJ to Southard, January 5 and March 6, 1827; and Southard to AJ, February 9, 1827, all below), and the Southard controversy, along with Hugh L. White's January 8, 1827, toast at Washington, threatened to draw James Monroe into conflict with AJ over the question of the supply of New Orleans (see John H. Eaton to AJ, January 27, 1827, below).

From Robert Butler

Tallahassee September 15th. 1826

Dear General,

Your kind letters of the 8th. and 14th. ulto. together with Mrs. Jacksons to Mrs. Butler all came to hand by the last mail;[1] and afforded us great satisfaction in knowing that all our friends were well and that the season promised fine crops—

I am much rejoiced to learn that Samuel[2] will be under your immediate guardianship and he has now arived at that age, when the necessity of his application to obtain a profession must be so apparent that I certainly anticipate the realization of my fondest wishes—Our little Daughter has been at the Hermitage and you say she is amiable; this is gratifying and I hope her present opportunity will result greatly to her improvement—[3]

You request my recollections, of what disposition was made of the proceedings against [Thomas] Maples[4]—I presume the proceedings were forwarded to the Adj. & Inspr. Generals Office, at any event the General Order Book of my Office which was sent to Washington would give the facts—I will make diligent search among the few papers I brought with me, and should they afford any light will give it you by next mail—"Drowning men will catch at straws" and the present case evidences an attempt at help from a broken reed—

I should have supposed that public opinion on that mans conduct would have induced him to have buried in oblivion the recollection of his opposition:[5] but the times are venal and resort to *every means* in the approaching struggle, will be had by the friends of the Administration—The state you found Louisiana in, the Ordnance mostly without carriages, and others sent from Pittsburgh with the observation that carriages could be made at New Orleans—The flints which fuzed the powder that destroyed the enemies of your country obtained by your weight of Character and decision from the Pirates of Barataria—the fact that upwards of three thousand men of your Army standing at the retired work between us and the City without a stand of arms, and lastly the famous Orders which was given to General Gaines to concentrate all the forces of the up Country at *Baton Rouge,* when he was to descend with overwhelming rapidity and destroy the enemy on their first landing (a copy of which you have)[6] must be a convincing proof to the world that Messrs Madison & Monroe (who were at the City of Washington in a state of despondence and Mr. Clay at Ghent playing cards), are entitled to the immortality of preserving Louisiana—surely Mr. Roberts will be *Canonized* for his discovery, or at least obtain a patent for it at Washington—I, who happened to be at New Orleans, and knowing all the difficulties which you had to encounter, have no hesitation in declaring with uplifted hands, before my God; that all the Heads of Departments from the President down, and Congress Assembled, with all the Robertss & [Abner] Laycocks of noted memory,[7] with all the Aid of an empty Treasury and disorganized army; without the simple fact of the aid of the *weigh[t o]f Character and personal exertions of [Andre]w Jackson, Louisiana would have fallen.* Your Count[ry] owes you a debt it never can pay—

Thank Providence we are all well—Mrs. B still on her feet[8]—Mrs. Call was threatened with premature delivery on last night, and the danger is not past, although she is much easier—[9]

Your friends are all well. Mrs. J. informs us that Capt. A. has been blessed with a fine son[10]—Give our Love to our kind friend Mrs. J. and all friends—God bless you both.

Robert

Politicks. Colo: [Achille] Murat & Judge [David Betton] McComb fought a duel on the 13t. Murat lost a little finger and the others shirt twice perforated between the hip & ribs—local politicks the cause—McComb a *White* man—[11]

ALS, DLC (34).
    1. Letters not found.
    2. Born c1808.
    3. Butler's daughter Sarah Jane (1811–78) was most likely attending the Nashville Female Academy.
    4. Jackson had apparently asked about the court martial proceedings of Maples and Jacob Smith, government contractors, who failed to deliver arms on schedule to his troops at Baton Rouge (*Jackson,* 3:249–50).
    5. Butler was referring to Jonathan Roberts, who had cast the only vote against AJ's nomination for president at the 1824 Harrisburg convention.
    6. James Monroe to Edmund P. Gaines, December 7, 1814, DLC (14).
    7. Lacock (1770–1837), a former Pennsylvania senator, had chaired the Senate committee that issued a report criticizing AJ's conduct of the Seminole campaign. See *Jackson,* 4:275–76.
    8. Rachel Butler gave birth to a son, William Edward (1826–36), on September 24.
    9. Ellen Call gave birth to twin daughters, who died in October.
    10. "Capt. A" was probably Andrew Jackson Donelson. His son Andrew Jackson (1826–59), had been born June 6.
    11. The specific cause of the duel between Murat (1801–47), a nephew of Napoleon, and Macomb (1793–1837), a judge of the Leon County court and supporter of Joseph M. White, has not been established.

From James Buchanan

Lancaster 21 September 1826

Dear General,

    Although I have nothing of importance to communicate; yet I feel disposed occasionally to trespass upon your time & indulge myself in the pleasure of writing to you.

    We are for once in a political calm in this State. Mr. Shulze will be reelected Governor without opposition: & upon the Presidential question there is not, out of the City of Philadelphia, a sufficient division in public sentiment to disturb our repose. In the large wealthy & populous county in which I reside, containing more than 70,000 people, I feel confident Mr. Adams could not poll 500 votes.

    There was a most artful & powerful effort made against you in this State during the last Spring. They did not dare to attack you personally; but levelled all their artillery against Mr. Calhoun, Mr. Randolph, Mr. M'Duffie &c but principally against the former; & they endeavored to make you answerable for his political offences, as presiding officer of the Senate. They have succeeded, to a considerable extent, in injuring the popularity of Mr. Calhoun; but their arrows have fallen harmless at your feet. Your popularity throughout the State of Pennsylvania is fixed upon sure foundations which your enemies have not nor ever will be able to shake.

Our society in this City has had a most agreeable addition in Mr. [Langdon] Cheves & his family. He has purchased a farm within a mile of Lancaster & has taken up his residence amongst us with an intention, as he says, of laying his bones here.[1] His sterling good sense & his agreeable manners have already made him a great favorite. Although he has been & still, I believe, is upon terms of personal friendship with Mr. Clay; yet he disapproves highly of his recent political course & does not hesitate upon all proper occasions to express his opinion.

Our season in this part of the world has been dry & in consequence the crops have not been so abundant as usual. There are many cases of sickness throughout our Country; but not many deaths. For several years past the Cities & large Towns in the Eastern portion of this State have been much more healthy than the surrounding Country.

I have spent a busy summer. The change from law to politics, & from politicks to Law, makes both pursuits very laborious. A man, in such circumstances as I am placed, cannot do himself justice at either. Instead of preparing in the summer for winter, I have often scarcely had time to read the common news of the day. Nothing but a belief, that it would have been deserting my post in the hour of danger, could have induced me again to become a candidate for Congress. I do not anticipate any very serious opposition to my re-election.[2]

Please to present my most kind & respectful compliments to Mrs. Jackson. Remember me to my friends Major Eaton & Gen: Houston. and believe me to be with the utmost affection & respect your very sincere friend

James Buchanan

ALS, DLC (34); AL draft, PHi (11-0369). Published in Moore, *Works of James Buchanan,* 1:216–17 (from AL draft), and Bassett, 3:313–14 (extract).
    1. Cheves (1776–1857), a former South Carolina congressman and former president of the Bank of the United States, remained in Pennsylvania until 1829, when he returned to South Carolina.
    2. Buchanan was reelected to Congress in October.

To Richard Keith Call

Hermitage Sept. 24, 1826.

Dear Call:

I have just recd. your letter of the 26th of July last[1] and regret to learn "that a long time has past since you have recd. a letter from me—" I assure you that I have answered every letter I have recd. from you, or Colo. Butler, and since the death of Mr. Kirkman I have wrote you often and I sincerely regret that they should be lost by the way. I have not recd. the promised letter from Colo. Butler—I fear it may be lost by the way—as one of his letters heretofore, which he informed me he had written has never come to hand. I hope you have received mine by Mr. Williams with a copy of the will of Mr. Kirkman[2]—I hope it may be convenient for you to come up, and be at our next court, I think it is important that you should be here and Mrs. J. and myself anticipate the pleasure of seeing Mary with you. It is rumored that Mr. [Thomas] Washington is paying his addresses to your mother-in-law and you and Mary may be in time for the wedding—this is the rumour, I give it to you as I have recd. it from Gen. Houston, as rumor, and as Mr. Washington is her lawyer perhaps she may yield to him the management of her estate.[3] It is just stated to me by Mr. J. D. Overton[4] that your sister Miss Kirkman is married to a Mr. Perkins[5]—Mrs. Kirkman had sent her on to Philadelphia to prevent her from marrying him, he went on and it is said they married, & I suppose banished—and if the codicil to the will can be established, disinherited—should the rumor of Mr. Washington and the old lady be true—she will find in Mr. Washington a true aid in husbanding the property to his and her—I am sure it is your duty to come up to court and bring Mrs. Call with you if you can, we will be happy to see you at the Hermitage where you will find a home so long as you can stay with us.

The Presidential campaign appears to be oppened thro the public journals, and Mr. Clay has made his tour to Kentucky to produce effect there, and as he supposed to make a favourable movement in favour of Mr. Cook in Elonois—he has failed in his object—he has made a little noise in Kentucky thro a few noisy portions and has failed to secure Mr. Cook's reelection—Mr. [Joseph] Duncan has beat him,[6] notwithstanding he carried another Jackson candidate, Mr. [James] Turney,[7] on his back, and Mr. [John] Scott is beaten three to one[8]—They have only succeeded in Louisiana in the election of Brent & Gurley—as [Major] Baker writes me[9]—they cannot carry the state, as it elects its electors, by general ticket[10]—I feel grateful for the good feelings of your citizens, expressed towards me thro your country—as it respects those gentlemen at Pensacola—I suppose they join into the cry of support of the powers that be regardless who *rules, they will be vicars of Bray* they love the loa[v]es and fishes and forget who procured for them their present Berths men who cry with the hounds and run with the hare never to be relied on— and [if] these gentlemen can approbate the principles [avowed] by Mr. Adams and the apostate course of Mr. Clay; for myself I regret not the loss of such political friends—they are a curse to any one—I have not seen account of the celebration at Pensacola I would like to have the [papers] that contain it.[11] The Presidential canvass will be warmly contested executive patronage with all entrigue & management of Messers Clay & Adams, will be wielded against the (undecipherable) of the people—but having lost Elonois and Missouri—and Mr. [Caleb] Atwater says,

Ohio[12]—without a third candidate, the election cannot be brought into the house.

Present Mrs. J. and myself affectionably to Mary, to Colo. Butler & his family—to Gov. Duvol and his—I would to write them by this mail, but am surrounded with business and company—Accept for yourself the assurance of our friendship & regard—It was rumored in Nashville you were dead your letter refuted it, & be assured we were rejoiced to receive it—yr friend

Andrew Jackson

Printed, *Taylor-Trotwood Magazine*, 10(April 1910):514–15 (mAJs).

1. Not found.
2. The other correspondence mentioned has not been found. Williams has not been identified.
3. Washington (1788–1863) was from Nashville.
4. Possibly a misreading for James G. Overton.
5. Call's sister-in-law was Jane Barbara Kirkman (1807–93); she married John Farrell in 1838. Perkins has not been identified.
6. In the Illinois congressional canvass, Duncan (1794–1844) defeated Cook, who had voted for Adams in the House, with about 49 percent of the vote.
7. Turney (d. 1833), a native of Tennessee and at this time Illinois attorney general, garnered only about 6 percent of the vote in the congressional election.
8. Scott obtained only 38.5 percent of the Missouri vote, losing to Edward Bates.
9. Letter not found.
10. According to reports, some disputed by administration newspapers, Edward Livingston, who had voted for AJ, won reelection over his opponents by more than 900 votes, while in the other districts Henry H. Gurley and William L. Brent, who had voted for Adams, each had a margin of fewer than 100 votes over the totals of their challengers.
11. AJ was referring the July 4 celebration at Pensacola, presided over by his "friends," Samuel R. Overton and Henry M. Brackenridge, at which pro-Adams toasts were given. The *Pensacola Gazette and West Florida Advertiser,* July 8, carried an account of the meeting. According to tradition the vicar of Bray maintained his position during the reigns of Henry VIII, Edward VI, Mary, and Elizabeth I by changing his religion to accord with the monarch's predilection.
12. The prediction of Atwater (1778–1867; Williams College 1804) concerning the election in Ohio was wrong: none of the seven congressmen "blacklisted" by Jackson supporters because they voted for Adams in the 1825 election were defeated. In 1829, AJ appointed Atwater to negotiate a treaty with the Winnebago Indians in the vicinity of Prairie du Chien.

To John Coffee

Hermitage Septbr. 25th. 1826

Dr. Genl

By our mutual friend Mr. [Francis] Kemper[1] you will receive your mare—She is in foal, and apparently in good health—I see rising on her jaw a small lump which I suppose is the remnant of her former complaint, and which, if it does not disapear, you must have burnt, with a sharp hot chissel—I wish you to have coalts from her—her filly by oscar, is a fine animal, and when matured will, I have no doubt make a first rate runner.[2]

Our crops generally are good, but we have experienced lately two much rain, which has much impeded our progress in getting them out—we have a good deal of sickness amonghst us; but it is mostly confined to those who have been exposed to the sun & moisture, & children—In the western District it has been very sickly and many deaths—our friends at present all well, but Saml. J[ackson] Hays who has been sick, but is mending.[3]

In my last I informed you of information I had recd. that Mr Winburn had a wish to give up his superintendence of Master A. J. Hutchings place[4]—that his sister was about to move.

Indeed I have some doubts whether he will be capable of manageing that establishment if his sister leaves that—I am fearful he is not a good stock raiser, as he has informed me, that he has not as much pork as will meat the family—but in his letter[5] he has made no mention of his wishes to leave the business—I recd. the information from the former overseer of Mr Booker—who wishes to be employed—If you have time before you set out to the treaty, please write me on this subject, and if necessary I will go out—I mean to be out the latter end of Novbr. or about the time you return.[6]

you will discover from the public journals that the Presidential Canvass has commenced with great spirit from the east, even in Boston, the former hotbead of Federalism has had a meeting[7]—and the secratary of state always comes in for his share of public censure—he, like Lucifer, is politically fallen, never to rise again—He is on an electioneering tour in the upper parts of Virginia—travelling for his *health* it being much *impaired by official duty*[8]—But it will not do—he never can raise himself again in Virginia—The administration will make great exertions to succeed—every engine that can be wielded will be used—as we have a right to expect from the falshoods & fabrications we have already seen published, by their *Tools*—I think Jonathan, must ere this, repent of his folly—he has been severely exposed—and the reply over the signature of Major Eaton, which will soon appear in the Eastern prints, will prostrate him forever.[9] indeed the four numbers which has appeared in the Cincinati Republican over the signature of *Vindicator* has put his falshood to rest[10]—but as most of the replies has been over anonimous names—it was thought best, as Mr Roberts has been a Senator, that a reply by a Senator who were both members during the discussion of the Seminole campaign would be more relied on, and better calculated to prostrate the *faction*

When you meet with Genl Hinds present me to him affectionately—I have no hope of your succeeding—if you succeed at all, you must succeed with both nations, and succeed I would, if they will sell—¿what is the vallue of the soil, compared to the vallue of the population that section of country will maintain—labour is the wealth of all nations—and it is your business to make a treaty the best you can obtain, and leave it with the senate and president to approve or reject.

Mrs. J. Joins me in affectionate regard to you, Polly & the children yr friend

Andrew Jackson

ALS, THi (11-0371). Published in Bassett, 3:314–15 (extract).

1. Camper (d. c1850), a native of Botetourt County, Virginia, resided in Lauderdale County and did various jobs at the Hutchings and Coffee plantations during the 1820s.

2. Oscar, undefeated before retired to stud, was a bay horse bred by Hubbard Saunders and raced by Roger B. Sappington.

3. Hays (1800–66), son of Robert, was AJ's nephew.

4. See above, AJ to Coffee, September 2.

5. Not found.

6. AJ left Nashville en route to Alabama about November 26 and returned on December 6; Coffee arrived home from the negotiations with the Choctaws and Chickasaws on November 26.

7. The report of the pro-Jackson meeting at Boston on August 31 had been reprinted in the *Nashville Republican* on September 23.

8. Clay had gone to Kentucky and returned to Washington via northern Virginia, stopping for about a week at the White Sulphur Springs and for a dinner at Lewisburg.

9. Eaton's letter *To Chandler Price, Chairman, Jacob Holgate, and Henry Horn, Secretaries . . . in Reply to Jonathan Roberts* (Philadelphia, 1826) first appeared in the Philadelphia *American Sentinel* beginning on September 26.

10. The essays by "Vindicator," appearing in the Cincinnati *National Republican and Ohio Political Register* from August 29 to September 19, meticulously refuted Roberts' criticism of AJ.

Adams' appointment of John P. Erwin as postmaster in Nashville in the late winter of 1826 created a political whirlwind. In the letter below, Jackson describes for Call one episode in the fall out from Erwin's appointment, a duel involving Houston, candidate for governor of Tennessee. In a protest from the Tennessee delegation, Houston and Eaton wrote Adams that Erwin was morally unfit for the post, he having previously stolen mail and more recently having declared bankruptcy to defraud his creditors. At first a dispute between Houston and Erwin, it exploded to include John Smith T (d. 1835), a notorious duelist from Missouri, formerly from Tennessee, and William White, judge advocate under Jackson during the Creek campaigns. Jackson's account provides not only details of the Erwin-Houston dispute; it also, and more importantly, outlines the two major factions in Tennessee politics in the election of 1828: the Jacksonians, running on the issues of public morality and subservience to the popular will, and the administration forces, led by "Erwin & Co.," which included Jackson's longtime enemy Andrew Erwin and his large family with alliances to Clay, a group intent on Adams's reelection and Clay's succession to Adams.

To Richard Keith Call

Hermitage Septbr. 30th. 1826–

Dr. Call

your letters of the 10th. & 18th. ult.[1] has been recd. with the enclosure—Major Lewis being about to set out to the treaty & Mr E[phraim Hubbard] Foster[2] being absent I filled up the letter of attorney to Mr John Bell[3] in whom I have great confidence—I instructed Mr Bell to have an interview with Mr Erwin, the surviving witness to the will, & to know from him at what time he became a witness to the will—whether, on the day it bears date, or otherwise. If Mr. Erwin will swear that he became a witness in July 1820, I have no doubt but the sanity of Mr Kirkman of that date will be established—In that case I have instructed Mr Bell to agree to a compromise placing You on the same footing as the other children and (without a law suit) making a fair distribution of the estate— Should it at any time hereafter appear that a fair disclosure of all the estate has not been made, you can by bill of disclosure bring it to light, and if I mistake not some Branches of the family will save you of this trouble— I shall be at Nashvill next week, & as soon as any thing is done in this business will advise you; what is annexed as a codicil, without signature or date, cannot be established or have effect. I have noted your information as it respects the Pensacola dinner—I have just recd a letter from Major Overton[4] explaining how he & Brakenridge came to be there & to preside—that they were invited guests—had been applied to, to preside, & had refused—but when they got there, the company insisted on their taking the chairs & were thus prevailed upon to preside without knowing what toasts were to be drank, & so soon as the regular toasts were gone through they immediately retired. *Thus the explanation,* and as every freeman has a right to do as he pleases, *I am content with it.* It was for this right you & I both fought.

Our friend Genl Saml Houston since his return has had some dificulty with the faction Erwin & Co at the head, and as is believed in Nashville the Govr. & Doctor [Boyd] McNairy[5] at the *tail* Saml has sustained himself well and by the result has added at least 20,000 votes to his canvass as Governor—This faction after having brought on John Smith T. as their assasin, got Genl White as his escort to accompany Smith to offer to Genl Houston a note from John P. Erwin which had been refused by Colo. [John] McGreggor[6] (Houstons friend) to be received through Smith in the morning. Houston was asked by Smith to speak with him, he walked with him near to where White was posted, when Smith offerred Houston the note, Houston said he would hand it to his friend McGreggor who would give him an answer, when Genl White observed, "Why Genl you surely will not deny but you have recd the challenge," When Houston replied yes Sir I do, but will with pleasure receive one from you—by this time McGreggor who had been absent came up & Houston handed him the paper when McG. asked Smith if it was the same note he had attempted to hand in the morning he answered yes when McG. Observed I then told you & now repeat, that we will receive no communication thro you and threw the note at Smiths feet—after many days consultation of the parties after Houstons reply thro the papers to Erwins publication[7] White challenged him, Doctor McN–Whites friend–the challenge promptly accepted & then the civil authority from the information of Judge [John] McN[airy][8] set to work to arrest Houston & White—*in this Scheme they were defeated, White* only was *arrested*—on last Thursday the met in Ky. and on the first fire White fell badly wounded, Houston untouched, to the great gratification of all the good & moral part of society. Thus ends the first *chapter,* & I suppose Houston will have peace—White I think will not die, and it will be of benefit to him—I do suppose there was more baseness in this thing, when it is unfolded, than in any thing of the kind before—*old Andrew* at the head, reporting that Houston had run away to avoid the fight &c &c &c—

you will see from the papers that the presidential campaign has been opened & is waxing warm My friends in Ohio has taken the field—and Newjersy is is in motion—Virginia is warm—Adams has no chance unless he can through his friends bring out Mr Clinton—their plan is, divide & conquor—By the resullt of the late elections & from a letter from Colo. Benton[9] Missouri, Ellonois, & Indiana are safe—and [Elijah] Hayward of Ohio[10] says that state is also safe—I give the information as recd thro my friends for I correspond on politics with none—

Mrs. J is in good health, has written twice to Mrs. Call without receiving any answer—I recd a letter from Gadsden complaining that he had recd no letters from me this summer—altho I had wrote him often, and Mrs J. is afraid hers has also miscarried.

Mrs. J & the Andrews unite with me in kind salutations to you, Mrs. Call, & daughter, wishing you health & prosperity your friend

Andrew Jackson

ALS, F (mAJs).
1. Not found.
2. Foster (1794–1854; University of Nashville 1813) was a Nashville lawyer and member of the state general assembly, 1829–31.
3. Bell (1797–1869; Cumberland College 1814), a Nashville lawyer and later congressman, represented the Call's interest in the Thomas Kirkman estate.
4. See Samuel G. Overton to AJ, August 28, 1826.
5. McNairy (1785–1856) was a physician, the brother of John.
6. McGregor (d. c1835) was from Rutherford County.
7. John P. Erwin's publication appeared in the *National Banner and Nashville Whig,* September 6; Houston's reply, in the issue of September 13.

8. McNairy (1762–1837) was federal district judge for Tennessee, 1797–1833.

9. Not found.

10. Hayward was originally from Massachusetts. In 1830 AJ appointed him Commissioner of the General Land Office.

To Robert Paine et al.

Hermitage Septbr 30th. 1826

Gentlemen

Your note of the 25th instant[1] is Just recd through the post office

Whilst I feel grateful for the honor intended me, I must decline your request—Was this great & good cause in need of this effort it should be yielded with much pleasure & promptness—but as this cannot be the case, there being so many Gentlemen much better qualified for public speaking than myself & more in the habit, I must be excused—having lost many of my teeth it is with great dificulty I can articulate, and not being in the habit of public speaking of late, it is very unpleasant for me to appear in that character I therefore resign to abler hands.

There is still a stronger reason for my declining, it is this, under existing circumstances, was such an address to go forth to the world, I might be charged by my political enemies with having come forth hypocritically under the sacred garb of religion thus to electioner—never having worn this mask I cannot permit myself to appear in an attitude which might justify my enemies in raising imputations so unpleasant.

Permit me to assure you gentlemen whilst for the reasons offered I decline the profered honor, that there is nothing that I can do with propriety that I will not do, to prosper the great & good cause of christianity & the true religion of Jesus christ by the spread of the gospel.

With great consideration & respect I am Gentlemen yr mo. obdt. servt.

Andrew Jackson

ALS draft with revisions in Andrew J. Donelson's hand, DLC (34). Published in Bassett, 3:315. Paine (1799–1882), a Nashville minister who was later president of LaGrange College and a bishop of the Methodist Episcopal church, chaired the committee of the Davidson County chapter of the American Bible Society, which invited AJ to address its anniversary meeting on October 20.

1. See Paine et al. to AJ, September 25.

From John Coffee

Coxes Creek, Sunday. 1st. October 1826

Dr. Genl.

By Mr. Camper I had the pleasure to receive yours of the 25th. Ulto.[1] and also my mare in fine order. I hope she is in foal. I thank you for this additional service, to the many heretofore recd. from you—About a week ago I went down to A. J. Hutchings farm and went through the crop and examined it well, the Cotton is indifferent owing to the droughth, it seems to have been very well cultivated, but most of it in the oldest land is very small and badly bowled, and the wet season had started it to a second growth, that was also injuring it very much, it was forward and they were picking it very fast. Winburn informed me that he had out at that time 35 thousand, since which he had a week's picking he must have by this time 45 thousand out, his calculations were from what he had picked that he would gather in about six hundred to the acre, when all done—he had at that time Gined his packing room full and was waiting to get Baging and rope to begin to bail. he will be done baleing as soon as he is done picking, or very soon thereafter, as he carries on both branches of business at the same time, he says his hands pick remarkably well, so much so, that he himself attends the Gin, and keeps all hands in the field. I bought Baling and rope, & sent it to him the day after I was there say on yesterday was a week ago, he would bale on monday last all that he had picked, and continue Gining—the Scotch Baging (which was the same price with the other) cost 30 cents a yard, and Rope 12½ cents p lb. I omitted to purchase for myself or that farm, untill very lately, when that was the best bargain I could get, taking enough for both farms—

The old ground corn was also rather light, but the new ground was very fine with a good crop of Pumpkins, the corn crop will abundantly supply the place but nothing more—he could not tell how many hogs he could command to make pork, but he said there would not be enough to supply the place, the hogs were very much scattered, running after the whiteoak mast that had begun to fall, and which is in great abundance this year—I think it unnecessary to make any provisions about the pork untill it is known the quantity that may be wanted, as it is likely to be very low here this year, I can get delivered at the place, at that season upon better terms than a contract can be made, or to have it driven out, and I hope to be here and will attend to it in due time—Winburn is very desireous to remain on the place at his old wages say $200. he is about to Marry one of Old Mr. Scrugs's daughters[2] a young girl of 16 or 17 years of age, and that is the reason his sister Mrs. Nicholson is about to move away, another of her brothers and herself are about to settle a new place in the woods and carry on a farm—I am at a loss to determine whether Winburn ought to be continued or not he is very anxious to do so, and I believe he is doing the very best he can with his judgment, but both him and his wife are young and will necessarily be at some loss to manage the young negroe family—in reply to that objection, her Mother is very near and possibly would counsel when called on for the purpose, this might be somewhat of a palliative, but not a compleat removal of the objection, and I would not consider him equal to such a man as Nicholson was, yet he will do the best he can I believe—The man you mentioned in your letter who had written to you, and who had overseed for Booker, has I am told engaged with James Jackson—but if it should be determined to turn away Winburn, and get another, I can employ a man by the name of Hudson in this neighbourhood at $300. and his family found,[3] who is an old overseer under an excellent name, he applied to me last year before Winburn had been engaged, and I mentioned him to you by letter, I think I should have then employed him but he was under a partial engagement with John Craig[4] & could not get off he has about as much family as Nickerson had, is a man about 35 years old from appearance is said to be a first rate overseer, he is a very decent man and so is his family as I learn, I think he would be able to manage affairs better than the other, and would be a more responsible person—but his family would be a little more expence, and his wages is $100. higher than the other—both of them seems desireous to continue on the place if employed, untill Andrew would arrive at age to take charge himself—under all circumstances possibly it would be better to employ Hudson, as he certainly would have more judgment in the management of the negroes and every thing else appertaining to the plantation—and if equal to his reputation as an overseer, he would relieve you measureably of resposibility—

I have given you as near as I can the history of the two men with the prospects before them, you can better determine which to employ than I can—If Winburn is to be employed you need not say so positively to him yet untill he brings his crop nearer to a close, and if he is not employed it will [be] more necessary to keep the information from him least he relax in his duty—therefore if you should wish to employ Hudson you may instruct me to that effect by a line and I will do it without giving the other notice of it, at least untill he progresses further with the crop. As I expect to set out to the treaty on the 11 or at furthest the 12th. of the month, the sooner you determine and write me the better, and if you conclude to employ Hudson, write such a letter as would do to shew to my neighbour Major Allen,[5] that in the event I should have started from home before it came to hand, I would request Mrs. Coffee to send for the Major and get him to see Hudson and close the contract for me, he is well acquainted with Hudson, and recommds his being employed, I will speak to Major

Allen on the subject before I leave home, provided I do not receive your instructions before I start—[6]

I observe you mention that you intend coming out about the time I return home if it is not necessary to come sooner on the business of Little Andrews farm—I dont believe that any thing will require you here on that account, at least earlier than the last of November, by which time I hope to have returned home—and if all things have gone on well perhaps we may be enabled to travel with you to Tennessee, as we wish to visit our friends there as soon as we can—

I wrote you in great haste a line by Mr. Eastin,[7] in which mentioned the birth of a daughter, and that Polly and the child was as well as usual at such time, she continues well in health, but for the last three days she has had a very sore Breast, it has given her much pain, but she thinks it will not rise to a head, so as to be opened, I hope it may not—the child is very well, (not yet named)—[8]

All our politicks here are turned to the Senatorial election next fall at Tuscaloosa to fill the place of Chambers who succeeded Kelly—[John] McKinley was the first announced on the list, he promises every thing required as to the Presidential election, and the amendment of the Constitution &c &c &c—Nick Davis, Clement C[omer] Clay, and lastly James Jacksons name has been announced as seekers for that appointment,[9] & I have been told that he Jackson claims the support of your friends, on the ground that he will support you if the voice of his constituents are such—which all know are so—thus we see how this man will bend with the currant, if necessary to his own popularity Kelly had been urged to come forward but he says he cannot on account of some very important suits in which he has been employed, but Col. [James W.] Exum has been to see me lately and thinks that Kelley may yet be brought out, if so no doubt of his success[10]—Judge [Richard] Ellis's name has also been announced of late, but I think it most probable if Kelley does not come out, that [Israel] Pickens will offer and be elected, and if so it will meet the wishes of many of your frinds[11]—Polley and our little children join me in tendering to Mrs. Jackson and yourself our respects, and best wishes—will thank you to give th[em] to Mrs. Donelson & Capt Donelson if you should see them—Dr. Genl. yours

Jno Coffee

P.S. I have so little hope of success at the pending treaties that I forgot to mention it to you before, but we will go and do all we can in the business. I mentioned to you by Mr. Eastin the wishes of Genl. Hinds as respects your influence,[12] I have no doubts of your high standing with that people, but on reflection I doubt the propriety of your interfering, where there is so little hope of sucess—but you know best what to do. J. C.

ALS, DLC (34). Published in Bassett, 3:316–18 (extract).

1. See above.
2. Not identified.
3. Possibly Joseph G. Hudson or Jeremiah Hudson, both from Lauderdale County.
4. Craig (d. 1836) was Florence postmaster at this time.
5. Probably Lewis Buckner Allen (b. 1784).
6. For AJ's instructions, see AJ to Coffee, October 5, below.
7. Letter not found.
8. Katherine Coffee was born on September 24.
9. Henry H. Chambers had died on January 24. McKinley (1780–1852) was elected in November and served until 1831. He later represented Alabama in the House of Representatives, and Martin Van Buren appointed him to the Supreme Court in 1837. Nicholas Davis (1781–1856), of Limestone County, was president of the state senate. Clay (1789–1866; East Tennessee 1807), a Huntsville lawyer and judge, later represented Alabama in both the House and Senate.
10. Exum (d. 1838), who had served as one of Coffee's deputy surveyors, represented Limestone County in the Alabama House, 1819, 1824, and 1826. By 1828 he had moved his surveying business to Florida, where AJ appointed him marshal in 1829.
11. Ellis (1781–1846), of Franklin County, was a circuit court judge. He soon moved to Texas, where he served as president of the 1836 constitutional convention and as a senator of the Texas republic. Former governor Pickens (1780–1827; Jefferson College 1802) had been appointed to replace Chambers as senator; he served from February 17 until the election of McKinley. Contrary to Coffee's speculations, only McKinley and Clay were formally nominated for senator.
12. Thomas Hinds had written Coffee on September 3 (THi), suggesting that, as the Chickasaws and Choctaws had such great respect for AJ, "if the Genl. would write a *Talk* to be sent to them in the way of advise pointing out their true Interest . . . it would come very much in aid of our exertions." AJ, however, declined.

To John Coffee, with Enclosure

Hermitage Octbr. 5th. 1826—

Dr. Genl

I am Just returned from Nashville where my time has been engrossed for the last Eight days, attending the examination at our College, and on yesterday, our commencement—where I was truly gratified with the examinations—& the performance of the graduates—but particularly, with the learned, pertinant, & eloquent address, of the President Doctor Lindsley—however, I shall not speak more of this address at present, as we have directed 500 coopies to be printed, and I will send you one[1]— The decorum of the students, and the result of the examinations, gave *full* proof of the ability of the professors, and the attention of the faculty to the youths intrusted to their care[2]—I can with truth say, this college has not its superior in any country, or clime.

I intended to have wrote you by Mr. Eastin but I could not obtain the opportunity—and this morning Major Lewis set out without me seeing him;[3] and todays mail brought me your letter of the 1rst. instant;[4] I hasten to answer it, in hopes, that it may reach you before you set out. On the subject of an overseer I will leave it to your Judgt. to decide knowing as I do, you can better Judge than I can—I am fearful Mr Winburn has not sufficient experience to superintend such an establishment, for surely with the quantity of corn he had this year, he ought, with attention, to have produced his *meat*—still, his wages is very moderate, and if he has energy & industry might improve—I believe there is no doubt of his *honesty*—still sir, as the other is recommended highly, altho his family is larger and his wages higher, still if Major Allen vouches for his *honesty*; in the end, he might be the cheapest—that farm ought to produce from the hands on it, at least, 120 thousand seed cotton, our duty to the child makes it necessary we should do the best for him that our Judgt may dictate—A. J. Hutchings will be fourteen years old next February—in the seven years to come, by making the contract with Mr Winburn there would be saved, say $1400 dollars—this to be sure would be a great saving, still, the question to be solved, is whether the capacity the experience, the industry & honesty of the other is such as might save more than that sum, *or make more*, in the seven years, yet to come, than would counterballance the saving of the $1400—if so—let Mr Hudson be employed. But on the other hand unless the *honesty* of Mr Hudson is well vouched for, let him not be employed—we know Mr Winburn, and believe him honest, and with the aid of old Mrs. Scruggs, the health of the negro children, with the attention of Mrs Winburn, may be well attended to. I would further remark, Whosoever may be employed it will be necessary, that he be obligated to take care of the negro children, & to cloath (as Mrs. Nicholson had done) the family, & raise their supply of meat; and that no stock, except what belongs to the farm, to be kept there—as I believe the stock sufficient for the support of the farm; from this, might be the *exception*, of a horse for the overseer. with these hasty remarks, I leave it to your Judgt. who you may employ.[5]

I cannot be out before the last of Novbr. as I have to be in Nashville on the 13th. of that month, as the fall session of our college commences on that day—I remark & note, your observations with regard to keeping for the present, from Winburn, whether he is to be employed or not; which I fully approve—to conclude I leave it to your Judgt. with the observations I have made to decide which you will employ—from the price of cotton $300 for the hands on that plantation *[is a]* large price—I give Mr Parsons but $350 *[a]* year, & unless cotton rises that will take ¼ of My crop to pay it.

We regret to learn that Mrs Coffee is not well, but hope for her speedy recovery, tender us kindly to her & family & believe me yr friend

Andrew Jackson

P.S. the inclosed will give you my views of your prospects of treating with the Indians—& on what basis you may rest the future hopes of obtaining their country A. J.

ALS, DLC (11-0375).
1. Philip Lindsley, *The Cause of Education in Tennessee: An Address Delivered to the Young Gentlemen Admitted to the Degree of Bachelor of Arts in Cumberland College, at the Anniversary Commencement, Oct. 4, 1826* (Nashville, 1826).
2. At the October 5 meeting of the college trustees, AJ was appointed to a committee to prepare a statement on the examinations. That report of October 6 appeared in the *Nashville Republican*, October 7.
3. Lewis accompanied Coffee to the Chickasaw and Choctaw negotiations.
4. See above.
5. Coffee continued Winborne's employment, at least pending the results of his crop, but before leaving for Alabama, AJ hired John W. Phillips for the position.

Enclosure: To John Coffee

[October 5, 1826]

Dr. Genl

Yours by Mr Easton has been recd;[1] assure Genl Hinds when you see him, that I would freely comply with his request, but there would be, under the circumstances in which I am placed, a delicacy that forbids it—It might be said by the administration I was intermedling in matters with which I had no authority, & if unsuccessfull fall under the censure of the administration—therefore I decline addressing my babo-she-lies[2]

I have no idea that you will succeed at present, but you may perhaps make a conditional treaty to be binding on the two nations should they be pleased with the country when it is explored by their chiefs selected for that purpose. It is your province to make a treaty if you can, & the best you can—If therefore they will yield their country at all, you will have to pay them *well*—If you find they alledge that they are unacquainted with the country, stipulate on what terms they will *exchange,* if they should be pleased with it when viewed by them, appoint an agent to accompany them, & stipulate that they shall have so many months to give their final approbation to this agreement—further stipulating that the approval of the President & Senate is to be had to this conditional treaty, in which, must be stipulated a sum to bear the expence of this exploration—to this they Indians may agree—but still this ought to be the last proposition—Unless the Indians are acquainted with the country you propose giving them in exchange, *they will not, nay, ought not,* to enter into a final treaty before they obtain this information, but an arangement may with justice to them be made on the condition they like the country when explored—This will test how far the President & congress will approve the treaty when absolutely made, on the application for the appropriation to defray the expence of exploring the country—your powers does not Justify such a conditional treaty, but if you can obtain no other—this of itself will Justify this thing, and may be the means of finally obtaining their country, and at a much earlier day than without it, because it will be the inducement for them to explore it when otherwise they would not. make a treaty, this is your business if you can & leave it to the P. & congress to approve.

I write in haste & for yourself & with a bad head ache—say to Major Lewis that I have had the interview with the Gentlemen, the result with one satisfactory, with the Govr. not as satisfactory as I could have wished, but still it may result in good.[3] Wishing you health & success in your treaty, with a tender of my good wishes to Genl Hinds, I am your friend

Andrew Jackson

ALS, THi (11-0349). Published in Bassett, 3:315–16 (extract).
1. Not found.
2. "Baboshila," the Choctaw word for "my brother."
3. AJ's "interview" may have been with Governor William Carroll and John H. Eaton concerning the upcoming senatorial election.

Samuel Lewis Southard (1787–1842; Princeton 1804) of New Jersey, appointed Secretary of the Navy by James Monroe in 1823, was continued in the post by John Quincy Adams. Around the first of July, while visiting friends near Fredericksburg, Virginia, Southard dined at the house of John Spotswood Wellford (1783–1846), a merchant. Also present was John Hooe Wallace (c1793–1872) a physician who had been a leader in the Virginia Jackson movement in 1824. When the conversation strayed to the Battle of New Orleans, Wallace's praise of Jackson's accomplishments struck Southard as unfair to then Secretary of War Monroe, and he launched into a spirited account of Monroe's services on behalf of that victory.

Wallace reported Southard's remarks to Samuel Houston shortly after the dinner and Houston repeated them to Jackson in October. Already sensitized by Jonathan Roberts's letter disputing the significance of his actions at New Orleans, Jackson viewed Southard's assertions as an assault on his honor. In the letter below, he formally asked Houston, who was about to return to Congress, to obtain a statement from Southard regarding the matter. After consultation with Jackson's supporters in Washington, Houston wrote Jackson on December 13 to suggest a different approach, but Jackson persisted and sent, through Houston, a letter to Southard on January 5, 1827. Southard's placatory reply of February 9, 1827, failed to mollify Jackson, who addressed a scathing response to Southard on March 6, 1827 (all letters below).

Jackson refused to drop his dispute with Southard, and he urged friends to collect information regarding comments at the Fredericksburg dinner and about his role in defending New Orleans. In Fredericksburg, Wellford gathered statements from those who had attended the dinner, which he displayed at his store. Wallace responded by obtaining copies of the Jackson-Southard correspondence from Jackson, which he showed around as well (see Wellford to Wallace, and Wallace, Fayette Johnson, William F. Gray,

Archibald Hart, William M. Blackford, and John Minor to Wellford, all March 22, 1827, DLC-34; Wallace to Houston, March 24, 1827, DLC-72; Washington National Intelligencer, September 12, 1827).

Meanwhile Southard was showing the correspondence to supporters in Washington, and Jackson's friends were doing the same (John Agg to Daniel Webster, October 30, 1827, DLC; Memoirs of John Quincy Adams, 7:260; Washington United States' Telegraph, July 11, 1827; Washington National Journal, December 18, 1827). On March 19, 1827, the United States' Telegraph warned Southard not to repeat his story, and in late June and early July 1827 the administration press briefly aired its view of the correspondence as "indicative of Gen. Jackson's violence and intemperance" (National Journal, July 9, 12, 1827; National Intelligencer, June 29), while the Telegraph responded that the correspondence, if published, would display Jackson in a favorable light (June 29, July 7, 11, 1827). At some point during the controversy, a portion of the Jackson-Southard correspondence was printed, though there is little evidence to suggest that it had wide circulation. The Carter Beverley affair quickly crowded the matter out of the newspapers.

To Samuel Houston

Hermitage Octbr. 23rd. 1826—

Sir

You are aware that I never have paid any attention to the slanders or falshoods propagated against me by the hired minions of the Govt. But when members of the cabinet become the assailants the respectable stations which they occupy, forbid the idea that their animadversion will be attributed to the same corrupt source, and it then becomes necessary for the individual who may be the subject of it, to notice the cause, and as far as possible prevent the injury designed to be produced by it. This observation is prompted by some information recently convayed to me thro a very respectable channel, from which it appears that the Sec of the Navy has been instrumental to the circulation of a fabrication calculated to give a wound to my character; and as I have hazarded much to acquire and maintain this character however humble it may be, I am unwilling that it should now be assailed by authority so high, without some inquiry into the cause. The facts are these, as given by my informant, who derives his information from my friend Doctor John H. Wallace of Fredricsburgh Va.: that at a public dinner given to the Honble. the Secy. of the Navy *"Mr Southard, while at table remarked to Colo. [William Fairfax] Gray of Fredricsburgh,1 did you ever learn that Genl Jackson on one occasion left the army and was returning home without leave, or orders, when Mr. Monroe, then Secy. of War, sent him a preremptory order, and compelled him to return; and that owing to this circumstance neworleans was saved?"* "no (replied col. Gray) where can that fact be had? It would be of importance to *us* if we could get hold of it." (Mr Southard said) *"I do not know, but such I am told is the fact."* This I pronounce a positive falshood: no circumstance like it has ever occurred; so far from it, that from the beginning to the end of the last war, when I had a camp, I never slept one night out of it; and I therefore request you to call upon Mr Southard and demand of him in my name in writing, from whom, he obtained this information so prejudicial to truth, and to my character, as I am determined to put a stop to this system of falshood contrived, and circulated for effect, whenever I can trace it to the Departments of the Executive Goverment.

You will please communicate the answer of Mr Southard to me, so soon as you have the interview with him, which I hope will be, as soon as you reach the city of washington—make a copy of this and preserve it, presenting this original to Mr Southard; say to him from me, that from the high & honourable station he fills I expect a prompt, and categorical answer from him. I am sir with great respect your friend

Andrew Jackson

ALS, DLC (72). Addressed to Houston, "present." Published in Bassett, 6:485–86.
1. Gray (1787–1841), anti-Jackson, was postmaster. Later he moved to Texas and served there as clerk of the House, secretary of the Senate, and clerk of the supreme court.

To Samuel Houston

Hermitage Octbr. 23rd 1826

Dr. Genl

Agreable to your request, I herewith send you my letter of the 22nd. of January 1822 to Mr. John Q. Adams then Sec of State[1]—also a copy of Genl [John] Armstrongs letter to me of the 18th. of July 1814, not recd until the 17th. of January 1815[2]—I have not time to send you a copy of my report to the Department of War detailing my movement on Pensacola in Novbr. 1814—you will find it on file in the Dept of War, it is dated the 14th. of Novbr. 1814, and my letter of Octbr. 26th. 1814, informing the Govt. of my intention of vissitting Pensacola with my reasons therfor.[3]

I send you the Sec of Wars letter of the 10th. of Decbr 1814 recd. on the 18th. of February 1815 and my answer thereto the moment it was recd[4]—This was the first and only communication I recd from the Govt. from the 20th of Novbr. 1814; on that date I recd and acknowledged the receipt of the dispatch of the 19th. and 21rst. of Octbr 1814[5]—I enclose you a copy of Lut. Harold Smith U. S. artillery dated at Staunton Febry 7th. 1815[6] This with the letter of Mr [Abram Rall] Woolly of the ordinance Department dated at Pittsburgh 18th. of January 1815[7] (which I have not time to copy) with the letter of advice accompanying it, with a list of supplies required in Septbr 1814 and which Mr Woolly assures me are given over for transportation to the quarter master for transportation & will be sure to reach me in 30th days, will afford you some evidence of the great exertion of the Govr. for the defence of the lower country—If men without arms or ordinance or fixed amunition, could defend the lower country, it would have been secure; The militia were ordered, when the enemy were on the coast—but where & when was it, that a supply of arms & fixed munitions were ordered & forwarded.

If you could read the dispatches from the Goverment up to the 21rst. of Octbr. and my answers up to the 20th. of Novbr. and my various communications, to that date—and my communications to the Goverment from my arival to the close of the Campaign—then the letter of Decbr 10th. 1814 recd. the 18th. of Febry 1815 and my reply, keeping in view Lt Smiths letter you can form a correct Judgt. of my situation & exertions & how much credit the Govt. is really entitled to, for their supplies and aid given me in the defence of the lower country

I wish you to examine whether my letters of the 10th. and 26th of Decbr 1814, and my letter of the 13th. of February 1815 are on file in the War Department;[8] this last letter is a full detail of my opperations from the time I reached Mobile untill the close of the War with my views, & reasons for my course—This letter of the 13th. of Febry I would wish you to read, and I want to be informed whether this is on file on the War Department; If these letters named are not to be found on file, Justice has not been done me, or is it intended to be extended to my memory when dead—and I would like to know this when living. In haste your friend

Andrew Jackson

ALS, DLC (72). Addressed to Houston in Nashville. Published in Bassett, 6:484–85.

1. See AJ to Adams, January 22, 1822. Houston probably made the request while at the Hermitage earlier in the day.

2. See Armstrong to AJ, July 18, 1814, (*Jackson,* 3:90). Armstrong (1758–1843) served as secretary of war from February 1813 until August 1814.

3. See AJ to James Monroe, October 26, (*Jackson,* 3:173–75), and November 14, 1814.

4. See Monroe to AJ, December 10, 1814; and AJ to Monroe, February 18, 1815.

5. See Monroe to AJ, October 19, October 21, 1814, (*Jackson,* 3:170–71).

6. See Smyth to AJ, February 7, 1815. Smyth (c1793–1852; Washington & Lee), later a Wythe County, Virginia, lawyer and editor, had been given the December 10 dispatch at Washington, but wrote that he had become sick en route and was forwarding it by mail.

7. See Woolley to AJ, January 18, 1815. Woolley (1784–1858) was deputy commissary of ordnance. He was dismissed from the army May 1, 1829.

8. See AJ to Monroe, December 12 (dated 10 in letterbook copy), 26, 1814, and February 13, 1815. Houston was unable to find the February letter in the war department, even though it was registered as received. It was then most likely among the papers of Daniel Parker, clerk in the department until 1822, as it is now.

From Samuel Swartwout

New York 24th October 1826

My dear Sir,

I avail myself of the opportunity afforded by Mr. [Francis Barber] Ogdens visit to Tennessee[1] to renew the assurance of my unalterable attachment and regard. I refer you to Mr. O for the particulars of our late defeat in New Jersey[2]—He will explain to you the cause of that disaster and the confidence entertained by the friends of just govt. of our success in 1828—Indeed, we were sensible ourselves of the weakness of our own ticket, that defeat was predicted before the poll commenced—But I will not dwell longer upon so unpleasant a subject—In the State of New York, a great change is working—The people are begining to see the necessity of controling those who have given such unequivocal evidence of their desire to control them and the next Congress will exhibit a change in the Administration party from that state—But I will leave politics for conversation and dwell upon a subject much nearer & dearer to your feelings—I perceive by the public prints that Mrs. Jackson has been in ill health, but I rejoice too to learn thro the same channel by your letter in answer to the invitation from your fellow citizens in Kentucky[3] that she is convalesent I rejoice to learn too that your own health is good and that that circumstance may materially affect the cause of the people in their determined efforts to restore the Govt. to the rank and purity it attained to during the Administration of Washington & Jefferson—The power & patronage of the Excecutive is so great, that none but a *pure* patriot can make head against the thousand corrupt sources of power which he can bring to bear directly upon the people—Live then my dear friend and enjoy the triumph that your name will enable the people to achieve—The battle of 98 must be fought over again and no man other than yourself can lead us up to the conflict & bring us triumphant out of it.

The Adams prints here have assailed DeWitt Clinton already—This will drive him into opposition to them and into friendly feelings for us— He holds aloof—not daring to trust himself with a declaration for or agt. the Administration But the period will soon arive when he will be compelled to declare for one party or the other and it is not difficult to tell which dilemma he will prefer—

But I must refer you to Mr. O. for more lengthy details. He will be enabled to present a perfect picture to you of all the conflicting interest of this large state & also of the prospects the *people* have of being felt & honored in the next congress & the next election for President—We are all confident of our cause. Mrs. S. desires me to present her respects to you & Mrs.

J. to which I beg permission to add my own affectionate regards, I remain my dear Sir, with the greatest truth your friend & Obt. Hmbl Sevt.

Saml Swartwout

ALS, DLC (34).
   1. Ogden (1783–1857) was a son of the revolutionary general Matthias and nephew of former New Jersey governor Aaron Ogden. In 1830 AJ appointed him consul at Liverpool.
   2. At the New Jersey state convention on September 20, Jackson and Adams supporters offered competing delegates from all but eight counties, with the result that the convention dissolved and both factions ran separate congressional slates. On October 12, George Holcombe, endorsed by both parties, and five Adams candidates won the election.
   3. See above, AJ to Thomas P. Moore, July 31.

From Richard Keith Call

Tallahassee 8th. Nov 1826

My Dear General
   Your favour of the 30th. Sept has been received.[1] I am pleased with the arrangement you have made, in constituting Mr Bell my attourney, and hope ere this that every thing has been adjusted with the old Lady.[2]
   The excuse of Overton and Brackenridge is indeed a lame one, even were it true, but I presume it is the best the nature of the case would admit of. I regret very much that neither of them had manliness enough to resent the insult offered to them as invited guests, by drinking sentiments, which no true friend of yours could have swallowed. The company must have been extremely rude indeed, after having invited them to preside, to wound the feelings of such worthy Gentlemen, by treating you with indignaty. But they both have *Philosophy* enough to beare with the infirmaties of their associates.
   I am truly rejoiced to learn that our friend Houston has acquited himself so well. He will now have honourable peace. No man ever embarked more folishly in a scrape than did Mr [William] White and none more richly deserved his fate. I presume he was the only one of the party who could have been prevailed on to enter the list.
   Our friend Gadsden was with us a few days since he is in good health. We entertain no doubt of his election to Congress in May next notwithstanding the duplicity and management of his *friend* Mr [Joseph M.] White.[3] In a former letter[4] I told you that this man was your friend while in your presence, or in the presence of your friends only, I have now the most convincing proof of this. Nine tenths of the people of this Territory are devoted to you, and while here he is no less so. Your old friend Col [John] McKee[5] was here when White arrived, and when he heared that he was a good Jacksonian in Florida, he expressed great surprise He observed "it was the greates[t] revolution he had ever known, and that at Wash-

ington he was the most humble slave of the administration." He further observed that the Administration party had given him $20,000 for a canal only for the purpose of keeping him in power.[6] Your letters to him were shown freely as he passed through this country, to convince the people that he was your friend.[7] I know this man perfectly, and intimately, and you may depend on it a more unprincipled fellow never lived. He is plausible, and will pass well among strangers but when known will be held in contempt by all honourable and intelligent men. I am rejoiced to find that no doubt is entertained of your success at the next Presidential election. Your friends in all parts of the union as far as I have heared, speak of it as an event beyond the possibility of doubt. My dear Marys health is quite restored and she speaks of carrying her daughter to see you and Mrs. Jackson in the spring. The Governors family will return to Kentucky at that period and I am [anx]ious for her to accompany them as [far as the] Hermitage, if she will consent to [go] without me. I have promised if she will do [so] to go for her in the fall. The Col and Mrs Butler are both well, but are still very severely afflicted by their late misfortune[8]

Please present us affectionately to Mrs. Jackson and the Andrews, and believe me dear General sincerely your friend

R K Call

ALS, DLC (34).
1. See above.
2. Ellen J. Kirkman, Call's mother-in-law.
3. Gadsden lost the Florida territorial delegate election to White in 1827.
4. Not found.
5. McKee (1771–1832) was an Alabama congressman.
6. The appropriation to survey a route for a canal across the Florida peninsula passed on March 3 (4 *U.S. Statutes at Large* 139–40).
7. Only one letter to White, that of December 29, 1825, has been found.
8. The Butlers' son Jackson Orleans Butler (1816–1826) had died on October 20.

To Richard Keith Call

Hermitage Novbr. 21rst 1826

Dear Call

I have just recd your letter of the 20th. ult. (having recd. heretofore, yours of the 3rd and postscrip, of the 13th)[1] giving me the maloncholy intelligence of the death of your two little infants, and Jackson Butler—we rejoice to learn that Mrs. Call is fast recovering, and whilst we simpathise with you & her on the loss of your little twin daughters, we rejoice at the happy prospect of Marys speedy restoration to health; and from their premature birth, we anticipated, from your first letter recd., that as one was gone, the other would soon follow—But instead of repining at the loss, we ought to rejoice at their change from this world of evil & of wo, to those heavenly climes where happiness forever raigns—let us remember "that god *doeth all things well*," and at the events of providence we ought to be at all times ready to exclaim, "the Lords will be done."

With all my Philosophy, and whilst I cheerfully submit to the will of providence, I cannot but regret the untimely fate of my little favourite namesake, he was a charming child, & I had written to Colo. Butler to send him to me last summer[2] & expected him up in Septbr or October. I anticipated much pleasure in superintending his Education—but providence has decreed otherwise, & I calmly yield to the decree and I trust and hope that the parents will summons up all their fortitude & submit to this calamity, with a proper temper and humility—The child is gone, providence has thus decreed, and he cannot be recalled and we ought to submit with proper humiliation, and I hope, & trust, they will do so.

I am happy that the unpleasan difference between you & Colo. White has been satisfactorily & honorably adjusted. My *friend,* we ought as we pass through life not *break* our *shins* against stools not in our way, when we can honorable remove them—and when we become acquainted with men in whom we cannot confide, pass thro life with them, having as little to do with *them* as possible, & saying as little about them as we can, so long as their conduct is such, as not to injure us, or ours. This unpleasant differrence having ended, as I hoped, and expected, when I wrote you,[3] and one remark in your letter, has induced me from the most friendly mo[*tives*] to make the above remark, you will receive it, as I intend it, *most* friendly.

Be assured my Dear Call, I know human nature pretty well—my course ever has been, to shew confidence in all men, repose it in none until I find, from experience, they are worthy of it—hence I have seldom been deceived by missplaced confidence and when I have found men mere polit[ic]ians bending to the popular breese, and changing with it, for the sake of self popularity I have ever shunned them, believing that such was unworthy of my confidence—but still, I treat them with politeness & hospitality when they call upon me—from these my general rule, you may be sure I am not often imposed upon by political men.

Before this reaches you, you will have heard, of Houston's *duel,* & Eaton's reelection without opposition—The faction in this State is buried, and harmony prevades the whole, and the Executive influence cannot revive it—*we will have peace & harmony.*[4]

I shall expect the promised account of the adjustment of y[o]ur differrence with Colo. White—whi[*lst I]* know you too well, and have great conf[*iden]*ce in your friends—Butler & [James] Ramage,[5] to whom present me; still I have a desire to hear how it has been adjusted knowing before I receive the details that it has been honorably done—you know, your charecter is dear to me.

Mrs. J. unites with me in love to you & Mary, to Colo Butler & Rachel & their family—with our blessing to all, your friend

Andrew Jackson

ALS, DLC (11-0393); Printed in *The Collector* (December 1901), p. 16 (11-0397).
1. Letters not found.
2. Letter not found.
3. See above, AJ to Call, September 5.
4. According to one observer, AJ personally lobbied the legislature to support Eaton over Carroll, arguing that despite Carroll's merits he was viewed as "the administration candidate" and his elevation would damage AJ's presidential prospects (James Campbell to David Campbell [1779–1859], December 19, NcD). Significant minorities in both houses of the Tennessee legislature attempted to postpone the senatorial election until after the expiration of Eaton's term in March 1827, but AJ's friends opposed, and on November 4 Eaton received fifty-two of the fifty-six votes cast.
5. Ramage, a naval lieutenant, and Butler served as Call's intermediaries in his dispute with Joseph M. White.

To Samuel Houston

Hermitage Novbr. 22nd 1826

Dr Genl

I set out tomorrow for the neighbourhood of Florence to make some arangements relative to the interest of my little ward, H. whose cotton Ginn & all the cotton has been consumed by fire—I therefore before I leave home trouble you with this letter.

I am anxious as early as your convenience will admit, that you should see Doctor Wallace & Colo Gray, and obtain their statement in writing of what the Sec of the Navy should have said, at the Public dinner given him at Fredericksburg va, relative to my leaving the army without leave or orders &c &c and communicate a copy to me and retain the original yourself—so soon as this is done present my note to the Sec[1] and transmit me his reply[2]—I trust you will attend to this thing promptly for me; for, I find the heads of Departments have been ranging the union & secretely intimating slanderous things of me—This I mean to Expose, & put down, one after the other, as I can obtain the positive proof—*Let it not be long before I hear from you.*

I have recd several letters from the western District since you left Nashville the *current* has *changed there,* and you will (unless a mighty change) receive an overwhelming majority[3]—The result of your Political quarrel, & Major Eatons reelection, has put down the faction, and uninimity & harmony will prevade our whole state.

Present me to Mr John Randolph & all my friends in the senate—If you find it convenient, you may suggest a desire I have of obtaining a good filly got by Sir Archey, & full bred by the dam side—knowing that he has the purest blood, if he has a filly of this description broke to the halter, that he can sell for $300 or under that sum, say a two or three year old, if he will deliver such a one to you, & you will bring her out, I will be prompt in remitting him the amount.[4]

Mrs. J. & all my family including Mr Earle unite in kind salutations to you—present us to Major Polk & Lady—and all the Tennessee delegation with such other friends as inquire for me respectfully yr friend

Andrew Jackson

P.S. please transmit under cover, the enclosed,[5] to its address A. J.
[P.S.] Capt A. J. Donelson who has engaged my stud coalts, desires me to say to you, if a faithfull good keeper of race horses can be got, he will give them good wages, a freeman of colour, who could be well recommended for his capacity & honesty would be preferred, from one hundred dollars to one hundred & fifty of standing wages would be given, besides other priviledges, but none except those well recommended would be employed, he must be sober, honest, & capable—under such recommendations, I will gurantee any engagement for the Capt, that you may make—A. J.

ALS, DLC (34). Published in Heiskell, 3:159–60, and in Bassett, 3:318–19 (extract).
  1. Possibly AJ to Houston, October 23, above.
  2. Houston replied to AJ's request on December 13, below.
  3. Letters not found. AJ was referring to support for Houston in the gubernatorial campaign, which he won in August 1827.
  4. After a successful racing career in Washington and Virginia, Sir Archy was put to stud in 1810, and he became the most distinguished sire of his era. When Randolph was unable to supply a filly of the desired age, AJ decided not to purchase.
  5. Not identified.

From "An Enquirer"

[November 1826]
Facts and Sudjestions
There was at Frankfort in the course of the last year an old ill looking Englishman named [Edward] Day.[1] his apparrel was thread bear rusty and dirty, his professed employment was a collector of debts for the Baltimore and Philadelphia merchants, he sometimes walk*[ed &]* was *[a mean]* squallid looking man, about 60 years old and rendered himself conspicuous and meritorious with the partizans of the collition by cours and harsh abuse of General Jackson.

As Day was an Englishman and no doubt partook of the national manifestations pride and hatred of his countrymen against General Jackson, as the commander of the American troops which inflicted on a regular Brittish army the most extraordinary and signal defeat which the nation had ever sustained, It was then believed by many that Day's enmity and abuse proceeded more from national pride and mortification on that account than any other cause or pretence, and that he was thus stimulated to lend himself or hire himself to the coalition or to some of their partizans, to endeavor to excite a public odium against Jackson who by being the commander of the brave men who had so much degraded the Brittish [army and] Nation.

Day being thus excited by Spleen and vengeance was a proper tool for the coalition, who also hated Jackson on account of his services merits and popularity, so that under the pretence of coming to the west to collect debts, he had travelled at leisure to get such testimony as might be picked up.

In this vindictive and diabolical ocupation this Day visited many parts of Kentucky, and passed through that part where Mrs Jackson formerly resided, he then went to Nashville in Tennessee and then to Natchez. after an absence of some time he returned to Frankfort having obtained as he said what [led] him to demonstrate that General Jackson and his lady had never been married. he brought with him copys of some records, from Mercer County stating that Mr. and Mrs. Roberts (now Mrs Jackson) had been divorced by a suit brought for the purpose, on the testimony of one Hugh MGary,[2] this record and some other papers, he Shewed in Frankford to the partizans of the coallition, by whom they were r[ead] and made subjects of much conversation, after a while they were carried to and left at Lexington, as it has been said with Mr. Henry Clay, who delivered them to Charles Hammond,[3] by whom they were published after being bragged about.

Thus it happened that an ill looking black hearted malignant a[nd vi]ndictive Englishman named Day who hated Jac[kson] on account of the victories over the Brittish troops at Orleans, has been used by [the coali]tion or their partizans, to obtain garbled [docume]nts, for the purpose of creating Odium and hatred against General Jackson and his lady, to gratify the malignant passions of the coalition, or to fill his own pockets.

Days appearance excited such an opinion as might be formed against a proud English misanthrope and miser, who would not spare his money except to execute a malignant act, and there were so many causes for his hatred to Jackson, and so much reason for believing that he delivered the records to Henry Clay in Lexington, and so many inducements to suppose that Charles Hammond received it from Clay, that the mind reflecting on the whole matter is apt to make these conclusions.

Hugh M'Gary the sole witness named in the record was well known to be an unprincipled scoundrel, which can be fully established in Kentucky.

An Enquirer

Let those who know more give the information

AD, T (11-0653).
    1. Not further identified.
    2. McGary (d. 1808), from Mercer County, Kentucky, had accompanied the Jacksons on their return from Natchez to Nashville in late 1791. On March 23, 1827, the *Liberty Hall and Cincinnati Gazette* printed a portion of the Mercer County records stating essentially what "An Enquirer" reported above.
    3. Hammond (1779–1840), editor of *Liberty Hall and Cincinnati Gazette,* had discussed the Jacksons' marriage while visiting Steubenville, Ohio, in October and had subsequently indicated that he would publish information regarding it at a later date (*Liberty Hall and Cincinnati Gazette,* November 14, 21). His records of the Robards' divorce did indeed come from Day, according to *Truth's Advocate,* January 1828, p. 17.

From James Knox Polk

Washington City
Decr. 4th. 1826.

Dear Genl—
    Congress has just convened, organized & adjourned until tomorrow. The message has not yet been recd. There is considerable anxiety among Mr. Adams's political friends as well as among the *factious opposition,* (as you know the prints by authority term us) to know what its complexion will be. Will the President still press the ultra federal policy which has heretofore marked his administration, or will he *from policy* recede? If he takes the former course, he has I think had abundant testimony that the great body of the people of the Union will not sustain him; and if the latter he subjects himself to the charge of inconsistency. It is possible he may give us an *electioneering,* negative sort of thing, the main object of which may be to promote his own views and those of his *dear Secretary.*[1] I have not since I saw you collected any political information, which would interest you, but what you have had an opportunity of seeing in the newspapers, and do not now address you for the purpose of communicating any, but merely to intimate to you, what may possibly occur, & of which it may be important for you to have early information. On my way through Virginia, to this place, I learned from a source in which I place confidence, that it was contemplated by some of the leading men of that state, about Richmond, to address you soon, for the purpose of ascertaining your opinions at large, in relation to the construction which you place on the federal consti[tu]tion, and more especially in relation to the power of making internal improvements, through the territory of the states, by the General Government. Your opinions on this subject I have no doubt have long since been settled, and when called on in a proper way I have as little doubt will be given independently—and regardless of consequences. Virginia you know is exceedingly sensative on this subject, and the only object I at present have, in writing you is, that you may not be taken unapprised, and be called upon for a hasty opinion. Without great care in the phraseology employed to convey our ideas, you know

the plainest sentiment in the English language may be perverted, and by the uncandid made to mean any thing but what it was intended to mean It may be that the call may never be made; but whether it should or not, I hope not to be deemed obtrusive in making the suggestion.[2] It can do no harm. The information though not given to me in confidence, I presume was not intended to be made public; I feel however unrestrained in communicating it to you, and for your greater satisfaction, will state it to you confidentially as I recd. it. At Abingdon in conversation with *Dr.* [Alexander] *McCall,*[3] he stated to me that such a call would certainly be made on you; that he had learned it from *Col.* [John] *Campbell* a very intelligent gentleman of that vicinity and one who was well acquainted with the views of the leading politicians of the state; and particularly of those in Richmond and its vicinity.[4] Whether the call will proceed from the *friends* of the administration, or from the *lukewarm,* I am unable to say. That it will not proceed from your friends I am satisfied—1st. because they have had ample opportunities in the whole tenor of your public life of understanding and Knowing your opinions upon this as well as all other great National questions, on which it has become necessary for you to either speak or act, and 2nd. because in Virginia, your friends have now, no occasion to make such a call, for Virginia, from information recd. from all quarters is now as determined in her opposition to the present administation, as Tennessee, Pennsylvania or any other state in the Union. Whatever therefore may be the design of some in Va. who have suggested this plan, with a view as I beli[e]ve to injure you in that state, the effort must be wholly abortive I must close this communication already swelled to a much greater length than I anticipated when I commenced it. It is written with the best design, and if the suggestion contained in it should possibly be of any service I shall be amply rewarded. In the progress of the Session if any thing of interest should occur, which does not appear in the Newspapers I will take great pleasure in communicating it, and shall be happy at any time you can find leisure to hear from you. I have the Honor to be Very Respectfully yr. friend & obt. set.

James K. Polk

NB. Our foreign friends here rejoice with us at the success of our friend Majr. Eaton. We consider it a great point gained.

ALS, DLC (34). Published in *Polk Correspondence,* 1:51–54.

1. Henry Clay.

2. The only inquiry found on internal improvements addressed to Jackson came from Thomas D. Arnold of eastern Tennessee.

3. McCall (1797–1869) had practiced medicine in Nashville before moving to Abingdon.

4. Campbell (1789–1866; Princeton) was a member of the Virginia executive council; in 1829 AJ appointed him Treasurer of the United States.

To William Berkeley Lewis

Hermitage Decbr. 12th. 1826

My Dear Major

Inclosed you will receive a copy of Mrs. Genl. [Sarah Michie] Smiths statement on the subject spoken of[1]—Capt Donelson is not acquainted with Mrs. [Mary Henley Russell] Bowen, and how her statement will be obtained I cannot devise,[2] unless you & Mr McLamore will ride up & see her; and perhaps neither of you are acquainted with her—Mrs. Bowens, together with Mrs. [Elizabeth Brown] Craigheads[3] & Mrs. Smith will be all sufficient—Mrs. Bowen is sister to Colo. [William] Russle, late of Fayette county Kentucky, deceased, and I believe sister of Genl [Robert Spotswood] Russle, step father of Mrs. Frank Preston[4]—The high character of these three ladies, & their numerous respectable connections, will carry credence with their statement wherever it is seen.

I am more anxious on this subject than perhaps I ought to be—but the Rascallity of the attempt to blacken the character of an ancient & virtuous female who has thro life maintained a good reputation & has associated with the best circles of society in which she has been placed, and this for the basest purpose, by a coalition at the head of which I am sure Mr Clay is—raises in my mind such feelings of indignation that I can scarcely control—but a day of retribution, as it respects Mr Clay & his tool Colo Hammonds, must arive should I be spared.[5]

you cannot confer a greater obligation on me than by obtaining Mrs. Bowen's statement—could I move in this thing, I would apply to her myself, but if I did, it might be used injuriously

I will come down & see Mr Overton as soon as I can make some arrangements about my cotton. I am very respectfully yr friend

Andrew Jackson

P.S. I have to send you the original which I have not time to copy—My Dr. Sir, will you have it copied, and the original I will get when I go down—or Capt A. J. Donelson will copy it when he goes down on Friday next—keep the original safe. A. J.

ALS, NNPM (11-0427). Published in Bassett, 3:323–24.

1. Smith (c1755–1834), widow of former senator Daniel Smith and Andrew Jackson Donelson's grandmother, had been a neighbor of the Donelsons and Jacksons. In her deposition of December 10, she detailed irrational and cruel treatment of Rachel Robards by her husband, the separation of the two, and the marriage of AJ and Rachel after receiving word of the Robards' divorce. She called Rachel a "Most prudent & virtuous female."

2. On December 21, Bowen (1760–1827), a niece of Patrick Henry and the widow of Sumner County pioneer William Bowen and mother of former Tennessee congressman John

H. Bowen, gave her deposition, attesting, from personal knowledge, to the cruel treatment Rachel Robards received from her husband and to the upright character of AJ and Rachel.

3. On December 2, Craighead (1755–1829), the widow of the Reverend Thomas B. and a sister of James and John Brown, former Louisiana and Kentucky senators and a neighbor of Mrs. Donelson in the 1780s, attested to Rachel's good character, "becoming" manners and action during the period of marriage, separation, divorce, and remarriage.

4. William Russell (1758–1825) was a regular army colonel, and Robert S. Russell (1762–1841), a Kentucky militia general. Mrs. Bowen's father, General William Russell (1735–93), was the stepfather of Sarah Buchanan Campbell Preston (1778–1846), wife of Francis Preston (1765–1835; William and Mary 1787), who had served with AJ in the Fourth Congress.

5. "An Enquirer," [November], above, reported that Charles Hammond and Henry Clay were behind the efforts to collect information on the Jackson's marriage, and AJ requested John H. Eaton to query Clay, who denied involvement (see Eaton to AJ, Dec 22, below).

From Samuel Houston

Washington
13th Dec 1826

Dear Genl,

On confering with Judge White Major Eaton, & some other especial friends of yours, and perceiving that the statement given to you[1] does not precisely accord with the detailed statement of Dr Wallace, I have thought it best not to hand your letter to Mr Southard but for the present to refer it back to you with a copy of the written statement of Dr Wallace.[2]

Your friends are of opinion that the better course, is for you to make no application yourself, but to permit it to come thro' some other channel. In conformity with this suggestion, I had prepared in my own name, a letter to the Secretary, a copy of which I inclose you as the better course;[3] I shoud prefer that it may meet your approbation, for the application to be made to Mr Southard; thro' me, acting as I shall state, at your instance, or *otherwise* as you may prefer[4]—It is now a desirable matter with all your friends, to keep you out of collision, as to things said and done; and for whatever action may be thought necessary, for it to proceed thro some friend. Political matters move on as promisingly as the most sanguine can desire!

I trust Sir that you will not for one moment suppose that my course has been dictated by an eye, to your political advancement, and that while I woud promote that, that I woud suffer your character, as a man, and Patriot to rest under imputations of dishonor! for permit to assure that no hope of earthly elevation for you, or myself coud induce me, to forget for one moment the personal relations in which I have the pleasing satisfaction, and the honor to consider myself in relation to you.

If you shoud write directly thro me to Mr Southard, I pray you to let it be in the mildest, calmest tone of expression—The very fact of his conduct and statement, will most effectually damn him, and those united with him.

Eatons letter in answer to Roberts,[5] and Genl [John] Adairs letter to Mr [Worden] Pope,[6] have a most happy effect, and whilst the administration are on their back: they wou'd be glad that something wou'd occur to divert for a spell, the public eye from them.

I will most promptly obey any directions which you may give me on this subject but trust it will meet your views for me to make the demand of Mr. Southard.

In a few days I will call, and look the Dept for your letters as directed by you and let you know the result of my search![7] Mr. Randolph has returned, and is one of the most cool & dignified men in the senate—I met him, when he asked me most kindly about Mrs J & yourself—when I presented you to him, he was much pleased, and asked me to express to you his thanks. The old Dominion will reelect him. I have no doubt[8]

Be pleased to present me to Mrs Jackson, & say to her that her friends here are very many, and express a confident hope of seeing her here before long!! I have the honor to be most truly your friend

Sam Houston

P S. Nothing will be done until I hear from you. Matters do not require expedition!

ALS, DLC (72). Published in Bassett, 6:486–87.

1. Presumably the account Houston related to AJ at the Hermitage on October 23.

2. Wallace's statement, November 30 (DLC-72), reported that Southard had said at the dinner: "*Mr. Monroe and not Genl. Jackson was entitled to the credit for the victory at New Orleans—That just before our troops were ordered to New Orleans Genl. Jackson left the army and was returning home when Mr. Monroe sent him a peremptory order to return to the defence of that place and That this with other energetic measures of Mr. Monroe was the salvation of New Orleans.*" For AJ's initial understanding of what Southard's comments were, see above, AJ to Houston, October 23. That letter was the one AJ intended for Houston to deliver to Southard.

3. Not found.

4. On January 5, 1827, AJ rejected Houston's plan and wrote directly to Southard.

5. *To Chandler Price, Chairman, Jacob Holgate, and Henry Horn, Secretaries . . . in Reply to Jonathan Roberts* (Philadelphia, 1826).

6. In response to a query concerning AJ's defense of New Orleans from Pope (1772–1838), a strong supporter of AJ and clerk of the Jefferson County, Kentucky, court, Adair (1757–1840), adjutant general of the Kentucky militia at New Orleans and former governor, praised AJ's defense of the city (*Louisville Public Advertiser*, October 28).

7. For AJ's directives, see above, AJ to Houston, October 23. Houston reported his findings to AJ on January [28], 1827, below.

8. Randolph lost in the January 1827 Senate race but won reelection to his old seat in the House in April.

To Samuel Houston

(Private)   Hermitage Decbr. 15th. 1826
Dr. Genl

The business of my little ward (Hutchings) drew me to Alabama shortly after you left me from whence I have Just returned—The Legislature of Alabama has chosen Mr John McKinley their Senator. James Jackson, Colo. N. Davis, Judge Clay, & Doctor [David] Moors names were before the people as candidates with Mr McKinley—finding Judge Clay the Strongest of the coalition, Jackson, Davis & Moore united upon Judge Clay against McKinley, and were defeated by three votes[1]—however it is said Judge Clay came forth publickly against the administration, but my friends it appears, had not as much confidence in his avowals, as they had in McK—you will therefore infer that Major McKinly has been elected by my political friends, and I hope he may realise their expectations— The major will be with you shortly, and you can soon Judge whether the confidence of the people is well founded or not—[Henry] Clay will endeavour to wield him to his views, but I cannot believe he will succeed.

As far as I could Judge from the voice of the people as I passed through Tennessee your popularity is daily increasing—but you will have to return early in the Spring and pass through the State.

We are now looking to the city for the President communication to Congress which will afford the type holders some employment, and develope to the Nation its political prosperity & situation—and give us a clear view of the panama Congress, as I see Mr Seargeant has Just *sailed before the meeting of Congress:* the necessity of this movement, must have been as urgent, as the cause of accepting the invitation to be represented there, a few days before the meeting of last Congress.

I am anxiously awaiting a letter from you, after your arival at the city, & having seen our friends of Fredrickburge Va—& presented my note to Mr Southard—I am determined to unmask such part of the Executive council, as has entered into the combination to slander & revile me; & I trust, in due time to effect it, and lay the perfiday, meaness, & wickedness, of Clay, naked before the american people—I have lately got an intimation of some of his secrete movements, which, If I can reach with posisitive & responsible proof, I will wield to his political, & perhaps, to his actual destruction[2]—he is certainly the bases, meanest, scoundrel, that ever disgraced the image of his god—nothing too mean or low for him to condescend to, *secretely* to carry his cowardly & base purpose of slander into effect; even the aged and virtuous female, is not free from his secrete combination of base slander—but *anough, you know me,* I will curb my feelings until it becomes proper to act, when retributive *Justice will vissit him & his panders heads.*

Since my return from Alabama I have recd a letter from my friend J[ohn] S[trode] Barber accompanied with his speech on Mr McDuffies proposed amendment to the constitution,[3] present him my respects & thanks for this letter & pamphlet, it has afforded me much satisfaction and the speech is fraught with much sound construction of our constitution, and real republican doctrine. when leisure occurs I will write him. present me to all my Tennessee friends & all members who inquire for me to Judge White & Branch of the senate—

When I wrote you last I made a request of you for Mr Donelson[4]—he has wrote you himself; if Mr Randolph has returned, and you should think it right, present him my compliments as an admirer of his independence & virtue, not as a flatterer, yr friend

Andrew Jackson

ALS, DLC (34). Published in Bassett, 3:324–25.

1. McKinley received 41 votes to Clay's 38. Jackson, Davis, and Moore (1784–1845), who had served as surgeon's mate at Huntsville during the Creek campaign, all voted for Clay.

2. AJ was probably referring to the disclosures above of "An Enquirer," [November].

3. Letter not found. Barbour (1790–1855; William and Mary 1808) represented Virginia in the U.S. House, 1823–33. His remarks supporting McDuffie's proposal were published as *Speech of Mr. J. S. Barbour, on the Proposition to Amend the Constitution of the United States, Respecting the Election of President and Vice President . . .* (Washington, 1826).

4. See above, AJ to Houston, November 22.

From Samuel Houston

Washington
18th Dec 1826

Dear Genl.

as I have leisure at this moment to state the reasons why I do not wish the letter enclosed published[1]—I have no doubt but the *minions* engaged will get themselves into some *ridiculous* scrape! They applied for a copy, and finding I wished one they declined taking one until I shoud get mine. My *eye* is on them, and I will not close it, while on the watch. I wish to hold back until they make some move, and then check them.[2]

I will wait anxiously until I hear from you relative to *Southards* case and do what you may *direct*! There is at this time trouble in the *Wigwam,* and the calmest course will be the best—It woud be possible at this moment to excite sympathy in behalf of the administration notwithstanding their corruptions—

Every thing is moving on in the best way possible to put down a most base, and corrupt coalition—It must & will fall—The Bourbons will fall!!!

I have no doubt but it is now the object of the administration and its minions to get you into a controversy with them and if not that to get insiduous fellows to address you, that they may have the letters published—or it may be that men (in the general state of local & national excitement) to subserve their individual interest & aspirations and to have it know[n], that they correspond with *you* regardless, of *you,* and the great cause, seek to bring you before the public in this way! But of all these matters you *[are better]* capable of judg*[ing than any other]* person can be!

In a fin*[al . . . I en]*close you a letter *[. . .]* wishes to write a *[. . .]* life.[3]

You will ple*[ase do me the]* honor of presentin*[g my kind]* Salutations to Mrs J*[ackson.]* W*[ith perfect Respect]* & *[Regard I am your friend*

Sam Houston]

AL fragment, DLC (75).

1. According to AJ's endorsement, Houston had enclosed a copy of Jackson's letter to John McLean (1785–1861), March 22, 1824 (*Jackson,* 5:379–80). In that letter, AJ recommended George Croghan for postmaster at New Orleans over Fulwar Skipwith, one of the leaders in the Louisiana legislature at the time of the Gulf invasion whom AJ accused of being willing to surrender to the British.

2. As Houston wrote AJ, Skipwith applied to McLean for a copy of the letter at the same time. In the *Richmond Enquirer,* June 26, 1827, Skipwith published a copy of AJ's letter, along with a defense of his conduct. Administration spokesmen subsequently referred to the comments on Skipwith as examples of AJ's personal vindictiveness, his tendency to military despotism, and his failure to comprehend civil institutions.

3. Probably Henry Lee to Houston, December 10, DLC (34), in which Lee discussed his plan to write a biography of AJ.

From John Henry Eaton

Washington City
Dec. 22—26

Dr Sir

Owing to the engagements of the Secty of State it has not been in my power until yesterday to confer with him on the subject, about which you desired me to see him.[1] It was the fourth time of application at his office, at each of which I found him absent with the President, or engaged with the British Minster. Yesterday I saw him, and the enquiry requested by you was made—

Mr. Clay very frankly, declared that the communication made to you, was altogether unfounded & untrue that he had seen Mr. Hammond whilst in his visit to Kentucky, he did not know of any meditated attack, such as your correspondent has alluded to; and certainly neither aided, or contributed, directly or indirectly in any thing such as is suggested. Asserted that much as any, he regretted that any thing should be attempted, by Editors of Papers in reference to other than public transactions, which were ever fair subjects for investigation—private matters never.[2] I entertain no question, from the frank manner after which Mr. Clay expressed himself, that the surmise of your correspondent, in reference to him is incorrect: that he has been in this affair, neither an agent, or actor, directly or indirectly concerned, for to this extent were the statements which were made to me, by him.

I stated the propriety of his giving me the statements offered in conversation in writing. He expressed a willingness to do so, & would prefer it if I would by letter to him afford a ground for replying—this I thought unnecessary & hence declined it, from a conviction that his disavowal made to me, & thus communicated, would be altogether satisfactory that he was without any agency in the vile course, for political purposes, which has been charged on Mr Hammond

J H Eaton

ALS draft, DLC (72).
　　1. Eaton was seeking information for AJ regarding Clay's possible involvement with Charles Hammond in threatening to discuss publicly the Jackson's marriage, as revealed above by "An Enquirer," [November].
　　2. Two days after Eaton's conference with Clay, Clay wrote Hammond regarding their meeting, whereupon Hammond addressed Eaton, denying, like Clay, any involvement in the matter (Clay to Hammond, December 23, *Clay Papers*, 5:1023–24).

To James Knox Polk

Hermitage Decbr. [2]4th. 1826

My Dear Sir
　　I feel greatly obliged to you for the information contained in your letter of the 4th. Inst,[1] which is Just recd. and I duly appreciate those feelings of friendship which dictated the communication.

I have no disguise with my friends, but am not in the habit of gratifying enemies—I have nothing in my political creed to keep secrete, it was formed in the old republican school, and is without change—I have no secretes, nor have I, nor do I wish to conceal my opinions on the powers of the general Goverment, and those reserved to the states respectfully, as it respects internal improvements, I never have witheld them when I spoke upon this subject—and I am sure I never will—and I am sure the general goverment has no right to make internal improvements within a state, without its consent first had & obtained.

I have seen the presidents message, glanced my eye over it, and find it quite a modest *thing* it shews clearly he has felt the lash for his former & winches under it—he still urges the wise policy of being represented at the national Congress in spanish america, without daining to give us his reason why at this late day it is so—he will *nominate now,* not appoint & commission, as was his languge last year, *happy change*[2]—but he accepted the invitation last year three days before the meeting of Congress, & our minister sails Just three days before its meeting, this year—dispatch, after such long delay, was necessary, particularly as Mr Seargent & Mr [William Beatty] Rochester had failed in their elections, and the sickly season had passed by.[3]

The election of Eaton has produced a political calm in our state, and am happy it is hailed abroad by the Republicans; I am sure at home its political benefits will be long felt.

It will afford me much pleasure to receive a line from you when leisure will permit, tho, this I am aware cannot often happen you must attend to your constituents—I saw your father on my rout to alabama, he was better, other friends all well   Judge [John] Haywood is buried to day.[4]

Mrs. Jackson Joins me in kind salutations to you & Mrs. Polk—with the request you will present us to Eaton, White, Houston & all the Tennessee delegation and other friends. yr friend

Andrew Jackson

ALS, DLC (11-0439). Published in *Polk Correspondence,* 1:63–65. Redated, based on date of Haywood's death.

1. See above.

2. In his annual message of December 5, 1826, Adams reported that he would "nominate" a successor for Richard C. Anderson, Jr., deceased, instead of sending a "commissioned" delegate to the Panama Congress as he had the previous year (*Register of Debates,* 19th Cong., 2nd sess., Appendix, pp. 1547–59; 19th Cong., 1st sess., Appendix, p. 3).

3. Rochester (1789–1838), a former congressman who had been appointed as secretary to the Panama Congress legation, lost the New York gubernatorial election in November. In the October Pennsylvania congressional election, John Sergeant, commissioner to the congress, had tied with the Jacksonian Henry Horn in a three-way contest. Sergeant subsequently won the congressional seat. Sergeant and Rochester departed for Panama on December 1.

4. Haywood (1762–1826), a judge of the Tennessee Supreme Court and one of the state's earliest historians, died on December 22.

To Henry Lee

Hermitage Decbr. 25th. 1826

Sir

Your letter of the 2nd. of octbr. last from Quebec with that of the 18th of Novbr. from Washington has been recd.: being absent on business to Alabama when they reached Nashville, will account to you for the delay in acknowledging their receipt.[1]

The historical facts detailed in yours of the 2nd of october are highly interesting. The name of [James] Wolf[2] must always live in the memory of every military patriot and every incident, therefore, of his life & death deserve attention. I tender you my hearty thanks for the gratifying detail which you have given me of his last moments.

Before the receipt of yours of the 18th of Novbr. I had seen announced in the news papers that you were about to write my Biography.[3] I will with great pleasure furnish you with any official public documents necessary to you for this purpose, that you cannot obtain from [Arsène Lacarrière] Latours history of the Southern Campaign[4]—the cause shewn by me on a rule of the U. States court at Neworleans, why a writ of attachment should not issue against me;[5] my memorial to the Senate of the United States on the subject of the report of its committee touching the measures of the Seminole War;[6] and the pamphlet written & laid on the tables of the members of Congress in 1819, titled, the Vindication of the President & his commanding Generals in the Commencement & Termination of the Seminole War by a citizen of Tennessee;[7] and the correspondence between the President, Secratary of State & myself on the subject of the affair with [José Maria] Calava (the copy of one of the most important communications from me to the Secratary of State you will find in the hand of Genl Houston)[8]—of this correspondence, all that you may not be able to lay your hands on in Washington, or obtain from my friend Major Eaton will be furnished on application—But further than this, notwithstanding the confidence which I repose in your pledge, I cannot speak of myself, or relate anecdotes of myself, which have not been recorded by others. Should I attempt this, the most secret recess, could not conceal my shame.

As to the praise bestowed upon the militia at the *Horse shoe,* & the complaint of Colo. [John] Williams, rumored to have been made, it will be sufficient to refer you to my communications to the Commandg. Genl [Thomas] Pinckney, & to the Sec. of war upon that Subject; also to Genl Houston who was an active agent in the affair, & got severely wounded there—From these sources you will at once discover upon what foundation rests this charge against me.[9]

It is true that I wrote hastily those letters to Mr Monroe to which you refer, & that I never calculated that they would be published[10]—the sacred confidence, however, which characterise them, served to increase the malignity of those who were anxious to destroy me, and the circumstance of incaution, & looseness, in the manner & substance, encouraged the hope, that their publication would effect all that was desired. But they have been mistaken, whether from a sentiment of disapprobation to the base manner by which I was thus brought before the Public, and from a conviction that the views submitted to Mr. Monroe were in the main right, or the contrary, rests with the people—When I take a view, now, of the differrence of duty operating on our citizens in a state of peace & war; the constitution declaring our militia the bulwark of our national defence, that in time of war the President is commander in chief, not only of the army and Navy of the U. States, but of the militia also, when *called into service,* and that he is charged with the national defence; I cannot see upon what constitutional grounds he can be refused the power of punishing all delinquents who fail to comply with the legal orders of the Goverment in the form & manner contemplated by the constitution and provided for by the Legislature in the rules and articles of war. It cannot be said that our goverment is constitutionally incompetant to its own defence and protection in a state of war, so long as these powers are admitted to be granted, & so long as in obedience thereto rules & articles for a state of war are declared to be in force, among which in the 56th. & 57th article I think it will be found written, that all who aid the enemy or who hold correspondence with him directly or indirectly; or who aid & comfort him in any way whatever, are made punishable with death by the sentence of a courtmartial. Now if there be no mistake about the powers referred to, & if there had been none in the public prints, when they charged the Hartford Convention with carrying on an illicit correspondence with the enemy, by its agents, with a combination to disobay the *calls* of the President for the Just quotas of militia thereby paralising the arm of the goverment and aiding & assisting the enemy by withdrawing themselves illegally, & in open violation of the *call* of the President from the ranks of their country, I ask if the conduct as charged against the members of the Hartford Convention, & the correspondence with the British agents (if true) did not bring them within the purview & meaning of the 56th & 57th rules & articles of war—if not then they are a dead letter & ought to be expunged. Surely it cannot be contended that when we are in a state of declared war & the president makes a legal call for the militia that he is not cloathed with the power thro the medium of the *law martial* to take cognizance of delinquents who fail to comply with the order—otherwise his power would be a mere letter, altho charged with the defence & preservation of the country, the force competant thereto, & authorised by law, might be witheld from him. These are my impressions of the powers of the Goverment when involved in war, and when all our energies must be brought into instant action, for its defence, preservation & safety—[11]

From these remarks your discriminating mind will easily collect to what extent my observations to Mr Monroe relative to the members of the Hartford convention went, and all that may be necessary to do Justice to the subject. I have not my confidential letters before me, & therefore forget the precise language used in them, but I have no hesitation in saying that if I had been placed in command in that section of country by the orders of the President, I should have at once tried the strength of the powers of the Goverment in a state of war—whether it was competent to wield its physical force in the defence of our country by punishing all concerned in combinations to aid the enemy & paralizing our own efforts. In this course if my Judgt. had been condemned, all good men & patriots would have at least commended the motives. Wishing you the Joys of the season I am very respectfully your mo. obdt. servt.

Andrew Jackson

P.S. I have not time to copy the above letter you will pardon interlineations & obliterations A. J.

Photocopy of ALS, NN (11-0442); LS draft, DLC (34). Published in Bassett, 3:327–29 (from LS draft).

 1. See Lee to AJ, October 2 and November 18. AJ arrived at Nashville from Alabama on December 6.

 2. Wolfe (1727–59), a British general, was killed in the battle on the Plains of Abraham near Quebec City.

 3. The Washington *United States' Telegraph,* November 20, carried one of the earliest announcements.

 4. Latour (c1775–1839), an engineer with AJ's troops at New Orleans, published a *Historical Memoir of the War in West Florida and Louisiana in 1814–15* (Philadelphia, 1816).

 5. For AJ's address to the U. S. District Court, Louisiana, [March 27, 1815], see *Jackson,* 3:321–36.

 6. Memorial to the U. S. Senate re Conduct during the Florida Invasion, [1819–20], *Annals of Congress,* 15th Cong., 2nd Sess., Appendix, pp. 1308–2328.

 7. Pseudonym for John Overton.

 8. Callava was governor of West Florida, 1819–21, and was the Spanish officer responsible for the transfer of the territory to the United States in 1821. Documents relating to the Callava affair can be found in *Jackson,* 4:36–105, *passim.* The document in Houston's possession was probably AJ to Adams, January 22, 1822, transmitted to Houston on October 23.

 9. Williams (1778–1837), subsequently among AJ's political enemies, commanded the 39th Infantry at the battle. Pinckney (1750–1828) commanded the Southern District. For the communications, see AJ to Pinckney, March 28 (*Jackson,* 3:52–54), and April 5, 1814, and AJ to John Armstrong, April 2, 1814.

 10. AJ to Monroe, October 23, November 12, 1816, January 6, March 18, 1817, (*Jackson,* 4:68–71, 73–75, 80–82, 102–103).

 11. AJ was referring to his letter of January 6, 1817, in which he wrote that, had he been in command during the meeting of the Hartford Convention, he would have punished its principal leaders (*Jackson,* 4:81). Critics had questioned the authority for such action (AJ having cited Section 2 of the act of April 10, 1806). In his letter above to Lee, AJ shifted the authority for his claim to Articles 56 and 57 of the first section of the act (2 *U.S. Statutes at Large,* 366, 371).

1827

To William Moore

Hermitage Janry 4th 1827

Dear Colo.

Your letter of the 8th ult.[1] did not reach me until last saturday, when it was handed me in Nashville; this will account for the delay in answering it.

I highly approve the caution you used with Mr Kendal, & the referrence you made to Major [Thomas Patrick] Moore & Major Eaton.

I have yielded to Major Eaton all benefit from my public papers, when he undertook to finish the history of my life begun by my aid de camp Major [John] Reid[2]—since there would be an impropriety in my yielding my consent to a Byography being written of me by any one else, except on the assent of Major Eaton all that I could do would be to permit a copy to be taken of my public document in my hands. Mr Kendal corresponding with Majors Moor & Eaton can obtain every information, & every public document necessary for such a work.

I have no doubt but such a work from the pen of Mr Kendal would be read & sought for with avidity by the Kentuckians & would produce a good effect—*he is an able writer.*[3]

I would like to hear whether he is progressing with the work, if he has wrote you, I would like to be informed—many of his Books could be sold in Tennessee, Alabama, Mississippi and Louisiana. I never doubted for a moment the result of the dispute between Major Moor and [Samuel] Oglesbay—I knew Major Moor had talents & energy, and he would prostrate all such corrupt panders of power, *hirelings* to slander & abuse virtuous men that will not be wielded to the corrupt views of Henry Clay[4]— I was gratified to find that all my anticipations in this office was realised in the result—and sooner or later all such corrupt panders to power as Oglesbay will receive the same meritted downfall—Moors energy & talents, will cause him always to triumph over vicious men.

Letters Just recd from the East says all things are going on well in Newyork Newjersy, Pensylvania, Maryland, & Virginia. Those from the north are equally sanguine; Kentucky & Ohio will not seperate from Virginia & Pensylvania, as the politicians of those states believe; time will prove the correctness of this belief.

Present me respectfully to your Lady[5] & believe me your friend

Andrew Jackson

Photocopy of ALS, T (11–0460). Moore (1786–1871), a colonel with the Tennessee militia, represented Lincoln County in the Tennessee legislature, 1825–29, and had served on the committee honoring AJ in Fayetteville in July 1826.

1. Not found.

2. Reid (1784–1816), AJ's aide in the Creek campaign and at New Orleans, had begun the *Life of Andrew Jackson,* which Eaton completed and first published in 1817. Eaton revised and reissued the work during the campaign of 1828.

3. Between November 7, 1827, and February 13, 1828, Kendall published serially a biographical sketch of AJ based largely on the Reid-Eaton work in his Frankfort *Argus of Western America*; in 1842, he commenced a second serial biography of AJ which he published in seven installments but never completed.

4. The Ogilsby-Thomas P. Moore dispute involved AJ's charge of cowardice against the Kentucky troops at New Orleans. In 1826, Ogilsby, a former Kentucky legislator from Shelby County, had publicly denounced John Adair for expressing a favorable opinion of AJ, whereupon Thomas P. Moore, under the pseudonym "Kentucky" had defended AJ's dealings with the Kentucky militia and excoriated Ogilsby as a political opportunist and tool of Adams and Clay (Frankfort *Argus of Western America,* November 1, 1826). Ogilsby responded, challenging Moore to a duel, but the two men never agreed on a meeting and, indeed, disagreed over who had initiated the challenge—Ogilsby insisting that Moore's article contained a challenge, which Moore denied.

5. Elizabeth Lawson Moore (1796–1854).

By the fall of 1826, administration backers, embellishing the "military chieftain" theme with episodes to illustrate Jackson's rash and violent behavior, had made his temperament an issue in the presidential campaign. One of the earliest stories circulated was that in 1819, when Jackson heard that the Senate committee chaired by Abner Lacock of Pennsylvania had adopted its report critical of his conduct in the Seminole campaign, Jackson, then in Baltimore, rushed back to Washington at night and appeared at the Capitol the next morning threatening "to cut off the ears" of Virginia Senator John Wayles Eppes (1773–1823; Hampden Sydney 1786) for casting the deciding vote on the report. According to the account, Commodore Stephen Decatur (1779–1820), either by threats or persuasion, prevented Jackson from carrying out his intentions (Milledgeville Georgia Statesman, October 31, 1826; Philadelphia Democratic Press, October 17; Jackson, 4: 275–76). In the letter below, Jackson recounted the event for George Wilson, editor of the Nashville Gazette.

To George Wilson

HERMITAGE, January 4th, 1827.

DEAR SIR:

I have just received your note of this day,[1] and give you the information required. I was not in Congress Hall during the discussion of the Seminole question. I visited no one except the President and Secretary of War—my official duty required that I should report myself to them. After the debate in the House of Representatives terminated, and before I left the city for New York, I visited the House of Representatives, and by motion a seat was prepared for me, which I occupied for about an hour.[2] After my return from New York I was not in the walls of either House of Congress, and not at all in the Senate.

I visited the President by special invitation and the Secretary of War in his office, both on business. But I dined with no one until the debate ended, and then only with the President. I believe this was after Congress adjourned.[3] As I was informed, there was no debate upon the report of the committee in the Senate, and, as you observed, there could be none unless on the motion to print, and this, if any, would foreclose any member from speaking to the merits.

I received intelligence of the report being made whilst I was in Baltimore, on my return, and on the day I dined with the citizens. At nine o'clock P.M., I rose from the table by permission of the company, took the stage and drove to the city before day. On the morning of the 2d of March I got the report, and the strictures on it appeared on the evening of the 3d.[4] On the 4th Congress was constitutionally dead. I never heard Mr. Eppes speak in public in my life. I never saw him to know him. I had no acquaintance with him. I went to the city to demand justice, not to beg favors; therefore, I visited no member of Congress, and no one but the Secretary of War and the President, to whom I was by the regulations bound to report; and after I had reported to them, then on special invitation and business. Yours, respectfully,

ANDREW JACKSON

Printed, Parton, 2:571 (11-0463)

1. Not found.

2. Debate in the House on the Seminole War lasted from January 12 to February 8, 1819, and AJ left Washington on February 11. The printed journal of the House did not record any motion regarding a seat for AJ on February 9 or 10.

3. AJ's visits were not restricted to Monroe and Secretary of War Calhoun. He met with John Quincy Adams on February 3, attended a "drawing room" hosted by Monroe the same evening, and dined with John Quincy and Louisa Catherine Adams on March 4, the day after after Congress adjourned (*Memoirs of John Quincy Adams,* 4:239–43, 282).

4. AJ's "Strictures on Mr. Lacock's Report on the Seminole War" was dated March 5, 1819, instead of March 3.

To *Samuel Houston*

Hermitage, Jany 5 1827. 10 oclock P.M.

Dr. Colo.

Your letter of Decbr 13th ult[1] is just handed me by Colo. McGregger, and I hasten to answer it by tomorrows mail.

The plan you propose of communicating with the Sec of the Navy I cannot consent to[2]—was he not a branch of the Executive goverment, I should leave him to my friends—but as he occupies an exalted Station he might answer you, that he could not reply to any individual but myself, and he might make a charge of a combination, formed against him by members of Congress, who could not demand of him a reply; that the subject solely appurtained to my military character—*to my call,* he can have no excuse, *he must reply*—I have therefore inclosed a note to him,[3] in its close, I inform him I have enclosed it to you with a request that you hand it, obtain his answer and forward it to me. you will find my note is calm & decorous, to which I have no doubt he will unhesitatingly reply. When he does, I wish you to keep a duplicate, least the original may be purloined on the way, and let Major Eaton see it—If the original does not reach me, I will request you to forward the duplicate.

I inclose Doctor Wallace letter to you having taking a certified copy of it,[4] and your note, stating you have shewn the statement of Doctor Wallace to Mr. [Fayette] Johnston,[5] who was present, and says it is correct.

I have recd. yours, inclosed in the report of the Sec of the Treasury, with a copy of my letter to Mr. McClain P. M. Genl. recommending Colo. Chroghn.[6] I only wanted this letter to have it by me, not for publication—I find it is right in these evil days, to be prepared to repel wicked slander, when coming from sources worthy of notice.

I thank you for convaying the respects of Mr Randolph, present him with my congratulations on his good health. I wish him a continuance of it.

Mrs. J. requests to be presented to you kindly with a request that you have the goodness to present her & me to Mrs Watson & the family—present me to all the Tennessee delegation & all other friends & receive my salutations. yrs

Andrew Jackson

P.S. I write in great haste, but take time to remark, that I have no doubt in your friendship, and that the view taken of the subject as it regards Mr. Sec. Southard, is your deliberate view of the propriety of the course you recommend. you know you have my confidence but upon a full view of this subject you will agree with me, that I am the only person who have a right to make [the request]—as a military man I am bound to make it, it is due to my fame & to my country, it is due to posterity—I am sure I will reach the source, and if I should find I have been reposing confidence in a hypocritical villain, it is due to my country to expose & unmask him—to do this, it is only necessary to publish to the world the whole orders and communications I recd. from the Dept of War during the late war. These are my reasons for adopting the course I have chosen. you will please deliver the letter & inclose me his reply. I send it open that you may read, shew it to Eaton, seal & deliver it. A. J.

ALS, DLC (72). Published in Bassett, 6:487–88.
1. See above.
2. See above, Houston to AJ, December 13.
3. See below.
4. See John H. Wallace to Houston, November 30, 1826.
5. Not found. Johnston was a Fredericksburg merchant and sometime councilman.
6. Not found.

To Samuel Lewis Southard

Hermitage Janry. 5th. 1827.

Sir

Being informed through a friend that at the table of Mr Jno. S. Welford of Fredericksburgh Virginia, the following conversation took place between you & Doctor J. H. Wallace,[1] towit, you asked Doctor Wallace upon what ground he supported the election of Genl Jackson to the presidency. with other reasons, the Doctor mentioned my services during the late war, to which you replied, *"that Mr Monroe and not Genl Jackson was entitled to the credit for the victory at Neworleans—that Just before our troops were ordered to Neworleans Genl Jackson left the army and was returning home when Mr. Monroe sent him a preremtory order to return to the defence of that place, and that this, with other energetic measures of Mr Monroe was the salvation of Neworleans.["]* Colo. Gray of that place who was present, asked *"where could that order be found* remarking—*that it would be of <service> importance"* Mr Southard said—*he did not know, but he had been informed such order was Issued and did exist.*

I have thought it my duty, not less to my own character, than to the high and responsible situation which you occupy, to address you stating the facts precisely as they have been communicated to me—A charge of so serious a nature as that implied in your declarations, as Stated, to Doctor Wallace, it cannot be expected of me to pass, without some notice, especially, as it seems to be adopted as true by an executive branch of our goverment—and as an act of Justice you cannot be surprised when I demand of you the name of your informer, or the source thro which you have felt yourself warrented in making this statement; which I am compelled from principles of truth, to pronounce false and unfounded, and that nothing during my military command ever happened like it—nor can it be said with truth, that I ever left my army, or ever slept one night beyond the limits of my camp, so long as I had one—or that I ever was on the sick report, or asked for leave of absence during the whole time I held a military command

I have enclosed this letter to my friend Genl Houston, with the request that he present it to you, and enclose your reply—which I have no doubt, you will promptly make[2] I have the honor to be very respectfully yr mo. obdt. Servt.

Andrew Jackson

ALS, ALS copy, and Copy, DLC (34, 72). Published in Bassett, 3:329–30.
    1. Houston had been AJ's informant. See above, AJ to Houston, October 23, 1826.
    2. See Southard to AJ, February 9, below.

From [Samuel Houston]

Washington
5th Jany 1827.

Dear General,

Owing to the peculiar situation of our Post office arrangements I have not ventured to write when I had matter to communicate, and when it wou'd have given me sincere pleasure to have done so. A private opportunity now presenting its self—will be embraced—promptly![1]

Two, kind favors have come to hand from you, one before you visited Ala' and one since your return! For each and both of them I thank you[2]— Since the receipt of the last I have not seen Mr Randolph, but will on to day, when it will be *fit* to execute your suggestions. When I have seen him he has always been very polite, and enquiring for you with much interest—I presented you to him, which appeared to give him much pleasure— The business part of your letters shall be attended to, with pleasure so soon, as his election is over—which is daily expected—

Mr R—— throughout the session has been truly dignified, and silent, and I have heard his friends say, that he will rest his claims to a reelection on his last winters acts—and says he will stand, or fall by them—which by the by, I deem manly & honorable. He has surely never been so much himself, as he is this session, he is amiable, kind, and courteous to all he meets with. Times have been squally at Richmond, but his friends here say he will be elected easily—and it will be over in a few days, from this time! The *powers that be here,* are greatly busied in trying to defeat his election, which will not help their cause in Virginia.[3]

Of matters generally at this place I have written to my friend Dr [John] Shelby, requesting him to let you see my *data* so far as they are assumed by me![4] Mr McKinly has arrived, and your friends here deem him—a good, and *true* man for the country! So far as I can judge, I woud say so too. Matters at this time here are surely favorable to a change in the administration, and as you will learn from my letter to Dr S—— they are so elswhere.

The baseness, and corruption of the present incumbents of power, woud displace men of more talent than what they possess. I have heard of some *schemes of Clay in the west,* and have no doubt if he shoud by his agent Mr Hammond, prossecute them, but what he will most tim[or]ously "meet retributive justice" and first from the hands, of an indignant and manly community!!! I have seen letters from Ohio, & Ky on *this* subject, and it was not until a week ago, that I knew of his Hellish designs; thro his base *pandors,* to be effected.[5]

You will see that they dare not attempt or rather, execute; what their *foul* souls have conceived—Tho' the game *is* desperate—Like the wounded serpent; when they find that, their adversary, is beyond the reach of their fangs, they will be compelld, in the anguish of disappointment to strike themselves; and of *their own* poison—perish!

You loose no friends—but gain daily! It will be so until the great day of deliverance to our country arrives—Dr. [John] Floyd of Va. is a devoted friend of yours, and indeed, *almost all* the Crawford men. Govrs. Branch, & [Gabriel] Holmes of N. Carolina with many others direct me to present their warmest regards to you![6]

The subject of a Horse *trainer* that Captain Donelson wishes to obtain I have in part attended to—tho have not Yet succeeded in procuring one—when I can, it shall be done! To day I send papers, on the subject of purchasing a fine Horse for a company of which I am one, to L[eonard] P[ope] Cheatham esq of Nashville[7]—shoud you be in Nashville soon I wou'd like you to see them—and join the company

AL fragment, DLC (34). Published in Bassett, 3:330–31 (extract).

1. Because of their suspicions that John P. Erwin was plundering their mail, AJ and his supporters frequently sent letters under cover to third parties whose mail was, they expected, less likely to be opened, directed their correspondence through post offices other than Nashville, used friends to deliver communications in person, and sometimes even hid letters in printed government documents. Houston probably enclosed the letter above in his communication to John Shelby (1786–1859), a Nashville doctor, and sent it by Thomas Washington.

2. Houston was referring to AJ's letters, above, of November 22 and December 15, 1826.

3. On January 13, the Virginia legislature elected Governor John Tyler (1790–1862, William and Mary 1807) to the Senate in Randolph's place.

4. Letter not found.

5. Houston was probably referring to Hammond's pledge to publish material about the Jacksons' marriage.

6. Floyd (1783–1837) and Holmes (1769–1829) were both in the House of Representatives; Branch, in the Senate.

7. Cheatham (c1796–1863, Cumberland College 1815) was a Nashville lawyer.

To *Samuel Houston*

Hermitage January 8th. 1827

Dear Genl

I wrote you on the 5th. instant,[1] advising you on that evening, by the hand of Colo McGreggor at 10. P. M. I had received yours enclosing me Doctor Wallace statement relative to the declarations of Mr Sec. Southard with regard to my self[2]—I sent my reply by the mail of the 6th. which I hope has reached you

I wrote in haste, having to send it to Nashville the next morning, and had not time, to take notice of your generous proposal, to make the call upon Mr Southard yourself, in your own name. whilst I feel weight of gratitude which your generous proposal has elicited, propriety compelled me not to accept it. I am the only one whose charecter by the charges made have been attacked. I only positively can be said to know the falsity of the charge made, and am the only one entitled to make a demand of Mr Southard of the name of his informer and if you were to make the call in your name, the reply would be, you could not be interested to know; here the matter must end, for if you went farther it might subject you to the charge of officiousness and a combination of *military chieftains,* to Bully the administration—I am charged with the heinous crime of *desertion*—I am the person directly injured, and I have a right to make the enquiry and demand a categorical answer. As this charge has been made by one of the Departments of the government, with a *seeming* knowledge that it is founded upon a written order it is due to my charecter, due to my country & to my future fame, that it should be promptly met by me and its falsity exposed—and I view it a happy circumstance, that I am still living to meet this wicked & unfounded charge intended to Destroy my fame, by a combination of men some of whom I fear, I have been reposing confidence in, whilst my friendship & confidence have been repaid by hypocrisy & deception—you have seen it *hinted* that there is more of my confidential correspondence—*and these are to see the light let them come,* I fear nothing from all the light that can be given to all & every confidential letter written to Mr Madison & Mr Monroe, nor shall these hints prevent me from probing to the quik the source from which Mr Southard has got his false sugestion ¿what must my countrymen think of me if I would be silent under such an imputation; the answer is plain that I am *mean,* & *cowardly,* & *indeed* still there must be some truth in the charge or I would investigate it—Investigate it must & shall be—My charecter is all I have, for all the d[an]gers & privation I have sufferred, I *will protect it.*

I am sorry I requested you to deliver the letter sealed; If not handed before you receive this, handed it open, as I wish his answer to be seen by you & Eaton, and his answer will be returned to you open; and at least, he will know, you are in possession of the subject matter it contains.

I enclose you a furlow of an old soldier George Wilson[3] who says he has never received his pay—he was disable when in service by a gun shot wound thro the arm, that has contracted his f[in]gers so that he has lost the use of them, will you attend to his claims there may be some evidence in the department that may entitle him to a pension—If he has not received his pay, the rolls of the Department will shew it—write me the result of your inquiry, & I will make it known to him.

I will be happy to hear from you often, & also to receive the promised letter from Major Lee.[4]

Mrs J. Joins me in best wishes for your happiness. your friend

Andrew Jackson

P.S. I have recd. a letter from Colo. R. Butler[5] with his congratulations upon your complete triumph over your enemies. A. J.

ALS, DLC (72). Published in *Cincinnati Commercial,* January 8, 1880 (extract).
1. See above.
2. See also above.
3. Wilson, from Knoxville, has not been further identified.
4. Letter not identified.
5. Not found.

From Edward George Washington Butler

Cincinnati,
January 11. 1827.

My Dear General,

After the receipt of your letter of the 22nd ultimo,[1] I requested Mr. [Moses] Dawson,[2] Editor of the "Cincinnati Advertizer," to procure for me, if possible, the Gazette containing the remarks to which you allude,[3] and the number of his paper containing "Jefferson's" reply thereto.[4] Some days after my request, Mr. Dawson sent me his country paper of the 1st. of November, containing a piece, signed "Jefferson," in reply to an attack of Hammond's on Colonel Benton,[5] touching his conduct towards you, with the remark that the number of the Gazette desired was not to be found, and that he could discover on his files no other communication from "Jefferson," in reference to Hammond's threatened attack.

I saw the exceptionable remarks in the Gazette, at the time they appeared, and, altho' they referred particularly to your letter to a gentleman in Kentucky, they were sufficiently rude and indelicate towards Mrs. Jackson[6] to have justified the punishment which he would have received, but for the remonstrances of your most estimable friend, Colonel [William] Piatt. I am now convinced that the Colonel advised the prudent and proper course, as he assured me, on learning your wishes, which I communicated to him *alone* that Hammond and his instigators are deterred from the promised publication;[7] and the good Colonel begged me to entreat you, by the friendship which he cherishes for you, and by the solicitude which he feels for the welfare of his country, to allow no consideration to induce you to notice any thing which may flow from the *Sources* or *Tributaries* of corruption. To this, my Dearest General, allow me to add my humble—my affectionate entreaties? The character of my Dear Mrs. Jackson has ever been above the suspicion of friends and honest men, and if the baseness of desperate and unprincipled wretches make it necessary at this late period of her long, pious, and exemplary life, to vindicate the actions of its earliest period, and to blast, by contemporaneous evidence, their villainous assailants, let the painful, yet proud task, be assigned, as I have reason to believe it is, to the Historian.

I communicated to my kind mother[8] the purport of my letter to you of the 13th ultimo[9] and in her last letter, she expressed her mortifi*[cation and]* regret at having done anything *[that]* could compromit you with an admin*[istration]* for which she has no respect, & *[she was]* solicitous lest I should ha*[ve given]* you the impression that *[Genl. W.]* had been *influenced* by *[the]* applications.

I believe I only gave it as a matter of opinion, that such applications had been made, and I am sure that you, or myself, would be the last to believe that Genl. W. had been improperly influenced by them.

I have been actually *required* to make this explanation, as my good mother makes it a point of duty to defend the General to the last ditch. She desires in her letters, which we receive twice a week to be most kindly remembered at the Hermitage. Our dear little boy[10] is improving in size & beauty beyond conception, & his mother often speaks of the pleasure it will afford her to present him to Mrs. J. & yourself, to whom she joins me in assurances of the most affectionate regard. Mrs. Gaines desires her kind regards, & we all beg to be presented to Mr. & Mrs. A. J. Donelson.

E. G. W. Butler

ALS, DLC (72). Published in *Cincinnati Commercial,* January 8, 1880 (extract).
    1. See AJ to Butler, December 22, 1826.
    2. (1768–1844).
    3. Jackson was probably referring to "Courtesy Requited," an article discussing Rachel Jackson, which had appeared in the *Liberty Hall and Cincinnati Gazette,* November 14, 1826.
    4. "Jefferson" has not been found.
    5. In the *Cincinnati Gazette* of October 10, 1826, Hammond had pointed out that in 1824 Benton had maintained that the House of Representatives was without question a safe and secure place to determine the presidential election. After reconciling with AJ, however, Benton argued that a presidential election in the House offered too many opportunities for intrigue and corruption. The November 1 issue of the *Cincinnati Advertiser* has not been found.
    6. See above, AJ to [Thomas Patrick Moore], July 31, 1826. In an editrial discussing AJ's reasons for not visiting Kentucky as disclosed in his letter to Moore, Hammond added: "I did speak, in the public reading room at Steubenville quite freely and plainly of both

Gen. Jackson, and the woman who he and others call '*Mrs. Jackson.*' . . . It is said . . . that I *traduced* the General and *abused* the woman. I spoke truths of both—truths which rest upon legislative acts, and judicial records, and which are of vital importance, in illustrating the true character of Gen. Jackson. These truths are now but little known. They are, in my judgment, deeply interesting to the public, and ought not to remain in almost total oblivion. At a proper time I shall take care to make them fully known, in a form that will admit of no question" (*Liberty Hall and Cincinnati Gazette,* November 14, 1826).

7. Piatt (d. 1834), a veteran of the Battle of New Orleans and living in Cincinnati at this time, was a Jackson elector in 1824 and 1828. It is not known how or by whom Hammond was "deterred."

8. His wife's mother, Eleanor Parke Custis Lewis.

9. Not found.

10. Edward George Washington Butler, Jr. (1826–27).

From Samuel Houston

Washington
13th Jany 1827

Dear General

Not long since I was in conversation with a Gentleman, when he stated to me that he had in his possession an original letter from Mr Monroe, to the Secy of War, dated Sept 1819, and went on to State the contents of the same, but did not, as well as I recollect, state to me by what means it came to him.[1] The envelope I recollect he stated was lost before it was put in his hands—I made him pledge himself, that he wou'd send me a copy, on his return home; which is some distance from this place. He has comply'd, and you will find the Copy herewith inclosed. The Original, he has pledged himself to place in *your own* hands, or to furnish it to me, for *that* purpose. Comments from me, on the subject of this letter wou'd be ridiculous, when offerd to *you,* who felt, and acted on that occasion. But I felt it to be my sacred duty, to obtain for you a Knowledge of the facts: so far as it has been in my power—No part of the letter was *Italicised,* but I will mark in *that way* such sentences, as struck me with *peculiar* force.

You may rest assured from the nature of this affair, that it will be kept profoundly secrete. The circumstances under which it came to me; are such as will not warrant the use of in any other way, than at present to advertise you of the fact; when the original is presented to you; you will then be enabled to pursue the course dictated by the fitness of the circumstances; and the relation, which you bear, to the individuals; concerned; but above all; to the *community* in which you are placed. For I do regard *you* as occupying a station; in the Republic at this moment, of the last— yes! vital importance to its *happy existence*; to say the least of it. Your virtues, your qualifications; and your distinguished services to the country; have rendered you the rallying point, of the friends of principle throughout the Union; and with you these friends must either *triumph, or fall*; and in *that fall,* (tho' it may be remote) certain ruin, is portended to our institutions—The Republicans ask nothing in return; but the pleasure, and joy, of seeing, the destinies of this country wrested from the hands of a corrupt Dynasty, and guided by an enlightened Patriot, who will regard the principles of our Goverment; and administer its laws agreeably to the constitution!

Your friends here are confident, & your enemies are decreasing in number! *Some* are desperate—I need not say *who*—the passing events will advertise you, as you see them in the news Papers!

Before this letter reaches you; you will have seen, an account of a *dinner* given here on the *"8th of Jany"*—The account given in the "Telegraph" is correct—but you can not conceive the happy effect of our friend Judge Whites *speech & toast* on that occasion[2]—It was beyond all doubt the happiest effort of kind, that I have ever witnessed—Its effect too, will be happy in the extreme, elsewhere.

You will perceive that in all parts of the country, it was a Day of joy, & rejoicing—It will increase every year, in a ratio not hitherto Known in the country—New York, has been where she ought to be, on the occasion;[3] and I have no doubt, but she will be at her *Post* on the P—— election!

As I know that you require of your friends at all times; to approach you as friends; and speak to you as men, in *candour,* and confidence: and as you will appreciate my *motives,* however ridiculous you may esteem my expressions; I will state to you the apprehensions of some who are really your friends, but who *do not Know You!* They are fearful, that you will let the administration; or their hireling miscreants, provoke you to some course; which; may eventually *turnout* to their advantage! and, in part this fear is induced; by the by, a Knowledge of the efforts, made by them to prostrate your friends; and thereby wound you; not only in your own prospects, but in your feelings; Your Known devotion to your friends, and to the countrys friends; has increased their hopes, of thereby prompting you to take the *arena,* and let yourself down to *their level!*

Your friends are known, they will be sustained; and your known confidence in them, will be the most efficient aid; which they can receive. By your maintaining the station which you have so justly gained & rightfully sustained—their efforts either of personal detraction, or political defamation, must recoil upon their authors, and leave you in the full possession of self approbation; and a nation's confidence. The views which I took in my letter to my friend Dr Shelby; I have no reason to disclaim;[4] from the late developements of the several *states* named in my letter—but on the contrary I am more, and more confirmed in my belief—The Message of Gov. Clinton, is out right against the administration,[5] and of Mr [Martin] Van Buren's opposition to it; I have no doubt.[6] Mr V. B—— will support you in all good faith. I have not spoken to him only in the way of politeness since we met, but your friends who Know him best are satisfied as to his course, and pleased with it. Virginia is right, and there is no doubt, but Mr Randolph was elected, to day. Genl Floyd of Virginia is among your most devoted friends; and is a *true man*—he goes the whole amount of his power—nor is it small. I Know of no man, more devoted to your success than he is.

The committee has not yet reported, in the V. Presidents case, nor do I suppose it will in less than ten days, owing to the many witnesses summoned to give evidence in the case[7]—I am satisfied tho I have not heard a word directly (nor have ever heard any member of the committee speak on the subject) that the V. President will be honorably acquited!

It has not been in my power, to obtain the Horse Keeper, which Capt. D wishes got, but I will not cease trying. To Mr R. I have not spoken about the *filly*, but so soon the election is over I will do so!

Be pleased to express in the most respectful terms, to Mrs Jackson my sincere wishes; for her health & happiness. To Capt D—— and lady & to yours son's please to present me kindly. With sincere wishes for your health; and enjoyment of many happy years. I am most respectfully & truly your friend

Sam Houston

P.S. your letter to major Lee, I rec'd and sent the same day to him.[8] H.

ALS, DLC (72). Published in Bassett, 6:489–91. John McKee of Alabama franked Houston's letter.

1. Henry Lee provided Houston with the letter from James Monroe to John C. Calhoun, September 9, 1818 (DLC-71). In the letter, Monroe directed Calhoun to get a statement from Jackson of his understanding of the orders under which he seized St. Marks and Pensacola in the spring of that year, since "our view, of his powers, is decidedly different" from his. It is not known how or when Lee got the letter.

2. In his speech, White lauded AJ's leadership both before and during the Battle of New Orleans: "He may well be said to have created, as well as concentrated, his army, at the time and place most proper. He himself supplied the implements of war which his government had not placed within his reach" (*United States' Telegraph*, January 11). White's toast was to "*The People of the United States*—In their unbiased decision, all may safely confide."

3. The January 8 *United States' Telegraph* reported that in New York City there would be "a military parade—several private dinner parties, a ball—and the Theaters will be embellished, and patriotic pieces performed."

4. Not found.

5. In his annual address to the New York legislature, DeWitt Clinton lamented that "party spirit has entered the recesses of retirement, violated the sanctity of female character, invaded the tranquility of private life, and visited with severe inflictions the peace of families . . . The cause of the alarming and portentous evil," he continued, "must be found, in great measure, in the incompetence and injudicious provisions relative to the office of chief magistrate of the Union" (*Daily Albany Argus,* January 1, 1827).

6. Van Buren (1782–1862) was senator from New York, 1821–28.

7. The House was investigating Calhoun's role in the Rip Raps Shoal scandal.

8. Probably AJ to Henry Lee, December 25, 1826, above.

From Hugh Lawson White

Washington January 17th. 1827.

Dear Sir,

On the 8th. Instant in this city some of those disposed to commemorate it, had a dinner, at which I was present, and in answer to a toast made some observations which you will have seen[1]—It was my wish to glance rapidly at some of the leading events of the last war, without saying aught in your favor which truth did not justify, and without in malice alluding to the acts of the Administration—I am this moment informed President Monroe feels himself not only injured but offended by what I said—and is preparing materials to shew, my *statements untrue*—Having said what I *then believed* and yet do *believe* was strictly true, in manner, and form, I shall certainly not change one Syllable, until convinced 'tis wrong—I ask the favor of you to run your eye over it, and if in any thing, I have done the Administration of that day, injustice, to point out in what that error consists.[2]

No matter by whom attacked, provided the man is respectable, I shall by all fair means sustain my statement without caring to whom it is offensive. With the highest respect I am, your Most Obt. Servt.

Hu L White

ALS, DLC (34). Published in Bassett, 3:331.
  1. White's comments had been published in the *United States' Telegraph*, January 11.
  2. For Jackson's response, see AJ to White, February 7.

From John Caldwell Calhoun

Washington
24th Jany 1827

My dear Sir,

I duly received Your letter of the 18th July last,[1] and, which I would have answered long since, had any event worthy of being communicated occurred. I cannot, however, to permit the opportunity, which the return of Genl. Coffee offers to pass without availing myself of it to renew our correspondence.[2]

He will make known the state of things here fully and accurately, which will supercede the necessity of details on my part; but I cannot but congratulate you and the country at the certain termination of the present corru[p]t state on the 4th. March 1829. I never did doubt its overthrow from the beginning, because I firmly relied on the good sense and virtue of the people. This great foundation of our whole system has at all times, and under all circumstances been the basis of my hopes and actions. It has never yet failed me, and, I feel assured, will not in this instance. Every indication is in our favour, or rather I should say in favor of the country's cause. The whole South is safe, with a large majority of the midle states, and even in New England strong symptoms of discontent and division now appear, which must daily increase. If events should continue to march on in the present direction, and I can see nothing to arrest them, the triumph of principle will be one of the most signal, that ever was achieved; and you will have the proud satisfaction of having restored in your name the great principles of popular rights, which have been trampled down by the coalition.

As to my self, it is my pride, that I have been the object of unceasing attack by the corrupt occupants of power. From the begining, I saw the real character of the coalition, and the means, which it would adopt to perpetuate its power, among which was, if possible, my distruction; but I determined to brave any danger on the side of liberty, and to sustain the whole weight of their attack, let the consequence be what it might to me. Finding all other attempts fail, a conspiracy the most base, and with the most profligate instrument, a man guilty of forgery, swindling and perjury, was artfully got up to blast my private reputation.[3] I saw the assassin's aim, and immediately appealed to the House, where alone, I could defend myself. A packed Committee was appointed, which has been sitting for three weeks, collecting irrelevant testimony, and hearing the testimony of a perjured wretch in order to bury the whole in an incongruous mass of suspicion, for the purpose of breaking the force of publick indignation. But it shall not avail them. Having through my whole life been governed by disinterested and patriotick feelings, I shall not permit my character to be stabed by conspirators, who would immolate me and my name, simply because I will not bow to power.

Make my best respects to Mrs. Jackson, and believe me to be with sentiment of great respect and esteem Yours &c

J. C. Calhoun

ALS, DLC (34). Published in Bassett, 3:332.

1. See above, AJ to Calhoun, [July 18, 1826].

2. Coffee had been in Washington to brief the government on the recent Choctaw and Chickasaw negotiations.

3. Calhoun was referring to Elijah Mix, a former navy master who, in 1820, had been implicated with Christopher Vandeventer (1789–1838, Military Academy 1809), his brother-in-law and chief clerk in the war department, in a scandal arising from a contract awarded for erecting fortifications at the Rip Raps Shoal. In late December, 1826, Mix had charged that Calhoun had benefitted from the contract and, at this time, the House was investigating the charges (Virginia *Alexandria Phenix Gazette*, December 28, 1826).

To *Samuel Houston*

Hermitage Janry 27th. 1827

Dr. Genl

At the request of an old Revolutionary soldier who resides in the County of Sumner, I enclose a narative,[1] which he has addressed to the Chief Justice [John] Marshal[2] with a hope that it will enable the Judge to Identify him in such a manner as with the evidence which may be found in the war office, will intitle him to a pension—one fact he wishes me to state, that you may make it known to the Judge, by which, he will be able to Identify him. that is to say—

William Bradford[3] Taylor by trade, made the last uniform suit for Colo. Thomas Marshal while living at Oak Hill that he ever wore[4]—This is the same man that is now applying for a pension, and Colo. Thomas Marshal was father of the Judge & Mr Bradford says the Judge will recollect him.

Will you try to obtain a pension for him—he has lost his sight, so that he is unable to follow his trade, and has a large family of young children by his last marriage, to provide for, & *is very poor.*[5]

I have not recd any letter from you since the one under cover to Colo. McGreggor.[6] all things are going on well here, as relates to yourself, no publications as was talked of—This I believed would not be hazzarded, when your enemies had every thing to loose by publicity to the unwarantable course that had been pursued by them.[7] Genl [Richard Gilliam] Dunlap from Knoxville was here the other day, & relates that your opponants will not obtain one tenth of the votes East of the mountains[8]—so soon as congress rises I would advise that you return to this state.

I will be happy to hear of my letter to Mr Southard having reached you[9]—whilst living, I wish to put down that vile slander, and expose the slanderer (be he whom he may) & if such order, as aluded to, is on file, the *Villain* who has placed it there, shall be unrobed whilst I am living—and the nation advised of the *Treachery* & hypocracy of their public functionaries—If it had passed unnoticed whilst I was living, when dead, it would have been said, if not true, why had this thing not been enquired into whilst I was living. We have an evidence in Mr Calhouns case, I admire his course, it was one worthy of him, his promptness in adopting it has astounded his enemies, *now says the hired presses*—It was improper to stir this thing in congress, it will delay public business &c &c. had he not, it would have been circulated like lightning, recorded in all the ministerial prints, and hereafter would be said, *If not guilty why had he not applied for investigation* he has applied, and I for one rejoice at it[10]—public officers, ought not only to be honest but unsuspected—and When any charge emanating from, or through, any of the departments ought to be investigated promptly—hence my anxiety to hear that my letter to Mr Sec Southard has reached you. Mrs. J. Joins me in good wishes believe me yr friend

Andrew Jack[son]

N.B. please give the enclosed letter to Judge Johnston if in the city—if not transmit it under your cover[11]
My friend Senator Read, has lost his election by a large majority, and the citizens of that state has established a press for the people—see circular[12]— A. J.

ALS, DLC (34). Published in Bassett, 3:332–33 (extract).
1. Not found.
2. Marshall (1755–1835) had been named Chief Justice of the United States in 1801.
3. Bradford (c1760–c1832) was from Shenandoah County, Virginia.
4. Marshall (1730–1802), a Revolutionary veteran and former Virginia legislator.
5. Bradford had married Nancy Boyles, his third wife, in 1810.
6. See above, Houston to AJ, December 13, 1826.
7. AJ was alluding to Houston's disputes with John P. Erwin and William White over Houston's protest to Erwin's appointment as Nashville postmaster. In August 1827, just before the Tennessee gubernatorial election, which Houston won, Houston and White published accounts of their duel.
8. Dunlap (1795–1841) was a Knoxville lawyer. He moved to Texas in 1837 and served as its treasury secretary (1838–39) and minister to the United States (1839–40). Newton Cannon was Houston's chief opponent in the gubernatorial contest.
9. See above, AJ to Samuel L. Southard, January 5.
10. AJ was referring to Calhoun's call for an investigation into the charges of Elijah Mix.
11. Probably William Johnson (1771–1834), a justice of the Supreme Court. Enclosure not found.
12. In early January, the Mississippi legislature elected Powhatan Ellis to the Senate over Thomas B. Reed, whom AJ considered an opponent to his election. The "press for the people" was the Natchez *Mississippi Statesman,* established in December 1826. By "circular" AJ probably meant "prospectus."

From John Henry Eaton

27 Jany 1827

Dr Genl.

Genl. Coffee goes tomorrow & will be able to tell you all & every thing of & about us, that I have no time to place in a letter. I have written you seldom & the reason is, that I am truly afraid to commit my letter to the P: Office, well knowing the vile system of espoinage that is afloat here, & every where.

Yr. friend J. Monroe, is greatly displeased at Judge Whites speech on the 8th. He brooks not the idea, that any one should claim from him honors on a/c of the So Campaign Coffee will tell you the particulars as we have them, how that he has complained, & has written to the Dept of war for papers & documents. For what end I know not; all I do Know is, that if he shall come forth, White will meet him at the threshold, & send him where he merits to go—to silent forgetfulness—no matter let him pass.

Yr letter requiring me to declare your willingness for all secrets 'twixt you Madison & Monroe has reached me safely, & will be acted upon when occasion shall make it necessary.[1] I *hope* the occasion may arise But Js. Monroe is as assuredly one of the coalition gentry as Clay Southard or Barbour; Have no confidence in him or about him; he is unworthy of it; & this for his long service & old age only, I would say to none other; yet I say it to you, that you may be upon your guard. Here, (I speak to you truly) almost with one consent, friends & foes, declare & admit, that nothing save death, can keep you from being elected: in this state of things all sorts of stratagem from sheep in wolves cloathing will be resorted to: be it so, I have no fears about you, I only name it, to put you on your guard, well knowing that no enemy has ever found its way into your camp, or can do so, unless where he approaches in the garb & character of a friend; & hence do I say, look sharply out. Be assured then, they will assail you in every way; & try if they cannot after some form or other arouse & commit you. I know them all, & well; & every thing I have to say is, be cautious—be still—be quiet; & let your friends fight the arduous battle that is before them; they will call for you when wanted, & until wanted, no matter if the battle rage at your very Markee door, lie still, & sleep on, until they say to you *rise up*—Even Hammond of Cincinati has written me, a very insiduous & friendly letter of which & all other matters Genl Coffee can tell[2] I enclose you a letter read it; & upon the enquiry presented about Dewit you will See the necessity of your old & usual caution.[3] I have confidence in Swartwout, tho I have also recd similar applications from other quarters to Know what you will do with him. In my answers I adopt your own opinions—I know not Jackson thinks well & favorably of him, but will never—never, make his way to the Presidency by bargain to any, or promises to any.

Most of the admn folks look sad & sorrowful & are I believe prepared to give up the [sh]ip, & very many put on solemn faces [who?] heretofore looked joyful. Considering me a friend of yours, there are some now who are quite kind & friendly & good humored, who but lately were erect & distant—No matter & be it so—all things are well & moving well, & all I have to ask of you is this—just weigh & bale & your Cotton & sell it; & if you see any thing of or about yourself just throw the paper into the fire, mind it not, & just go on to weigh the Cotton

To Genl Coffee I refer you for a thousand particulars that I have not time to write thine truly

Eaton

ALS, DLC (72). Enclosure: Samuel Swartwout to Eaton, January 2.
   1. Not found.

2. On January 3, Hammond wrote Eaton, after being prompted by Clay, that Clay had not supplied him with documents about the Jacksons' marriage, but he refused to rule out a public discussion of the materials he had collected from other sources. "I meditate no attack upon Mrs. Jackson," he wrote, but "I do not view the character of the general in a light so favourable as you and many others do, and I propose to use the affair in no other manner than to elucidate my estimate [of] that character" (OHi; *Clay Papers*, 6:5–6.).

3. Swartwout had written that some of Clinton's partisans indicated that they would possibly support AJ for president in exchange for AJ's endorsing Clinton for the vice presidency.

From Samuel Houston

Washington
Jany [28] 1827.

Dear General

By the mail of last Wednesday I had the pleasure to receive your favo'r of the 8th Inst, stating, that you had written to me by mail on the 6th.[1]— which communication I am truly sorry to say has not been heard of by me; except from yourself. In my letter to you: I think that I mentioned to you there wou'd be safety at least in having your letter mailed at Jefferson![2] I have despaired of ever receiving the letter refer'd to in yours of the 8th.

I did not advise you immediately of its failure knowing as I did that letters sometimes passed each other on the road—but when it did not arrive by the next mail I have determined to let you know of it by Genl Coffee who will leave here to day!

I will go forthwith to the Post M. Genl, and start an inquiry into the matter and if possible *ferret* out the wretch! who has been guilty of this *espoinage*. I doubt not but Erwin is the fellow. Major Graham has in his possession, evidence of *misconduct* on part of Erwin, in the Post office and if he wou'd forward it to me properly attested, my opinion is that Mr McLean wou'd put every thing on his part at hazard by removing Erwin forthwith from the office. I hope you will see Major Graham on the subject, and forward to me the evidence, that I may at *least* submit it to the Department.[3]

To receive your reply to this letter I will wait some two or three days after the rise of Congress shoud it be necessary! And I pray you to mail your letter at Jefferson, inclosed to the Post Master Genl, or if to me that you will have the superscription in some hand writing, not your own! It is too well known![4]

Under the frank of Col McKee I wrote to you, and sent the copy of a letter refer'd to in a former communication to you[5]—Whether or not, you will get it Heaven only can tell!

There is nothing said here of your "confidential correspondence seeing the light"[6]—but I have not in my life seen a cause rising so fast as *that of the people is, nor,* one sinking faster, than the cause of a *wicked,* and *corrupt coalition.* Every movement tends to its more complete over-throw—Genl Coffee can give you particulars; which are too numerous to place on paper! The elections in Deleware, Missouri, and the certainty, that Van Buren, and the probability that Ellis of Mississippi, will be elected, has struck consternation into the "Wigwam"—and desperation is their only hope!![7]

Mr Randolph bears himself in the most manly, and noble mood, and is far above his former self! His enemies tremble, while his friends are delighted with him! [Samuel McDowell] Moore who attacked him in the legislature of Virginia has got into difficulties, and will be compell'd to challenge Dr [George William] Crump; and no doubt will get worsted![8] Moore is a distant connexion of mine, as also of Col. Benton's by his wife[9]—neither of whom will take any part with him, but leave him, with Mr Clay, and his friends to take care of!

I have spoken to Mr Randolph on the subject, of the *Archy filly,* that you wished to purchase of him—He says that he has none of three years old nor, under four, as I understood him to say—perhaps he has year-lings—for his four year old Filly, he asks $400.00 I will expect you to write me on this subject—It has not been in my power to hear of a good Groom, which can be had—Shou'd I hear of any I will forthwith apply to him, for Capt Donelson. Mr Randolph requested me whenever I wrote to you to present his kindest and best wishes to you—at the same time, he was very kind in his inquiries for your health!

It has never yet been in my power to find your letter on file in the war Dept of the 13th of Feby 1815.[10] The list which I sent to you by Mr Washington thro' Dr Shelby; contained a list of letters sent by you to the war Dept and those rec'd, but they are not on file[11]—I have now ordered a list to be made out of those on file, intended for you, with a list of all letters sent to you![12]

I regret that I did not send my last communication to you thro' Col McGrigor, instead, of sending it under the frank of Col McKee:[13] No letter to or from you is safe in the Nashville Post office!

I trust that you will write to me at length, in reply; Having it mailed at Jefferson, being first inclosed to the Post Master Genl—retaining a note of the date, and by whom placed in the office—It is possible that yours mailed at Nashville on the 6th. may yet come to hand—if it shou'd I will advise you of it instantly—[14]

Inclosed you will receive all the intelligence, which I can obtain on the subject of George Wilsons claim—It will be sufficient to enable him to give a specific shape to his application![15]

You will please do me the hono'r to make my acknowledgements to Mrs Jackson for her good wishes & present to her my most respectful and sincere salutations—To Capt Donelson & lady—also to your Sons present me! With perfect Respect & Regard I am your friend

Sam Houston

ALS, DLC (34). Published in Bassett 3:329 (extract). Houston actually addressed his letter to Daniel Graham (1789–1869, North Carolina 1812), a former secretary of state and comptroller of Tennessee. Graham subsequently placed it in the hands of John Coffee, who then delivered it to the Hermitage.

1. See AJ to Houston, January 5 and 8, both above.
2. A post office in Rutherford County.
3. Houston had earlier alleged that Erwin had "*purloined* a newspaper from the Post office in Nashville before his appointment" as postmaster ("To the Public," September 12, 1826, *Writings of Sam Houston,* 4:7). It is not known whether Graham's evidence concerned this occasion or another.
4. In his answer of February 15, below, AJ enclosed to Houston another copy of his January 5 letter to Southard, addressed in his own hand and mailed from the Nashville post office.
5. See above, Houston to AJ, January 13.
6. Houston was quoting loosely from AJ's letter above of January 8.
7. Martin Van Buren won a Senate seat in New York, as did Thomas Hart Benton in Missouri, Powhatan Ellis in Mississippi, and Louis McLane (1786–1857) and Henry Moore Ridgely (1779–1847) in Delaware.
8. In the Virginia House of Delegates, Moore (1796–1875) had spoken against Randolph's reelection and, with Randolph defeated, Crump (1786–1848) resigned his seat in the U.S. House of Representatives to make way for Randolph to succeed him. Afterwards, Crump challenged Moore to a duel, but no report of a duel between the two has been found (*Richmond Enquirer,* January 16).
9. Moore's aunt, Nancy McClung Moore, was first cousin to James McClung (b. c1728), Houston's uncle, as well as to Mary McClung McDowell (c1734–1827), a great aunt of Benton's wife, Elizabeth McDowell Benton (1794–1854).
10. In his request for a copy of the letter on October 23, 1826, AJ had mistakenly written February 13, 1815, for February 18.
11. "Genl Jacksons Letters, &c" [1826].
12. "List of Letters from Genl Jackson to the Department of War on the files of 1813–1822," [Feb 1, 1827].
13. See above, Houston to AJ, January 13.
14. The letter arrived in Washington on February 2, according to Houston's endorsement.
15. Houston enclosed for AJ Peter Hagner's letter of January 27, detailing the procedure Wilson should follow in filing his claim.

To James Buchanan

Hermitage Janry 29th. 1827

Dr Sir

your favour of the 19th.[1] has been before me for some time, but observing in the papers the obituary notice of your brother[2] whose illness took you from the city, I have delayed acknowledging its receipt untill advised of your return. I pray you to accept my sincere condolence for the serious loss you have sustained in the death of your brother.

I suspect the administration begin to perceive the necessity of public confidence without which it is an arduous undertaking to execute the solemn duties confided by the constitution to the chief magistrate. The Panama "*bubble*" & the loss of the trade with the British West Indies are the result of this defect in the Cabinet, for it cannot be supposed that such reputed diplomatists would have committed errors so obvious had not some influence stronger than the public good operated upon their minds[3]—My hope, however, is, that the wisdom of Congress may remedy these blunders, and that my friends the *"factious opposition,"* may in your own language never forget the support due to the Country. I had predicted that from the movements of Seargeant and Rochester that the Panama subject was done with, and that the charge of *factious opposition* would be hushed, but it appears I was mistaken—Tacubaya is to be the Theatre on which these mighty projects are to be unfolded[4]—alas, what folly & wickedness.

Present me to my friend Mr Kremer & believe me very respectfully yr. Mo. obdt. Servt.

Andrew Jackson

ALS, PHi (11-0480). Published in Bassett, 3:333 (extract).
1. Not found.
2. William Speer Buchanan (1805–1826, Princeton 1822), a lawyer, died at Chambersburg, Pennsylvania.
3. AJ was referring to the response of the Adams administration to the British orders in council suspending trade between the United States and the British West Indies.
4. Sergeant and Rochester were en route to the adjourned meeting at Tacubaya.

To Andrew Jackson, Jr.

Hermitage Janry 31rst 1827—

My Son

I have recd. your note of yesterday by George, and I have no doubt, but the attendance on Mr [Robert] Goodacres lectures on Astronomy will be beneficial;[1] having obtained, as you must, some idea of the Theory, the explanation by Mr Goodacre with his instruments must make the subject plain to your understanding—believing this, I enclose you four dollars, that you may purchase a Tickett of admission to his lectures; I am certain from observation that you will receive much benefit by attending them. Should doctor Lindsley think, that it would be beneficial for Hutchings also to attend them, by applying to Mr Josiah Nichol, and shewing him this letter he will advance him four dollars to purchase his tickett of admittance.

I should have been down to day, but I have been much afflicted with headache—which prevents me. I am happy to be informed that you are progressing *well* in your studies. My greatest anxiety is, that you should become a thorough scholar, & so conduct yourself as to become respectable in society—This will be to me, a sufficient reward for the expense of your education.

It would be gratifying to me to receive a letter from you often, that I might be the more able to judge of your improvement, in writing, & diction.

I will send for you whenever you wish to come up, & can obtain leave of absence from College I am with great affection your loving father

Andrew Jackson

P.S. if the waters should subside before friday I will send a boy for you A. J.

ALS, DLC (34).
    1. Note not found. Goodacre was at this time making a tour of the United States, delivering his series of lectures in major cities.

From Hugh Lawson White

Washington Feby. 2nd. 1827.

Dear Sir,
    General Coffee will I hope see you on his return home and be able to inform you what was passing here when he left us.
    On the day he set off I was favored with a communication from the late P.—U. S. in which he complains that I had done him injustice in some remarks which I made on the 8th. January.[1] His communication is very lengthy—I have sent him an answer[2]—So soon as I can copy I will send them to you.
    His letter is respectful and apparently friendly—Mine is respectful and frank:[3] but as I said nothing but what I believed to be true I could of course take nothing back—In my own mind I immediately connected this with the Fredericksburg story,[4] and imagined it might be the commencement of an attack upon that point.
    I am at all times inclined to be watchful if not suspicious and at present it is necessary to be more so. I have no doubt attempts have been, and will be made, to get you to *write,* or *say* something, from which at the same time you will please *one section* of *country,* you will *injure yourself* with another.
    You shall hear from me again before long. With sincere esteem, Your Mo. Obdt. Servt.

Hu. L. White

ALS, DLC (34).
    1. James Monroe to White, January 26, 1827 (DLC-72).
    2. White to Monroe, January 29, 1827 (DLC-34).
    3. Eaton assisted White in preparing the response to Monroe. On January 29, before White composed his response, Eaton wrote John Coffee at Baltimore, then en route home, asking for further information on arms for the defense of New Orleans in 1814–15.
    4. White was referring to Southard's comments at Fredericksburg the previous summer.

From John McLean (1785–1861)

Post Office Department
3 Feby 1827

Sir:

The enclosed envelope was handed me yesterday by Gen. Houston, with the seals unbroken as he received it from the post office.[1] As the packet was delayed in its transmission several days longer than the ordinary course of the mail, and as the hand writing on the envelope does not appear to be yours, some suspicion is entertained that the packet may have been purposely delayed, its contents examined, and a new envelope substituted. I will therefore thank you to inform me whether the endorsement made on the enclosed paper was made by you or your order, and if not, I wish the affidavit of the person who conveyed it to the post office, to accompany your answer.[2] The object of this enquiry you will at once see is of a public nature, and seems to be necessary to the preservation of the integrity of the department. I have the honor to be with great respect your obedient servant

John McLean

Please to return the envelope

ALS, DLC (34); LC, DNA-RG 28 (M601-34).
    1. The envelope was from AJ's letter to Houston, January 5.
    2. AJ's response, March 7, appears below.

To *Samuel Houston*

Hermitage February 4th. 1827—

Dear Genl

I have had the pleasure to receive yours of the 13th. ult. with its inclosure[1]—for which receive my thanks. The date of the inclosure, the time when it was thought proper to have the executive construction placed upon the record, of the archives of the nation, being long after the execution of the orders, and my communications shewing the understanding which I had placed upon them, whilst executing them;[2] *bears an aspect,* that I am *sorry to see*; and the attempt to coo me as to the responsibility every way belonging to the executive, shews a *diplomatic maneuvre under the imposing aspect* of *friendship* that I never expected from that quarter—*still it benefitted nothing*—for when the faithfull historian takes up the documents to give a faithfull relation of those things to posterity—if the enclosed document should not be found upon the records of the war Department, it will be found in my Beaurau, with the letters written in pursuance to the plan it proposes—and altho I would have assumed any responsibility that would have bestowed a benefit to my country—When those benefits were from *imbecility* to be taken from it—those to whom responsibility belonged, & who surrendered the *benefit & security* to our frontier, must bear its own responsibility—and it will find this ground I have maintained, and I am still able to maintain—This the then executive well knew, and as it appears from the inclosure, I was under kind expressions of friendship, to be courted out of—*it did not take*—The document shall remain in confidence untill I see you—Tho, this with the declaration of the Sec of the Navy at Fredericks-burgh Va, when his informant is obtained, will give a clue to the course the Richmond Whig whose Editor is a personal friend of the writer of the letter inclosed has pursued;[3] and will open a door at a proper time, to give a history of these opperations, with the conduct of the Executive; and afford a clue, why the orders, Issued in July 1814, by the then Sec of War, authorising me to take possession of Pensacola was witheld, untill after peace was declared.[4] O, Tempora, O, mores.

Your celebration of the 8th was a sp[l]endid one—the speach of my friend Judge White, well timed, eloquent & appropriate—It will have its effect all over the union, & must prostrate those hidden Slanderers, who breath & exist upon the Treasury pap—I feel much gratitude for this act of kindness, and I beg you to present me to him.

I regret Mr Randolph has lost his election—it will be such a gratification to the administration, altho add nothing to its strength—if an opportunity offers, present me respectfully to him—and to all the Tennessee delegation & other friends in congress.

Mrs. J., Mr A. J. D. & my son who is with me Join in good wishes for yr health & happiness—expecting to See you shortly in Tennessee, where your early return will be joyfully hailed, believe me your friend

Andrew Jackson

ALS, DLC (72).

1. See above.

2. The enclosure, Monroe to Calhoun, September 9, 1818, questioned the authority under which AJ had seized Pensacola on May 24 of the same year. For AJ's interpretation of the orders, see *Jackson,* 4:235–39.

3. John Hampden Pleasants (1797–1846) was editor of the *Richmond Constitutional Whig.*

4. AJ did not receive the orders of July 18, 1814 (*Jackson,* 3:90), until January 17, 1815.

From Arthur Lee Campbell

Louisville Feby. 4th. 1827.
Dear Genl.

I have given you the annexed list,[1] for the purpose of enabling you, if you should think proper, to write to certain men in this state, and at the same time, to give you the best data now at command, from which to estimate your present strength in Kentucky.

To defeat, or check the purposes of the Aristocracy, it became indispensibly necessary for the Republicans, to have recourse to extraordinary means and exertions—I therefore originated, and with the cooperation of about half a dozen, intelligent and zealous friends, carried into full and successful operation last year, a plan, or System of Committees, from a Principle or Central Committee at Louisville, down to Sub-Committees into every ward of the Town, and Captains Company in the Country—In the execution of which, our Sub-Committees not only kept the secret so well, that our adversaries remained entirely ignorant and secure, until overwhelmed in disgraceful [ruin] but likewise went so far in detail, in the [regu]lar reports, as to give the names of each voter, how each would vote, both on the local and National questions. By which I find, that in Jefferson and Oldham Counties (which vote togeather) Seven eighths of the New Court, and three eighths of the Old Court voters, will at this time support you for the next U. S. Presidency.

The organization of this Committee Plan, so as to embrace the whole State, has already been commenced by your friends, and it is expected to be in full and successful operation, before the next August elections, with a view not only to your elevation, but likewise to the resuscitation and success, of our local Republican cause or question. With the highest respect & esteem I am your Sincere friend

A. Campbell

ALS, DLC (34). Published in Bassett, 3:333–34 (extract).
1. Campbell enclosed a list of the members of the Kentucky House and Senate, identifying each as a supporter of either Adams or Jackson.

From John Henry Eaton

Washington
4— Feby. 1827— Sunday night

My dear Sir

Your several letters have been recvd.[1] and while I confess myself indebted to you for more letters written by you than by myself, must plead as excuse for my silence, the apprehensions I have at addressing any thing to you, of that confidential kind often which in writing I should desire to express myself. The truth is, that at no period of the French History since the revolution has there been a system of espoinage practiced to an extent surpassing the present co-alition times. why it happens, & how it happens, I cannot tell, but by referring it to the consideration, that when the men at the head of power, & patronage become corrupted, & corrupt, it is idle to expect that every subaltern shall not partake of the corporation & character of the heads themselves: What letters I do write of private or even apparently a confidential character, I am constrained to place under cover to some other than it is addressed to, or else to conceal it, by enveloping it in a document of some kind Your letter for example to S. H. enclosing yours to S. was delayed two weeks and reached here, on a day when the mail was not regularly due The endorsement on the back of the letter, assuredly is not your writing & hence the conclusion that it has been intercepted & re-enveloped again at some other point.[2] No matter, there was no secret about it, that any one, could benefit by, & none certainly that any one can venture to speak of. The superscription of the letter, was a good imitation of your hand; but agreed by judge White & myself not be yours. The explanation however, which it may be in the power of Mr Secty S. to give on this matter, genl. H. will I suppose communicate. We had arranged and determined however for judge W. to deliver it, on acct of his superior discretion, had it not been for a remark of yours that it would be handed by genl. H—that expression rendered it necessary that H. should be the organ of communication

By this Mail you will receive a Copy of Mr Monroes letter to judge White,[3] on the subject of his great exertions made in defence of Orleans. Whether Southard will be content to forbear any confession which may go to injure his old master & patron I know not; but from the context of the labored essay to H. L. W. there can be no difficulty I apprehend in believing that Monroe is the author of the whole matter. In referring to his letter of the 7 of Dec, which my recollection bears testimony never came to hand, or if it did, not till after you had been at N. Orleans 7 days before it was written contains the remarkable expression that you "were directed to repair to N Orleans."[4] This you will remember is the identical expression which Mr Jona. Roberts makes use of. Now it is very common & quite natural for great men to think alike about matters but then it is neither, natural or common for them to adopt expressions so literally alike as these. The consequence is, as I always believed that Jona was the catspaw of men greater than himself, & by whom he was made a Tool to his own destruction. Poor old Mr Monroe his vanity has long lain ahead of his judgment; & his great solicitude seems now to be to claim what never was his, credit for deeds never performed. Well! it is an innocent sort of ambition, & while he seeks not to decry others, be him indulged, tho I know full well, that with posterity, & even by the present race, such aspiring will serve no other end, than to render him effectually ridiculous.

The answer of judge W. will also be sent you: it will afford Mr. M. nothing of consolation or blarney; & if more for his benefit be necessary it will become his proper course to appeal to the public journals We fully calculate that he will do so,[5] & in that event White feels concerned that you shall stand away from the conflict, and not interfere in a matter, which he claims exclusively to be his own, & which he is confident of managing, with justice both to you, & to himself, & with entire clearness to the public. He would take it, unkind in you to interfere, and arrest from his hands a business which by his dinner speech of the 8, he considers his, not yours; & so I hope you will consider it.

This matter is but proof possitive of what I have always said to you, that this Mr. M. is not & never was any friend of yours; about him is nothing but weakness & deception; & according to my humble conception of things, throughout his friendly feeling has been that of self interest. If this be so, then is there a greater necessity for you occasionally as time may permit to place upon record & in your own hand, as posthumous matter every incident relating to your public life, that those to whom you may confide the great & important trust may possess the means of repelling any future assaults which the malevolent & designing may think proper to wage

There are no circumstances better calculated to give you a stronger evidence of the fears & apprehensions which your name inspires than those repeated assaults which the little & the great are pleased to urge against you. If you were not supposed to be in their way, they would let you alone, & permit your name & fame to pass; but as it is, apprehending thro you, entire discomfiture & defeat, there is nothing they will not do, & nothing they will not say to affect, & if possible to injure you. Every battery that can be turned upon you, or upon your friends will be made to operate; for in the contest before them, not merely is defeat seen, but the utter destruction of all future hope & expectation In this state of things, rest assured that every thing that ingenuity can work out, or detraction suggest, or falshood urge, will be attempted while your friends, not *you* must meet & mingle in the conflict. Could they excite you to any act, by which to maintain before the people that you were a man of rashness, nothing would delight them more it would be music to their Souls.

But however much they may assail, whether publickly, or privately even, there is this recollection always to be borne in mind, that in your success the great republican cause—the security & triumph of the Country is involved; & that apart from yourself there is none other that can combat for the tarnished & lost honors & principles of the Constitution. Be their charges & accusations then, of whatever character & description they may, you should sit patiently, & while they passed in at one ear, permit them *hastily* to pass out at the other: to be thought of no more. Upon yourself I think depends not the abstract question who shall be President; but a much higher & more important one; the question of the freedom of the Constitution & the happiness of this Country in times that are to come. Were it the mere matter, who shall be President, I should indeed prefer on your own acct, to see you at ease on your farm, rather than here, surrounded by bustle & trouble; but this is not the question; it is matter of higher import, & greater consideration; it is one which in my humble opinion involves the interest of the Country, perhaps her essential security. In the guidance of such men as now preside I have no confidence; & yet give them another election, & what may they not attempt, judging of them, by what they have already done in their little & short career. At a moment so critical you are at hand to be rallied upon; & yet will a man who was without your popularity before the people of this Country, & it would be altogether vain & idle to contend with the intrigues & patronage of present rulers. Hence do I say, be their course towards you what it may—abuse public or private—detraction small or great, heed it not, & hear it not. Let them go on it will presently all fail, & by putting down the clan, your triumph will be complete, & their mortification exemplary. The very parasites who now know nothing too harsh to be urged, will then become singers & praisers of you, & of every thing you do My word upon it, even Hal. C. will become a convert, & as a pretext for it, will alledge your administration unexceptionable & superior to all he had anticipated. One thing is most obviously certain, that there is nothing in all their collected & digested catalogue, that can be made to do you any the least injury. You have been abused & slandered so much, that now the people will hear nothing more, & still less will they believe any thing abusive of you: to be sure things may be said calculated to awaken in your own bosom, a momentary feeling; but then it should be but momentary, leaving all and every thing as you should to the tribunal of public sentiment You have waded swamps & slept on the cold ground—encountered cold & hunger, and even met abuse in its most angry forms; all of which you bore, & why; because your Country & her interest stood before you, dependent upon you for safety; but believe me; your Country does not now demand less, your bold exertions, & cautious prudence, than she did in 1813–14 & 15. The danger was then, to be sure more imminent, & more immediate & apparent, but not a jot more serious; if so, the same sacrafices & the same forbearance are at present not the less demanded at your hands. In your Country then let all the considerations of *self* be buried, for thereby, & by no other means can her interest, her happiness & security be attained. Apart from you, & the end can not be effected; the co-alition to the ruin of the Country must again triumph, which, may Heaven forbid

At this moment I think the Presidential question dependent wholly & entirely upon your health & life; these being preserved the game is over. They may put Mr Clinton up or not as they please the result will still be the same Including N. Jersey South to Georga I am confident & satisfied that you will not loose more than 5 votes, & most likely but three in Maryland in all 104 votes this side the mountains; to say nothing of N. Y. where are conceded to you from 18 to 25 even in the event Clinton shall run, & almost the entire state, if he should not be a candidate. Already do the coalition wear the aspect of deep despondency, and have longer faces than any I have seen except on those which some of your friends put on, the fell 9th. of Feby 1825 when corruption rode triumphant thro the streets of this City. Hourly your strength is growing & increasing, & from every point out of N England the accounts declare that you are going far ahead of the patronage gentry here. My faith is such, & my information so versant & possitive that I do, not at all question it; & in the end veryly believe that Adams & Clay will be driven into the States of N. England dependent for support there *only*. Quietness, forbearance, & modest unassuming demeanor, is all that your friends are now under the necessity of practicing. Tis the course I hope & believe they will pursue.

I have recvd a letter from Mr. Ch. H. of Cincinati, dated the 3d of Jany. My interview with Mr. H. C. was on the 21st between 2 & 3 O Clock. If then he wrote to H——d the next day, 22d—it would have reached him the 30 or 31—From Mr. H——d writing me, on this subject I entertain no doubt but that Clay desired him to do so, stating what had taken place; for we never interchanged a letter before, & his object is to satisfy me that C had nothing to do in the matter He says by way of appology for writing to me, that he had heard that I believed so, or had said so; its all false—Clay wrote him I have no doubt thus to address me; the exact correspondence of dates in my interview on the 21 of Dec, & his letter on the same subject only 12 days after, it only requiring nine to go to Cincinati makes the matter too palpable not to be understood.[6] About this tho & many other matters genl Coffee will have told you, before this reaches you.

Upon this subject I would beg leave to say, that it is one, upon which, altho I very well know your feelings must be awakened, yet is it one, about which judgment and not feeling [s]h[ou]ld be exercised. Can a man undertake to resent these things which the humble minions of patronage, & promise, urge against him; and even if he should resent them, like the Hydra in ancient story, where one should be put down, a dozen would rise in his place. Again would I repeat, that let malice and detraction urge whatever it can, & all that the most vindictive feeling shall suggest, the course for you to steer is not to know it even; to leave it with your friends; & for this very plain reason, that your name, & prospects under existing circumstances belong not to yourself, but to your Country The great cause of her security, & her redemption from the foul & wicked usurpation that has been practiced towards her, renders it obvious, that the course of Him, who alone is competent to arrest & put them down should be such as may be calculated to maintain & to preserve the varied opinions, of all, of all classes & descriptions of the Community. Irritation of feeling, resentment even at wanton aggression, would every where carry with it this answer, he should not have minded the assaults of any portion of this corrupt crew: he belonged to, & was claimed by the Country, & for the great interest & purposes of the Country & should leave those abuses of him to those who know, & respect him—*the People*. Such would be the language of the people, while friends having greater cause might more loudly & correctly complain, as well on their own acct, but more especially for and account of the Country, which should be, & ought to be, the great & paramount interest; & beneath which should be buried every thing of private & personal consideration

Mr. Calhoun is yet before his triers, nothing in the shape of a report yet produced, or as I believe likely to be produced, until it shall be too late to have any thing done with it in the House.[7] Next to Lacocks course in the Senate on the Seminole question I think it one of the meanest basest acts of any legislative body. A single charge is made imputing corruption & dishonesty, he being party to a large contract entered into as agent of the govt. Forthwith an enquiry is demanded, about which any County Court Jury would have arrived at a conclusion within a week at farthest, lo & behold week after week, without even yet the prospect of a close, have the Committee been sifting & probing & delaying with a view, for none other can be conceived of, to draw around the V. President a cloud of suspicion, & in the end to adjourn & leave this cloud still hanging over him. It is cruel & unmanly, & such as I hope & trust no friend of ours would extend even to such a man as H. Clay. Nothing better tho, was from the first anticipated, when it was found the kind & materials after which the Committee was composed. Upon it, not a single personal friend of Calhoun, & with the exception of Floyd & [John Wilson] Campbell the devoted friends, & blind adherents of the administration.[8] He has been passed into the hands of his enemies, & denied an impartial jury even, a right secured to the humblest culprit of the Country. And all this is for political ends, & for political effect. I pray then any reasonable man to say, what is to be expected, or indeed hoped for, under an administration whose agents shall be thus disposed to act. Can any man calculate, that he will not be assaulted, or trust to any thing else for deliverance, than his uniform deportment, & general good character? To these, & these only can he, & must he look at a time like the present, when the prostration of character, & feeling outraged is the great turnpike which it is fondly hoped shall lead them forward, not to the advancement of their Countrys interest, but in fact to their own contemptable, personal benefit. Give us office & power is their maxim— their creed & their practice; & how obtained they care not, even if it be over the mangled corpses of the fairest characters that can be found

The very day when Calhouns business came before the House Clay was seen in the lobby whispering & managing. The Speaker[9] poor devil was mean enough to lend himself a helper in the dirty work and hence acting under his masters orders no doubt, gave a Committee who have been ransacting the whole affairs of the war Dept from the period Calhoun came into it, when but a single isolated point or matter was submitted; all that the Session may close upon the scene when it shall be altogether too late, to have the mass of immaterial matter so arranged, & so presented as that any body can by possibility understand any thing about it. Again I say it is that contemptable course that honorable men should spurn; & such a one, as that the President & Secty of safe precedents[10] who sanctions or encourages, should not merely be put down for, but should be in fact despised

Such are the men & such the practices more dangerous to the Liberties of this Country, than would have been the conquest of Louisiana, that it becomes necessary to supplant, & who must be supplanted; & while all agree that there is none other in the Country than can effect this, or in so imminent a degree merits to effect it, to you must occur the necessity of that course which shall maintain that confidence & regard which every where thro this nation is awarded—that nothing may transpire affording to enemies the means of assailing that purity of character & purpose which has so constantly been manifested

I have greatly I feared fatigued you. My rule however is, that we always venture to be at the trouble of reading what another is at the trouble of writing, inasmuch as the latter is rather the worse of the two. There are many other little matters I could trouble you with, could I consent to annoy you so far but will not. It is already nearly 12 O clock at night Sunday. I am wearied & so too must you be—

Be pleased to present to Mrs. Jackson my earnest & sincere good wishes for her continued health & happiness & believe me truly Your friend

J. H. Eaton

ALS, DLC (72).
    1. No letters from AJ to Eaton for December 1826 or January 1827 have been found.
    2. Eaton was referring to AJ's letter of January 5 (above) to Houston, enclosing his letter of the same date to Southard (also above). Houston had already taken up the matter of mail tampering with McLean, who wrote AJ on February 3 (above) about the suspect writing on the envelope.
    3. Monroe to White, January 26 (DLC-72).

4. Monroe to AJ, December 7, 1814, (*Jackson*, 3:200–201). AJ reached New Orleans on December 1, 1814.

5. White to Monroe, January 29 (DLC-34). The White-Monroe correspondence did not get into the newspapers.

6. Eaton's speculation was correct. On December 23, 1826, two days after the interview in which Clay denied any part in providing information to Charles Hammond about the Jacksons' marriage, Clay wrote Hammond about the meeting and asserted that he knew nothing about any impending revelation. Hammond then wrote Eaton on January 3, supporting Clay's claim of non-involvement (OHi; *Clay Papers*, 5:1023–24).

7. Eaton was referring to the House investigation into Calhoun's alleged involvement with the Rip Raps Shoal scandal.

8. Campbell (1782–1833) represented Ohio in the United States House. When the committee reported, Campbell and John Floyd issued a minority report (see *HRDoc* 79, 19th Cong., 2nd sess., Serial 159).

9. John W. Taylor.

10. Clay. The characterization drew from Clay's 1825 letter to his constituents.

From Samuel Houston

Washington
4th feby 1827

Dear Genl.

Your favo'r of the 5th Ult[1] came to hand on the 2nd Inst. after being delayed some 10 Days at last—When it reached me, seeing the post mark of Nashville on the letter I was about to tear off the invelope, but on looking at the superscription, I was satisfied that it was a forgery. I gave it back to the Post Master, with the seals unbroken, made him seal it with wax, endorse upon it when it was recd, took it myself to the P. M. Genl and in his presence broke the seals—He was satisfied, that it was a forgery.[2] He is determined to probe the matter to the bottom—so I *guess,* our post master will go over *board.*

The letter inclosed for Mr Southard[3] I presented, on yesterday with a belief that a copy had been sent to him from Nashville, or that the original had been seen by him—for these reasons first the invelope taken off at Nashville, a new one put on, Post marked; an attempt to counterfeit your hand writing, and then inclosed here, and sealed—droped in the Post office, for it happened to come to me, on a day when the Western *mail* did not arrive—These are my opinions and reasonable too, I think!

When the letter was presented Mr S—— read to where Mr Welfords Name was mentioned, and remarked "The Genl is under one mistake, for I never dined with Dr Wallace at Mr Welfords." I made no reply when he read the letter I said to him "it was at *wine* drinking after dinner," he at first said Wallace was not there, but after some time seemed to think he had been He stated that he "had talked to Wallace about you some hours at a Mr Hooes, and at Fredericksburg"—but seemed to say that he doubted that Wallace was not to be trusted. He did not deny the fact charged; but said he wou'd reply to you, which I presume will be on tomorrow—I need not say to you that he was greatly embarrassed: for that he was there is no doubt! It was evident in his *countenance*. I approved highly your letter to him and have no doubt but your course is right, if any movement was to be taken in the matter.

The list of letters sent to you by Dr Shelby's hand, was of all the letters rec'd at the Dept from you.[4] I now have a list of all on file in the Dept. from you.[5] For many are missing. Yours of the 16th Feby 1815 is to not the fore;[6] I will search again for it, and take the list home with me.

I have other papers, which I woud send, but prefer to take them myself in person. The *"invelope"*—I will take in my own care, & let you say whether or not, you write the superscription upon it. That will put matters at rest.

The Post Master General has pursued a manly course, & will do it; at the hazard of his place!

Two days since we had some *sparring* in the Hall. of Reprs. you will see by the inclosed Intelligencer that I was drawn into it to a small extent, but if I shoud get another opportunity, I will touch—them in *another sort*[7]

The answer of Mr S— will be taken by me to Nashville tho I may inclose you a copy—I do not know that it was necessary to retain a copy of yours to him as I presume you had done so: but to "make surety doubly sure," I took one, and had it compared by Judge White, & Maj Eaton!

All matters move on here as I wou'd have them to do, if I had my wishes, in the way of puting down a corrupt aristocracy, who rely solely for power, on the influence of patronage! Desperation now seems to characterize every act of the *ministry*!

You will please accept my grateful acknowledgements, for your renewed expressions of confidence. Make my most respectful, salutations to Mrs Jackson, and say to her, that very many of her friends have commissioned me to present her with their best regards. Mrs W's family,[8] Col Towson & lady, amongst the first. Your friends make daily enquiries for your health, and *[exp]*ress the warmest regard, & hopes *[for the] success* of pure principles *[. . .]* I am Most truly your obt servt & friend .

Sam Houston

ALS, DLC (72). Published in Bassett, 6:491–92.
1. See above.
2. For McLean's inquiry about the case, see above, McLean to AJ, February 3.
3. See above, AJ to Samuel L. Southard, January 5.
4. "Genl Jacksons Letters, &c.," [1826].
5. "List of Letters from Genl Jackson to the Department of War on the files of 1813–1822," [February 1, 1827].
6. AJ to James Monroe, February 16, 1815. Houston probably had trouble finding the letter because it was not in the register, Letters Received by the Secretary of War.
7. Houston enclosed the February 3 *National Intelligencer,* which covered the House debates on a resolution asking the secretary of state for a list of newspapers awarded contracts to print federal laws. Houston spoke in favor of the resolution, attacking the administration's alleged use of such patronage for political ends.
8. Elizabeth C. (Love) Watson.

To *Samuel Houston*

Hermitage Febry 7th. 1827.

Dr Genl.

I have just recd. a letter from my friend Judge White,[1] informing me, that his address at the festive board, on the 8th of January last when I was remembered in one of the regular toasts, has given great offence to Mr. Monroe and he is preparing for the public, a reply. Why or where-fore Mr. Monroe should thus get offended I am at a loss to conjecture. when he comes forth I will see the cause he assigns, and however I may regret to appear before the public—still if he ascribes acts of his own, in defence of the lower country, not fairly belonging to him, Justice will promp me to reply—The application to Mr. Sec Southard may have come to his knowledge and this assumed offence, may be put forth in terrorum, to shield Mr. Southard from his situation[2]—but be this as it may, I hope you have presented my letter to Mr. Southard,[3] and required his reply—I write this, that if you have not upon the receipt of this, that you forth-with do so—This is necessary, if no use ever should be made of it. It may be that Mr. Monroe has heard of it—if so—the greater necessity for the delivery of my letter to Mr Southard, that I may if occasion should re-quire, have his informant, and be prepared to shew the possitive falshood of the declarations he has made let them come from what quarter they may. you may rest assured, that there has been already two much delay in delivering my letter, having heard it, delay may be construed into a proof of the truth of his declarations—and as I am now living, I am able to shew the possitive falsety of his Statement, and it is my duty to do so, whenever the proper period may arrive. The copy of the letter you in-closed to me the other day,[4] gives such evidence of hypocracy & diplo-macy that when the original reaches me, I will be prepared at some fit moment to give to the nation a true picture of base ingratitude, & wicked deception—I therefore enjoin it on you, before you leave the city to de-liver, if you have not done it before, my letter to Mr. Southard and re-quire his answer—If he refuses to answer, note it in writing in his pres-ence, & send it to me by some safe hand. I have been looking for your letter for some mails past, and am without information of my letter en-closing the one to Mr. Southard having reached you. attend to this busi-ness for me, and you will much oblige yr. friend

Andrew Jackson

ALS, DLC (72). Letter endorsed as "(private)" on envelope page. Published in Bassett, 6:492–93.
    1. See above, White to AJ, January 17.

2. As AJ suspected, Southard wrote Monroe about the dispute with AJ on February 4, the day after Houston delivered AJ's letter of January 5.
3. See above, AJ to Southard, January 5.
4. James Monroe to John C. Calhoun, September 9, 1818 (DLC-71).

From John Henry Eaton

W. City 8 Feby. 1827—

Dr Sir

I have recd. your letter,[1] & in reply, (enclosed to Miss Lewis) you will if not intercepted on the road, receive a long & confidential letter.[2] You will also have by the same mail two communications from a Mr. Vincent Grey of Havanna of the Island of Cuba[3] on the business of secrecy heretofore unknown, & until now untold.

Your communication on the subject of internal improvements has reached me in *safety*;[4] this word I oft repeat in my letters because under the present system of espoinage now so often practiced upon; & indeed so frequently complained of, it is always matter of uncertainty with me, if what I write shall meet its destination; & therefore is it; that no certain calculation forms itself in my brain on placing a letter in the Po office that it will reach its destination. I am forced therefore not merely to seal my letters *particularly* & with care but often, when I would attempt security, to address them to others under cover, than those for whom they are designed.

Your letter I say has been recvd & read. I am glad to be possessed of the sentiments it contains. To Judge White it has been shown, & to none else; & those were his remarks, which I offer to you because they have force & reason & good sense . . . ["]The generals views says he, are certainly good; but then upon this subject there is no necessity of his giving any opinion. He is called upon by no one, & if he should be, let him not answer, for inasmuch as his votes upon this subject are matters of publicity & known, none should ask for information about that, which his public life already sufficiently dis[c]loses. His friends will not care to enquire, & those who shall enquire will do it for no other view than to See if something against him can not be produced and made public. I could wish therefore that the general should not in any way commit himself in opinion upon any subject, that when he comes in, he may be entirely free to shape his course accordingly as his views in referrence to the best interest of the Country may dictate to him to be right" I think the reasoning good, & such as should have its effect; for indeed such are the views or rather conduct of many that for political interest & gain to themselves they would rejoice in any thing to be said, or published by you out of which they could make a noise. I shall therefore show your views to none, but retain them as a relick of my own; & I hope that should any one write you on this, or any other political subject, you will forbear to place your-self upon paper, resting in confidence in this, that the application is for occult purposes & to be used if possible against you. There is nothing in the shape of ingenuity to divine, that they will not essay against you, & for this obvious reason, that they now plainly & certainly discover that you must & will consign them to retirement & private life. I know of nothing that can prevent it, if health is preserved; & as the Country & its interest is vitally concerned I again say, what heretofore I have said to you, that to forbear all political letters, enquiries & discussion is the true policy. Be still—Be at home is the great & open path to tread, heedless of whatever may be said or done by any of the *"corrupt crew"*

No tidings yet of Calhouns Committee[5]—nothing known, of when they will report: it is said that it will now be in a day or two *[alt]*ho it is mere rumor: Soon as they do, I will *[se]*nd you, what they may say—

I sent you to day the Presidents declaration of War against Geo— it produces no ferment here; it is understood to be a tub to the whale, to divert public opinion from them. None are so silly to believe that this Civil administration, & Civil Cabinet, who so oft have denounced mil. chieftains will raise the sword against a Sovereign State: the thing is too preposterous & absurd for belief[6]—Will he send his little army of 6,000, they will be eat up before they get to Georga. while the mila of the So & west will never arm in such a cause. How idle then for peaceable men like our present rulers who so often have denounced mil. chieftains to talk of war, & upon their own citizens. If the laws be not strong enough let the laws be amended & the Judiciary settle the matter—not the *bayonette.*

AL fragment, DLC (34). Published in Bassett, 3: 341–42 (extract).

1. Not found.

2. See above, Eaton to AJ, February 4. The same packet also contained Eaton's letter of February 5 to AJ.

3. See Gray to AJ, December 30, 1826, with enclosure, Gray to Baring Brothers, November 20, 1814.

4. Not found. AJ probably composed the internal improvements communication in response to Polk's warning of December 4, 1826, above.

5. The investigation into the Rip Raps Shoal scandal.

6. In his message of February 5, Adams informed Congress of his instructions that "if the legislature and executive authorities of the State of Georgia should persevere in the acts of encroachment upon the territories secured by a solemn treaty to the Indians, and the laws of the Union remain unaltered, a superadded obligation even higher than that of human authority will compel the Executive of the United States to enforce the laws and fulfill the duties of the nation by all the force committed for that purpose to his charge. That the arm of military force will be resorted to only in the event of the failure of all other expedients provided by the laws, a pledge has been given by the forbearance to employ it at this time" (Richardson, *Messages and Papers of the Presidents*, 2:373).

From Samuel Lewis Southard

Washington 9 Feby. 1827

Sir,

Your unsealed letter, of the 5th Jany,[1] was handed to me, in my office, on the 3d of this month, by Genl. Houston, with the remark, that he had recd. it, as an enclosure, from you, on the preceding day. Disposed to regard it *only* as an enquiry, dictated by the persuasion, that you have been injured; and feeling that I have done you no intentional wrong, I cheerfully give such explanation as is in my power.

About the first of July last, I was at the private table of My friend John S. Wellford, in Fredericksburg, in company with five or six of his immediate neighbors, who, I believe, had been invited to spend an hour or two, with me, after the cloth was removed. There was much conversation on a variety of subjects, occasionally political. That part of it, which related to Mr. Monroe & yourself, was, probably, the foundation of the tale which has been borne to you. You will perceive, from the time & place, that it was, in no aspect, *official*. I do not profess to have a very distinct recollection of every part of it—particularly of the language used. No effort was made to retain it in my memory, because I was not aware of the presence of any one, who would seize such a time & occasion to treasure it up, for future use. I can rely on my memory however, for the substance of what was said.

I cannot recollect that I asked Dr. Wallace upon "what ground he supported the election of Genl. Jackson to the Presidency"—The question would have been superfluous, as the Doctor's habit of talking upon that subject, has rendered the enquiry unnecessary, for anyone who has fallen in with him, at least, since his visit to Washington during the winter before last.

I am also satisfied, that he did not then, or at any time, state "other reasons," besides "your services during the late war"—as I feel very sure, that he has never, in my presence, given any other than one reason, for his choice—The battle of New Orleans.

I have no hesitation in denying to you, the statement of my remarks, as they are presented in your letter—And assuring you, that I have never charged you with neglect or desertion of your military duties—Nor denied to you, the merit & glory of fighting the battle of N. Orleans. But as a conversation relating to that subject did occur, at the private table of Mr. Wellford, and as it may have been misunderstood, & has certainly been misrepresented, I think proper to give you my recollection of it—& feel the more confidence in my correctness, because I then intended to express what I have frequently expressed elsewhere, & what I have always believed to be in conformity with the truth of history.

The conversation was, on this point, commenced & principally sustained by others. In its progress some one, probably Dr. Wallace, remarked that the battle of N. Orleans, was proof that Genl. Jackson was fit for any station. Some other answered, that fighting no one battle could be proof of fitness for high civil stations. The reply was, that it was not the fighting of the battle alone, but also providing the materials & preparing the means for it—that this had been left to his unaided exertions—the War Dept. having neglected to make the preparations & left him, without arms, means or money. I think I had not, before this, taken part in the conversation—but considering this view of the subject, as extremely unjust to Mr. Monroe who had been Secretary of war at the time, to whom I have long professed a strong personal attachment, and for whose virtues I felt reverence, as I did gratitude for his services to the Country—I thought it my duty to say, in substance; that my impression of what had occurred, at that period, was different—that I did not think Genl. J. had been left in the manner represented—that all which could be done, had been done, after Mr. Monroe came into the Dept. that his exertion & devotion to his duties, at that time, had nearly destroyed his life—that he early discovered or foresaw that N. Orleans would be attacked—& informed Genl. Jackson of it—and provided such troops & arms, as he could to meet the emergency—that he had learned that Genl. J's health was bad, & he & the President were extremely anxious, lest this cause should induce him to return to Tennessee, or he should remain so long in Florida, as to prevent him from reaching N. O. in time to prepare for its defence—that urgent & pressing letters were sent to hasten him to that point—And that I believed the means provided, the information given & the Orders sent, enabled Genl. Jackson to fight the battle & to fight it successfully—that without Mr. Monroes exertions, it could not probably have been won, as it was won. But I did not deny to you, the merit of fighting the battle well; or making every possible exertion to prepare for it—nor fail to give you, the high praise which was your due. My object was to vindicate Mr. Monroe, and was not then, nor has it been, at any time, to depreciate your military exploits. They form a part of our national glory which I have no inclination to tarnish.

It is not improbable, that Col. Gray did ask where the letters or orders which I mentioned, were to be found—and that I did answer, that I could not tell, except it might be in the War Dept—but that I understood, & had no doubt, that they did exist.

You will not, after this narrative, expect me to give the name of any informer. My information, whether correct or otherwise, was derived from the various sources, verbal written & printed, from which my knowledge of the history of that day is drawn.

As you request, I shall enclose this letter to Genl. Houston, that he may forward it.[2] I am, Sir, respectfully &c

Sam L. Southard

ALS, Copies, and Extract, DLC (72, 34); Presscopy of ALS, T (mAJs). Published in Bassett, 3:342–44 (from DLC-34 copy).
  1. See above.
  2. Southard sent his letter to Houston, but Houston refused to accept it sealed, whereupon Southard mailed it directly to AJ.

From Alfred Balch

Tuesday Morning [February 13, 1827]

Dr Sir,
  Enclosed I send you a letter from Col Benton[1]—From it, it is clear that the situation of the administration is perilous in the extreme.
  I feel myself flattered by the kindness, unworthily perhaps, manifested towards the Biographical sketch which I wrote at the request of some distinguished citizens of Virginia, who caused it to be inserted in the Richmond Enq[uirer.] I am told that ten thousand copies have been distributed in Maryland Va. & New York—V. B. will cause an edition to be printed in Albany & distributed all thro the upper part of the "great state"[2] yr friend

A Balch

ALS, ICHi (11-0454).
  1. Not found.
  2. Balch's sketch, a ten-page pamphlet entitled *Gen. Andrew Jackson,* was first published in the *Richmond Enquirer,* November 24, 1826.

From Ralph Eleazar Whitesides Earl

14: Feby. 1827.

Dr. Sir,
  Th[omas] H. Fletcher is appointed Attorney for the district of West Tennessee—[1]
  This is all right? Because it is in perfect consistency with the balance of the coalition appointments—For instance says Mr. Fletcher, (in a speech on the measures taken by the Legislature of Tennessee 1825, recommending you for the Presidency)—
  "That the will of the people was unheeded—that the voice of the nation was stiffled—and that Adams became our President. In the cup of bitterness, this to me, was the bitterest drop of All."[2]
  Some extracts of a Simular nature might be taken from his "Political horse race" if it was necessary.[3]
  The inclosed Letter is from Col. Benton to Mr. Balch[4]—Respectfully

R. E. W. Earl.

ALS, DLC (34).

1. Fletcher (1792–1845), former state legislator from Franklin County, held the post until 1829 when he resigned. He had been the nominee of the Andrew Erwin anti-Jackson faction for the post.

2. In his speech, Fletcher stated that he personally favored William H. Crawford but, since the majority of votes had been cast for Jackson, he should have been elected president (*Nashville Republican,* October 15, 1825).

3. Fletcher's "Political Horse Racing, & Presidential Contest" was a popular pro-Crawford piece published in the *Richmond Enquirer,* June 13, 1823 (reprint edited by Joseph C. Clifft, Knoxville, 1995).

4. Not found.

To *Samuel Houston*

Hermitage Febry 15th. 1827.

Dr. Genl

I have this evening recd yours, sent under cover to Major Graham,[1] it was handed to me by Genl Coffee who reached Nashville on yesterday.

I regret very much that my letter to Mr Sec. Southard, of the 5th. of Janry last under cover to you, has not reached you.[2] I regret this the more, from information recd by Genl Coffee, of my friends address on the 8th. of January,[3] having aroused the ire & displeasure of my old friend James Monroe, I am sure he cannot be serious, for he does know that Neworleans, was left destitute of the proper means of defence, & that if the enemy had not been driven from Pensacola, before I left Mobile for orleans, that Mobile would have been taken, and the British would have reduced the lower country by forming a lodgement on the missippi river at the cheksaw Bluffs[4]—whether the want of the means of defence, was owing to the neglect of the Department of war, or to the subordinate officers, is for them to determine; I have never yet heard of any of the ordinance Dept. being arrested, for their disobedience, & it is certainly true, we had neither arms, flints, entrenching tools, nor ordinance of large caliber, or in sufficient number for ample defence—

I hasten to inclose you a duplicate to Mr Southard which I request you to deliver open, and demand his answer, should he refuse, note his refusal in wr[i]ting in his presence, and advise me of it—I send this by the mail from Nashville endorsed by my own hand, taking the postmasters receipt for it—If it does not go Safe we can then ferret out the purloiner I have to repeat, on its receipt, please to hand it without loss of time.

Say to Judge White I recd his letter[5] & mailed the answer at the fountain of health on the 12th. enclosing copies of such documents as may answer his views for the present.[6]

you say you cannot find my letter to Mr Monroe, of Febry. 13th. 1815—Its date is the 18th. of Febry 1815—it was wrote on the receipt of his Duplicate of the 10th. of Decbr 1814, which was recd at 9 oclock P.M. of the 18th. & his of the 10th. of Decbr 1814. was the first letter I had recd from the Dept of War, from the time I left Mobile which was on the 22nd. of Novbr. 1814—The original letter was placed in to the hands of a Doctor Cousens who got as far as Nashville,[7] and another Duplicate to the charge of Major [Alexander Campbell Wilder] Fanning[8] who did not Join me If he did, it was not untill after the declaration of peace— altho, *all marked by express*—the one that reached me first, was placed in the hands of Lt Smith of artillery, he took sick at Staunton Va, wrote & informed the Govr. of it, asked advice as to the dispatches—he wrote that he had recd. orders from the Dept. of date the 30th. of Janry, to forward the dispatches by express I am thus explicit that you may examine for his letter to the Dept. and the letter of the Dept. to Lt Smith of the 30th. of January or of the 31rst. Not having his letter before me, I cannot with positiveness say which—but I have Lt Smiths letter on file, which I view a happy circumstance—My letter of the 18th. of Febry was put into the Post office by Colo. R. Butler, it must be there if not *burnt*—

I have recd the copy of the letter you allude to, under cover of the Frank of Colo. McKee[9]—and it fills the measure, of every thing communicated to me by my annonimous *friend* in 1821 a copy of which, with the frankness of a friend, I sent to Mr Monroe[10]—I thank you for this copy—if *necessary,* and I cannot obtain the original, I shall ask the Sec. & Mr Monroe, the one whether he *wrote* & the other whether he *recd,* such a letter. I have the letters to which it refers, and when compared with the hypocritical intention of the writer to *coo* me out of the principles upon which I had acted and that I might assume that responsibility which rested upon the President, the most friendly terms of expressions were used—but I thank my god who guides me, having always acted upon principle, & always taking truth for my guide, I gave him a reply that facts warrented, & real principle dictated but the intention must have been to have entrapped me—*it failed*—

I have not recd the list of letters you say you sent me by Mr Washington thro Dr. Shelby—I will thank you for the list of all letters recd. from me & those sent to me which are on file in the Dept. of war.

I receve the salutations of Mr Randolph with the kindest feelings, & beg you to reciprocate them—I am happy to learn that he bears the loss of his election with his usual magnamity—all his friends expected this—

I thank you for the Trouble you have taken about the archy filly—as Mr Randolph has no three year old—I shall not ask you to seek farther— I knew if he sold one, its blood would be relied on as genuine, and I wanted it for my son—

Capt Donelson was here this evening, & desires his, & his ladies, compliments to you and adds, if you can procure without too much trouble a good keeper for him you will lay him under obligations—he would have wrote you, but is engaged copying for me, he has some good coalts, had he a *good keeper,* without which, he had better not have them.

I shall give the intelligence you have transmitted to George Wilson soldier—

Expecting to see you soon, with the best wishes of Mrs. J. & myself & sons I am your friend

Andrew Jackson

ALS, DLC (72). Published in Bassett, 6:493–94 (extract).
1. See above, Houston to AJ, January [28].
2. Houston received the letter on February 2.
3. Hugh L. White's speech at the Washington celebration of the anniversary of the Battle of New Orleans.
4. The Chickasaw Bluffs are on the Mississippi River, at the present site of Memphis.
5. See above, Hugh L. White to AJ, January 17
6. AJ to White, February 7.
7. Probably Dr. William R. Couzens of Washington, D.C. Couzens did not go through Nashville, but rather to Milledgeville, Georgia, where Benjamin Hawkins forwarded the letter to AJ.
8. Fanning (c1788–1846; Military Academy 1812), a career officer, was breveted major for his defense of Fort Erie in the War of 1812. Fanning carried the letter of December 7, not the one of December 10, 1814.
9. Monroe to John C. Calhoun, September 9, 1818 (DLC-71).
10. "Friend" to AJ, Oct 29, 1821 (*Jackson*, 5:112–14).

To Hugh Lawson White

Hermitage Febry 16th. 1827—

My Dear Sir

Genl Coffee reached me last evening and shew me a note recd from Major Eaton addressed to him at Baltimore, advising that Mr Monroe had sent you a long letter, supposed for the press, "claiming for himself great merit on account of the orleans affair," and complaining of your expressions, "that he Jackson had supplied the implements of war which his govt. had not placed within his reach." This he says imputes to him ["]neglect—"[1] I sincerely regret the imbecility of this old man to attempt to stir this matter, for he does know as well as I do, that there was shere neglect somewhere, in leaving neworleans in the destitute state of defence it was. <left; I was constantly writing to the Dept of war, from the time I reached Ft. Jackson on my way to Mobile on the subject of the invasion made & intended to be made on the lower country & the necessity of preparing for defence—still it was neglected.> The Dept. was advised from time to time of its want of arms, ordinance & stores, still the supplies were not forwarded—I send you a copy of my letter to Mr Monroe of the 3rd. of January 1815[2]—This with those mailed for you on the 11th. instant, at the fountain of health, will enable you to reply. This letter with the certificate of Major Lewis[3] & others heretofore sent you will determine how far the vigilence of Mr Monroe deserves praise, or censure &

how far your expressions complained of are untrue—blame rests between him & his subordinate agents of supply, & I have said before, altho requested by me, the subagents were not brought to account for this criminal neglect, but Capt Woolly, continued on the peace establishment When necessary more can be furnished—yours respectfully

A. Jackson

ALS draft, DLC (34).
1. AJ was quoting from Eaton's letter to John Coffee, January 29 (DLC-34).
2. See *Jackson*, 3:228–29.
3. See AJ to White, February 7, and William B. Lewis to AJ, February 10.

From John Donelson (1787–1840)

February the 26th. 1827

Dear Uncle

Your favour by Capt Crawford of 30th January was duly receiv'd.[1] Since that time have been to the plantation several times. I have seen the girl that you speak of twice in the house suckling Mrs. Philips' child but think that she is not kept for a nurse. I have taken up an Idea that Mr. [John W.] Phillips will not prove a first rate maneger he appears to me to be good natured easy kind of man that is never in much of a hurry though it is hard to Judge of man unless we could be with him a good deal and see how he dose things.[2] It Seems to me that the gin house should have been rebuilt in less time than it has they have not yet got the shed raised nor the gin house covered.[3] The statement that I gave you by Capt. Crawford about the cotton was true it was not delivered untill about a week after I wrote you; there was within a few pounds of 1000 out of which Mrs. Philips took two hundred and twenty eight pounds for spining. Mr. Winbourn delivered twenty three thousand one hundred and eighteen pounds of cotton out of which I made 14 bales of cotton weighing 5618 pounds. I had loaned them 94 pounds which I retained making in all of neet cotton 5940 pounds. I shiped the 14 bales with mine on board the Pioneer and wrote to White to be governed by your instructions. The 22 bales made at home went on the same boat, she had been detained on account of the water. The rope gave out and I had to put hoops on two or three bales they done very well here *but* will not do for repacking at orleans. I borrowed one coil of Rope of Mr. Winbourn after the gin was burnt which I owe for. There is nearly one piece of bailing left that I will use and pay for—Eliza's health is still very bad she is able to sit up the most of the day and has rode out twice. Mary [Donelson Coffee] is well and Unites with Eliza and myself in love to Aunt and you. yours affectionately

John Donelson Jr.

N.B. I sent a boy inn with R. Childress[4] for sister Catharine [Donelson Martin] Should he not get there in time I wish you would let them know that he is on the way. J. D.

ALS, DLC (34).
1. Letter not found.
2. Phillips managed Andrew J. Hutchings's plantation during 1827.
3. Hutchings's gin and cotton had burned the previous fall.
4. Not identified.

To William Berkeley Lewis

H. Febry [2]8th. 1827.

Dr. Major

I have recd through the Postmaster Genl, Mr Sec Southards answer to my letter to him thro Genl H.[1] I have prepared an answer, and wish to forward it by next Sundays mail.[2] before I do, I would be glad to see you and have conversation with you on one point—I cannot come down, [h]aving no horse that I can ride—Will you come up—and brin[g] with you the letter, that will enable me to write to Mrs. Ayers,[3] and if you come please bring with you any letters & papers that may be in the post office—I am respectfully yr friend

Andrew Jackson

ALS, NNPM (11-0484). Published in Bassett, 3:344–45 (dated February 18).
1. See above, Southard to AJ, February 9, and AJ to Southard, January 5.
2. See AJ to Southard, March 6, below.
3. Not identified.

To Hardy Murfree Cryer

(Private)   Nashville March 1rst. 1827.
Revd. Sir

I have just recd. your note (confidential) of the 23rd ult.[1] I intend to be at your next Sumner circuit court, and intend being at your house on Sunday night preceeding.[2]

I regret that there should be any thing intended like parade, at any rate I hope there will not be any speechmaking. It will be pleasant to me to meet & shake by the hand my old acquaintance in that friendly sincere manner that republicans should meet, and have a review of the Genls Brigade or any portion of it, but as I have been called by the coalition, "the Military chieftain," I have no wish that any thing like speech making should constitute any part of it—I mean for publication[3]

I regret to learn the indisposition of your lady[4] & hope for her speedy recovery, with my prayers for the same, & best wishes for yourself, believe me yr friend

Andrew Jackson

P.S. Should any thing occur to prevent me from being at your house as intended I will advise you.

ALS, John P. Mullins (mAJs).
1. Not found.
2. AJ planned to attend the Sumner County court to help defend William Brackin's title to land that AJ had sold to him in 1812.
3. On March 13, AJ visited Gallatin, where there was a dinner in his honor *(National Banner and Nashville Whig,* March 17). The "general's brigade" was likely the Sumner County militia, commanded by Robert Desha (1791–1849), a general in the state militia and brother of Kentucky governor Joseph Desha.
4. Neé Elizabeth L. Rice (c1793–1833).

To Samuel Lewis Southard

Hermitage 6th. of March 1827—

Sir

I have recd your letter of the 9th. ult. in answer to mine of the 5th. of January[1] under cover of your subsequent letter of the 16th. of February.[2]

On the receipt of the written statement of Dr. Wallace, affirmed to be substantially true by Mr Johnston who was present,[3] I addressed you and from the high & dignified station which you then, & still hold, I had a right to expect a frank & candid answer giving the source thro which you derived information so positively expressed, & where the order Issued by Mr Monroe, that brought me to Neworleans was to be found. This from one of the heads of the Department of our goverment was not too much to look for. I had not asked for your historical knowledge, or for your opinion of Doctor Wallace, or of Mr Johnston *who is not a neighbour of Mr Willford* as advised, or any other gentlemen who were present, believing that all must have been gentlemen & men of truth who were associated with you at the party. I asked you for a frank answer, not an argumentative one which to my mind always carries with it the want of sincerity. As you are at the head of that chivalric corps, the Navy, to whose exploits the glory of our country is so much indebted, I believed that you would have answered Just as one of those high minded honorable men would on such an occasion, but I have been disappointed. You deny any intention, however, to injure me, whilst you profess to have no distinct recollection of the language used. Whether the *unofficial "aspect" of the [*"*]time and place"* shall excuse your memory, or weaken the statement of the Doctor, it is not my business to determine;[4] I cannot suppose that you meant to intimate that the stamp official or unofficial can affect the obligation of honorable men on all occasions to speak truly and act Justly, whether at wine drinkings or at the bureaus of state—It is a matter of much regret to me that the variance between your statement, & that of the gentlemen named, does not enable me to act understandingly on the subject; it was to avoid this situation, that I requested Genl Houston to receive your statement, and thus save me the trouble of sending a copy to those gentlemen, which Justice now requires should be done. I feel sorry therefore that you could not deliver your communication unsealed to Genl Houston.

As my inquiry was dictated by the persuasion that my character was injured by the statement presented thro Dr Wallace; & its *only* object to expose those who wilfully misrepresented it, especially should they be high in authority like yourself, I shall add a few remarks upon your historical knowledge, & your reply to the question you acknowledge to have been asked by Colo. Gray, & your answer. Had your recollection not proved very bad as it relates to the history of the times & to myself *"verbal, written, & printed,"* you would have known that I solicited the Govt. as early as June 1814, when I forwarded to it information of the assemblage of a British force at Pensacola, for permission to drive them from that rendezvous before their reinforcements could arrive, & to disperse the Indians whom they had organised there; & altho, the order requested was Issued in July 1814 it never reached me till after the declaration of peace. From your *"verbal, written, & printed"* information, you might also have ascertained, that I kept the Govrt. advised of the preparations of the British in Pensacola to attack Ft. Boyer & thro that point to invade the country, & that I again entreated the Govt. for orders to attack them—no answer from the Govt— That after the British did actually attack Fort Boyer & invade the country, & were repulsed, I again made the same entreaty of my Govt.—but it was still silent. I then informed it of the meditated attack by great Britain with all its combined force as early as the 27th. of august, when I appealed to the patriotism of my old Volunteers under the command of that brave officer Genl Coffee (having ordered before, all the Troops authorised by the Govt.) and with this force called for on my own responsibility marched to, & expelled the British from Pensacola; by which movement I frustrated the original plan of invasion thro Mobile, & by thus clearing my left flank of the enemy, was enabled to move to Neworleans, ordering on Genl Coffee's command to Baton Rouge; These were the men called, armed, and equiped, at my own responsibility, that enabled me to save Neworleans. Tho my friendship has been as sincere for Mr Monroe as yours or any other mans can be, I will ask in what history *"verbal, written, or printed,"* have you learned that he had any agency in all this, except writing to me on the 21rst of octbr. not to march on Pensacola, that the Govt. was about to negotiate with Spain &c &c and I would ask you as a military man Whether negotiation then with Spain would have prevented invasion on the part of great

Britain had I not have driven her force from Pensacola & destroyd her Indian allies—But these facts were forgotten in your *unofficial* zeal, & in your *wine drinking*. I cannot but marvel what connection there is between Mr Monroe and the Presidential canvass in your mind, that at this period you should seek to adorn him with plumage which I know he could not consent to wear—To proceed however with the historical facts *"verbal, written, and printed,"* So soon as I had cleared my left flank of the enemy, having ordered Genl. Coffee across to Baton Rouge, without the *["]means provided, the information given, or the orders sent,"* of the Govt. I repaired to orleans reaching that place on the first day of Decbr. 1814. Now I hazard the assertion, without the fear of contradiction, that you have never seen, read, or been verbally informed by Mr Monroe, or any other person of truth, that ever Mr Monroe wrote, or sent me an order prior to the date of my arrival at Neworleans; & that from the 20th. of Novbr. 1814 untill the 18th. of February 1815 I ever recd a single line from the Department of War: and as you are so conversant with history *"verbal, written, & printed."* I regret in your Zeal for truth that you did not read mine in answer to the letter of the 10th. of Decbr 1814 that moment recd. But further, on my arrival at orleans I found the arsenal empty of all the materials for vigorous & ample defence against such an overwhelming invading <army> enemy, well armed, and supplied for attack—no arms, & what was still worse, no flints for the few arms to put into the hands of the militia. What was to be done? Requisitions had been made in Septbr. 1814 & acknowledged, and the agent at Pittsburgh had promised to have them forwarded, still the Steam Boat arrived from Pittsburgh with no arms, no fixed ammunition, no flints, no ordinance, or ordinance stores, & the report was that those supplies altho offerred to be brought by the Steam boat at 75 cents pr. Cwt was entrusted to a pedling merchant at 50 cents pr Cwt. with the permission to sell, or barter, his goods on the way, all which, as you have read much, you might have seen on record in the war office where the trial of Mr Maples before a courtmartial ought to be found.[5] Thus situated, I was advised that the Barritarians[6] had flints & some arms, and were willing to surrender themselves and all their Supplies on condition of promise of pardon on good conduct. I directed Mr Livingston My voluntary aid to accept them, & give the pledge. This was done & I obtained 7500 pistol flints, which were put into the arms obtained for the militia and contributed much to the defence of the city. Now I will again ask what agency had Mr Monroe in all this that it should be said his energetic orders raised the *means for the defence* of Neworleans. These means were procured by myself & my agents, & enabled me to make the defence I did. I would be the last man in the Union to Strip Mr Monroe of the credit to which he is entitled, & have no doubt he Issued orders for the requisitions, & for the supply of arms, but in a military point of view it is not only necessary for the Superior to order but to see his orders executed. Besides, the Govr. did know & was informed in the latter end of Septbr. or first of Octbr. 1814 that the Tenneseans & Kentuckians would march, but could not be armed—in consequence the 5000 stand was sent to pittsburgh & might have been brought to me in due time in the Steam boat; but for the pittance of 25 cents pr Cwt were detained,˙ & our country thereby Jeopardised, and would probably have been lost, had it not have been for the providential supply obtained from the Barritarians.

I have therefore to *request* when on your electioneering tours, or at your wine drinkings hereafter, you will not fail to recollect these historical facts which indeed you ought long since to have known from the *verbosities, writings, & printings* of the times—and that you will not forget to state that I never abandoned the eagles of my country in the day of trial & danger; nor ever failed to take upon myself the responsibility of driving from our shores, or from those of a faithless neutral, our declared enemy when I found it necessary for the safety of my country; and altho I admire the zeal you display for your friend, yet it ought to be recollected that an honorable man will never do injustice to another in that zeal. I am sure Mr Monroe from his love of truth (or I am much mistaken in him) would be the last man to say that he had given or written me an order to repair to Orleans of prior date to the time I reached that place as I always kept him advised of my situations, intentions, & movements, and mine of the 14th. of Novbr. 1814 from Pierces Blockhouse & 20th. of Novbr. from Mobile,[7] as is believed, must have reached him before the 10th. of Decbr was written, from the then expedition of the mail—mine being sent by express to the direct line of mail, which at that time travelled at the rate of 100 miles in 24 hours, & the distance to the city 1200 miles.

Having given you a *few* of the *"written, printed & verbal"* facts of the time alluded to, I close this correspondence, and am yr. mo. obdt. Servt.

Andrew Jackson

ALS copy, Copy, and LS draft in Andrew J. Donelson's hand with corrections in AJ's hand, DLC (34, 72); Copy, Tx (11-0493). Published in Bassett, 3:345–48.
1. See above.
2. See Southard to AJ, February 16.
3. John H. Wallace to Samuel Houston, November 30, 1826 (DLC-72).
4. AJ's quotations throughout this letter were from Southard's of February 9.
5. Thomas Maples's court-martial for failure to deliver arms, March 2, 1815.
6. Pirate followers of Jean Laffite (c1780–c1826).
7. See AJ to Monroe, November 14, 1814; and November 20, 1814 (*Jackson*, 3:191–94).

To John McLean (1785–1861)

Hermitage March 7th. 1827.

Sir

your letter of the 3rd. ult.[1] has come to hand with its enclosures, and altho the envelope of my letter of the 5th. of Janry to Genl Houston,[2] has much mistery about it, and the paper, such as I had none about the house at the time, still, I might have used the envelope of the letter Just recd from Genl. H. to enclose mine to him—If the address on the envelope is genuine it is my own hand writing, not that of another by my directions—The address "Honble.," instead of, "Genl," and the word, "Senator," instead of, "member in Congress," has not been my usual mode of address [to] Genl Houston—still, as I wrote in haste, & in the night, this singularity might have happenned, and when I look at the writing, there is something so much of the general character of my hand, that I would not for any consideration say that it was not mine, and particularly under the present circumstances of this case, one thing I am certain of, and the enclosed certificate of Capt A. J. Donelson[3] will prove, that the letter of the 5th. to Genl Houston was mailed at Nashville on Saturday the 6th. of January last—

I was impressed with the belief, that I had endorsed on it, "Pension claims," or directed Capt. D. to do so, that it might pass through the postoffices, in safety to its address—The envelope before me, has no such endorsment, still, I cannot say that the direction of the letter is not mine, as I might have intended to put such an endorsment on it, for the purpose mentioned, and in the hurry of the moment, have forgotten it—I therefore return all the papers you enclosed to me, under the impression that no forgery has been committed, determined hereafter that all letters of importance wrote by me sent through the mail, shall be noted in such a way as forgery, if committed, shall be detected.

It is to be regretted, that any cause for suspicions & complaints, <should rest on, & be made> against the safety of our mails, but it is a fact, that many of my letters have not reached their address, and of late, I seldom write by mail—unless on private business—but, as I have no secretes, <the purloiners, cannot> no one can profit by the espoinage, nor do me much injury—circumstances has occurred since I wrote the letter of the 5th to Genl Houston, to raise a suspicion, that its contents had been known by some others, before it reached the Genl at the city[4]—still I have no suspicion that it was opened at Nashville, if opened at all; time may develope, whether these suspicions are well grounded—I have adopted the precaution of late, to have receipts taken of all letters of importance when deposited in the post office

Whatever delay has happened in the transmission of this letter is chargeable to the postoffice, as I am certain I sent it by Captain Donelson on Saturday the 6th. and he reported that on that day he put it in the mail at Nashville, & Mr Irwin, as Capt Donelson informs me, recollects it. I am Sir very respectfully your Mo. obdt. servt,

Andrew Jackson

ALS draft, DLC (34).
1. See above.
2. Envelope not found.
3. Not found.
4. AJ probably had in mind Houston's February 4 account, above, of the comments Southard made when Houston delivered AJ's letter to him that suggested that Southard already knew the contents of AJ's communication.

From Henry Lee

Westmoreland. Va. 12th. March 1827

dear Genl.

Your letter of the 25th. Decr.[1] last reached me in due time, & was no less valuable than acceptable. I am glad that my Quebec correspondence answered my hopes, and gave pleasure to you. I now send you by my friend Mr. Clarke,[2] a genuine fragment of the Rock, against which Genl. Wolfe leant when he Uttered that glorious exclamation upon learning that the french fled—And by which he was supported when he breathed his last.[3] And I also take the liberty to present you with a chrystal found in the face of Cape diamond, the high promontory on which Quebec is situated, and at the base of which our own [Richard] Montgomery fell.[4] These relics or mementos of two "military chieftains" I trust will be acceptable to you and I should be pleased if they Could be in some shape or other appended to your person—by being infixed in the hilt of your sword, the head of your cane, your watch seal, &c &c.

The accompanying correspondence will evince the jealousy & prevarication, with which my attempt to obtain information respecting the public & national part of my work, has been repelled by the "Earl of Empty Barrels"[5]—under the dictation no doubt of the whole Coalition. I have resolved in consequence, to adopt the step advised by Genl. Houston, and other of your friends & to visit your neighbourhood; where I hope to arrive in the course of the month of may, that I may have access to your military papers, and get such explanations on points of my narrative as Yourself & your officers will best be able to furnish.[6] Homer travelled for wisdom, from Greece to Egypt, & I may afford to journey from Virginia to Tennessee for truth. Under the hope that in nothing I may contravene your wishes I remain dear Genl your faithful Sevt.

H. Lee

ALS and cover with ANS by AJ, DLC (72, 34). Endorsed: "Major Lee letter enclosing his correspondence with the Sec of war on the subject of having access to my correspondence with the sec of war; which, the Sec refuses to grant, but permits mutilated accounts of mine to be sent to Mr. Hammonds—this Shews the coalition & combination of the Executive branches to slander me, & to keep their offices locked against my friends A J."

1. See above.
2. Not identified.
3. The alleged last words of Wolfe, who died leading his troops to victory over the French in 1759, were, "What, do they run already? Then I die happy."
4. Montgomery (1738–75) commanded the American invasion of Canada in 1775.
5. The enclosures were Lee to James Barbour, December 8, 1826, and Barbour to Lee, December 13, 1826 (both DLC-72). In these letters Barbour refused Lee, then beginning his biography of AJ, access to war department files. Jacksonians seized the epithet "Earl of Empty Barrels" to refer to Barbour from his toast at a July 4, 1826, dinner: "Let the people judge of their servants, in whatever grade, by their deeds rather than by what they say of themselves, or others say of them—always remember the quaint adage, that 'an empty barrel sounds loudest'" (*National Intelligencer,* July 7, 1826).
6. Lee did go to Nashville in May and remained in the area, with some interruptions, until January 1829.

To James Allen

(Copy)   Hermitage March 31rst. 1827—
Dr. Sir

I have recd your letter of the 22nd instant[1] and feel greatly obliged for the information communicated by it. It breathes such evidence of candour & honest sentiment, that notwithstanding my hitherto determination to interefere in no wise with the presidential election, or to write upon the subject to any one, I am pursuaded in this case, the most scrupulous will acquit me of all sinister motives, when repelling charges of so heinous a charecter as those stated by you to be made by Messhrs. [Richard Aylett] Buckner & [Francis] Johnston.[2]

At the tribunal of the people it will be acertained that I never have solicited the office of president of the U. States—There frank and flattering call placed me before them as a candidate for that distinguished station; and hence my determination ever has been to leave to their unbiassed Judgement the selection regardless of the abuse and slander heaped upon me by the minions of power & the panders of corruption. But in this class of wretches I could not have calculated to find any who enjoyed the confidence & respect of the people. I had a hope for the honor of the country that no man who occupied the exalted station of a member of congress could be made to *lie* or gainsay, as occasion might require, in order to maintain the power of a coalition whose object seems rather to be my destruction than the advancement of the interests of their Country

I could not have believed that men elevated as Messhrs. Buckner & Johnston have been were so lost to all respect for truth & charecter as to take up Jessee Bentons pamphlet[3] for the purpose of vending *tissues* of falshood and calumny to the credulous & unwary. Such, however, appears to be their conduct, and if, the truth, which is mighty & will ultimately prevail shall consign them to infamy & disgrace along with poor Jessee, they cannot blame me. It can be no apology for them to plead that they are not the authors of the charges—neither was poor Jessee. He only put his signature to the pamphlet, controuled by the same influence which dictated the famous letter of my military friend H. at Washington Pensylvania, the same influence which now operates upon the honorable Messhrs. Bukner & Johnston as the wire upon the puppets.

The charge relative to the execution of the six militia men, is the only allegation of Mr Buckner which you say you are not prepared to refute from a knowledge of the facts, or from documentary evidence. I shall therefore first bestow some time upon it.

at the close of the Creek war the Forts in that nation were ordered to be occupied & garrisoned—for this purpose Col P Pipkin was ordered with a Regt of drafted militia for six months into the service of the U states. Whilst stationed at Fort Jackson on the 19th or 20th of Septr. 1814 a mutiny took place headed by a Captain, & in the presence of the Col. forced the guard, seized the provisions, burned the bake house & marched off forcibly leaving the Col destitute of provisions, & without a competent garrison in the midst of the Creek nation stirred up to hostility against us at that time by the agents of the British: at a period too when the British with an overwhelming army were preparing to invade the lower country. It was reported to me about the time of my appeal to your venerable patriot Shelby, when I made the requisitions on Tennessee for aid in so solemn a crisis. Orders were immediately given for the apprehension of the mutineers, Col Pipkin being instructed to join me at the *Cut off* with the remainder of his Regt and Genl Coffees volunteers from Tennessee on the march to Pensacola where the British were rendevoused. The mutineers becoming alarmed, all except nine of the ringleaders returned, were pardoned, and remained with their Col during the whole of that campaign. These ringleaders were taken, & brought to Mobile after I had left that section of command; and when I was at New Orleans were tried by a Courtmartial at Mobile, and condemned to be shot—three were pardoned, having been recommended to mercy by the court which tried them, the ballance were shot, but not as Mr Buckner falsely pronounces in his stump speech for crimes committed after their term of service had expired; but for crimes of the deepest dye, perilous to the country—at a time when every patriots arm was stretched; when every nerve of the Govt was strained to defend our liberties & our country from conquest & subjugation. It was at this period, too, the Hartford convention were giving to the enemy every encouragement of success either by a division or conquest of the States. These facts are on record, and ought to have been known to Mr Buckner before he undertook the commission of traduction & slander. The mutiny, the order for the apprehension, the trial &c. are, or ought to be on file at Washington; or, if not, a copy of the record can be had from the papers of my Adjt Genl. Thus you see, Sir, with the exception of my being commander of the division, Mr Buckner had as much to do with the execution of these men as I had. It is well there are virtuous & good citizens who have independence & strength to check the career of the wicked and ambitious, & in whose support and approbation there is ample reward for patriotic service. The man who knows me not, and can yet charge me with a crime which from the known history of the times must be untrue, and whilst the allegation is scarcely made has the hardihood to say *he has sent to Tennessee for proof*, would not only rob me of my hard earned reputation, but betray his country if he had the power.[4]

Inclosed I send a reply made to Jesse Benton's pamphlet on its first appearance,[5] which I have no doubt Mr Buckner has seen, & he must have been very negligent indeed if he has not read the report of the Senate, my reply & memorial, where many, if not all, the charges are proved to be false.[6]

You say that Majr [Joel] Yancey[7] informed you that Frank Johnston told the people in his stump speech (on the same day Mr Buckner spoke & made his charges, 32 miles apart) that I left Congress about the time the sedition & alien laws passed, meaning to insinuate that I would have voted for the law if I had been there. This statement Mr Johnston knew to be false when he made it. All my public life gives evidence of my opposition to the alien & sedition laws as well as the general administration of John Adams.[8] My votes in the senate will shew that upon all questions I voted with the republican party, with [Henry] Tazwell, [Stevens Thomson] Mason & others: and being continually in the then minority I resigned to make room for Genl [Daniel] Smith whose age & weight of character I thought would add to the republican strength.[9] You add that Frank Johnston further stated, I had drawn pay as Genl for staying at home, & for seven servants, meaning to insinuate that I recd pay for seven servants. This is another wilful misrepresentation, & I challenge with boldness Mr Johnston to the production of any account in which I have ever charged for seven servants. I never have drawn a cent of public money in my life to which I was not both justly & legally entitled. Let us examine the charge of staying at home. I returned from the creek campaign in May 1814, recd. the appointment of Major Genl, unsolicitted by me, with orders to proceed to the south in June. I recd the submission of the Creeks in July 1814, and never saw my family until after the close of the War. I returned to Nashville in May 1815, & there established my Head quarters. In octbr I went to the City of Washington, arriving there with my family in November when my life was despaired of. I left there the 24th Decbr. under orders, and reached Nashville 2d February 1816; & on the 9th of that month proceeded to the lower country, & took a recognizance of the whole coast & inlets for the purpose of selecting scites for the erection of Fortifications. I returned to Nashville in the latter end of May 1816, where my attention was called to the defence of the North Western frontier then likely to be attacked by the Indians. In Septr of that year I was ordered as one of the commissioners to hold a treaty with the Chickasaws, Creeks & Cherokees which I did, reaching Nashville in December 1816, from whence I was ordered to explore the country for a proper scite for a Foundry & arsenal, & to lay out, & cause to be surveyed & opened a military road from Nashville to Orleans—this was done. In the fall 1817 I was ordered as one of the Commissioners to hold a Tr[e]aty with the Cherokees: this service was not long performed, when I recd an order to proceed to Fort Scott, collect a sufficient force, & put a speedy end to the war with exemplary punishment for the unprov[o]ked crimes of the enemy. I performed this duty worn down with sickness privations & fatigue; so much so that my friends did not expect me to recover; yet I reached Nashville in June 1818. In the fall of that year, associated with the venerable sage & patriot Gov. Shelby, a treaty was held with the Chickasaws by which we obtained a cession from them of all the lands north of the southern boundary of Tennessee. From my return to Nashville in that year, I was employed in superintending the military road, removing intruders from the Indian lands, & by the duties of my division, being under confidential orders preparing for the defence of the lower country expected to be invaded. In the month of Octr 1820, I, with Genl Hinds, held a treaty with the Choctaws, and shortly after recd orders to march for & receive possession of the Floridas—this brings me to the first of June 1821 which terminated my military service. With those services which I have enumerated, the additional duty of superintending my division, occupied every hour of my time. During my whole military command, I never had a furlough, was always under orders, and altho' in wretched health was never on the sick report. I often suggested my wish to resign, but was always prevented by the request of the President. So much for the charge of Mr Johnston, of staying at home, & of drawing the pay of a *sinecure*.

I have been thus particular to put it in your power to correct the misrepresentations of Messrs. Buckner & Johnston whom I know to be the mere panders of the coalition of which you speak. It cannot be possible if their real characters are unmasked in time that the high minded people of Kentucky will deem them worthy of their confidence.[10]

With sincere thanks to you, Sir, allow me to assure you, that altho' personally strangers, I duly appreciate the favor conferred upon me by the opportunity afforded of opposing to the calumnies of my enemies a naked statement of the truth. Truth has been my shield in all the perils which I have encountered for the cause of my country. I shall never part with it for the sake of office. Allow me to subscribe myself Yr. very obliged & Humble sert.

(Signed) Andrew Jackson

AL copy (partly in Andrew J. Donelson's hand) and Copy, NN (11-0519, -0537); Draft in Donelson's hand with corrections by AJ, DLC (72); Copy in Donelson's hand, THer (11-

0529). Published in Bassett, 3:349–52, 6:500–504. Allen (d. 1836) was a brigadier general in the War of 1812 and at this time represented Green County in the Kentucky Senate.

1. See Allen to AJ, March 22.

2. On March 19, Buckner (1763–1847) and Johnson (1776–1842), Kentucky congressmen, in separate speeches, charged AJ with unjustly executing the six militiamen, padding his military expense account, leaving the Senate previous to the enactment of the Alien and Sedition Acts and thereby giving implicit support to those measures, and supporting a property qualification for the franchise at Tennessee's first constitutional convention.

3. *An Address to the People of the United States* (September 1824).

4. For the events involving the six militiamen, see *Jackson*, 3:133–36.

5. The enclosure was probably Samuel R. Overton's "Mr. Benton's Pamphlet" published as a broadside under the pseudonym "Truth" by the *Nashville Gazette*, October 12, 1824.

6. The Lacock Committee Report (*Annals of Congress*, 15th Cong., 2nd sess., pp. 631–74), the March 5, 1819, "Strictures on Mr. Lacock's Report on the Seminole War" (*National Intelligencer*, March 9, 1819), and the Memorial to the U.S. Senate re Conduct during the Florida Invasion, [1819–1820].

7. Yancey (1773–1838), a Kentucky state senator challenging Johnson's reelection, won the seat in congress.

8. The Alien and Sedition Acts of 1798 gave the President broad authority to detain and deport aliens he considered dangerous, made it much more difficult for foreigners to become United States citizens, and made it illegal to publish "false, scandalous, and malicious" writings against government officials (1 *U. S. Statutes at Large* 566–72, 577–78, 596–97).

9. Tazewell (1753–99; William and Mary, 1770) and Mason (1760–1803) were from Virginia; Daniel Smith (1748–1818), Tennessee.

10. Drawing heavily on AJ's letter, Allen published, over the name "An Old Fashioned Republican," a refutation of the charges made by Buckner and Johnson, asserting that their "speeches were tissues of falsehood, slander, and abuse" (Frankfort *Argus of Western America*, May 9). When Buckner took umbrage at the article, Allen denied any intention of attacking Buckner's moral character (Frankfort *Commentator*, September 8).

To Arthur Lee Campbell

Hermitage, March 31st. 1827—

Dr. Sir,

I have received your kind favour of the 18th. instant, and yours of prior date therein alluded to[1]—I have no apology for not answering the first but the press of business, and my unwillingness to write on politicks—my letters are sometimes interrupted on their passage—sometimes published, and become the subject of unpleasant remarks by my enemies, and mutilated for their own views of deception to pervert my meaning and opinions and hold me forth as using expressions I never made or opinions I never held. I have therefore declined answering political letters.

The idea given me in your letter before me of the 18th. comports with the rule I have long since adopted—I give no pledges on any subject—If elevated to the Presidential chair it shall be by the free will of the people who have the sovereign right to call me there—my duty to them, to remain free & unpledged and go there with clean hands without bargain, pledge, or management, and if, I ever be there, it will be agreeable to this rule laid down.

I would visit Kentucky with much pleasure, but when I see with what propriety the public journals have lashed the heads of departments for their electioneering tours last year, I cannot subject myself to such imputations when my politics are so much at variance with such a course— wherever business leads me, *there I will go,* and I will visit Kentucky with much pleasure when I can without the imputation of electioneering tour.

Accept the assurance of my great respect and believe me your most obdt. servt.

Andrew Jackson

Copy, DLC (11-0548). Published in Bassett, 3:45–46 (dated March 31, 1821). Endorsed by Arthur L. Campbell: "The foregoing (copied by my son) is a literal copy of an original letter from Genl. Andrew Jackson to me."
1. Neither letter found.

From Henry Johnson (1783–1864)

New Orleans, March 31st., 1827.

Sir,

I take particular pleasure in transmitting to you the copy of a resolution in which the Legislature of Louisiana have expressed the wish, that the illustrious defender of New Orleans should participate in the celebration, at this city, of the next anniversary of the glorious victory achieved under his auspices.[1]

Permit me to add, Sir, that your presence here, on the return of that auspicious day, would be hailed with enthusiasm by the whole population of Louisiana—

I have the honor to be, with the highest consideration, Sir, your obedient servant.

H. Johnson

LS, DLC (34). Published in Natchez *Statesman & Gazette,* May 3. Johnson was governor of Louisiana, 1824–28.
1. The resolution (DLC-34) of the Louisiana General Assembly requested the governor to invite Jackson to attend the celebration.

To John Coffee

Nashville April 3rd 1827—

Dr. Genl

yours of the 29th. ult.[1] reached me last evening, detailing the murdrous attack upon Capt J. Donelson—I feel gratefull & thankful to a kind providence for his preservation, as there can be no doubt but this fellow was excited by others to commit a wilful murder.[2]

The Capt had wrote me[3] to Attend to the taking of some Testimony, to prove that the Capt was with us, at the time this fellow *swears* he was at *Alabama* The Testimony of three witnesses prove this beyond any doubt—This must have come to their knowledge, and finding there was no longer safety behind the perjury of suborned witnesses the attempt by the murder of the Capt to shield them from infamy—The gods are Just, and will expose their infamy & I hope the Capt will survive, to attend to the Suits with energy & effect.

I recd your letter by Major Chambers boy, with my horse, & only regretted that you thought any apology necessary for his detention.

I have noted your remarks about the Overseer at A. J. Hutchings farm Should you find him unfit, or indolent, or inattentive, turn him away & employ young Mr Winburn.[4] Mr. Phillips has covenanted that his wife is to perform the same services toward the care of the negro children and their spinning & cloathing as Mrs. Nicholson did, I fear this will not be complied with—and if not the sooner a bad overseer is turned away the better—I have had a Just experience in the conduct of Persons who, I have discovered to be, the greatest villain on earth—he left me & brought Suit against me, I entered into the defense as Capt D. ought, and brought him to know that peace & honesty was his better course, and he agreed to reduce fifty dollars of his wages, pay all costs & dismiss his Suit[5]—upon this proposition I closed with him forever with the determination to turnaway every overseer on their first Misbehaviour—it is the only safe course—but if Phillips will hold out, and make a good crop, it will be well to let him continue to the end of the year—[6]

all friends are now in good health, hoping to see you & family at the Hermitage soon, with a tender of respects to all, your friend

Andrew Jackson

ALS, THi (11-0552). Published in Bassett, 3:352–53 (extract).
    1. Letter not found.
    2. The stabbing of John Donelson (1787–1840) grew out of a dispute regarding payment for land sold in 1820 and Donelson's charges that several witnesses in the case, many of whom were among James Jackson's relatives, had committed perjury.
    3. Letter not found.

4. Probably Jesse Winborne, who had previously served as overseer on Andrew J. Hutchings's plantation

5. Person had been AJ's overseer from 1823 through 1826. In early 1827 AJ had dismissed him and docked his wages for damages to property at the Hermitage. For the resolution of the dispute between AJ and Person, see Memorandum, [cMarch 19].

6. Phillips remained as Hutchings's overseer until the end of 1827.

The letter below relates to the defense of Jackson by the Nashville Jackson Corresponding Committee against the charges made by Buckner and Johnson of Kentucky and reveals, in part, the consultation that Jackson had with the committee in the drafting and publication of its reports. The "Vindication" finally appeared in print on April 25.

To William Berkeley Lewis

Hermitage 5th of april

Dr Major

Since I returned home I have been looking over Colo. Pipkins evidence he says, on oath, speaking of the block house that it was *demolished*,[1] from which I suppose it was intended, *pulled down*—in one of the reports[2] it is stated *burned* now I wish you to use language that the Colo. has used—*demolished*—it will meet the *case*[3]—yrs in haste

Andrew Jackson

ALS, NNPM (11-0556); Copy, NN (11-0558).

1. The record of Pipkin's testimony in the courts martial of the six militiamen and his usage of "demolished" appears in *ASP, Military Affairs*, 3:705.

2. Pipkin's reports have not been found.

3. In his affidavit of April 16 (*Maryland Republican*, July 3, 1827), Pipkin again used "demolished" in accordance with AJ's recommendation. It is highly likely that Lewis prompted Pipkin on the usage.

From Hugh Lawson White

Knoxville
April 7th. 1827.

Dear Sir,

Your favor of the 30th. Ult.[1] was received yesterday. That containing the Documents concerning the War in the lower country was received in Washington in due course of mail[2] and a Duplicate accompanied by your favor under date of the 5th. March[3] was received as soon as I reached home. To you it is unnecessary for me to make any apology for not answering those communications immediately.

Your kind sympathies for my domestic afflictions have all the effect that a cordial of that description can have upon wounded feelings.[4]

From your old friend M———e I received a very lengthy reply to my answer to his first letter, of which I did not think it worth while to advise you, as it contains nothing of consequence which was not to be substantially found in the first. I immediately gave to it such answer as it seemed to merit and there the matter rests.[5] His and mine are both in kind terms. The real object I always suspected was to get some excuse for coming before the public, and my wish always is to furnish no reasonable pretext for a controversy, to the end that if forced to contend before the tribunal of the Sovreign people I may in truth as well as appearance be in the right.

That every means have been, and will be, employed, to destroy you and all those who advocate your pretensions no reasonable man need doubt. That *money* and *offices* can do much there is too much reason to fear; and every thing which the judicious use of them can do, will be tried, with untiring zeal, in the whole course of this spring and Summer I most firmly believe.

It is a fearful and unequal contest—*money office,* the hope of office and every thing which can be included under the term patronage on the one side, confronted by nothing but intelligence and virtue of the people on the other: but he is unworthy of public employ who will *faulter* for a moment. *Discretion, firmness* perserverance and union will carry us successfully through or leave us all honorably at home to attend to our own concerns, under nominally a Rep[ub]lican government: but practically a monarchy of the worst stamp. That any falsehood they chuse to invent can be proved either upon you or any of your friends I am well aware; and every man may prepare his mind for the worst. It is a poor battle in which none are killed or wounded—if defeated we can bury our dead and dress our wounded at leisure. If victorious we have the highest consolation, to wit, that the slain and mangled have suffered in the best of causes.

I hope to be in Nashville in a few weeks and will bring *[with]* me the correspondence with your old friend M———e and have much to say.

Present us all kindly to your good lady and believe that I am, with great Sincerity Yr. Mt. Obt. Servt.

Hu. L. White

Note Colo. Williams yesterday avowed candidate for Senate to the legislature.[6]

ALS, DLC (34). Published in Bassett, 3:353 (extract).
1. Not found.
2. See AJ to White, February 7.
3. Not found.
4. White's daughter, Lucinda, had died on March 20.
5. Monroe to White, January 26 and February 9, and White to Monroe, January 29

and February 21 (DLC-34, -72, *Writings of James Monroe* 7:104–12, and DLC-Monroe Papers).

    6. In January, John Williams had returned from a diplomatic mission to Guatemala.

To John Coffee

Hermitage april 13th. 1827

Dr. Genl

We have not heard from Capt Jack Donalson for some days, hope he is recovering & that Eliza health is improving—present Mrs. J. & myself affectionately to them.

When leisure permits will you have the goodness to inform me whether Mr Griffin has paid the ballance of the price of Negro George, if he has not, whether suit has been brought vs him—If suit has not been brought, & he has not given other assurance of payment than his word, if you have heard where he resides I will try & have him sued where he has removed—If he has business that will lead him *[b]*ack to your county, have a writ issued to await his arrival—it is useless *[to]* rest on his promise any longer.[1]

The Messhrs. Winstons sold their fathers place here to Mr. Wm. Ward, and I have taken the contract off his hands—the land is to be survayed & convayed the first of May next, when the consideration is to be paid[2]—I wish you to send me the amt of the bond due by Colo Winston to me, with the time it became due—I believe the two bonds are for $1066.66/100 due first of March 1827. & first of March 1828[3]—If I am incorrect, please correct me—I have had a laborious task in getting the place in order for a crop—has at length succeeded, & have it all under good fence & in corn & oats, and in a few weeks will have a good pasture for my out stock & mares.

I am anxious to see you and your family here—Mrs. Call is with us, will leave us next week—The old *Turk*,[4] has not even enquired after her health—*What Savages*—

Mrs. J. unites with me in good wishes to yo*[u]* & family—friends all well, in hast*[e]* adieu—

Andrew Jackson

ALS, THi (11-0564).

    1. No writ or suit against William Griffin has been found.

    2. William C. Ward had contracted to buy the property of Anthony Winston (1750–1827) in Davidson County, but had transferred the contract to AJ; and on October 22, 1828, the Winston descendants deeded the property to AJ.

    3. Anthony Winston (1782–1839) owed AJ for the Big Spring farm near Tuscumbia, Alabama.

    4. Ellen J. Kirkman, Mary K. Call's mother.

To Henry Johnson (1783–1864)

Nashville April 18th. 1827—

Sir

Your letter of the 31st. ulto.[1] transmitting to me the copy of the Resolution of the Legislature of Louisiana, expressing the wish, that I should participate in the celebration of the 8th. of Jany. in the year 1828 at the City of New Orleans, has been received.

I pray you to convay to the Legislature of the State of Louisiana, the great pleasure it will afford me in complying with their expressed wish, upon this occasion; and assure them, that nothing but the interposition of divine providence will prevent me from uniting with them, and the citizens of Louisiana, my associates in arms, & in those privations, & dangers, which rendered glorious the day, intended to be celebrated.

For the kind manner in which you have been pleased to communicate to me, the Resolution of the Legislature of Louisiana, be pleased to accept a tender of my sincere thanks.

I have the honor to be with great respect your obedient servt.

Andrew Jackson

ALS copy and ALS draft, DLC (34). Published in *Natchez Statesman & Gazette*, May 3.
  1. See above.

From Edward George Washington Butler

Cincinnati, April 27. 1827.

My Dear General,

I have received your letter of the 13th Instant, and regret to inform you that your suspicions, in regard to the letter of a previous date, are realized.[1]

Excepting your letter of the 13th Instant, I have received no letter from you since early in January,[2] and feel myself peculiarly fortunate in being allowed to peruse it. As [Joseph] Fouché[3] was commended for his uniform villany, I know not whether to commend Mr. Ervin for his close imitations of that accomplished spy, or for the few honest deviations from his path.

In reference to Genl. Gaines, the history of the late difficulty, to which Genl. [Thomas] Cadwallader alluded, is this:[4] a few days before Genl. Gaines' departure for New-Orleans, he enclosed to several of his friends the pamphlet, a copy of which I sent to you, containing the report of the Board of officers in reference to Genl. [Winfield] Scott and himself, with a portion of their correspondence with the General-in-Chief, and some extracts from the laws & regulations of the Army, &c.[5] On the receipt of this pamphlet, it appears that Genl. Scott addressed the Secretary of War a communication, in reply to which the Secretary assigned the want of authentic evidence of Genl. Gaines' agency in the publication of the pamphlet as the reason for not bringing him to trial, under the 1497th paragraph, of the Army Regulations, which commences thus: "publications relative *[to]* transactions between officers, of a private or personal nature, are prohibited."

Genl. Scott finally applied to Mr. Barbour to free him from the restrictions of the above paragraph; and, on being answered in the negative, he published a pamplet of eighty odd pages, styled "A letter to the Secretary of War," &c, which is characterized principally by insinuations against that office, and the most unrefined and unquallified abuse of Genl. Gaines.[6] The General has not yet seen the pamplet last mentioned, and I, therefore, know not what course he will pursue towards Genl. Scott. Of this, however, I am satisfied, that Genl. Scott is not to be quieted by letters, nor pamphlets.

I was grieved to learn from Mr. Washington Jackson,[7] a few days ago, that Capt. Donelson had been severely stabed, and wait with anxiety for an answer to my inquiries concerning him. Mr. Jackson presented to me an account of $74.15, being the sum, and interest of $50, remitted to me at West Point, which, he assured me, had not been paid by you, owing to its having been presented after you had ceased to be my Guardian. I, therefore, paid it.[8]

[W]hen my Sister Eliza [Donelson] was in Tennessee I requested her to ascertain of Mr. Earle wha*[t]* would be the probable cost of a portrait of my Father,[9] and of yourself, stating that I was desirous to obtain my fathers immediately, and yours as soon as my finances would allow. As she neglected my requests, I wrote twice to Mr Earle, making the above inquiry in reference to my father's portrait, but have received no reply. I presume I must attribute this apparent rudeness to the *shock* which my *inquiry* must have given "to the feelings usually cherished in that profession," as the *literary* Mr. [Edward] Everette said, in his report on the subject of the National Paintings.[10] If *you* can venture to touch on this subject to Mr. Earle, I will feel greatly obliged to you. I am extremely anxious to have my Father's portrait; and, as he has the original, I am reduced to the necessity of renewing my application. I went on the principle that no man should contract a debt, without first ascertaining his ability to meet it; but, if you think it proper, I beg you will order the portrait, without any *inquiries,* as its cost cannot be very considerable. Genl. G. returned early this month,[11] and he & Mrs. G. desire their most friendly regards. Frances' health is much improved, and the boy is growing to the astonishment of his friends. He sends his most affectionate & dutiful regard to Mrs. J. and yourself, for whom his mother joins me in sincere and affectionate regards. God bless you, Sir,

E. G. W. Butler

ALS, DLC (72).
1. Letters not found.
2. Probably AJ to Butler, December 22, 1826.
3. Fouché (c1759–1820), Napoleon's minister of police.
4. Cadwalader (1779–1841, Pennsylvania 1795), a director of the Bank of the United States in Philadelphia, had recently visited Nashville to establish a B.U.S. branch there.
5. The disagreement between Gaines and Scott (1786–1866) arose over the question of precedence in the army, with Scott claiming superiority because his brevet rank as a major general during the War of 1812 antedated Gaines's by about a month, and Gaines arguing that his longer service gave him preference. In February 1825 a board of officers led by Jacob J. Brown decided that Gaines was entitled to precedence (DNA-RG 107, M222-24), but that failed to settle the controversy. Gaines's pamphlet has not been found.
6. *Letter to the Secretary of War; or, Review of the Controversy on a Question of Rank between Generals Scott and Gaines* (New York, 1827).
7. Jackson (1784–1865), a Philadelphia merchant, was James Jackson's brother.
8. The account dated from January 11, 1819.
9. E. G. W.'s father, Edward Butler (1762–1803), a revolutionary war veteran, had settled in Springfield, Tennessee, before his death.
10. Everett (1794–1865; Harvard 1811) was a congressman from Massachusetts. In 1826, he chaired a House committee that examined the possibility of offering a premium for the best design for historical paintings for the Capitol rotunda. His report concluded that this approach was not a good way to get fine paintings, in part because it ran contrary to "the feelings usually cherished in that profession" about how to commission art. Instead the committee urged the government simply to hire an artist with a good reputation to do the work (see *HRDoc* 9, 19th Cong., 2nd sess., Serial 159).
11. Gaines had been on an inspection tour through Florida and Louisiana.

In February 1827, the Jacksons' marriage became a public issue. Though Jackson's opponents had conducted a whisper campaign on this subject for some years (see above, AJ to William Berkeley Lewis, December 12, 1826), heretofore they had not publicly broached it. On February 12, however, Thomas Dickens Arnold (1798–1870), a Knoxville lawyer running for Congress, published Thomas D. Arnold to the Freemen of the Counties of Cocke, Sevier, Blount, Jefferson, Grainger, Claiborne and Knox *(Knoxville, 1827). In it, he described Jackson as "a lump of naked deformity," and declared, "Gen. Jackson spent the prime of his life in gambling, in cock-fighting, in horse-racing, and has all his life been a most bloody duelist, and to cap all his frailties, he tore from a husband the wife of his bosom, to whom he had for some years been united in the holy estate of matrimony." Arnold concentrated on the last accusation, going so far as to allege that one of Jackson's friends had boasted that Jackson had "driven Roberts off like a dog, and had taken his wife" (p. 17). Administration newspapers soon picked up this charge, spreading it far beyond East Tennessee.*

Charles Hammond, a Cincinnati newspaper editor with close ties to Henry Clay, also entered the field. He had been hinting for months that he had information that would embarrass the Jacksons, and Arnold's publication may have forced his hand. On March 23, Hammond's Liberty Hall and Cincinnati Gazette *asserted that "in the summer of 1790, Gen.*

Jackson prevailed upon the wife of Lewis Roberts of Mercer county, Kentucky, to desert her husband, and live with himself, in the character of a wife." Hammond continued these attacks right up until the 1828 election in subsequent editions of his newspaper, a campaign magazine (Truth's Advocate and Monthly Anti-Jackson Expositor, *January–October 1828), and a pamphlet* (View of General Jackson's Domestic Relations, in Reference to his Fitness for the Presidency *[Washington, 1828]).*

Once published, the marriage allegations required an immediate answer. On April 7 the Nashville Republican *put aside "delicacy" to reply to "the innuendoes and insinuations . . . of the Coalition prints" with an account of events surrounding the marriage. In Kentucky, Thomas P. Moore produced another defense based on documents gathered in that state (Frankfort* Argus of Western America, *April 18). The most important response, however, came from a group of Jackson's supporters in Nashville who, on March 17, organized the Nashville Committee, under the leadership of John Overton. To fulfill its stated purpose "to detect and arrest falsehood and calumny, by the publication of truth . . . connected with the fitness or qualifications of Andrew Jackson to fill the office of President of the United States"* (National Banner and Nashville Whig, *March 24), the committee immediately set about collecting statements on the marriage from those who had lived in Middle Tennessee and Kentucky at the time. A* Letter from the Jackson Committee of Nashville, in Answer to One from a Similar Committee at Cincinnati, upon the Subject of Gen. Jackson's Marriage: Accompanied by Documents in an Appendix, Thereto Annexed *(Nashville, 1827), published in early June, formed the basis of rebuttals that appeared in Jackson papers throughout the country. The committee's work did not end with its publication on the marriage; throughout the rest of the campaign, it worked closely with Jackson to respond to other attacks on his character and history.*

To Richard Keith Call

Hermitage May 3d. 1827—

Dear Call,

I have no doubt thro the newspapers, you have seen the base attempt, by Clay & his panders, to harrow up the feelings of Mrs. J & myself—This unheard of procedure in any civilised community, was well calculated to harrow up my feelings, but situated as I am for the present, my hands are pinioned, as it is evident that it is the last effort of the combined coalition to save themselves & destroy me—they calculated that it would arouse me to some desperate act by which I would fall prostrate before the people—in this they shall be disappointed, but the day of retribution & vengeance must come, when the guilty will meet with their Just reward—This base attack was first Issued from the press of the scoundrel Hammond, and reiterated through all administration prints[1]—it has recoiled upon them, by a united indignation of every Just man in society—& in Ky. I am told, will prostrate Clay, for all believe that he is the author of this base & cowardly procedure—he keeps himself under the cloak of Hammond who, he knows is beneath, any other notice than a cowhide—

I regretted that whilst your dear Mary was with us,[2] so much of my time was taken up by the calls of my friends abroad, & here, for documents & Statements to enable them to meet this attempt of the secrete assasin to wound *[female]* reputation, & feeling, by raking up transactions that had slept *[fo]r* thirty odd years, when allmost all the cotemporaries of the day slept in their silent tombs, but providence has spared as many of the most creditable, & respectable, as will fully refute this base attempt to stain the reputation of Mrs. J. & harrow up her feelings in her declining years—when this is done, then my friend, the *blood* of this secrete mover behind the curtain must *attone* for this wicked attempt.

I sincerely regretted my Situation at the time your dear Mary left us, we went with her as far as Judge Overtons, nothing but the situation I was placed in prevented me from conducting her as far as Mr Jones[3] in alabama—*it was impossible* the *committee were waiting information,*[4] the duty I owed to my own & Mrs. J. fame, required my attention—*I could not accompany her*—how grating this to me.

My letter enclosed to Mr Jones to hand you, will have given you the pleasing information of that due respect which was paid Mrs Call in Nashville[5]—nothing but the situation we were placed in at the time Mary was with us, prevented Mrs. J. & myself from giving her a final blow out at the Hermitage—you must vissit us next year when we will attone for this should it take the last shot in the *locker*.

I hope Mary, & the sweet little daughter, will have Joined you in good health before this reaches you to whom present us affectionatly & let us hear from you—In haste adeu. yr friend

Andrew Jackson

P.S. I will attend to the estate of Mr. K. place it where the setting aside the pretended codici*[l]* will leave it—Then, unless the Executors notify you to attend & receive your proportion it will be an investment carrying 6 pr.ct. interest for your children.[6]

present us affectionatly to Colo. Butler & his family A. J.

ALS and Copy, NHi (11-0571). Published in Bassett, 3:354–55.

1. As early as November 14, 1826, Hammond had threatened to discuss irregularities regarding the Jacksons' marriage; and, on March 23, he published a lengthy account. About the same time, both the *Richmond Whig* and the *National Journal*, both leading Adams papers, published extracts from Thomas D. Arnold's pamphlet discussing the marriage.

2. Mary Call had been at the Hermitage in April.

3. Not identified.

4. Nashville Committee.

5. In his letter of April 23, AJ wrote Call about the "splendid ball" given Mary in Nashville, where she, with the Jacksons, had spent the previous eight days.

6. The final settlement of the Kirkman estate did allow Mary Call's portion to pass to the Call children.

To William Berkeley Lewis

Hermitage May 5th 1827

Dr. Sir

When genl Houston was here he informed me that you had recd a letter from Doctor Wallace[1] on the subject of Mr Sec Southards declarations at Mr Wellfords Fredkg Va. I would like to know its contents, before I forward to the Doctor the correspondence between myself & Mr. Southard on this subject—[2]

I should have been down this week to have seen you, but had no horse without stopping a plow—My riding horse being absent on a Journey—another reason, I do not wish to be seen mingling with the membe[rs] of the Committee *now*[3]—I hear Major Eaton is on his way home—this I am glad of—I wish to see him. I am respectfully your friend

Andrew Jackson

ALS, NNPM (11-0577). Published in Bassett, 3:355.
1. Not found.
2. No correspondence from AJ to Wallace has been found.
3. The Nashville Committee was preparing its report on the marriage issue.

From Richard Gilliam Dunlap

Kingston Ten—
May 12th. 1827

Dr Sir

Having on my way home some leisure this evening, I will give you a slight sketch of the politi[c]al disturbances of the place so long cursed with faction. Soon after Colo Williams became a candidate he was much flattered by the people—This nerved the Colo. to dare to meet and crush, political objections to his election—He moved high on the traiterous tide of new & old but noisey friends—Every day seemed to brighten his prospects—hope almost seemed to rest on reality—But the lean, hungry and impatient *Cassius,* could no longer be silent—with roman fierceness he took the field and now boldly & ably defends & supports the cause of his Country, in his choice of men as well as measures—already the bright elements of the Colos hope seems to be troubled and Clouded—At first the Colo, with a view to paralise the judges influence, tryed to make his opposition personal—about to meet a *Lawyer,* he shifted his course, as appeared, to have the war as a struggle between the houses of Yorke & Lan[c]aster; and his friends becoming sick & weary in this struggle, are now modestly *sliding* the Colo into the safe harbour of the *true faith.* What will be the certain course of the Colo's zigzag route—I can not tell, but his ultimate distiny will not require the aid of proficy to divine.[1] Mr Arnold has a new edition of his *cheerished* slander in print—The wires are beginning to work, but the friction will either burn up or wear out the macheniary[2]—An administration paper from Wheeling va. has been kindly sent to many of their worthy coadjutors of Knoxville & vicinity[3]— but some were labiled wrong & fell into the enemies hands—These papers are proping the tottering tabernacle of mercenary slander—If the administration can not have Skylights to awe and *benight* the people, they will not muzzel the press, while it plays so well in detraction on the chief of their fears.[4] Mr [Pryor] Lea will be the choice of the district by present sings [signs]—Arnold looses votes with the same facility that he makes a noise. [William B.] Reace & Lea are the formidable compctitors.[5] Your refusal to answer Arnold letter as he alledges, is by the generous ignorant deem'd a sufficient reason for his change of opinion—If you have no objection I should like to know whether you ever received his letter—If you have, you have served him right—If you have not, some changes may be made and they will be for Lea's benefit.[6] It is passing strange that Arnold's friends in the main are all Jackson men—no prominent man opposed to your election supports Arnold, such men rally to the *new flag* raised by Mr Reace. Please present my respects to Mrs Jackson and accept my ernest wishes for your ultimate happiness. Your friend

R. G. Dunlap

Colo Cannon has made favorable impression in Roane Knox, & Washington Counties—He has done something in all—Genl. Houston presence is indispensible here—altho I have no doubt he will receive a majority in every County in E. T.[7] R. G. D—

ALS, DLC (34).
1. John Williams, an Adams backer, was a candidate for the Tennessee state senate, seeing that post a springboard to replace his brother-in-law Hugh Lawson White, a Jacksonian, in the United States Senate. In the course of the campaign, White announced that he would not vote for Williams, thus, as Dunlap saw it, defending the American republic as Cassius (d. 42 BC) had the Roman. Dunlap also likened the struggle to that of the War of the Roses in fifteenth-century England.
2. Arnold's revised work, *Arnold's Review: To the Freemen of the Counties of Cocke, Sevier, Blount, Jefferson, Grainger, Claiborne, and Knox* (Knoxville, 1827), reaffirmed his commitment to internal improvements, asserted that AJ had supported the tariff, and discussed the Jacksons' marriage.
3. Probably the *Wheeling Gazette.*
4. "Skylights" referred to Adams's description of observatories as "light-houses of the

skies" in his first annual message to Congress (*Register of Debates*, 19th Cong., 1st sess., Appendix, p. 7).

5. Lea (1794–1879), a Jacksonian, won the congressional election with 3,688 votes. Arnold garnered 3,316 votes, and Reese (1793–1859), a Knoxville lawyer, 2,272 votes.

6. In both of his pamphlets, Arnold claimed that he had written AJ on October 24, 1826, asking him to clarify his position on the tariff and internal improvements, but AJ had not replied. In his reply to Dunlap on May [23], below, AJ insisted that he had never received Arnold's letter. Only a newspaper printing of Arnold's letter has been found.

7. Cannon was Houston's chief opponent in the gubernatorial election. In late July, Houston made a tour of East Tennessee and, in the August election, he won all but three of the nineteen counties.

From John Overton

Travellers Rest. 14th May 1827

Dear Sir

In the *defence,* now in progress by the Jackson Committee it may be necessary to state explicitly, that Hugh McGary, (the witness on the divorce)[1]—*never saw you and Mrs Jackson together either before or since he came in Company with you both in Septr. 1791 in company with nearly 100 assembled for protection in the trip from Natchez to Nashville*

Such I believe to be the fact and if so, please to communicate it. This letter, nor your answer is intended for publication, but your answer may be necessary to satisfy some of the Committee[2]

Majr. Moore of Harrodsburg has been addressed on the subject of this same Colo H. McGary—and requested to examine the Clerks office of Mercer County. K to know, if there is any deposition of his on file there, and if so to send us a Copy Respy as usual

Jno. Overton

ALS, DLC (34).

1. The March 23 *Liberty Hall and Cincinnati Gazette* had identified McGary as the witness who testified to Rachel's adultery in Lewis Robards's divorce proceedings against her.

2. According to AJ's endorsement, he wrote Overton that McGary "never saw Mrs J. & myself together only in the wilderness with Capt [John] Caffery [1756–1811, AJ's brother-in-law] & a hundred more relates the Col. running from the Indians & reducing him to the ranks." The *Letter from the Jackson Committee* adopted AJ's statement, reporting that McGary had seen the Jacksons only in September 1791, when they believed themselves legally married.

From Anthony Butler

Fleurissant 17. May 1827.

My dear Sir,

I have the pleasure of acknowledging the receipt of yours of the 24th ulto.[1] by our last Mail—so great an interval had passed since I had heard from you by letter, that I considered the circumstance as indicating some untoward event. I regret to find that my apprehensions are realised, and that your adversaries have adopted a mode of attack so well calculated to wound the generous sensibilities of your nature by the assault on Mrs. Jackson—As it regards political effect it will serve you, and produce a reaction against the authors whose consequences will be terrible—six months will prove to them, that even were there colour for such calumnies the public temper would sympathise with you on this occasion, and discountenance and denounce their nefarious proceeding—but with the facts all against them, and the course they have adopted resulting from malignity falsehood and corruption, and designed to sustain an unholy ambition, the people will see and understand the motive and the object, the Men concerned and the means employed, and assign to them their just reward *now* and *forever*.

That I once respected Mr. Clay very highly you have cause to know, for you will recollect the efforts once made by me under the sanction of that man to reconcile the differences between you and himself, originating as I believed (innocently on his part) from the part he performed on the Seminole question as a matter of duty[2]—this was the character he gave to it in the conversations with me, and such I described it to you—Your explanations and some facts you communicated, gave the question a different aspect, and as those facts were some of them communicated to Mr. Clay with your permission for the purpose of affording him the means of explanation, and as that explanation was not satisfactory to me, I desisted from further efforts to effect the reconciliation—My judgment however still accorded to Mr. Clay patriotism and a respect for the principles of our Government—In the result of the Contest for the presidency in 1825, I was forced to withdraw from Mr Clay—all regard—all respect—every thing like confidence in his political principles—patriotism or respect for the Constitution—in short I was compelled to see in him a man reckless of all consequences, and ready to employ any means when his own ambition or his selfish purposes were to be promoted, and I was prepared therefore to expect the use of all means to retain what he had acquired, except indeed an attack on femal reputation and feminine sensibility—I confess I did not expect this, it is done however, and the course proves that like [Aaron] Burr he would make any effort, adopt any plan and use any instrument to regain what he has lost, and even jeopardise the integrity of the Union to subserve the purpose if the hopelessness of such an attempt, was not already *History* to admonish him.[3] In this State I can render you no service—because every thing is already done to my hand; yet I believe you know and will credit me when I say, that it would afford me *gratification* to serve you even by *sacrafices* if sacrafices were necessary. Before your letter arrived I had heard a rumour, a sort of subdued murmur from the few who are opposed to you here, that "*some things would come out soon to change public opinion*—and to shew the impropriety of placing you in the Executive Chair"—I denounced the suggestions—and defied the charge, they were called on to state upon what facts their opinions were founded, and then for the first time I heard Mrs. Jackson had been *slandered* in some Newspaper, and that I would see the whole affair developed after a while—but as they professed disinclination to detail what their own Newspapers' contained, and as my Newspapers were all of a different character, it was not untill by the Mail which brought your letter, I also was informed by my Kentucky as well as by my other newspapers, of the course your enemies had adopted, and the character of the charges made: I concur with you most decidedly in the opinion that Mr. Clay prompts every thing that appears in Hammonds paper—I know their intimacy I am acquainted perfectly with Hammond's subserviency to him, and the readiness therefore with which he would perform any dirty work assigned him by Mr. Clay. It will no doubt be difficult if not impracticable to trace these things to the true source, and I shall congratulate the Country if you are fortunate enough to do so. The Administration are playing a desperate game, and no doubt each member has assigned to him such duties as he can perform best—principle is out of the question—fairness, truth and honour does not belong to the vocabulary—yet with the use of all their means, and without any restraint from principle in the mode of their employment I feel confident the people will put them down.

If your Committee of investigation in Nashville publish, send it me whether in pamphlet or any other form—I wish to have the facts so that I may stop the mouths of the few malcontents here. I intended to have said something more to you about Texas, but my letter has extended already beyond my usual limits and I shall reserve that subjec[t] for another occasion. If you can ferret out Clay and any other of the Cabinet I pray you do not spare them—such a pen as is used by some one in Virginia, under the signature of "*A Member of the Jackson Convention*" would be valuable in chastising Mr. Clay and others of his faction. The publication I allude to is made in the U. S. Telegraph 14th & 15th. April.[4]

I pray you to present to Mrs. Jackson the respectful and cordial salutations of Mrs. B— and myself, and be assured of the sincere regard of yours always

A. Butler

ALS, DLC (34). Fleurissant was probably Butler's farm in Lawrence County, Mississippi.
    1. Not found.
    2. In early 1819, Clay, as speaker of the House, spearheaded the congressional investigation into AJ's 1818 invasion of Florida.
    3. Butler was referring to the course followed by Burr (1756–1836; Princeton 1772), Thomas Jefferson's first vice president, after the 1804 election.
    4. "A Member of the Jackson Convention," from Orange County, Virginia, had identified Clay as the author of an editorial in the *National Journal* critical of the February 14 Jackson convention in Fredericksburg, Virginia. On April 19, the *Journal* dismissed the claim as a "shallow falsehood."

From Henry Banks

Frankfort Ky. May 18th. 1827.

My Dear Sir;

I hope that you have recd. my last letter,[1] which enclosed one to General Overton, and that my solicitude and conduct relating to the contents of the one to Genl. Overton, are not unacceptable to yourself, to Mrs. Jackson, and to him.[2]

Since my last I have ascertained by a voluntary declaration made by Mr. John Smith who resides about 8 miles from this place on Elkhorn, which corresponds with the contents of mine, in regard to the declarations of Mr. W. Short. Mr. Smith is a connection of Mr. Clay by having married a Miss [Chenoe] Hart, a near relation of Mrs [Lucretia Hart] Clay. Mr. Smith is very decidedly opposed to the coalition.[3]

Mr. Thomas [Davis] Carneal who resides near to Cincinnati in Campbell County in Kentucky, has publicly held some conversation of the same character.[4]

Mr. Humphry Marshall[5] who resides here, a strong coalition man, has publicly said, in a Barber's shop in this town, that he often visited old Mrs. [Rachel Stockley] Donalson[6] the mother of Mrs. Jackson near Danville to see persons who boarded there, where he frequently saw Mr. and Mrs. Roberts (now Mrs. Jackson) and also saw and was well acquainted with Mr. [Peyton] Short, that her conduct was modest, unassuming, unsuspicious and decorous—That during those visits he neither heard of nor suspected, that there was reason to doubt her virtue and modesty. That after Mrs. Roberts retired to Tennessee and became acquainted with General Jackson, he believed that they went to Natchez for the purpose of being married there, according to the rites of the Catholic Church—that they were married as he understood after the passage of the law of Virginia, relating to a divorce between Roberts and herself[7]— That after they returned, he heard of no censure, but that Mrs. Jackson being desirous to join the Presbyterian church, the clergyman who he believes was Mr. [Thomas B.] Craighead, was desirous, that they should be again married by him; and they were married by him, whereupon she became a member.[8]

Some persons who introduced this subject to me in a jeering manner, appeared to be disappointed and confounded by my answers and by the voluntary and unexpected avowals of Messrs. Carneal and Marshall.

I think it my duty and I take great pleasure to name these things to you, and embrace the only mode which exists by which I can transmit such strong and honourable Testimony—to demonstrate the innocence and virtue of an injured and calumniated female, and to disgrace the authors of the most audacious and viprous calumny which ever existed.

Although I am in low and debilitated health, yet my publications show that I pay honourable regard to my voluntary engagement—long since made, and that the motives and emotions are strong indeed.

I am now preparing at intervals according to my health another pamphlet in which I propose to close my remarks against the town of Lexington, and to commence personally with Henry Clay whom I have long known. I am afraid that I shall not be able to do justice to this undertaking, but I will do my best. The pamphlet or pamphlets as they appear will speak for themselves.[9]

I am my Dear Sir with the highest Esteem and utmost confidence, the same Philo-Jackson whose pamphlets have done so much in Virginia and elsewhere for the cause of public merit and private virtue.

Henry Banks

My relations and friends in Virginia are generally, I believe entirely, the supporters of Genl. Andrew Jackson.

I shall be glad to receive the papers which contain the different Reports of Genl. Overton, I wish to notice them in a pamphlet in reply to Mr. [Robert] Wickliffe's which I propose to publish some time in August.[10]

If my testimony is thought desirable by the Committee, I shall not be unwilling to make an affidavit or give my signature and will make preparations accordingly. H. B.

The next Argus will contain some very flattering accounts[11]

LS, DLC (34).
1. Not found.
2. See Banks to John Overton, May 10.
3. Smith (1765–1851) was a Franklin County, Kentucky, planter and former state legislator. His wife (1779–1870) was first cousin of Mrs. Henry Clay (1781–1864). Instead of W. Short, Banks meant Peyton Short (1761–1825), whom he discussed in his May 10 letter to Overton. According to Banks, Short, who came from a prominent Virginia family and represented Fayette County in the Kentucky Senate, 1792–96, first aroused Lewis Robards's jealousy.
4. Carneal (1786–1860) was a member of the Kentucky Senate, 1821–29.
5. Marshall (1760–1841), cousin of John Marshall, represented Kentucky in the United States Senate between 1795 and 1801 and wrote *The History of Kentucky* (Frankfort, 1812), the first formal history of the state.

6. (1730–1801).

7. For documents relating to the Robards's marriage and divorce, see *Jackson*, 1:423–28.

8. Craighead (c1750–1824; Princeton 1775) settled in Davidson County in 1785. The Jacksons were married by AJ's brother-in-law Robert Hays, a justice of the peace, not by Craighead. Mrs. Jackson was a regular member of Craighead's congregation by the late 1790s.

9. In March Banks had issued *A Reply to a Scurrilous Publication, in the Kentucky Whig . . . Against Sundry Persons* (Frankfort, 1827), a vituperative attack on the "Literati, or the billingsgate gentry, of Lexington . . . the subjects, or idolaters, of Mr. Henry Clay." He continued his charges with at least two additional pamphlets similarly titled.

10. Wickliffe (1775–1859), a lawyer and member of the Kentucky Senate, had published in the spring his *Address . . . to His Constituents* (Lexington, 1827), in which he announced his opposition to AJ, citing AJ's political alliance with opponents of the tariff and internal improvements. Banks's reply has not been found.

11. On May 23 the Frankfort *Argus of Western America* carried an account of a Jackson meeting in Frankfort and also reports of a Mercer County militia muster supporting AJ for the presidency.

To Edward George Washington Butler

Hermitage May 21rst. 1827—

Dr Edward

yours of the 27th ult. has been recd,[1] & I am pleased to learn that mine of the 13th[2] reached you, as mine of a prior date, it appears, was arrested on its passage—I hope this will be permitted to reach you.

Genl Gains passed thro Nashville the other day, left for me a package, which, with your information, fully explains the information given me by Genl. Cadwallader—Genl Gains has promised to call at the Hermitage on his return, when I shall have the pleasure of seeing him.

I have seen Mr. Earl, on the subject of your father's portrait. He assures me it shall be attended to; that it is nearly finished, & shall be compleated as early as possible—He will charge you as he does others—I have paid him at the rate of $50 pr portrait—Mr Earl promises to write you by tomorrows mail, to which I more particularly refer you.[3]

On the subject of the demand of Washington Jackson I have only this to observe—that his brother James at the time you were at West Point held in his hands all my funds and was instructed to pay to Washington Jackson & Kirkman any sum they advanced you or A. J. Donelson—in the year 1824 I settled with James Jackson & closed our accounts having given him credit for all sums advanced by him to those Gentlemen—and it is strange indeed, that the sum of fifty dollars alluded to, had been omitted to be furnished James Jackson before the settlement between him & Washington, & then between James and me—I have paid every cent that I ever heard was advanced to you & A. J. Donelson by Mr Kirkman & Washington Jackson—some years after we had closed all our business, & after the whole connection had fallen out with me, Mrs. Kirkman one day in the street sent one of her lackies to me with this account against you, I replied to him I had long since closed all accounts for money advanced to you & A. J. Donelson, & would have nothing to do with her or her accounts—This Spring when I was informed Washington Jackson was in Nashville (altho I did not see him) I was there at the post office, when the same puppy came to me & in the presence of several presented the same account, saying it was done at the request of Washington Jackson[4]—I said to him you recollect Sir when you presented this before I told you I had long since closed all those accounts & it is strange that this, if Just, had not been forwarded, That I had paid James Jackson every cents that I had ever heard or been advised had been advanced to you, that I should have nothing to do with it—That I was surprised Mr W. Jackson had not presented this to me himself, instead of sending it by a lackey & if ever he attempted again to call upon me with that account I would insult him—To say to Mr W. Jackson I was astonished that, as he was in Town he did not call on me himself, that I had long since closed all acpts of this kind with Mr James Jackson and unless he was here, I should not have any thing to do with it—I have only to add, that if ever it was made known to James Jackson, it was included in our settlement, and when you come here we can find it out by looking over the accounts—I have no doubt but it was included in our settlement, as every cent advanced in Philadelphia to you, was immediately forwarded to James, & I was charged with it, *in mony matters their memories were good & nothing omitted.*

Mrs. J & myself are much gratified to hear of the good health of Frances & *the boy growing finely,* we will be happy to greet you welcome at the Hermitage. & ask to be presented to them affectionately & to Mrs. Gains with our best wishes to yourself. yr friend

Andrew Jackson

ALS, NcD (11-0604).
1. See above.
2. Not found.
3. See Ralph E. W. Earl to Butler, May 22 (LNHiC).
4. For Washington Jackson's statement of funds advanced to Butler and Donelson, see Account with Kirkman & Jackson, January 11, 1819.

To Richard Gilliam Dunlap

(Copy)   Majr Lewis. 23d May 1827
Dear Sir,

I have this moment recd your letter of the 12th inst from Kingston;[1] & feel greatly indebted for the information it contains. It seems to be true that all the means which wickedness & falshood can invent, are now employed against me by the friends and supporters of the present administration; but

I thank my God that truth is mighty & will ultimately prevail. Let the great wire workers push forward their tools upon the stage—the unity & concert with which they execute the biddings of their master may catch for a moment the attention, but can never win the applause of the public.

You say that my refusal to answer Arnold's letter[2] is the alledged cause for his change of opinion of me, & his unfounded slanders. I never recd a letter from him in my life that I have any recollection of. The young gentlemen who, in my absence, receive all my letters[3] have no knowledge of any such letter, nor is there such a one to be found in my file of papers. And if a letter, of the character ascribed to this, had been received from him, I certainly might have treated it with silence without meriting all the obloquy & abuse which has been levelled at me by Mr Arnold—What right had Mr Arnold, a boy of yesterday, to interrogate me on my political opinions—opinions which have been uniformly acted upon & which were well known & well established before he was born? The very pretense exposes the *pliant conscience* of this young man, which no doubt was his fittest recommendation to the service in which he is now enlisted, & where *Swiss like* he will fight as long as he is well paid.

You are at liberty to state in any way you may think proper, that such a letter as that described I never recd from Mr Arnold. Nor, as far as I recollect, did I ever receive any letter from him on any subject whatever. I speak with the more confidence having examined with care the various files of my letters, and ascertained from the young gentlemen who attend to them in my absence, that no communication from him has ever been seen—I could not consent to reply to such a creature as he is in the newspapers. The man who is capable of fabricating such a tissue of falsehood and calumny as that to which he has subscribed his name, <cannot claim this privilege> is already lost to public shame.[4]

You will excuse my haste. I have just stopped to acknowledge the receipt of your letter, & reply to your query concerning Mr Arnolds letter—It is a mere pretense—a flimsy covering for his baseness—The traitor, of our revolution, Benedict, would have been more magnanimous[5]—With great respect yr Mo obdt Servt

Andrew Jackson

LS copy in Andrew J. Donelson's hand with minor additions in AJ's hand, DLC (34). William B. Lewis's plantation, Fairfield, was located off the Murfreesboro Road, about two miles from Nashville's courthouse square.

1. See above.
2. Thomas D. Arnold to AJ, October 24, 1826.
3. Andrew J. Donelson, Benjamin F. Currey, and Ephraim H. Foster.
4. AJ was referring to Arnold's pamphlets and perhaps other publications.
5. Benedict Arnold (1741–1801).

To William Douglass (d. 1831)

Hermitage May 30th. 1827—

My Dear Sir

I have recd your letter of the 6th instant by your son;[1] I assure you it will give me pleasure to render him any Service or attention in my power.

I have attended the examinations of the Students ever since Doctor Lindsley presided over the College, and with truth can say, that the Students did honor to themselves, & the institution, & gave conclusive evidence of the ability & attention of the professors—Your son on every examination, gave evidence of both talents & application—I have no doubt he will graduate at our next commencement in October, with credit to himself, at which, I would be happy to see you, when I would expect the pleasure of seeing you at the Hermitage.

In the choice of a profession for your son, I would recommend you to let him pursue the bent of his genius, & choose for himself—he has capacity, with application, to succeed in any profession—from what I know of him he possesses that necessary ambition to excell in whatever he undertakes, I would therefore approbate his studying of law, this being his choice, affords evidence, that it is best suited to his taste & to his genius.

I have recd the newspaper & pamphlet you have mentioned,[2] but until the receipt of your letter, did not know to whom I was indebted for them—for this act of kindness I tender you my thanks—These publications conclusively shew the want of principle of the authors, & with what facility they can misrepresent things, & propagate falshood, knowing it to be such—*Swiss like* they will *fight or lie* for those who pay them best, & as long as their employers pay them *well*—poor men, I lament their want of principle & proper regard for truth—Truth is mighty and will ultimately prevail, when the slanders, propagated by these hired panders of power against me & my family, will recoil upon their own heads, & fall harmless at my feet—Under present circumstances, it is gratifying to me to be informed that I still retain the good opinion of your good Citizens, which is evidence that the tissue of slander and misrepresentations of my enemies, has had no injurious effect in your state against me, & is recoiling upon the head of my slanderers.

Mrs. J & myself are happy to hear from Mr [Gideon] Blackburn[3] & his family & to receive their salutations present us respectfully to them.

Should fortune throw Mrs. J & myself near you, it will give us pleasure to vissit you, & your family, to whom present us affectionately—& with regard to your son, it will at all times afford me pleasure to serve him, in any way I may have it in my power, & only regret that I have not had more of his company at the Hermitage.

accept assurances of my great respect & believe me your friend

Andrew Jackson

ALS, ViRVal (11-0608). Douglass was a Louisville, Kentucky, businessman.

1. Not found. Douglass's son, George Lattimore (1808–89; Nashville 1827), returned to Louisville to engage in law and business.

2. Not identified.

3. Blackburn (1772–1838), a Presbyterian minister living in Louisville at this time, had been a missionary to the Indians in Tennessee and had served under AJ as chaplain on the Natchez expedition in 1813.

From Richard Gilliam Dunlap

Knoxville Ten
June 4th. 1827

Dr Sir

your letter from Majr. Lewis's was rcd. last evening[1]—I shewed it to Judge White—& doubt the propri[e]ty of makeing any publication of your name &c—at this time, as it might seem that such authority was realy necessary to put down the vilest slanders that ever agitated an honest but disturbed community—But I feel no fear, from such a contemptable source.[2] Every thing is to be brought into requisition even the tomb of the departed is to be raked & filtched of its peace & honor and have them converted into calumny, to sustain the tottering & falling powers, that are with the foulest means corrupting the publick—Judge White informed me that you may be prepared to meet the storm, that Dr. [Francis] May *(after you and him became cool with each other about a certain lot in Nashville),* had written to Colo Wm P[reston] Anderson, that in the duel between Dickerson & yourself, that your pistol snaped, and that you immediately cocked it and killed him, which throws dishonor on your conduct[3]—Sometime since Anderson gave those letters to Colo. Williams It is conjectured that they will finally be used in the present struggle with a view to tarnish your fame—The Judge says that he understands that you have the certificates of those gentlemen, who kncw all about this transaction, that will fully acquit you of all blame and place this charge on the ungovernable temper of Dr May, who always spoke from *passion* about men.[4] In the event of the explosion of this foul plot, its thought advisable that you forward this evidence to some friend at this place, in order that your frends may meet & crush this last effort, of the dying hopes, of hireling corrupt and desperate minions, who have sallied *for pay* to the support of the usurpations, of the advocates of alarming power. This may not happen, but you are too skillfull a general, to be taught, that there is no danger to be apprehended from *timely* preparation.[5]

The Judge laments with bitterness of heart, that an attempt to injure you, will be made, which, as he says must affect the memory of one of the members of his family, who has bid adieu to the troubles of life—But he has taken his stand & like a roman martyr, is ready to die on the alter of publick purity & freedom, rather than fold his arms and witness with apathy the death of republican principles. I'm in much haste, we have been attending to tax gatherings for two weeks & will only finish in two more. Your friend

R. G. Dunlap

ALS, T (11-0679). Endorsed by AJ: "Genl Dunlaps letter, look at & extract from it." Extract published in *Knoxville Register*, July 16, 1828.

1. See above, AJ to Dunlap, May 23.

2. Dunlap was referring generally to the anti-Jackson activities of John Williams and specifically to his role in spreading rumors about irregularities in the Dickinson duel and to Arnold's second pamphlet.

3. May (d. 1817), Hugh Lawson White's brother-in-law, served as AJ's surgeon in the Dickinson duel. Shortly before his death, he wrote two letters—September 16 and 17, 1817—to Anderson (c1776–1831), a son-in-law of John Adair with whom AJ had a quarrel at the time, to suggest that Adair gather information about the duel, citing the "snap as a fire" matter to show that AJ had not behaved properly during the duel. May's most damning passage described how Thomas Overton, AJ's second, used threats to extract a favorable statement regarding AJ's behavior from Hanson Catlet, Dickinson's second. Anderson, like May, had been AJ's friend, but the relationship had deteriorated. Anderson and May acquired title to the land on which stood the Nashville Inn, a concern owned by the estate of William Terrell Lewis (1757–1813), a Nashville businessman and planter for whom AJ was an executor. Anderson and May sued Lewis's estate and lost not only the case but AJ's friendship.

4. Certificates of Hanson Catlet (d. 1824) and Thomas Overton, June 25, 1806 (*Jackson*, 2:104–105), and the deposition of George Ridley, June 25, 1806.

5. A story, said to have originated with John Williams, was at this time circulating in East Tennessee to the effect that Dickinson had fired into the air before AJ shot him. This was not true—Dickinson had wounded AJ—and the July 18 *Knoxville Register* pointed this out and printed the Overton, Catlet, and Ridley documents. Jackson most likely forwarded the affidavits to Dunlap or someone else.

In early March, Carter Beverley (1774–1844) of Virginia visited the Hermitage on a tour through the western states. On March 8, he wrote his friend Richard Shippey Hackley (b. c1770), a brother-in-law of ex-governor Thomas Mann Randolph and former consul at Cadiz, who was at this time residing in Fayetteville, North Carolina. In his letter, Beverley related that Jackson "told me this morning, before all his company, in a reply to a question I put to him concerning the election of J. Q. Adams to the presidency, that Mr. Clay's friends made a proposition to his friends, that if they would promise for him, not to put Mr. Adams into the seat of Secretary of State, Clay and his friends would, in one hour, make him, (Jackson) the President. He most indignantly rejected the proposition, and declared he would not compromit himself" (United States' Telegraph,

April 13). Hackley shared Beverley's letter with Edward Jones Hale (1802–83), editor of the Fayetteville Carolina Observer, *who published an extract from it on April 5.*

Beverley's letter caused quite a stir. Jacksonians had made the cry of "corrupt bargain" a staple of their rhetoric since 1825, but heretofore Jackson himself had not publicly entered the debate. At first, Clay refused to credit Beverley's account of his conversation with Jackson (Report of Interview, [cApril 15], Clay Papers, *6:448–49), whereupon Beverley asked Jackson for verification, which he provided in the letter below. Clay then denied Jackson's charge and demanded that Jackson produce evidence to back it up. Jackson responded by naming James Buchanan as the messenger who carried the offer of Clay's friends, and Buchanan replied with an ambiguous letter that Jacksonians claimed proved the bargain and Clay's supporters asserted exonerated the secretary of state. Throughout the remainder of the year, the debate on the alleged offer continued.*

In subsequent decades, the Beverley affair continued to haunt its principals. In the 1844 presidential campaign Democratic newspapers resurrected it to embarrass Clay, and twelve years later opponents of Buchanan's presidential ambitions used the episode against him.

To Carter Beverley

Hermitage, June 5th. 1827.

Dr. Sir:

Your letter of the 15th ulto. from Louisville, Ky, is just received,[1] and in conformity with your request, address my answer to Wheeling, Va.

Your enquiry relative to the proposition of bargain made thro Mr. Clay's friends to some of mine, concerning the then pending Presidential election, were answered *freely & frankly* at the time; but without any calculation that they were to be thrown into the public journals; but facts cannot be altered; and as your letter seems not to have been written for publication, I can assure you, that having no concealment myself, nor any dread arising from what I may have said on the occasion & subject alluded to; my feelings towards you are not the least changed—I always intended, should Mr Clay come out with his own name, and deny having any knowledge of the communication made by his friends to my friends & to me, that I would give him the name of the gentleman thro whom that communication came.

I have not seen your letter alluded to as having been published in the Telegraph;[2] altho that paper, as I am informed, is regularly mailed for me at Washington; still I receive it irregularly, and that containing your letter has not come to hand, of course I cannot say whether your statement is substantially correct or not. I will repeat however again the occurrence, and to which my reply to you must have conformed, and from which, if there has been any variation, you can correct it. It is this. Early in January, 1825, a member of Congress of high respectability visited me one morning, and observed he had a communication he was desirous to make to me; that he was informed there was a great intrigue going on, & that it was right I should be informed of it; that he came as a friend, and, let me receive the communication as I might the friendly motives thro which it was made he hoped would prevent any change of friendship or feeling with regard to him. To which I replied, from his high standing as a gentleman & member of Congress, and from his uniform friendly & gentlemanly conduct towards myself, I could not suppose he would make any communication to me, which he supposed was improper; therefore, his motives being pure, let me think as I might of the communication, my feelings towards him would remain unaltered. The gentleman proceeded. He said he had been informed by the friends of Mr Clay, that the friends of Mr Adams had made overtures to them, saying if Mr Clay and his friends would unite in aid of the election of Mr Adams, Mr Clay should be Secretary of State—That the friends of Mr Adams were urging as a reason to induce the friends of Mr Clay to accede to their proposition; that if I was elected President, Mr Adams would be continued Secretary of State (inuendo; there would be no room for Kentucky|)]—That the friends of Mr Clay stated, the west did not wish to separate from the west; and if I would say, or permit any of my confidential friends to say, that in case I was elected President, Mr Adams should not be continued Secretary of State, by a complete union of Mr Clay & his friends, they would put an end to the Presidential contest in one hour—And he was of opinion it was right to fight such intriguers with their own weapons—To which, in substance, I replied: "that in politicks, as in every thing else, my guide was principle; and contrary to the expressed & unbiassed will of the people, or their constituted agents, I never would step into the presidential chair["]—and requested him to say to Mr Clay & his friends, (for I did suppose he had come from Mr Clay; although he used the term Mr Clay's friends) that before I would reach the presidential chair by such means of bargain & corruption, I would see the earth open & swallow both Mr Clay & his friends, and myself with them: If they had not confidence in me to believe, if I was elected, that I would call to my aid in the Cabinet men of the first virtue, talents and integrity, not to vote for me. The second day after the communication & reply, it was announced in the newspapers, that Mr Clay had come out openly & avowedly in favor of Mr Adams.[3]

It may be proper to observe, that the supposition that Mr Clay was privy to the proposition stated, I may have done injustice to him: if so, the gentleman informing me can explain. I am, very respectfully, your most obt Sert

Andrew Jackson

A true copy of the original in my possession, recd. from the Genl.

Carter Beverly
Virginia, Wheeling
25 June, 1827

Copy in unknown hand with ANS from Duff Green, June 30, sending the copy to James Buchanan for comment, PHi (11-0683). Published in contemporary newspapers (some as dated June 6) and in Bassett, 3:355–57.

    1. Not found.

    2. On April 13, the *United States' Telegraph* reprinted an extract from Beverley's March 8 letter to Hackley.

    3. Though Clay announced his support for Adams on January 24, 1825, the first definite notice of that support in a Washington newspaper did not appear until the *Washington Gazette* attacked Clay's course on January 27, 1825. Buchanan stated that his meeting with AJ took place on December 30, 1824, but John H. Eaton asserted that the meeting took place on January 19 or 20, 1825 (Moore, *Works of James Buchanan*, 1:263–67; *Nashville Republican*, September 18).

From Robert Young Hayne

(*Confidential*)   Charleston 5th. June 1827.
My Dear General.

    Nothing has prevented me from writing to you long since, but the belief that you must be *oppressed* by the number of your correspondents. You know me I trust too well, to attribute the omission to any want of attachment, to your person, or *your cause*—the cause certainly of the whole country. I have determined however to write to you now, because I think it important that you should be made acquainted with the views and feelings of your friends in various quarters of the Union, in order that you may be enabled to decide on your own course, with all the lights which a variety of opinions can afford. I know that you always judge and act *for yourself,* and therefore feel the less scruple, in presenting my views, knowing that they will be carefully examined and will receive neither more, nor less weight than they are justly entitled to. The *great contest* is obviously becoming every day warmer. It is now manifest that the men, who have usurped the reins of government, do not mean to surrender it, without a desperate struggle—and that they are determined if possible to sacrifice to their vengeance all those, who venture to oppose them. They are playing a desperate game, and their motto is "to conquer or die." Hence it is, that they have let loose "the floodgates of their wrath," against yourself, Mr. Calhoun,[1] and many others of your best friends, and so little discrimination do they make, that they do not hesitate to brand our estimable and excellent friend Judge White, as one of "the worst men in the worst Senate the Country has ever seen.["]² The spirit thus displayed originates from the consciousness of error. The men in power *know*, that they have done you personally, and done their country *wrong,* & that they have been detected and exposed; Hence the bitterness of their anger, and the recklessness of the course they are about to pursue. They are actuated by a spirit not unlike that which inspires a criminal flying from justice, who turns on his pursuers, and to save himself from exposure and merited punishment, attacks indiscriminately all who are in pursuit. There is another circumstance to be taken into the account. Mr. Adams, who is not a practical man, has been persuaded to rely on Mr. Clay, as the only pillar that can sustain his administration. He has therefore practically yielded the reins of government to him, at least so far as relates to the new Department, of *political management. We* know Mr. Clay well enough, to understand the course that will be pursued in matters where his will is law. Altogether unprincipled, ambitious, daring, bold, and without the smallest regard either to the Courtesies or descencies of life, he inspires his political followers with a spirit not unlike that, which distinguishes a *savage warfare*—"sparing no age, sex, or condition"—There is still another motive that lurks beneath, the unmanly and ungenerous course of the Administration, it is the desire to betray you into some indiscretion. They have taken pains to impress the public mind with the belief that your *temper* unfits you for civil government, they know that a noble nature is always liable to excitement—and they *have put,* and will continue to put into operation, a hundred schemes to betray you into some act, or expression, which may be turned to their own advantage. If I am not much mistaken, I have now exposed the true springs which direct the movements of your political opponents. If I am right, we may pretty clearly discover, their future course of conduct, and by prudence and wisdom, not only avoid the snares, set for us, but cause them to be entangled in their own nets. It is certain, that far from abating in their violence, they will henceforth display greater and more undiscriminating fury, and as it is not in the nature of man to remain unkindled in a common blaze, we may be assured that the contest will wax warmer to the end. For this we must all be prepared. Every man must be resolved to take his share, of the slander, and abuse which will be levelled at him, and to act his part manfully in the fight. But more than this will be necessary, we must each of us, in his own person set an example of prudence, and self command and endeavour to give a tone to all around us, which will in itself go far to secure the victory. In your own personal conduct, your adversaries will endeavour to find something to assail—hitherto they have failed, and I have no doubt they will fail forever, if you are only sufficiently on your guard, not to be tempted to give utterance to the feelings of indignation which their conduct is so well calculated to produce. Mr. Clay *will use every effort to draw you into some public controversy,* whether on the question of *the Tariff,* or *his intrigues,* or any other matter, is to him not very material. He would thus divert public attention, from himself & Mr. Adams, present you, perhaps, as an accuser, and at all events, insist that you were endeavouring to advance your own claims, & had relinquished the high ground of leaving your cause in the hands of the people. I doubt not that you will have *his partizans,* paying their respects to you *at the Hermitage,* and leading the way to the expression of your opinions on points capable of misrepresentation. Something has been already done in this way, and more will be attempted.[3] In the mean time the administration presses will be loud in their calls for your opinions on the Tariff, internal improvements and other questions, on all of which Mr. Adams is as silent as the grave, and concerning which your opinions have been fully and clearly expressed in your *public and recorded acts.* Mr. Adams and yourself stand on equality as the only Candidates for the Presidency—Will he answer questions? If so I should be glad to put him a few Interrogatories—But it is beneath *his* dignity it seems to respond to such questions—& let me ask whether one who has acted the part you have done, & whose principles have been uniformly displayed by your actions are to be compelled to vindicate those principles from the misrepresentations of every Newspaper Editor who has been paid to slander you? In relation to the two great questions of the *Tariff* and *internal improvements,* your opinions can need no elucidation. During the two years of your service in the Senate, and frequently since, your opinions have been publicly expressed. But does it follow that any one disposed to afford a moderate protection to American Industry or to enter upon a few great works of National Improvement, should support *every measure* which bears *the name* of a Tariff Bill—or Internal Improvement? The truth is, that the Administration have determined, if possible to ride into power on these *popular Hobbies,* and as they intend to use them only *for their own advancement,* it is perfectly immaterial, what the character of the particular measure may be, which they are called upon to support. They have in fact, *perverted the whole system* of internal improvement into a scheme of buying up the people, with their own money—while Mr. Clay's *American policy* has degenerated into a plan for granting to a few overgrown Incorporated Companies *in New England* an exclusive monopoly of the home market. The Bill of the last session, was in its character *prohibitory,* encreased the Tax in exact proportion to the *poverty* of the person on whom it was to operate, and above all was calculated and *intended* to crush all the small manufacturers in the union while it gave a monopoly to the large companies. *This last feature* in the Bill will be found in the provision which leaves the Woollen goods, free from any encrease of duties 'till the last of August—the consequence of which must have been a great influx of foreign fabrics until that time, the consequent fall in prices, & the ruin of all who should be compelled to sell before that period, while immense fortunes would have been secured to *the rich* who could keep their goods on hand until the time, when they would have had a monopoly.[4] Now the people of the South (as you know) are opposed to this system in any shape, but they can and always will distinguish, between those who supported the Tariff of 1824 (as modified in the Senate,) and those who advocate such a Bill as that of the last session, between one (who like yourself) looks to the moderate protection of manufactures, without oppressing any branch of Industry, and one (who like Mr. Clay) wishes to form a party, & for purposes *purely selfish,* converts, the whole system of Internal Improvement & the Tariff into a political engine, of management, intrigue and corruption. I repeat, the high and honorable ground on which you have always stood, of affording judicious protection to all the great interests of the Country, suppressing none—must sustain you against the misrepresentation of your enemies, and though we at the South, deny the power of Congress to legislate on these points, yet, we feel that our interests would always be safe in your hands.[5]

Notwithstanding the boastful language of the partizans of power, you may be assured that the cause of the people is safe *in this quarter of the union.* Of all the Southern States, I consider Louisiana alone as at all doubtful. *South Carolina* is as fixed as "the everlasting hills which cannot be moved," and if New York can be retained in *her present temper* the contest will not be doubtful. But the victory is not yet won. There will be a fierce and hard battle during the next session of Congress—and the utmost zeal, firmness, and prudence will be necessary on the part of all your friends and supporters. One of the difficulties in our way, and not the least, is the party differences which have heretofore divided those who now find themselves united against the administration. Where bad men coalesce—it is necessary that the good of all parties should combine. Where a fatal attack is about to be made, on the purity of our institutions, and the attempt is openly made to subvert the rights of the people, it behooves all who are desirous of maintaining these main pillars of our political edifice, to forget minor differences, and unite in one great and common defence. But still to maintain harmony among persons of various opinions so united, it is necessary that the spirit of mutual conciliation should be carefully cherished. In looking through the U. S. I can find no man but yourself, who as the great leader of such a party, can harmonize the elements of discord, and give energy, unanimity and success to those who are fighting the battles of liberty and the Constitution. On your life and health my dear Sir, at this time, may depend the future prosperity and glory of your Country. May the God of mercies have you in his holy keeping, and may the remainder of your days be blessed, with peace, prosperity, and honor!

Having trespassed far beyond the limits I had assigned to myself, I must conclude by requesting that mine and Mrs. Hayne's affectionate remembrances[6] may be presented to Mrs. Jackson, and to assure her and yourself, that all of my family, (even our little boys who still remember and speak of you,) will always cherish for both of you the highest respect & esteem. Yours sincerely

Robt. Y. Hayne

P.S.

My brother & his Lady spend their summer in Charleston. They are well, and desire to be kindly remembered to Mrs. J. and yourself—

ALS, DLC (34). Published in Bassett, 3:357–60. Hayne (1791–1839), Arthur P.'s brother, had represented South Carolina in the United States Senate since 1823.

1. In mentioning "wrath" against Calhoun, Hayne was probably referring to the Rip Raps Shoal investigation.

2. On April 5, at a public dinner in his honor in Knoxville, Hugh L. White remarked that if the people were "sufficiently virtuous and enlightened to govern themselves" they would vote against Adams in the next presidential election. On May 24 the *National Journal* denounced this sentiment as "worthy of the Senate's worst days and worst members."

3. Hayne was possibly referring to Carter Beverley.

4. The woolens bill of 1827, providing increased duties on manufactured woolen goods imported into the United States, was defeated with Calhoun casting the deciding vote.

5. AJ and John H. Eaton had voted for the 1824 tariff in the Senate, providing the only southern support for the measure in the upper house and the margin of passage (see *Jackson,* 5:412–13, 464–66).

6. Née Rebecca Motte Alston, Hayne's second wife.

Account with Decker & Dyer

Nashville June 5th. 1827

Received of Genl. A. Jackson twenty five Dollars for a Parrot[1] bought for him by Mr. Decker

Decker & Dyer

ADS, DLC (34). Decker & Dyer was the Nashville confectionary firm of John Decker and Isham Dyer.

1. Named "Poll," the parrot, bought for Rachel, was still living at the time of AJ's death. According to an eyewitness account, "Poll" had to be removed from the house during AJ's funeral because of its loud cursing.

From Charles Pendleton Tutt

Locust Hill near Leesburg Va. June 6th 1827

My Dear Sir

A clerk in the War Department informed me a few days since that it was in contemplation by the administration to make an attack upon you in congress at the next Session, that various extracts from your accounts as an Indian Commissioner have been made out at the request of those in power with the view as I understand to contrast your accounts with Genl Browns,[1] and to found upon those garbled extracts a motion before Congress for further enquiry, calculating that much injury will be done to you

ANDREW JACKSON

THE OLD HOUSE OF REPRESENTATIVES

JOHN QUINCY ADAMS

JOHN CALDWELL CALHOUN

RACHEL JACKSON

SHADRACH PENN

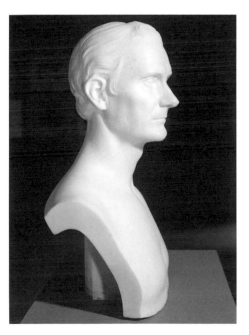

DUFF GREEN

JOSEPH GALES

CHARLES HAMMOND

HENRY CLAY

JOHN MCLEAN

SAMUEL LEWIS SOUTHARD

JAMES BARBOUR

JAMES BUCHANAN

JOSEPH DESHA

DEWITT CLINTON

GEORGE MCDUFFIE

Symptoms of a Locked Jaw

RICHARD III

ANDREW JACKSON

RACHEL JACKSON

John Patton Erwin

James Shelby

Leslie Combs

TRUTH'S ADVOCATE

AND

MONTHLY ANTI-JACKSON EXPOSITOR.

CINCINNATI, OHIO, MARCH 1828.

5000 COPIES
Of this work are circulated Monthly.

CONDUCTED
BY AN ASSOCIATION OF INDIVIDUALS.

No. III.

TABLE OF CONTENTS.

CINCINNATI:

MORGAN, FISHER, & L'HOMMEDIEU, PRINTERS.

1828.

*TRUTH'S ADVOCATE AND MONTHLY
ANTI-JACKSON EXPOSITOR*

ANDREW JACKSON

ANDREW JACKSON

before the charge could be refuted by an examination, which of course would be delayed as long as possible; under such circumstances would it not be adviseable in you to apprise some friend in Congress of the fact, and to give them such information upon the subject as will enable them to put down the vile slander, the moment it is ushered into existence. I had heretofore viewed the Secy at War as a high minded honorable man who would not have countenanced such a course, but I much fear that the administration has so entangled him within its web, that like all new converts, his zeal to sustain their cause has been such as greatly to impair his sound discriminating Judgment, indeed I regret to be compelled to say to you, that *he is up to the Hubb* in all executive measures, Electioneering and all others; formerly he did manifest some regard for you, and some consideration for your friends. The administration are now playing a desperate game, the whole force, power, patronage and funds of the government are employed to put you down, and to ensure their own election, all means however base and dishonorable they may be, will be resorted to with alacrity by them to effect their object, to countervail which it is absolutely necessary that every friend of yours should be on the alert; we have only to pursue a firm and temperate course, and we have no cause to apprehend the result, Justice & truth will, nay must prevail; do not my Dear Gen. permit the base and dastardly course of your Enemies, to betray you to manifest publicly any excitement upon the occasion, leave the Vindication of all their charges to your friends they are fully competent to the Task—and will cheerfully undertake the refutation of all their calumnies. The course the administration party is pursuing towards you, for its depravity, is unparalleled in this and I believe in any other country.

Every thing is going on well in Virginia notwithstanding our section of it has been well engineered with many promises of roads and canals to every mans Door.

I wish to God I could sell my property here so as to enable me to settle in your neighborhood. Mrs. Tutt and the children are all very desirous of doing so but to [sell] lands here at present is out of the [quest]ion, and I am too poor to remove [with]out selling here. Mrs. T. and my children beg me to give their love to Mrs. Jackson and yourself.

Be pleased to remember me most kindly to Mrs. Jackson and tell her that the Pipe she presented to me and which I valued so highly, I presented to a distinguished friend of yours in New Hampshire, under a pledge that no Enemy of yours should ever use it.

God bless you both my Dear Genl. and believe me to be very sincerely yr friend

Chas. Pen. Tutt

ALS, DLC (34).
    1. As early as April 1827, administration newspapers had been criticizing AJ's federal

accounts while major general in the army; and on June 1, Clay forwarded to Charles Hammond Jackson's accounts while serving as governor of Florida (*Clay Papers*, 6:631–32).

From Duff Green

Washington 9th. June 1827.

Dear Sir

The espionage upon my correspondence and the laborious detail of the duties which devolve on me have prevented me from Communicating with you often—The opportunity which offers by Mr [Michael T.] Simpson who visits your part of the Country as a confidential agent of the Department to which he is attached[1] and the peculiar relation in which we both stand to the public at this moment makes it proper that I should suggest the course that I would prefer the investigation, likely to arise out of Mr. Carter Beverly's letter, should take—It is my intention to lay before the public the facts & circumstances demonstrating the corrupt understanding between Mr Clay & Adams, and if possible provoke an appeal on the part of Mr Clay to the House at its next session. This I think will be much better than leaving the subject where it now is or of permitting yourself to be brought before the public through the newspapers as the accuser of Mr Clay more than you now are.

Many reasons urge upon my mind the propriety of this course. If we succeed in getting an impartial or an independent speaker he can organise a Committee which will draw to light much hidden matter and compel witnesses to testify who cannot otherwise be brought to disclose what they know. The fact that Mr Adams has rewarded [Philip Swenk] Markley[2] will do much in making out the case for he is the person through whom Mr Clay operated on Buchanan—Buchanan will not make a statement against Markley and must be drawn out by a committee. I shall not give the names of the parties in the disclosures which I have to make And place it upon the ground that it is due to Mr Clay that he should call for an investigation by a Committee.[3]

So much for this matter and now Sir permit me to congratulate you & the Country for that ardent patriotism and discriminating intelligence which marks the discussions in the public Journals devoted to the cause of the people and with which I consider your election so completely identified. Whilst your enemies have assaulted your public & private character & have gone so far as to invade your private Sanctuary and assailed your amiable partner you have found Consolation and protection in the confidence & virtue of a grateful and intelligent people

I have had many opportunities of ascertaining public opinion in the different states. The Republican party will be joined by the Clintonians in New York and arrangements are making among the leading Republicans of the north to rally with those of the north & south in the support of your election.

By some it is supposed that you will have a powerfull opposition organised against you and that your administration will be embarassed at every step [in] its operations—This seems to be the policy of the Amalgamists of Boston who despairing of the Reelection of Mr Adams have resolved to make for themselves a great New England party to the aid of which Mr Clay intends to bring his western interests.[4] Our republican friends in New England look to this state of things and desire that the canvas shall be so conducted as to enable them to stand with you on the old basis of the Republican party. I am at the same time delicately situated because a large portion of the Republican & Patriotic Federalists South of New York particularly in Delaware & Maryland are with us and altho the difference between these men is as marked as it could be yet names have charms which it is difficult to break. You will the better understand the guarded position I occupy. You owe to your Country that Major Lee should be permitted to develope fully the services you have rendered.[5] You must have ample proof in your possession that Mr Monroe deserves no thing from your forbearance.[6] Public expectation will be much excited and his work will be greedily sought for—it *[is his]* intention to throw it into every section of the Country imme*[diately.]* I do not regret the Violence with which you have been assailed because it will illicit enquiry & place this election on its proper ground before the public.

You will appreciate the embarasments which surround me unaided as I am by that advice and necessary counsel which would guide me from committing many errors—I have endeavored to make my paper the organ of correct principles & have carefully avoided the falsehood which characterise our opponents—In truth I have endeavored to prove myself opposed to them—Remember me kindly to Mrs. Jackson to Mr & Mrs. Donaldson. and accept assurances of unabated respect of

Duff Green

ALS, DLC (34). Published in Bassett, 3:360–62.

1. Simpson (d. 1836), an agent for Postmaster General John McLean (1785–1861), was at this time in Tennessee perhaps to look into the matter of espionage in the Nashville post office. In late June he visited AJ at the Hermitage.

2. In March Adams appointed Markley (1789–1834), who represented Pennsylvania in the U.S. Congress, 1823–27, naval officer at Philadelphia. AJ removed him in March 1829.

3. On July 2 Green published a long piece on the "corrupt bargain" in the *United States' Telegraph* and a week later made a direct call for a congressional investigation of the matter.

4. The Amalgamists were those political leaders in Massachusetts who, with leadership from Daniel Webster, urged the old Federalist and splintered Adams Republican factions to unite both at the state and federal levels behind the Adams administration. The Adams Republicans had recently split over the charter of the Warren Bridge Corporation, allowing the construction of a toll-free bridge across the Charles River, which Governor Levi Lincoln had vetoed.

5. Lee was writing a biography of AJ, an effort that Green backed. Lee never finished it,

but it became the basis for Amos Kendall's serial biography in the early 1840s, also never completed.

6. Green was referring to the ongoing dispute over the roles of Jackson and Monroe in the defense of New Orleans in 1814–15.

"A Female Friend" to Rachel Jackson

(Copy)   Washington city June 10. 1827
Madam,

Pardon a lady for addressing you on a subject of a delicate nature but believing that every illiberal attack upon the female character ought not to be viewed with indifference by any, I view it as a duty to apprize you of a fact that perhaps few besides myself has come to the knowledge of.

You no doubt have seen the brutish attack upon your reputation, with the real intention of thereby injuring the standing of the General with the public and altho the attack with the *real authors* will ultimately fall to the ground

You may then Madam rest assured that the *real* instigators, managers, and directors of this attack, made through the Cincinatti paper, is John McClean Post master General and Mr. Clay—the *first* the active agent— Previous to the last Election he suggested and urged that mode of attack on your husband, but the coalition then thought it unnecessary—It was kept back for a forlorn hope and the present trip of the Post master Genl. to Ohio is but an excuse to see how far this project is likely to succeed and to direct its application—He is constantly detailing his stories of your illiterate chat as he calls your remarks and it is the constant theme with others about him who obtain their observations from his stream of scandal—on its being suggested to him that the Genl. might be elected, by a confidential friend he replied that he will soon throw dust in his eyes sufficient to do any impression away, that the Genl. had his vanity and of course his weak side—

A female friend

I have forwarded this to Nashville by a private conveyance

ALS, DLC (11-0694).

By late spring 1827, the Adams faction, under Clay's guidance, had directed an arsenal of charges against Jackson, covering almost every aspect of his past, both as a public servant and as a private citizen. In the letter below, Jackson conferred with William B. Lewis on responding to the recent report that Thomas Jefferson had lacked confidence in Jackson's ability to serve as president.

The origin of this account of Jefferson's attitude was difficult for the Jacksonians to trace, as were most of the stories of Jackson's "crimes," indiscretions, and questionable leadership qualities. It was Jackson and Lewis's understanding that the disclosure of Jefferson's attitude was made at a dinner party. "It seems that Mr. Lewis Williams, . . . being invited to dine with Mr. Secretary Barbour, where, also, was found Mr. Coles, Governor of Illinois, heard the latter say, that he had heard Mr. Jefferson say, after the late Presidential Canvass, 'that Gen. Jackson's extraordinary run was an evidence that the Republic would not stand long.'"

Further disclosures about the report revealed that Congressman David Trimble of Kentucky who, hearing of Coles's comment, asked Williams for confirmation of the statement, then repeated it in a speech to his constituents, whereby it reached the newspapers. Coles maintained public silence on the matter until the fall of 1827, when, prompted by a query and continued public debate, he wrote that it was he who, on a visit to Monticello in August 1825, remarked about Jackson's significant vote in the previous presidential election and his fear for the Union, a sentiment which Jefferson endorsed by saying that Jackson's showing "had made him doubt of the duration of the Republic." Jefferson had added, according to Coles, that Jackson lacked the "temper, the acquirements, the assiduity, the physical qualifications for the office," that he had failed in his civil offices, and that "there are one hundred men in Albemarle County better qualified for the Presidency." With this confirmation from Coles, the administration forces continued to discuss the matter until the election the following year (Niles' Register, December 29, 1827, pp 281–83).

To William Berkeley Lewis

June 13th. 1827—

Dr Major

Since I returned home I have laid my hand on Mr Jeffersons note to me recd in Decbr 1820[1]—I enclose it that it may be stated by the Editor that it is in the proper hand writing of Mr Jefferson[2] I pray you preserve it carefully, & return it to me—It may be well contrasted with the certificate of Lewis Williams[3] &c—Genl Duncan can give you the standing of Mr [Edward] Coles[4] in Elanois, & how far he would be creditted there— Mr Coles has the appointment, to inspect the land offices, It is fair to conclude that he is only now performing his obligations entered into as part consideration fo[r] this appointment—The information communicated by Major Lee, of the expressions of his family of his favourable sentiments of me, may be fairly brought into view,[5] without giving the name of Major Lee.

I enclose Genl Winchesters letter giving the date of the fall of Ft.

B[owyer] & of his situation,[6] the other letter I have not laid my hand on yet—return this letter with

AL signature removed and Copy, NN (11-0696, -0698).
   1. Jefferson's letter to AJ, November 22, in which Jefferson complimented AJ on the vindication of his actions in Florida, was actually 1819 instead of 1820 (*Jackson*, 4:337).
   2. The letter appeared in a *Nashville Republican* editorial, June 19.
   3. Lewis Williams (1782–1842), congressman from North Carolina, was the brother of John Williams of Tennessee and the brother-in-law of John P. Erwin.
   4. Coles (1786–1868), governor of Illinois, 1822–26, was private secretary to Jefferson during his presidency.
   5. See Lee to AJ, July 1, 1826. The *Nashville Republican* editorial did not mention the Lee letter.
   6. See James Winchester to AJ, January 15, 1815. In referring to the Winchester letter, AJ was preparing materials to combat the alleged Binns forgery of the John Harris letter of January 15, 1815 (*Nashville Republican*, July 7, 1827).

From Maunsel White

New Orleans June 14th. 1827—

Dear Sir,
   I am now in rect. of your esteemed favors of 10th. 16. & 28 May.[1] & feel much gratified that my course has met your approbation. & the result is that I have at last Obtained my price for your Cotton. say 9 Cents all round, I dare not hold on any longer, & truly when it was brot. out for Examination I feared for some which was negligently handled, yet after considerable Obstinacy on the part of the Enemy, I succeeded in getting in the Whole, When we began to Weigh it I was surprised to find it loose 12, 14 & 20 lb. Bale I immediately Changed the Pattent Balances got others & tried it in every way, seeing that nothing could change our Weights to corrispond with yours. I waited on the Messr. Dicks[2] who recd. the Cotton you sold, at home, I asked them how it held out, & they shewed me that it lost 9 lb pr. Bale on an Average, & Laughed at me, for not being aware that nearly all Cottons which had lain here any length of time & which was put up as planters generally do put up their Cottons in damp Weather, loose considerably, if stored in Open sheds and any way exposed to the dry Scorching weather which we have had here for nearly two Months. I then continued to Weigh it & it looses nearly 12 lb. pr Bale on an Average, but to shew the powerful effect of the dry weather, It will be manifest when I inform you that a few Bales which lay at the Bottom of the Pile stowed away where sun or air could not get at them well, lost very little indeed in Comparison—Mr. Foristal the Broker[3] who bot. it from me, weighed it like gold, for I stood by the time. I could not have supposed that the Weather would have had such an effect. I knew that cotton would loose from 6 a 8 lb. in three months & much less in pro-

portion afterwards & in very damp Foggy weather will again, gain, it seems to be something of the nature of a sponge, with more attraction.

The next question is. are your Ballances Correct, here we have them regulated twice a year, agreeably to the standard. at any rate so it is & I feel much Mortified that they have not held out. enclosed, I Send you the Accot Sales Nt proceeds $3062 $^{55}/_{100}$ & by Mr Stacker[4] who leaves here in a few days I shall Send you the Balance I shall owe you—I was afraid to hold up any longer, for fear of letting the sale slip thro my Fingers, besids having Got. ¼ of Cent more than my Neighbours, owing however to a little liveliness in the Liverpool Market which I fearing would again subside, I was determined to embrace, I know of no price now abroad which will Warrant, more's being given. it is your Name alone therefore that has sold yr Cotton.

I have only to add that your Friends here will be overjoyed to see you, & one good thing is they are Sin[c]ere—& Speak with enthusiasm of the contemplated Meeting[5]—I have not seen Mr. [John Devereux] Delacy yet altho I called several times at his Lodgings,[6] be assured it will give me great pleasure, to shew any civility in my power to any of your Friends— & if I were not well assure'd that you will be provided with Lodgings, I would ask you to honor my humble dwelling during yr stay with yr. Friends here—with my best Wishes for yr success, & yrs & Mrs Jacksons welfare I remain yr Frd & obdt.

Maunsel White

ALS, DLC (34). Published in Bassett, 3:363–64.
1. Not found.
2. James and Nathaniel Dick (1781–1839), New Orleans merchants.
3. Probably Edmond Forstall.
4. Either Samuel (b. c1790) or John Stacker (1790–1869), brothers, steamboat owners and ironmasters in Stewart and Montgomery counties, Tennessee.
5. AJ had accepted an invitation to visit New Orleans for the January 8, 1828, celebration of the thirteenth anniversary of the Battle of New Orleans.
6. Delacy (c1781–1837) was a North Carolina attorney, who was on business in New Orleans with letters of introduction from AJ.

To *William B. Keene*

(Copy)   Hermitage June 16th 1827.
Dr. Sir

Your letter of the 5th ult.[1] has reached me: and I assure you it affords me much pleasure to learn the good feelings of your citizens towards me— this, under the torrent of the vilest Slander wickedness & falsehood can invent, daily poured out against Mrs Js character as well as my own, is the more grateful.

When the midnight assassin strikes you to the heart, murders your family, & robs your dwelling, the heart sickens at the relation of the deed: but this scene loses all its horrors when compared with the recent slander of a virtuous female propagated by the minions of power for political effect.[2] It is a case unheard of before in civilized life, and I would fain hope, is the only one of the kind which the faithful historian will record, as having occurred in enlightened America, in the 50th year of her independence, under the administration of Messrs. Adams & Clay—

The tree is known by its fruit—the man by his conduct. Apply this rule to the present administration of the General Government, and if it be the fact that its patronage as seen & felt in the selection of its officers, in the appointments of publishers of the laws, & in its various means of influencing the public sentiment, is chargeable either with the fabrication or circulation of this vile slander of Mrs J & myself, where does the moral place it? the country will decide.

As for my own part, I am content to accept with gratitude, such evidences of the continued kindness & confidence of my fellow citizens as that which you have communicated from Kentucky. Never having entertained a doubt of the high minded virtue & patriotism of her citizens, I feel assured they will ever protect the cause of truth with that liberty—

Mrs J physician[3] has advised her to visit the Harrodsburgh springs this season for her health, & we were preparing for the journey when an act of Providence interposed, which will postpone, if not prevent it, this season. By a stroke of lightening she is left without a carriage horse, & myself without a riding horse.[4]

I beg you to say to that portion of my friends in Kentucky which you may see, that it would afford me much pleasure to visit them, & I intend so to do when I can with convenience & under circumstances that cannot justly charge me with electioneering views or interference with your state policy & elections. Accept assurances, &c

A Jackson

Copy in Andrew J. Donelson's hand, DLC (34). Endorsed by AJ: "Doctor W. B. Keene letter 5th. of June, Georgetown Ky. to be answered—given to Mr. E. H. Foster. In answer say the pleasure it would afford to visit my friends in Ky intended to visit but cannot say where it will be in my *power or not*." Keene (b. c1775), a native of Maryland, practiced medicine in Georgetown, Kentucky.

1. Not found.

2. Among other things, the Frankfort *Commentator* had recently compared Rachel Jackson to a "*dirty, black wench!*" (as quoted in Frankfort *Argus*, April 18).

3. Miles Blythe McCorkle (d. 1869).

4. The Jacksons did not visit Kentucky in 1827.

To John Overton

Nashville June 16th. 1827

D. Sir,

Will you be so good as to inform me whether you did not write the original publication, made in the Impartial Review, of June 28th. 1806 and that the certificates and extracts published are correct copies from the originals, and also whether they together with other publications relative to the duel which was fought between myself and Mr. Charles Dickerson, was not handed to you by your brother Genl. Thomas Overton, who was my friend on that occasion, for your inspection and safe keeping. At the time you wrote the publication above alluded to, you must recollect that I was still indisposed from the wound I recd. from the fire of Mr. Dickison.[1] Your early compliance with this request will very much oblige Your friend

Andrew Jackson

ALS, THi (11-0704). Published in *THQ*, 6(1947):173.
1. On June 23 Overton responded in the affirmative.

Henry Clay, who was perhaps more closely identified with the protective tariff than any other politician, hoped to turn its popularity in the North and West to the administration's advantage. This tactic, however, had a serious weakness—as a senator, Jackson had voted for the 1824 tariff, the chief piece of protective legislation. Indeed, Jackson had been one of the few southerners to back the measure, and his support had been key to its passage. On May 5, John Binns's Democratic Press, *a paper closely allied with the administration, alleged that Jackson, in a confidential letter to political allies in Virginia, had promised them that he would strive to roll back protection. The source of this intelligence concluded, "ONE THING IS CERTAIN—EITHER VIRGINIA OR PENNSYLVANIA WILL BE COMPLETELY DUPED." On May 11, Thomas Ritchie (1778–1854), editor of the* Richmond Enquirer *and no friend of the tariff, replied in his paper that he had heard of no such communication and that Jackson would never write anything so underhanded.*

To deal with the issue, John H. Eaton drafted two letters, both written on the same sheet of paper. The first, dated June 23 and signed by John Overton, asked Jackson if he had changed his attitude towards the tariff since 1824. The second, dated June 24 and signed by Jackson, below, replied negatively.

To John Overton

Hermitage 24 June 1827

Sir—

I have recd your Note of Yesterday:[1] the question you propose to [me?] is a simple one, and I reply to it with pleasure—

The letter written to Dr. [Littleton H.] Coleman of No Ca. was in reply to certain enquires submitted to me by the Dr. in 1824 when the tarriff of that year was pending before Congress.[2] The opinions then expressed were such as were had in referrence to what I considered the general interest and advantage of the Country, & from a knowlege of the manifold inconveniences which had been experienced by us during the late war, when for many articles, essential to our defence & well being in a state of war, we were compelled to be dependent upon our enemy. Nothing has transpired since to alter or change any opinion that is there expressed, nor with me, has any alteration taken place.

Andrew Jackson

LS draft in John H. Eaton's hand, THi (11-0712).
    1. See Overton to AJ, June 23.
    2. Coleman (d. 1824) was a physician from Warrenton, North Carolina. For AJ's letter of April 24, 1824, to him, see *Jackson*, 5:398–400.

To Henry Daniel

Hermitage June 25th. 1827.

Dr Sir

Your letter of the 9th Inst. has been recd.[1] in which you ask of me some explanation relative to the duty imposed in 1824 on cotton Bagging. I have a thorough recollection of the circumstances of that Bill, & particularly of the proceedings which took place as to the article of Bagging.

When the Bill came to the Senate from the House of Representatives my attention was directed principally towards those items which I considered assential and necessary to our prosperity in times of war, where of Hemp, & articles made of Hemp stood prominent. Duck was necessary in war, as constituting a material article in the preparation of our ships. With a view to an uniform & equal operation of the Tarriff, in different sections of our country, it seemed proper that a relative and corresponding duty should be placed on all & every article of which Hemp was the material part: & this object appeared to have been regarded by the House of Representatives, looking to the shape in which the Bill came to the Senate.

An increased duty on Russian & Holland Duck going to effect the ship-

ping interest of New England was objected to: the amount at which it had
been placed by the House of Representatives was stricken out, & *the ad
valorum* duty reduced to 15 pr cent. Acting with a view to uniform Justice
between the north & south, I could not discern the propriety of placing Duck,
needfull to our merchant ships, at a low rate of duty; & Bagging made of the
same material at a more advanced duty. You will accordingly find that on
the first application to reduce the 4¹/₂ cents duty on Baggin I voted against it;
& did likewise vote against reducing Russian & Holland duck to the
advalorum duty of 15 pr cent. Senate Journal 1823–24 pages 361–368. The
motion to reduce however succeeded, after which time I deemed it right & so
voted to make a correspondent reduction on Bagging. The two Houses remained divided between 4¹/₂ & 3¹/₂: This in the end was settled by a committee of conference at 3.³/₄ to which I agreed, & for which sum I voted; &
likewise for the entire bill on its final passage.

Another consideration operated: The House of Representatives had
placed the duty on Hemp at 2 cents a pound. This the Senate had stricken
out & reduced, contrary to my vote & wishes, to I think $35 a ton, mak-
ing about 25 percent deduction. Uniformity being assential & right, it
seemed to be proper, that as the raw material was reduced, so likewise
should there be a correspondent reduction on the manufactured article.

These are concisely the considerations & reasons which operated upon
me on that part of the Tarriff of 1824 about which you have solicited my
views & opinions.

Wishing you health & happiness I am very respectfully yr most obdt.
servt.

Andrew Jackson

ALS, John Tuska (11-0715); Draft in John H. Eaton's hand (DLC-34). Published in Bassett,
3:365–66 (from Eaton's copy). Daniel (1786–1873), former Kentucky state legislator, had
recently been elected as a Jacksonian to the Twenty-first Congress.
    1. See Daniel to AJ, June 9.

From Carter Beverley

Virgna. Wheeling
27th. June *1827.*

Dear Sir

Since the date of my letters two days ago, one inclos'd to Mr. James
Edmonson[1] of Nashville wi. sundry documents, (& the postage pd. upon
it,) & the other directed to you,[2] I have recd. a letter from the Hon'ble
Judge [Alexander] Caldwell[3] of this place, directed to Mr. Noah Zane,[4] a
resident here also, & inclos'd to me by his letter[5]—It is a full detail of Mr.
Clay's denial on Sunday last, before them all, of the whole of the charges
contain'd in your letter, both agt. him and his Friends[6]—I have sent an

attested copy of it by this day's mail, to Mr. Duff Green of Washington City, to appear immediately in the Telegraph.[7]

Your declarations are pretty generally believ'd; & Mr. Clay & the Administration are daily sinking in the public opinion—Under the whole aspect of the business, the people will not disbelieve the *fact,* that strong attempts *were projected among* them, to get you over to them—Moreover, they believe in the negotiation between Mr. Adams & him—Your candor & openness to me in your letter, gives great satisfaction, & the prompt manner in which you met my letter from Louisville is equally pleasing to them[8]—The partizans of the *Coalition,* had commenc'd a report, to impress the community wi. a total disbelief of me; & had gone so far, as to say, that you *never would in any shape reiterate the subject of my letter to my Friend in Fayette-Ville*[9]—The arrival of yr. letter consequently, threw them all into deep consternation; especially, as the morning after, Mr. Clay was to be here, & did arrive—The course taken wi. your letter by Mr. Zane, was a scandalous & unprecidented liberty—I have expos'd both him, Mr. Clay & the Junto upon their conduct regarding it; & sent it to Mr Green to appear in the Telegraph, that the public may view the grossness & vile impudence of their conduct, & that you may be satisfied of the advantage taken of my confidence in Mr. Zane, a man far advanc'd in life as he is, & of very high character.[10] A Gentleman has just arriv'd in this neighborhood from Florida, a Mr. Floyd;[11] and openly states, after reading a copy of yr. letter to me, that he hear'd Colo. Gadsden in Florida, say distinctly, that he had communicated to you, exactly what you wrote me; Floyd is consider'd a young man of considerable respectability, & he is Relied, upon *for this fact.* Colo. Gadsden was a member *then* from South Carolina, & he is a man whose character stands high; of course, Yr. letter is most importantly supported *at once.* This additional matter, is making great way among the people here, & every credit given to the charges—

That you may be fully & fairly convinc'd, that I have been most innocently drawn into this business, I beg leave to quote to you, part of a letter just recd. from my Friend in FayetteVille N. C. upon the subject of my letter to him, & his disclosure of it—[12]

I trust, should any apprehensions have at all crept upon yr. mind, as to my honorable intentions towards you in this unlook'd for, & accidental business; you will readily throw it off, & believe that it was unsought for, & altogether unexpected by me: The zeal & honor of my Friend, embolden'd him, from his high opinion of yr. integrity & good Judgement, to develope it—Your letter to me exculpating me so frankly, & so greatly to yr. Credit, affords me the very utmost relief. I have been most severely goaded indeed, by a junto of low-liv'd hireling Printers in every direction of this Western, & North Western section of the Union, and by a numerious body of time serving creatures to the Coalition—They are however now Completely prostrated, & are put down, & I trust & hope most effectually & permanently, wi. their whole & entire corrupt Body.

The people are speaking strongly & confidently of this matter being brought fully & fairly before the next Congress[13]—That Mr. Adams ought to be impeach'd, and made to answer to the Nation for so great a degredation upon the people: He stands charg'd wi. gross & foul corruption; & ought to be held accountable for it—This idea is gaining ground very rapidly—I see that Ritchie of the Richd. Enquirer, has already hinted at this Course, as one that ought, & will be taken.[14]

Mr. Clay acknowledg'd here at Mr. Zane's House on Sunday, that he had long heard of *your* free speaking, & *charges* upon him, reiterated by yr. Friends; but, that he never could *before,* get at it in any tangible form—He now had at last gotten it under full authority, & was enabled thereby to confront it—

I told the Gentleman, (who told it to me, Colo. Moses [W.] Chaplane) a lawyer of high respectability, & who mention'd it to me, before a Mr. Forsythe a merchant here, and Mr. Moses [C.] Good, a young Lawyer of high character here; that I beg'd him to recollect what he said; for, he would perhaps, have to repeat it hereafter[15]—He said he should not forget it—Thus, you see how very artful Mr. Clay is; for he has all along known of these charges upon him, & he has fain'd ignorance & want of proof; when he *well knew,* you would have, at *any moment* given it to him from under yr. own signature—I mention this, to show you, how cunningly this creature & his coadjutors & supporters have acted, & will endeavor to persist in, agt. you—They ought to have no quarter given them, but be prostrated if possible.

I must now refer you for all further particulars to the Telegraph, & the other News Papers; for you will, I apprehend, 'ere this reaches you, see the whole matter spread before the Community, wi. severe editorial remarks upon the Chief & his Coadjutor.

My Sincere respects to Mrs. Jackson I am Dear Sir, wi. very sincere respect & esteem Yr. Mos. Obt. Set.

Carter Beverley

ALS, DLC (34). Published in Bassett, 3:366–69.

1. Edmonson, formerly a Louisville and Cincinnati hotelier, had just moved to Nashville.

2. Letters not found.

3. Caldwell (1774–1839, Canonsburg College, Pa., 1797) had been appointed judge of the federal district court for western Virginia by Adams in October 1825.

4. Zane (1778–1833), banker, steamboat owner, bridge builder in Wheeling, served in the Virginia state senate, 1812–16.

5. Letters not found.

6. En route to Kentucky, Clay made a brief stop at Wheeling and visited Zane, who showed him AJ's June 5 letter to Beverley. Caldwell, along with Moses W. Chapline and Richard McClure, who had also been at Zane's house during Clay's visit, later issued a public statement describing Clay's denial of any knowledge of or involvement in the purported deal offered to AJ in 1825 (*National Intelligencer*, August 8). Clay formally denied

AJ's charges regarding the "corrupt bargain" in his letter to the public, June 29, (*Clay Papers*, 6:728–30).

7. On July 2, Duff Green published an abstract of the certificate sent by Beverley.

8. See above, AJ to Beverley, June 5.

9. Beverley was referring to his March 8 letter to Richard S. Hackley, which made public AJ's allegations of a bargain offered by Clay's allies in 1825.

10. Zane had asked to borrow AJ's June 5 letter to Beverley and pledged to return it. Zane then showed the letter to Clay and, against Beverley's wishes, had two copies made and gave one to Clay. Clay forwarded a copy of the letter to Charles Hammond. Beverley condemned Zane's actions and sent copies of his correspondence with Zane regarding the incident to Green for publication (*United States' Telegraph*, July 2).

11. Not identified.

12. In his letter of June 14 (DLC-34), Hackley took full responsibility for allowing the extract from Beverley's letter to him to be published in the Fayetteville *Carolina Observer*.

13. See, for example, above, Duff Green to AJ, June 9.

14. On June 12, the *Richmond Enquirer* urged that AJ and Clay make clear their respective claims regarding the "corrupt bargain" and that a more formal investigation then be undertaken, perhaps by Congress. It did not, however, mention impeachment.

15. Chapline (1789–1840) represented Ohio County in the Virginia House of Delegates, 1818–21, 1835–36. Forsythe has not been further identified. Good (d. 1873) later served in the Virginia state senate, 1839–42.

To Charles Pendleton Tutt

Hermitage June 30th. 1827—

Dr. Sir

yours of the 6th. instant has Just reached me,[1] & be assured, I feel very gratefull for the information it communicates.

Whilst the conduct of the sec of war, which you detail, inspires only feelings of contempt for the man, I can assure you it would give me much pleasure (& I am sure it would my friends) to see all my accounts in the Indian, as well as every other department of the govt., exposed to public view, and fairly contrasted with Genl Brown accounts, or any other officer of the army or the goverment—I defy all the panders of power to injure me by exposing all & every transaction with Govt. during my whole life—whenever I had the disbursing of public mony it will be seen, that I used it with oeconomy & Justly.

My friends in next congress will, I trust, call for a full investigation of my accounts & others—This I expect the sec of war has heard of; & the inuendoes are intended for effect, perhaps, to keep my friends from making the call for those accounts. My friends have been prohibited from a view of my correspondence with the goverment, fearing, as it is alledged, that they would have a view of others, against which "(the Honble. Sec) *has insuperable objections.*"[2]

In my public acts, as well as private, I have always viewed honesty the best policy & pursued it—Therefore I fear nothing that can be extracted from my accounts—If mutulated, or forged, accounts are given out, such as was handed to Frank Johnston it is as easy to detect them as those given to Frank, in which there appears to have existed nearly seven thousand dollars of an Error.[3] This was an intentional error, I have no doubt, and for the purpose which was attempted; but it has recoiled on their own heads—Rest assured I am prepared at all points, & my friends need have no fear of the result.[4]

Mrs. J. begs me to say to you, that the use you have made of the pipe, meets her entire approbation, she unites with me in a tender of our best wishes to you, your lady, & family, & desires me to add that it would afford her great pleasure, as it would myself, to have you & your family as neighbours in this country. accept assurances of my great respect & Esteem

Andrew Jackson

ALS copy, DLC (34). Published in Bassett, 3:369.

1. See above.
2. The term "insuperable objections" came from Secretary of War James Barbour to Henry Lee, December 13, 1826, in which Barbour denied Lee access to war department files (DLC-72). Congress did not investigate AJ's accounts.
3. While campaigning for reelection to Congress in Kentucky, Johnson had accused AJ of padding his expense accounts while in the army and as governor of Florida.
4. On June 16, the *Louisville Public Advertiser* published a report, based on certified copies of accounts provided by federal auditors, demonstrating that AJ had received $38,878.88 for his military services between 1814 and 1821—$6,984.23 less than Johnson had claimed, and $413.16 less than paid over the same time to General Jacob Jennings Brown for roughly comparable duties.

In the brief note below to Peter Force (1790–1868) and other editors and writers of the Washington National Journal, *Jackson vented his anger at the charges the administration presses had made against Rachel Jackson, and in 1828, that paper published a transcription of the item to show Jackson's illiteracy. Several of Jackson's friends examined the item and concluded that the writing looked like Jackson's, but Jackson denied ever sending the inscribed pamphlet to Force. At one point in the campaign, the Jacksonians learned that the inscribed pamphlet with a document in Jackson's hand from the war department files was being circulated in Virginia, all to prove that the handwriting was indeed Jackson's.*

To [Peter Force et al.]

[cJune 1827]

When the midnight assasins plunges his dagger to the heart & riffles your goods, the turpitude of this scene looses all its horrors when compared with the act of the secrete assasins poinard levelled against female charecter by the hired minions of power.

AN inscribed on *A Letter from the Jackson Committee of Nashville, in Answer to One from a Similar Committee, at Cincinnati upon the Subject of Gen. Jackson's Marriage* (Nashville, 1827), DLC (mAJs); Printed, Washington *Daily National Journal*, February 21, 1828 (mAJs); *Truth's Advocate and Monthly Anti-Jackson Expositor*, March 1828 (11-0612); *U.S. Telegraph Extra*, April 26, 1828, p. 32.

To John Coffee

Hermitage July 1rst. 1827—

Dr. Genl

Yours of the 21rst ult is Just recd;[1] I regret to hear of your misfortune in the loss of your seamstress;[2] but those losses we must expect, & have philosophy anough to meet them—I have lost another horse yesterday & console myself by reflecting If I had none I could loose none, but being blessed with a good supply, I ought & am content with all things that providence dispenses to me—I am happy to learn that you & your family have reached home in safety.[3]

The season with us has continued wet & cold untill last monday—my crop is unusually foul; my cotton has been injudiciously worked, contrary to my orders, the overseer[4] had directed the hands to cover the grass in the cotton, the rains washed the earth, & left the grass in fine condition to grow, this has occasioned me much trouble in forty acres of my cotton—I am getting through it—my cotton is Just beginning to grow, I have one field of 32 acres that is good, I believe the best in the neighbourhood—my corn has been well plowed about 120 acres in good order the ballance wants the hoes to clear the hill—The rust has injured our wheat, some not worth cutting, mine, if it was not for the quantity of cheat, is good—I have my rye & wheat cut & my oats ripe, which appears to be much in the way of laying by my crop—The loss of so many of my horses has reduced my plows to 15. with those I hope to be able to lay by my crop in good order—I have cotton knee high with many forms, no blooms yet.

I am glad to hear you have got your coalt out safely—feed the coalts on meal & water mixed with salt—This will do them more good than the milk from the mare, by feeding the mare *well*, & giving the coalts *meal & water*, they will *grow finely*—I wish you to raise him *well*—as I believe him the finest coalt I have ever seen.

My political enemies, appear to be somewhat palsied by the exposure their falshoods have experienced—It raised a little alarm & bustle in the war office when Major Eaton called for a copy of all my accounts. he has obtained a regular certified copy of all my accounts, which when compared to that furnished Frank Johnston, there appears a differrence of nearly seven thousand dollars[5]—This when fairly before the nation, must forever dam the sec of war as a dishonest & dishonorable man—it proves that there is nothing too base for them to do, to injure me, & thereby retain their power—the people are too honest to support such a course. I fear nothing from the attack made by Col Williams on Judge White,[6] all his, & the panders of powers vials of wrath, cannot injure the Judge, he will prevail over his enemies, if truth can prevail over error & vice & wickedness then will the Judge come forth triumphant, & our next Legislature will elect him, if not by a unanimous voice, by at least 9/10 of all the members—I hope Williams will loose his election, if so, he is down never to rise more[7]—The friends of the administration & the heads of it, are making a desperate struggle, they stop at nothing, their whole view the retention of power regardless of the means used to retain it—men without truth & principle for their guide, may flourish for a moment, but must fall at last, & like the fall of Lucifer, will be thei[r] fall, never to rise more.

I am not going to Ky. My pri[n]ciples will not permit me to do any act that will *Justly* lay me under the imputation of electioneering for office—I have not heard of J. J. passing on to Ky.[8] he can do me no harm any where, altho if he could, I have no doubt he would do so.

I have recd a letter from Judge White enclosing one from Wm H Crawford to him, on the Presidential Election in which he says, if it was not the fear that I would take Mr Calhoun into the Cabinet, both the north & south would unite in my support, & *adds proof,* that Calhoune was as much my enemy as Clay, until him & Adams fell out—*can this be*—The Judges answer & mine a proper one, "that I had, nor would have no understanding with any man, or set of men, on that subject; that if elected, I must go into the office untramelled in any way, free to choose my Cabinet—without restraint, from those whose virtues combined with talents were thought most worthy.["][9]

Mrs. J. Joins me in best wishes for your & families welfare & happiness—your daughter is in good health & now with her grand mother[10]—your friend

Andrew Jackson

ALS, DLC (11-0725).
    1. See Coffee to AJ, June 21.
    2. Probably Coffee's slave Bettey.
    3. The Coffees had visited the Hermitage in early June.
    4. Ira Walton was AJ's overseer from January through August, when AJ dismissed him for killing the slave Gilbert.
    5. For discussion of AJ's accounts, see above, AJ to Charles Pendleton Tutt, June 30.
    6. Williams had attacked White for accepting business from the state of Tennessee while serving in the U.S. Senate and for receiving extravagant compensation while president of the Bank of the State of Tennessee (*Knoxville Register,* June 6, 13).
    7. Williams won election to the state senate and White, reelection to the U.S. Senate.
    8. In his letter of June 21, Coffee informed AJ that James Jackson had just left for Nashville and Kentucky.

9. See White to AJ, June 19, enclosing Crawford to White, May 27, and White to Crawford, June 19. AJ was quoting loosely from White's letter to Crawford.

10. Mary Donelson Coffee (1812–39), a student at the Nashville Female Academy, was visiting her grandmother, Mary P. Donelson.

To Robert Mills

Hermitage July 8th 1827.

Dr Sir,

I have recd your favor of the 15th ulto.[1] accompanied with a map of the district of Lancaster within which I was born.[2] For this flattering evidence of your regard be pleased to accept my sincere thanks.

A view of this map pointing to the spot tha*[t]* gave me birth, brings fresh to my memory many associations dear to my heart, many days of pleasure with my juvenile companions: but alas, most of them are gone to that bourne where I am hastening & from whence no one returns. I have not visitted that country since the year 1784. Most of the names of places are changed; all the old generation appears to have passed away, & to be succeded by another more numerous and often differently named. The crossing of the Waxaw creek, within one mile of which I was born, is still, however, I see, possessed by Mr John Crawford, son of the owner (Robert) who lived there when I was growing up & at school. I lived the*[re]* for many years, & from the accuracy with which this spot is marked in the map, I conclude the whole must be correct. With great respect I have the honor to be Sir, your very obliged servant

Andrew Jackson

Photocopy of LS in Andrew J. Donelson's hand, NcSal (11-0734). Published in Bassett, 3:371. Mills (1781–1855), an architect, was a member of the South Carolina Board of Public Works. In 1836, AJ made him Architect of Public Buildings for Washington, D.C. He designed the Treasury Building, the Patent Office, the Post Office, and the Washington Monument.

1. Not found.

2. The map was taken from Mills's *Atlas of the State of South Carolina* (Columbia, S.C., 1825). Subsequently, Mills sent AJ a complete copy of the *Atlas*.

From Duff Green

Washington 8th. July 1827

Dear Sir.

The multiplied duties of my office have kept me so much engaged that I have not indulged myself in writing letters as I should do. You have been of the number neglected. You will however permit me through you to tender to Mrs Jackson the congratulations of a sincere friend on the satisfactory and conclusive vindication of her innocence which has been presented to the public by the Nashville Committee.[1] To a lady of her great sensibility the knowledge of her own innocence would bring much consolation but that sensibility must have been the more acute when she saw that the envenomed shaffts of malice were aimed at her on your account. Let her rejoice—her vindication is Complete—the voice of slander is hushed—and she must be gratified to know that your magnanimity to her is rightly appreciated by an intelligent public—That so far from impairing the confidence of the people in you this attack has made you many friends. I am aware of the delicacy of the subject and under other circumstances would be last to intrude such remarks upon your notice but I have not been without my share of difficulty in this matter. I saw the necessity of bringing home the matter to Mr Adams' own family and by threats of retaliation drove the Journal to condemn itself.[2] This you have no doubt seen & understand—The effect here was like electricity. The whole Adams Corps were thrown into consternation—soon They had no doubt that I would execute my threat and I was denounced in the most bitter terms for assailing *female* character by those very men who had rolled the slanders on Mrs. J. under their tongues as the sweetest morsel that had been dressed up by peter Force & Co during the whole campaign—It was plainly hinted that my paper must not be taken at the public offices and *some* of those who had been suspected of Jacksonism were weak enough to discontinue, and some others to threaten me with a meeting of Your friends to disavow any aprobation of my remarks unless I would make some apology!! I put them at once at defiance—told them that they had done nothing for the support of the cause—that I had never looked to their fears or their hopes for counsel, and that I looked to the people and *not* to the attachers of the palace for approbation—The gentlemen were check mated and some of them have bowed to me most politely since—especialy if no spies are near when we meet—

I find that I have dwelt much more at large on this unpleasant topic than I intended. One great object in addressing you this is to say that I suspect that Mr Monroe is apprised that you have discovered his treachery to you and is desirous to lend the influence of his name to promote the reelection of Mr Adams I am told that numerous documents in relation to the Campa[i]gn of 1814–15 have been furnished him from the War Department and that he & Southard have been in active correspondence[3]—Is it not probable that the late notice of your correspondence with Southard, in the National Intelligencer is intended to provoke a publication on your part, so as to give Mr Monroe an opportunity to come out?[4] If this conjecture be right it would appear to me proper that Monroe's former treachery (for I can call it by no other name) should be exposed—How much did the sight of that letter change my opinion of the man!!

I have written to Doctor Wallace to send me a copy of your Correspondence, that I may be prepared to act[5]—I shall endeavor to do the best I can and altho I will not unnecessarily bring Mr Monroe into the Controversy—if he obtrudes himself he will find me prepared to do him ample justice—

I feel the want of confidential friends and advisers. I have a few fast friends who are true and ready to aid with advice but there are but two or three in whose opinions I Can Confide. The atmosphere is infected—those in office br[*eathe*] upon permission of the President and his influence is felt in every workshop in the city—It will not do for me to receive my impulses from such sources. I should soon sink even below Gales & Seaton were I to do so. Your friend

D Green

ALS, DLC (34). Published in Bassett, 3:371–73.

1. *A Letter from the Jackson Committee of Nashville . . . upon the Subject of Gen. Jackson's Marriage . . .* (Nashville, 1827). Green published the Committee's report in the *United States' Telegraph* on June 22.

2. On June 16 and 18, in the *United States' Telegraph,* Green warned that he did not wish "to bring the female character of this country into public discussion." He added that "it was not our desire to trace the *love* adventures of the Chief Magistrate, nor to disclose the manner, *nor the time,* at which *he,* his brother-in-law, and his father-in-law before him, led their *blushing* brides to the hymenial altar." But in light of the attacks on the Jacksons, "we feel that forbearance, under such circumstances, almost ceases to be a virtue; and we say to those men—beware how you touch upon this subject." Green did not carry through on his threat, but he continued to criticize the administration press for its efforts to cloak Louisa Catherine Adams with republicanism and "to demonstrate how much better qualified she was to discharge the duties of the drawing room, than the unassuming plain, old house-wife of the Tennessee Farmer" (June 20).

3. In writing of Monroe's "treachery," Green was referring to Monroe's letter to Calhoun, September 9, 1818, which Lee had apparently shared with Green.

4. On June 29, the *National Intelligencer* referred to rumors that AJ had challenged the Southard to a duel. Since February, Southard and Monroe had been corresponding on the question of the defense of New Orleans. All along, however, Monroe had declined to have his name brought before the public.

5. In the July 11 *Telegraph,* Green reported that he had copies of the correspondence between AJ and Southard and indicated that he might publish it shortly. Only a fragment of a printing of the Jackson-Southard correspondence has been found (T). It is not known if this was issued by Green.

To Robert Young Hayne

Hermitage July 9th. 1827—

My Dear Sir

The confidential letter of the 5th ult you had the goodness to write me under cover to our inestimable friend Judg White[1] has Just reached me, I feel flattered by the candeur & friendship, with which your letter is marked—the advice given is that of friendship fraught with much wisdom, and is such that I altogether approve.

It appears we live in evil times, when those exalted to high dignified & honorable stations have abandoned the course dictated by truth & honor, and move on to self agrandisement regardless of the use of means by which it may be acquired. What wickedness would not men commit who, for political effect would falsly assail female charecter that they might rule. I have always thought Clay corrupt, that he would do any thing to promote his own views—but I was not prepared to believe, untill I recd the proof, that the Secrataries of War & Navy, were base anough to enter into his views, become his panders, secretely to slander me, but it appears I put too high a value on their honor & attachment for truth—Under all circumstances that surround me, I confess it requires much philosophy to bear things with calmness & equanimity of temper—My political enemies have not Judged of me rightly—they cannot provoke me to an act of rashness—should the uncircumcised philistines send forth their Golia[t]h to destroy the liberty of the people & compel them to worship Mamon, they may find a David who trusts in the god of Abraham Isaac and of Jacob, for when I fight, it is the battles of my country. I am calm & composed, trusting in the Lord of hosts, I believe him Just; and therefore look forward to a time when retributive Justice will take place, & when Just attonement can be *required and enforced.*

Against spies I have been guarded, and it may be ultimately found they have been caught in the nett spread for me in an ungarded hour as it might have been thought in my own domicil. you have no doubt seen a letter published in the public Journals said to have been written by a gentleman who had vissitted me, with many others, relative to a narative I had given in answer to a question asked about the truth of the intrigues practised on the last Presidential election—sometime since I recd. a letter from a Mr Carter Beverly stating that he was the writer of that letter, that when written he had no idea that it would get into the newspapers, but as it had, requesting me to advise him if there was any error in his statement— Viewing t[he] whole ground, & not having seen th[e] statement as published, I forthwith ans[wered] his letter giving him the statement I had made, and such as I am fully able to substantiate, closing my letter thus "Whenever Mr. C. will over his own signature deny that he had any knowledge of the propositions made by his friends to mine, I will give him the channel thro which the communication was made." When my answer was written, I did expect it would be shewn to Mr Clay, I am Just informed that this is the fact, & Mr Beverly has given him a copy of my letter to him This is as it ought to be[2]—Mr. C. it is said, is very wroth & threatens as loud as the champion of the Philistines did of old—Mr Clay is now in a dilema—If he does not make the call for the channel thro which it was communicated it will prostrate him—if he makes the call, I will throw him on his beam ends, I think, from which he will find great dificulty to right his vessle—he is in a dilema not foreseen by those who asked me the question if they were his friends & Spies upon me.

I have always made it a rule when I speak, to speak the truth—when the question was asked me, silence would have been reported as a denial of those things that had appeared in the papers in *[regard to Mr. Clay th]*erefore the question *[being asked in my ow]*n house, A reply *[was given to it, bu]*t could not expect *[it to]* appear in the newspapers, but I conclude all things will eventuate in good—What course Mr Clay may adopt know not & feel quite unconcerned about—from the irratation of Mr. C. upon seeing my letter as reported I would suppose the *Galld. Jade Winches*[3]

permit me to say, I admit of no political fathers of confession, I make no answers to any inquiries of that kind, if the good people of the U. States have not, from my votes & letter to Doctor Coleman[4] & others which have been published, confidence in my attachment to my country, & if elected that I would not pursue that course best calculated to promote its Independence & prosperity, surely nothing I could say would be believed *now by my enemies,* my friends have no questions to ask me, & my enemies I never gratify—If I go into the Presidential office it will be without commitment in any way, free to call to my aid such a cabinet, composed of the most virtue, talents & integrity, that I can select—I will not be in the Presidential chair by any other means but by the *unbiassed will of the Sovereign people.*

Mrs. J. requests to be presented to Mrs. Hayne affectionately, informs her she has recd. the inestimable present sent her under care of our good friend Judge White[5]—will write her shortly—present my kind salutations to Mrs. Hayne & your Sweet children, to Col Arthur P. Hayne & his lady, and believe me *[. . .]*

AL (signature removed), NcD (11-0737).
1. See above.
2. For a report of how Clay gained access to the June 5 letter, see above, Beverley to AJ, June 27.
3. "Galld Jade Winches" comes from Shakespeare's *Hamlet,* Act III, Scene 2.
4. AJ was referring to his views on the tariff as outlined in his letter to Littleton H. Coleman, April 26, 1824 (*Jackson,* 5:398–400).
5. On March 1, Rebecca Hayne had sent Rachel Jackson a present of card racks and a watch case.

To Ezra Stiles Ely

Hermitage, July 12, 1827

Having been educated & brought up under the discipline of the Presbyterian rule (my mother being a member of that Church) I have always had a preference for it. Amongst the greatest blessings secured to us under our Constitution, is the liberty of worshipping God as our conscience dictates. All true Christians love each other, and while here below ought to harmonize; for all must unite in the realms above. I have thought one evidence of true religion is, when all those who believe in the atonement of our crucified Saviour are found in harmony and friendship together.

My enemies have charged me with every crime but hypocrisy: I believe they have never alleged this against me: and I can assure you no change of circumstances, no exalted office can work a change upon me. I will remain uniformly the same, whether in the chair of state, or at the Hermitage. My habits are too well fixed now to be altered.

Printed extract, *Nashville Republican*, April 1, 1828 (mAJs); Heiskell (2nd Edition), 2:406 (11-0746). Ely (1786–1861, Yale 1803) was a Presbyterian minister in Philadelphia.

The disclosures in Jackson's June 5 letter to Carter Beverley gave Henry Clay the excuse he wanted to discuss openly the "corrupt bargain" that had dogged him since 1825, and on June 29, he responded. In the letter below to James Buchanan, alleged to be the intermediary who made the overtures from Clay to Jackson and his supporters, Jackson sought evidence to confirm the accusation he had made to Beverley, documentation he would use in his response to Clay's denial of the whole matter.

To James Buchanan

Hermitage July 15th. 1827—

Dr Sir

You will see from the enclosed publication of Mr Clay[1] repelling the statement made by me respecting the propositions said to have been made by his friends to mine & to me & inten[d]ed to operate upon the last election for President, that it becomes necessary for the public to be in possession of the facts. In doing this you are aware of the position which you occupy, and which I trust you will Sustain when properly called on. Ever since the publication and the enquiry before the House of Representatives in January & February 1825[2] questions have been propounded from various sources calculated to draw from me the information I had upon that unpleasant subject—Many no doubt with sinister views placing me in selfish connections with the facts, from my accustomed silence have sought to fortify the charecter of Mr Clay: But in a number of cases where enquiry seemed to be prompted by a frank & generous desire to obtain the truth I felt myself bound to answer in a corresponding spirit; and accordingly the statement made by you to me has been on several occasions repeated, as it was to Mr Beverly who vissitted me at my house where he found a number of his friends & relatives Having tarried all night, in the morning conversing on politics, the question so often put to me before was asked by Mr Beverly—It was answered—Mr. B. went to

Nashville & wrote to his friend in No. Carolina who it appears published his letter[3] On the 15th. of May last he wrote me from Louisville[4] requesting to be informed whether the statement made by him was correct & observing that his letter was not intended for publication—not having seen the letter as published there was no safe alternative for me but that adopted of making the statement as you will see in the inclosed paper.[5]

I shall now in reply to Mr Clays appeal give my authority accompanied by the statement you made to Major John H. Eaton & to Mr Kreamer & leave Mr Clay to his *further enquiries*[6] He cannot be indulged by me in a paper war or newspaper discussion—Had his friends not voted out Mr McDuffies resolutions, when Mr Clay threw himself upon the House the truth or falshood of these statements would have been made manifest & the public mind now at rest upon this subject. That they did will appear, referrence being had to the National Journal of the 5th. of February 1825—You will recollect that Mr McDuffie moved to instruct the committee to enquire whether the friends of Mr Clay have hinted that they would fight for those who pay best, & whether overtures were said to have been made by the friends of Mr Clay offering him the appointment of Secratary of State for his aid to elect Mr Adams, & whether his friends gave this information to the friends of Genl Jackson & hinted that if the friends of Jackson would close *with them* &c. &c. giving the committee the power to examine on oath[7]

I have no doubt when properly called on you will come forth & affirm the state[ment] made to Major Eaton, then to Mr Kreamer & then to me, & give the names of the friends of Mr Clay who made it to you

I will thank you to acknowledge the receipt of this letter on its reaching you I have the honor to be with great respect yr Mo obdt. Servt.

Andrew Jackson

ALS, PHi (11-0748); ALS draft fragment, DLC (35). Published in Bassett, 3:373–74.

1. Henry Clay's June 29 "Address to the Public," published in the Lexington *Kentucky Reporter,* July 4.

2. AJ was referring to the disclosures of George Kremer and the subsequent investigation of them by the House.

3. Beverley to Richard S. Hackley, March 8, published in the *Fayetteville Observer,* April 5.

4. Letter not found

5. This enclosure was probably AJ to Beverley, June 5, above.

6. See AJ to the Public, July 18, below.

7. George McDuffie offered the amendment described by AJ on February 4, 1825, during the debate on whether the House should investigate George Kremer's charges. McDuffie considered the amendment necessary to limit the investigation and prevent it from becoming a de facto proceeding against Kremer for libel, which he regarded as beyond the authority of the federal legislature (*House Journal,* 18th Cong., 2nd sess., Serial 112, p. 204).

To William Berkeley Lewis

July 16th. 10. P. M.

Dr Major

I have recd. your two notes of this day[1]—If it is necessary Mr [Allen A.] Hall shall have a copy of the declarations of Mr Southard,[2] but I have not time to send a copy now, but I think the Telegraph will Attend to the Intelligencer—and it is not necessary to fill their mouths with two hot potatoes at once—however, should you want it, write me by George & a copy shall be sent you.

On the other subject, I am happy you accord with me—I cannot see any ground for the committee to notice Mr Clays appeal, it would place them, as well as me, in an awkward predicament—I will make the reply myself,[3] there leave it, & hereafter if any thing should arise worthy of the notice of the committee, and which it can with propriety take under consideration, it can do so—It is late, & I wish you good night

Andrew Jackson

P.S. Should you see Judge Overton make known to him this my determination & it corresponds with Major Eatons views. J—

ALS, NNPM (11-0751).
1. Not found.
2. Hall (c1803–67) was publisher of the Jacksonian *Nashville Republican and State Gazette*. He had probably requested a copy of Samuel L. Southard's letter above of February 9.
3. For AJ's reply of July 18 to Clay's public letter of June 29 on the corrupt bargain, see below.

To the Public

Hermitage, July 18th, 1827.

A letter addressed by me to Mr. Carter Beverley, of Virginia, has lately, without any consent, agency, or wish on my part, found its way into the newspapers, accompanied by a statement over the signature of H. Clay, contradicting and denying, not any thing I have written, but that which he himself makes me to say.[1] It is not the interpretation given by him to my letter, but my own language and own statement, that I am called upon to defend, and expect to vindicate.

To explain the manner in which my opinions have found their way into the journals of the day, seems, in the first place, to be due both to the public and myself. Mr. Beverley, being on a visit at my house, requested to know of me, other gentlemen being present, whether the overtures heretofore imputed to Mr. Clay were well founded, and if I had a knowledge of any of the facts myself. I answered him candidly; being unable, as well as unwilling, to refuse telling things I had heard and knew to be true. A letter detailing our conversation, shortly afterwards obtained publicity in the "North Carolina Journal," printed at Fayetteville. On the 15th of May last, from Louisville, Kentucky, a communication was addressed to me by Mr. Beverley, stating, what before I had not known, that he was the writer of this Fayetteville letter. He explained the reasons for his having repeated the conversation, and requested to be informed, if in any thing he had mis-quoted or misconceived my meaning. Under such circumstances, concealment and silence might have seemed mere affectation, or indeed something of a different and even worse character. Publicity having been given to the conversation, and an appeal made to me for its accuracy, I felt it to be due to Mr. Beverley, that nothing of fabrication should be imputed to him, and to myself, that what I had stated should be correctly understood. Accordingly, on the 6th of June and in reply to his of the 15th of May,[2] I addressed him a letter of which the public are already possessed. How, and by what means, it found its way into the columns of a newspaper, Mr. Beverley has explained:[3] he states to me, that he gave it into the hands of Mr. Noah Zane, of Wheeling, Virginia, at his own earnest request, for perusal, under a pledge of honor, that it should be returned; and with no expectation that any copy of it was to be retained. That on his applying for, and demanding the letter, it was refused to be restored, until two copies should be made. He proceeds to say:

"Mr. Zane, an old and most respectable gentleman, asked the loan of your letter as a favor; and, contrary to all custom and propriety in such cases, he, in conjunction with Mr. Clay and his friends, took copies of it, without my knowledge or privity in any way, and without asking my leave to do so. Soon as I understood that such was the use they were making of it, I demanded of Mr. Zane the letter, and remonstrated against the unprecedented course they were taking. He refused to restore it to me, most peremptorily, until they had satisfied themselves by furnishing to Mr. Clay one copy, and reserving another for their own use."

The original conversation referred to, and the above extract of a letter from Mr. Beverley at Wheeling, dated 25th of June, 1827,[4] are presented to show that I have not, as is charged "placed myself in the attitude of a public accuser," and that whatever publicity has been given to this transaction, has arisen from no agency or procurement of mine; and that Mr. Clay, in fact, has, himself, held the matter up to public gaze. In doing this, he should have quoted what I had written accurately and fairly; for then, the text and his commentary would have suited together; at present his contradiction is of something suggested by himself, and is not contained in my letter.

The statement contained in my letter to Mr. Beverley, is this: That in

January, 1825, a member of Congress, of high respectability, visited me one morning and observed—"he had been informed by the friends of Mr. Clay, that the friends of Mr. Adams had made overtures to them, saying, if Mr. Clay and his friends would unite in aid of the election of Mr. Adams, Mr. Clay should be Secretary of State; that the friends of Mr. Adams were urging, as a reason to induce the friends of Mr. Clay to accede to this proposition, that if I was elected President, Mr. Adams would be continued Secretary of State (inuendo, there would be no room for Kentucky)—that the friends of Mr. Clay stated, the West did not wish to separate from the West, and if I would say, or permit any of my confidential friends to say, that in case I was elected President, Mr. Adams should not be continued Secretary of State, by a complete union of Mr. Clay and his friends, they would put an end to the Presidential contest in one hour; and he was of opinion it was right to fight such intriguers with their own weapons."

This disclosure was made to me by Mr. JAMES BUCHANAN, a member of Congress, from Pennsylvania, a gentlemen of the first respectability and intelligence. The evening before, he had communicated, substantially, the same proposition to Major Eaton, my colleague in the Senate, with a desire warmly manifested that he should communicate with me, and ascertain my views on the subject. This he declined doing, suggesting to Mr. Buchanan, that he, as well as himself, could converse with me, and ascertain my opinion on the matter; though, from his knowledge of me, he thought he could well conjecture my answer—that I would enter into no engagements whatever. It was the morning succeeding this interview, after Major Eaton had objected to converse with me on the subject, and before I had set out from my lodgings for the Capitol, that Mr. Buchanan came to visit me, and when the conversation I have stated took place. The answer returned, has already been published, and need not here be repeated.

To be thus approached by a gentleman of Mr. Buchanan's high character and standing, with an apology proffered at the time for what he was about to remark to me—one who, as I understood, had always, to that moment, been on familiar and friendly terms with Mr. Clay, assuring me, that on certain terms and conditions being assented to on my part, then, "by an union of Mr. Clay and his friends, they would put an end to the Presidential contest in one hour," what other conclusion or inference was to be made, than he spoke by authority, either of Mr. Clay himself, or some of his confidential friends? The character of Mr. Buchanan, with me, forbids the idea that he was acting on his own responsibility, or that, under any circumstances, he could have been induced to propose an arrangement, unless possessed of satisfactory assurances, that, if accepted, it would be carried fully into effect. A weak mind would seldom or ever be thus disposed to act; an intelligent one, never.

Under all the circumstances, appearing at that time, I did not resist the impression that Mr. Buchanan had approached me on the cautiously submitted proposition of some authorized person; and, therefore, in giving him my answer, did request him "to say to Mr. Clay and his friends," what that answer had been. Whether the communication was made to Mr. Clay and his friends, I know not; this though, I do know, that while the opinions and course of Mr. Clay as to the election, were but matter of conjecture with many, at and before this time, very shortly after this conversation took place, his, and his friends' opinions became, forthwith, matter of certainty and general knowledge. Still I have not said, nor do I now say, that the proposal made to me was *"with the privity and consent"* of Mr. Clay, nor neither have I said that his *friends in Congress made any propositions to me.* These are Mr. Clay's interpretations of my letter to Mr. Beverley, and not what my letter itself contains. What I have stated are the facts of a conversation between myself and a member of Congress of high respectability. The conclusion and inference from that conversation—the time, manner, and all the circumstances, satisfied my mind that it was not *unauthorized.* So I have thought, and so I still think; and yet I again repeat, that, in this supposition I may have possibly done Mr. Clay injustice. If he shall be able to sustain the averments he has made, and acquit himself of any participation and agency in the matter, I beg leave to assure him, that, so far from affording me pain, it will give me pleasure. I certainly can have no desire that the character of my country, through the acts of a prominent citizen, shall rest under any serious imputation; for the honor of that country, I should greatly prefer that any inference I have made may turn out to be ill founded.

Mr. Clay declares his great satisfaction that this matter has at last been brought to light, and to public consideration. He feels rejoiced "that a specific accusation by a responsible accuser, has at length appeared." To this, a passing notice is due.

It must be recollected, that in consequence of a letter from Mr. George Kremer, in January, 1825, an enquiry was set on foot in Congress upon the application of Mr. Clay himself.

On this memorable occasion, of guilt imputed on the one hand, and innocence maintained on the other, Mr. McDuffie, it will be recollected, submitted for consideration to the House of Representatives, as matter of instruction to the committee, the following resolution: "That the said committee be instructed to inquire whether the friends of Mr. Clay have hinted that they would fight for those who would pay best, or anything to that effect; and whether overtures were said to have been made by the friends of Adams to the friends of Mr. Clay, offering him the appointment of Secretary of State for his aid to elect Mr. Adams; and whether the friends of Clay gave this information to the friends of Jackson, and hinted that if his friends would offer the same price they would close with them; and whether Henry Clay has transferred, or resolved to transfer his

interest to John Q. Adams; and whether it was said and believed, that, as
a consideration this abandonment of duty to his constituents, Clay was
to be appointed Secretary of State; and that the said committee be authorized to send for persons and papers, and to compel the persons so sent
for, to answer upon oath."

Now here is a resolution, officially submitted, covering more than the
ground of my communication to Mr. Beverley: and resting in connection
with an accusation publicly charged in the newspapers: and yet Mr. Clay,
at this late period, professes to be rejoiced, that "a specific accusation by a
respectable accuser has at length appeared." Certainly more than two years
ago, an accuser respectable, and an accusation specific, were both before
him—were both within his reach, and might have been met, had he been at
all disposed to the interview, or rejoiced at the prospect of meeting an accuser. Had Mr. McDuffie believed the charges groundless and untrue, he is
a man of too high sense of honor to have pressed upon the consideration of
the committee, an instruction clothed in the pointed phraseology that this
is, nor can it be inferred that, in a matter so serious, the friends of Mr. Clay
would have voted against extending this asked for power to the committee.[5] An innocent man, before an impartial tribunal, fears not to meet the
exercise of any power that competent authority gives: and far less should
he distrust that exercise, when in the hands of correct and honorable men.

Innocence never seeks for safety through covert ways and hidden am-
buscades; she fights by day and in the open plain, and proud in her own
strength meets her enemy fearlessly. In the proposition submitted by Mr.
McDuffie, there was nothing to alarm, nothing that innocence should
have doubted about; it was neither more nor less, than a call of the attention of the committee to particular inquiries, with an application for
power to ferret out the truth, through an appeal to the oath of those who
might be called upon to depose before them.

Without documents, and unacquainted with the number of Mr. Clay's
friends in the House, I cannot assert that *they* were in opposition to Mr.
M'Duffie's resolution. Yet it is obvious that the influence he possessed, would
have been amply sufficient to produce a different result, had Mr. C. been at
all desirous that a different one should have been produced. The resolution
contained strong imputations, and serious charges—Mr. Clay and his friends
were both implicated. Can it be presumed, under such a state of general excitement, that if Mr. Clay desired it, he could not have found present and at
hand, some friend to ask in his behalf, that the resolution should be adopted
and full powers extended to the committee! And, moreover, can it be thought,
that such an indulgence, if desired by Mr. Clay, or any of his friends, could
or would have been denied? And yet, it was denied, inasmuch as the resolution was rejected, and the power asked for, refused to the committee. A solicitude to find "a specific accusation, by a responsible accuser," could not
have been so seriously entertained then, as it is earnestly expressed now, or
else so excellent an opportunity being afforded to encounter both, both could

not have been so carelessly regarded—so contemned, and so thrown away. A controversy with me can no more disclose or render apparent Mr. Clay's innocence, than could the controversy placed within his reach two and a half years ago; and yet, while the one was avoided, or at any rate not embraced with a zeal corresponding with the necessity of the occasion, at the prospects presented by the other, exceeding joy seems to be manifested. Then, as now, *a specific accusation,* was before him.

One further remark and I am done, with a hope that, on this subject, I may not be under any necessity of again appearing in the newspapers. In saying what I have, all the circumstances considered, I have felt that it was due to myself and to the public. My wish would have been to avoid having any thing to say or do in this matter from an apprehension well conceived, that persons will not be wanting, who may charge whatever is done, to a desire to affect others, and benefit myself. My own feelings though, are of higher importance and value to me, than the opinion of those who impose censure where it is believed not to be deserved. I have been actuated by no such design, nor governed by any such consideration. The origin—the beginning of this matter, was at my own house and fire-side; where, surely, a freeman may be permitted to speak on public topics, without having ascribed to him improper designs. I have not gone into the highways and market places to proclaim my opinions; and in this, feel that I have differed from some, who, even at public dinner tables, have not scrupled to consider me as a legitimate subject for a speech, and the entertainment of the company.[6] And yet, of this, who has heard me complain? No one. Trusting to the justice of an intelligent people, I have been content to rely for security on their decision, against the countless assaults and slanders, which are sought so repeatedly to be palmed upon them, without seeking to present myself in my own defence; and still less, to become "the responsible accuser" of Mr. Clay or any other person.

ANDREW JACKSON

Printed, *United States' Telegraph,* August 7 (first published in the *Nashville Republican,* July 21, not extant); ALS draft with printers's and other revisions in unknown hand, NjP (11-0754); Extract, MB (mAJs).

1. See above, AJ to Beverley, June 5. The Lexington *Kentucky Reporter,* July 4, had published AJ's letter to Beverley from a copy furnished by Clay, along with Clay's "Address to the Public," June 29.

2. AJ's letter to Beverley was dated June 5, not 6. Beverley's of May 15 has not been found.

3. Beverley's account of the events in Wheeling involving AJ's letter, along with the letter, had appeared in the *United States' Telegraph,* July 2.

4. Not found.

5. McDuffie's resolution to instruct the select committee of the House of Representatives to investigate the specific charges George Kremer had made failed to pass the House (*Register of Debates,* 18th Cong., 2nd Sess., pp. 463–86). As speaker, according to AJ, Clay could have insisted that the select committee be so empowered, but he did not.

6. AJ was alluding to Samuel L. Southard and his comments at a dinner in Fredericksburg.

Rachel Jackson to Elizabeth Courts Love Watson

Hermitage July the 18 the 182[7]

My Dear friend

it is a Long time since you wrote me a Line But haveing so favourable an oppertunity by Major [Benjamin Fort] Smith[1] I Cold not Deny my self that pleasure: for rest asured my Dear friend you ar as Dear to me as a Sister—I am denyd maney pleasurs & Comforts in this Life and that is one and Sister Hays and her famaly your Famaly with Hers would have been my joy in this world but alas you ar all far from me, well the Apostle Say's I Ca[n do all] things in Christ who strentheneth me[2] I Can say my soule Can be a testimony to the truth of that Gospel for who has been so cruelly tryed as I have my mind my trials hav been severe—the Enemyes of the Genls hav Dipt their arrows in wormwood & gall & sped them at me Almighty God was ther Ever aney thing to Equal it my old acquentan[c]es wer as much hurt as if it was themselves or Daughters—to think that thirty years had past in happy social friendship with society, knowing or thinking no ill to no one—as my judg will know—how maney prayers have I oferd up for thir repentencenc—but wo unto them if offencces Come theay have Disquietd one that theay had no rite to do theay have offended God and man—in as much as you offend one of the Least of my little ones you offend me[3]—now I leave them to them selves I feare them not I feare Him that can Kill the Body & Cast the Soule into Hell fire—o Eturnity aw[ful] is the [error?]—this has been a subject my Dear friend that I fear has paincd your Sympathizeing friendly Disposition toward your friends—let not your Heart be troubled—I am on the rock of agees—in the world I have tribulation—jesus says in me you shall have peace, my peace I gave unto you not as the world gives &c &c[4] your Brother & famaly ar all well ar liveing in stile a fine firtile plantation fine large brick ho[u]se with Every Com[fort.][5] Nashville has gon beyond description in point of improvement in good fashion Dress is fineer then aney wher I Ever was the theatre & parties has brorne down the Church—the pastor of the presbeterian Church has been dismised is now in pittsburgh[6] religion has got a wound but, I thank God He has promised that the Deep watters shall not overflow us nor the flames shall not hurt he will be with us in all our afflictions[7]—how is my Dear Mrs [Jane Love] forest & famaly Dr [Thomas] & Mrs [Harriet Love] Sim Colonel Graham & famaly[8] Colo Towsen Mrs Towsen Dr Marrible tould me what true friend she was to me in this time of persicution—I pray god to bless her Days on Earth that theay may be happy—Can I Er forgit you all no—Mrs Call has paide us a visit & returned She had her Daughter with her she had twins but lost them will be confined in September again[9]—her mother never saw her we stayed A week in Nashville She had nearly as much attention paide to her as was to Gel Lafaett a committee of jet men of the first respectability waited on Her with an address She answerd them appropriately the Ball was splendid attend by at Least #100 Ladese the party spirit her Mother aidied in giting an opposition party but failed, the Mother againt the Daughter, the Matrons wept for it when theay saw so fine a woman abandoned by her mother; she is happy with Husband & Daugter—I have seen Sister Hayes once Since I saw you—how is my Dear M[ay] Elen[10] tell her W D is married she would not Come out to Tennissee[11]—I wish she would Come & see me poor Dear John[12] how is he grown I suppos[e] I had a hope when I last saw you of haveing the happyness of having you beside me a neighbour but in that I am disappointed—well I remember you allways & Should I not see you here I hope to see you with Jesus in the new jerusalem, we shall hav no more sorrow no malevolent Enemes ther to harm us—farwell my much Loved friend & sister To Mary Harriett Eliza Olivia Mr Andrew J Watson all the Connection[13]

Rachel Jackson

Mrs. Lee & Husband is boarding at the springs 1 mile from here theay stayed a few Days at the Hermitage[14] She will not see aney Companey appears somewhat deraingd—She is invisable to all but myslf is very fond of me I go & see her occasionally oh that I that I cold pour the wine & the oile to her wounded Spirit—adieu adieu Dear friend forever R J

Mr J is not well at present but surround with Crowd from one weeks End to an other as one Carriage full goes another Comes well I am fond of Society maney friends but will theay Bear the test—in times of trial a Volum I hav to write you my Son is one of the sweetest youths in the wourld

Andrew J Donelson's his Love to you all

ALS, CtY (12-0055). Published in Bassett, 3:415–16 (extract dated 1828).

1. Smith (1796–1841), a veteran of the War of 1812 and at this time Chickasaw Indian agent, was leaving on a trip eastward that included Washington.

2. From Philippians 4:13. Jane D. Hays lived in Madison County, Tennessee.

3. Rachel Jackson was alluding to the discussion of her marriage to AJ in the newspapers; her scriptural reference was probably to Matthew 18:6.

4. From John 14:27.

5. Charles Jones Love (c1777–1837) and his family lived at "Mansfield," near the Hermitage.

6. Allan D. Campbell, the pastor of the First Presbyterian Church, had been dismissed for organizing a nondenominational Sunday school in Nashville, the city's first Sunday school.

7. A paraphrase of Isaiah 43:2.

8. Jane, Elizabeth Watson's sister, was the widow of James Forrest. Sim (1770–1832), married to Harriet Love (d. 1831), another sister, was a member of the Jacksonian Central

Committee in Washington and AJ's physician during his first term as president. Graham was married to Jane Love Watson (c1810–69), one of Elizabeth Watson's daughters.

9. Mary K. and her daughter Mary E. Call had visited Nashville in April. In the fall, Mrs. Call gave birth to Mary Jane Call (1827–34).

10. One of Elizabeth Watson's daughters.

11. William Donelson (1795–1864), the Jacksons' nephew, married Elizabeth Anderson (1809–41), the daughter of Stockley Donelson's widow Elizabeth G.M.D. Anderson, on June 14.

12. John L. (c1812–35), one of Elizabeth Watson's sons.

13. All were Watson's daughters and son.

14. Ann Robinson McCarty Lee (1797–1840) and Henry resided at the Fountain of Health while Henry was working on his biography of AJ.

On July 22, as the 1827 congressional campaign neared its end in Kentucky, William Owens, a former state senator from Adair County and candidate for Congress on the Jacksonian ticket, asked Jackson for information regarding the execution of the six militiamen in February 1815. Owens's opponent in the campaign, Richard A. Buckner, had made Jackson's military record a key issue in the campaign. He had charged Jackson with inhumanity and despotism as evidenced in Jackson's disregard to the plea for clemency and pardon in John Harris's alleged letter of January 15, 1815. In addition, Jackson had allowed those soldiers in Philip Pipkin's regiment convicted of mutiny and desertion to be executed after the Battle of New Orleans and the arrival of the news of peace.

*While vacationing at Robertson's Springs north of Nashville, Jackson responded in the letter below to Owens's request for information. Owens immediately published Jackson's account, but it failed to swing the election in his favor. Buckner won and shortly addressed his constituents condemning Jackson's intrusion in the Kentucky congressional campaign as "unworthy and contemptible," unfit for a presidential candidate (*Frankfort Commentator, *September 8).*

To William Owens

Robertson Springs. July 26, 1827.

Dear Sir:

Your letter of the 22d, instant was handed to me, late last evening, and I hasten to answer the enquiries, as requested, in regard to the case of Harris and the other five militia men who were executed at Mobile.[1]

The regiment to which these unfortunate men belonged, was received into the service by the orders of the general government, was mustered for a six months tour, and was paid accordingly, for said service, as will appear by the muster and pay rolls, and by Colonel Pipkin's report to me.[2] These rolls with Col. Pipkin's report; the proceedings and sentence of the court martial detailed for the trial, and all the circumstances connected with the subject, are, or ought to be, on record at Washington

City, where I have no doubt Mr. Buckner has had a full opportunity of examining them. I confidently assert that they stamp the allegations of Mr. Buckner with falsehood.

The letter which Mr. Buckner now makes use of, in order to injure my character, is well ascertained to be a forgery. It was first published by Binns, editor of the Democratic Press, purporting to be a letter from the unfortunate Harris to me.[3] Now this man never wrote but one letter to me, that I ever saw, or heard of before this publication, and in that he acknowledged himself to be guilty of the enormous crimes charged against him, and stated his willingness to meet the just sentence of the court.[4] If Mr. Buckner was as desirous to cull the truth from the archives of the nation, as he is to pluck from me my hard earned reputation, he would have seen that Gen. Winchester, who commanded at Mobile at the time that this *Binn's* letter is dated, made several communications to me after that date, and before he had any knowledge that the battle of New Orleans had been fought. Does not this circumstance show the imposibility of Mr. Harris having this knowledge at the time stated, and still more that he could have gained it in time to have made it a ground of application for mercy. The letters of Gen. Winchester to me show that he did not receive intelligence of the victory until the 17th January;[5] this forged letter gives the intelligence to Mr. Harris two days before. Strange indeed, that Mr. Harris closely confined in jail should be so much earlier informed than the commandant of that post.

It would give me great pleasure to send you printed copies from the documents in my possession, properly certified, proving what I have here asserted, but it is impossible that this can be done within so short a period as that requested.[6] I trust, however, that the statement here made will be sufficient, with all honourable men, to counteract the false impressions sought to be forced upon the freemen of Kentucky by Mr. Buckner. As a public or private man, speaking of transactions which concern the reputation and character of others, every manly feeling should remind him, that he ought to be guided by established facts, not by the *hearsay* of a party; and when he thus produces facts, or the least plausible ground upon which to bottom such charges, as those which you have recited, I pledge myself to be at all times ready to meet him at the bar of my country.

It may be proper to remark in conclusion, that the finding of the court, proves conclusively that those men were legally in service—or, otherwise, that they must have been acquitted. I approved of their condemnation, because they were the promoters and ringleaders of the mutiny and desertion, committed at a period, when the safety of our Southern frontier was threatened—at a period, which called for the most energetic measures, and when every nerve of the government was stretched in the defence of our liberties. When they violated the law in such atrocious manner; the public good demanded their sacrifice. Had they have done their duty as faithful soldiers their country would have rewarded them with its protection and gratitude. I am Sir, your most obedient servant

ANDREW JACKSON.

P.S. It will be recollected in the Revolutionary war, at a time of great trial, General Washington ordered deserters to be shot without trial. Capt. [Philip] Reed under this order, having arrested three, had one shot without trial, and his head brought to the General; but he, General Washington, reprimanded Reed for not shooting the whole three.[7] Gen. [Nathanael] Green, near Ridgly's mill, South Carolina, says Gordon's history, had eight men hung, on one pole for desertion. Johnson's life of Green says five, without court martial.[8] I only approved of the proceedings of a court composed of men who were the friends and neighbours of those to be tried by them. Respectfully,

ANDREW JACKSON.

Printed, Lexington *Kentucky Gazette*, August 3 (mAJs); Draft (dated July 25), DLC (34). Published in Bassett, 3:375–76 (from *Niles' Register*, September 8).
    1. See Owens to AJ, July 22. For a discussion of the issue, see *Jackson*, 3:133–36, and above, AJ to James Allen, March 31.
    2. Pipkin's report has not been found but on April 16, 1827, he published his recollections of the events (*Louisville Public Advertiser*, May 5).
    3. John Harris to AJ, January 15, 1815 (spurious). In the letter Harris asked AJ to "take pity on your poor, forlorn, friendless fellow creatures." Should clemency be impossible, Harris wrote, "permit your poor suffering broken hearted fellow creature to go home and see the blue hills and the green fields of Tennessee, and his poor miserable wife and child, before he is shot." With prescience, Harris continued, "should it turn out, that the peace was signed a'ready, how it would grieve your noble heart, to think you had signed a death-warrant in time of peace."
    4. Letter not found.
    5. See James Winchester to AJ, January 22 and February 3, 1815.
    6. Owens had requested AJ to have 1,000 copies of his reply printed.
    7. Reed (1760–1829) later served as colonel in the War of 1812 and as U.S. senator and representative from Maryland. Washington's orders had been introduced into the debate on the Seminole War in 1819, and Reed had then entered the debate in AJ's behalf by discussing the orders and his action. In 1827 as the issue reemerged, he again wrote on the matter (*Annals of Congress*, 15th Cong., 2nd sess., pp. 1061–64; Frankfort *Argus of Western America*, August 8).
    8. Greene (1742–86) led the American forces in the southern states during the last years of the Revolution. AJ was referring to William Gordon, *History of the Rise, Progress, and Establishment of the Independence of the United States . . .* (3 vols. New York, 1789), 3:193–94, and William Johnson, *Sketches of the Life and Correspondence of Nathanael Greene, Major General of the Armies of the United States . . .* (2 vols. Charleston, 1822), 2:97–98.

To John Coffee

Hagan Springs July 30th 1827

Dr. Genl

I have recd yours of the 15th. instant,[1] & I was so continually crouded with company until I left home for this place, that I had not time to reply to it—here we will remain untill we refresh ourselves with some rest.

I regret to hear you have experienced a drought to the injury of your crop; when I left home we were dry, and altho there has been generally fine seasons last week, still in our neighbourhood, I learn, we had none; of course, are sufferring; My Cotton crop & corn promised well when I left home, I fear the want of rain will injure both—the corn most, as it is Just filling.

you will have seen my reply to Mr Clays appeal to the people; and his speech, to the citizens of Ky., at a dining near Lexington—In this speech, he has shewn much warmth & lack of common sense—he has under all his boasting, plainly discovered how much he feels under these disclosures[2]—*The galled Jade winches*—I have given to the nation my author—There I leave it—There is nothing in his speech that makes it necessary I should reply to it—untill it does become *absolutely necessary,* I shall not appear before the people again—I have said to them, "that I hope it may not again become necessary to appear before them." There is nothing in Clays speech that makes it necessary, and he has been so unguarded, he has left himself open on all points, to attack—The Journals will goad him to death—he will have to defend, I am not his accuser, I only tell what was communicated to me, give my informant who is respectable; and leave Mr Clay, & him, to settle this matter you will observe he carefully avoids saying any thing about Mr. McDuffies resolutions voted out by his friends & denies having any knowledge of Govr Branch's charge of corruption, bargain & intrigue, in the Senate when his appointment was called up for approval[3]—These two things, will be sounded in his ears untill these falshoods uttered in late his speech will crush him—Rowan who was present, heard the speech, voted for clay, who, Clay now says, he could not trust, as well as others, will feed the Journals for months—What must the world think of Mr Clays veracity when it is told, that Branch made one of the strongest charges in the Senate, that has been heard any where; Mr. C says, he had instructed a friend in case charges were made in the Senate to call for investigation instead of his friend calling for investigation, Govr. Branch was answered by a call for the question, and a silent vote was taken on the approval, and no one attempted to reply to Govr. Branch[4]

Mr Clay must have been unfortunate in the selection of his friends, it appears on all occasions they were asleep, never having communicated to him any thing.

It is said our congressional election is waxing very warm—Mr James Jackson has taken the field—he was at the adams dinner 4th. of July[5]—has become, it must be supposed, a compleat convert to Mr Clays american system—*he is a thorough tariff man*; and no more of his *sh[irt] tails* will be used, instead of domestic cotton Bagging—he has offerred, as it is here stated, to bet from one to $5000 dollars that Bell will beat Grundy—and ten thousand, that Adams will be elected—I expect it will be a close election, but I have always thought, & now think, Grundy will be elected.[6]

Mrs. J & my best wishes for you & family & all friends—write me how your coalt gets on. your friend

Andrew Jackson

ALS, DLC (11-0780). Hagan's Springs, also known as Tyree Springs, was a sulphur spa in Sumner County, close to the Robertson County line.

1. Not found.

2. See above, AJ to the Public, July 18; Clay to the Public, June 29, and Toasts and Speech at Lexington Public Dinner, [July 12], (*Clay Papers*, 6:728–30, 763–79). At the public dinner in Lexington, Clay proclaimed AJ's charges in the letter to Carter Beverley "destitute of all foundation."

3. For discussion of the defeat of McDuffie's resolution, see above, AJ to James Buchanan, July 15, and AJ to the Public, July 18. In the debate on Clay's confirmation in the Senate, Branch warned that by confirming Clay the Senate condoned at least the appearance of corruption. Branch published a copy of his speech in response to the Jackson-Clay debate on the subject of confirmation (Raleigh *Star and North Carolina State Gazette*, August 30).

4. Clay claimed to have been ready for an investigation, even asking Senator William Henry Harrison of Ohio to call for an enquiry should any challenge to his nomination appear, because he did not trust John Rowan, the only Kentucky senator present, to carry out the task. Yet, Clay asserted, "I was afterwards informed that, when it was acted upon, Gen. Jackson and every other Senator present was silent as to the imputations now made . . ." (*Clay Papers*, 6:773).

5 About sixty-five people attended the Adams celebration in Nashville on July 4 (*National Banner and Nashville Whig*, July 7).

6. John Bell defeated Felix Grundy for the U.S. Congress. Both professed support for AJ, though AJ made no secret of his preference for Grundy.

From James Buchanan

Lancaster 10 August 1827.

Dear Sir/

I received your letter of the 15th. ultimo on Tuesday last. Your address to the Public[1] also reached me upon the same day in the Cincinatti Advertiser. This communication made it necessary for me to publish in detail the conversation which I held with you, concerning the Presidential election, on the 30 December 1824. I shall enclose to you in this letter that part of the Lancaster Journal containing it.[2]

I regret beyond expression that you believed me to be an emissary from Mr. Clay. Since some time before the first Harrisburg Convention which nominated you, I have ever been your ardent, decided, & perhaps without vanity I may say, your efficient friend. Every person in this part of the state of Pennsylvania is well acquainted with the fact. It is therefore to me a matter of the deepest regret that you should have supposed me to be "the friend of Mr. Clay." Had I ever entertained a suspicion that such was your belief, I should have immediately corrected your impression.

I shall annex to this letter, a copy of that which I wrote to Duff Green, on the 16th. October last.[3] The person whom I consulted in Pennsylvania was the present Judge Rogers of the Supreme Court—then the Secretary of State of this Commonwealth.[4]

The friends of the administration are making great efforts in Pennsylvania. We have been busily engaged during the summer in counteracting them. Success has I think hitherto attended our efforts. I do not fear the vote of the State, although it is believed every member of the State Administration, except General [Isaac Dutton] Bernard[5] is hostile to your election. Your security will be in the gratitude in the hearts of the people.

Please to present my best respects to Mrs. Jackson and believe me to be very respectfully your friend &c

James Buchanan

ALS, DLC (34); ALS draft, PHi (11-0785). Published in *Works of James Buchanan*, 1:269.
1. See above, AJ to Buchanan, July 15, AJ to the Public, July 18.
2. In his public letter in the August 10 issue of the *Lancaster Journal*, Buchanan wrote: "I called upon General Jackson . . . solely as his friend, and not as the agent of Mr. Clay, or any other person. I never have been the political friend of Mr. Clay, since he became a candidate for the office of President . . ."
3. Buchanan to Duff Green, October 16, 1826 (DLC-34). In that letter Buchanan, responding to a previous query from Green, discussed his visit to Jackson in December 1824, averring that "I had no authority from Mr. Clay or his friends to propose any terms to General Jackson in relation to their votes, nor did I make any such proposition."
4. Rogers was the person from whom Buchanan sought advice before he contacted the Jacksonians in December 1824 regarding the appointment of Adams as secretary of state should Jackson be elected president.
5. Bernard (1791–1834), a veteran of the War of 1812, was at this time secretary of state for Pennsylvania. He won election to the U.S. Senate in 1827.

To Duff Green

Hermitage August 13th. 1827—

Dr Sir

I have the pleasure to acknowledge the receipt of your two letters of the 8th. & 18th ult,[1] the latter in answer of mine of the 29th. June last—[2]

The manner you have treated the Beverly business is proper, & one which I approve, Mr Clay must throw himself on some tribunal cloathed with power to investigate this matter & to coerce the attendence of witness & examine upon oath, or sink in the estimation of all the honest & virtuous portion of society[3]—The course of my friends, ought now to be as heretofore on the defensive; should the administration continue their systematic course of slander, it will be well now & then to throw a fire brand into their camp by the statement of a few facts, but female charecter never should be introduced or touched by my friends, unless a continuation of attack should continue to be made against Mrs. J. and then only, by way of *Just retaliation* upon the *known guilty* my great wish is, that it may be altogether *avoided,* if *possible,* by my friends, *I never war against females* & it is only the base & cowardly that do—your course, has hitherto been, approved by my friends, & must continue to be approved, so long as you adopt truth & principle for your guide, never departing from either.

Before this reaches you, you will have seen my reply to Mr Clays appeal to the people[4]—His speeches to dinner parties before my reply was recd,[5] gave evidence of his intention to forestal public opinion, by making up an Issue for himself that my statement did not warrent, & displays his inward dread of the disclosure to the public of the individual who made to me the communication. They are also proof to me that he knew as well as I did the gentleman who had made the communication to me. I had no fear but Mr Buchannan would come out when properly called on, and his letter to you is a clear pledge that he will—he cannot do otherwise, having first made the communication to Eaton, then to Kremer, they refusing to communicate, then coming to me[6]—in short Mr. B. knows that Mr McDuffies resolution was based upon this information & the declarations of Frank Johnston,[7] in the presence of Col [James T.] Sandford, made to Kremer.[8]

¿will Clay make the Call upon Buchannan? If he does will not Mr B. reply, place yourself before a tribunal competant to investigate, & to send for persons & papers, & interrogate upon oath, before which I will detail all I know, & have communicated to Genl Jackson, with the source from whence I derived my knowledge and induced me to make the communication to Genl Jackson. or what will be his course. If Mr Clay places himself before a proper tribunal to investigate; there must be circumstantial, presumptive, & positive proof, sufficient to authorise a Jury to convict on a charge of murder. Trimbles speech to his constituents, Frank Johnstons declarations, Moors, Calls & others information;[9] & lastly, Clays being appointed sec of State must be viewed as the positive proof of the bargain, & this act, as its full & compleat performance.

I have recd several letters disclosing channels thro which testimony can be had, one, if true, that fixes upon clay proof that will convince worlds of his corruption I have Col Sandfords statement.[10]

I never have heard that, Major Eaton was hurt at any conduct of yours.[11]

I have said to Major Lee that he can have copies of any correspondence of mine with the goverment, not confidential; If, as you intimate, Mr Monroe does come out, then these documents may be given to the public—I act on the defensive,[12] The copy of the letter of Mr M to the sec of war on the subject of his view of the orders to me, & to which you alude, which was forwarded by Genl Houston, is not, as to me, confidential—Major Lee having given me the original, & taken the copy he can do with as he pleases.[13]

When you have Leisure I will be glad to hear from you. with my best wishes adieu.

Andrew Jackson

P.S. I have recd. several letters from my friends in Ky. approving of my reply to Mr Clay.

ALS copy, DLC (34). Published in Bassett, 3:376–78.

1. See Green to AJ, July 18, and above, July 8.

2. Letter not found.

3. In an editorial on the Beverley issue in the *United States' Telegraph* on June 8, Green had advocated an investigation by the House of Representatives at the upcoming session of Congress.

4. See above, AJ to the Public, July 18.

5. Jackson was referring to Clay's speech at the public dinner in Lexington on July 12.

6. On July 11 Buchanan had written Green: "I have *a very distinct* recollection of the only conversation I ever held with General Jackson, concerning the last Presidential election, prior to its termination, and when compelled to disclose it, I need not say that I will speak the truth." Green had published that letter in the *United States' Telegraph* of July 16. On August 8, Buchanan issued a fence-straddling statement, whereupon the Jacksonians began to collect affidavits to substantiate the corrupt bargain charge. These documents were subsequently published by the Washington Central Committee (*United States' Telegraph— Extra*, May 10, 1828).

7. Kremer claimed that Francis Johnson told him in early 1825 "that if Jackson should be elected, it is said Adams will remain Secretary of State, and in that case nothing could be done for Kentucky; and we wish to know if we aid in electing Jackson, what the friends of Jackson will do for Kentucky."

8. Sandford (d. 1830), a farmer from Columbia who represented Tennessee in the Eighteenth Congress, allegedly overheard Johnson's remarks (*Washington Gazette*, February 28, 1825).

9. Trimble, a Kentucky representative who voted for Adams in the House, had said in a speech that he could not have voted for AJ because "Gen. Jackson would not, and Mr. Adams would, appoint our friend, Henry Clay, Secretary of State" (see statement by Jacob Frizzle et al., November 2, 1827). An undated statement by William Howard et al. attributed to Francis Johnson the words, *"if Mr. Adams was elected President, Mr. Clay would be Secretary of State*; but that, *if General Jackson was elected President, Mr. Clay would not be Secretary."* Thomas P. Moore reported that Johnson had read him a letter from John J. Crittenden stating "that Gen. Jackson was his (Mr. C.'s) first choice after Mr. Clay; but, that if Mr. Adams would appoint Mr. Clay Secretary of State, or place him in his cabinet . . . then it would be an easy task to reconcile his constituents to a vote in favor of Mr. Adams" (Moore to John P. Van Ness, March 4, 1828). Richard K. Call wrote that in 1825 "a gentleman, in whose sagacity and means of being correctly informed, I had much confidence, suggested to me, that from his knowledge of the value which Mr. Clay set upon the office of Secretary of State, and its

patronage, that he was convinced that Mr. Clay had determined to dispose of his interest in a manner that would secure him that station" (Call to Van Ness, February 4, 1828). All of the above documents were published in the *United States' Telegraph—Extra,* May 10, 1828.

10. Statement and letters not found.

11. AJ was referring to the friction between Eaton and Henry Lee over Lee's proposed biography of AJ.

12. Green was concerned that Monroe would issue a pamphlet concerning his role in the defense of New Orleans in 1814–15, possibly provoking a public dispute with AJ.

13. Monroe to John C. Calhoun, September 9, 1818.

To John Overton

(Private)   Hermitage August 15th. 1827—
Dr Sir

I was at Nashville yesterday, heard you had not returned, or would have went to see you, so soon as you return, I will be glad to know it—I wish you to see the Frankfort Commentator as soon as you return, there is something on the subject of the Dickerson affair therein stated, highly dishonorable to the memory of your brother, which I know to be false, which ought to be noticed for this purpose I would like to see you, & Genl Walter Overton, as soon as you get home[1]—you will find the paper in the hands of Major Wm B Lewis. I begin to think that the lying rascals live in Nashville & are companions of Col Andersons.[2]

I would be glad to know whether you have recd an answer to your letter from Major Barry, if you have, I would be glad to be informed the tenor thereof.[3] Major Eaton writes me that a gentleman from Kentucky has stated precisely what Sharp wrote me on that subject. With good wishes to you & family respectfully yr friend

Andrew Jackson

ALS, THi (11-0793).

1. On July 28, the Frankfort *Commentator* published a report that Thomas Overton, John's brother and AJ's second, had used threats to extract a favorable statement from Hanson Catlet, Dickinson's second, about the duel. For Thomas Overton's statement and Catlet's affidavits, see *Jackson,* 2:104–105.

2. The Frankfort *Commentator* merely identified its source as a gentleman of "high and unblemished respectability."

3. Overton, perhaps inspired by what AJ had heard from either Leander J. or Fidelio C. Sharp, had apparently asked William T. Barry about a Jackson meeting at Fowler's Garden, near Lexington, Kentucky, on July 21. When Barry, the designated speaker for the occasion, arrived too late to give the keynote, the organizers turned to former senator John Pope (1770–1845), a Jackson supporter but also a brother-in-law of John Quincy Adams, to deliver the main speech. Barry characterized Pope's speech as able, but "too tender of Adams" (Barry to Overton, August 30, THi). Pope's speech appeared in the *Louisville Public Advertiser,* August 15.

The congressional elections in Kentucky in the summer of 1827 proved to be a testing ground for the presidential election the following year.

In the letter below, Jackson called William B. Lewis's attention to disparaging charges regarding his military career from John Flournoy Henry (1793–1873), a physician from Scott County and the incumbent seeking reelection to Congress. Henry's Circular (Hopkinsville, July 1827) was an omnibus attack on Jackson's military career in the southern campaign, elaborating on his government accounts, on the execution of the six militiamen, on the dispute regarding terms of service, on his dismissive attitude toward Kentucky troops, and on the imposition of martial law in New Orleans.

For some time Jackson and Lewis had been working on a response to the discussions of Jackson's military career; and the pamphlet from Henry, who lost the election, gave focus to the report they issued shortly through the Nashville Committee.

To William Berkeley Lewis

August 16th. 1827—

Dr. Sir

I never saw Mr Henry's circular untill last evening—Have you seen it? I think it requires some notice.

I have at length found my letter Book, which contains the Sec of Wars order to Govr Blount Dated War Dept. Jany 11th. 1814[1]—Major Genl Pinckneys letter of instructions of 22nd. april 1814[2]—Gov Blounts letter & order to me of the 20th. of May 1814 which begins thus—Sir In compliance with the requisition of Major Genl Pinkney that the posts at Fts Williams &c &c &c ought to be kept up &c &c &c. you will without delay &c &c order 1000 *Militia Infantry for the term of Six months unless sooner discharged* &c &c &c. These troops will be required to rendezvous at Fayettevill on the 20th. of June next—and be at their post between the 1st. & 10th. of July next &c &c &c. *you will order the muster master to muster them into service* &c &c &c[3]—This will put an end to all dispute upon the legality of the service of these militia—and as Mr H. says application has been made at the War [Dept] & no authority for this call can be [found] there; it affords aditional proof, to what I already profess, that the Sec of War is aiding & abetting in these slanders.

When I finish, I will submit the comments to your inspection, in the meantime you can thro the repu[blican] make such remarks on the letter as you may think proper.[4] I have no doubt but a copy can be had from the Boyd Junto[5] Nashville. I am respectfully yr friend

Andrew Jackson

ALS, NN (11-0796).
   1. See John Armstrong to Willie Blount, January 11, 1814 (DLC-8).
   2. See Thomas Pinckney to AJ, April 22, 1814.
   3. See Willie Blount to AJ, May 20, 1814.
   4. A brief editorial on the terms of service, perhaps by Lewis, appeared in the *Nashville Republican* on August 21.
   5. AJ was referring to Boyd McNairy and his associates, probably including William P. Anderson, who were instrumental in discussing AJ's role in the Burr business, his involvement in slave trading, and his duel with Dickinson.

To John Overton

Hermitage August 18th. 1827.

Dr Sir

I enclose you a letter, containing the peace aluded to in my note to you the other day[1]—The statement your deceased brother is made to make, is the vilest forgery, & falshood ever penned—I have no doubt but it is furnished from Nashville or its neighbourhood. To put this down, & that the villains should be unmasked, I would suggest, that it might be proper for Genl W. Overton to demand of the Editor his author, *and coerce it*; in this way, such dishonorable *tales* as it relates to the memory of your deceased brother ought to be put down—The whole statement is a base fabrication by the forger, & if the Editor, has not fabricated it, himself, he ought to be made to give up his informant, & in time, they may discover whether Jackson has a *tremulous hand*. Respectfully yr friend

Andrew Jackson

ALS, THi (11-0803). Published in Bassett, 3:378.
   1. Enclosure not found. For a discussion of the report in the *Frankfort Commentator*, July 8, see above, AJ to Overton, August 15.

To John McLean (1785–1861)

Hermitage August 21rst 1827—

Dear Sir

The enclosed papers will shew you the means resorted to by the minions of the Coalition to annoy me, and if possible create the suspicions in my mind that you have been base enough to assail female charecter, for political effect.[1] In this I assure you they are mistaken. Whatever may be my impressions of the agency wh*[ich]* Messhrs. Clay, Barbour & Southard have had in the many private & false statements circulated against me, I have too exalted an opinion of you to suppose that you could be persuaded to unite with them. My object in forwarding these papers is, to bring to your view the corrupt use to which the post office is here converted, that if possible, the proper remedy may be applied. under the management of Mr. Curry no such abuse existed; and perhaps, it is the first instance where the franking privilege has been employed to keep in concealment anonymous slanders.

*[You will find I ha]*ve traced it to the Gallatine postoffice from the west, & back to Nashville. I conjecture it is of Kentucky or Nashville growth, emanating from the panders of Mr. Clay, for I am sure there is no other source base anough to originate such dirty work; and I know there is none which wickedness could suggest that they are not capable of attempting[2]

If it be true, as from the authority of several members of congress from Kentucky & other sources, I am inclined to believe it is, that the secratary of war is sustaining the attack made on me in consequence of the execution of the six militiamen at Mobile, upon the ground that in the Department of war no order can be found ordering into service the command of Col. pipkin for six months &c;[3] I am at no loss for the motive of this slander upon you. all the departments must be united, or otherwise the exception unperceived by my indiscriminate suspicion.

When you have examined these papers & taken order upon them, be pleased to return the anonymous letter, as from its mark I discover the paper to be British manufacture, which, with other circumstances *[ma]*y be of use in detecting the author. with the assurance of my high respect and continued regard I am yr mo. obdt. servt.

[Andrew Jackson]

P.S.

The results of the elections in Kentucky prove that the highminded freemen of that state, will no longer yield to the mandates of *a dictator* or be transferable at his *will*. Happy omen for the durability of our goverment, but unpropitious to the reign of the Dictator & his coalition.[4]

Truth and honesty are the only sure guides to lasting public confidence, in this land of freedom & virtue. A. J.

AL (signature removed) and Copy in Andrew J. Donelson's hand with AJ postscript, DLC (11-0806; 34).

1. AJ enclosed "A Female Friend" to Rachel Jackson, June 10, above, and other items not identified.

2. In his response on September 22, McLean accused Caleb Atwater, a rival for the leadership of Ohio's Jacksonians, of mailing the "Female Friend" letter.

3. On the issue of the terms of service of the militia, see above, AJ to William B. Lewis, August 16.

4. AJ was referring to Clay and other Adams supporters. In the August congressional elections, Jacksonians won seven of Kentucky's twelve seats in the U. S. House of Representatives. Only three of the eight congressmen who had voted for Adams in 1825 remained in office (Richard A. Buckner, Robert P. Letcher, and Thomas Metcalfe), and three of AJ's most persistent critics, David Trimble, Francis Johnson, and John F. Henry, lost.

In late summer 1827, the corrupt bargain charge overshadowed all other issues in the presidential campaign. In his July 18 letter to the public (above), Jackson identified James Buchanan as the intermediary from the Clay faction. This disclosure prompted Buchanan to tell his side of the story on August 8 to the editor of the Lancaster Journal, *where it was published two days later.*

In his discussion, Buchanan admitted that he had contacted Jackson previous to the 1825 presidential election regarding the role that Clay might play in a Jackson administration, but insisted that he was not an emissary from either Clay or Clay's friends. Both Jacksonians and Adams-Clay partisans claimed Buchanan's statement vindicated their respective interpretation of the corrupt bargain charge; but, to bolster their claims, both sides sought evidence to corroborate their respective stories. In the letter below, Amos Kendall made his initial contact with Jackson offering advice in dealing with the issue.

From Amos Kendall

Frankfort Ky Aug. 22d 1827.

Dr. Sir,

Although I have never had the pleasure of a personal acquaintance with you, there are some circumstances of a peculiar nature which induce me now to address you.

I have been somewhat embarrassed and much vexed at the course which has been taken by some of your friends relative to the "bargain" &c. Beverly, with the best intentions, has certainly been guilty of great indiscretion, and it seems to me that your friends of the Telegraph are not doing much better. However, they may be better judges than I am. But I fear that the investigation upon that line, that is, through Markley, will do no good.[1] You will see by our papers what took place here in January 1825.[2] It has been brought out to sustain you in the position to which you have been, as I think, unfortunately, brought by your friends. Mr. Clay never treated me confidentially in relation to his arrangement with Adams, and if he had done so, I should either have disclosed it long ago out of an impression of duty to my country, or never have divulged it at all. But I am one of those who were told here by one of his friends, as I think about the 20th day of January 1825, that if Mr. Adams should be elected he would make Mr. Clay his Secretary of State,[3] and I was three times solicited to write to Mr. [David] White, our representative, to vote for Mr. Adams on that account.[4] Thus urged I did write, informing Mr. White, as near as I can recollect, that you were unquestionably the choice of Kentucky as you were of myself; but that it was possible the state might be reconciled to another choice if Mr. Clay were placed at the head of the cabinet. Many others instructed him directly to vote for Mr. Adams. Having been one of Mr. Clay's family,[5] I should at least have been silent in relation to this transaction, but for the discovery, or at least the conviction, that Mr. Clay was willing to gratify his ambition at the sacrifice of every tie, regardless of every obligation whether to his friends or to his country. I know not from what source the information relative to the arrangement with Mr. Adams, came; but I now believe that it came from *Mr. Clay himself.* So confident am I, that I would risk my honor and my life upon the result of a thorough investigation. It must have come from him before the 10th of January as the letters got up here were written in time to reach Washington before the election. I write this for *your own eye only.* You can found on the information such suggestions to your friends as you may think proper; but I never shall disclose to mortal man the avenue through which this evidence can be procured, unless called on in the name of my country.[6]

In a few days you will receive an invitation to a public dinner in this place.[7] Whether you accept it or not, it is my earnest desire and that of your friends, that you should visit Kentucky this fall. We have gained a victory, which, if followed up, will be decisive of the vote of this state.[8] The country is eager to see you. It cannot now be said, that your object is to operate on our elections; yet, your presence here would have a greater effect on public feeling than if you had come before the election. Then you would have appeared as one struggling for mastery in a doubtful contest; now, you would come as a victor. The country would flock around you as did the people after the battle of Orleans, and the impulse to the good cause would be decisive. Let me entreat you to gratify our wishes— it would save your friends immense labor and almost finish the war in Kentucky. We should meet you at our dinner with the most ardent enthusiasm; but if you do not deem it expedient to join with us on an occasion so joyous, it is our most decided opinion, that your presence in Kentucky would not be improper and would redound much to your own advantage and to the success of those principles for which we are all contending. Very respectfully Your friend

Amos Kendall

ALS, T (11-0814).
1. Since July 21, the *United States' Telegraph* had focused its discussion of the corrupt bargain almost exclusively on the role of Representative Philip S. Markley. According to the *Telegraph,* Markley had told Buchanan that Clay's friends would probably "act in concert at the election" and could elect either Adams or AJ, but that they would not support AJ if he "had pre-determined to prefer another to Mr. Clay" for secretary of state.
2. One report on the events in Frankfort, mainly involving efforts to swing Kentucky's vote in the House for Adams in order to secure a position in the administration for Clay, appeared on August 22 in the *Argus of Western America,* Kendall's paper, copied from the *Kentucky Gazette.*
3. The friend of Clay's was probably Francis Preston Blair (1791–1876; Transylvania 1811), at this time a co-editor of the *Argus* and later editor of the leading Jacksonian newspaper in Washington, the *Globe.*
4. White (1785–1834) served a single term in the House from Kentucky, 1823–25; he

did cast his vote for Adams in the election, following receipt of a letter from Kendall, also discussed in the editorial copied in the *Argus,* August 22. In a public letter to Clay in the September 26 *Argus,* Kendall described the circumstances of his letter to White.

5. When he first moved to Kentucky in 1814, Kendall served as tutor for the Clay chil dren.

6. In early 1828, the Kentucky Senate investigated the corrupt bargain charges and called Kendall to testify. He did, claiming to have learned before the election that Adams, if victorious, would appoint Clay secretary of state, but he did not disclose the name or source of his information.

7. See Kendall to AJ, August 27, below.

8. Kendall was referring to the recent Kentucky congressional elections.

From Amos Kendall

Frankfort Ky Aug. 27th 1827

Dr Sir,

I have the honor to inclose you an invitation to the public dinner which is to be given by your friends in the vicinity of this place on the 10th September.[1] It would be gratifying to the committee to hear from you as soon as your convenience will permit.[2]

Buchanan's statement has been received here by the Adams men with much exultation; but their joy has very much abated. "Sweet in the mouth" they find this document "bitter in the belly." We ask them, do you admit Mr. Buchanan's statement to be true? This leads them to re flect on its contents, and to save the honor of their party in Congress they are obliged to answer no. He substantially confirms your statement and perhaps says as much as he could do and save himself from reproach.

Your friends here are in the highest spirits. One convert within my knowledge has been made to your cause by your answer to Buchanan as detailed by himself. We do not doubt of carrying Kentucky entire; but we shall have a tremendous contest next year. Clay would rather die than be defeated.

Since I wrote you the impressions conveyed in that letter have received additional confirmation.[3] Scarcely a room for doubt remains in my mind—indeed none—that Mr. Clay himself, before the middle of Janu ary, informed his friends here of the arrangement with Mr. Adams. The evidence can be reached by the strong arm of government but not with out it. With the highest respect Your friend &c

Amos Kendall

ALS, T (11-0825).

1. See Matthew Clark et al. to AJ, August 27.
2. AJ declined on September 4.
3. See above, Kendall to AJ, August 22.

Early in the 1820s Jackson bought a number of single male slaves in Virginia, specifically for his Evans Spring farm and later the Big Spring farm, both in northern Alabama. Among them was Gilbert, whose death at the overseer's hand is reported below. He ran away from Alabama in March 1822 but was recovered. About January 1823, Jackson moved him, along with all his other Alabama slaves, to the Hermitage, where Gilbert ran away again in August 1824 and again was recaptured. Gilbert's final escape was in June 1827. When he was returned in August, Jackson ordered the overseer, Ira Walton, to whip him in the presence of the field hands. The details of the ensuing events come almost entirely from Walton's deposition, published in 1828, as part of Jackson's defense against accusations of slave trading and mistreatment made by Andrew Erwin. According to Walton, he had bound Gilbert's hands in front of him and, accompanied by Joe (c1816–30), drove him through a wooded area toward the field where slaves were working. Gilbert loosened his bonds, attacked Walton with a chunk of wood, and in the fray, Walton drew a knife and inflicted several wounds, which felled Gilbert. When Jackson was informed, he sent for Dr. Miles McCorkle and had Gilbert moved to the Hermitage, where he died a few hours later.

Jackson promptly dispatched Walton to the coroner with the letter below, and a nine-man jury, consisting of nearby neighbors, assembled over the body, and determined that Walton had acted in self-defense.

To William Faulkner

Hermitage August 28th. 1827

To the coroner of Davidson County
Sir

An unfortunate occurrence has taken place to day on my farm, between my overseer, & one of my negro men, which terminated in the death of the latter. Notwithstanding I believe the fatal stab was given in self defence, still as I wish Justice to be done, I request a coroner inquest over him, and notify you thereof. I am very respectfully your mo obdt. Servt.

Andrew Jackson

ALS, THi (11-0828). Endorsed in Andrew Jackson Donelson's hand with names of the jurors: "Dr. Sanders Edward Hobbs Ti[moth]y Dobson Wm Donelson James Martin John Cook Wm. Watson Andw. J Donelson Levin Donelson." Faulkner was a Davidson County justice of the peace.

The death of Gilbert was brought into the presidential campaign by Jackson's old nemesis Andrew Erwin, who, on August 2, 1828, published in the National Banner and Nashville Whig, *a long article that almost immediately circulated as a pamphlet titled "Gen. Jackson's Negro Speculations, and His Traffic in Human Flesh . . ." In a concluding paragraph he wrote: "Lastly, I never had a slave brought before me for offending against whom I gave an unmerciful sentence, such as you are said to have done at or near your own fire side at the Hermitage of late, in the attempt to execute which, it is said your own slave was killed, and all hushed up without any proceedings in court against the man, who, it is said, in executing your order, or on the way to do it, killed said slave." Jackson's "unmerciful sentence," as broadcast by the Erwin camp, was for 1,000 lashes, alarming Gilbert into rebellion and ending in the overseer's killing him in self-defense (John P. Erwin to Samuel Shock, August 5, 1828, T). The letters below, along with Ira Walton's account of the incident, appeared in the* Nashville Republican *on August 12, 1828, in response to Erwin's polemic. On August 15, 1828, the* Republican *exonerated Jackson in the affair: "We do not see how Gen Jackson can be considered in the slightest degree censurable for this unfortunate occurrence," the editor wrote. "We heard the matter spoken of at the time, but never were informed of the particulars. We did not even know that it had ever been investigated by the grand jury, although he believed, from the beginning, that whatever might have been the conduct of the overseer, the General was entirely free from blame. This appears to have been the fact, and we cheerfully give an opinion decided and unequivocally in his behalf."*

To Andrew Hays

Hermitage, August 30, 1827.

Sir–

You have been already apprised of the unfortunate affair which took place on my farm on the day before yesterday, in relation to the death of Gilbert, who was slain by Ira Walton, my overseer.

You have also been apprised that a jury of inquest has been held over his dead body, by the Coroner of the county; and that the jury reported that Walton killed him *"in his own defence."* I communicated to you yesterday, all the facts relative to that unfortunate event. I wish to know of you, from the statement of the facts I have detailed, whether you think, from a consideration of them, there has been such a violation of the laws as requires a further prosecution of the matter.

I have discharged Mr Walton from my service; he remained here until released by the finding of the jury, since which he has been going at large. If you should be of opinion, from a consideration of the case, that he should be held to answer at the next circuit court, let me know as soon as your convenience will permit. I have no wish to prosecute Mr Walton should you think justice does not demand it, but being the guardian of my slave, it is my duty to prosecute the case so far as justice to him may require it; therefore submit the matter to your consideration, as attorney prosecuting for the government for your advice on the premises. I am very respectfully, Your most obedient servant,

Andrew Jackson

Printed, *Nashville Republican,* August 12, 1828. Hays was state prosecutor for the Fourth Circuit Court and a member of the Board of Trustees for the University of Nashville, 1820–31.

From Andrew Hays

Nashville, August 31, 1827.

Dear Sir—

I have received yours of the 30th inst.[1] and have given that attention to the matters therein contained which their importance requires. You are fully aware that the finding of the jury, summoned by the coroner, is no bar to the further prosecution of the offence; the finding is a *prima facie* evidence of the innocence of Mr Walton. But my opinion is, from the full consideration of the evidence, that there exists a considerable doubt as to the absolute necessity of killing the slave Gilbert, at the time that he received the mortal blow. Although he behaved very much amiss, it would seem to me that the distance of the place where he was found from the place where the scuffle took place, as well as from the place of the wound in Gilbert's back, afford a strong presumption that he was stabbed in the back whilst running, and not in the first scuffle; and among other circumstances which induce me to think that it is not a case of justifiable homicide, is, that his hands were tied; and I do not believe they ever were untied. The rule of law is, that if the homicide is ever brought home to a delinquent the *onus probandi* of the circumstances of excuse or justification are imposed upon him. Without an expression of any positive opinion of his guilt or innocence, (which would be improper in me at present) I have no hesitation in saying, that I think that public justice, as well as your duty as a master and guardian of your slave, requires that you should have Mr Walton before the circuit court to answer a bill of indictment for the death of Gilbert.[2] Yours &c. Very respectfully,

Andrew Hays

Printed, *Nashville Republican,* August 12, 1828.
1. See above.
2. According to Hays's 1828 account, Jackson caused Walton to be re-arrested, and he was bound over to appear at the November term of the Fourth District Circuit Court. Hays

prepared an indictment for murder and sent it before the grand jury. After two days of deliberation, the jury brought in the bill of indictment endorsed "Not a true Bill," and Walton was discharged from further prosecution. The court's minute book records only the grand jury's decision (Davidson County Circuit Court, Fourth Circuit, Minute Book F:524, November Term 1827, TNDa).

To *William Berkeley Lewis*

Hermitage Septr 1rst. 1827—

Dr Major

The late unfortunate occurrence between my overseer & one of my negro man, in which the latter was slain, has occasioned me to discharge my overseer: Having borrowed five hundred dollars of him to meet an engagement last Spring, he has called for his mony & I must return it.[1] I have it not ready for him—can you aid me with convenience, if so, it will oblige me, if you can advance me one half the loan I made you, it will place me clear of pressure.[2] Should this be inconvenient, I must have recourse to a loan from the bank, which I have no inclination for, if I can av[o]id it—

The unacountable statement of Mr Buchanan will require my attention.[3] I have been waiting for papers in the hands of Judge overton—who I have expected at home ten days ago. has he arived, if he has, & you see him, please say to him to send me Judge [Jacob C.] Isaack's statement[4]— I am respectfully yr friend

Andrew Jackson

P.S. I would like to see you, A. J.
If Major Lewis will send me my papers of to day by Dunwody who is in Nashville, he will oblige A. J.

ALS, NNPM (11-0838).
1. See promissory notes from AJ to Walton, January 29 and May 12.
2. Records of AJ's loan to Lewis have not been found. AJ repaid Walton on September 20.
3. For a discussion of Buchanan's report to the editor of the *Lancaster Journal*, August 8, see above, Buchanan to AJ, August 10, and AJ to Duff Green, August 13.
4. In his letter of August 25, Overton wrote that he had obtained a statement on the corrupt bargain from Isacks (1767–1835), congressman from Sparta, Tennessee, and that he would deliver it to AJ on his return to Nashville. In his statement of August 12 (*Nashville Republican*, September 18), Isacks confirmed AJ's account of Buchanan's visit to the Jacksonians in 1824–25 to discuss Clay's role in the forthcoming administration.

To Amos Kendall

Hermitage Septbr 4th 1827—

Dear Sir

Your letter of the 27th. ult[1] enclosing me an invitation from the committee of arangement to a public dinner to be given by my friends in the vicinity of Frankfort on the 20th. instant, was recd yesterday; & as requested, I hasten to answer it.[2]

It is with regret I am compelled to inform you, that from circumstances which at present surround me, & over which I have no control, I am deprived the pleasure of participating with you in this festival. I regret this the more, as it is the anniversary of Perrys glorious victory on Lake Erie, & which led to the subsequent triumph of our arms on the Thames, principally achieved by the bravery of the Kentucky Troops & their gallant & experienced commanders. On this occasion, tho absent, my heart will be with you.

I recd your letter sent under cover to my young friend Saml J. Hays, for which I thank you.[3] It is recd in the confidence in which it was written, & shall be so preserved. It is a valuable key, & should Mr. Clay place himself before a tribunal with power fully to investigate, must lead to the development of new & additional matter.

I have seen Mr Buchanan address,[4] it is such a production as surely, I had not a right to expect from him; but we live in days of wonder—Mr. B. situation tho was a delicate one. It would be now only necessary for me to publish Major Eatons statement[5] & Mr Kreamers,[6] contrast them with his, & it would appear that his recollection had materially failed him, Surely no one could believe that Mr. B. would go to my friends make statements to them, to communicate to me, & when they had refused, come to me himself, then make a different one; and that I should understand the statement made to me, as my friends did, that, which was made to them. And could it be, that Mr. B. would approach me so guarded & cautiously barely with a view to make the inquiry, whether the rumor abroad was correct, that I had said if elected, I would appoint Mr Adams secratary of state—This was a question that might have been asked by any one, without delicacy, and which I would any where have promptly answered. This however is a subject of much delicacy, & is one upon which I will deliberate fully before I act.

Amonghst all the scenes of intrigue, management, & slander, with which I have been, and am still surrounded, my great consolation is, that I receive the protection & maintain the confidence, of the virtuous intelligent citizens of my country. accept assurances of my high respect, & believe me to be yr mo obt servt

Andrew Jackson

ALS and ALS copy, DLC (78, 34). Published in Bassett, 3:381 (extract) and in *Cincinnati Commercial*, February 4, 1879.
1. See above.
2. See Matthew Clark et al. to AJ, August 27, and AJ to Clark et al., September 4.
3. See above, Kendall to AJ, August 22.
4. Buchanan to the editor of the *Lancaster Journal*, August 8.
5. Eaton's statement appeared in the *Nashville Republican* of September 18.
6. Either Kremer to AJ, March 8, 1825, above; or Kremer's pseudonymous letter of January 1825, published in the Philadelphia *Columbian Observer,* January 28.

From Caleb Atwater

Columbus Sept. 4. 1827

Dear Sir,

I arrived at home, a few days since, & am here, attending court. I found no letters from New York, but a Mr. Wilcox, a friend of your's, directly from Connecticut,[1] informs me, that Gov. Clinton has written many letters to his friends there, in your favor, and that, there is a considerable party springing up there, for you. This may be relied on. I wish to say, in confidence, to you, that I saw a man in Tennessee, who is a *double spy on you.* He was appointed, since the last election, to an office, in a Department, through the influence of *Mr. Clay*—he wrote *against you* for months, in the N. Journal! until, Mr. Clay, *pretended,* that he had caught him writing in the Telegraph, for Calhoun! and had him turned off. Next, I learned, that he was seated by *your side,* and letters began to arrive in Ohio, from Tennessee, extremely unfavorable to you, & the holy cause! Your friends began to feel uneasy, & I was induced to make a long & tedious journey, at an unseasonable time of the year, having in view, among other things, the discovery of the traitor! And when I saw him, as I did, & do still believe, I did, I confess, that my feelings were suppressed with difficulty. You inquired "what was the matter? I appeared to be in "health." I waved the question, and was silent. *He is a spy—a double one*—for Clay—and for McLean & Calhoun! Such is my deliberate opinion. Any man, who violates all moral principle, so far as to destroy his wife's sister—so far as to write on *both sides,* at the *same time*—will do any thing else. No matter, what may be a man's genius and classical attainments, if he lacks principle, what is he?[2]

I thank you for your kindness and hospitality, and send my best respects, to your venerable and pious lady—to your kind, and amiable family. My own health is somewhat impaired, by my journey, though I hope to escape a fever. My children are unwell, though the general health of the country is good.

I have written to the *friend, in Philadelphia,* I mentioned to you.[3] It was a prudent letter, tho' drawn up, in warm language.

I have visited our friends, every where, on my return—they are in high spirits.

I hope, the purity of my motives, will form an apology for saying, that but one man, can injure your election, *by writing*—shall I name him to you? I will not, but one thing appears to me, to be certain, that a candidate for President, can do nothing for himself, *directly,* though indirectly he can, through his friends; and warmer ones—more zealous ones, more intelligent and patriotic ones, no man ever had than you have. The patriotism, the virtue, the talents are with you—will not that suffice? Trusting yourself in the hands of such friends, and in the hands of that great and good Being, who has hitherto watched over this beloved country, for good, leave your cause, and that of our beloved country, to your friends, and to your GOD.

Remember the Immortal Jefferson, in '98, and during many years—accused of every crime, and his friends libelled in every possible way, yet who slanders Jefferson now? who dares abuse his friends? "Respice finem:" says a maxim of antiquity.[4] "The storms of these wintry times, will soon be over;" and the civic wreathe, will entwine your brow; and the very sycophants, who now libel you—who libel even *me,* every week and every day, for being your supporter, will flock around you, bending and bowing before you, while myself, who have passed through all manner of persecution, on account of my attattchment to you, shall be silent—at home, unknown, and forgotten. Let it be so, but for Heaven's sake, for y[our] country's sake, do remember, that, but one man, ca[n] write you down—his name is—Andrew Jackson. My great anxiety for your success—my abundant zeal, (in this case, *super* abundant, I hope,) must plead my excuse, for this hint. Thousands, yes, tens of thousands of your friends, think as I do, on this Subject. I am requested to say, what I have, to you, by all your friends, wherever I have been. Leave all to us, who support you. Can we do more? I promise you, that every friend you have, in Ohio, who can get to the polls, shall go there, and vote for you. In the meantime, all shall be done, that can be, for you. If I can raise the means, I will visit the Eastern states this autumn—all that I can do, shall be done, though you will not know of my doing any thing, perhaps. May GOD prosper our righteous cause and may you put your trust in him. Success to the Hero of Orleans.

Caleb Atwater

ALS, DLC (34).
1. Possibly Norris Wilcox (b. c1798), a Hartford County deputy sheriff whom AJ appointed federal marshal for Connecticut in December 1831.
2. Atwater was referring to Henry Lee, who had received a minor job in the post office department in 1825 through the influence of Calhoun and Chief Justice John Marshall. Lee had resigned that post in 1826 and, in May 1827, had arrived at the Hermitage to write a biography of AJ.

3. Not identified.
4. "Respice Finem" (Aesop's Fables XXII, 5) means "consider the consequences."

"*General Jackson*"

[cSeptember 4, 1827]

Some of our pretended friends seem much to regret, that General Jackson should have written to Mr. Carter Beverly on the subject of bargain and sale which was going on in Washington City in the winter of 1825. I, for one, do not regret General Jackson's having written to Mr. Beverly: let motives be what they may, "truth is powerful and must prevail."

General Jackson has never placed his name in black and white, that it did not elevate him in the eyes of his countrymen. He is a republican of the *true* principles of 98, and will speak out when it becomes necessary. No secret springs, nor "midnight tapers," nor closed doors, nor back stair arrangements, are the movements at the hermitage. Frankness and candor are the predominant features of republicanism; so it is with Andrew Jackson; he is a man who never conceals. There is nothing within his own breast, but what he is willing his God and country should know; particularly when the rights and privileges of that country are endangered. There are certain times and circumstances, (which the present period offers) when men should "cry aloud, and spare not." He never writes on trivial occasions; it is only when palpable corruption comes within his knowledge. This is one out of many of the fundamental principles by which he is actuated—and who among them can lay claim or tythe to the gratitude we owe him for services rendered to the country at the most dismal period of its history?

In purity of purpose and integrity of action,— in a heroic contempt of all that regards himself when the interest of his country is concerned, his equal is to be found no where but in the pages of history, and I doubt if it is to be found there.

Such a man is General Jackson; and fortunate will it be for the People of the United States, if they shall have the wisdom to elect him their chief magistrate.

A REPUBLICAN.

Printed, *Nashville Republican,* September 4, 1827; Extract and abstract, Swann Auction Galleries, Catalogs 35, 1943, and 68, n.d. (11-1000). The original manuscript for "A Republican" has not been found, but both Swann catalogs describe the manuscript as being "written for publication in the 'Nashville Republican.'" Catalog 35 describes the manuscript as being in Jackson's own hand while issue 68 refers to the manuscript as having "many corrections in Jackson's hand."

From Martin Van Buren

Albany Septr. 14th. 1827

My dear Sir

I am reminded by a letter from your friend & neighbour Mr. Balch[1] of the propriety of apprising you of the State of public opinion with us. It was my intention to do so as soon as I could possess myself of the requisite information. I have recently been through many of the Counties respecting which I felt the most anxiety, have seen most of the leading men from others & the Legislature are now & have for some days been in session. From the information thus derived I am sure I cannot be mistaken in believing, that we shall be able to give you a very decided majority of the votes of this state, if nothing turns up hereafter to change the present aspect of things. I do not think I should hazard any thing in saying two thirds. at all events we can settle the question unless we are greatly disappointed in other states. Nothing that can be done by the people at Washington, or by any particular influence that can be brought to bear upon us at home, can prevent this result—if it is prevented it can only be by some indiscretion of our own. This is not the opinion of the friends of Mr Adams & a short time since the public indications were certainly very different. The politics of this state like those of Pennsylvania & most of the northern states are yet governed by old Party feelings. For four fifths of the time since 1800 the old Republican Party has possessed the power of this state. It does so now to a greater extent (the Govr. alone excepted) than it has done for many years. Until within the last two months, it for reasons (unnecessary to state) paused on the Presidential question. Upon that hesitation & the general avowal of the old Federalists in favour of the administration, it was, that its friends counted so confidently upon the result in this state. The scene is now greatly changed & will soon be altogether so. Out of the fifty Republican Presses we have in the State very many have already come out in your favour, & the rest with at most three exceptions will do the same soon. The Legislature have come in in fine feeling, & the Republicans throughout the State are avowing themselves in your favour, & making your support the Party Standard. At the ensuing fall elections they will literally put to rout the discordant factions by which they have heretofore been opposed and thereafter rally under one common standard on national politics. All that is necessary to secure this gratifying result is that we be let alone. Attempts will doubtless be made to entangle your friends in the Vice-Presidential & other questions but they will I am persuaded have good sense enough not to meddle in them. I have no other feelings in relation to the Vice Presidency than as it may operate on the main question. Let it be left to the natural course of public sentiment & it will fare best. It is as far as I can see the only point upon which we can have difficulty & the true policy in regard to it for the present, clearly is, to let it alone.² one word more & excuse me for the liberty I take in refering to it. I can well appreciate your feelings under the torrents of malignant vituperation to which you have been exposed, & I am sensible of the difficulty of avoiding replies to direct applications which are (sometimes with the best intention but not infrequently from mere vanity on the part of their authors) made to you from different parts of the Union. But I think I hazard nothing in saying that for the future the case must be an extreme one that can make frank explanations from you personally necessary. The obvious design to bear you down by calumny has produced a great re-action, & I am quite certain that they have so much overacted their parts as to render their past as well as future vituperation entirely harmless. Our people do not like to see publications from candidates. It is a singular point that in almost every case in which they have (with us) been attempted on the eve of an election they have operated agt. the cause they were intended to serve. Do not infer from this that it is my intention to complain of the past. On the contrary I am clearly of opinion that all that has been done was not only proper but unavoidable & has been useful. Although our friend Buchanan was evidently frightened & therefore softened & obscured the matter still the <incontrovertible> fact of your entire aversion to all & any intrigue or arrangement is clearly established, & nothing could be of more value, or more acceptable to the people—The sentiments contained in your letter to Dixon in 1801 & of your 4h of July toast at Nashville are those best adapted to the feelings and opinions of our people.³ Make my best respects to Mrs. Jackson & believe me to be Your sincere friend

M. V. Buren

P.S. As the publication of any opinions from me would only furnish texts for misrepresentation here, I beg that it may be avoided.

ALS, DLC (11-0853). Published in Bassett, 3:381–82.
    1. Not found.
    2. Some of AJ's New York supporters favored Clinton over Calhoun on the Jackson ticket.
    3. AJ to William Dickson, September 1, 1801 (*Jackson,* 1:256–57), in which AJ indicated his support for limited government, had been widely reprinted during the 1824 presidential campaign, and in 1827 it reappeared in the September 13 *Albany Argus & Daily City Gazette.* AJ's July 4 toast was: "The memory of the illustrious patriot, and sage of Monticello."

To John Coffee

(Private)   Nashville Septbr. 29th. 1827.
Dr Genl

I recd. your kind letter[1] by due course of mail, but when recd, & ever since, I have been surrounded by company, & with other pressing business, that has engrossed all my leisure time, the answer has been therefore delayed untill now.

I have been from the first, well apprise[d] of the course, & system adopted, by H Clay & his panders—Their object, by slandering me, to draw the attention of the public from their corruption, bargain, & intrigue, and keep myself & friends always on the defensive. My friends have thought it best, now & then, to carry the war into the enemies camp, and expose their corruption to the view of the public, & employ their time in defence—for it was soon found, that refuting the various slanders were useless; no sooner refuted, but the same falshoods were reiterated—The people now understand their wicked course, & refutation of the charges are only ma[d]e the better to expose, the wicked and unjustifiable course adopted by Clay & his associates—for myself, I intend not to appear before the public unless it should in the investigation of the Carter Beverly & Buchannan business, become necessary for me to do so; and I am well advised, if this should become necessary, that I have the means of full exposure within my reach, but was I to come out again, & give the statement of Mr Kremer to the public,[2] it must destroy Mr Buchanna[n] this, if it can be avoided, I have no wish, altho. he deserves it, should be done, the object of Mr Clay would be promoted by a contest between Mr. B. & myself; because it woud draw the attention of the public from his corruption in obtaining the appointment he holds, to the contest between myself & Buchannan, about immaterial things—The statement of Buchannan substantially is the same that I have made, except the date & place where, in which he is mistaken as is shown by Major Eaton[3] —Mr. B. was alarmed, & has done himself no credit—still, for the present I will be silent—Information from all quarters are pleasant, & shew that the people understand the corruption that have been practised, & [t]hey are determined to manage their business in their own way.

The course adopted by the Legislature here, have been well calculated to correct erroneous opinions abroad & has left Col. Williams to brood over his situation, having Just found his real weight of charecter. Judge White was elected by a unanimous vote again to the senate for six years from the 4th. of March 1829—The Colo. I do believe wishes he was not in the Legislature—This is part of his punishment, for aiding in writing, & circulating Arnold pamphlet.[4]

A Resolution has been adopted, voting you a sword; This is what ought to have been done in 1815—but better now than never.[5]

I shall be out as early as I can, I expect the pleasure of *[your co]*mpany to orleans in Janry next, to set out the latter end of Decbr. next.[6]

My crop is very short, I have not had as much rain as was necessary to *[br]*ing up my rye, & my stock has been sufferring for grass for six weeks.

I am glad to hear that your Motherless coalt is still living—a good rye lott, will give it size, with good feeding on oats & corn. I refer you to Stockly, for the news of this place, with our best wishes to you, your Lady, & family believe me your friend

Andrew Jackson

P.S. Miss Mary is in health, as is Mr McL. family, he is not returned but is daily expected—all friends well. A. J.

ALS, DLC (11-0880). Sent by Stockly Donelson.
 1. Not found.
 2. See above, Kremer to AJ, March 8, 1825.
 3. AJ had stated that Buchanan visited him in late January 1825; Buchanan, that it was late December 1824. Eaton wrote that the meeting with AJ took place not on December 30, 1824, as Buchanan recalled, but sometime during the week of January 15–22, 1825, about the same time that Clay's decision to support Adams became public (*Nashville Republican,* September 18).
 4. Either *Thomas D. Arnold's Review: To the Freemen of the Counties of Cocke, Sevier, Blount, Jefferson, Grainger, Claiborne, and Knox* (Knoxville, 1827) or *To the Freemen of the Counties of Cocke, Sevier, Blount, Jefferson, Grainger, Claiborne and Knox* (Knoxville, 1827), or both.
 5. On September 25, the Tennessee House of Representatives voted to consider granting Coffee a sword to honor his services during the Creek War and the New Orleans campaign but did not act further on the matter.
 6. AJ visited Florence, Alabama, in late October, returning to the Hermitage on November 6. On April 18 he had accepted the invitation to attend the January 8, 1828, celebration in New Orleans. Coffee did not accompany AJ to New Orleans.

To Richard Keith Call

Nashville Octbr. 2nd. 1827—

Dr. Genl

your letter to myself, & Mrs. Calls to Mrs. Jackson,[1] have been duly recd. We have been in this place of bustle for some days—The Legislature has Just convened, the examination at our university is going on, & its commencement is tomorrow—The various elections for speakers, of the senate & House of Representatives, and senator to congress, has excited some interest, all squinting to the presidential election—These with public dinners, weddings, &c &c, has, with my other concerns, busily occupied my time since the receipt of your last[2]—that the departure of our mutual friend Col [Richard C.] Allen[3] tomorrow Just whispered to me brings to my mind the propriety of answering your friendly letter by him, & seize a moment for that purpose.

The late minister to Gatamala, *Col Williams,* returned from his mission in time, to offer for state senator, & was elected; in the Canvass, he made a severe attack upon Judge White, came on to the Legislature, big with his *outfits,* to revolutionise every thing in favour of the administration—he was to be speaker of the senate; Col Brady, speaker of the House of Rep, with this influence, he was to oust White in the Senatorial election for the U. States senator. How he has succeeded in this *grand project,* the following concise narative will shew. Genl [William] Hall is speaker of the senate,[4] Doctor Camp is speaker of the House of Rep, Genl Brady getting only 13 votes[5] and Judge White Senator by a unanimous vote of all present[6]—it must follow as a matter of course that we will have peace in Israel for some time, and the Col has found that he has overated his own importance. He looks as much depressed in spirits as Mr Clay is said to have been on hearing of the result of the Kentucky elections—From every quarter the politi cal Horison looks clear & the signs of the times (as Joe Gales would say) are very ominous of the fate of the present dinasty.

For the further political news of this place, I refer you to our mutual friend Col. Allen, as I have not time to for further comment.

I sincerely regret that it will not be in your power to meet me at Orleans on the 8th. Janry next; Col Butler writes me[7] that the same causes that prevent you, will also prevent him from meeting me there—whilst I sincerely regret this disappointment in seeing you, still my Dear Genl, I applaud your course; you are a public officer & while such, your first duty is your countries, and you owe to her, & to yourself, first a faithfull performance of the duties assigned you, and all feelings of friendship ought to bend to duty[8]—I fear it will not be in my power to vissit Tallahassee from Neworleans—every floodgate of slander, as you must have seen, has been opened against me & Mrs. J. The War Department encourages, as far as it dare, some of them, and those official documents, within my own possession, are the only defence on which I can rely, as the *[office]* of the Department of war appears to have lost all necessary vouchers for my defence against the various calumnies fabricated by the panders of power, therefore, when I am absent these cannot be had, as I have no confidential person to leave them in charge.

Inclosed I send you the amount of the costs in the case of Mr Kirkman *will* and whilst I approve your honorable feelings that dictated your order of dismissal, still, if left to me, the Exetrs should have paid the costs, by setting aside the codicil.

What the lawyers will charge, if any thing, I cannot say—I have spoken to Mr Foster & Bell upon the subject, & lastly, put your letter into their hands requesting a dismissal & forwarding you the amount of costs—the inclosed is all furnished as yet.

Mrs. J. unites with me in our best wishes for the happiness of you, Mary & the sweet little daughter, Mrs. J. will write Mary shortly—your friend

Andrew Jackson

ALS, PHi (11-0886).
1. Neither letter found.
2. AJ attended the wedding of Washington Barrow to Ann M. Shelby, John Shelby's daughter, on September 27, a public dinner for Hugh L. White on October 1, and a meeting of the University of Nashville's trustees and the school's commencement on October 3.
3. Allen (d. 1841) was a Florida land surveyor and speculator.
4. Hall (1775–1856) was from Sumner County.
5. According to the *National Banner and Nashville Whig*, September 22, John H. Camp defeated William Brady for House speaker by twenty-six votes to eleven votes, not thirteen, as AJ reported.
6. Although there was some debate concerning the propriety of reelecting White two years before his current term expired, the state legislature did so unanimously on September 27.
7. Letter not found.
8. Call was receiver for the West Florida Land Office at this time, and Butler, surveyor.

From Duff Green

Washington 22nd. October 1827

Dear Sir

In the Telegraph of the 20th. I have convicted Mr Barbour of a participation in the infamous charge propagated by the Adams presses about the six militia men in which I have taken the liberty to suggest a visit to this city during the next session of Congress for the purpose of supplying that part of your official correspondence which has been withdrawn from the files[1]—It would be placing yourself under obligations to Mr Adams to petition him for the privilege of entering the department & you could not go there without a resolution of Congress or one branch of that body authorising You to do so without meeting Mr Barbour on terms unpleasant to you—Not so if the resolution authorises you to examine the records in that department.[2]

It is due to yourself, it is due to your friends & to your country, that your official correspondence be made perfect. for I am advised that Mr Monroe has been furnished with copies from the department preparatory to an attack which they intend to make and for which your correspondence with the Secretary of the Navy is to be made the pretext—

The fact that you cannot safely trust your Official correspondence with this administration is so intimately connected with the distrust of the people that the public sympathy will attend you where ever you go and the good sense of the people will sustain you in your appeal to Congress. I wish you to think well upon this subject. You can see all its bearings and I hope will visit us immediately after your return from New Orleans, whither the hearts of a grateful people will attend you.

Our prospects from the north are most flattering—We are now confident that you will recieve at least 30 votes in New York. A majority of the legislature of Maine are in your favor and the whole Republican Party of the north are preparing for an union upon you. I do not expect that you will get any votes in New England except in Maine, New Hampshire & perhaps a part of Vermont Yet such will be the strength of your friends as to silence all opposition to your administration and to enable you to take your measures with a sole eye to the public good uninfluenced by any dread of consequences—

We have had some little difficulty with Dewitt Clinton which I hope will pass off without injury.[3] Major Eaton's letter[4] is well received it is an able production highly creditable to him and gratifying to his friends. Judge Barry & our friends in Kentucky are doing well, and my advices from Ohio all concur in placing that state with the West. I have not heard the entire result of the local elections but hope much that our majority in both houses will enable us to select Jackson men as speakers for both houses.[5]

Pensylvania has done well, I have an extensive Correspondence in New Jersey Our friends claim that state, with an increased majority, and have no fears for the result. We are certain of 9 if not the entire vote of Maryland, and you have nothing to fear from Delaware—

Please to excuse this hasty scrall—& make my best wishes to Mrs Jackson & my friends Mr & Mrs. Donaldson. Say to my friend Lee that I have received his apologetic letter—& will attend to his request. your sincere friend

D Green

ALS, DLC (34).
1. Green published correspondence with the war department concerning AJ's orders in the fall of 1813 and Barbour's failure to produce the requested documents, claiming that they could not be found.
2. Instead of a congressional resolution authorizing AJ to search the records of the war department, the House authorized its Committee on Military Affairs to investigate AJ's orders and the execution of the six militiamen. The committee demanded and got the requested documents and issued its report on February 11, 1828, exonerating AJ on the six militiamen question.
3. At issue was the question of AJ's running mate—Clinton or Calhoun. On October 22, Green argued in the *Telegraph* that although Clinton had given public support to AJ, his friends in Congress had voted with the administration, and many pro-Clinton newspapers in New York also supported the administration. He warned that the equivocal stance of many of Clinton's supporters, coupled with the intention of some to make him vice president, "placed him so much in the same relation to Gen. Jackson that Mr. Clay held to Mr. Adams previous to the late election" that Jacksonians could not support Clinton for vice president.
4. Discussing Buchanan's account of his meeting with AJ previous to the election in 1825.
5. Jacksonians elected Andrew Stevenson (1784–1857) of Virginia Speaker of the House

in December, and Samuel Smith (1752–1857) of Maryland President Pro Tempore of the Senate in May 1828.

From Martin Van Buren

Private   City of New York Nov 4—1827
my dear General

You must excuse me if my anxiety to avoid any movement that may impair our present good prospects leads me to say what under different circumstances might seem officious. I see by the Telegraph that it is desired to bring you to Washington next winter[1] and my reading of the paper is confirmed by letters from the Editor of that paper to those of the Argus & Enquirer in this state. The reasons agt. such a step are manifold & to my mind conclusive. To that effect have our editors written to Genl. Green. I forbear to assign those reasons because I cannot but think that it will strike you as it has me. Should I be mistaken in this I would be happy to be heard before a decision upon the point is made.

You have doubtless seen the nomination of Gov Clinton in this State. At this distance from the scene of action I cannot with certainty define its object. It is either a small continuance from Washington under the auspices of Gnl Brown (who resided in that County (Jefferson) or it is a bonafide attempt on the part of the Govrs. friends to feel the public pulse or it is got up by them to give him an opportunity to obtain the merit of declining.[2] I have no evidence that Gov Clinton had any hand direct or indirect in the matter & I am perfectly satisfied that (unless it should take to an extent not to be anticipated) he cannot be so mad as to enter the field under existing circumstances. But come it from whence it may or be it persisted in as it may you may positively rely that it could do us no possible injury but on the contrary secure us *every district* in the state. The reason for this is very simple. The party that has heretofore supported Gov Clinton was composed of the old Federalists consisting of about eighty or ninety thousand electors & some portions of the old Republican Party that have from time seceded with prominent individuals. The present question has completely severed & destroyed their combined weight. About 7/8ths or perhaps nine tenths of them are warmly and virulently for Mr Adams on Federal & other grounds & the residue will go with us if Mr Clinton is not a candidate. Of Consequence if both ran we should have the entire democratic vote & their accustomed opponents would divide between Clinton & Adams, the larger portion going for the latter. Of the result of such a contest there cannot be the shadow of a doubt as we are able to carry the election as matters now stand in a larger majority of the districts by our own strength (that is what is called abroad Bucktail but is here the old Republican Party) & would fall but a few short in any of the districts. You & your friends therefore may dismiss from your minds the subject of this nomination all together & with perfect safety.

Our election commences tomorrow. In this City it will be unusually animated but we shall succeed here as we will throughout the state. My full belief is that we shall carry our Bucktail Jacksonian Senator in every district in the State. But one is in my judgment at all doubtfull. Of the assembly we shall elect three fourths certain & I believe more. Both parties have made their selections of candidates almost exclusively from what is known with you as the Bucktail party. This is produced by the decided ascendancy which that interest has obtained in the state & which is felt by all. But those who are seduced to go on the administration tickets are generally men who have been disappointed & are consequently disaffected and if not they loose their weight in the party from the moment of their seduction.

Of New Jersey it is impossible to speak with certainty. If no *horse race law* or other local question interferes our chance is I think the best, but the state is always an uncertain one. But happen what may in that quarter I am entirely confident that all that is necessary to make the election perfectly safe is that we be discreet.

Remember me kindly to Mrs. Jackson & Major Eaton & believe me to be Very sincerely your friend

M. V. Buren

ALS, DLC (11-0907). Published in Bassett, 3:383–84.
   1. See above, Duff Green to AJ, October 22.
   2. A convention in Steubenville, Jefferson County, Ohio, had nominated Clinton for president; he did not announce that the did not want the presidency until mid-November.

To Henry Lee

Saturday Novbr. 17th. 27—

Dr. Sir

your note[1] by Mr Saunders of this day has been recd.—by Doctor Hogg, I send you two Books containing the documents imbracing the Subjects of the Seminole campaign, Calava, & Judge [Eligius] Fromentine.[2] you have my memorial to congress,[3] & my reasons offered to the U States Court at Orleans, Shewing cause, why an attachment should not be Issued against me for contempt[4]—In which, you will find ample materials for a reply to the charges of chapman Johnston & Co.[5] I shall endeavour to Spend this evening with you, or tomorrow I am yrs respectfully

Andrew Jackson

I send you the enquirer[6] J

Photocopy of ALS, T (11-0924).

1. Not found.

2. Fromentin (d. 1822) was a Federal district judge for West Florida. For a discussion of the Callava–Fromentin affair, see *Jackson*, 5:93–101. AJ probably sent copies of the documents attached to the November 17, 1818, message of the president (*Annals of Congress*, 15th Cong., 2nd sess., pp. 2136–2278) and the January 28, 1822, report of the secretary of state on the Callava affair (*HRDoc* 42, 17th Cong., 1st sess., Serial 65).

3. Memorial to the U.S. Senate re conduct during the Florida invasion, [1819–20].

4. AJ to the United States District Court, Louisiana, [March 27, 1815], (*Jackson*, 3:321–36).

5. Johnson (1779–1849; William and Mary 1800) was a Virginia lawyer and a member of the state legislature. AJ was referring to the resolutions adopted by the Richmond anti-Jackson convention of October 24 detailing his alleged abuses of the law in New Orleans and in Florida. In the *Nashville Republican* of December 21, Lee, under the pseudonym "Jefferson," issued the first of two responses; the second came in March 1828. Subsequently, the two were printed as a campaign pamphlet: *A Vindication of the Character and Public Services of Andrew Jackson, in Reply to the Richmond Address, Signed by Chapman Johnson, and to Other Electioneering Calumnies* (Boston, 1828).

6. AJ probably sent Lee the October 26 *Richmond Enquirer*, containing the report of the October 24 meeting.

From Alfred Balch

26th. Nov 1827.

Dear General,

You will perceive from the enclosed what are the views of two intelligent men, residing more than a thousand miles from one another concerning your prospects.[1] Whilst the prospects are bright to the north—all the efforts of yr friends will be required in the south. The truth is many below hate our Government hence their hostility to you. There lies the secret. I have it from the very best & highest authority that orders have been issued from Washington to New Orleans—to spare no exertions to parry the effects of your intended visit. You may *rely* on this statement & act accordingly—Between ourselves, our *ex* Governor[2] I *know* has at last become convinced of what he might long since have known that he will get no living from this administration—This truth he has at last reluctantly acknowledged to me. You may Judge of his feelings & you may see them if he accompanies you.[3] It is said that he has influence below. In the Richmond Enquirer of the 13th. you will see a letter from a Gentleman about Govr Clinton. If you have not been otherwise informed, I can state that the substance of that letter is correct & if deemed necessary a similar assuran*[ce]* will be transmitted here from Govr C. for your eye in a few weeks—[4]

The contest grows warmer & war*[mer]* every hour & your friends are on the alert in every direction. If they fail it will not be for want of skill or courage. Of course you will be absent on your journey[5] as short a time as possible consistently with your objects. Events are happening so rapidly that you may be wanting at your own head quarters to meet emergencies. Yr friends in Congress would be glad, if you could return by the early part of February at Farthest yr friend

A Balch.

ALS, DLC (35).
1. William Lord Robeson to Balch, November 11, discussing Louisiana, and William T. Barry to Balch, November 19, discussing Kentucky (DLC-34, -35).
2. William Carroll.
3. Carroll had supported Clay in the 1824 presidential election. He accompanied AJ to New Orleans for the January 8, 1828, celebration.
4. The *Enquirer* reported that Clinton "would not consent that his name should be used as a candidate in opposition to that of Gen. Jackson."
5. Balch referred to Jackson's impending trip to New Orleans, which lasted from December 27, 1827, to January 26, 1828.

To Andrew Jackson, Jr.

Hermitage Novbr. 27th. 1827—

My son
I have recd your kind letter,[1] & send you the air gun requested—The Book I cannot find, but as you will be up on friday, you can get it.[2]

The ideas you have expressed relative to the benefits resulting from education are proper, & the first pride of my heart that you possess them and it is only by practising on the principles you have laid down that you can attain a proper standing in society & be ranked amongst its ornaments. Youth is the only time to acquire knowledge, that will be useful in the meridian of life, and enable you to fulfil the duties through life with honor to yourself & usefulness to that society with whom you may be placed—Having discovered the great benefit resulting from education, your application will be redoubled to obtain it, & you are sure to succeed. you are still young, and having formed those correct ideas expressed in your letter I have no fears but you will become eminent. I have again to recommend that you spend all your time you can spare to composition & elocution; to become eminent in both requires much study & practice—To become an orator, or handsome speaker, you must practice much, it is this alone that will give you a good attitude & graceful delivery, writing is mecanicle, & to become a good compositor requires much practice & study—Having formed a proper ambition to excell, you will succeed—& that you should excell, is the first wishes of my heart—you shall have all opportunities that I can afford you.

say to my child Hutchings, for being bequeathed to my direction by his fathers will,[3] I view him so, how much anxiety I have about him fearful he may do something that may disgrace him, or lessen his respectability in society—say to him he is no more in the years of boyhood, but approaching that of man hood, that it behoves him to assume that upright & dignified conduct of a man, & to abandon all boyish tricks—That instead of idling away his time on foolish conduct, he ought to apply himself diligently to his studies with a view to excell his fellows, in education & correct demeanor—It is by this course alone he can become respectable in society & useful to himself, & country—Let him reflect on his fathers last injunctions to me—oh said he, bring my child up with good morals, learn him in his youth the value of honesty, & a go[o]d ch[arac]ter, [& often] bring to his mind the value [of a g]ood education, accompanie[d] with religion morality, & sobriety of conduct—tell him often, how I have regretted the want of education & how much I wish him to possess one—how it would harry up his fathers feeling in the dust, if he was [to] do any act to disgrace himse[lf] & produce his expulsion—Let him read this letter, & say to him I hope he will conform his conduct to the admonition it contains.[4] say to Hutchings I will send for him & you on friday I am My dear son yours affectionately

Andrew Jackson

P.S. I write in haste & with candle light—& cannot see well, & have no time to correct—A. J.

ALS, DLC (35).
    1. Not found.
    2. Andrew Jackson, Jr., was attending the University of Nashville.
    3. Will of John Hutchings, November 7, 1817.
    4. Andrew J. Hutchings, also attending the University of Nashville, was suspended for bad conduct from the school in March 1828. He was reinstated for the summer and following session but was again dismissed later in 1828.

From John Branch

Senate Chamber
Dec. 11th. 1827

My Dear Sir,

I have this moment been informed by Maj. Eaton that a safe opportunity is afforded to write to you as freely as I think.

Permit me then to say that the Republic is safe, and that in regard to the Coalition that their days are numbered & their destiny fixed. *Tekel tekel mene Tekel* is inscribed on the wall in such legible characters that he who runs may read[1]

The election of Stephenson D. Green etc etc speaks a language that cannot be misunderstood.[2]

All that we have to do is to act calmly & dispassionately and to adjourn as soon as a proper regard to the public interest will permit. Some of our friends are aspiring, particularly those who formerly espoused the cause of Calhoun and Crawford and there is some danger that unpleasant feelings & jealousies may be excited.[3] But Sir nothing can arrest the progress of public sentiment, and *some of our friends* are whipd into the ranks under a full conviction of this truth. This is however inter nos.

Present me in the most polite and friendly terms to Mrs. Jackson and accept for yourself my undiminished confidence & esteem. Adieu

Jno Branch

ALS, DLC (35). Published in Bassett, 3:385.
　　1. A paraphrase of "Mene, Mene, Tekel, Upharsin," Daniel 5:25. In using the phrase regarding the writing on the wall that Daniel had translated for the Babylonian king, Branch was suggesting that the prospects for the Adams-Clay coalition were doomed.
　　2. When the Twentieth Congress assembled on December 3, the Jacksonian majority elected Andrew Stevenson Speaker of the House, and the Senate elected Duff Green printer on December 4.
　　3. Some Jacksonians wanted Calhoun's name dropped from the ticket as the vice presidential candidate.

To *William Berkeley Lewis*

Decbr. 19th. 1827

Dr Major

Yours of yesterday is this moment recd.,[1] Mr Earle did not reach me last evening.

I shall not be down untill I leave home for N. Orleans. I will be happy to see you & Mr [John F.] Clay[2] at the Hermitage on any day it may be convenient for you to visit me.

I shall leave to you all arrangements for the Journey, & for our passage & supplies—My *health is not good,* however, I complain not, because I know, it would be grateful to my enemies, & I hope with care it may be restored—

I rejoice to hear that Mr. S. is appointed speaker. It is evidence at least that congress has some respect for itself, by placing a man of good morals over it yr friend

Andrew Jackson

ALS, NNPM (11-0967).
　　1. Letter not found.
　　2. Clay was a horse trainer and owner in Davidson County.

To John Coffee

Hermitage Decbr. 22nd. 1827—

Dear Genl

I have recd your letter of the 16th. instant,[1] & whilst I sincerely regret the misfortune, which will create great labour & anxiety to you, still, I can see no so[urce] for apprehension on your part, of any blame or censure that can attach to you or your clerks—The precaution you have taken in forwarding affidavits to the commissioner of the land office, shewing the transaction, as i[t] happened, was certainly proper, & will close the door against misrepresentations, should it be attempted—But your charecter, & that of Mr [James Harvey] Weakly, and your other clerks, stand too fair to be injured by those individuals around you, who would be base anough wilfully to misrepresent[2]

I would recommend you, to commit to record, all the transactions relative to the Cypress land company that can be recollected—The bonds destroyed, &c &c, call upon all to renew them, & on failure to comply, to bring suit to recover the amount due, this will be the only safe course for the commissioners, and the only one that can bring the business to a speedy close.[3]

your survayors business will occasion the Goverment (not you) some expence, as I suppose it will be their duty to send you on duplicates of all survays made & not ordered for sale, or un[so]ld unless these are in the Registers office The Govrt., must be at the expence of clerk here, to have them copied for your office—On the subject of all expence to be incurred in this way, I would recomm[en]d you to write to the commissioner of the land office & have his instructions.

I sincerely regret this occurrence, as it will necessarily prevent me the pleasure of your company to Neworleans—but you cannot—ought not, to leave home *now*—your whole attention must be draw[n] to the duties of your office as survayor, & to close the business of the Cypress land company—The latter will be most apt to produce dificulty—your survayors office can produce to you no real injury, in any way except the labour that it may produce to you—but the other may, without great care and attention—as there may be some unprincipled men concerned, that may delight in perplexing the commissioners, *now,* when all the papers are destroyed.

I am pleased that Phillips is gone—I was uneasy that he was there, when I found he was without honest principles, from the statement of Mr Easton[4]—I hope [George J.] Jourdan will turn out better[5]—I would like that the whole of the cotton should be got to markett and out of the way of the farm as soon as possible;[6] I think that cotton must take a rise in the spring—I have made but 48 Bales weighing 24,300 <ginned> Baled from 130 acres, last year from 120 acres I sent to markett 56,000 Baled[7] & my present crops is equal to any of my neighbours—I am compelled to sell or I should hold on until april or may—it must *rise*.

I shall leave Nashville in all next week, perhaps the 29 or 30th. instant—I dread the season but it is too late to recede.

We hope your Dear little Rachel has recovered from her attack—We salute you all Kindly, & believe me yr friend

Andrew Jackson

ALS, THi (11-0974). Published in Bassett, 3:385–86 (extract).

1. Not found.

2. On December 14, fire destroyed the building in Florence in which Coffee housed the records of the Alabama land office and of the Cypress Land Company. Weakley (1798–1856), later surveyor general for Alabama, was at this time Coffee's chief assistant in the surveyor's office.

3. Founded by Coffee, James Jackson, and AJ, among others, during the boom of 1818, the Cypress Land Company laid out the town of Florence. Having sold much of its land on credit, the Panic of 1819 thoroughly deranged the company's affairs, spawning a series of court cases, many of which rested on records that the fire had destroyed. But as it turned out, copies and duplicates of documents for some of the most complex cases were already in the hands of lawyers or of the founders. The company finally wound up its affairs in 1851.

4. William Eastin had reported to AJ questionable financial practices in Phillips's management of the Hutchings's Alabama farm, and he had been fired.

5. Jordan was overseer until at least 1831.

6. For the sale of Andrew J. Hutchings's cotton, see Maunsel White to AJ, January 26, 1828. AJ took his own crop with him to New Orleans on the *Pocahontas*.

7. AJ mistakenly wrote 56,000 for 36,000.

1828

On December 27, 1827, Jackson departed Nashville for New Orleans to celebrate the thirteenth anniversary of the Battle of New Orleans. He traveled aboard the steamboat Pocahontas, chartered for him by citizens of the city, and enjoyed the company of a large entourage of family, friends, and political supporters from throughout the Union.

Eight days later, on January 4, 1828, the boat docked at Natchez, and that afternoon and evening, the citizens hosted a dinner and a ball in his honor. On the following morning, the entourage left, having been joined by a delegation from New Orleans.

On January 8, the Pocahontas arrived at New Orleans, where a flotilla of steamboats with veterans of the War of 1812, delegations from other states, and citizens of Louisiana met it and escorted it to Chalmette, site of the January 8 battle, down river from the city. There, troops fired a hundred-gun salute and Jackson and the state delegations exchanged greetings. From Chalmette, the party returned to New Orleans to attend the theater and a public dinner. The festivities continued until Jackson left shortly after midnight on January 12, stopping at the plantation of Samuel McCutchon (1773–1840) to recuperate before his final departure on January 14.

Jackson's response to the welcome from the New York delegation appears below.

To James Alexander Hamilton, Saul Alley, and Thaddeus Phelps

[January 8, 1828]

Gentlemen:

The congratulations of my fellow-citizens of the city and county of New York, presented here, and on the return of this day, accompanied with such unqualified assurances of their confidence and favor, fill me with no ordinary emotions.[1] Sensible only of having discharged the duties allotted to me, as a citizen of our common country, with an honest zeal to preserve and advance its prosperity, I was not prepared for the flattering distinction which you have conferred upon my exertions. I receive it as an evidence of the liberality and kindness of those who have authorized you to express it,

· 407 ·

and who, because Providence assigned me an instrumentality in the glorious struggle of the Republic, are pleased to number me amongst its benefactors. I am more than compensated for my services, Gentlemen, in being allowed to accept the tokens you present, of the approbation of so numerous and patriotic a portion of my fellow-citizens. This is the highest reward to which a citizen can aspire under our government, where by the spirit of its constitution, the people control its operations, and are devoted to its service. I pray you, therefore, to assure your constituents of the high gratification your salutation has afforded me, and that I shall ever retain a grateful recollection of the signal mark of their regard.

It is true, Gentlemen, that this fair portion of the West was rescued from the grasp of a foreign foe, by the assumption of power, on my part, at variance with the regular operation of our sacred constitution and laws; and you have done justice to the necessity which dictated it. Acting upon the principles that the safety of the people is the supreme law, and that it was better they should attempt a glorious deliverance from the dangers which threatened them, by a suspension of their invaluable rights, than contend for their *shadow* amidst the arms of the enemy, and thereby sacrifice the substance forever; I shrunk not from the responsibility which the crisis devolved on me. Had I done otherwise I should have thought myself a traitor to my country.[2]

I receive with gratitude, the high estimate, which as individuals, you, Gentlemen, are pleased to give to my official conduct. That our government was constituted for the happiness of the people and that its offices are the instruments of their will and created for their welfare, are maxims which I learned from the fathers of our revolution. I am now too old to depart from them. They spring from the same source with the great principle which cannot be too solemnly impressed upon the attention of the American people. It is the channel of sovreignty, through which their renovating influence is conveyed to every department of the government, and the weak points in the system detected and fortified, so as to contribute to the defence of liberty. That you should consider my humble example as in any degree illustrating the value of this principle is an honor which I shall ever prize.[3]

This medal commemorating the completion of the Erie canal, and the resolutions refering to it, are received with feelings of peculiar satisfaction.[4] A work displaying in such an eminent degree the resources of your state, gives to the councils from which it eminated, and by which it was prosecuted a claim to lasting recollection. It presents to her sister states a model of improvement worthy of their imitation, and deserves to be celebrated by the fine arts.

The kind manner, Gentlemen, in which you have performed the duties confided to you on this occasion, has impressed me with the most lively sentiment of affection and regard; of which I beg you to be assured, with the offer of my sincere prayers, that you may be safely restored to the bosoms of your families and friends.

Printed, Natchez *Statesman & Gazette,* January 24 (mAJs, 11-1025). AD drafts and Copies, DLC (33; 11-1028, -1031, -1035). Hamilton, Alley, and Phelps were the delegates from New York's Tammany Society: Hamilton (1788–1878; Columbia 1805) was a lawyer and the third son of former treasury secretary Alexander Hamilton; Phelps (c1784–1847) and Alley (c1777–1852), a state legislator, were merchants.

1. See Hamilton, Alley, and Phelps to AJ, January 8.

2. AJ was responding to Hamilton's brief remarks concerning AJ's imposition of martial law in New Orleans.

3. AJ was replying to Hamilton's commendation of AJ for "resigning the various civil and military offices conferred upon you whenever in your judgment the public interest did not imperiously demand your services." In one draft of his address, AJ at this point endorsed the concept of "rotation in office," though he did not use the phrase in the final version (11-1031).

4. On behalf of the New York City Common Council, Hamilton had presented AJ with a medal commemorating the completion of the Erie Canal and a copy of Cadwallader David Colden's *Memoir Prepared at the Request of a Committee of the Common Council . . . and Presented . . . at the Celebration of the Completion of the New York Canals* (New York, 1825).

To Edward Livingston

(Private)

Captain McCutchings
Janry 12th. 1828

Dr Sir

Having a moments leisure after my visit to orleans, I employ it in writing you—I shall not attempt to give a description of the good feelings with which I was saluted by the citizens of orleans, & my old compatriots in arms, believing you will receive it from more able pens; all I have time to say at present, is, that I am truly gratified with my visit. It inspired me with emotions more easily conceived than expressed—The splendour of the scene of the Steam Boats, the waving of the various flags from the shipping, & else where, the cheering of the citizens on the plains where we met the enemy & saved the City, were well calculated to inspire feelings inexpressible; all I regretted that you were not with us, and that your letter, containing your sentiment, did not reach orleans untill the 9th, but I am informed by Major Davezac, who read it to me, that it will appear with the proceedings.[1]

Major Davezac informs me, that from a letter recd from Mrs. Livingston, you have not recd my letters—I have answered promptly, all your letters that came to hand, but the last This you wrote me from the city, after the election of the Speaker of the house of Representatives, which I recd on my passage to Neworleans[2]—I sincerely regret that my letters have not reached you, as it appears, Mrs. Livingston is fearful, that I have heard something, that has weakened my friendship for you—be assured, this is not the fact; I only write to my friends & in answer to their letters, having long since known that there were a system of espoionage introduced in some lines of the post, equal to that during the war in France, therefore, I trust nothing to the post office, that I would fear for the whole world to Know.

At the request of an old soldier who states his claims upon our goverment, I inclose his statement to you,[3] knowing with what pleasure you will procure him aid if you can—I do this more to gratify him than under a hope that you can obtain, any relief for him, but on his solicitation, I could not forbear forwarding it to you.

When a Leisure moment occurs I will be happy to have a line from you—It gives me pleasure to find your popularity has greatly increased in Louisiana, whilst your Colleagues has Sunk, you will find this, from the public expression of the Citizen almost every where. I refer to the paper

Mrs. J. unites with me, in the most affectionate regard, to you, your Lady, & amiable daughter, with our best wishes for your happiness, and believe me yr friend

Andrew Jackson

P.S. I write in great haste, & as it is *for your own eye,* you will pardon all incorrectness A. J.

ALS, NjP (mAJs). Published in Bassett, 3:388–89 (11-1056).
1. Livingston was in Washington for the First Session of the Twentieth Congress. His toast was published with the account of AJ's visit: "Louisiana—the only State that has received the thanks of the confederacy—she deserved them by her energy and attachment to our republican institutions—she will shew her gratitude to the hero who led her brave citizens to the attainment of this proud distinction" (*Mobile Daily Register,* January 24).
2. Only Livingston to AJ, May 21 and November 11, and AJ to Livingston, December 6, all 1827, have been found.
3. Not identified.

By 1827, the presidential campaign was conducted not only at the state, county, city, and precinct levels but in the halls of Congress as well. In the letter below, Robert Desha (1791–1849), a veteran of the War of 1812 and member of the House of Representatives Committee on Military Affairs from Sumner County, Tennessee, informed Jackson of the efforts of his opponents to influence the outcome of the forthcoming election by publishing documents relating to the execution of the six militiamen, a longstanding issue in the campaign.

For some time, Jacksonian partisans had been clamoring for the release of all the documents relating to the executions in the war department files, but the secretary of war claimed that several letters could not be located. But on January 11, John Sloane (1779–1856), an Adams supporter from Ohio, introduced resolutions calling for the secretary of war to lay before the House the documents relating to the matter. Following the adoption of his resolution on January 16, the war department submitted all the requested documents to the House Committee on Military Affairs, including those earlier reported missing. The submission, however, was in a numbered, not chronological, sequence, an arrangement unfavorable to Jackson.

On February 11, the House committee, with a Jacksonian majority and chaired by James Hamilton, Jr., of South Carolina, issued its report favorable to Jackson. Considerable debate over the printing of the report and documents ensued on the House floor, with the Adams Republicans insisting that, if printed, the documents be arranged in the order they were numbered and received from the war department, and the Jacksonians, demanding that the documents be printed chronologically. The two factions eventually compromised, both agreeing to the printing of the report with the documents attached, printed chronologically, but retaining the sequence numbering assigned by the war department. Jacksonians gave the committee Report . . . on Correspondence and Documents from the War Department in Relation to . . . the Trial of Certain Militiamen (HRep 140, 20th Cong. 1st sess.) *widespread circulation during the remainder of the campaign.*

But the Adams partisans were not to be outdone. Shortly, Sloane published his View of the Report of the Committee on Military Affairs *(Washington, 1828), and Adams presses issued their numbered account as the* Official Record from the War Department, of the Proceedings of the Court Martial, which Tried, and the Orders of General Jackson, for Shooting the Six Militia Men, Together with Official Letters from the War Department (Ordered to Be Printed by Congress), Showing that These American Citizens were Inhumanly & Illegally Massacred *(Washington, 1828). Adams partisans gave these, too, widespread circulation.*

From Robert Desha

Washington Jany 21st 1828

Dear Genl.

You will have seen ere this reaches you H. Clays Book[1]—and the letter of the unprincipled fellow, Brent of Louisiana,[2] and also the toast that was drank at the Dinner in this place, at the Celebration of the 8th Jany— offered by myself when this letter made its appearance in Clays Book[3]—I did not feel myself Justifiable nor did your friends here (who are numerous) that I should—act differently—My object was, as expressd frequently—to *insult him*—and contend, as does your friends, that as your personal as well as political friend, I had a right if I thought proper to thro. the language he applies to you in his own teeth—You will see in the public prints how he gets off—Public Sentiment appears to have settled down to his disgrace here—and will I have no doubt throughout the U States—[4]

You are advised before this reaches you of the Resolution introduced by Slone of Ohio—calling on the Sect. of war to furnish the house with all the information in his office touching the court martial convened for the trial of the Six Militiamen and the executions &c. If you have any papers in your possession which would thro. light upon this subject would it not be well to forward them to some of your friends here.[5] This enquiry at this time proves clearly that it is for Political purposes, and not for the interest of the Nation—

I recd. a few days—ago a letter from Capt. [Jesse] Haney requesting that I should try to get Your young horse—for the races next fall—If you have not disposed of him—I would be glad to get him—and will have him trained at my own expense.[6] The Capt and myself will have there five three year old Colts but we want one four year old for the races next fall—Yours I think a fine horse if he has a fair chance—Your Friend

Robt Desha

PS—your friends here are fine, and cant be opperated on by Clay who you know is a great intriguer—Write me if you have leisure we are anxiously looking for the proceedings at New Orleans—on the 8th Jay—

ALS, DLC (35).

1. Henry Clay had just published his *Address . . . to the Public; Containing Certain Testimony in Refutation of the Charges Against Him, Made by Gen. Andrew Jackson, Touching the Last Presidential Election* (Washington, 1827). AJ saw the Clay publication about January 24.

2. Brent's June 4, 1827, letter to Tobias Watkins, calling AJ's claims on the corrupt bargain "the fabrication of a desperate man, who, to obtain his object, dares to assert what he knows to be false," appeared in Clay's *Address,* p. 47–48.

3. Desha's toast was to "*Edward Livingston, of Louisiana.* The first and only *Honor* in the Louisiana political *pack:* though beaten in the presidential game, by the KNAVE from that State, he shall shine conspicuous, while the KNAVE 'will stand before the world, as a proven base calumniator, unworthy of public or private confidence, and avoided by every man who has a respect for virtue and honor'" (*United States' Telegraph,* January 12). Livingston had voted for AJ in the 1825 presidential election in the House, but Brent and Henry H. Gurley, his colleagues from Louisiana, had voted for Adams, giving him the state's vote.

4. In response to Desha's toast, Brent wrote that "it never was my intention . . . to wound the feelings of any of Gen. Jackson's friends." He then pronounced Desha's toast as "dishonorable, and at war with every gentlemanly feeling." Desha replied, implying that Brent was merely trying to avoid his obligation to challenge him (*National Journal,* January 15; Washington *United States' Telegraph,* January 16).

5. AJ did indeed send documents relating to the six militiamen to James K. Polk, March 23, and to John H. Eaton, March 28.

6. Haynie (c1769–1842) was a Sumner County horse breeder whose mare, Maria, had beaten AJ's horses repeatedly between 1811 and 1815. Desha was probably referring to Bolivar, which AJ did not sell. Haynie, however, trained him in the fall of 1828 (*Nashville Republican,* March 5, 1830).

To William Robinson

Hermitage Febry 3rd. 1828—

Dr Sir

your favour from Oak grove of the 7th. ult[1] was received at Nashville after my return from Neworleans, and it afforded me much pleasure to be informed by your communication, that notwithstanding all the vile calumnies my enemies heaped upon Mrs J. & myself we are still held in the estimation of a majority of the good people of Virginia—Their approbation amidst the mass of misrepresentation & calumny employed against me is doubly cheering.

I feel grateful for the kind expressions of your regard for Mrs. J and myself—We enjoy good health, and are gratified to learn that your family have been blessed with this greatest of gifts. We saw your niece & nephew Mrs. & Mr. Butler in Orleans, and request with our kind salutations to Mrs & Mr Lewis, to say to them, the excursion seemed to be of service to their daughters spirits,[2] and no doubt will enable her to visit them with her health fully restored.

Major & Mrs. Lee[3] are living with a neighbour of mine. Mrs. Lee has not enjoyed good health at times her mind appears somewhat deranged, she cannot be persuaded to visit her kind neighbours & mix in company, her health lately is believed to be better and I hope she may regain her spirits & with it her health will be restored.

I do not think it very strange that Sec. Clay, & Mr. [Tobias] Watkins[4] "appear honored by each others confidence," birds of a feather, says the old adage, flock together, their interest & feelings are the same, they are both labouring in the same cause, that is, to keep themselves in office & in power, and only think of the means that will ensure the end, regardless of either tru*[th]* or Justice as relates to those who may oppose their views, or stand in the way of their ambition.

Mrs. J Joins me in respectful compliments to you, with our best wishes for your health & happiness, believe me yr friend.

Andrew Jackson

ALS, CU-BANC (11-1091).
1. Letter not found. Oak Grove is a town on Mattox Creek in Westmoreland County, Virginia.
2. Frances P. L. Butler had lost her first son, Edward G. W., Jr., the previous year.
3. Ann Lee was Robinson's niece.
4. Watkins (1780–1855; St. John's 1798), a physician, linguist, fourth auditor of the treasury, and writer for the *National Journal,* had gathered much of the material that went into Henry Clay's *Address . . . to the Public.* In 1829 AJ dismissed him from office, and soon thereafter the administration successfully prosecuted him for embezzlement.

From John Coffee

Coxes Creek near Florence
6th. Feby. 1828.

Dear Genl.

By the newspapers from Nashville I see that you and Mrs. Jackson has reached home in safety and health,[1] for which I rejoice, as I was under some dread that some accident might happen you, and thereby deprive the nation of your future service, as well as the loss to your numerous friends and your family; But I hope and trust that you are under the guidance of a kind providence that will sustain you many years for the benefit of mankind, and to enjoy your later days in peace and tranquility, beyond the reach of base slanderers, and rotten hearted politicians—

I had expected that your reception at New Orleans would be marked with strong expressions of gratitude, by the Citizens of that Country, but it has so far exceeded my most sanguine expectations, that I only wonder how those people can feel composed towards their representation who so basely represented them at the last election for P. but it will not be so again, they will surely keep an eye to their public servants in future and hurl them from Office the moment they depart from their duty—It has been extremely gratifying to your real friends, that Louisiana seems awakened to a proper sense of their duty and sees her own interest. Your reception at New Orleans will add much strength to your cause in other states, when it is seen that the people that were with you, in the most trying scenes of peril and danger, and at the moment you had to adopt the strong measures (that your enemies lay hold of to weaken you) you did for their safety—when it is seen that those same people hail you as their saviour, and ascribe all honor and praise to you that can be allotted to any mortal man, it will open the eyes of the lukewarm and such as are too careless to investigate any subject untill it burst upon them as this transaction has done—the dye is cast, and the present rulers see it, And hence the course of policy lastly adopted, to endeavour by stratagem to arouse your passions & get you to notice them in some way, in any way, they care not how, all they wish is to get in collission with you, they have all to gain & nothing to lose, and you all to lose and nothing to gain— therefore I hope and trust that you will be and remain yourself, that you will not notice them, nor any of them, in any manner, or way whatever— this is the earnest wish of all your real friends, and I hope it meets with your views also. I see Mr. Sloane's resolution calling for the papers & documents of the six Militia Men has passed—I have no doubt but if any thing amongst them in your favour, which can be, *will* be suppressed. therefore would it, not be well to place in Major Eatons hands, copies of all the documents in your reach that will tend to throw any light on the subject. I presume no harm can arise if all is brought forth, but by keeping back some, they may disfigure the transaction in some way, and shew it to your prejudice—

We have had but few days without rain this year, consequently not much done on farms. this day week I was at A J. H. farm, I am well pleased with the movements of Jordan, he appears steady and attentive, and things begin to look better than when he went there, he has to repair much of the fences before he can make a crop, and to run a cross fence through the farm to seperate his oats from his corn land, to enable him to pasture the stubble, and he is taking out some of the dead timber in the cleared land, particularly out of the last two years clearings. he has built a very good stable two pens and a passage, this is the first stable that was ever built on the place. I have advised him not to cl[ear more] land untill he gets his fences made, least the s[torms] should continue bad and make him too backward in planting his crop—I have purchased for the place four mules—I sent Winburn to Maury County, and bout three mules of two years old each, and one that is three years old, the whole cost $220. making an average of $55. for them all round,[2] they are good young mules, and will supply the place with a sufficiency of work horses for the present—and from the two young Mares they can raise mules in future to keep up the farm without any further purchase of horses—I shiped the Crop of Cotton to Maunsel White in time to be there before you reached New Orleans. I instructed him to ask advice of you when you reached there, and to pay over the proceeds to you if he should sell while you were there. I expect he mentioned it to you—I made out the accounts of A. J. H. and entered them on the books on my return home as I promised you I would do and there is yet in my hands after paying for the mules, $1133. which the vouchers will shew—[3]

Our family enjoy good health, Mrs. Coffee unites with me in a tender of respects to Mrs. Jackson & yourself—Dr. Genl. yours—

Jno Coffee

ALS, THi (11-1098).
   1. The Jacksons had reached Nashville on January 26.
   2. For the purchases, see receipts from Jesse Winborne, January 14, and from John W. Byrn, January 15.
   3. On the sale of Andrew J. Hutchings's cotton, see Maunsel White to AJ, January 26.

To *Samuel Houston*

Hermitage Febry 13th. 1828

Dr Sir

The letters & inclosures from Mr Beverly forwarded under cover to you have been recd.[1]—The are returned to you again, with the request, that you return them to Mr Beverly with this remark. That he surely [*ca*]nnot expect me to become the organ [*thr*]o whom, the eclarcisements of his disputes [*w*]ith any one, is to be made—our acq[*uain*]tance is too limited to authorise such a request, (only having seen him once when he called at my house as a stranger, to visit me[)]. This limited acquaintance, is not such as to Justify such a request—you may add, that I have nothing to do with Major Lee, or his writings. The Major, when he writes, is like all others, responsible for it, & to him directly, & not through me, he must appeal—That I never saw, nor do I k[*now*] untill it was in print the peace signed Jefferson, & whether Major Lee is the author or not, he must apply to others, & not me, to obtain this information[2]—I shall have nothing, in any way, to do with it.[3] I am respectfully your friend

Andrew Jackson

Photocopy of ALS, Tx (11-1113).
1. In the packet sent to Houston, Beverley had enclosed his letter of January 20 to AJ and letters to Henry Lee and to Allen A. Hall and John Fitzgerald (not found) of the *Nashville Republican*, detailing his umbrage at Lee over comments regarding the corrupt bargain charge in the piece "Jefferson" in the December 21, 1827, *Republican*.
2. AJ had furnished Lee with documents and materials for the Jefferson essay, as revealed in his letter above to Lee, November 17, 1827.
3. In accordance with AJ's instructions, Houston returned the letters to Beverley on February 18 (*Writings of Sam Houston*, 1:122–23).

To *George Washington Campbell*

Hermitage Febry 14th 1828—

My Dr Sir

I have Just recd. the letter you had the goodness to write me by Mr Donelson on the 12th. instant, with enclosures,[1] for which I thank you.

The reply you have made Mr. [John] M[ontgomery] is such as I approve, & which I would, had I been present, requested you to have made[2]—Indeed, under existing circumstances, delicacy & propriety would admit of no other. My real friends want no information from me on the subject of internal improvements, & manufactories, but what my public acts has afforded, & I never gratify my enemies—was I now to come forth, and reiterate my political opinions on these subjects, I would be charged with electioneering views for selfish purposes: I cannot do any act that may give rise to such imputations.

Plans have been formed by my enemies, resolutions written & forwarded by men calling themselves a committee appointed for that purpose, to inveigle me into a reply, but still, I could not be got out, because my opinions were before the public, and I was convinced, my friends could not wish me to reiterate my opinions, for surely, no honest man having the good of his country at heart, believing that I would change my opinions for selfish views, could support me, and I was determined not to furnish food for my enemies to annoy me with.[3]

I thank you kindly for the trouble you have taken, I return you inclosed Mr Montgomeries letter.

Mrs. J. Joins me in kind salutations to you, your Lady, Miss Stodard[4] & family and beg leave to remind you of your promise—we will be happy to see you at the Hermitage. With high consideration and respect I am your friend.

Andrew Jackson

ALS, NjMoHP (11-1115). Published in Bassett, 3:390–91 (extract). Campbell (1769–1848; Princeton 1794) had served as a representative and senator from Tennessee, state supreme court justice, United States secretary of the treasury, and minister to Russia.

1. In his letter of February 12, Campbell had sent an extract of his letter to John Montgomery.

2. Montgomery (1765–1828), a brother-in-law of Albert Gallatin and former congressman from Maryland, was mayor of Baltimore, 1820–26. In his reply, Campbell had referred Montgomery to AJ's votes on the tariff and internal improvements in the Senate and to AJ's 1824 letter to Littleton II. Coleman (*Jackson*, 5:398–400).

3. See, for example, George McCook to AJ, January 4, and James B. Ray to AJ, January 30. AJ's February 28 reply to Ray virtually reiterated what Campbell had written.

4. "Miss Stodard" was presumably a relative of George W.'s wife, Harriet Campbell (1789–1849), née Stoddert.

To Wilson Lumpkin

(private)   Hermitage Febry 15th 1828
Dr. Sir

My absence on a visit to Neworleans where I had been invited by the Legislature of the State of Louisia, to be present at the celebra[tion] of the 8th of January last, prevented me from receiving your kind letter of the 1rst. ult.[1] untill a few days past—for this mark of your attention I make you [a] tender of my thanks.

I have read with much pleasure the address to your constituents,[2] which you did me the honor to enclose, and particularly, that part of it, which relates to the Indian tribes. The present situation of those east of the Mississippi require the immediate attention of Congress; I am sure, they cannot be long fostered and preserved where they now are—They can only be perpetuated as tribes, or nations, by concentrating them west of the Mississippi upon lands secured to them, forever, by the united States, where its homanity, & liberal protecting care, can be extended to them; and where they can be shielded from the encroachments of the whites, without violation to state rights, or the rights of citizens; where only they can prosper, & be perpetuated—as a nation—I am happy that this subject has been taken up by Congress,[3] & I am pleased to find you are on this committee.

The friendly Sentiments convayed in your letter, I shall ever cherish with grateful recollection

Wishing you health & happiness, and a pleasant session, believe me very respectfully Your mo. obdt. Servt.

Andrew Jackson

ALS, Gilder Lehrman Collection, NNPM (mAJs). Lumpkin (1783–1870), representative from Georgia, was a member of the Committee on Indian Affairs.
1. Not found.
2. Not found.
3. On December 13, 1827, Lumpkin had introduced a resolution in the House directing the Indian affairs committee to inquire into the expediency of removing all the various tribes of Indians within the states or territories of the United States to an "eligible situation" west of the Mississippi River.

To John Coffee

[cFebruary 20–24, 1828]

Dr. Genl.

I have received your letter of 6th. instant,[1] and rejoice to find that you & family enjoy health—ours were very good, when we returned home; Mrs. J. is still good, but mine, has been a little impaired, by hard & close labour, & confinement, still, I trust providence will spare me untill my enemies are prostrate. Truth is beginning to shine forth, and it will soon display the association of corruption, in all its deformity—The Testimony before the senate in Kentucky, has *pinned* to the letters of Clay himself, to Mr Blair, *that if Adams was elected, Clay, would be sec of State*; & Blair solicited Kendal to write to White to vote for Adams, *as it was assertained, if elected, Clay would be sec of State*—I refer you to the Ky Argus for details.[2] Thus the light begins to shine—I[t i]s hinted from Washington that $70,000 has been used out of the contingent funds, & only $20,000 of which there is the least semblance of vouchers for—The Ballance I suppose as I have thought throut the year was distributed at the Ky elections & elsewhere & paid for published calumnious pampht.

against Mrs. J. & myself—A confidential letter from a member of congress says, that it is said, there is heat in the wigwam, & warm & blasfamous words has passed between Clay, & Adams[3]—The Committee is expected to report in a short time—It has leaked out from one of the Committee, that the fact I have stated is true—a short time will develope all matters, & things, about this corruption, at present, *it is confidential.*[4]

I am happy to hear that the overseer at Hutchings place, promises well.[5]

I have recd a letter from Mr Thos. Simpson, Mr. N. P. Cyrus & Doctor W[estern] T[erritory] Rucker, wishing to obtain part of one of my Lots to build a Masonic Hall,[6] I have said, if the Lot selected is mine, & not one given to one of my young friends, they shall have ¼ or ½ of a Lot, for one hal[f] I paid for it—that is to say, I wil[l] deduct one half of the original sum th[e] Lot [co]st me, apportioning the cost of the whole Lot by the ¼ or ½ which ever they may choose, but, in their selection, it must be so made, as to equalise the part taken to the part left me—I authorise you to make the erangement with them, as I know such a building will add to the prosperity of the Town. Indeed, If you think I ought, I will give them ¼ of a Lott gratis, and authorise you, if ¼ will satisfy them to give it, but if they take a half Lot, they pay me one fourth what the Lot originally Cost—

All friends are well except Mrs. E. Donelson, who, I expect cannot remain with us long.[7] Mrs. J. has rejoiced greatly on hearing Polly had Joined the Church, I rejoice also, it is what we all ought to do, but men in Public business has too much on their mind to conform to the rules of the church, which has prevented me hitherto[8]—Mrs. J. & myself salutes you & family in affection, your friend

Andrew Jackson

ALS, THi (11-1119). Published in Bassett, 3:387–88.

1. See above.

2. The Frankfort *Argus* of February 6 and 13 reported the details as AJ described, but the Kentucky Senate, where the resolutions to investigate the "corrupt bargain" originated, exonerated Henry Clay, unconvincingly for Jacksonians.

3. Letter not found.

4. AJ was referring to the investigation into the expenditures in the state department by the House committee chaired by John Blair of Tennessee. The committee found that, indeed, there had been, between 1825 and 1827, some $19,760 spent out of contingent expenses for foreign intercourse for which there were vouchers, and $16,300 without vouchers. The routine investigation did not, however, uncover documentation for the large outlays for publishing which it anticipated, only minor infractions and some laxity in record keeping (*HRRep* 226, 20th Cong., 1st sess., Serial 178).

5. George J. Jordan had recently been hired as overseer at the Hutchings plantation.

6. Letter not found. Simpson (c1797–1868), an Irish immigrant, was the partner of merchant John Simpson; later he worked as a land agent. Rucker (1798–1831) was a physician in Florence. Cyrus has not been identified. The Florence Masons did not select any of AJ's lots for their lodge.

7. Elizabeth R. Donelson died on March 28.

8. AJ attended services regularly, but he did not formally join the Presbyterian Church until 1838.

From Hugh Lawson White

Senate Chamber Feb. 22. 1828

Dear Sir,

Inclosed you will find a paragraph which I cut out of the National Journal of yesterday morning.[1] It struck both Eaton and myself as matter of great singularity that you should write such a note to such people, and to satisfy my own curiosity upon the subject I determined to call at the Printing office and ask a sight of the note itself—Accordingly in Company with Colonel Polk I did call late in the evening and asked a sight of your note and ultimately prevailed upon Mr. Force to shew it to us. That which is represented as a note from you turns out to be some writing on the title page of one of the pamphlets published by the Nashville Committee—On the outside the page are these words, "To the Editors of the Washington Journal." On the inside the same page are the contents of the note without either date or signature—The ink has of course spread pretty much on such paper—After I had examined it Mr. Force asked me if it was not your hand writing—I told him, if I were to say *I thought it was I should not tell truth.* He then asked me if I would say it was not your hand writing—I told him by taking the reverse of what I had before stated he had my answer and that I could add that in my opinion I could easily find a dozen persons who could write as much like you as that. Still it might be yours as I had not been accustomed to see your writing on such paper—Polk still more decidedly negatived the idea of its being yours—Force says he is able to establish it by the most satisfactory evidence to be yours.

For myself I view it a matter of small importance any way and do not suppose you would be inclined to trouble yourself about it.

One letter of mine I should like to hear you had received. It is dated in January.[2] With great sincerity your friend

Hu L White

ALS, DLC (35). Endorsed "answered from Major Searcys March 14th. 1828—"
1. The paragraph was that above, To Peter Force et al., [cJune 1827].
2. Letter not found.

In 1828, administration forces charged Jackson with complicity in the venture of Aaron Burr involving the West in 1806. Burr's goals remain in doubt even today, but at the time some suspected him of disloyalty to the Union. While in the West, Burr met several times with Jackson and even purchased some boats and provisions from him before sailing with a small company down the Mississippi River. Shortly after he arrived in Mississippi Territory, civil authorities arrested him (see Jackson, *2:110–60, 164–70).*

In early 1828, Jackson's opponents in Virginia began to circulate privately a letter from Nathaniel W. Williams (c1779–1833), a Tennessee circuit court judge and a cousin of Jackson's bitter political enemy, John Williams. Williams's letter of December 18, 1827, addressed to his nephew Nathaniel W. W. Kerr in Pittsylvania County, Virginia, stated that "it is madness to think of Jackson for President of the United States. This Burr matter I cannot be mistaken about; my eyes and ears are my wittnesses. He (Jackson) offered me a commission of Captain in Burr's army, or told me I could get one if I would accept. And during this affair he said to me, in the presence of Judge ——— [(]who though now says he does not remember it) [']depend upon it, gentlemen, the division of the United States has taken deep root; you will find a number of the Senate, and a number of the members of the House of Representatives, deeply involved in this scheme[']" (United States' Telegraph, July 26). Upon learning of Williams's charge, Jackson promptly wrote him the letter below.

Though claims of Jackson's involvement with Burr initially appeared only as rumor and gossip, the charge reached the newspapers by May 14, when Bedford County physician James Loudon Armstrong (1782–1868) stated in the fifth of his "Tennesseean" revelations that the "first cause" of his opposition to Jackson was Jackson's "friendship and intimacy with Aaron Burr, in 1805-6—the man who was so strongly suspected (even at that time) of being a traitor to his country" (Lexington Kentucky Reporter, May 14). Within a couple of months, Nathaniel W. Williams had published his correspondence with Jackson in the Knoxville Enquirer, adding an undated statement reaffirming the charges against Jackson first aired in Williams's letter to Kerr (reprinted in Washington National Intelligencer, July 26).

To Nathaniel W. Williams

HERMITAGE, Feb. 23, 1828.

Sir:

Having received a letter from a highminded, honorable gentleman of Virginia, who loves *truth* and knows how to appreciate character, I lose no time in laying before you the postscript of his letter,[1] which is in following words, to wit: "It may be well to say that a letter was handed about at the *Adams Convention*,[2] I hear, accusing you of being concerned in Burr's conspiracy, upon the authority of a Judge Nathaniel Williams, of your State. The report is, that this Judge Williams writes, when a young man, he applied to you (then a Judge) to sign his license as a lawyer; that you did so; but recommended to him, as you conceived him to be a man of promise, to push his fortune, by joining Burr, *who was then in your house*, promising, if he would do so, to procure him a commission as a captain in Burr's army. This story is going the rounds from the Adams

Delegates, who have returned home, notwithstanding they ought to know that you was the first person to put Governor [William Charles Cole] Claibourne on his guard,[3] against the schemes of Burr. *Verbum sat.*"

The records of the country contradict this statement, as it is well known that I resigned my appointment of Judge before Colonel Burr *ever was in the State of Tennessee.*[4] I cannot, then, for one moment, permit myself to believe, that you, elevated as you are, to a seat on the judicial bench of Tennessee, could give your authority to such an unfounded falsehood. Duty to myself as well as justice to you, therefore, require that I should, without delay, advise you of this libel upon my character, so that you may at once declare whether you are, or are not the author of this calumny, before I expose it as such.[5]

I am, and have been, well advised of a secret combination of a *base and wicked few* in Tennessee, whose object is to slander me,[6] but, until *now* I have never heard, or had the least intimation that you were of that *group*. Nor do I now believe that you, who must be so well satisfied of the falsehood contained in the postscript of the letter referred to above, as well as the rectitude of my conduct since your acquaintance with me, could be so lost to *virtue* and to *truth* as to have originated and put in circulation so base a calumny. With this impression I send J. W. D[aniel] S[mith] Donelson to you with this communication, having no doubt, as an honorable man, that you will send me a frank and prompt reply.[7]

(A copy Signed,) ANDREW JACKSON.

Printed, Washington *National Intelligencer,* July 26 (mAJs, 11-1139). Published in Bassett, 3:391–92 (from LS copy, not found). The version printed by the *Intelligencer* and most widely distributed was issued by Williams. On August 1, the *Richmond Enquirer* published a slightly different version that Jacksonians claimed was more authentic. Except where noted, the alterations involved punctuation, grammar, and minor word changes not affecting the substance of the letter.

1. AJ was referring to William B. Banks (1776–1852), a brother of Henry Banks and former Halifax County, Virginia, legislator.

2. Banks had sent AJ a copy of the postscript to the Williams letter, which had circulated in the Virginia anti-Jackson convention in Richmond in early January. His letter to AJ has not been found, but he acknowledged sending the extract shortly after the Jackson-Williams correspondence was published.

3. AJ warned Claiborne (1775–1817), governor of the Orleans Territory, 1804–12, about Burr on November 12, 1806 (*Jackson,* 2:116–17).

4. No record has been found that AJ signed Williams's law license, but he, along with others, did sign his bond as clerk and master in equity for the Winchester District on October 20, 1806, between Burr's third and fourth visits to Nashville. AJ resigned from the bench in 1804.

5. For Williams's reply, see below.

6. The *Richmond Enquirer* added the word *"secretly"* before "to slander."

7. Donelson (1801–63; Military Academy 1825), AJ's courier whom he referred to as "J"[unior] "W"[arden], was AJ's nephew and Andrew J. Donelson's brother. The *Enquirer* also printed the complimentary closing: "I am, very respectfully, Your ob't servant."

From Nathaniel W. Williams

Sparta, Feb. 27th, 1828.

SIR: I have just about fifteen minutes since received, by Mr. Donelson, your letter of the 23rd inst.[1] in which you state, as by letter from Washington, "It may be as well to say that a letter was handed about at the Adams Convention, I learn, accusing you of being concerned in Burr's conspiracy, upon the authority of a Judge Nathaniel Williams of your State. The report is that this Judge Williams writes, when a young man he applied to you, then a Judge, to sign his license as a lawyer; that you did so, but recommended to him, as you conceived him to be a man of promise, to push his fortunes by joining Burr, *who was then in your house*—promising, if he would do so, to procure for him a commission of Captain in Burr's army. This story is going the rounds from the Adams delegates who have returned home, notwithstanding they ought to know that you were the first person to put Governor Claiborne on his guard against the schemes of Burr—*verbum sat.*"

I can frankly deny ever having written the letter (or anything like) the one spoken of by the gentleman who wrote you from Washington. I did write a letter to a relation of mine, Nathaniel W. W. Kerr, at that time in Richmond. The letter, if seen, would show that it was designed as a confidential one. I do not at this time remember accurately what the letter did contain. I believe, though, I can remember a part, if not the whole, of what I intended at the time—and I will state it; as it is but just that what has been, by my means, privately circulated, should be publicly avowed under the necessities of this case.

"Some time after Burr had passed Nashville once or twice to the lower country, *some time* before Mr Jefferson's proclamation,[2] in riding from General Jackson's house to Nashville, Gen. Jackson, in reference to that conspiracy, or what was afterwards called by others a conspiracy, Gen. J. said to me, that I could, if I would accept, obtain a commission of Captain.

Afterwards, (some time afterwards, how long I cannot tell,) during the sitting of the County Court of Sumner, at a time when Patton Anderson[3] told me either that Burr or Adair,[4] or both of them were at Gen. Jackson's house—in a room of Edward Crutcher's tavern,[5] as I believe, General Jackson said to me, (I think Judge T[homas] Stuart[6] present at the time,) 'take notice, gentlemen, (or remember, gentlemen,) the division of the U. States has taken deep root. You will find that a number of the members of the Senate, and a number of the members of the House of Representatives are deeply involved in the scheme.'"

I am not certain that the above was contained in my *private* letter to my relation Mr. Nathaniel W. W. Kerr. But as I have made those *private statements* privately, it is but just that I should now avow them.

I am in hopes, sir, that this letter will be altogether satisfactory to you, for General Jackson may be assured that no man can be more justly bound to him than myself, (the Presidential question aside,) for the great services conferred by him on my country. I have the honor of being, most respectfully, your humble servant.

Signed NATH. WILLIAMS.

Printed, *Richmond Enquirer*, August 1 (mAJs). Extract, Washington *United States' Telegraph*, July 26 (11-1150). Published in Bassett, 3:392–93 (extract). The *Richmond Enquirer* printing was certified by William B. Lewis as a "correct copy," and Jacksonians distinguished this printing from the corrupted extract previously published by Williams, which omitted the first paragraph quoting AJ's letter.

1. See above.
2. Burr had visited Nashville in May and August 1805, from September 24 to October 6, 1806, and again in mid-December of the same year. Jefferson issued his proclamation denouncing Burr's alleged conspiracy on November 27, 1806, but the document did not reach Nashville until after Burr's final departure in late December 1806.
3. Anderson (d. 1810), William P.'s brother, supposedly recruited troops for Burr's expedition.
4. Adair was William P. Anderson's father-in-law.
5. "Edward Crutcher" was a probably printer's misreading for Edmund Crutcher (1774–1846), at that time a resident of Gallatin and sheriff of Sumner County.
6. Stuart (1762–1838), formerly U.S. district attorney for West Tennessee, was elected judge of Tennessee's Fourth Circuit Court in 1809 and held the post until 1836.

From Thomas Stuart

Murfresborough, March 1st, 1828.

DEAR SIR:

In answer to your letter of Feb'ry 28th, 1828,[1] in which, among other things, you enquire whether I ever heard Gen. Jackson offer to obtain a commission for Mr. Nathaniel Williams under Burr or any other person, &c. &c. I respond that I never did, that to the best of my recollection, I never was at Gen. Jackson's house when Burr was there, nor do I remember of ever being there with Mr. Williams. I never heard General Jackson say to Judge Williams, nor to any other person, that Burr wanted men to join him in any project whatever; nor did I ever hear General Jackson say any thing in relation to Burr or his views, from the time he first came to Nashville until after he was a prisoner. I do not exactly remember the time Burr came to Nashville, but it was after he ceased to be Vice President, and had killed Hamilton, and no suspicion was entertained by any body, so far as I knew, that he was engaged in any illegal, or treasonable project. The citizens of Nashville gave him a public dinner a[t] which I was present. I presume Gen. Jackson had resigned his office of Judge, some years before Burr first came to Nashville; of course he must have signed Mr. Williams' license, and held a conversation with him, before Burr's conspiracy was set on foot. If I had ever heard such conversation as that above stated, it would have excited my curiosity to know what Burr wanted with an army, and when, in a short time afterwards, his treasonable projects were talked of, I should have recollected it so strongly, that I would not afterwards have forgotten it. I recollect that after the public began to talk of, and suspect the unlawful view of Burr, a certain Mr. [Seth] Pease[2] came to Nashville, sent, as I understood by the Post Master General, to enquire into some matter, relating to the Post Office, he consulted me as Attorney of the United States for this District, and after that business was ended, the conversation turned upon Burr's conspiracy; he asked me if I thought Burr had many friends in this country who would be likely to join him? I told him no, I thought few or none; that a majority were republicans, who were displeased with Burr for intriguing to be elected President by Congress, when he had been voted for, by them, as Vice President. He asked if there were not a considerable number of Federalists, who would favour him as they had heretofore done in the Presidential election—I replied, their number was considerable; but, so far as I knew or believed, he would get no support from them; they disliked his political opinions, they doubted his integrity, and they disliked him because he had killed Hamilton, and I did not believe they would support any man against the lawful Government of the country. He enquired if I was well acquainted with Gen. Jackson; on replying in the affirmative, he said he had been informed that Burr and Gen. J. were on terms of great intimacy and friendship—that he Burr lived much at Jackson's house. I replied, that there need be no fears from that quarter; that the house was open to all respectable strangers, and he was in the habit of treating all with hospitality, attention, and politeness, and this he would continue to do so long as Burr acted correctly; but the moment he would venture to develope his treasonable purposes, General Jackson would come out openly against him: that General Jackson had been highly gratified at the election of Mr. Jefferson, and displeased at the attempt to elect Burr president; that he was a man of strict honor and integrity and no fears need be entertained of him—upon which he left me apparently well satisfied.

Now, if I had heard Gen. Jackson offer to procure a commission for Mr. Williams so shortly before, under these circumstances, I must have recollected it. Your's Respectfully

(Signed) THOMAS STUART

Printed, *Richmond Enquirer*, August 1, 1828.

1. Not found. In his letter to William B. Lewis, March 3, 1828, below, AJ noted that he had forwarded Stuart's letter of March 1 to Lewis.

2. Pease, originally from Suffield, Connecticut, was nominated as surveyor general of the territory south of Tennessee by Jefferson in 1807. In 1816 he was assistant postmaster general.

To William Berkeley Lewis

Hermitage March 3rd. 1828—

Dr Major

I send inclosed the Honble N. Williams letter in reply to mine of the 20th. ult.[1] When you read it, and compare it with mine which is inclosed, you will see how prone he is to misrepresentation, even when my letter was before him—I state my "information is recd from *a high minded Virginian &c &c*," the Judge says, "in which you state to have recd. *by a letter from Washington,*" now I stated no such thing, in my letter to him. This poor devil being caught in his vilany, will make any shift to screen himself from being *damd.* for willful lying—He now says, it was after Burr was gone, or while Adair was here, in his letter, first, he says; it was at my house, when he applied for *his license,* when Burr was at my house, & when I signed them—In his first Judge Stewart was present, *now,* he thinks so—Tell me in your reply; does not his letter bear the impress of falshood on its face.

The first time Burr was here, he had Just left the Vice Presidents chair, he came without the least suspicion around him, of plans, or conspiracies, and was given a public dinner in Nashville; when he returned in 1806, he was followed by rumors of plans, & conspiracies, took lodging at the Tavern at clover Bottom, where Genl Adair must have met him in the latter end of Octbr. or first of Novbr remained two or three days & went on—in a few days after Col Burr descended the river—about five or six days after I recd. the information that occasioned me to write to Govr Claibourne, Jefferson, and Genl Smith then in the U. S. Senate—My letter to Govr Claibourne bears date the 12th. of Novbr 1806—[2]

I inclose the extract from the Journals of the senate shewing the date of the acceptance of my resignation as a Judge;[3] the extract from the Tennessee reports of it being made in June,[4] on which is indorsed, the date that Burr *killed Hamilton* taken from [David] Ramseys history[5]—from all of these, together with Judge Stewarts reply to my letter, (which I hope you have recd)[6] Major Lee can answer Mr Millers;[7] with the assurance from me that his honor emphatically lies, when he says, I either told him he could get, if he would accept, or that I would get for him commission of any kind from Burr

If it is thought best to inclose Mr Miller a copy my letter, with a copy of Williams answer, you must have the goodness to copy them, & return me the originals with Judge Whites letter, and Judge Stewarts answer—as I wish to write Judge White so soon as I get Judge Stewarts answer.[8]

I have searched every where & cannot find my letter to Genl Pinckney, reporting the affair of the horse shoe[9]—I have found mine to the Sec. of war & to Govr Blount of the 2d. april 1814 which I inclose you, and as in neither there is any mention made of *[any]* Indians being destroyed the day after the battle,[10] and the facts, as recollec*[te]*d would not have Justified such statement, I infer that, that part is fabricated for effect—I will write to the s*[ec o]*f War *[or to]* some friend to procure me a copy from the sec of war—

have several extra numbers of Jefferson published for circulation[11]—I will want a few for distribution—detain George, untill you can Copy such as you think proper & send the papers by him to me. *[In has]*t*[e]* I am very respectfully yours &c

Andrew Jackson

P.S. say to Major Lee Mrs. Lee has not wrot—I sent twice, for her answer, she is confined to her room[12] Λ J

ALS, NN (11-1157). Published in Bassett, 3:394–95 (extract).
1. See above, AJ to Williams, February 23, not February 20; and Williams to AJ, February 27.
2. See AJ to Thomas Jefferson, [cNovember 5], AJ to Claiborne and to Daniel Smith, November 12, all 1806 (*Jackson*, 2:114–15).
3. The *Journal of the Senate . . . of Tennessee* (Knoxville: 1804), p. 10, recorded AJ's resignation as July 24, 1804.
4. John Overton, *Tennessee Reports . . .* (Knoxville, 1813), 1:xi, gave AJ's resignation as June 1804.
5. AJ was referring to *History of the United States, from . . . 1607, to . . . 1808 . . .* (3 vols., Philadelphia, 1817) by Ramsay (1749–1815), a South Carolina physician active in revolutionary and federal era politics.
6. See above, Stuart to AJ, March 1; AJ's letter to Stuart has not been found.
7. Not identified. Documents not found.
8. Only one of the letters in the exchange with White, AJ to White, March 30, below, has been found.
9. In an effort to dramatize AJ's inhumanity, anti-Jacksonians had charged that, on the day after the Battle of Horseshoe Bend, his troops had killed sixteen Creek warriors found hiding along the banks of the river. For AJ's letter to Thomas Pinckney, March 28, 1814, see *Jackson*, 3:52–54.
10. See AJ to John Armstrong and to Willie Blount, April 2, 1814. AJ's letter to Blount, March 31, 1814, did discuss the battle and the killing of the Indians.
11. Henry Lee's *Vindication of the Character and Public Services of Andrew Jackson in Reply to the Richmond Address* (Boston, 1828).
12. Lee was probably at Lewis's plantation working on campaign materials. His wife, Ann, was probably still at the plantation of Charles J. Love, near the Hermitage.

From John Henry Eaton

Washington 4 March 1828

Dr Genl

Yr Letter and the enclosure was recvd.[1] I had asked for it, by request of Mr Calhoun and of course it was shown to him, that by comparison of dates and expression it might be determined if the Copy corresponded with that of the 9 of Sept 1818. They do correspond in every thing

In conversing with Mr C on this subject & at which interview both judge White & myself were present, we can perceive nothing to induce any belief that there is substantially any difference on this matter; & that looking to the whole affair there is no room for the slightest misinterpretation. Of one thing, looking over the whole ground I feel fully confident, that, this letter of the 9 of Sept. has been conveyed, thro him who sent it to you, by some one who entertains towards you nothing of friendship & who hoped, by the means employed to arouse a displeasure between yourself and Mr Monroe, that thereby injury might be produced to yourself.[2] Pardon me for saying so, but rest assured that you cannot be too much on your guard at all points. No stone will be left unturned to produce effect; & the garb of enmity & friendship will be alike assumed, if there be a hope of any resulting benefit to their cause, & injury to you. That the letter was placed in the hands of genl H[ouston], to be placed in yours that a scism, & consequent injury might be produced I verily believe. There is nothing that could so gratify *some* as to see you, in a public controversy, more especially with such a personage as Mr M—— that you should under any & all circumstances avoid such a *dissasterous* state of things, is what I hesitate not to suggest and do readily believe your own better judgment will accord to as correct

Much as you are acquainted with mankind, & their variant and governing rules of action, yet being at a distance from the theatre of motive, impulse & design, you can form no correct estimate of the numerous secret strings that are touched & worked upon. The whole machinery is, & will be kept, in operation, for the present year, & no effort spared to arouse & bring you forth into some sort of scrape. On this subject I have only to repeat, that which before I have <often> taken the freedom to suggest to you, that reserve and silence, & forbearance under any & all circumstances is the true path to tread. Let them write, indite, abuse, & say whatever they may, you owe it to your friends, to leave the entire defence to them. They would prefer greatly that in the news papers, the name of Andr. Jackson, should not appear even to an advertisement and with a view to this object, that you should write to no one, meet no argument, and answer inquiries for no one, no matter how exalted they may be. Your tarriff notions may & possibly will be asked, on that a very laconic note might be given refering to your old letter of 1824 to Dr Coleman as containing your views.[3] You must excuse the freedom I take, & I know you will, inasmuch as you will understand the motive which dictates it.

The Seminole war having long since passed by, & public judgment fully and fairly pronounced, I should consider it matter of regret that any circumstance whatever should arise to bring up again a matter of discussion. For any distrustful timidity that Mr Monroe might have felt on this subject, much allowance is to be made. It was the first year of his administration and he feared any position before the public the tendency of which might be to endanger his election. I cannot tho perceive any reason to infer aught of duplicity or double dealing, which the tenor of his letter to Mr. C of the 9th. Sept, apart from the rest of the correspondence might seem to authorise. Mr M——— letter to you of the 19 July 1818 takes the ground asserted in that of the 9th. Sept: that altho the order of the 26 of Dec 1817 did not contemplate, & of course did not convey the full powers asserted, yet that the exigencies & necessities of the case in connection with the general authority given in the order, did sanction and justify all that was done;[4] and judging by the tenor of the entire correspondence, the desire of Mr M. in suggesting this correspondence between yourself & Mr C was that upon reflection you might in your communication mark out a course, beneficial to the administration and to yourself; & to maintain that altho the orders contemplated no such exegencies as did arise, yet as they were general discretionary & unlimited, soon as those exegencies had arisen, your authority & power to pursue the course you had done, became proper and right, with the exception solely of not retaining the posts and thereby affording to Spain a cause of war Now to attain this, & to place the question exclusively on this ground, the effect of which should be as it was thought fully to sustain you; and at the same time to leave the Administration on higher vantage ground in her negotiation with Spain, was this correspond[ence] proposed between yourself & Mr. C———, that from the Documents of the Department the ground of defence broadly & fully might appear Accordingly by Mr M. in his letter of the 20 Octo 1818, that is suggested as the course to be pursued by you.[5] On the whole I cannot but think that the course is frank open & friendly on the part of Mr M. and was so intended: and that in giving construction to the order of Dec. 26 there is but a slight & very slight shade of difference 'twixt you & him. You maintaining that the order *directed* you to do all that was done, & he, not that the order did *direct*, but that the circumstances & necessity under which you acted, in connection with the order, justified all that had been done. These are nice distinctions, & constitute mere matter of opinion, & do not in my belief amount to any thing that may be considered at all material.

The communication of this letter thro Houston rests I have no doubt upon some intrigue; & that it came into his hands by some one standing behind the scenes, whose hope & calculation was, that a rupture between you, & Mr M might be produced. A means of tracing this business to its source would be to ascertain how he Mr C. came to find out, that the letter was in your possession:[6] this being ascertained it might be discovered how the letter got first out of the possession of the war department, & in that way the thing might be traced to its source

You are now fully possessed of the information that this letter of the 9 of Sept was addressed to Mr C. I suggest to you then, if it would not be well for you to say thro me, to Mr. C. that the impressions entertained by you on perusing it, is now removed by the communications made to you by judge White & myself, & that the letter will be held in private, and delivered over at some future time, when it may safely be done.[7] I would not that you should enclose it here for fear that it may be intercepted. And I would not either that you should write particularly about it more, thro fear your letter may be arrested on the way. Such are the spies of the present day, & numerous under currents which prevail, that I should conceive it most politic for you seldom or ever to write, and then to speak with great care & caution of *men or measures*. Leave all these matters to the judgment care & caution of your friends, and suffer nothing to reached thro your writings or declarations over & about which foes may cavil, & make news paper abuses out of, to annoy & to harrass you & your friends. Many to whom you may write, will not only speak of, but will show your letters, and thereby will they find their way before the public. All we want, & most ardently desire, is that you may rest quiet, still and silent let the storm pelt as it may. The result is now certain—we have no doubt it, and you must calculate with certainty that furious & vile assaults will be made & repeated against you, & against your friends. These friends will wage back the war, and keep up a necessary, calm & firm defence, wishing always that you may be silent let what will arise. This course ought to be adhered to as rigidly as tho you were the now incumbent of the office, abiding a reelection: that being the case you would maintain a rigid silence; it is no less proper as you now stand before the public to do so

As regards the tarriff about which I dare say, many inimical to you, will seek your opinions Beverly like by letter, I repeat, & again suggest, if a laconic, very laconic note referring to your votes in the Senate heretofore, with the letter addressed by you to Dr. Coleman as the outline of opinion then entertained and not yet altered would not be ample & sufficient—Upon so complex & difficult a subject no man can venture to go into detail, or do more, than speak in terms the most general: this you did do in your letter to Coleman, while your votes in 1824 give opinions more in detail, than the letter did

The members from Tennessee, have it in contemplation to publish at this place a Pamphlet over their own names stating in detail, and answering fully, all and every the charges and accusations that have been made against you.[8] The manuscript is nearly completed & ready for the press. I mention this to show the readiness & determination of your friends here, to meet fully whatever in your behalf may se*[em]* to them to be necessary to be done. A production of this sort we conceive, will prove beneficial, as coming under responsible names, in whom the public will have confidence as to the truth of what may be declared very truly yours

J. H. Eaton

You are breaking rapidly into the enemies strong holds Genl [John] Chandler[9] speaks confidently of four votes in Maine. The Legislature of that state decidedly with you have adjourned. A paper was secretly & privately circulated to approbate the present Administration, when only 60 names out of 152 could be procured. The 11 of this month the contest for Govr takes place in N Hampshire & will be decided wholly in reference to the Presidl question. [John] Bell the Adams, & [Benjamin] Pierce the Jackson Candidate.[10] Both parties are confident Binns 6 militia, & 6 Coffins have fairly inundated the state.[11] Thousands of the Richmond address have been circulated from this place under members franks, & Clays pamphlet in abundance.[12] They are vastly a head of us in money matters: where it comes from the Lord knows. In the Telegraph of to day, you will see Mr Madison & Monroes letters refusing to be on the Adams ticket. Their replies are written 22 Feby the day after notice had been given them. Keeping back the annunciation by the Chairman Judge Brooke, Clays old & faithful ally, was a stratagem to catch N Hampshire[13]

The investigation in Kentucky has been so full and final that I cannot perceive that the Central Comme. at this place need to redeem their pledge in exposing the error of Mr. C pamphlet. In addition to that already eked out at Frankfort, there is some here quite material, & perhaps the Committee may republish in Pamphlet form what has transpired along with the testimony here at this place. I hardly think any thing more on this subject need be written or said, altho I am satisfied the Committee will do it. The witholding Blairs letter and releasing him from the confidential ground he occupies, produces a most terrible influence: but without this there is enough, amply enough to satisfy every body who can be convinced.[14] Some partisans you know will believe nothing, scarcely that which they themselves may see & know

The Administration crowed loudly at first, that the death of Mr Clinton would greatly aid their cause;[15] they now find that that is a circumstance that is to do them no good: it is the other way. Clintons friends take their bragging, & comforting <themselves> of the Admr folks at his death, as unkind to their deceased friend; & will not think any the better of them for it With sincere regard

Eaton

ALS, DLC (72). Endorsed: "Major Eatons answered 30th March—Substantially as Judge Whites See. Copy to White March 30th. 1828—"

1. On January 21 Eaton had requested a copy of James Monroe to John C. Calhoun, September 9, 1818, which AJ had forwarded in his letter (not found).

2. The Monroe letter had been sent to AJ by Henry Lee.

3. See AJ to Littleton H. Coleman, April 26, 1824 (*Jackson*, 5:398–400).

4. See Calhoun to AJ, December 26, 1817, and Monroe to AJ, July 19, 1818 (*Jackson*, 4:163–64, 224–28).

5. In his letter of October 20, 1818, Monroe had suggested the exchange between AJ and Calhoun.

6. Calhoun knew as early as February 1827 that the September 9, 1818, letter had left his possession (*Calhoun Papers*, 10:268–73).

7. See AJ to Calhoun, May 25, below, for AJ's conclusions about the subject.

8. The publication has not been identified.

9. Chandler (1762–1841), a brigadier general in the U.S. Army during the War of 1812, was senator from Maine, 1820–29.

10. Pierce (1757–1839), a lawyer and father of Franklin Pierce, lost the New Hampshire gubernatorial election to Bell (1765–1836), a businessman.

11. *A Brief Account of the Execution of the Six Militia Men* . . . [New Hampshire, 1828] and *An Account of Some of the Bloody Deeds of General Jackson* (Philadelphia,1828).

12. The "Richmond Address" was that of the Virginia anti-Jackson convention, which met in January 1828; and "Clay's pamphlet" was his *Address . . . to the Public . . .* (Washington, 1827).

13. The Virginia anti-Jackson convention had placed the two ex-presidents at the head of its slate of presidential electors.

14. On January 8, the chairman of the Jackson central committee in Washington, former New York Congressman John Peter Van Ness (1770–1846; Columbia 1789), promised to respond to Clay's pamphlet denying the "corrupt bargain" (*United States' Telegraph,* January 11). The committee redeemed that pledge in the May 10 *United States' Telegraph— Extra,* printing a long refutation of Clay's charges that included an account of the Kentucky Senate's hearings.

15. Clinton had died on February 11.

To William Berkeley Lewis

Hermitage March 8th. 1828

Dr Major

My friends in Murfreesborough and its vicinity, on hearing of the secrete slander circulated by Judge Nathl. Williams, became aroused with indignant feelings against the slanderer, had a meeting, appointed a committee to wait upon & invite me to a public dinner on the 15th. instant, my birth day. I could not do otherwise than accept this invitation[1]—will you go up with me—I shall leave home on Thursday evening, and go as far as Mr Kibbles,[2] and leave there after breakfast, & stay, by request, at Mr [William W.] Searcys,[3] and ride into Murfreesborough on Saturday morning—If you can go Major Donelson & myself will meet you at any convenient point, and at any time, it may suit your convenience; either at the Hermitage, or at any other intermediate point; I will be glad to hear from you—I send for Mr Earle to day, and he may accompany me, to Murfreesborough[4]

I have wrote to Judge White under cover to the Postmaster Genl. to ensure its safe passage, fearful that your letter may have been purloined on its passage.[5]

I wish you would send me by Mr Earle a Dozzen of Jeffersons reply to the Adams Meeting address by Chapman Johnston of Richmond.[6] I wish to send them from the fountain of health Eastward & Southward—I wish one hundred extras, circulated to every printer & Jackson Committee in Ky ohio Indian[a] Illinois, Mississippi Louisiana and alabama—and to the north Pensylvania Virginia, Maryland, New Jersy, Newyork and New Hampshire. Those you may send me I shall distribute in Virginia and Ky.

I hope we shall hear from the City & get the report of the Committee on Military affairs, on the subject of the Six Militiamen.[7] I am anxious to see it I am very respectfully your friend

Andrew Jackson

ALS, NNPM (11-1164).

1. See William Mitchell et al. to AJ, March 4, and AJ to Mitchell et al., March 5.

2. Kibble was probably Walter Keeble (d. c1844), who lived in Jefferson, Rutherford County, between the Hermitage and Murfreesboro.

3. Searcy (1769–1846), a long-time resident of Rutherford County, had served in the Tennessee General Assembly, 1821–23.

4. Lewis and Ralph E.W. Earl attended the festivities at Murfreesboro, but the account in the *National Banner and Nashville Whig,* March 29, did not note the presence of Andrew J. Donelson.

5. See AJ to John McLean, March 7. The letter to White has not been found.

6. Chapman Johnson's address to the people of Virginia, January 12, had been printed in *Proceedings of the Anti-Jackson Convention . . .* (Richmond, 1828), pp. 11–24. Henry Lee as "Jefferson" replied to that address in the March 7 *Nashville Republican,* and that essay was later published, with Lee's earlier "Jefferson" piece, in *Vindication of the Character and Public Services of Andrew Jackson . . .* (Boston, 1828).

7. The *Report . . . Correspondence and Documents from the War Department, in Relation to the Proceedings of a Court Martial, Ordered for the Trial of Certain Tennessee Militiamen* (Washington, 1828; *HRRep* 140, 20th Cong., 1st sess., Serial 177) had been released February 11.

To Richard Keith Call

Hermitage March 20th. 1828

My Dear Call

Yours of the 22nd. January last by Mr. [Robert White] Williams has been recd.[1] and I intended answering by him—He left Nashville yesterday, I was invited by the citizens of Rutherford County to partake of a public dinner on the 15th. instant, my birthday, and did not have it in my power to get to see him before he set out, as I had intended. A few days before Mr. Williams arived I had been called on by the Clerk for the Court fees; I had paid it, Mr Williams, repaid me the amount, & I handed to him the receipt.[2] I assure you, had it not have been that I was under great pecuniary pressure, I should not have recd it—but having no source of revenue but my farm, & my crop last year falling very short, not equal to my expence, I f[ou]nd myself, the first time in ten years, behind my accounts, I therefore recd it.

I have seen, & have on file, your letter to Genl D. Green & again repeat my thanks to you for this act of Justice[3] I believe I have named to you in a former letter, that Mrs. S[usan] [Wheeler] De[ca]ture had, unsolicited, wrote me on this subject,[4] & completely shews, from the whole tenor of the commodores expressions relative to me, the baseness of that unfounded calumny—It will be published in due time, but her claim pending before

Congress,[5] I have witheld it from the public altho, authorised by her, to use it as I please, least it might prejudice her claim with the administration folks.

Mr Clay's Book has fell still born from the press,[6] it has done him great injury—His imprudent friends in the Senate of Kentucky, know*[in]*g they had a majority brought in a resolution to whitewash Adams & Clay, or more properly speaking Mr Clay, for they are not for Adams, This ended in examining witnesses at the bar of the House, and has produced a full answer to his *Book* by proving the *Bargain,* "that if Mr Adams was elected president, Clay would be secratary of state["]—and Trimble, Metcalf, and Frank Johnston, gave this as the reason to their constituents, why they voted for Adams.[7] This at once destroys those Gentlemens certificates, & proves the Bargain, & has had a great recoil against Clay in Ky. you will see the Whole procedings published in the papers—Clay will have to call out Mr. Blair to publish the confidential correspondence, or he is politically dead forever—This he will not do, as it is believed, as it would doubly dam him.

It would have given Mrs. J & myself much pleasure to have had it in our power to have visitted you & Mary, & our other friends in Tallahassee, when we were at Orleans, but we could not—It was necessary we should be at home—It is well known that some of the administration have been engaged in circulating slander against me; & the Sec. of war witholding documents, that would disprove many of their slanders, it was necessary therefore that I should be at home, to furnish my friends with the necessary documents when called for—You will see in the report of the Committee on military affairs on the six militiamen, the most disgracefull attempt was made by a sec. to mislead the people, by *"shuffling"* the documents, & placing what ought to have been no 1, No 6—it having no relation to the subject of the detachment to which Harris, & the others belonged—The trick was discovered by the Committee, & the wikedness of the attempt exposed.[8] Mr *Sec* Clay, has sent forth all his subalterns to circulate slander against me, in this corps, is the redoubtable Andrew Erwin, & Patrick H. Darby—*birds of a feather will flock together.*

I would be much gratified, as would Mrs Jackson, if you & Mary would visit us next fall, rember your & Marys promise—or winter, & let us see the little stranger & your elder daughter—Major Clements who is now with me, says they are both sweet children, and by him we were gratifyed to learn, that you all enjoy good health, & providence smiles upon you with plenty. Mrs. J. Joins me in our sincere prayers for your happiness, & that of your dear family, thro life with a happy immortality beyond the grave yr friend

Andrew Jackson

P.S. Mrs. Jackson requests me to say to Mary, that her dear grandmother,[9] is always inquiring after her health with many good wishes for her happiness, & would be glad to hear from you all by letter—we will expect to see you all at the Hermitage next fall—with all our best & fond wishes adieu *[A J]*

ALS, ICHi (11-1177).
    1. Letter not found. Williams (d. 1864), a native of Middle Tennessee, was a clerk in Robert Butler's surveyor's office in Florida.
    2. The court fees stemmed from litigation regarding the settlement of the estate of Call's father-in-law, Thomas Kirkman.
    3. On December 23, 1827, in response to the charge that AJ had threatened to "cut off the ears" of Senator John W. Eppes in March 1819, only to be prevented from doing so by Commodore Stephen Decatur, Call, one of AJ's aides at the time, had written Green, denying the story. The *United States' Telegraph*, January 12, had published his letter.
    4. See Susan Wheeler Decatur (d. 1860) to AJ, January 22.
    5. Her claim was for prize money for the frigate *Philadelphia*, which her husband had recaptured from the Barbary pirates in 1804. She did not receive an award until 1856.
    6. *An Address of Henry Clay to the Public* . . . (Washington, 1827).
    7. For discussion of the "corrupt bargain" issue before the Kentucky legislature, see above, AJ to John Coffee, [cFebruary 20–24].
    8. For a discussion of the document "'shuffling,'" see above, Robert Desha to AJ, January 21.
    9. Barbara Carroll Kirkman (c1746–1842) resided in Nashville.

On January 30, after other newspapers rejected his materials, Dr. James L. Armstrong of Bedford County, Tennessee, commenced a series of articles under the pseudonym "Tennesseean" in the Lexington Kentucky Reporter *cataloging reasons why Jackson should not be elected president. His inaugural piece dealt with the execution on March 14, 1814, of John Wood (c1796–1814), also of Bedford County, for insubordination and mutiny. According to Armstrong, the execution of the six militiamen in Mobile was nowhere near "as appalling and cold-blooded" as the Wood case. In the first place, Wood had not deserted in late 1813, as Jackson declared. In fact he had volunteered for service and was committed to serving. Secondly, he was on guard when charged with his insubordination and mutiny and chose to obey the orders of his immediate commander rather than another officer. Finally, according to Armstrong, his "doom" was sealed before the trial commenced, mainly because Jackson had determined to use Wood to set an example.*

In the letter below to William B. Lewis, Jackson discussed Armstrong's charges.

To William Berkeley Lewis

Hermitage March 22nd 1828

Dr Major
    I have seen the Louisville advertiser in which the case of Wood is commented on,[1] and confirms me in the opinion, that nothing should now appear over the signature of Col [Joel] Parish [Jr.],[2] than the order for the

Genl Courtmartial, the detail of its members, and Judgtment of the court, with my approval, & order for its execution; with my genl order read to Wood, in presence of the whole army, at the place of his execution[3]— This with the republication of [Samuel H.] Millers statement in the Louisville paper,[4] & Adgt. [Thomas] Camps deposition[5] (& one other that you may select if you conclude that any is necessary for the present) will be sufficient—leaving the ballance, for a replication, if any should become necessary. These slanderers, with all the engenuity of Andrew Erwin at their head, will fear to come forth, least the evidence on record will contradict theirs—The record of the proceedings ought to be kept from the eye of all Andrew Erwins pimps & spies, and if they come out with certificates, they may be caught as they are now, falsifying the record, which will prostrate them—In haste yrs

Andrew Jackson

P.S. I have Just recd the report of the Committee on military affairs it is short but well drawn[6]—I am preparing some documents to forward to Col Polk, to enable him if there are any discussion of the subject to do Justice to the cause—J—

ALS, NNPM (11-1188).
1. *Louisville Public Advertiser*, March 15, a Jacksonian paper.
2. Parrish (d. 1834), one of AJ's aides-de-camp during the Creek War, was at this time cashier of the Nashville branch of the Bank of Tennessee.
3. See order for, and proceedings in, the court-martial of John Wood, both March 11; and AJ to John Wood, March 14 (*Jackson*, 3: 48–49), all 1814. In early April, Parish published the documents AJ suggested.
4. Miller was a mounted rifleman in AJ's army in 1814 and at this time lived in Green County, Ohio. His statement, published in the *Louisville Public Advertiser*, March 15, declared that Wood had deserted once before and had been pardoned by AJ before committing the offense for which he was executed.
5. Camp (d. 1816) was the officer Wood allegedly refused to obey. Camp's deposition (not found) was probably his testimony before the court-martial.
6. *Report . . . Correspondence and Documents from the War Department, in Relation to the Proceedings of a Court Martial, Ordered for the Trial of Certain Tennessee Militiamen* (HRRep 140, 20th Cong., 1st sess., Serial 177).

To James Knox Polk

(Private)   Hermitage March 23rd. 1828
My Dear Sir
    I have the pleasure to acknowledge the recpt. of your letter of the 3rd. instant.[1] I assure you, there was no necessity for an apology, for not writing me earlier in the Session. I am well aware of your situation; a representative of Congress, who attends to his legislative duties, has but little time for corresponding with his friend. I sincerely thank you for the com-

munication before me, & will always feel honored by your letters, altho, I do not expect many from you

I have recd. to day the report of the Committee on military affairs on the 6 militiamen, that you had the goodness to forward me.[2] My thanks are due to them for the Justice done me. The sec. of war must surely hang his head and blush, when he finds he is detected in the dishonorable course he has pursued on this occasion, while Justice will approve the detection of this *vilany* to tarnish innocence, when he ought to have been its protector; a[n]d an honest public will approve the exposure of this *vile tri[c]k* by this high minded, honorable Committee—The sec being thus exposed, will he not go & hang himself? he must have great impudence indeed, if ever after, he can look an honest, and honorable man in the face.[3]

When I forwarded the documents to Col [James Coffield] Mitchell,[4] I was going to certify them myself, but I thought it was best that they should be certified by one who had once acted as my aid dc camp—you may safely vouch for their correctness, they were compared with the originals, all now on file in my office, by myself.

I send you enclosed a few more Documents to which I place my own certificate—a Duplicate of letter from Majr Genl Thomas Pinckney to Governor Blount, dated 23rd Decbr 1813—2d. Genl Pinckneys order to me of 21rst april 1814—3rd. his letter of instructions referring to his order 22nd. april 1814—4th. Extracts from Genl Pinckney letter to, & requisition on Govr Blount of 10th. of January 1814.[5] These to Govr Blount will shew the construction which Genl Pinckney gave the act of Congress, "that all requisitions must be for six months unless sooner dis[c]harged by the president of the U. States."

Genl Pinckney Instructions, & order, inclosed of date 21rst & 22nd. of april 1814, shew that the Posts in the Creek nation were by him, ordered to be maintained & Garrisoned by the troops under my command—they were so garrisoned, and Col [Samuel] Bunch left in command,[6] and agreable to his order the ballance of the Troops mustered & dis[c]harged, when my command, & services ceased, being discharged with the Troops. The time at which the services of Col Bunch, & his men, would expire, was reported to Govr Blount, & Genl Pinckney, & it was left to Genl Pinckney who remained in command, to give the necessary instruction for relieving Col Bunch[7]—the were given, & Col Pipkin was ordered into the field with 1000 men in pursuance of Govr Blounts order to me of the 20th of May 1814 and my order of the 24th of May 1814[8]— as Majr Genl of the 2nd Division Tennessee militia being the legal organ thro which the order of the Govr. could be made known to my Division.

Should there be any debate upon this subject, I wish some of my friends to call for all communications between me & the sec. of war upon this subject, from Novbr. 1813 *[to]* the end of the Creek war—and all correspondence between Gen*[l]* Pinckney & myself, & between the sec of war, & Genl Pinckney, upon the subject of requisitions.[9] The history of the

South cannot give one instance where Militia were called for under the act of Congress, for less time, than six months—The act itself was declarative of the length of service, "six months unless sooner discharged, by the President," and all Governors on whom requisitions for militia were made under it, was bound to order them for six months, unless specially directed otherwise by the President. and this was the uniform practice under the act of Congress of 1812—

Judge Nathl Williams, from what I hear, is on the stool of repentence—and has wrote to his friends in Virginia not to permit my friends to get a copy of his letter—I enclosed Judge White some time since a copy of my letter to his Honor. & his reply, & a copy of Judge Stewarts letter[10]—These compared with his letter to his friends in Virginia, will forever dam him, as a vile lieing *Valet* & Slanderer. My friends has written for a copy of his letter, *[i]*f it can be obtained, all will be published, & I expect at our next Legislature he will be impeached for misbehaviour[11] quere on the same ground could not an impeachment be sustained against some of the Vi[r]ginia Judges that composed in part, the Adams Richmond meeting.

I have recd some communications from Newyork since the death of the much lamented Clinton—his death it is said, will not add to the strength of Mr Adams in that state.[12]

Note, I only write when called upon by the Legislature of a State—Indiana by resolve of its senate, enjoined on the Governor to address me on my *political faith,* & he sent me a string of Interrogatories, as long as a bill in chancery, to which I replied in a Laconic stile,[13] referring him to my letter to Dr Coleman[14] & my votes in the senate—he was ordered by the resolution, to publish the resolution, his letter, & my reply, if I made one—I saw in the whole transaction the finger of Mr Clay, & met it—Whether this foolish proceeding, will be published or not I cannot say—But if there is any thing said about it in the news papers, I mean to publish the whole[15]

With my respects to the Whole Tennessee delegation & all other inquiring friends I am very respectfully yrs

Andrew Jackson

P.S. I have thought on reflection it would be well to send enclosed, a copy of Blounts order to me of 20th of May 1814, certified by myself—it is important that this order should be spread upon the record with the other documents—It is enclosed[16]—J.

ALS, DLC (11-1192). Published in *Polk Correspondence*, 1:169–71.
1. Not found.
2. *Report . . . Correspondence and Documents from the War Department . . .* (Washington, 1828; *HRRep* 140, 20th Cong., 1st sess., Serial 177).
3. Secretary of War James Barbour had submitted the documents to the House in a

numbered, not a chronological, order, seeking, so AJ argued, to tie unrelated events together to AJ's detriment.

4. Mitchell (1786–1843), from Athens County, represented Tennessee in the U.S. House of Representatives, 1825–29. The documents have not been identified.

5. AJ's certified copies remain in the Polk Papers, DLC.

6. Bunch (1786–1849), a Grainger County farmer, later served in the U.S. House of Representatives, 1833–37.

7. On May 1, 1814, AJ had informed Blount that the term of Bunch's troops would expire between July 1 and July 11. His report to Pinckney and Pinckney's order for the relief of the troops have not been found.

8. See Blount to AJ, May 20, and AJ to 2nd Division, May 24, both 1814.

9. On March 4, pro-administration congressmen introduced a resolution asserting that the six militiamen had been executed unjustly and offering compensation to their widows and children, but the House voted 124 to 50 not to take up the matter (*House Journal*, 20th Cong., 1st sess., Serial 168, pp 375–77). Congress made no further calls for documents on the subject.

10. See AJ to Nathaniel W. Williams, February 23; Williams to AJ, February 27; and Thomas Stuart to AJ, March 1, all above. AJ's letter to White has not been found.

11. In 1829 the Tennessee legislature did impeach Williams for alleged swindling of an ailing widow and for undue political partiality in court. Williams insisted that the charges were politically motivated and escaped conviction when the Tennessee Senate by a one-vote margin decided that a guilty verdict required the assent of two-thirds of the whole Senate rather than two-thirds of those voting.

12. See, for example, James A. Hamilton to AJ, February 17, and Henry Post, Jr., to AJ, February 25.

13. Ray (1794–1848) was governor, 1825–31. See James Brown Ray to AJ, January 30, and AJ to Ray, February [28].

14. See AJ to Littleton H. Coleman, April 26, 1824 (*Jackson*, 5:398–400).

15. In late March, Ray transmitted the correspondence for publication in Indiana newspapers, and both Jacksonians and anti-Jacksonians republished the letters during the 1828 campaign.

16. On April 5, the House Committee on Military Affairs issued a copy certified by Blount (*HRRep* 225, 20th Cong., 1st sess., Serial 178), and Polk used that copy in his April 11 defense of AJ (*United States' Telegraph—Extra*, April 30).

*On February 7, almost a month after he introduced resolutions for the war department to release documents relating to the execution of the six militiamen, John Sloane proposed anew that the secretary of war provide the House "with copies of all letters and correspondence between the secretary of war and General Andrew Jackson, from the commencement of the Creek war, until the 1st March, 1815, on the subject of the draft, service, and discharge, of the several corps of Tennessee militia." The following day the House adopted the resolution, and, on February 14, Barbour complied (*HR Journal, 20th Cong., 1st sess., Serial 168, p. 263*). In the letter below, Jackson critiqued Barbour's report.*

To John Henry Eaton

Hermitage March 28th. 1828—

My Dr Major

I have Just seen a report of the *Sec* of *War* endorsed "*Correspondence—Sec* of *War and Genl Jackson* Letter from the Secratary of War transmitting copies of all the letters and correspondence between the Secretary of War and Genl Andrew Jackson from the commencement of the Creek war to 1rst. of March 1815"[1]—Now it would appear from its endorsment that the whole correspondence was to be found within, but instead of this being the case, when it is opened, I find but four letters from the Sec of War to Genl Jackson the first dated Febry 4th. 1814 and last 20th of Augt. 1814,[2] and my letters commencing 16th. of Decbr 1813 and ending 10th. of August 1814,[3] not one in 1815 & not one fourth of the letters in 1814—How does this happen ¿Why has not *all* the correspondence within this period of time, been laid before the nation—as there has been a part? does the Sec of War expect to shield himself, by alledging that these are all that relates to militia drafts—This wont do, for there is but one of the Secretarys & one of mine that relate to this subject. Indeed a reason may be found from the note made on my letter of the 31rst. of Decbr. it is this "This letter not on the files of the Department."[4] If that is not on file, where was it found, had it been taken out, & by whom. I have to request that, on the recpt of this, you take Judge White and call upon the Sec of War for an explanation of this business and enquire whether this letter was found out of his office and in whose possession. I have in my possession, a roster of all the letters of mine on file in the *War* office, certified by *Mr. Vandeventer.*[5]

When you make the enquiry requested, I think it would be well, that some of my friends in the House of representatives make a call by resolution, for all the correspondence between me and the *Sec* of War from the declaration of war with great Britain to its close ending with the first of June 1815 and give the result of the enquiry as the reason—and all the correspondence between myself & Genl Pinckney,[6] and between Pinckney & the Sec of War, from the commencement of the Creek war to the first of June 1814—This will give a full view of the term of service of the Militia under the acts of Congress of 1812—to which may be added a call for the instructions given to Govr Blount & requisition on him in 1812 to hold his quota of militia ready for Service for Six months tour—This is the only order from Sec of War to Govr. Blount that designates the term of service *six months*—Genl Pinckney specially directed him that all requisitions under the acts of Congress must be considered for Six months—Indeed the act was declarative and all requisitions under it by the president must be considered for Six months unless expressly limited by the requisition of the president for a less term—As a garbled statement of the correspondence has by the Sec of War been sent to the world—I wish the whole to appear. I am informed that my enemies are still, under the rose, whispering the Story of Decatur & myself. I enclose you a copy of a letter, recd from Mrs Decatur to me, with my answer,[7] for your disposal in such way as you may Judge proper; it was unsolicited by me, and you will see she has authorised me to use it as I please

As the news papers has given currency to the resolution of the Senate of Indiana requiring the Govr of that State, to put interrogatories to me,[8] respecting my political faith, which he did do, and as my friends have expressed some anxiety on this subject, I enclose you a copy of my reply for your, & their Satisfaction[9]—I Suppose the reason why the Governor has not published his letter & my answer, before now, is that the whole was laid before Mr Clay for his *fiat* on the subject—The moment I recd the Govrs. letter I saw Clays finger in it—The Govr letter to me, would disgrace any man, when laid before the public—the first comment that is made in the news papers, I will have the whole published, not without.

Write me on the recpt of this—you may rest assured that the Sec of War intends something by the garbled correspondence he has laid before the public, it may be that he wishes to keep from the public eye my letter of June 1814 to the Sec of War, & his order authorising me to enter Florida which was witheld until after the peace—This correspondence is highly proper to appear at the present moment, and my report to the Sec of War of the Various Battles in the Creek nation, and if there is any thing said on the subject of the report of the M. committee on the Six Militia men, I trust some of my friends will call for the whole correspondence which I have requested. Mrs. J. Joins me in good wishes, & believe me your friend

Andrew Jackson

ALS copy, DLC (35).

1. *HRDoc* 146, 20th Cong., 1st sess., Serial 172.

2. There were five, not four, letters: John Armstrong to AJ, February 4, May 24, June 25, July 12, August 20, all 1814.

3. AJ to Armstrong, December 16, 30–31, 1813; April 25, May 8, June 13, July 24, 31, August 10, 1814.

4. The reference was to a copy of a letter from Willie Blount to AJ, November 24, 1813 (*Jackson*, 2:460–61).

5. The Vandeventer roster, February 1, 1827, merely listed the dates of the letters, not the writer or the recipient, and nothing is listed for November 24. Vandeventer found seven letters from AJ to the war department before December 16, 1813; thirty nine, from December 16, 1813, to December 29, 1814, all but one of which were in 1814; and forty-seven letters in 1815.

6. For the correspondence with Pinckney, see *Jackson*, 2 and 3.

7. In her letter of January 22, Susan Decatur stated that her husband and AJ has always been on friendly terms. AJ's reply has not been found.

8. See James B. Ray to AJ, January 30.

9. See AJ to Ray, February [28].

To Hugh Lawson White

Hermitage March 30th. 1828—

My Dear Sir

I have Just recd. your letter of the 2nd instant,[1] & thank you for it; & permit me to assure you, I duly appreciate your motives.

one of the most painful occurrence of my life would be to have cause to change that good opinion, and feelings of friendship I have always entertained for Mr. M. I cannot disguise tho, when the letter alluded to reached me, it smelled so much of deception that my hair stood on end for an hour—I am happy to receive the explanation given,[2] but I cannot refrain from making the remark, that it is unfortunate that my communications of such importance have been lost, & more recently, the documents mislaid, "in the dark recesses of the war Department—"[3] However I am willing to receive any apology for the past, as I always intended to act on the Defensive, & I hope nothing may hereafter occur *at wine drinkings* <*or 8th. Janry speeches,*> &c, &c, to arouse my suspicions of the sincerity of my friend Mr. M. as I have a great desire to carry my good opinion of him to my grave. I am told he & his son in law has been for the last six months engaged in writing, a Book.[4]

When I first recd a copy of the letter of the 9th of Sept. 1818, I was induced to believe from my inquiries, that it had been obtained by the friendship of Mr. C. that I might be placed on my guard & Judge of the sincerity of the professed friendship of Mr. M—as the letter had no marks that it was either confidential, or private, I supposed this probable; but I had doubts of its being genuine, & to put this to rest the original was in due time placed in my hands, as had been promised to put an end to my credulity & the copy first sent me, taken by the individual who handed me the original—It is due to Mr. C. as well as myself that a call should be upon him to know from whom he got the intelligence that I had this letter in my possession, and if without his consent it was furnished, I can soon get into this mistery—I wish you & Major Eaton therefore to see Mr. C. and make the inquiry sugested—and if the original was addressed to him, & has been taken *secretely* out of his bureau, it shall be safely preserved & returned to him, thro any safe channel, he may suggest.[5]

There is mistery in this thing, I would like to unravel it, and will, so soon as I receve your answer after seeing Mr. C. Mr. C. can say who had access to his papers that would do such an act without his consent—In haste respectfully yr friend

Andrew Jackson

ALS draft, DLC (35). Published in Bassett, 3:396–97.

1. See White to AJ, March 2.
2. In his letter of March 2, White recounted his conversation with Eaton and Calhoun on the subject of the September 9, 1818, letter from James Monroe to Calhoun.
3. AJ was referring to "Correspondence—Secretary of War and General Jackson . . ."
4. In response to the AJ-Southard affair, Monroe and his son-in-law George Hay (1765–1830) had started a work defending Monroe's management of the war department during the Gulf campaign, but they had since abandoned the project.
5. In his letter of April 30, below, Calhoun wrote AJ that he had no idea how the letter left his possession.

To John Coffee

Hermitage April 8th. 1828—

Dr Genl

yours of the first instant[1] has been recd. when it will be in my power to leave home I cannot say, but the necessity I have for mony, will urge me out, at as early a period as the call from my friends for documents to meet the virulent, & reiterated falshoods of my enemies, will permit. I do hope that my friend Col [Anthony] Winston will not disappoint me. My wants require the whole debt, & I have been disappointed in the recpt of mony I had loaned, which makes the pressure great, to meet expences over which I have no controle.[2]

When I go out, it will be impossible for me to tarry beyond the time necessary to settle up the business with A. J. Hutchings estate, & see his farm & overseer. It would afford me pleasure to vissit my friends at Courtland, but propriety, as well as the want of time forbids me—pending the present canvass.[3]

The Coalition are makeing their last, and desperate struggle—Forgery, & falshood, are their means, & it requires vigilence to detect & expose them—Evan our Doctor Armstrong has enlisted under their banner to lie for them, & is wielded by the pander of Clay, *Andrew Erwin*—They will meet their fate by exposure shortly—

We have lost Mrs. Donelson, She died on the 28th. ult. & has left a distressed family—I regret to learn the ill health of your servant, *Bundy,* but with attention, to keeping his bowels open & bathing him in bitters erbs, & salt, & rubbing him well with flannel & a brush, you may restore him, as his lungs cannot be yet much affected[4]

I have no doubt you have heard that A. J. Hutchings has been suspended, for bad conduct. I have had him ever since, at a school in this neighborhood, & will endeavour to get him again into College,[5] but I fear when out of my sight he will not be controlled, his conduct has given me much pain—Indeed this, with my other perplexities, has been as much as my fortitude can well bear—To be in a situation that I can neither speak, or punish those calumniators, is unpleasant; they know it, or I am sure such men as Doctor Armstrong would not hazard the risque to come forth to lie for Andrew Erwin about me—But providence I hope will prolong my days, untill I can both speak & act, when an awful retribution upon the heads of the leaders, & exciters, will come—upwards of 15,000 copies of the vilest slanders from the pen of Hammond have been republished at the city, & fran*[ked]* by the members of Congress, over the whole Union[6]—such profligate conduct as this, to be countenanced by our executive Govrt. & aided by the franking priviledge of members *[Co]*ngress, if not frowned down by the indignation of a virtuous people, then will Mr Adams have reallised, what has been ascribed as his motives, "that he would Join the republicans, & urge them into such measures as will disgust the people with their present goverment, & incline them to accept one similar to that of england—"[7]

Your friends are well, & Mrs. J. Joins me in affectionate respects to you, your lady & amiable family—Your friend

Andrew Jackson

ALS, THi (11-1204). Published in Bassett, 3:398–99 (extract).
1. Letter not found.
2. Winston (1782–1839) had bought half of AJ's Big Spring farm in Franklin (now Colbert) County, Alabama, in late 1822, and the other half sometime after October 1823, and he was still paying off the debt. Winston paid $500 on his debt to AJ at this time and the balance in November.
3. Illness prevented AJ from going to Alabama, and he sent in his stead Andrew Jackson, Jr.
4. Bundy (d. 1828) did not recover from his illness.
5. Hutchings was probably attending William McKnight's school. AJ managed to get him reinstated at the University of Nashville for the summer term, but he left the school permanently in 1829.
6. *View of General Jackson's Domestic Relations, in Reference to His Fitness for the Presidency* (Washington, 1828), which dealt with the Jacksons' marriage. Jacksonian presses accused John Sloane of Ohio, Henry R. Storrs of New York, and others of distributing the pamphlet (*Cincinnati Advertiser*, April 23; Washington *United States' Telegraph*, May 3).
7. AJ was loosely quoting from Samuel D. Ingham, *An Exposition of the Political Character and Principles of John Quincy Adams* (Washington, 1827), p. 12.

From James Knox Polk

Washington City
April 13th. 1828.

Dear Sir

I have received your letter of the 23rd of March with its enclosures.[1] I thank you for them as they may be of service should we have a discussion on the subject of the "six-militia-men" of which there is yet no certainty. I received a note a few days since from the Editor of the Baltimore Republican,[2] stating that the Adams-men continued to use the idle story of the "six-militia-men" as their principal weapon to your prejudice in the State of

Maryland, and requesting me to furnish him with any additional information in my power. I have answered his letter, summing up in as concise and clear a manner as I could the prominent facts connected with their service and execution. It will be published with my name.[3] I think the great error on our part has heretofore been, that the communications to the public on this subject have been too voluminous, and too much encumbered with documents to be readily comprehended by the casual reader. Hamilton's report[4] is very clear, but could not go minutely into the circumstances. I have procured a statement from Mr. Livingston,[5] fixing the precise time at which the rumour of peace reached you at N. Orleans, in order to put to flight the statement that has been often made, that the execution took place after the news of peace arrived. I have like wise obtained from Maj. F[rancis] W. Armstrong[6]—now at this place, and who was an eye witness at the execution—a statement containing important facts, as to the situation of the army at the time and the importance of the example. Judge White and myself have obtained from Genl. Gaines a statement of other executions which took place during the War and his views on the subject. All these will be published. Governor Blount's order to you and your order to your division—I have vouched to be correct. On consultation with friends it has been concluded that it will not be expedient to publish Genl. Pinckney's order of the 10th. of January 1814,[7] as it would require explanation to show that Col. Pipkin's regiment—were the troops embraced in that order. Such is no doubt the fact, but Pinckney's order is dated in January—1814—and calls for 1500 men to be *immediately* called into service. Gov. Blount's order was not issued until May—and is for 1000—and not 1500—men. At first blush therefore there might seem to be some discrepancy. Another main consideration is, that it is not necessary to make out the case. Should there be any debate on this subject I will make a call for the other documents—you suggest.

I have heard nothing recently of Judge Williams and his *Burr* story. The Coalition I think will not venture to use it. They have as yet said nothing about it in their newspapers. I would suggest as my own and the opinion of our friends here, that it would not be necessary for us to give publicity to the refutation of the calumny, until they shall attempt to use it. It will then be time enough. I am satisfied it has done no harm and can do none.

It is the evident policy of the administration to keep us constantly on the defensive. My opinion is we should "carry the War into Africa."[8] Not by asserting falshoods—as their habit is, but facts, many of which exist to their prejudice. We should defend only when necessary, and assail when proper, and when supported by truth. The Adams leaders have manifested such an utter disregard for truth, that they have in a great degree destroyed the effect of any thing they can now say.

Your friends here highly approve the course you have taken in answer to the Indiana resolutions. It was a political maneuver intended if possible to ensnare you. No doubt Clay was at the bottom of it. We have not yet seen it published, and Maj. Moore and Mr. Wickliffe of Kentucky, doubt whether Gov. Rhea (being disappointed in its contents) will publish it until the meeting of the Legislature next winter.[9] They think as I do that it may be important in the Western States, that it should be published, after giving sufficient time to the Governor to publish it if he intends to do so. They request me to suggest—should you prefer that course that you should transmit copies to some of your friends here, to be in their discretion published at the proper time, if from circumstances they should deem it advisable to do so. You will think of it, and do as you think best.

The Report of the Committee on retrenchment has not yet been made, but will I understand be a valuable document.[10] It will furnish the administration during the summer, employment in defending and explaining. If I am not wrongly informed it will exhibit a most profligate expenditure of the public money, out of *contingent funds* &c.

All is yet well in New York, and our friends from that state, say no ch[ang]e can take place there to your prejudice. Notwithstanding all we have recently seen in the administration papers, of a re[volu]tion there, it turns out to be a mere delusion. In the local elections—[of?] supervisors and town officers, which have just taken place, even [in the?] anti-masonic-district, the republican ticket has prevailed by increased majorities.

We must expect an excitement during the summer never before witnessed by the country. The administration will make a last desperate struggle to obtain their ill-gotten power. We must be prepared to meet it. Your friends are alive to your interest, and will be upon the alert in every part of the Union.

God knows when we will finish the tariff.[11] Thus far in the discussion they have effected nothing politically by it, nor will they. We will not probably adjourn before the last of May, or first of June. Very Respectfully Your friend & obt. Sert.

James K. Polk

ALS, DLC. Published in *Polk Correspondence,* 1:175–78.

1. See above.

2. Dabney S. Carr.

3. Polk's article for the *Baltimore Republican,* "The Six Militia Men," was reprinted in the *United States' Telegraph—Extra,* April 30.

4. *Report . . . Correspondence and Documents from the War Department,* HRRep 140, 20th Cong., 1st sess., Serial 177.

5. Livingston's statement was published in the "Six Militia Men" article.

6. Armstrong, from Franklin County, remained in the army until 1817.

7. See Thomas Pinckney to AJ, January 10, 1814.

8. A reference to the final phase of the Second Punic War between Rome and Carthage, when Scipio attacked Carthage, forcing Hannibal to abandon his assault on Italy and return to Africa, where Scipio decisively defeated him.

9. See James Brown Ray to AJ, January 30, and AJ to Ray, February [28].

10. The House Select Committee on Retrenchment issued its report on May 15 (*HRep* 259, 20th Cong., 1st sess., Serial 179).

11. The tariff bill, the "tariff of abominations," passed Congress on May 13, and Adams signed it on May 19.

To John Coffee

Hermitage april 24th. 1828—

Dr. Genl

I have recd your letter of the 13th. instant,[1] & intended setting out on Sunday next for your house, but from a very sudden attack of the bowels, & I might add severe, I find I cannot be able to ride that Journey so early, and send my son out to receive the amount due from Col A. Winston which I hope he will be able to meet—nothing but dire necessity pressing me, would induce me to call upon him, after the receipt of your note giving his reply to Mr Kemper:[2] he has heretofore been so punctual—from the debts owing me in this state, I cannot collect one dollar; & the most of it borrowed mony—I owe in bank, due the middle of the succeeding month $650 that I must meet—for the last two years I have had no control over my expences, and it has exceeded my means.

I have been somewhat astonished at the result produced by your examining the accounts [of] A. J. H. estate[3]—it is strongly impressed on my mind, there must be an error somewhere—When I sold to Col Winston it appears from memorandom I then made,[4] that the amount of the negroes to be recd. with the amount to be paid to old Smith was about the amount in my hands, & would close my then account with the estate—However, there may not be a mistake, & I shall be out at as early a day, as my health, & the political situation with which I am at present surrounded, will permit: In the mean time if a Leisure moments presents, run over the accounts of the cash on hand at his death; the proceeds of the plantation unite them; and then the cash paid for land, for negroes, for horses, the mony paid to Mrs. H—To old Smith &c &c—and draw the ballance—If there is not an error some where then have we been error, & kept in error, or all the memorandom I have taken, when we brought up the Books are wrong, & it may be, there was an error of which you speak—but I think upon recurring to the papers, there could not, as the only thing that was necessary & Just, was to deduct the expence of the farm at Meltons, from amount of proceeds of crop, & credit the estate with one half, which was its due—I will be out and attend to this, as early as I can, for really the result has surprised me, & I must meet it early—I cannot sleep in debted.[5]

I enclose The Winstons Deed to me, I wish you to hand it to my son, & direct him to have the acknowledgement of all the subscribers to it, in his presence, & some other, that will be in at Nashville to prove it, that it may be admitted to record[6]—If my friend Kemper could go over with him, as he intends spending part of the summer here, it would oblige me much—

If you could spare the time, to go over with Andrew to see Col Winston you would lay me under obligations—I inclose the sheriffs receipt for the Taxes paid,[7] for the year 1826—This will be deducted out of the debt I owe the Estate for corn & Hoggs bought at the sale, & is the Tax upon the negroes, as well as the land I bought.

I refer you to Andrew for the domestic news—The papers will give you the rascally working of the sec of war— ¿What can a people expect, when its rulers, & agents are corrupt, & will wantonly depart from their duty & introduce private letters in their reports, which have no relation to the objects of the resolution making the call for information—The Honble sec will meet with his reward, "The Just contempt of every honable man in the community."[8]

Mrs. J. Joins me in good wishes—I write in pain—your friend

Andrew Jackson

P.S. I furnish Andrew, with funds only to carry him out, calculating on his receiving part, if not the whole, of Col Winstons debt; you will please, from the sum recd, give him as much as will pay expences home, & let him put up the ballance securely in his side pockett or britches—Young Mr [Charles Leslie] Savage[9] may be returning to College, I wish they Could travel together—When you see Capt [Samuel] Savage present me kindly to him A. J.

ALS, THi (11-1220). Sent by "Mr A. Jackson Jnr." Endorsed: "answerd on the 1st. May 1828, and enclosed $500–"
1. See Coffee to AJ, April 13.
2. Probably Francis Camper.
3. The reexamination showed that AJ owed the estate $2,607.30³/⁴, plus $971.92, the proceeds from Hutchings's 1827 cotton crop.
4. Memorandum not found.
5. On May 1, Coffee reported that his accounts included only one advance of $976.18 from AJ to buy land for Hutchings and did not include the money that AJ had loaned to Hutchings's grandmother to buy land. On December 16, AJ and Coffee apparently reached a partial settlement that left AJ owing $471.09³/⁴ to the Hutchings estate. AJ did not finally close out the account until early 1832 (Coffee to AJ, February 6, 1832).
6. AJ had bought the farm of Anthony Winston (1750–1827) in Davidson County.
7. Not found.
8. In his report, on Indian affairs, March 27, informing Congress of Thomas L. McKenny's decision to remove authority from the Cherokee John Ridge, Barbour had included AJ's private letter of October 15, 1812, to George W. Campbell (*Jackson*, 2:334–36), in which AJ strongly condemned Silas Dinsmoor (1766–1847; Dartmouth 1791), the Choctaw agent who had demanded a passport from AJ as he passed through the nation with some of his slaves. Shortly after the publication of the report (*HRDoc* 219, 20th Cong., 1st sess., Serial 173), the Washington *National Journal* (April 3) also printed AJ's letter to show his intemperate nature.
9. Savage (d. 1834; Nashville 1830) was a student at the University of Nashville.

In the letter to James Alexander Hamilton below, Jackson made one of his rare references to the affair of William Morgan (c1774–c1826), a Batavia, New York, stonemason, who disappeared following his threat to reveal the secrets of freemasonry. Jackson, however, did not publicly enter the debate on the merits of the political movement, Antimasonry, or of masonry.

To James Alexander Hamilton

Hermitage April 29th. 1828.

Dear Sir,

I have the pleasure to acknowledge the receipt of your favor of the 2d inst.[1] calling my attention to some communications which I thought had long since been forwarded, to the corporation of New York, to the Republican meeting of the citizens whose representative you were at New orleans & to Mr [Thomas M. W.] Young who presented me with a hat—[2]

You will receive herewith enclosed copies of those letters which were written shortly after my return from New Orleans,[3] and which from their being filed I think were entrusted at the time of their date *[to]* the mail from Nashville, but as some mistake of this kind may have occurred in the arrangement of my papers which you know must have accumulated very much during my absence, I must beg you to attribute their failure to this cause—

In answer to your inquiries on the subject of my connection with masonry, I have to observe that I presided several years as Royal Arch Mason in the grand Lodge of Tennessee, but have not attended the sessions for two years or thereabouts—I have not attended the Chapter for many years, say fifteen or twenty—[4]

It will be a stain on our history to have it said that any administration with the view of sustaining its power should take advantage of the mysterious fate of Morgan—Such an unhallowed use of power can scarcely be credited here—But I will not comment on the subject, nor advert to the disclosures which have been recently published—

Mrs Jackson is well. My own health is improving altho I am still a good deal debilitated.

We unite in a tender of our sincere wishes fo*[r the]* health of yourself & family, which I beg you to acc*[ept]* with the assurance of my continued regard & est*[eem]* your very obt servt.

Copy in Andrew J. Donelson's hand, DLC (35). Published in Bassett, 3:399 (extract).

1. Letter not found.

2. Young, who ran a hat factory in New York City, has not been further identified.

3. AJ enclosed copies of his letters, February 1 or thereabouts, to William Paulding, mayor of New York, and to Young. AJ's letter to the Tammany Society, which Hamilton represented at the January 8 New Orleans celebration, has not been found.

4. AJ had been a member of the Harmony Lodge of Tennessee, which ceased operations in 1808. He was admitted to the Grand Lodge of the State of Tennessee in October 1822 and was named Grand Master of the Grand Lodge at the same time, serving until October 1824. AJ participated in masonic ceremonies of the Grand Lodge until as late as October 1826.

From John Caldwell Calhoun

Washington
30th April 1828

Dear Sir,

I received a short time since a letter from Majr. Lee at Nashville, of which I enclose a copy with a copy of my answer.[1]

The correspondence requires no explination, farther than to remark, that the Majr. in his letter to Mr Monroe,[2] to which he refers in his to myself, requests him to inform him what construction the executive gave to the orders, under which your operations in the Seminole campaign were carried on, and that his request to me refers to information on the same subject.

With you, I cannot have the slightest objection to correspond on the subject, if addition information be desirable

I learn from Judge White, that you wish me to indicate the conveyance, by which I may desire the return of Mr Monroe's letter to me of the 9th Septr. 1818. I know of no other, which will probably offer, but the mail, and you will be pleased to return it by that conveyance, under cover to my address, and enclosed to the Post Master General, to be forwarded to me in case, I should have left the city before its arrival.

I am at a loss to conjecture, how the letter was taken out of my possession.[3] It was doubtless the work of an enemy for the foulest purpose, but whether the motive was to serve those in power by sowing discord among their opponents, or to put you off your guard against old enemies by pretending to guard you against friends, whether it was enmity to you to Mr Monroe, or myself, I know not, as I am ignorant of the channel through which it reached you. The mystery ought to be unveiled, and for that purpose Judge White has my permission to make known to you, in what manner, I had the first intimation, that the letter was out of my possession. If it be material to the unravelling of the plot, I doubt not, tho the communication was strictly confidential, but what my informant[4] would assent to the disclosure of his name. He is a gentleman of the highest honor and is among your most steadfast friends. In order to have all possible light on this mysterious subject, I would be gratified to know the channel through which the letter passed to you, if it can be made known by you without impropriety. With great respect I am &c

J. C. Calhoun

ALS, DLC (35). Published in Bassett, 3:400.

1. The letter from Lee to Calhoun has not been found. In his response, [cApril 30] (DLC-35), Calhoun refused to discuss with Lee AJ's orders during the Seminole War unless AJ requested him to do so.

2. Lee to James Monroe, March 30 (Monroe Papers, DLC).

3. In February 1827, Calhoun learned that the September 9, 1818, letter was missing from his files.

4. Not identified.

To James Knox Polk

Hermitage May 3rd. 1828

My Dr. Sir

I hasten to acknowledge the recceipt of your letters of the 13th. & 15th. ultimo,[1] which has this moment reached me. I am happy to learn that mine of the 23rd. of april was safe to your hands with its enclosures,[2] I had some solicitude on this subject.

The six militiamen appear to be the little hobby of the coalition, they will ride it, so long as they can impose upon the credulity of the ignorant, by false colourings, & mutilated facts—This was the great object of that *degraded man,* the sec. of war, in the arrangement of the papers communicated to Congress—This act alone, is sufficient to consign him to the everlasting contempt of all Just, highminded, & honorable men, & for which, the President, if he had possessed virtue, would have removed him from office—but it really appears to me, that the members of the administration are lost to all sense of Justice, honor, & magnanimity, or respect for their own, or our national character—The plan therefore that you have sugested is the only one that can fairly meet, and effectually put down their *hobby.* When you carry the war "into affrica," truth, & principle, must be the *watchword,* this alone, is what ought to be relied on for success, this will give it—the people only want light, give it them, and they will hurl the present rulers from their confidence, & on their "native dunghills set them down." It is certainly true my friends have acted thus far on the defensive, this was right, but from the unprincipled course pursued by the coalition, it is time to carry the *war* into *africa,* and by adhering strictly to facts, the cannot cry persecution—I expect Clay intends to visit Kentucky this summer, he will endeavour to raise this cry, to enlist in his favour, his old friends, but he will be met with argument founded in truth, that must prostrate him—The report of the Committee which you sent, & I have recd. will be a mountain in his way, the people will see with what profusion, the public mony has been spent, & taught to know, that a great part has been given to such wretches as John Binn, Hammonds, &c &c, this, with a virtuous people, will have its effect.[3]

I think your reflections on the subject of the Burr business, is correct, no defence, without a charge, ever ought to be attempted—Richey, is in possession of the documents, he will move when it is thought necessary, *he is prepared,* as I am advised—[4]

Before this reaches you, you will have seen my reply to the Governor of Indiana, published in the various papers, the Louisville advertiser, & Cincinnati advertiser &c &c.[5] The moment I saw it, I saw plainly the finger of Clay in it, for altho, he possesses some cunning, he has not common sense to mask his intrigue so, that he is free from detection—I knew, he expected, I would not permit myself to be thus interrogated, & they would wield my silence against me—I answered, & am happy, it meets the approbation of my friends.

I have been seriously afflicted with a return of my old bowel complaint, from which I am Just recovered, but am much debilitated—Mrs. J. Joins me in kind salutations to your lady—have the goodness to present us to Mr & Mrs. Hayne Mr & Mrs Livingston, & daughter & to all our delegation, and accept for yourself our kind salutations, & believe me your friend

Andrew Jackson

P.S. present me to Mr Calhoun, Hamilton & McDuffie, and say to my friend Eaton I have not heard from him, for some time—Mrs J. & myself tender him our kind regard.

ALS, DLC (11-1234). Published in *Polk Correspondence,* 1:180–82.
    1. See above, Polk to AJ, April 13; and Polk to AJ, April 15.
    2. AJ meant his letter of March 23, above.
    3. AJ was referring to the "Report of the Committee on Expenditures in the State Department" (*HRRep* 226, 20th Cong., 1st. sess., Serial 178) which Polk had sent in his letter of April 15.
    4. William B. Lewis had sent materials on the "Burr business" to *Richmond Enquirer* editor Thomas Ritchie soon after Nathaniel W. Williams made his disclosures. On June 17, Ritchie labeled Williams's charges "idle and baseless"; and on August 1, the paper published a reply to Williams's claims by "Brutus" that drew on material sent by Lewis. The Jacksonians' main response to the Burr charges, however, appeared in the *Nashville Republican,* September 12.
    5. See James B. Ray to AJ, January 30, and AJ to Ray, February [28]. The *Louisville Public Advertiser,* edited by Shadrach Penn, and the *Cincinnati Advertiser,* edited by Moses Dawson, were among the leading Jacksonian papers.

To Hardy Murfree Cryer

Hermitage May 5th. 1828

Dr. Sir

I received your letter of the 21rst. ultimo,[1] by Dunwodie, & was happy to hear that your hea[l]th was improving, may you continue to enjoy that blessing.

I sincerely regret your pecuniary embarrassments, & I would to god, I had the means to relieve you—I have not; my own, for the first time since I got clear of my securityship, twelve years ago,[2] are more than I can meet, bad crops, & low prices of produce, have left me indebted, & without funds—Indeed for the last few years, altho I practice oeconomy, still I have no controll of my expences, but my Dr. Sir do not loose heart; you have friends & if they have not mony, they have credit & property & will aid you in the time of need, as much as they can.

I send two mares with their young coalts to Sir William, you will find the Cotton mares, very indifferent, and even discouraging to put her again to a fine horse, but hope she will do better from Sir William, than she has from the Stockholder—I send a dollar for the groom—I have been making enquiry for a purchaser for your negro wench & children, but can hear of no purchaser in this neighbourhood—indeed there is no one here who has any mony, all are hard pressed, and I have no doubt but money will be more dificult to be raised this, than it has been for many years—I have not been able to collect one dollar, out of all the debts owing me, & to meet some pressing engagements have been obliged to go into Bank.

I have been severely attacked lately with a return of my old complaint, from which I have recovered, but am still much debilitated—with care, I hope, soon, to regain my strength.

Mrs. J. Joins me in kind salutations to you & your family yr friend

Andrew Jackson

ALS, THi (11-1237). Published in Bassett, 3:401 (extract, dated May 3).
1. Not found.
2. AJ was referring to the Allison land claim (see *Jackson*, 4:315–18).

To John Henry Eaton

Hermitage May 6th. 1828—

My Dr. Major

It is some time since that I have recd a letter from you; from a letter recd. from a friend I understand you have been lately in philadelphia with your niece, who, I regret to learn, has been in bad health lately.[1]

There has been shewn me a letter from a *high minded honorable Virginian* dated the 15th. april 1828[2] from which the following is an extract.

"I cannot however omit mentioning one circumstance to you, to show what mean artifices the Adams men resort to—John Taliaferro[3] who has now *openly* become one of the most violent and virulent of Genl Jacksons enemies, fearful I suppose that the newspapers will not give sufficient currency to the note which the Editor of the N. Journal says he recd. from Genl Jackson,[4] is circulating that together with a general order, in manuscript[5]—He has thus become a voucher for its authenticity, and with those who have confidence in him it must do the Genl. material injury—I find the secrete of his zeal to be, that he is an applicant for the Treasurership, which has been promised him, but as old, Mr. [Thomas Tudor] Tucker 'obstinately refuses to die' he may be disappointed."[6] Was not this letter from the highest source for respectability, I could not bring myself to believe that members of Congress could descend to such *pitiful meaness,* which conduct like this discloses but when I reflect that some members have so much degraded themselves as to become the *common sewers* through which the vile slanders against Mrs. Jackson has been circulated throughout the united States, by prostituting the franking privilege <to this *vile, pitiful,* as well as, *wicked* purpose, & [so far?] unknown before to the history of the christian world,> I cannot forbear, from the high character of the writer, to give due credit to this statement, of the conduct of Mr Taliaferro. I therefore have to request, that you shew this letter to him, and demand a copy of the note, & Genl Order in Manuscript, which he is circulating, and by that means, vouching for its authenticity, & transmit them to me—That I never wrote, & sent, a note to the Editor of the Journal at Washington is true, and how the original of one of my Genl Orders could get into the war Department, & into the hands of Mr Taliaferro, I cannot conjecture, not having seen either its tenor, or date—Therefore, I have a right to demand not only a copy of these papers, but to be informed how Mr Taliaferro came to the possession of them, & request you will have the goodness for me, & in my name, to make this demand of Mr Taliferro—If he refuses to comply with this reasonable request, please *note it* in writing, & communicate the same to me, as early as you can—but I trust he will not refuse giving you a copy, & informing how, & where he became in possession of them.

I am very desirous to be informed of the tenor & date of this spoken of, Genl Order, that I may compare it with the original, and be prepared to shew to the world, that it is either a forgery, or acknowledge its authenticity—Fortunately, I hold a certified roster from Major Vandeventer, of all letters & orders of mine that was in the war office & on file in 1825[7]—Therefore, this will check Mr Barber and John Binns & Co in their *villany,* should it be attempted to be practised against me. expecting to hear from you on the recpt. of this, I tender to you Mrs. J & my kind salutations & believe me yr friend

Andrew Jackson

P.S. I have Just heard from Franklin, your mother,[8] Doctor [Edward] Breathet & family[9] are well—I have Just recovered from a severe attack of my bowels—I pray you to make the call upon Mr Taliaferro. I have no doubt, but I will get the sec of war in a dilemma, from which he will find it, not an easy task to extricate himself.

ALS copy, DLC (35). Endorsed by AJ: "Copy to Major Eaton May 6th. 1828—the one sent altered a little in commencement & conclusion—"

1. In the fall of 1827, Eaton had taken his niece, Mary Ann Lewis, William B.'s daughter, to Georgetown to attend school. Eaton's visit to Philadelphia likely involved arrangements for publication of a new edition of his *Life of Jackson,* which came out in the summer.

2. Not found.

3. Taliaferro (1768–1852) represented Virginia intermittently in Congress from 1801 to 1843.

4. See above, AJ to Peter Force et al., [cJune 1827].

5. General order not identified.

6. Tucker (1745–May 2, 1828), who had represented South Carolina in the Continental and United States Congresses, had served as treasurer of the United States since 1801.

7. "List of Letters from General Jackson to the Department of War on the files of 1813–1822," [cFebruary 1, 1827].

8. Elizabeth (c1753–1843).

9. Breathitt (d. 1837), a physician, had married Mary Eaton (d. 1847), John's sister, in 1815.

To Richard Keith Call

Hermitage May 12th. 1828—

My Dr. Genl

Since your kind letter informing me that you had forwarded a reply, to the polite notice Mr Clay had taken of you in his book, to the central committee, I have had no letter from you[1]—that I acknowledged on its receipt[2]—from a letter from Col Butler by Mr James R Donelson, of the 23rd. ult. we are informed you, & Mary & the sweet little daughters are all well[3]—Col. Butler has named, that you & Mary are not satisfied with [th]e likeness of myself Mr. Earle sent you—shortly after it had reached you, Mrs J. received a letter from Mary[4] giving that information, Mr. Earle was shewn [the] letter, & wrote you, that the one Mrs. Call had selec[ted] but which had been sent on to Philadelphia, to Mr. [James Barton] Longacre, to have an engraven from it,[5] should be sent you, the moment it could be brought [here] & I know Mr Earle wrote Mr Longacre to return it [to] him, the moment the engraving was comp[leted] the proof sheet has reached Mr Earle, & he is daily in expectation of receiving the original, when he assu[re]s me, it shall be forwarded to you, & instructions given as to the disposition of the one you have.

I have seen nothing yet from the central co[m]mittee at Washington[6]— have you any informa[tion] whether it intends coming out or not—really [if] I knew nothing about myself, but what I see in [the] administration papers, I would conclude I w[as a] mere devil incarnate—but really, I cannot belie[ve] it is a real likeness—¿Have you seen the sec of wars s[tack]ing up the documents; & his hunting up my private letter to Judge Campbell, & reporting it, as a public document[7]—surely the heads of departments must have become desperate to resort to such pitiful meaness as this, to support a sinking administration, & must have but little common sense, not to know, that such means will hasten its downfal, as no honorable man, be his politics what they may, will not despise those capable of descending to such pitiful means, to support them—such conduct is degrading to the american character, & Mr James Barber begins to feel how much he has degraded himself, this I think is equally degrading to his circulating Binns forged letter[8]—before long these men must cry out for the mountains to fall, & cover them from their disgrace.

I have Just recd a letter from [James McMillan] Glassell informing me he is maried to the niece of my friend Swartwout—*[I]* have wrote, congratulating him on this Joyous *[o]*ccasion,[9] if an opportunity offers write him a note for me congratulating him on his happy change of life, & presenting them with Mrs. J. & my best wishes for their happiness—

I have wrote Col Gadsden often, without reply—I have wrote him twice since my return from Neworleans.[10] Should you see him, present us affectionately to him, & his lady.[11]

Mrs. J. & myself calculate certainly on seeing you & Mary next fall at the Hermitage—write me on the recpt of this, present us affectionately to Mary, & kiss the daughters for us, & accept for yourself our best wishes for your welfare & happiness your friend.

Andrew Jackson

ALS, DLC (12-0001).
1. See Call to AJ, March 11. In his *Address of Henry Clay . . .* (Washington, 1827), Clay related a story that Call, on his way to Washington in 1824, had remarked that AJ's supporters did not expect Clay's assistance in the election in the House. In his letter of February 4 to John P. Van Ness, chair of the Washington Central Committee, Call denied the statement (*United States' Telegraph—Extra*, May 10).
2. Letter not found.
3. See Robert Butler to AJ, April 23.
4. Not found.
5. Longacre (1794–1869), a prominent Philadelphia artist, issued an engraving of AJ based on one of Earl's portraits in May 1828. See Illustrations.
6. In January the Jackson committee in Washington had promised a refutation of Clay's pamphlet on the "corrupt bargain." The committee's report was published in the *United States' Telegraph—Extra*, May 10. In addition to the chairman John P. Van Ness and the secretary Henry C. Neale (d. 1836), register of wills for the District of Columbia, the Washington Central Committee included Philip Stuart (1760–1830), a veteran of the Revolution and the War of 1812 and a former Maryland congressman; Thomas Sim; Henry Ashton (d. 1834), whom AJ appointed marshal for the District of Columbia in 1831; Henry Mason Morfit (d. 1868), a lawyer; William Jones (1790–1867), a physician, who became Washington postmaster in 1829; Duff Green; Thomas Corcoran, Jr. (c1794–1846), Jones's brother-in-law; and Joseph Watson, a land and pension agent, whom Jackson later appointed agent to examine receivers' offices in Ohio and Michigan.
7. The "stacking up the documents" was a reference to James Barbour's sequential numbering of documents sent to Congress instead of submitting them in chronological order. The George W. Campbell letter was that of October 15, 1812 (*Jackson*, 2:334–36).
8. In 1827 John Binns published a letter purporting to be from John Harris to AJ, January 15, 1815, which Jacksonians denounced it as a forgery (see above, AJ to William Owens, July 26, 1827). Jacksonians charged that Barbour had distributed pamphlets containing the letter while stopping at Bedford Springs in the summer of 1827 (Washington *National*

Intelligencer, November 28, 1827; Washington *United States' Telegraph,* December 14, 1827).

9. Letters not found. Glassell (1790–1838) had served as one of AJ's military aides, 1816–18, and was still a captain in the army. He had married Eudora Swartwout (1798–1875), the daughter of John (1770–1823) and Mary Smith Swartwout (1772–1857), and Samuel Swartwout's niece.

10. Letters not found.

11. Gadsden's wife was the former Susanna Gibbes Hort (1786–c1858), daughter of William Hort (1750–1826).

To John Coffee

Hermitage May 12th. 1828

Dr. Genl

I had the pleasure by the hand of my son to receive your two letters of the 1rst.[1] and 2nd. instant with five hundred dollars inclosed[2]—for your kind attention to him, and the business entrusted to his care, I feel under great obligations to you.

I much approved your accommodating Mr Easton, it was an accommodation to him, & the check answered my purpose[3]—The sum recd. from Col. Winston, will enable me to meet my debt in Bank, & enter my three youths in College for the next session,[4] and the debt I owe Mr Josiah Nichol must remain unpaid,[5] until the Cols. convenience will enable him to pay the ballance—you may assure the Col. when you see him I am hard pressed[6]—My expences have been beyond my Control, & under my present situation I must have mony, but he must be indulged, as I am sure he would pay the whole, had he it in his power, and will do so, as soon as he can.

I sincerely thank you for your letter of the 2nd. of May—it contains information that may be useful, altho, I have got Nathl Williams in an awkard situation. I was furnished by a Gentleman in va. with an extract of his letter to his friend detailing my agency with Burr; this I made the basis of my letter to him; a comparison of his answer to me,[7] with his letter to his friend, blasts him forever—I have *[written for]* a copy of his letter,[8] whether I will obtain it or not, is yet very doubtful, the Judge has become alarmed & wrote to his friend that his letter was *entirely confidential,* & to destroy it. It is perhaps, the first *confidential slander* ever introduced before a large convention. On this Burr business, my friends at Washington & Richmond, are prepared to meet it, whenever the attack is made—My letters to Claibourne Jefferson, Campbell, & Genl Smith,[9] with the certificate of [Willis] Aulston[10] obtained by Judge White, places me on safe ground from the secrete attacks of these vile miscreants, the Williams.

The patronage of the goverment for the last three years has been wielded to corrupt every thing that comes within its influence, & was capbable of being corrupted, and it would seem, that virtue & truth, has fled from its embrace—The administrators of the Govrt. has stained our Nationational Character, & it rests with the people to wash it out, by a full expression of their disapprobation—The present is a contest between the virtue of the people, & the influence of patronage—should patronage prevail, over virtue, then indeed "the safe precedent," will be established,[11] that the President, appoints his successor in the person of the sec. of State—Then the people may prepare themselves to become "hewers of wood, & drawers of water,"[12] to those in power, who with the Treasury at command, will wield by its corrupting influence a majority to support it—The present is an important struggle, for the perpetuity of our republican goverment, & I hope the virtue of the people may prevail, & all may be well—From the signs of the times, it appears, that the influence of the administration is on the wane, and the cause of the people will prevail.

I have had a severe attack, am recovering and in a few more days I hope I will regain my former strength when I intend to visit you, & have the accounts of Hutchings estate brought up & closed—I have been obliged to labour too hard—My friends were determined to meet the various slanders that were Issued against me. The various calls for information, I had to meet, and altho, I had adopted the firm resolution not to notice them myself for the present, still when Mrs. J. Character was so basely attacked, it was more than my mind could bear to hear it, and not redress it, with that punishment it deserved—I hope providence will spare me to that day, when I can freely act, when retributive Justice will await the actors in this vile procedure—This granted, I will set my house in order, and leave this world in peace.

My bad luck in horses continu, on yesterday morning was found dead one of my most favorite mares leaving a coalt about three weeks old, she had been Just brought home from the horse, and was not discovered to be unwell until found dead.

I have Just started my three youths to College this morning, I hope Hutchings will do better—he has promised me that he will, & I have a hope he will realise it.

Mrs. J. Joins me in a tender of our kind salutations to you & your amiable family, & to Capt Jack & Elisa. your friend

Andrew Jackson

ALS, THi (12-0005). Published in Bassett, 3:402–403 (extract).

1. See Coffee to AJ, May 1.
2. Letter not found. Andrew Jackson, Jr., had been to Alabama to collect the debt owed AJ by Anthony Winston (1782–1839).
3. Coffee had given William Eastin $200 of the $500 from Winston and received in exchange Eastin's check to AJ for $200.
4. The names of only two of the three students in college, Andrew Jackson, Jr., and Andrew J. Hutchings, are known for sure. The third may have been Lyncoya.
5. As of May 12, AJ owed Nichol $1,093.46¼.
6. Winston discharged the balance of his debt in November.

7. See above, AJ to Williams, February 23, and Williams to AJ, February 27.

8. AJ's letter has not been found.

9. For AJ's letters to William C. C. Claiborne, Thomas Jefferson, George W. Campbell, and Daniel Smith, all in late 1806 and early 1807, see *Jackson*, 2:114–20, 147–50.

10. On February 11, Alston (1769–1837), a North Carolina representative, related a conversation with Jefferson during the Burr crisis: "I this day received a letter from him (Gen. Jackson,) informing me that he had seen Burr, and that Burr said his enterprize was sanctioned by the government, and he, Jackson, had been tendered a high command by Burr, and asked of Mr. Jefferson the views of the Government, tendering his services, if wanted, to make a descent upon Mexico, as stated by Burr, but if Burr was not authorized by the government to carry on his enterprize as stated, then he, Jackson, was ready to arrest him" (*Nashville Republican,* September 12).

11. In his *Address to the People of the Congressional District . . .* (1825), Clay had described Adams's elevation to the presidency from the post of secretary of state as "conformity to the safe precedents" established by the examples of Jefferson, Madison, and Monroe.

12. From Joshua 9:21.

The tariff proved to be one of the more troubling issues in the campaign of 1828, as friends and foes alike tried to get Jackson to clarify his views on the subject. Jackson, however, refused to write or say anything beyond referring his interrogators to his votes in Congress and to his letter of April 26, 1824, to Littleton H. Coleman (Jackson, 5:398–400). Many Jacksonians wanted to avoid the issue since their coalition was made up of opponents and advocates of the tariff.

The Twentieth Congress, controlled by Jackson supporters, had to confront the issue, however. The bill that passed in mid-May pleased few, and some contemporary observers held that it had been designed to bolster support for Jackson in the middle states. When the bill became law, with unanticipated support from New York senators, its high duties on flax, hemp, and iron, and lowered tax on woolen goods, provoked many to christen it a "tariff of abominations," particularly in some southern states.

From John Branch

Washington City
May 23d 1828

My Dear Sir,

In a few days Congress will adjourn after a protracted Session of near six months. You may well imagine that many of us who have families are all anxiety to be off. I cannot however depart without saying to you that the prospects are as cheering nay more so than when we first assembled. The new tariff has however depressed the spirits of our southern friends no little, and will I fear produce a sensation in that portion of our union, which if followd up by new exactions on the part of the Governmt must terminate in results deeply to be deplored by every friend to the harmony and union of these States. For my own part it shall be my purpose rather to allay than to foment them.

Both parties have striven to operate on the public mind by legislative enactments. Our friends I am frank to say have fought their opponents with their own weapons and are therefore not exempt from their full share of those undue influences. If the alternative was presented to me of either perpetuating this corrupt dynasty or suffering my votes in Congress to be influenced by considerations connected with the pending Presidential election I certainly could not hesitate which of the two to choose. Of two evils I would choose the least; for I verily believe that if by any means Adams & Clay succeed, that the subversion of the liberties of this people would inevitably ensue. Every thing therefore dear to freemen is at stake.

But Sir I am not one of those who think that the *politicians* in Congress or out of Congress can vary the result. If elected which I trust in God you will be You will owe your election to the people, Yes, Sir to the unbiased, unbought suffrages of the independent, grateful yeomenry of this Country. You will come into the Executive Chair untrammeled, free to pursue the dictates of your own judgment. Many of the *would be* leaders are but humble followers of the people and while they profess to lead, are themselves led. It is really amusing to look on at the game that is playing by those in power; every stratagem every trick & device is resorted to to perpetuate their ill gotten power, when detected in one they fly to another, and as the game is drawing to a close they often present a ludicrous appearance.

It is now pretty well ascertained that Barbour will be sent to England, [William Henry] Harrison to Columbia and P[eter] B[uell] Porter Secretary at war.[1] Webster no doubt desired the mission to England, but the proof of the corrupt bargain between him & Adams is too strong to justify a belief that he could pass the ordeal of the Senate.[2]

[William] Gaston of N. C. was, I have cause to suspect kept in a state of expectancy, otherwise I am very confident that he never would have worshiped at a shrine which I know he detests He therefore has none of my sympathy[3]

I will not burthen you with a long letter, but will conclude by a request that you will present me in the most polite terms to Mrs. Jackson, and accept for yourself my best wishes for your health & happiness

Jno Branch

P.S. You have an independent, firm delegation from your State ardently devoted to the cause of the people, and permit me to say none more so than your immediate Representative Colo Bell

ALS, DLC (35). Published in Bassett, 3:403 (extract).
    1. Just days before Congress adjourned, Adams nominated and the Senate confirmed

Barbour minister to England, Harrison (1773–1841), veteran of the War of 1812 and senator from Ohio, minister to Colombia, and Porter (1773–1844; Yale 1791), also a veteran of the War of 1812 and leader of the Clay forces in New York, secretary of war.

2. On February 5, 1825, Daniel Webster had written to Henry R. Warfield (1774–1839), a Federalist congressman from Maryland, urging him to vote for Adams and assuring him that Adams would treat Federalists fairly (*Webster Papers,* 2:21–22). Warfield and a majority of the Maryland delegation then supported Adams, giving the state's vote in the House. By 1828, the outlines of Webster's letter were general knowledge, and Adams had warnings from many quarters that appointing Webster minister would fuel accusations of another "corrupt bargain."

3. Gaston (1778–1844; Princeton 1796), a lawyer and former Federalist congressman, had delivered the opening address at the North Carolina anti-Jackson convention in Raleigh on December 20, 1827 (Washington *National Intelligencer,* December 29, 1827). The administration considered him for the post of secretary of war before settling on Porter.

To John Caldwell Calhoun

(Copy)   Hermitage May 25th. 1828
Dear Sir,

Your letter of the 30th April 1828, with Majr Lee's of the 30th to you, and your reply, has been recd.[1]

These letters seem only to require from me the remark that Majr Lee has never seen Mr Monroe's private correspondence with me, and that he is, therefore, left to place such a construction upon the public documents as he may conceive they justly deserve.[2] Indeed that correspondence can be of little use in the interpretation of the orders by which I was governed, as on this subject it manifests nothing but an opinion entertained by the executive after they had been executed. Majr Lee has, however, shewn me a letter from Mr Monroe to him, in which he refers to this correspondence, and from which it may be inferred that he is desirous it should be made public. If this be the fact I can assure him that I have no objection to it.[3]

I can have no wish at this day to obtain an explanation of the orders under which I acted whilst charged with the campaign against the seminole Indians in Florida. I viewed them, when recd. as plain and explicit; and called for by the situation of the country. I executed them faithfully, & was happy in reply to my reports to the Department of War to receive your approbation for it. If doubts as to their import had occurred, I should have asked for explanation before I undertook their execution, but none did occur, nor did I suppose that any could be entertained by others, until I recd. the letter of the 19th July 1818 from Mr Monroe,[4] to which you have referred, & upon which I shall make a few remarks as Mr Monroe has also referred to it in his communication to the Majr.

To this letter I replied in August detailing at some length the views which I entertained of your orders, and referring to my communications from Florida where it is said that the measures I had adopted were in pursuance of *your instructions, under a full conviction that they alone were calculated to give peace and security to our frontier.*[5] Mr Monroe's answer contains this remark "that the best course to be pursued seems to me to be, for you (meaning me) to write a letter to the Dept of War in which I would state, that having reason to think that a difference of opinion existed between you and the executive relative to the extent of your powers, you thought it due to yourself to state your views of them and on which you acted. This will be answered so as to explain ours in a very friendly manner by Mr Calhoun &c &c."[6] This letter was recd. on the 13th November, and in my answer to it of the 15th. I referred him to my dispatches from Ft Gadsden and particularly requested his attention to the closing paragraph where I expressly state that all my measures were in conformity to your instructions, and that of course if the ground be then taken that I had transcended my powers, that document would shew that I believed I had not.[7] The fact is I never had the least ground to believe that any difference of opinion between the goverment & myself existed on the subject of my powers: so far from this, to the communications which I made shewing the construction which I placed upon them, there was not merely no difference of opinion indicated in the replies of the executive, but (as far as I received replies) an entire approval of the measures which I adopted—There can be no question that those measures are sustained by the principles of international law by which of course they were governed the moment I entered the foreign territory, and that the orders entrusting to my discretion *"the speedy termination of the War, with exemplary punishment for crimes so unprovoked, and security to our bleeding frontier,"*[8] anticipated this step, I had a right to believe, not only from an obvious construction of them, but from your approbation of my conduct. As Mr Monroe, however, seemed anxious to have on record some views of his own on the subject, my letter of the 15th Novbr. was concluded with the observation that "if the Secy. of War should address me a letter upon this subject I would answer it fully and promptly—"[9] This letter never was received; and I have of course rested satisfied with the belief that I had executed my orders to the letter and spirit, and had obtained the approbation of my country.

After the free and confidential correspondence with Mr Monroe (as in part stated) I must confess that the knowledge of the letter of the 9th Septr. 1818 supposed to have been written to you, taken in connection with Mr Southards wine drinking speech and other rumors of the day, truly astonished me. I am not yet free from surprise, and upon some other occasion may ask you for an explanation. But I certainly can wish none in relation to orders which I think every military man will say were faithfully executed.

Agreeably to your request I enclose the letter alluded to of Mr Monroe which I suppose to have been directed to you. *I send it precisely as I recd. it:* Tho' I had before recd. a copy from a high and responsible source who could have had no agency in obtaining it, with the promise that the original should be sent to me. *I thought it a forgery:* but in the mean time the original came as enclosed, and was handed me by a Gentleman who as far as I know or have been informed never was employed in the War Dept, and if he is honest could have had no unfriendly views to you. When the copy was first sent, it was intimated that it was with your privity as from the signs of the times it might be necessary for self defence. It may be possible that the Gentleman who informed you of its having been sent me, can explain how it came into my hands.[10]

I have before stated that Majr Lee has shewn me yours & Mr Monroe's letters to him, and appears to have a desire to enter into a correspondence with you both on the subject of those orders. Should it meet your wishes I can have no objection: or if Mr Monroe requests it every private and confidential letter that ever passed between us shall be cheerfully laid before the nation. As Mr Monroe has referred the Majr to this correspondence if convenient, I will thank you to communicate to him my feelings on the subject; but without his request I shall not expose this correspondence to Mjr. Lee, or any one else[11] I tender you my best salutation and am with great respect. &c yr friend

Signed Andrew Jackson

LS copy in Andrew J. Donelson's hand with revisions in AJ's hand, DLC (35). Published in Bassett, 3:404–406.

1. See above, Calhoun to AJ, April 30; and Calhoun to Henry Lee, [cApril 30], (DLC-35). Lee's letter to Calhoun has not been found.

2. AJ was referring to correspondence regarding the Seminole War.

3. In his letter to Lee of April 23 (*Writings of James Monroe*, 7:165–67), Monroe reiterated his position that AJ had exceeded his orders during the Seminole War, but that conditions in Florida, unknown to the administration, had justified his deeds. In his [cApril 30] letter to Lee, Calhoun stated that he understood that Lee did not have access to AJ's private correspondence.

4. See Monroe to AJ, July 19, 1818 (*Jackson*, 4:224–28).

5. See AJ to Monroe, August 19, 1818 (*Jackson*, 4:235–39). The italicized text was an approximate quotation from AJ's letter of May 5, 1818, to Calhoun (*Jackson*, 4:196–201).

6. See Monroe to AJ, October 20, 1818.

7. See AJ to Monroe, November 15, 1818 (*Jackson*, 4:246–48). The dispatch from Fort Gadsden, along the Apalachicola River in Florida, was AJ to Calhoun, May 5, 1818.

8. AJ quoted loosely from an order from John C. Calhoun to Edmund P. Gaines, January 16, 1818 (DLC-23), a copy of which the war department transmitted to AJ.

9. AJ quoted loosely from his letter to Monroe, November 15, 1818. Monroe answered on December 21, 1818, agreeing that a further response was unnecessary (*Jackson*, 4:257–59).

10. Houston sent AJ a copy of the September 9, 1818, letter from Monroe to Calhoun in January 1827, and Henry Lee most likely gave the original (not found) to AJ in the late spring or early summer of 1827 when he arrived at the Hermitage. The source of Calhoun's intelligence about the letter is unknown.

11. Calhoun communicated AJ's wishes to Monroe on July 10 (*Calhoun Papers*, 10:398–99). By then, Monroe had already sent Lee a summary of his correspondence with AJ on the Seminole War and indicated that the originals could be found among public documents (*Writings of James Monroe*, 7:169–73).

From James Hamilton, Jr.

Washington May 25h. 1828—

My Dear Sir.

I do myself the honor of enclosing you a speech[1] in which however much you may differ from me in some mere matters of doctrine as to the political economy of the question, you will I am sure do justice to the honesty & sincerity of my feelings—The truth is that this infamous Administration has pressed this most iniquitous Tariff against the South with I believe the express hope of driving us into Rebellion by which they thought they would obtain the votes of Penylana, Ohio & New York, but I am sure the good sense & Patriotism of So. C. will induce it to take no strong measures until your election is put beyond a doubt. I regret that your tariff friends yielded to the popular delusion. They have taken a step which they will find it difficult to maintain & have to retrace—

The Slip cut out of the Telegraph I hope will be gratifying to you. I was delighted that the old Gentleman should have come out—for, the administration papers with their usual falsehood have represented him by a strange sort of perversion against *me* as well as yourself.[2]

You will perceive that after the close of the next Congress I shall leave it, whilst it would have been eminently gratifying to me, to have supported (what I know will be altogether worthy of support) your administration in the House of Representatives. I nevertheless owe a duty to a large family which I can not neglect—At home however much may be done & I trust the truly national character of your administration, will furnish me with the resources of sustaining & doing justice to it, in the Legislature of our State to which I propose when I leave Congress of having my services transfered—[3]

We were greatly concerned to hear of your having a serious attack of your old complaint—We implore you to take the best care of your health—On your Life we believe depends the existence of this Union, for the people of the South, *at least,* will not stand the corruption profligacy & misrule of the present administration for another four years. Pray make my best respects to Mrs Jackson, & tell her we shall expect her to take good care of you & not to allow you to ride in warm weather on horseback in the sun. I pray you Dear Sir to be assured of the great respect & esteem with which I am Your friend—& obt Sert.

J. Hamilton Jr.

My direction will be Charleston So. C.—for the first of the summer, after which if it should be changed I will communicate either with Major Eaton or yourself.

ALS, DLC (35). Published in Bassett, 3:404 (extract)

1. *Speech of Mr. Hamilton of South Carolina, on Mr. Randolph's Motion Indefinitely to Postpone the Tariff Bill, Delivered in the House of Representatives of the United States, 19th April, 1828* (Washington: Green & Jarvis, 1828).

2. Hamilton was referring to an article in the *United States' Telegraph*, May 24, in which his father declared his support for AJ and denied ever having criticized AJ for his statements about Nathanael Greene's treatment of deserters in the American Revolution.

3. Upon his retirement from Congress, Hamilton was elected governor of South Carolina.

From Thomas Pinckney

Charleston S. C. 26 May 1828

Dear Sir,

I am very sorry that it is not in my power to comply with the request contained in your favor of the 22d of last month[1] by forwarding to You a copy of your dispatch to me of the 28th. of March 1814.[2] At the close of the last war an order was issued by the Secretary of War directing that all the military correspondence and documents relating thereto should be transferd to the department at the seat of Government:[3] in conformity whereto all your official letters to me must have been sent to Washington, together with all the contents of the Adjutant Generals and inspectors Offices of the District in which I commanded. But, although much debilitated by sickness and old age, I hasten to answer your letter which (though with the Nashville post mark of the 1st. May) has but recently reached me, in order to assure you of my conviction that your letter, as published in Niles' Register,[4] must be an accurate copy of what you wrote on the battle ground the morning after the Action: although it must appear presumptuous for a man in his seventy eighth year to prefer the result of his recollection to that of one 12 or 15 years younger. But I will explain to you the grounds of this preference, from whence you can draw your own inference: Your doubts appear to be founded in part on the circumstance of the 16 Indians killed on the morning on which you wrote; of which you have no recollection:[5] but I not only perfectly recollect the fact having been made known to me either by your dispatch or by the relation of Officers who supported you in that decisive victory, but I well remember that it was the subject of much conversation as a conspicuous instance of the savage principle of neither receiving nor giving quarter. From the verbal accounts these 16 Indians were reported to have posted themselves in a thicket within the inclosure, from whence they early in the morning fired upon our people; and although repeatedly urged, in their own language, to surrender; with a promise of quarter & good treatment, they persisted in their resistance, until it became necessary to destroy them; as they could not be left or permitted to escape to continue their depredations on our frontier. And you will observe that the above is alluded to in my letter to Governor [Peter] Early as the cause of the extensive slaughter of that tremendous day.[6] Another reason is that I perfectly remember the sentiments contained in my letter to the Governor of Georgia and although I have not my letter book at hand, I believe that letter as reported in the Register to be correct. I have also a perfect recollection of the "hasty sketch of the situation in which the enemy were incamped and of the manner in which you approached them" as stated in that dispatch.[7] It may be observed also that as the letters were published in the Register on the 23d of April of the same year no motive could at that time have existed for altering the original document: To which I may add that my Secretary was remarkable for the fidelity and accuracy of his transactions: and that one of my aids, then with me in the Creek nation, but now in this City, perfectly remembers the transactions of the Indians killed on the 28th of March, as related by the Officers of your Army whom we joined at Fort Jackson.

But I presume another ground exists for your doubts on this subject which your delicacy may have prevented you from objecting to me: otherwise you might very well have enquired how I could have been so inattentive to all military usage & etiquette as to forward a copy of your dispatch to the Governor of Georgia, which ought not to have been communicated but through the department of war. This is accounted for as follows: When in conformity to the orders of the President I assumed the general direction of the Creek war, I found the only troops at my disposal, for this purpose, consisted of the Militia of the adjacent States. An intense interest in the events of the war was naturally excited in those States, particularly among the relatives and friends of those actively engaged in the contest; and thinking that, in our circumstances, the public service would not suffer by deviating, in favor of these feelings, from the usuall routine; I solicited & obtained from the War department permission to publish at once on the spot, the official communications I might receive of the events occurring in the different detachments of the Army under my direction.[8] I trust, my dear Sir, you will appreciate the motive for my troubling you with this tedious detail and beg you to be assured of the continued respect and regard of your faithful Servant.

Thomas Pinckney

ALS, DLC (35). Published in Bassett, 3:406–407 (extract).

1. See AJ to Pinckney, April 22.

2. See AJ to Pinckney, March 28, 1814, (*Jackson*, 3:52–54).

3. Pinckney was probably referring to the general order from Daniel Parker, April 17, 1815 (Orderly Book of the Adjutant General, Vol. 391, 7th Military District, Division of the South, p. 192, DNA-RG 98).

4. AJ's letter of March 28, 1814, had been published in *Niles' Register*, April 23, 1814.

5. The March 28th, 1814, letter to Pinckney had mentioned the killing of sixteen Indians who had refused to surrender.

6. Pinckney's letter of April 2, 1814, to Early (1773–1817; Princeton 1792), of Georgia, attributed the heavy losses of the Creeks at Horseshoe Bend to their refusal to surrender. The Jacksonians' definitive response to the massacre charge, authored by Samuel Houston with testimony from many of AJ's subordinates, argued that all killings following the

main assault were justified by continued Indian resistance and emphasized that the sixteen Creeks fell in a battle with the Cherokees (*Nashville Republican & State Gazette*, September 26).

7. Pinckney was quoting from AJ's March 28, 1814, letter.

8. On February 28, 1814, Secretary of War John Armstrong gave Pinckney approval to publish official communications (DNA-RG 107, M6-7).

While Jackson generally declined to respond publicly to attacks or to interrogatories, he did work closely with the Nashville Committee in its preparation of defenses. In the case below, he sent materials for a response to Dr. James L. Armstrong's list of "juvenile indiscretions," published in the Lexington Kentucky Reporter, *June 11, and he also assisted the committee in its response to the charges of murder in the Dickinson duel.*

To William Berkeley Lewis

June 19th. 1828—

Dr. Sir

I herewith send you the papers relating to the affair with Dickinson,[1] &c, in this bundle, will be found also the papers with regard to Natha[nie]l McNairy as I suppose.[2] I also send the papers relating to the [John] Sevier[3] & Benton affairs &c[4]—I wish you to keep them yourself, & keep them safely—

I find Judge Whites & [Spencer] Jarrnagans were confidential they are destroyed,[5] but Judge [John] Overton can give such facts of Col Williams conduct in this affair of seducing the child of Doctor May to participate in this thing[6] as will be necessary in connection with Genl Dunlaps letters[7] to convince the world of his baseness & connection with Col A[nder]son in this matter, as may be necessary to convince every one of the channel thro' which Doctor Armstrong has been furnished with his information.[8]

you will find the meeting with D. was on the 30th. of May 1806—the certificates of Catlett & Overton on 25th. of June[9]—surely there could not have been much dificulty in obtaining them, as their could have been no use for them untill the publication of [Joseph] Erwin.[10] I barely note this to draw your attention to Dr Mays letter to Anderson as published—[11]

From Dunlaps letter you will see the propriety of accompanying the short notice taken of this matter, with the statement of May & Anderson suit &c &c[12] If necessary I will come down—advise me—The ladies are waiting & I must close yrs

Andrew Jackson

ALS, T (12-0020).

1. For the documents relating to the Dickinson duel, see *Jackson,* 2:77–105, *passim.*
2. McNairy (1779–1857) was a Nashville lawyer. For the papers found regarding AJ's quarrel with him, see *Jackson,* 2:89–91.
3. Sevier (1745–1815) was a former Tennessee governor. For the materials relating to the disputes with him, see *Jackson,* 1:489–506.
4. For documents relating to the fight with the Bentons, see *Jackson,* 2:408–27, *passim.*
5. Jarnagin (1794–1851) was a Knoxville lawyer who had read law in Hugh L. White's office.
6. According to AJ's recounting in his letter to William B. Lewis of June 22, below, John Williams had, in 1817, induced Anthony May (1804–25), son of Francis, to make copies of the letters from May to William P. Anderson.
7. See above, Richard Gilliam Dunlap to AJ, June 4, 1827.
8. Jackson continued to suspect that Williams had provided copies to Armstrong, who had published them in his "Tennesseean" essay, No. VI, in the *Kentucky Reporter,* June 11.
9. Jackson was at this point attempting to rebut Williams's contention that the affidavits of Catlett and Overton were obtained by coercion.
10. Erwin (c1761–1829), the owner of the horse Ploughboy whose forfeiture to AJ's Truxton set into motion the events that led to the duel, was Dickinson's father-in-law. His statement attacking AJ's conduct both before and during the fatal affair was issued on June 21, 1806, only four days before the date on Catlet's certificate (Bassett, 1:147–49). May's letters asserted that it had taken Overton eight to ten days to extract the statement from Catlet.
11. The charges in the May letters of September 16 and 17, 1817, were, first, that Thomas Overton had used threats to extract a favorable statement regarding the duel from Catlet, Dickinson's surgeon and second in the duel; and second, that John Overton's published account of June 28, 1806, suppressed the portion of May's statement that raised the issue of AJ's pistol's snapping without a fire.
12. See above, Dunlap to AJ, June 4, 1827. On June 27, 1828, the *Nashville Republican* (not extant) published a defense of Jackson's action in the Dickinson duel, presumably written by Lewis (reprinted in the *Knoxville Register,* July 16).

On March 25 the United States' Telegraph *claimed that the charges made by "Tennesseean" in the Lexington* Kentucky Reporter *were part of an effort by "the coalition . . . to divert public attention from themselves" and attributed authorship to Andrew Erwin, in its view Clay's pawn. Erwin, the* Telegraph *added, was not to be believed: he had been branded a slave smuggler and perjurer by the attorney-general (*Jackson, 4:286–87, 329–33).

*In response, Erwin claimed that he was "entirely unconnected" with the "Tennesseean" publications and was innocent of the charge of slave smuggling: the Georgia legislature had restored the smuggled slaves to his partner William Bowen, not to him. Erwin then took the offensive by warning Jacksonians that "their own idol was once himself engaged, to a considerable extent, in this traffic of human flesh" (*Kentucky Reporter, *May 21). He founded the charge on a memorandum in one of Jackson's bank books and on the record of the settlement of accounts with Horace Green and Joseph Coleman, Jackson's one time business partners (*Jackson, 2:261–63, 286–90).

Jackson had deposited the bank book, along with some other papers,

*in the Bank of Nashville for safekeeping during the Seminole campaign
and had left them there until he heard that his opponents were plundering the items for evidence against him. Jackson reclaimed the documents,
but Erwin already had a copy of the item he shortly published in support
of his allegation. At that time, the Jacksonians, denying Erwin's claim,
created a diversion by asking how Erwin got a copy of the memorandum
from the bank book. As the documents below suggest, that ploy deeply
divided the officers of the bank and much of the Nashville community, as
the anti-Jacksonians and the Jacksonians made further accusations and
developed defenses.*

To John Coffee

Hermitage June 20th. 1828—

Dr. Genl

When I last wrote you, I expected to have been with you ere this, but
the administration is making their last, dying, desperate struggle, and you
will see from the newspapers that all their corrupt tools are, & have been
at work—you will see in the reporter, the long rumored letter of Doctor
May procured by Wm. P. Anderson & Col Williams[1]—if wrote by May,
it displays a depravity more than common in the basest of the human
race, & displays another viper I have cherished in my boosom. It will be
promptly noticed, and the memory of May handed down to everlasting
dishonor, and I trust I will be able fully to expose Williams, & Anderson
in this thing.[2]

I am told by my son that James Jackson has shewn a disposition to be
friendly with you—If so, should an opportunity offer, to introduce a conversation with him on this subject, he was then friendly with me, & intimate with May, & heard him often extoll my conduct on that occasion
as honorable & fair in the highest degree—If, on conversing with him, he
speaks freely of the subject & recollects the Doctors declarations, you can
say to him, that Justice, truth, & magnanimity would say to him to give a
statement in writing of the Doctors uniform expressions on this subject.
if he does, send it to me, but *do not ask him for it.*[3]

How hard it is to keep the cowhide from some of these villains—I have
made many sacrafices for the good of my country—but the present, being
placed in a situation that I cannot act, and punish those slanderers, not
only of me, but Mrs. J. is a sacrafice too great to be well endure*[d]* yet a
little I must bear with it—To be told throu*[gh]* the prints by such a villain
as Andrew Erwin that I told him in 1811—that I was in the negro t*[rade]*[4]
is really too much, he knows my hands are bound, he does this to vex me,
and being detected in a lie, shifts his ground, and gives his own assertions
for proof—If my directions are complied with, he will get a reply which

he deserves—I fear our Editors want a little more energy—still I hope this fellow Erwin will be fully met.[5] The other case I am sure will be.

I have Judge Overtons statement of the uniform statement of Doctor May, his situation is a delicate one, and I will not use it if I can help it[6]—Therefore have brought to your view James Jackson—he being unfriendly with me, would have a good effect, and at once stop Patrick H. Darby & such other Corrupt Tools in Kentucky[7]—But from experience I know the corruption of the times, and act with great caution with James Jackson on this subject—

I will be to see you as soon as I can, in the mean time please close up the accounts with little Hutchings Estate as you find Justice to him requires—I have not had time to read the acts of Congress, I think there is a law passed, with regard to relinquished land—I know you attend to these laws, say to me in answer, if there is, & in what time the entry is to be made, that I may look round & be prepared with the funds to meet it[8]—For, from the pressure upon my friend McLamore I would not now ask him for what he owes—and Doctor Hogg, is in the same situation—[9]

I have a promising crop of cotton & corn, a good rain is wanted now, if it should be seasonable, I will raise as much as year before last—

with our love to Polly & the children & kind wishes for yourself, I am your friend—

Andrew Jackson

P.S. Mrs. J. Capt. A. J. D. & Mrs D. is at Nashville, went down yesterday to see Stockly maried[10]—I was pleased to learn from Capt Thos. [Booth] Jones[11] that all things were going on well at little Hutchings farm.

ALS, THi (12-0021). Published in Bassett, 3:409–410.

1. AJ was referring to the letters of September 16 and 17, 1817, published in the Lexington *Kentucky Reporter,* June 11.

2. William B. Lewis's response to Francis May's charges appeared in the *Nashville Republican,* June 27, and was reprinted in the *Knoxville Register,* July 16.

3. On July 2, Coffee wrote that he could not approach James Jackson on the subject.

4. Erwin had published that assertion in the June 20 *National Banner and Nashville Whig.*

5. On July 4 and 11, the *Nashville Republican* countered Erwin's charges, stating that in the Coleman, Green and Jackson business, AJ was security only.

6. A summary of the statement of Overton, who was married to May's widow, appears in AJ to William B. Lewis, June 22, below.

7. Darby, in his Frankfort *Commentator,* had published material on the Dickinson duel in 1827.

8. AJ was referring to a bill to allow those who, in the wake of the panic of 1819, had relinquished land bought on credit from the federal government to repurchase this property. The bill did not pass. The Hutchings estate had relinquished five tracts of land in 1821 (*Jackson,* 5:83).

9. McLemore had borrowed $1,000 from the Hutchings estate in June 1826, and Hogg owed the Hutchings estate about $1,500.

10. Stockly Donelson married Phila Ann Lawrence (1809–51).

11. Jones (c1800–c1868), a veteran of the Creek War, at this time lived in Lauderdale County, Alabama.

To William Berkeley Lewis

Hermitage June 22nd. 1828

Dr. Major

I recd. on the evening of the 20th. your note, same date,[1] by Mrs. J. with the K. Reporter, for which I thank you—When I read the letters signed F. May I could not help weeping over the corruption of human nature[2]—To behold in them the basest falshoods, for the vilest purpose, and from one I had a right to expect Justice, for to him, I had extended the arm of friendship, and protected him in my house when exiled and friendless, & surrounded by enemies,[3] and this too, because I would not become *a villain*, & aid him & Col W. P. Anderson, to cheat orphants, out of a large property, & support their spurious claim bought, as he told me, for $100, $50 of which paid in a horse[4]—What an accomplished villain he must have been, & aided, by still greater villains if possible, Wm. P. Anderson & Col John Williams, men combined secretely to assasinate my character & this too after Genl Overton was dead, for had he been living, These vipers dare not thus to have assailed his honor—I do think the letters are the most self damning evidence that I ever saw, here again is the adage proven, that "Truth is mighty & will prevail—"

I should have wrote you this morning was prevented by Mr Haskell calling[5]—however, it affords me the opportunity to send you Col [Edward] Wards statement of the uniform relation of this matter by Genl Thos. Overton, his friend & neighbour.[6]

The certificates of Capt [Andrew] Morrison & Major [John Pryor] Hickman, are important,[7] & I sincerely thank you for your attention—for altho, as you observe, Mays letters consign his memory to everlasting infamy, they are important to do Justice to Genl. Overton & Catletts memories—These arch fiends, Williams & Anderson has let this sleep untill *all are dead*. These fellows must be brought forth in bold relief—I suppose Judge Overton has given you a statement how Col Williams came by them, and how he induced one of Dr. Mays sons, to copy, & certify that it was a true copy from the original in his fathers hand writing. how the youth on reflection became alarmed fearing his uncles pursuasions had led him to do an act that was wrong, under this impression, his coming from school to consult with his uncle Judge H. L. Whites, upon the subject—The Judge upon hearing the youths story, told him, he had done wrong, & might bring disgrace upon his fathers memory, as his father had not only certified to the upright & Honorable conduct on my part in this affair, but had represented on all occasions to have been fairly & honorably conducted, and told the youth to go to his uncle, demand the letters, & destroy them—that the youth went to his uncle Col. Williams, demanded the letters, & his uncle refused to give them up—They are now before the public—¿can any thing exceed this in baseness: nothing, except the Cols. producing his wife certificate to free him from the detection of a falshood he had uttered against Judge White, to be used against her brother, this to be sure has not its paralel in baseness; and I hope will be brought into view, there is proof positive of this fact, and the detail of the first, I had from the lips of Judge White.[8]

I inclose two letters of Judge Overtons to me[9] for your perusal—that extracts may be used, if thought necessary, but his name witheld—you will preserve them safely, & let no person see them but Major Lee, and this only, if you think it discreet—John Williams conduct must be stated in bold relief—his conduct, and his whole Conduct—I will be responsible for the facts I have here stated, he deserves no mercy, nor ought lenity to be extended to Anderson or May—I will barely add, that Anderson & Col. Williams are both Master Masons—and this two, ought to be stated, it will damn him in East Tennessee where the craft are numerous—

I enclosed to you the other day Genl Dunlaps letter, *use it*.[10] I have reflected since I saw you, whether it would not be better for Major Lee to remain, and finish the narative of my life, & have it ready to present to the public on the close of the Election for President, when he could take a full view of all these matters, and present to the public such testimony as would consign to the contempt of all good men those minions of corruption, & base calumniators, by notifying the public that it would appear at that time, and the reason why it is posponed, <is> that it may be read by all, clear from the imputation, that it has been written for political effect—a debt I owe to myself, & the morals of the country has brought me to the conclusion to have it written, and I think thousands of copies would be sold[11]—for when the political heat is over, all good men will wish to know the truth—Name this idea to Major Lee.

I intend riding down early monday morning, or writing you, when I shall not forget the Bank business[12]—& shall speak more to you on the subject of the history—write me a note by return of bearer your friend

Andrew Jackson

P.S. Tell Hall to have a number of extra papers printed;[13] they must be sent to every state in the union—I enclose you a letter recd. from Ohio[14]— A. J—

ALS, NN (12-0024).
    1. Not found.
    2. On June 11, the Lexington *Kentucky Reporter* had printed the letters to William P. Anderson from Francis May, AJ's surgeon in the Dickinson duel.
    3. AJ was referring to the occasion in 1804, when May killed a medical colleague in a duel.
    4. AJ was referring to the May-Anderson suit against the William T. Lewis estate.

5. Probably Joshua Haskell (c1786–1840), judge of the eighth circuit of Tennessee, 1821–36.

6. On June 21, Ward wrote that Thomas Overton had never said anything about a pistol snap (*Knoxville Register,* July 16).

7. In his certificate Morrison (d. 1832), who operated the suspension bridge across the Cumberland River in Nashville, declared that Hanson Catlet had described AJ's behavior in the Dickinson duel as honorable (*Nashville Republican,* October 3). The statement from Hickman (1788–1840), who later represented Davidson County in the Tennessee General Assembly, 1835–37, has not been found.

8. John Williams's wife was Malinda White (d. 1838), the sister of Hugh L. White. The details of John Williams's "falsehood" have not been established. The commentary on the May letters published in the *Nashville Republican* on June 27 (not extant but reprinted in *Knoxville Register,* July 16) did not discuss the White incident, but it did detail Williams's dealings with young May, giving White and John Overton as sources.

9. Not identified.

10. See above, Dunlap to AJ, June 4, 1827.

11. Henry Lee soon left Nashville for the east coast and failed to complete his biography of AJ.

12. The "Bank business" probably pertained to AJ's 1811 bank book, which Andrew Erwin claimed contained proof of AJ's involvement in the slave trade.

13. AJ was referring to the article in Allen A. Hall's June 27 *Nashville Republican,* which defended AJ's behavior in the Dickinson duel and denounced the accounts of Anderson and May.

14. Not identified.

To John Branch

Hermitage June 24th. 1828

My Dear Sir

Your letter of the 23rd. ult. I have recd.[1] and hope this will find you at home amidst the sweet embraces of your amiable family, relaxed from the turmoils of political strife with which you have been surrounded during a protracted session of six months. I feel well assured that nothing could be more painfull to you, and every member of your body, whose paramount object is the public good, than to witness those scenes which are produced by the influence of executive patronage, operating upon the unprincipled aspirant for office, who would rather excite the angry passions than harmonise for the common good, by a strict adherence to the principles of virtue, honor, & Justice—

But my Dear Sir, I do not yet despair of the republic. I trust there is sufficient virtue in a great majority of the american people, to check the present system of corruption, in endeavouring to effect every thing by intrigue slander & management; and I shall live to see the day, when virtue shall resume its former umpire in the consels of the nation; when the public good will be the sole end & aim of the Legislature of the Union; When our national character, will no longer be stained, by charges against an itinerant cabinet travelling through our country, circulating forgeries & calumnies against individuals;[2] appropriating mony out of the contingent fund, for printing pamphlets, containing the most infamous slanders against female reputation;[3] and to close the scene, members of Congress prostituting their franking privilege, in circulating those slanders.[4]

Virtue, I trust, will once more arise from her lethargy & dispel those corruptions, with all the train of ills; <when the happy genius of a Washington & a Jefferson will again preside over our destiny> When the Constitution will be so amended as to preserve to the people their rightful sovereignity, & restore in practice the proper checks & ballances; when the public debt will be paid, and the executive department of our goverment freed from the corrupting influence of a monied aristocracy; When Congress will legislate with an eye single to the public weal, and limit by special acts all appropriations, and compel every officer in the goverment annually to account to Congress how the funds entrusted to his care have been applied.

Then, and not until then, will our national character be freed from the charges of corruption which is now imputed to it—keep our officers free from temptation, & they will be honest.

My health is good—Mrs. Jackson Joins with me, in a tender of our kind salutations to you & your amiable family very respectfully yr friend

Andrew Jackson

ALS draft, DLC (35).
1. See above.
2. Noting especially Samuel L. Southard's visit to New Jersey on the eve of 1826 elections in that state, James Barbour's visits to Virginia and Maryland, and Henry Clay's western tours, the Jacksonian press referred repeatedly to the "itinerant cabinet" to indicate that the administration was neglecting business for electioneering.
3. The Jacksonian press regularly complained that Clay used the state department contingency fund for partisan purposes. The House had investigated the matter and, in its report (*HRRep* 226, 20th Cong., 1st sess., Serial 178), found several irregularities, but it did not accuse Clay of abuse of office.
4. Beginning in late April, the *United States' Telegraph* had published complaints that congressmen David Woodcock, Henry R. Storrs, and Henry C. Martindale of New York; Isaac Pierson of New Jersey; Elisha Whittlesey of Ohio; John Culpepper of North Carolina; Clement Dorsey of Maryland; and Thomas Metcalfe and Robert P. Letcher of Kentucky, among others, were using the franking privilege to distribute campaign documents against Jackson. Most of the discussion focused on the distribution of the *Official Record from the War Department of the Proceedings of the Court Martial Which Tried, and the Orders of General Jackson for Shooting the Six Militia Men* . . . (Washington, 1828), which masqueraded as a government document and facilitated the franking. Some instances were also noted when documents on the Jacksons' marriage had been franked.

To Samuel Houston

Hermitage June 28th. 1828

Dr. Sir

I am anxious to hear the result of the affair between Col Parish & Doctor McNairy with the current news of Nashville[1]—I suppose the last republican contains something interesting, I have sent for it.[2]

When will you be up—recollect I set out on the first proximo, & tarry that night with my old friend Col [David] Campbell,[3] will Mr Earle be with you—I would like to see my old friend Judge Overton before I set out, if he does not accompany me, if you see him, please say so to him.

give me the news of your City, and accept of the kind salutations of Mrs J and myself & believe me your friend

Andrew Jackson

Photcopy of ALS, Tx (12-0033).
   1. Parrish was cashier of the Nashville branch of the Bank of Tennessee and McNairy was president of the Nashville Bank.
   2. Jackson was referring to the article on the Dickinson duel in the *Nashville Republican* of June 27.
   3. AJ had accepted an invitation to attend the Fourth of July celebration in Carthage, Tennessee, spending the night with Campbell (1782–1841), a Sumner County planter.

To William Berkeley Lewis

Hermitage June 28th. 1828—

Dr Major.

I am unadvised whether Mr E. H. Foster has furnished you with the statement promised.[1] If he has, please send me a copy of the one stating the conduct of the President & Cashier of the Nashville Bank, Dr McNairy & [Wilkins] Tannyhill,[2] exposing my Bank Book to Andrew Erwin & Co—*This I want.*

I wish you to send me about a Dozzen of the Nashville Republicans.[3]

Will it be in your power to accompany me to Carthage. I leave home on the evening of the first of July, & will tarry that night at Col Campbells.

If you have time write me, and give me the current news of Nashville I am respectfully yr friend

Andrew Jackson

ALS, NNPM (12-0035). Published in Bassett, 3:411.

1. AJ had probably sought a statement from Foster, a director of the Bank of Nashville, about how Erwin got a copy of the May 18, 1811, memorandum in his bank book. Foster's statement has not been found, but he did continue to support AJ in the campaign, even publishing a letter from John R. Lucas (d. 1831), a Limestone, Alabama, physician and acquaintance of Richard Apperson, who sold the slaves to Coleman, Green, and Jackson, asserting that Apperson had related to him at the time that AJ was merely security in the transaction, not a principal (*National Banner and Nashville Whig,* September 20).

2. Tannehill (1787–1858), AJ's successor as Grand Master of the Grand Lodge of Tennessee, a merchant, former mayor of Nashville, and president of the bank, admitted that he "did 'exhibit' [the book] to five or six persons, amongst whom was *a firm and decided friend of Gen Jackson,*" not with any intent to try to influence the election but to show the select few that the *Nashville Republican* had been too hasty in its denial of AJ's involvement in the slave-trading enterprise (*National Banner and Nashville Whig,* July 18). Presumably Foster was the Jacksonian present when Tannehill showed the bank book. McNairy denied having any role in the exhibition.

3. Probably the June 27 issue on the Dickinson duel.

To James Hamilton, Jr.

Hermitage June 29th. 1828

My dear sir,

I have had the pleasure to receive your kind letter of the 25th. ult.[1] with its inclosures, for which I thank you. I have read your speech with much attention, and permit me to assure you, if we differ in some matters of doctrine as to political economy, I am sure it is an honest difference of opinion, and I will always do Justice to your sincerity.[2]

I regretted to see the subject of a Tariff question discussed under the strong feelings of political excitement that prevaded the whole nation, & congress. To regulate a Judicious tariff, is a subject of great dificulty at all times, & ought to be discussed, with great calmness & due deliberation, with an eye to the prosperity of the whole Union, & not of any particular part viewing the whole as one great family, & extending impartial Justice to every branch, with feelings of Mutual concession, extending to all equal benefits, and each bearing a Just portion of the burdens the Tariff may impose—Whether the late act will operate equally upon every section of the union, can only be tested b[y] experience.

There is nothing that I shudder at more than the idea of a seperation of the Union. Should such an event ever happen, which I fervently pray god to avert, from that date, I view our liberty gone—It is the durability of the confederation upon which the general goverment is built, that must prolong our liberty, the moment it seperates, it is gone. The State goverments hold in check the federal, & must ever hold it in check, & the virtue of the people supported, by the <independent> sovereign States, must prevent consolidation, & will put down that corruption engendered by executive patronage, wielded, as it has been lately, by executive organs, to perpetuate their own power. The result of the present struggle

between the virtue of the people & executive patronage will test the stability of our goverment, and I for one do not despair of the republic; I
have great confidence in the virtue of a great majority of the people, and I
cannot fear the result—The republic is safe, its main pillars virtue, religion & morality will be fostered by a majority of the people, the designing demagogues who have attempted to retain power by the most corrupt
means will be driven by the indignant frowns of the people into obscu-
rity, & if ever thereafter remembered will be, as a Silla or caribdis.[3]

I sincerely regret the determination you have taken to withdraw from
public life; you cannot be spared from the councils of the nation; your
services are still necessary to aid in bringing back the administration to
the virtuous precepts of a Washington & Jefferson, in renewing the land
marks of the constitution, between the states and general goverment,
<which may be necessary to prevent consolidation> and to aid in the nec-
essary amendments of the constitution.

I sincerely thank you for the slip cut out of the Telegraph—your father
in his reply has displayed the true roman, he loves his friend, but he loves
truth more—I was truly gratified upon receiving it, and was much astonished that Col [Marinus] Willett should have been the author of such a
production[4]—present me affectionately to your father, say to him his reply has added to his fame, it is approved by all, whilst all honest patriots
must disapprove Col Willetts conduct, his publication must forever tarnish his fame. I hope you have recd the reply made to Col Willetts publication in the Nashville republican.[5] it nails his falshood to the counter, it
was sent you by Major H. Lee.

My health is good—Mrs. J. makes to you a tender of her affectionate
regard, & desires me to say to you that she will comply with your instructions as far as she has the power, & unites with me in kind salutations to you & your amiable family Sincerely yr friend

Andrew Jackson

ALS draft, DLC (35). Published in Bassett, 3:411–12.
    1. See above.
    2. In his speech against the tariff, Hamilton warned: "My constituents believe, as a sov-
ereign party to the compact of this Union, that South Carolina never did confer upon this
government the power to tax the industry of her own citizens for the exclusive benefit of the
industry of the citizens of the other States."
    3. Scylla and Charybdis were mythical monsters that imperiled shipping from opposite
sides of the strait separating Sicily from the Italian peninsula.
    4. Willett (1740–1830), a comrade of Hamilton, Sr., in the Revolutionary War, had
reported that Hamilton had said to him in 1826 that the comparison of AJ's execution of
the six militiamen to Nathanael Greene's execution of deserters during the Revolution was
a slander upon Greene. Hamilton's letter denied such a statement.
    5. The reply appeared in the June 6 issue of the Nashville Republican.

To Ralph Eleazar Whitesides Earl

Hermitage July 10th. 1828—
Genl A. Jackson with compliments to Mr. Earle, requests his attention to getting Doctor [James R.] Putnam[1] to finish my teeth—If the Doctor should want my presence the Genl will thank Mr. Earle to say to the Doctor he must ride up on tomorrow or Saturday

AN, InHi (12-0044).
   1. Not further identified.

*Even though settled, the Allison case continued to vex Jackson. James L. Armstrong's second and fourth "Tennesseean" articles condemned his conduct in the matter, claiming that in suing Andrew Erwin and others for title to the lands in middle Tennessee, Jackson had tried to reclaim lands that he himself had sold to Erwin years before (*Lexington *Kentucky* Reporter, *February 13 and April 9; Jackson, 2:62–63, 296–97; 4:315–18; 5:259–63, 307–309, 357–59; and above, AJ to John Coffee, May 19, 1825).*

Jacksonians issued a comprehensive reply to these charges in the May 16 Nashville Republican, arguing that Jackson's claim, based on David Allison's debts to him, was both legally and morally strong, that his lawsuit against Erwin had instead been to clear titles for purchasers of the land. Indeed, Jackson had been generous to Erwin, settling for just $10,000 (all of which went to AJ's partners). According to their story, Jackson settled for that sum because of an emotional appeal from Erwin's wife, Jane Patton Erwin (1770–1859), who tearfully pleaded with Jackson that to pay more would bankrupt Erwin. Erwin, however, denied his wife's role, asserting in the July 11 National Banner and Nashville Whig *that "neither she nor myself, nor any member of my family ever solicited any favors." In his denial, Erwin ignored a May 1827 testimonial by James Jackson, a party to the settlement, who stated that "Gen. Jackson compromised his half of the property by giving it up to Mrs. Andrew Erwin, in the event they could settle with me for the other half" (*Frankfort Commentator, *January 19, 1828).*

To *William Berkeley Lewis*

Hermitage July 10th. 1828—

Dr Major.

I never before late last evening saw A. Erwins piece in the Banner of the 8th.[1] however despicable I viewed him to be, I did not believe he was so regardless of truth, as I see, from his statement there, he must be. That he would deny the statement, tears, & supplication of Mrs. Erwin, on the subject of the suit, & her declarations, that she had been informed of the propositions of compromise, but being unable to meet it, they and all their Tenants would be ruined, he being present the whole time, convinces me, that he is the basest of the base—It was Mrs. Erwins tears that drew from me the reply "that I never could sleep sound upon my pillow, & reflect that for ten thousand dollars so many were in distress,["] therefore as my first object was to secure my tenants that Mr. Erwin had been trying to harrass & disposess, that so far as I was interested I would relinquish, being one half the twenty thousand dollars, which was seized on by Mr Erwin, & requested I would thus write upon the memorandom of compromise, which was to remain in the hands of Judge McNairy but had been put into the hands of Erwin, as he said, to shew his tenants—Judge McNairy has the paper in his possession, & I have no doubt recollects, my stating the case to him, & I have no doubt, that Erwin also has made a similar statement to him—please ask him, if Erwin did not so state to him, as I had, the manner & cause of the compromise—I have no doubt but the Judge recollects it—The Judge has the paper containing the terms of compromise, & my note on margin made at the stone fort,[2] *that I would relinquish my interest $10,000,* if he would settle ballance with James Jackson—I wish you to see Judge McNairy, & converse with him on this subject before the paper of tomorrow comes out—

I send inclosed a statement of Major A. J Donelson, that can be used as you may think best[3]—The publication ought to conclude with severity[4]—by observing, having shewn that Erwin is a base liar, & unworthy of the least credit, no more shall the columns of the republican be poluted by noticing any thing he may say, he stands charged on the records of the nation, by the atto. Genl U. States with corrupt perjury,[5] & the documents here appended shews, he lies with the same fearless boldness, as an honest man speaks the truth, having exposed his baseness no farther notice will be taken of him in our columns by us, leaving him & his coadjutor Dr Armstrong to the contempt of an honest public who has consigned them to infamy—In haste your friend

Andrew Jackson

ALS, NN (12-0045). Published in Bassett, 3:412–13.

1. The *National Banner and Nashville Whig* of July 8 is not extant but the issue of July 11 reprinted Erwin's piece.

2. Stone Fort, an abandoned Indian site in Franklin County, near the border of Bedford County, on the northernmost fork of the Duck River. AJ was in the area to attend Erwin's taking of depositions when the two agreed on the compromise settlement.

3. Not identified.

4. On July 11, the *Nashville Republican* published a long denunciation of Erwin, and it followed up with another attack on August 8.

5. For a discussion of Erwin's slave smuggling, see *Jackson*, 4:286–87, 329–33. The opinion of Attorney General William Wirt (1782–1834) on Erwin's slave smuggling and his defense appeared in *Message from the President of the United States, Transmitting . . . a Report of the Attorney General, Relative to the Introduction of Slaves into the United States, Contrary to Existing Laws* (Washington, 1822; *SDoc* 93, 17th Cong., 1st sess., Serial 60).

From John Caldwell Calhoun

Pendleton 10th July 1828

Dear Sir,

I have received your letter of the 25th May[1] inclosing the letter of Mr Monroe to me of the 9th Sept. 1818. The delay incident to the passage of a letter from Nashville to Washington & thence to this place will explain the long interval between the date of your letter and this my acknowlegement of it.

The more I reflect on the subject, the more am I convinced, that the letter of the 9th Sept. was intended by those, who took it out of my possession, as the instrument of a dark and dangerous intrigue, alike hostile to you and myself.[2] The first object certainly was to bring you and Mr Monroe into conflict; but I feel not less confident, that its ultimate was to bring you and myself into the same state, and that for the special benefit of those at the bottom of the scheme. I cannot doubt, but a part of the plan was to follow it up with secret and slanderous representation of my conduct. Knowing that my whole course had been open and strongly marked, the contrivers of this wicked scheme clearly saw the necessity of keeping my name at first out of view, and to attempt in the first instance to direct your suspicion against Mr Monroe. With this object, the letter was doubtless mutilated by tearing off the cover, so as to leave it uncertain, to whom it was addressed; and to the same motive must be traced the unfounded intimation, that the letter was communicated to you with my connivance, and with the intention of guarding you against treachery imputed to Mr Monroe; a course of conduct, which if true, would prove me to be equally cowardly and base. There need no other proof of the dark design at the bottom of this affair, than the fact, that while these insidious intimations were made to you, the whole affair was studiously concealed from me. I was even ignorant, that the letter was out of my possession; and by mere accident, I obtained the clue, which has given me the little that I know about it. I was thus kept in the dark, while the plot rested on a supposition highly injurious to my character.[3] It presupposes, that while Mr Monroe, under the garb of friendship, had formed an artful plan to entrap you into a correspondence, with the view of shifting the responsibility from himself by sacrificing you, that, I was to be the instrument in so base a transaction. Lost indeed would I have been to every sentiment of honor and virtue could such a proposition be made to me, without instant denunciation of its Author. The mail that brought the letter would have returned with my resignation, and an eternal barrier would have been placed between us.

Far otherwise was my construction of the object of the letter. I never doubted, that it originated in motives at once friendly and patriotick; and that its object was to place your conduct, as well as that of the Government on the high grounds, on which it ought to stand, by each side presenting fully and distinctly on the records of the government its views in regard to the orders, under which you acted. Any discussion of them now, I agree with you, would be unnecessary. They are matters of history, and must be left to the historian, as they stand. In fact, I never did suppose, that the justification of yourself or the government depended on a critical construction of them. It is sufficient for both, that they were honestly issued and honestly executed, without involving the question, whether they were executed strictly in accordance with the intention that they were issued. Honest and patriotick motives are all, that can be required, and I never doubted but that they existed on both sides. I will write to Mr Monroe on the subject to which you refer,[4] and should I receive an answer will forward it immediately.

You will see by the papers, that the Tariff of the last session excites much feeling in this, and the other Southern atlantick States. The impression, as far as I have observed, is nearly universal, that the system acts with great severity against the staple states, and that it is the real cause of their impoverishment. Under such impressions, it is not surprizing, that there should be some excess of feeling, but it would be wrong to infer, that it indicates a want of attachment to the Union. The long cherished attachment to our institutions is not so easily weakened, but as strong as it is, an impression of long continued wrongs would not fail to shake it. The belief that those now in power will be displaced shortly; and that under an administration formed under your auspices, a better order of things will commence, in which, an equal distribution of the burden and benefit of government, economy, the payment of the publick debt, and finally the removal of oppressive duties, will be primary objects of policy is what mainly consoles this quarter of the Union under existing embarrassment. That your administration may be the means of restoring harmony to this distracted country and of averting the alarming crisis before us is my sincere prayer. With sincere regard your friend

J. C. Calhoun—

ALS, DLC (35). Published in Bassett, 3:413–15.
1. See above.
2. See above, Houston to AJ, January 13, 1827, and Eaton to AJ, March 4, 1828, for a discussion of the September 9, 1818, letter.
3. In February 1827 Calhoun learned that the letter was no longer in his possession (*Calhoun Papers*, 10:268–73).
4. AJ had asked Calhoun to intercede with Monroe to let Henry Lee have access to the correspondence between Monroe and AJ.

To William Berkeley Lewis

Mr. Hagan's July 16th, 1828

Dr Major

I have recd by the hand of Mr. [James] McCully your two letters of the 15th. & 16th. instant.[1]

Having duly observed their contents, I cannot withold my thanks for the information given, and the admonition offerred; I freely acknowledge it is good;

I have heard of the publication of Judge Williams,[2] and did expect, that it would have been noticed by the committee in Richmond.[3] This not being the case, I think it right & proper that some notice should be taken of it—[4]

The papers will be sent you, or I will meet you tomorrow evening at my own house—I hold the certifi[cate] of Major J[oel] Dyer of Carthage,[5] which will be proper to accompany the notice taken of the Judge—It would not be proper for me to leave here to day, for it would be at once said I had gone to meet McNairy,[6] but I can send Mr Saml. J. Hays who is here, by home for the papers, & have them to you by tomorrow evening. write me this evening by the mail. I shall be at home certainly on saturday.

Since I recd your letters, I am informed the Whig & Banner is here, I have not seen it, But when an opportunity offers will read it calmly & soberly,[7] for you & my friends may rest assured, that I will notice nothing untill the month of November passes, beyond that period I give no pledges—If my name can save the republic, with my silence & sufferings, it shall be done, but I assure you it is the greatest sacrafice I have ever made for my country, altho I have risqued much in her cause, & suffered many privations—These cowardly miscreants, know my hands are tied, therefore come forth as champions of the coalition, ready to lie, or swear for it, as occasion may require—

upon reflection, I have determined to send Mr Hays home for the papers, with directions to take them to you—

Genl Desha being here has agreed to go to Nashville, by him you will receive this your friend

Andrew Jackson

Note—The papers with the signature of Major Archibald [Waller] Overton, are not to be used[8]—or at least his name is not—but the facts, without referring to him, may, if thought proper, be referred to.

Genl Desha has read to me the production of McNairy. In reply to him, it will be well to notice that part that refers to my having no concealment—the answer that my bank Book was placed in the hands of the Editors for the inspection of all & every one who might choose to see it, or to take true copies from it with the date of the entries—This the Doctor knew—as to the alusion of his information of things, that it wou[ld] be unpleasant to me & my frie[nds] to have revealed—it may be replied, that surely the man that could have, & loan pamphlets of the vilest slander on female character can have nothing to reveal, that has not long since been agravated ten fold by falshood, & secretely sent abroad to the panders of power to be circulated where deetection the Doctor thought was not possible—But the mask will be taken off him.

Mr E. Foster must now come forth, & Doctor [James] Roan—Roan will state that I gave him the statement long before Tannyhill shew him the Bank Book that I had no interest in the negroes, was security, when I paid the mony took a transfer of them on the day, the entry is made in the Bank Book—[9]

ALS, NN (12-0051). Mr. Hagan's referred to Hagan's Springs, also known as Tyree Springs, in Sumner County, about twenty miles from Nashville.

1. Not found. A native of Ireland, McCully arrived in Nashville in 1822 claiming to be a grandson of one of AJ's uncles. He subsequently married AJ's widowed niece Mary Caffery Knox (b. c1788) and settled in northern Alabama.

2. Williams had published a statement, adding three new charges to those already leveled at AJ regarding his relationship with Burr: (a) that AJ had defended Burr long after most other Nashvillians had turned against him; (b) that with Coffee he had provided Burr with boats and provisions for the trip down the Mississippi River; and (c) that he had sent his nephew Stockley D. Hays along with Burr to New Orleans (Washington *National Intelligencer,* July 26).

3. The Richmond Committee had been appointed by the legislative convention in Richmond on January 14 to nominate AJ for president, and included eleven prominent Virginians, many of whom were also members of the Richmond Junto.

4. On August 1, "Brutus" responded in the *Richmond Enquirer* to the charges of AJ's complicity with Burr, using corrected copies of AJ's correspondence with Williams (certified by Lewis) as well as Thomas Stuart's letter above of March 1, which Lewis requested back, probably in response to AJ's concern. On September 12, the Nashville Committee in the *Nashville Republican* elaborated on the matter of AJ's relations with Burr.

5. The certificate of Dyer (d. 1836), a Smith County blacksmith and former state legislator, has not been found. AJ had been at Carthage in Smith County for the Fourth of July.

6. On July 15, the *National Banner and Nashville Whig* (not extant) had printed the statements of Wilkins Tannehill and Boyd McNairy defending their conduct with respect to AJ's bank book, and McNairy accused AJ of trying to suppress information contained in the book. AJ apparently feared that, by going to Nashville immediately after McNairy's publication, he would start rumors that he intended to challenge McNairy to a duel.

7. Jackson was probably referring to the July 15 issue, which carried the Tannehill and McNairy statements.

8. Overton (1783–1857; Transylvania), a cousin of John Overton and brother of Samuel

R. Overton, was a lawyer who represented Smith County in the Tennessee Senate, 1823–25, and in the state House, 1829–31. The "papers" have not been identified.

9. Roane (1790–1833), a son of former governor Archibald Roane, merely stated that McNairy and Tannehill had shown him AJ's bank book in the spring (see Roane to AJ, September 14).

From Ralph Eleazar Whitesides Earl

Nashville 17th. July, 1828.

Dr. Sir,

No doubt you have seen this man of war's *bold* Epistle addressed to you in the Whig and Banner of Tuesday last[1]—How *brave* how *pitiful,* that this *pretended fighting* character should attack one who is tied hand and foot—*poor contemptable retch,* who does he think is a going to wedge war against a *Poltroon* and *coward*—No! had he not have known the situation in which you was placed before the Public, and the impolitic measures it would be for your friends to make a fuss at this critical moment, he would as soon thought of runing himself into the fire of a furnace, as to have come out on you in the manner he has done—*Thank God* the day of *retribution* is close at hand when *such scoundrels as Boyd McNairy* will meet with their proper doom.

I beg you will take the *cowardly production* from whence it came and treat it accordingly, *with contempt*—Hall will manage him—[2]

May God prolong your life and that of Mrs. Jackson's for many years to come is the sincere prayers of not only myself, but *millions of the American People*—Truly your friend and Obedt Servt.

R. E. W. Earl

ALS, DLC (35). Published in Bassett, 3:415.

1. Earl was referring to Boyd McNairy's public letter of July 14, in which he denied any role in the disclosure of AJ's bank book and argued extensively that AJ was involved in slave trading.

2. On July 18, the *Nashville Republican* printed its defense of AJ against McNairy's claims.

The 1828 presidential campaign dredged up quarrels that had lain dormant for years. William Martin (1765–1846), a Sumner County planter and former state legislator, had disagreed with Jackson in December 1813 over Jackson's views regarding the terms of service of the Tennessee volunteers. Martin, a lieutenant colonel of the troops, had urged Jackson to release his men from service since they had served a year's enlistment. Jackson, however, had contended that Martin's troops had signed up to serve one year in combat if needed, and they had not fulfilled that obligation since they had been released from service for several months after the

Natchez *expedition and before the commencement of the Creek campaign. At the time, Jackson considered the clamor for discharge mutinous.*

In October 1827, Martin wrote the editors of the Washington National
Intelligencer, *announcing his support for Adams (*National Intelligencer,
*December 13, 1827), because of Jackson's tyrannical bent. Jacksonians
responded by circulating the story that Martin "had wanted to run away
from the Creek nation, but Gen. Jackson would not let him" (*National
Banner and Nashville Whig, *July 25, 1828). In reply to this charge, Martin published his letters to Jackson of December 4, 8, and 28, 1813, and
from Jackson of December 6 and 8, 1813 (Jackson, 2:467–77), denied
that his troops had been mutinous, and asserted that his interpretation of
their term of service, not Jackson's, was correct (*National Banner and
Nashville Whig, *July 25). The Martin contention, only briefly mentioned
in the letter below so angered Jackson that he responded with a public
editorial in the August 5* Nashville Republican, *published under the
pseudonym of "A Volunteer." The feud with Martin dragged on into
1829, when Martin published* The Self Vindication of Colonel William
Martin Against Certain Charges and Aspersions Made Against Him by
Gen. Andrew Jackson and Others . . . *(Nashville, 1829).*

To William Berkeley Lewis

H— July 28th. 1828

Dr. Major

I have been reflecting on the subject you named, relative to the Burr
business, and have come to the following conclusion—That a plain statement of the facts in reply to Judge Williams under the Editorial head
might be proper, adding thereto, Judge Stewarts, Judge O. and Major
Dyers statement to shew what kind of man he is; that he is prone to lieing,
& evil in his ways;[1] This being done, it may then be proper for me, to
take a general view, of all the slanders that have been propagated against
me[2]—I do think it would be improper for any notice to be taken of this
Burr slander by the Committee, as such; it would be giving too much importance to this slander. I have thought it might be well to notice Col
Martin, I have the documents to nail him to the counter with his two
coadjutors Erwin & McNairy, as a base calumniator—before it goes to
the press you shall see it.[3] In haste yr. friend

Andrew Jackson

Please send my papers pr. boy J.

ALS, NNPM (12-0059). Published in Bassett, 3:416.

1. Instead of the approach suggested by AJ, the Nashville Committee itself issued a report on the Burr business on September 12 in the *Nashville Republican,* without the statements of Thomas Stuart, John Overton, and Joel Dyer.

2. On August 8, concerned that AJ might be preparing to issue a statement in his own defense, Lewis began soliciting opinions "from some of our safest and most prominent friends in other States," including Martin Van Buren, as to whether AJ should publish a reply to the "most material" of the charges against him. Van Buren advised against such a publication, and on September 27, Lewis informed him that "the project had been abandoned" (Van Buren Papers, DLC).

3. Jackson was referring to his "A Volunteer," published August 5 in the *Nashville Republican.*

On August 2, the National Banner and Nashville Whig printed Andrew Erwin's long public letter documenting Jackson's "negro speculations." Erwin's account was an elaboration of one of the themes developed in the "Tennesseean" essays, which Erwin had been accused of writing.

With documentation from Jackson's bank book and letters, Erwin's account detailed the business of Coleman, Green & Jackson, claiming that Jackson was not just security for the venture but that he was from the first a full-fledged partner, and later sole proprietor, in the cotton and slave-trading enterprise. For proof of his charges, Erwin produced a letter from Horace Green attesting to Jackson's active involvement in the venture and one from Robert Weakley (1765–1845), a Davidson county planter and former state legislator and congressman, recounting his conversation with Jackson at the time about the business and about Jackson's encounter with Silas Dinsmoor at the Choctaw Agency as he was returning the slaves to Tennessee. Erwin also detailed a slave purchase, with the idea of resale, from John Brahan, and another involving the purchase of a slave named Charles (b. 1793) from Dr. Benjamin Rawlings (d. 1825) of Sumner County.

Erwin's rambling account concluded with a discussion of the "murder" of Gilbert at the Hermitage in the summer of 1827, an event, Erwin wrote, "hushed up without any proceedings in court against the man, who . . . in executing your order . . . killed said slave."

In the letter below, Jackson discusses the Charles and Gilbert episodes and offers advice for a response to Erwin's claims.

To William Berkeley Lewis

Hermitage August 5th. 1828—

Dr. Major

yours of yesterday was recd.[1] read, & disposed of as requested—The case of the negro boy is as follows—[Benjamin] Rawlings & Bradford had purchased a large quantity of goods from Jackson & Hutchings in 1823 & 1824—They had failed in their payments and in the year 1826[2]—in closing the account, and being unable, as Dr. Rawlings said, to do it in cash, he proposed to give in part a negro boy—The negro boy was recd. & the account with Rawlings & Bradford closed—This negro boy was kept at the Clover Bottom at our store—Col Anderson, as I was informed by him, Coffee, & Hutchings, for I was not present—had made a race with Capt [Daniel?] Ross for a considerable amount,[3] when they were about to put up the stak[es] which was to be in cash or negroes as I understood, Anderso[n w]as deficient in his stake, Capt John Caffery having sent his negro boy to the store for some articles, Anderson, took & staked up the boy on the race—Anderson lost it—Cafferys boy not returning home as expected, the Capt went after him, found his boy & ordered him home—Capt Ross urged Anderson to pay up the vallue of the boy or produce another, and Anderson applied for the boy Bought of Dr Rawlings & he was loaned to him, he was to return the boy or pay a stipulated price for him—some time afterward, the sore on the boys leg broke out & Capt Ross returned the boy to Anderson & he sold him, as I understood, to [George Michael] Deaderick & [Hinchey] Pettyway,[4] & Mr Pettyway took him down the river, & perhaps sold him, but his leg growing worse Pettyway was obliged to take him back, brought him up & delivered him to Anderson, who took him to Doctor [William] Ward[5] instead of tendering him to Dr Rawlings, where the boy died—you have a knowledge of the ballance, Anderson was largely indebted to me individually, and the night before I descended the river with my Volunteers in Janry 1813, we came to a settlement, when Anderson insisted that Jackson & Hutchings should permit him to bring Suit in their name against Rawlings on the warranty of this boy—which I agreed he might do, if he would give in writing that he would exonerate Jackson & Hutchings from all costs Anderson did so in your presence—the suit being alone for his benefit—I cannot lay my hand on this paper, but you must recollect perfectly the circumstance—Anderson Brought Suit, and as I was advised, was lost on the ground that he ought to have tendered the boy to Rawlings & not delivered him to Ward, who swore that his death was not caused by the sore leg, but from disease engen[der]ed in the lower country—Anderson from his writen obligation was to pay all costs, & I had some dificulty with him about the costs & had wrote a bill in chancery praying an injunction he plead poverty but acknowledged the debt when demanded him the same mony, the amount, not recollected, to pay the cost[6]—Take Pettyway statement in writing.[7]

I enclose to you the papers relative to the prosecution of Walton for killing Guilbert[8]—you will hand them to Andrew Hays Esqr. I hope he will give this pander Erwin an expose that will lay him up as the vilest lier on earth & regardless of what he says.[9]

I have addressed a letter to [Robert] weakly, which I send open for your perusal, before it is sent,[10] & that of A. J. Donelson—I want his answer, for hereafter, as much as now—The Col has become a volunteer in this business he must now speak the truth in his answer, if he does not, their are living witnesses to correct him—[11]

I may go down & see you on thursday, will do so unless I hear your health is restored—yr friend

Andrew Jackson

ALS, NN (12-0120). Published in Bassett, 3:418–19 (extract).
1. Letter not found.
2. AJ mistakenly wrote 1823, 1824, and 1826 for 1803, 1804, and 1806, respectively. Rawlings (d. 1825) practiced medicine in Sumner County.
3. Ross lived in Nashville.
4. Deaderick (c1756–1816) was a Nashville merchant and banker; Pettway (1776–1856), a Davidson and Rutherford County planter.
5. Ward (d. 1836) lived in Rutherford County.
6. For the case, see *Jackson & Hutchings* v. *Benjamin Rawlings,* April 1, 1816. When AJ paid the $352.12½ court costs in 1820, Anderson paid half; no record of any subsequent payment by Anderson has been found.
7. Pettway's statement of August 5 backed up AJ's account of the events.
8. Probably AJ to [William] Faulkner, August 28; AJ to Andrew Hays, August 30; and Hays to AJ, August 30, 1827, all above.
9. In the August 12 *Nashville Republican,* Hays stated that, far from hushing up the case, AJ had pressed for further investigation, even after the coroner's jury had cleared Walton. As a consequence, Hays prepared an indictment of Walton for the Davidson County Circuit Court, but the grand jury chose not to indict.
10. See AJ to Weakley, August 5, below.
11. On June 14, Weakley had written Erwin that he had heard, but did not know, that AJ, Horace Green, and Joseph Coleman owned the slaves that AJ brought back from Natchez in December 1811. He also described what AJ had told him about the confrontation with Silas Dinsmoor on that trip.

To Robert Weakley

Hermitage August 5th. 1828

Sir

Retired as I have been upon my farm, attending to my domestic concerns, interfering with none, and mixing not in the politics of the day, or the affairs of others I was astonished to see in the Banner & Whigg of the 1rst. instant your name embodied with a vile & wicked association of detracters long since formed to endeavour to injure my character abroad, the shafts of these base calumniators falling harmless at my feet, it is not my intention to inquire whether in thus lending the weight of your name to this unholy work, you intended an injury to me, I leave you to explain. As your name has been used by Erwin to injure me abroad,[1] I wish you to be more explicit in your statements. I wish you to state how long you have lived near me, & whether since your first acquaintance, you ever knew me to buy a negro with a view of selling him again for profit, or ever knew me engaged in any speculations in negroes to the lower country or to any other place.

In your note appended to Erwins publication you say, "in the year 1811 or 12 you understood that Mr. Horrace Green took a number of negroes to Natchez for sale, that those negroes were the property of the late Joseph Coleman of Nashville, Genl. Jackson & the said Horrace Green." Now, I call upon you to state from whom, and at what time you recd this information, as in your note you positively say you have no knowledge of this fact yourself—That the statement that I had any property in said negroes, or stood in relation to those contracts, for the cotton tobacco & negroes but that of security for Capt. Joseph Coleman, I do assert is untrue, or that I had any property in them to the 20th of Novbr 1811, is also untrue, on that day I had to pay the first instalment of the debt I stood bound for Capt. Coleman as security, & finding I would have to pay the whole debt, took from him a transfer of the property and undertook the responsibility of the whole debt for cotton tobacco & negroes, and forwith proceeded to the lower country, at a most dangerous period, Tecumsa being then with the Southern tribes, to receive the property out of the possession of Green, who, it was said, was squandering it, by card playing—on the 12 of Decbr. 1811 reached Natchez when for the first time I saw the negroes, and on the 13th recd. from Green the whole negroes unsold & immediately set out with them on my return to Nashville where I arrived in Janry 1812—such were the facts, as always related by me, and makes it necessary that you should state from whom, & when, you recd. the information that I had any interest in those negroes before the 20th. of Novr. 1811.

You further state in your note appended to Erwins publication that I informed you that I had gone to [*the*] lower country without a passport, and the [*morning I*] had to pass the agency, (I suppose you mean upon my return, I had no negroes with me as I went down but my boy) I armed my negroes *&c &c*—Why you did not give the reasons I assigned for so arming the negroes, I cannot conjecture, and I have to ask you in reply, to state explicitly whether my reasons were as follows. Did I not inform you that the Sub agent Smith[2] (Dinsmore not being there) had collected about 400 armed Indians with about sixty whitemen, to stop or destroy me, if I attempted to pass the agency without exhibitting a passport, did I not tell you that being a peaceable citizen travelling a road obtained from the Indians by treaty, for the free & unmolested use of every honest Citizen, that the agent had, or could have no authority, to require of any citizen a passport for travelling that road, that the demand was an act of usurpation, and I could not yield my legal rights to the demands of any self created despot, be him, in the character of an Indian agent, or any other— That the free & unmolested right to travel that road was a vested right in every citizen, and the president of the united States could not divest them of this right, or no other branch of our Goverment, the treaty being the supreme law of our land—and I was determined to exercise this right, and resist & put down, at the risque of my life, this petty usurper, and particularly, as at this perilous period, he had armed the Indians to support him in these acts of tyranny upon our peaceable citizens; These were the reasons I gave you, for arming my negroes; & I ask you to state, did not my conduct in this meet with your, & the approbation of all our good citizens, & did you not join in denouncing these acts of tyranny committed by the agent, to the great oppression of our citizens travelling that road, and applaud me in resisting his lawless acts & having him removed. I wish you to be explicit in your answer to this part of my inquiry. I wish you to add whether the Choctaw agent was not the only Indian agent that assumed the power of calling on the citizen for a passport, & if he had none, to stop his servant untill he sent & obtained one, & was it not the general belief that the agent by this means had a large house built, & a plantation opened for which he charged the Goverment a large sum of mony, and that many families were detained in the wilderness by the agent, and by such detention suffered many priva[tions], vexations & great expence.[3]

you have been pleased to bring into the view of your letter a negro sold by you to Genl. Brahan & by him to Capt. Coleman. I call upon you to state whether I ever had any right or interest in said negro in my life— and whether you do not know of your own knowledge that this negro was brought up by Major Hutchings with his & mine from his farm in the lower country, & delivered either to you, or Capt. Coleman on our arival at Nashville & that I never had any interest in said negro, John amp, as you call him—I wish you to be explicit on this head, as Erwin has used this, to shew that this was one of the negroes I had traded in— Set forth what became of this negro.

As your note appears to have been written at the request of some one, will you have the goodness to name who,[4] as it has been intimated to me, that it was not at the request of Erwin, but another. I am sir, yr. mo. ob. Servt.

Andrew Jackson

ALS draft, NN (12-0123). Published in Bassett, 3:419–21.

1. AJ was referring to Andrew Erwin's public letter to AJ in the August 2 *National Banner and Nashville Whig,* which included Weakley's letter of June 14.

2. Not further identified.

3. For AJ's contemporary comments on his encounter at the Choctaw Agency, see *Jackson,* 2:277–80, 334–36.

4. No response from Weakley has been found.

To William Berkeley Lewis

Hermitage August 13th. 1828

Dr Major

I find Doctor McNairy has come out at full length on the Burr business, and has published two letters of mine, one with, and one without date— The one in September 1806 was the time Burr came to this country and a dinner was given to him, the other if wrote by me, must have been written shortly after Col Burr sent to me the mony for the purpose of procuring some Boats & provision[1]—Capt Donelson has written you, or Major Graham to see these letters, & inform me of the date of the one, as to where & to whom these letters were written,[2] & inform me by return of the boy

I have seen Colo Anderson letter to the Reporter, in which he states that there are but three men now living who were present on the ground when Dickison & myself met[3]—The Col has stated a wilful lie in this, "he say Elisha Green was on the ground."[4] This he has been informed by Genl Overton & myself many times that Green came upon the ground & was run off by Genl Overton—The proper answer to Anderson's statement will be the publication of Corban Lees statement to whom he has referred, or *as much of it* as shews the depravity of Anderson, and his coadjutor,[5] with a few comments on the sentiments contained in them compared with the first statement of May, and his statement, that a snap was to be a fire[6]— adding a few comments on the *high Character* of Col Williams, & how his name has been drawn into this business—It is strange indeed if Col Anderson furnished Col Williams with copies of these letters how did it happen that Col Williams got his nephew Antony May to copy & certify that they were true copies from the originals, in his fathers hand writing.[7]

The Col has confessed his depravity—he has acknowledged that he has been detailing these secret slanders over Kentucky for years it is well known he is a master mason, and a mason who would violate his solemn obligation by thus secretely slandering a brother, would be guilty of perjury, or any other crime.

I enclose you a paper containing a statement on oath of Genl John Coffee & myself when garnisheed, at the suit of [Harman] Blanerhasset in the Natcheys,[8] for the information of the Committee, please shew it to them—

I am anxiously awaiting the communication of the Jackson Committee for the Lord sake if they are comin[g out] let it be spedily, as I cannot mo[ve un]til they decline acting, and if they do not, I must come out over my own Signature.[9] Let me hear from you by return of the boy yr friend—

Andrew Jackson

(When you read burn this)—

ALS, NN (12-0131). Published in Bassett, 3:421–23.

1. On August 12, the semi-weekly *National Banner and Nashville Whig* (article copied into August 16 weekly issue) published Boyd McNairy's letter supporting Nathaniel W. Williams's allegations regarding AJ and Burr. The two letters were AJ to [William P. Anderson], [cNovember 20, 1803] and September 25, 1806 (*Jackson*, 1:397–98; 2: 110).

2. Instead of writing Lewis or Graham, Andrew J. Donelson requested McNairy to turn the letters over to Samuel B. Marshall. McNairy declined, but agreed to let Donelson see the letters but not the addressees' names (Donelson to McNairy, August 15 and 16, and McNairy to Donelson, August 16 and 19, Donelson Papers, DLC).

3. Lexington *Kentucky Reporter*, August 6.

4. Green (c1760–1830) was a friend of Dickinson.

5. Lee was the trainer of Joseph Erwin's Ploughboy.

6. In 1806, May had stated, "I never entertained any other idea than that it [the duel] was fairly and honorably settled" (*Nashville Republican*, October 3), but his 1817 letters to Anderson asserted that AJ had acted dishonorably by recocking and firing after his pistol had snapped (Lexington *Kentucky Reporter*, June 11).

7. In his letter, Anderson stated that he had given copies of the May letters to Williams eight or nine years previous, but he denied that Williams had any agency in their publication.

8. See John Coffee and AJ to the Adams County Superior Court, March 25, 1813 (*Jackson*, 2:398–400). Blennerhassett (1765–1831), an Irish immigrant who financed in part Burr's 1806 expedition, had sued Burr to recoup his investment, naming AJ as a garnishee.

9. The Nashville Committee published a response to the Burr charges in the *Nashville Republican*, September 12.

A persistent theme in the campaign of 1828 was Jackson's tempera-ment—his opponents contended that he was so volatile as to make him unfit for the presidency. That had been the essence of Clay's "military chieftain" characterization in 1825, and it was the same that the sons of Isaac Shelby, Jackson's fellow negotiator with the Chickasaws in 1818, made late in 1828.

According to the family of Isaac—his son Thomas Hart Shelby (1769–1867) and his son-in-law Charles Stewart Todd (1791–1871, William and Mary 1809)— Jackson's "rash, hot-headed temper, if it had not been re-strained, would have cost the nation double the sum for which the [Chickasaw] land was ultimately purchased"; and Jackson "had so per-mitted the integrity of his principles to be the dupe of an intrigue as to propose, on behalf of his personal friends, then present, to secure for them a reservation of the Big Spring, and a valuable tract of land around it" (Supplement to the Address of Henry Clay to the Public . . . *[Washington, 1828], pp. 9–11;* Kentucky Reporter, *July 16).*

William B. Lewis, one of the friends accused of involvement in the scheme to acquire the reserve, responded to the charges, stating that "ei-ther Governor Shelby's recollection must have entirely failed him, or that his remarks have been incorrectly reported" (United States' Telegraph, *August 7). Meanwhile, Jackson himself joined in the defense strategy, as in the letter below, by soliciting confirmations for Lewis's observations from others present at the negotiations.*

Lewis's comments regarding Governor Shelby outraged the oldest son

James (c1782–1848), a farmer in Fayette County, Kentucky. On September 19, he wrote Jackson asking for an explanation of Lewis's statement. Jackson, however, failed to answer the letter, whereupon Shelby sent another to Jackson on October 6, through his friend, Leslie Combs (1793–1881), a Kentucky militia officer, lawyer, and friend of Clay.

Accounts of the meeting between Combs and Jackson differ. Combs insisted that he received little cooperation from Jackson and his associates. According to Combs, he asked Jackson to permit his friends to speak about the Chickasaw negotiations, and Jackson agreed. But when Combs wrote James Jackson, who was in Nashville at the time, James Jackson replied that "whatever may exist of a private character with Gen. Jackson or any other individual and myself, they alone have a right to call on me to disclose" (James Jackson to Combs, October 11, DLC-35, published in James Shelby, Chickasaw Treaty: An Attempt to Obtain the Testimony of James Jackson . . . [Lexington, 1828], p. 7). Jackson, however, refused to provide the written request that James Jackson required. Combs also called on William B. Lewis to obtain a copy of the secret journal of the Chickasaw negotiations, but Lewis only allowed him to read the journal, referring him to the original in the war department in Washington for a copy.

Once again irritated when the Adams Republicans published the story of Combs's efforts, Jackson nevertheless followed his friends' advice and remained silent. Privately, however, he called Combs a "pimp" and expressed a desire to "cowhide" him.

To Richard Keith Call

Hermitage August 14th. 1828—

My Dear Call

On last evening I recd. yours by Major Clements,[1] and am happy to learn that your Mary & the sweet little ones are in good health.

I am happy the address of the central committee at the city of Washington has reached you;[2] taking this into view with Kendals fifth letter to Clay, and it is conclusive of the Bargain.[3]

The whole object of the coalition is to calumniate me, cartloads of coffin hand bills, f[o]rgeries, and pamphlets of the most base calumnies are circulated, by the franking privilege of members of congress, & Mr. Clay, even, Mrs. J. is not spared, & my pious mother, nearly fifty years in the tomb, & who, from her cradle to her death, had not a speck upon her character, has been dragged forth by Hammond & held to public scorn as a prostitute who intermaried with a negro, & my eldest brother sold as a slave in carolina. This Hammonds [da]re not publish in his vile press, but keeps the statement purporting to be sworn to (a forgery) and shews it secretely[4]—I am branded with every crime, and Doctor McNairy, &

Col Erwin, & Anderson & Williams are associated for this purpose. I have for some time knew that they were the Issuers of old slanders that appeared abroad, but it is only lately that they have been unmasked, & was not my hands tied, & my mouth closed, I would soon put an end to their slanders. This they know, but suppose when the elections over all things will die away—*not so,* I look forward to the first of Decbr. next with much anxiety[5] The day of retribution must come. I am charged with Burrs conspiracy & every other crime, was Anderson & McNairy as clear of purjury as Master Masons, as I was of the Burr conspiracy, it would be a pleasant thing for their conscience.

I believe you were at the chikesaw treaty—If so, I wish your attention to a publication of Thomas Shelby son of the Govern Shelby & Mr Todd soninlaw to the Govr. These men detail a conversation of their father, & Thomas Shelby Speaks of things to which he was a witness—Surely when you see it you will be of opinion that Govr Shelby could never have stated such things, if he did, he has stated a *positive & wilful falshood.* These statements were made on the eve of the Kentucky elections at the instance of Clay who is there, & for political effect, every virtuous & patriotic act of my life is charged upon me as a crime, & if the whole weight of E[x]ecutive patronage, with the contingent funds wielded in the most corrupt manner by so many pandors does not prostrate me, then I have right to exclaim "truth is mighty & has prevailed." I have enclosed a news paper to Col Butler with some strictures on Thomas Shelbys falshoods supported by the facts subscribed to as true, by Governor Shelby on the Secrete Journals;[6] & you will have seen Major Lewis letter published in the Nashville republican on this subject.[7] I wish you & Butler to look at it, & send me such a statement as the truth will warrant.[8]

My Philosophy is almost worn out, but all my enemies expect is, to urge me to some rash action, this the cannot do until the election is over, if my hands are not tied by the event, there will be a final settlement.

Mrs. J. unites with me in affectionate regard to you & yours & request you to present the same to Col Butler & his yours truly

Andrew Jackson

ALS, ViHi (12-0135). Published in *Virginia Magazine of History and Biography,* 29(1921):191–92 (dated August 16).

1. Letter not found.
2. The Washington Central Committee address had been published in the May 10 *United States' Telegraph—Extra.* It mainly consisted of documentary evidence supporting the "corrupt bargain" charge.
3. In his "fifth letter" of July 4, Kendall referred to the Clay-Francis P. Blair correspondence before the election and to his own correspondence to prove that the Kentucky delegation's vote in 1825 for Adams was with the clear understanding that Clay, in exchange, would be appointed secretary of state. (Frankfort *Argus of Western America,* July 9).
4. According to Hammond, he had the original affidavit of William Rodgers, from Clark County, Ohio, formerly from North Carolina, giving details of AJ's parentage. AJ apparently had heard Hammond's modus operandi was to send out copies of the Rodgers

statement asking for "satisfactory information" on the subject. For example, he sent one to William Gaston, former Federalist congressman from North Carolina and member of the state's Adams committee, through Tobias Watkins in Washington, with the request that Watkins peruse it before he forwarded it. In that letter of July 7, Hammond wrote Gaston that he was seeking "to obtain some further information of that distinguished individual, with respect to whom I begin to believe there have been as many impostures palmed upon the world, as were ever invented by the disciples of the prophet of Mecca" (Gaston Papers, NcU). Eventually Jacksonian presses published Rodgers's certificate, calling it a "vagabond production," unprecedented even in the "annals of Grub-Street" (Portsmouth *New-Hampshire Gazette*, August 26).

5. AJ was anticipating the casting of votes for electors in the state capitals.
6. The "strictures" appeared in the July 25 *Nashville Republican*.
7. Not found.
8. For the statements of Call and Butler about the treaty negotiations, see Call to AJ, August 25, and Butler to AJ, September 15, as well as Butler's undated statement in the *United States' Telegraph*, October 6, backing up Lewis's account.

In the letter below, Jackson was assisting Grundy, a member of the Nashville Committee, in preparing the Committee's defense of his role in the Burr business and in the Dickinson duel.

To Felix Grundy

Hermitage Augst 15th. 1828—

Dr. Sir

yours from Franklin of the 14th. instant[1] has been recd. The letter without date which you have seen published by Dr McNairy is one of Date, when seen, of Novbr. 1803[2]—*unless altered by the Doctor*; none ever was written by me, such as the one published that in truth can be attached to Burr or his Boats. But on the 12th. of Novbr. 1803, I recd. an order from the war Department of date 31rst of octbr. requesting me to have in readiness 22 Boats by 20th. of Decbr. 1500 militia provisions &c &c for the defence of Louisiana, on that occassion,[3] I wrote such letters & sent expresses in every direction over west Tennessee; This is one of the letters with its date suppressed villanously to attach this transaction with Burr—

Application was made by Col W[illiam] Williams,[4] the day after the publication was made, to see these letters, but the Doctor refused, saying that they could not be seen unless their *authenticity was denied*. Capt. A. J. Donelson went to Nashville yesterday to ask a sight of them, & to possitively declare that the one without date was a possitive forgery when applied to Burr but a genuine letter if it had reference to the Public Boats ordered to be built in the fall 1803—*"Truth is mighty & will prevail,"* against wickedness, forgery & fraud. I think the *thief* is caught at last.

providence has been kind to me. I had once like to have lost all my old papers, and at another time, Call & Mrs. J. had prepared to burn them, as I fortunately got home, & preserved them.

You have seen Col Anderson publication in the Lexington reporter[5]— he says "apply to Corban Lee obtain his deposition, he is an honest man, that there is but three of the parties living who were upon the ground, Green, Lee & myself &c &c." Now the Col *knows* Green was not on the ground, the full statement by Corban Lee reached me through a friend the other day, his statement mentions who were upon the ground, and contradicts May statement positively, says everything was conducted on my part fairly & honorably, & refers to his former statement to Capt [George] Ridly,[6] in due time the Col will be laid along side of his co workers, branded with infamy & disgrace—Before the *little* Doctor gets out of the *scrape,* he will wish he had let the Tennessee farmer alone on his farm & not have disturbed him.

I neither attemp to dot my i's nor x my t's, in haste yours,

Andrew Jackson

P.S. You may assure my friends, that these malignant shafts of calumny will still fall harmless before me.

I do not despair of the republic, nor yet of Barrys Election, I never did despair A. J—

ALS, NcU (12-0140). Published in Bassett, 3:423 (extract).
1. Letter not found.
2. The letter was AJ to [William P. Anderson, cNovember 20, 1803] (*Jackson,* 1:397–98).
3. Henry Dearborn to AJ, October 31, 1803 (*Jackson,* 1:392).
4. Williams (1776–1862, Harvard 1799), former state legislator, was a Davidson County lawyer and planter.
5. Lexington *Kentucky Reporter,* July 16.
6. The *Philadelphia Democratic Press,* July 23, 1827, had published an informant's report that Corbin Lee, then residing in Maryland, had denied a statement made to Ridley that AJ had acted honorably in the Dickinson duel. On August 29, 1828, however, the *Nashville Republican* published a July 18 letter from Lee, in which he reaffirmed his statement to Ridley. In his deposition of June 25, 1806, Ridley (1738–1836), a revolutionary veteran, had testified that Lee had told him that AJ acted "with a great deal of honor" in the Dickinson duel.

To William Berkeley Lewis

August 15th. 1828 Hermitage

My Dr Sir

I have Just returned from Capt. Donelsons he is not at home, & I send George down with a letter to you, with two enclosed that I found on a search yesterday in my old papers & think they will be serviceable to explain Burrs expressed views, & his authority under the Govrt.[1]

Upon mature reflection it strikes me that the letters published by McNairy, if written by me, must have been to James Jackson, & the one without date must have been written at the time[2]—Burr forwarded the mony with his letter to have Boats built & a supply of pork & meal laid in[3] At that time James Jackson was hard pressed & had like to have broke, being friendly with him, and yielding him all the pecuniary aid I could at all times, it is Just such a hasty scrall as I would write to a friend who I thought could be benefitted by such a contract by bartering his goods for those articles, & thereby relieve himself from his embarrastment.[4] This at the time was believed to be a fair mercantile transaction, no secrete in the business & from the letter I enclose you from Burr believed to be in furtherence of the views of Goverment and as such ought to be viewed by the Committee in their comments upon the transaction & which will be supported by Genl Coffees affidavit in the suit Blanahasset sent you the other day. These Boats were built & the letter written when there were not the least suspicion around Burr & when from his letter he was supposed to be in the Confidence of the Goverment—But the moment that suspicion arose that his views were hostile to the Goverment, & he had been acting deceptiously with his friends, what was my conduct, & that of all his friends here Genl [James] Robertson Overton &c &c &c[5]—our countenance was withdrawn, and when I recd the first intelligence from Mr [Anthony] Hopkins of his intention against our Goverment, I wrote to Claibourne, Jefferson, Campbell & Smith.[6] Here is ample means to meet this secrete attempt to assasinate my character, & from a man that owes every thing to me—This letter from Burr was shewn to every person that desired it—If I am right in my conjectures of it being written to J. Jackson, what *a villain he is,* but I am at his defience, he knows the moment I recd. the information that Burr was engaged in a plan not sanctioned by the Goverment I at once would have nothing, to do with him—If the letters are not to James Jackson, I have no idea to whom else, unless Mr. John Shute who was in that day a Boat builder.

If my friend Eaton is with you I will ride down tomorrow to see him,[7] advise me yr friend

Andrew Jackson

P.S. I had been employed by the Govrt. in 1804[8] to build Boats for them, & when I recd Col Burrs letter & mony I did believe—from his letter I enclose to you, that the Goverment had instructed him to apply to me to have them built—I enclose you a roster of the Boats built for the United States & sold by their directions in Febry 1804 & to whom sold— I have Just laid my hand on this paper & open this letter to inclose it.[9]

ALS, NN (12-0144). Published in Bassett, 3:424–25.
1. Only one of the enclosures, Burr to AJ, March 24, 1806 (*Jackson*, 2:91–93) has been identified.

2. The letters were to William Preston Anderson, not to James Jackson.

3. For Burr's accounts with AJ, see *Jackson*, 2:113–14, 121–22. His letter has not been found.

4. At this point, AJ was discussing his letter to Anderson of [cNovember 20, 1803] (*Jackson*, 1:397–98) mentioned in his letter above to Grundy and described as dealing with boats for the war department, not for Burr. For the business directed to James Jackson and which did involve outfitting Burr, see Account of Jackson & Hutchings with James & Washington Jackson, December 17, 1806 (*Jackson*, 2:123–24).

5. Robertson (1741–1814), one of the founders of Nashville, was a vice-president at the dinner honoring Burr in September 1806. He was later called as a witness for Burr's trial but did not honor the subpoena.

6. For the extant records regarding Hopkins's visit to Nashville, see *Jackson*, 2:113–14, 121–22. For AJ's letters to Thomas Jefferson, William C.C. Claiborne, Daniel Smith, and George W. Campbell, all in late 1806 and early 1807, see *Jackson*, 2:114–20, 147–50.

7. Eaton had been expected home about August 14 or 15, but he did not arrive until the 20th.

8. AJ mistakenly wrote 1804 instead of 1803.

9. See Memorandum of the sale of boats, February 18, 1804.

In mid-July, William P. Anderson released a previously unpublished portion of Francis May's letter of September 16, 1817, a section that accused Jackson of collaborating with Robert Hays to defraud creditors (Lexington Kentucky Reporter, July 16). According to May's account, Hays, before he declared bankruptcy in 1807, had transferred funds to Jackson with which Jackson bought Hays's slaves at a contrived auction, thereby aiding Hays in shielding that property from his creditors.

That charge, along with the earlier one that Jackson had acted dishonorably in the Dickinson duel, proved particularly irritating to Jackson, who sought to minimize the impact of the claims by casting doubt on Anderson's character and credibility.

To William Berkeley Lewis

Hermitage August 16th. 1828

Dr Major

The inclosed copy of a letter of Mr Francis Woodward formerly of the united States army will give a true character of Col Anderson & shew what credit is due to his statement of *Dr Mays letters being genuine*; it will not do to take his evidence in the case, he is too deeply interested, & he who, would hire a man to commit *forgery* to exonerate himself from a *Just debt* would commit *forgery for vengeance sake*.[1] My opinion is therefore streng[t]hened that Anderson has forged these letters. Can it be that May would be so base as to endeavour to destroy unjustly the character of Col [Robert] Hays & his family with it, with whom he had always been on friendly terms, & the most intimate habits of friendship with the Col Hays & family during his life, & apparently with myself—These letters appear to be written for the use of Genl Adair in his dispute with me,[2] but was never used, nor did I ever hear of them until I recd. a letter from Knoxville, said to be written by the suggestion of Judge White in 1827[3]—if I had, heard of them before brought before the nation as President, Anderson would not have been in this world, or I would have been in my grave.

I wish you to shew Woodwards letter to Judge overton, if he wants a copy, let him have one, the letter is addressed to Col Harmon A. Hays & in the possession of Mr Saml Hays.[4]

Will the committee take this subject into view ¿or will it be managed by Hall? inform me—[5]

The statement of all present including May have certified to the fairness of the whole of this business on my part, Lee shews green was not on the ground as Anderson has stated.[6] Anderson knew when he was making the statement it was false, for I have heard Genl Overton & May both tell Anderson how Genl Overton run Green off the ground—Green and several other *Bullies* came up with Dickeson, & at once they were dismissed—It was this same Green that Brought the intelligence to Nashville, that Dickesons pistol had went off *[by]* accident, & the ball struck the earth half way between him & me, & thus it was believed, & so would Green have sworn, altho not present, had it not have been for the wound on my breast; When Green reached Nashville the Federal court was sitting Green stepped up on the bench gave the intelligence to the Judge & altho in the middle of a cause instantly adjourned, & Dr. Boyd & him were the first signers of the application to put the paper in mourning.[7]

The Col has in his address introduced the letter of May to prove that I secretted Hays property & that Hays committed perjury by takeing the oath of insolvency, a baser lie than this never was told & I have the documents to prove it. I bought in the property with my own mony subject to a morgage & the debt due Cafferry for the land Bot of him, & the negroes I bought with my own mony which I have never received one cent, part of which I borrowed from the store say $750—[8]

Let me hear from you. I hope Eaton has arrived in good health, I would be glad to see him.

I forgot yesterday to propose a bottle that Barry was elected. I propose it now, will you take me.[9] yours sincerely

Andrew Jackson

P.S. I hope the documents sent you yesterday was satisfactory—I expect McNairy may have altered the date, if it bears any other date but Novbr. 1803 it is a forgery—Why does the rascal withold it from view; he must have altered the date & the chemical operation has not been well performed, he fears detection, or it bears its proper date Novbr. 1803 A. J.

ALS, NN (12-0160). Published in Bassett, 3:425–26.
1. In his letter of August 15 to Harmon A. Hays, Woodward, from Wilson County, a

lieutenant and regimental quartermaster in the William P. Anderson's 24th Infantry during the War of 1812, related that, in 1823, when the federal government sued Anderson to collect $15,000 that he owed on his military accounts, Anderson asked him to forge receipts for $10,000 in exchange for $500 to $1,000 in cash. Woodward wrote that he refused the offer.

2. AJ was referring to his earlier dispute with Adair, Anderson's father-in-law, over the performance of Kentucky troops on the right bank of the Mississippi River during the Battle of New Orleans.

3. See above, Richard G. Dunlap to AJ, June 4, 1827.

4. On August 13, AJ had asked Harmon A. Hays (d. 1835), a nephew of Robert Hays, to solicit the statement from Woodward.

5. On November 11, Samuel J. Hays published Woodward's letter in Allen A. Hall's *Nashville Republican* as part of his defense of his father's reputation against the charge of fraud. Four days later Woodward complained that Harmon Hays had coerced the letter from him, but Woodward affirmed the truth of the charges against Anderson.

6. At this point, AJ was discussing the Dickinson duel.

7. The reference was to John and Boyd McNairy.

8. See bill of sale for fifteen slaves belonging to Robert Hays to AJ, March 7, 1807, and conveyance of fifteen slaves from AJ to Severn Donelson in trust for Jane Hays, May 11, 1807.

9. William T. Barry, the Jacksonian candidate for governor in Kentucky, lost the election to Thomas Metcalfe.

To William Berkeley Lewis

Hermitage 19th. of August 1828.

Dr Major

Some notice ought to be taken of McNairys publication in this days republican, to convey to the public that it will meet with a full reply.[1] The coalition have "bearded the lion in his den," and the public will expect him to act promptly.

I have said to you, & now reiterate, that the letter published & without date by Dr. McNairy must refer to the public Boats built in fall 1803 & when applied to Burrs Boats is a forgery. My letter speaks of a draft on N. orleans or bank bills—Arangements were made with [George Michael] Deaderik[2] to furnish the mony here, & take the draft on Govt. as cash was needed here, Boat yards to be established workmen to be hired, and provisions to be furnished for them, therefore agreed to advance $3000. Now it is impossible that it could have related to Burrs Boats, or why say "drafts upon Neworleans," when Burr had sent the Ky. bank bills & they were lodged with Coffee & Hutchings in the store who was to conduct the business as a mercantile transaction for profit. I never wrote or spoke to any one on the subject of engaging them to build Boats for Burr in my life. again, it appears by the published letter, that I was confined to the sum of $3000—therefore it could not relate to Burrs Boats & provisions because, Burr had deposited a larger sum than that, & a sufficient sum to cover the Boats & provisions ordered to be furnished, therefore drafts on Orleans were or could not have been necessary, which makes me positive that it could not relate to Burrs Boats if I was not well convinced from other reasons that I took no agency in the building of Burrs Boats whatever.

The great misfortune has been that the calumnies has always had two or three weeks the start of their refutation, and if the Committee are not ready to come out (if the do intend) the greater necessity that some notice should be taken of it in to days republican. If the Committee have declined, then some notice should be taken of it untill I can come out myself, which I will be compelled to do, altho from the stand I have taken, there will be great delicacy, and it is a very doubtful question, whether I ought until after the Election is over—Should then the Committee have declined, let the order of the sec of war be published and let it be accompanied, with the refusal of McNairy to shew the letter only in a mutilated state, or to permit it to be known to whom written—& then pronounce it a forgery when it is made to relate to any other subject than the Boats built in the fall of 1803—This will give time for me to make an address to the public, but the committee under all circumstances ought to say something on the subject first—

There is only now a few weeks before the election will be over, & this is why the Burr business is seized on, every other thing having failed—I would like to hear from you shortly. I would have come down but you said you would send for me if you wanted me. your friend

Andrew Jackson

ALS, NN. Published in Bassett, 3:427–28.
    1. The *Nashville Republican* of August 19th pledged a full reply on Jackson's relations with Burr and continued to discuss the issue in brief notes until the Nashville Committee issued its report on September 12. Eaton, in particular, advised Jackson to remain quiet on the matter until the Committee issued its report.
    2. Deaderick (c1756–1816), longtime friend and occasional business associate of Jackson's, was a merchant and banker in Nashville.

To Richard Mentor Johnson

[September 1, 1828]

My Dear Sir

I have received your kind letter of the 22nd. ult[1]—and hasten to reply to it.

The result of your elections has been as favourable to the cause of the people as could have been expected, when the active & conspicuous part Mr Barry had taken in your relief & new Court System is taken into view. [John] Breathits election was a surer test of the wish of the people on the great national question which was agitated, and the number in your legislature opposed to the administration, shews that the majority of the people are decidedly against it—[2]

Had you my Dr. Sir reflected that I am not a candidate for the Presidency by my own volition, but by the selection of the people, you would not for a moment entertain the idea, that it would be proper for me now to adopt the electioneering pursued by our travelling cabinet.[3] I have long since announced my principles to the nation and in pursuance of them have *[been]* silent amidst the violent torrents of the vilest calumny ever heaped upon man, leaving to the virtue of the people my Justification. Being thus brought out by the people, it is for them without any agency of mine to sustain me, for I will not *abandon principle* to secure to myself the highest *Boon.*

When we see a travelling Cabinet ranging over the continent, wielding its patronage for the purpose of corrupting the election franchise and thereby inflicting a wound on our national character not easily to be washed out, it behoves me at least, to shew by my acts that the professions I have made were based upon principle, & that I will not depart from them. My enemies would delight to see me *now* entering upon an electioneering tour, it would realise the saying ascribed to Mr Adams, "that he would turn democrat & urge them into such extravagance that the whole people would become disgusted with our goverment, & cry out for a change."[4] The people having taken me up must determine the canvass themselves, without any agency of mine. If they succeed, then it can with truth be said, that virtue has triumphed over the corrupting influence of executive patronage & designing Demagogues. *The people must themselves Triumph,* a great principle is at stake, & if they do, then it can be said all power flows from them & when their agents violate their declared will, they will be hurld from their confidence, then will our republican form of goverment endure forever, but if the dictation of designing demagogues be acknowledged, freedom & independence are gone—I do not despair of the republic.

I salute thee affectionately & tender to you my best wishes, yrs

Andrew Jackson

ALS draft, DLC (35). Published in Bassett, 3:431.

1. See Johnson to AJ, August 22.

2. Though the Jacksonian candidate for governor in Kentucky, William T. Barry, had lost his election, Breathitt (1786–1834), the Jacksonian nominee for lieutenant governor, had won.

3. Out of his postured contempt for electioneering, AJ declined Johnson's invitation to visit the Harrodsburg Springs in Kentucky.

4. Probably a paraphrase of the sentiments ascribed to Adams in Samuel D. Ingham, *An Exposition of the Political Character and Principles of John Quincy Adams* (Washington, 1827).

From Alfred Balch

3d Sept. 1828.

Dear Sir,

Enclosed you have letter from my friend Benton.[1] You will perceive that the Bill to graduate the price of the public lands has laid [David] Barton low.[2] From all I can learn after much anxious enquiry, I have no doubt but that Missouri & Illinois will go for you by an overwhelming & Indiana by a decisive majority. The scale in Ky. is nearly balanced—but *circumstances* are decidedly in favour of our success.

Mr Clay will put Judge Clarke aside next summer go to Congress & lead the opposition!![3]

Judge Overton has talked to me a good deal about the mode in which this very small affair of Burr should be disposed of. In this stage of the contest—& at this particular moment I consider it a sm[all] affair. In those states which are considered doubtful it may have some little effect but it will be very little. I am told there are some of the Committee who are for a very laboured effort on this matter—

I believe that the majority will not support such a course. A very mild appeal—treating it as a mere neighborhood matter & placing the whole affair very much in our own personal knowledge and uniform understanding will be the best disposition of it—

To labour the question that you were concerned in any improper or unlawful enterprize will be injudicious & wholly useless No body beleives it but he who is now has been & will be against you. yours truly

Alfred Balch

ALS, DLC (35).
    1. See Thomas H. Benton to [Balch], August 17 (DLC-35).
    2. In the congressional canvass in Missouri in 1828, Spencer D. Pettis, a proponent of Benton's bill for "graduating" the price of western lands, had won the election over Edward Bates, the administration candidate endorsed by Barton (1783–1837), Benton's Senate colleague and opponent of the graduation bill.
    3. James Clark, who held the seat in the U.S. House occupied by Henry Clay before 1825, remained in Congress until 1831. Instead of reclaiming his place in the House, Clay entered the Senate in November 1831.

To William Berkeley Lewis

[September 13, 1828]

Dr Major

I return the letters enclosed for my perusal as requested, tendering my thanks for their perusal.[1]

I am sure the course recommended is right—to come out at this late period would be ascribed to electioneering view[s] & handled accordingly to the benefit of the coalition.[2]

I have recd the republican & view the expose of the Committee full and convincing.[3] I only regret that Mr Hall could not in the same paper have made a few comments on the subject & passed in review Dr McNairy[s] letter without date, giving the order of the sec of war of 1803[4]—and the certificate of Mr [Lucius Junius] Polk[5]—I am in haste yr friend

Andrew Jackson

ALS, DLC (72, 12-0179).
    1. In his letter of September 13, Lewis had sent AJ letters (not found) from Martin Van Buren and Samuel D. Ingham.
    2. All of AJ's chief advisers recommended that he not reply personally to the various charges made against him by partisans of the administration.
    3. The September 12 *Nashville Republican*, covering AJ's involvement in the Burr venture.
    4. On September 26, most likely in compliance with AJ's wishes, the *Nashville Republican* stated that the undated letter was from 1803 and dealt not with Burr's expedition in 1806 but with supplying boats to the war department.
    5. Polk (1802–1870, North Carolina 1822), cousin of James K., was a Maury County planter. In his "certificate" of September 7, Polk wrote that William P. Anderson, to whom the undated letter of [cNovember 20, 1803] was addressed, had stated that the communication "had no reference to Burr's conspiracy." A month later, Anderson confirmed that he had made such a statement, but declared that he had been wrong, and that McNairy's interpretation of the letter was accurate (*Nashville Republican*, September 26; *National Banner and Nashville Whig*, October 18).

To William Berkeley Lewis

Hermitage Septbr. [14] 1828—

Dr Major

In the hurry & bustle of my company leaving me on last evening I have sent you a letter I did not intend, in lieu of Mr Inghams that I thought I had inclosed you—I now by my son inclose it to you, the one I sent instead of Mr Inghams, you will please retain until a safe opportunity offers for its return.

I am this morning engaged watching over an unfortunate individual, whose spirit is about to take its flight from its earthly tabernacle, from one in the last stage of consumption, sent here on Saturday last by Col Weakly in a carriage—The trip from the Cols here, entirely exausted him, & in a few hours his pulse must cease to beat—I suppose the poor fellow in a state of delirium requested to be brought here, but it is strange to me why the Col should suppose I was more able to watch over a dying man than he. For this I cannot account—so it was, and humanity compelled me to take him in, & render to the distressed, all that a good Samaritan could do, in a few hours the unfortunate being will be at rest, & I will discharge faithfully the last act that humanity can bestow. I barely name this to account to you for the mistake I have committed, as the attention to the sick, & my company, occasioned it[1] yours respectfully

Andrew Jackson

ALS, NNPM (12-0196).
1. Joseph Hughes (c1778–1828) died the next day at the Hermitage.

From James Shelby

Richland near Lexington Septr 19. 1828

Sir

It is with deep regret I have observed that the name and memory of my deceased Father have been assailed in the course of the public controversy which has been excited in relation to the Chickasaw Treaty of 1818 and some of its incidents.[1] The sacred obligation of defending a fathers memory from unmerited imputations makes it my duty to seek a thorough exposition of the transactions in which it has been implicated.

Having learned that Col. Butler, R[obert] P. Currin esqr.[2] and Mr. James Jackson were present at the negociations of that treaty or have some knowledge of the circumstances and transactions connected with it, I design to apply to them for information. Without your concurrence my application will, probably, be ineffectual, as these Gentlemen, who are reputed to have been your friends, may feel restrained by obligations of a confidential nature from making a full disclosure on the subject.

You can, probably, remove all those considerations which may bind them to silence, by simply furnishing me with an expression of your willingness that they may disclose all the facts within their knowledge.

To obviate all possible difficulties I request that General Jackson will be pleased to say in answer to this letter whether he has any Objections to these Gentlemen making a full disclosure of the circumstances and transactions to which I have alluded.

I take it for granted that with your assent they will speak; that without it they will be silent. Furnished with the Evidence of your assent I shall immediately apply for the information. My object is to elicit the whole truth in order that in it's pure & perfect light the conduct & character of my honored father may be seen and judged.

Trusting, Sir, that you will afford me all the facilities for this investigation which your consent to the disclosures of others can give I have the honor to be respectfully Your most obedient servant

James Shelby

P.S.
The bearer has been requested to await the receipt of your answer.[3]

ALS and Copy, DLC (72). Published in Lexington *Kentucky Reporter,* October 29.
  1. Shelby was referring to William B. Lewis's public statement re Isaac Shelby (*United States' Telegraph,* August 7).
  2. Currin (d. 1857), a merchant in Williamson County, had joined with William B. Lewis and James Jackson to secure a lease of the Chickasaw salt lick reserve on the Big Sandy River, when AJ and Shelby had failed to secure a cession from the Chickasaws. This deal had been a focus for earlier attacks on AJ's handling of the treaty talks (see *Jackson,* 4:320–21).
  3. Thomas Gott (b. c1804), the bearer of the letter, resided at this time in Warren County, Kentucky.

From Arthur Peronneau Hayne

Private.   Fort Moultrie, Sullivans Island.
                                              So. Ca. 20th. Septr. 1828.

My dear General:
    I have received your last Kind letter[1]—& for which be pleased to accept my most sincere thanks. I would certainly have answered it some time ago, but I know full well, how numerous the calls upon your time must be, particularly in writing letters & in receiving Company; under these circumstances I could not reconcile it to my feelings for the present, to continue our correspondence, *more especially as I feel the most perfect Confidence that our beloved Country is to be blessed, in having you for our next President.* I have supposed of late, that your friends should write you as seldom as possible—for among other considerations, I am perfectly convinced, that many of your letters at certain Post Offices are opened & read.

    You inform me, that the letter I wrote you by Genl. [Eleazar Wheelock] Ripley while at NewOrleans last Winter has just been received.[2] My only regret on the occasion is, that you could for a moment have supposed, your not having received that letter—and my not having received your Note from Natchez,[3] could have produced any unpleasant feeling on my part. Such a thought, never flashed across my mind, even for a single moment. A friendship formed, in the *hour* of *trial* & *danger,* & of *14* years standing, must go along with us to the *grave.*

There is unfortunately a good deal of excitement in our State, & at the South generally, on the subject of the late Tariff. It is my most earnest wish, that for the present, you would neither write or express any positive opinion upon this subject, for any opinion or expression, much less letter of yours would be seized upon to produce a schism among your friends. So soon as the proper period arrives, so soon as the true sentiments of Carolina are known, on this subject, I will place in your possession, all the *Data,* necessary to enable you, to understand every thing; & then, ere long, I trust, you will in your *Official Capacity,* be called upon to place your opinions & views, before the people of our beloved & common Country. In the mean time, I can only say you stand, & maintain yourself among us like the *"Rock of Ages." South-Carolina, one & all is for Jackson & the Union.* So anxious do I feel on the subject of the Tariff, that if my family were in Charleston, (where the *Strangers Fever*[4] at *present is,* & on account of our *Daughter,* who is *perfect Stranger,* we have been induced to repair to this place; were it not for this circumstance,) I should be tempted to ride to see you at the Hermitage, for a few days; giving myself time enough to be present at Columbia our seat of Government, during the meeting of our Legislature; which will take place about the 20th. of Novr. The great Question, with us, *Is, What is to be done? & I would fairly, directly, & Confidentially put that Question to you.* Sound judgment, & great delicacy would be required, in the management of such an Affair. The object, of such a scheme, wd. be public good. I would present myself at Columbia early in the Session—it would be known, that I was just from under the Roof of Genl. Jackson—*& without even mentioning his name, your opinions & views through me, wd. be known, & would necessarily produce a powerful effect.* Genl. Pinckney, who is my next Door neighbour thinks it wd. have a good effect, could this plan be executed. The Genl. takes a deep interest in your election.[5]

Mrs. Hayne & Frances unite with me in most affectionate love to Mrs. Jackson & yourself. Be pleased to present me respectfully to all my friends. I remain Dear General, your faithful friend.

A. P. Hayne

ALS, DLC (35). Published in Bassett, 3:436 (extract). Fort Moultrie was in the Charleston Harbor.

1. Not found.

2. See Hayne to AJ, December 27, 1827. A New Hampshire native and former brigadier general in AJ's Southern Division, Ripley (1782–1839; Dartmouth 1800) had settled in Louisiana after leaving the army in 1820 and was one of the committee that met AJ in

Natchez and escorted him to New Orleans in January 1828 (see Ripley to AJ, and reply, January 4). Hayne had attended the January 8 festivities in New Orleans.

3. Not found.

4. Yellow fever.

5. Hayne was a member of the South Carolina General Assembly, 1828–29. In November, the Assembly met to consider responses to the tariff. The next month, a special committee reported and the legislature ordered printed John C. Calhoun's *South Carolina Exposition and Protest, Reported by the Special Committee of the House of Representatives, on the Tariff* (Columbia, 1829).

From *"One of the People"*

[September 24, 1828]

Dear Sir,

Our country has been so generally exempted from the crimes of ambition, that we are perhaps too little apprehensive of them. The coalition have now no chance to defeat you—if you live. Do you think there is any crime that the friends of your opponents are incapable of committing?

Caution is said to be the parent of security. Take care of your health. You are now the only hope of the nation; for the people cannot be united on any other man. I pray you take care of yourself, & guard against poison & the dagger

Be always prepared to give yourself a vomit The most speedy is 15 grains of white vitriol (sulphate of zinc) or 15 grains of blue vitriol (sulphate of copper). Remember that Henry 4th of France and William of Nassau founding the Republic of Holland were assassinated[1]

On the 15th of October a statement of your good health should be published, & sent to every post office of the Union.[2]

One of the people.

ALS, DLC (36). Postmarked "Wythe C. H. Va. Sep 24."

1. Henry (1553–1610) of France and William the Silent of the House of Orange-Nassau (1533–84).

2. Some of AJ's supporters feared that the administration might spread rumors about AJ's health—even announcing his death just before the election—"to prevent the people from voting for him" (William B. Lewis to Martin Van Buren, September 27, Van Buren Papers, DLC). Henry Lee feared the forgery of letters from AJ's confidants reporting his death (Lee to AJ, September 17). Beginning on September 3, the *Cincinnati Advertiser* cautioned its readers in each issue not to believe such reports, and other Jackson papers picked up the practice. On October 17 and 28, the *Nashville Republican* published notices that AJ was in good health to rebut any rumors to the contrary.

From John Henry Eaton

Private   Fairfield. 25 Sept—28
Dr Genl—
I have talked with McLemore & Lewis, both discreet men you know
They say, & I do most heartily agree, that we had better let the Woodward Story alone,[1] Anderson, in so great a warfare, is too small game.
"Why raise a tempest for to drown a fly" As Randolph would say, it is
turning aside from the tired Fox, to chace a Rabbit
Anderson is out[2]—McNairy is out & why?[3] To turn public attention
from his *undated* published letter,[4] which plain as day, without adverting
to a single fact as coming from you, or through you I will show does not
relate to Burr. I shall prove it by the undated letter itself—irrefragably
prove it—[John] Fitzgerald[5] is <Due> here (2 Oclock PM) waiting for the
manuscript which will appear to morrow—[6]
On sober reflection, let us let for *the present* the Woodward affair
alone—I am afraid of it, & with McLemore & Lewis think for the present
it should be let alone; & too that Saml Hays should be silent.[7] Four weeks
from this time, When it cannot operate out of the State will be time
enough, & then there can & will be no objection to it For the present, Let
us let that part of the matter rest; the pill for Anderson is bitter enough
without the Woodward matter which just now may do harm & certainly
can do no good The other parts of W P As publication Hall & Fitzgerald
[w]ill attend to next week At present McNairy & the Burr affair for which
they would decry us is the most important yours truly

                                                        Eaton

I write in a wonderous hurry

ALS, DLC (72). Sent via "Mr. B F Curry."
1. For a discussion of Francis Woodward's comments about William P. Anderson, see
above, AJ to William B. Lewis, August 16.
2. In the September 20 *National Banner and Nashville Whig,* William P. Anderson had
reiterated his attack on AJ's conduct in the duel with Charles H. Dickinson.
3. Eaton was referring to Boyd McNairy's circular of September 22—McNairy was candidate for presidential elector on the Adams ticket—defending his support for Adams because Adams had more experience in civil government than did AJ and detailing examples
of Jackson's extravagance in his Florida accounts (*National Banner and Nashville Whig,*
September 27).
4. AJ to Anderson, [cNovember 20, 1803] (*Jackson Papers,* 1:397–98).
5. Fitzgerald, formerly a printer in New Orleans and Mobile, became a partner at the
Nashville Republican in April 1826; in June 1829 he was appointed postmaster at Pensacola.
6. Eaton's article, in the September 26 *Republican,* declared that the undated letter
pertained not to the Burr affair, as McNairy had asserted, but to the purchase of boats by
the war department in 1803.

7. Hays waited until November 11 to defend his father against Anderson's charges that AJ and Robert Hays conspired to defraud Robert Hays's creditors in 1807. In his defense, he published the Woodward letter (*Nashville Republican,* November 11).

From Hugh Lawson White

At Home
Octo. 4th. 1828.

My Dear Sir,

On monday last I reached home, after a four weeks absence to the Harrodsburg Springs, in company with my son, who I thought too weak to be alone. He, it is feared, has but a slender chance to reestablish his health.[1]

I have abstained writing you often since my return from Washington, for many reasons, but chiefly, because I confidently expected until lately to see, and spend some time with, you during the summer or fall—That expectation is now abandoned. The approaching Courts in Knoxville will occupy the interval between this and setting out for the City. My news from all quarters teaches me to look with much confidence to a successful result in the pending election—Yet the enemy are so untiring in their efforts, so full of invention and so destitute of every thing like moral restraint that if your friends relax there is no telling what changes may take place.

In Kentucky I saw many friends, they say they fought the battle of the *23rd. Decr.* in August, and will do their duty on the *8th. of January,* which is to be in Novr.[2] They count with much certainty on a decided Victory—Tis said Judge McNairy has taken the water and passed off in the Gulph Stream—I hope it is not so: but if it should be we must do without him—'Tis a pity he had not taken his appropriate place at first— His importance has been increased by putting him on Our Committee.[3] Every thing is kept pretty snug here—In this county we have at least *five* to *one* and in the District I think *ten to one* at least.

Pardon the suggestions which follow, they are intended as mere hints for your own mind to operate upon—Ought you not at your leisure moments to be reducing to writing your thoughts upon the Cardinal points of your Administration supposing you elected? Fix in your mind those who would form your Cabinet—If elected immediately make known to them what would be your policy and know whether they could give it their cordial support—I am of opinion you could expect no benefit from any man whose judgt. would not approve your policy—

Some plan of this sort digested in due time, *by yourself, and kept to yourself,* would enable you to select a suitable cabinet of proper materials, and would put it in your power in due season to spread your political views before the nation, in such manner as to have the best effect, and without having put you in haste on any subject.

Should you be elected I feel deep solicitude that the government should in all respects be administered upon principles which the present and future ages will approve, and upon such principles as will best secure the blessings of Civil liberty to the Sovreign people themselves. This solicitude is felt on account of the public, and on account of *you individually*—As to myself, individually it is of but little importance to me what is to happen—Out of twelve children I have now but Six left, and the eldest of them, at this time, seriously threatened. I can therefore say safely "all is vanity and vexation of spirit."[4]

Still I am not soured with the world nor am I disposed to play the part of a monk, we were put here for activity and usefulness and while here I am not disposed to avoid the discharge of duty in any respect.

In the Senate, if I approve your policy I would give it my humble support—If otherwise I would yield the berth to some other—To be your political opponent, in a public station, I would not, and to support that which I did not approve, you know, I could not.

If elected when will you be in Washington? Ought you not to be there pretty early?[5]

Present me in such terms as will be most acceptable to Mrs. Jackson, and believe that I am with great sincerity Your friend

Hu. L. White

ALS, DLC (35). Published in Bassett, 3:436–37.
1. James White, Hugh Lawson's second son, who had been a lawyer in Huntsville, Alabama, died later in the year at Tuscaloosa.
2. In the August election for state offices, Kentucky Jacksonians had gained control of the legislature and lieutenant governorship.
3. John McNairy had been a founding member of the Nashville Committee but had by this time left it. An unsigned August 18 letter, attributed by Jacksonians to Andrew Erwin, asserted that evidence of AJ's involvement with Aaron Burr had convinced McNairy to resign. The October 17 *Nashville Republican*, however, denied this, declaring: "The truth is, he is displeased, because we demolished his brother Boyd."
4. White was quoting Ecclesiastes 1:14.
5. AJ arrived in Washington on February 11, 1829, the same day Congress formally counted the electoral votes.

From Leslie Combs

Nashville 14th Octr 1828

Sir,

I did myself the honor, on Saturday evening after my return from the Hermitage to address a letter to James Jackson Esqr,[1] in which I endeavoured to detail substantially the conversation I had just held with you, so far as to indicate your willingness to have no concealment about your transactions with him or any other person, relative to the Chickasaw treaty of 1818 made by the late Gov Shelby & yourself.

You will perceive by his answer of which I have considered it my duty to enclose you a copy,[2] that he does not regard the verbal permission granted by you, in our conference for him, to make a disclosure of any thing in his power coming from you relative to said treaty or its incidents as Sufficient to authorise him as an honorable man to make a *public* developement of facts of a *private* character & therefore declined to do so without you would *Call* on him to disclose them.

So far as I have had any agency in this unpleasant affair, I have endeavored to govern myself by the Strictest rules of delicacy & propriety and I beg you to believe I would not willingly give you pain or do any thing, which (as a man of honor) I did not feel myself bound to do, acting for the representative of Gov Shelby—

As Majr W. B. Lewis has made a statement & as I understood from you that Col Butler of Florida would soon make one,[3] may I not be permitted respectfully to submit to your consideration whether there is not a propriety in your making the desired *call* on James Jackson Esqr, who is thought by my principal to be possessed of information & papers important to be communicated.

My friend Mr Benjamin M. Hinchman[4] will do me the favour to recieve your answer and if I am furnished with the necessary authority I will send a confidential friend or go, with any Gentleman you may designate to Alabama & obtain a full Statement from Mr Jackson[5]—I have the honor to be very respectfully Yr. Mo. Ob. Servt.

Leslie Combs

ALS and Copy by Benjamin F. Currey, DLC (72). Published in *National Banner and Nashville Whig,* October 29.
1. Not found.
2. See James Jackson to Combs, October 11, published in *National Banner and Nashville Whig,* October 29.
3. William B. Lewis had written the editors of the *Louisville Focus* on July 12 to defend AJ's conduct at the Chickasaw negotiations. On September 15, Robert Butler had notified AJ that he would send his remarks to Duff Green. Those were subsequently published in the *United States' Telegraph,* October 6.
4. Not identified.
5. AJ refused to write directly to James Jackson, but on October 29 he asked John Coffee to get a statement from him.

From Thomas Cadwalader

Philada. 15. Oct: 1828.

Dear General,

Our Election has closed most triumphantly—the *right* tickets have succeeded throughout—for Congress, Assembly, & City Councils. Sergeant is beaten by 557 votes—the City & County together give majorities of between five & six thousand—The vote for Electors on the 31st. will be even more decisive from the dispiriting effect of this overwhelming victory.[1]

We have no Accounts yet from Jersey—this being the 2d. & last day of their election. That ground is *debateable,* & we can well spare its votes—if we get them, it will be, to me, an agreeable surprize.

Having had a particular agency in selecting the first list of Directors of the Office of the B. U. S. in your quarter, I feel very anxious to know how far public opinion approves of the Administration—

Complaints have been made to me that "the men are unpopular"—that "the Prest: is selfish, without the least influence, except that which his Official station gives him"—that "he has a numerous train of Relatives engaged in Commercial pursuits, & the Bank is made an instrument for the promotion of their private interests, without regard to the effects upon the Community, or the Bank itself—" &c: &c. that, "with the exception of Geo. W. Campbell, there is not an individual in the Direction who has the least influence beyond his own shop upon the public square[2]—they consist for the most part of men who would not dare to express an independant opinion, if they were capable of entertaining one." "Our friend Major L. is removed, in order to make way for a man recently accused and convicted (in public opinion) of fraud for a series of years, by the use false weights at his Cotton Gin—" &c: &c:— "this change however is made by the suggestion of the Prest: & Cashr. for the purpose of procuring *business men*! this excuse for getting rid of an independant man is too flimsy to gain credit any where but in Phila."[3]

Should you favor me with any communications on a subject in which I feel interested personally, as well as in my character of Director of the Parent Bank, I need hardly say that I should receive them as strictly confidential—and they would be considered as additional obligations to those under which your former kindnesses have laid me.

Mrs. Cadwalader[4] unites in Compts. to Mrs. Jackson—I remain dear General with the most sincere respect & regard Yr. ob Servt:

T: Cadwalader

ALS, DLC (35). Published in Bassett, 3:438–39.

1. In the Pennsylvania presidential canvass, AJ carried the state with 66.7 percent of the vote.

2. Josiah Nichol was president of the Nashville branch of the B.U.S., and the cashier was John Sommerville (1770–1846), former cashier of the Nashville branch of the Bank of the State of Tennessee. The original board in 1827 consisted of Nichol, James Bell, James Erwin (1788–1861), Robert Buchanan, Robert Farquharson, George Crockett, George W. Campbell, William B. Lewis, Ephraim H. Foster, Alexander Porter (d. 1833), Joseph Vaulx, and Harry R. W. Hill. Bell (d. 1842) was a commission merchant. Buchanan (d. 1829) was a draper. Farquharson (c1776–1856) and Porter were former directors of the Nashville branch of the Bank of the State of Tennessee, and Farquharson was a justice of the Davidson County court. Crockett was probably the Nashville merchant. Vaulx (c1799–1878) was a dry goods merchant who had formerly been in business with Nichol's son, William Nichol (1800–1878). Hill (1797–1853) operated steamboats and was at this time in partnership with the younger Nichol. Foster and William Nichol were also brothers-in-law.

3. By July 1, Lewis, Foster, and Porter had been replaced by John Harding (1777–1865), a Davidson County planter; Joseph Anderson, a Nashville merchant; and James J. Gill (c1790–1853), the partner of Porter's son James A., in the mercantile firm of Gill & Porter.

4. Née Mary Biddle (1791–1850), a cousin of Nicholas Biddle's, president of the Bank of the United States.

From Benjamin McCarty, Sr.

State of Indiana Franklin County Octr 17th 1828

Sir

Permit me to address you after an elaps of about thirty years. Since I saw you last in Knoxville East Tennessee I living At that time in Granger county near Rutledgeville, having At that time a personal acquantance with you, and my desire for your welfare in the national contest for the presedency induces me to address you, and In doing so permit me to remark that it is verry Important for you to succeed in the states of Kentucky and Indiana and If you should, your Election, I think is safe. Indiana, At the last Election, was for you but owing to the paternage of the president and Clays friends, It is now somewhat doubtful. Kentucky from the best Information I can obtain, is About equally devided. Knowing as I do, that It is not your wish to seek an office but from the Abuse you have recieved from your enemies And the duty you owe your warm friends that are so Anxious for your Success, And it becoming the Custom of the day, I think you Ought, As it is now At the eve of the Election to pass through part of Kentucky and if you could arrive in Indiana About the time of the Election in that part of it that is bordering on the Ohio river that it would be of Service & perhaps Secure booth States, but if it should be out of your power or you may think differant from me and should only arrive in Kentucky nothing shall be lacking in Indiana on my part and Sons as I have a number of them and some in public Stations, one of them Genl Jonathan McCarty[1] was An Elector for you At the last Election and would have been now had he not have been A Candidate for A Seat in congress. but Owing to the presidential Election being made a Test he was beeten by the Adams candidate John Test[2] by A Small Majoriety but I have no doubt he would have beeten Mr. Test had it not have been that the quakers all voted against him. As you know, they are opposed to a Military Chieftain As Mr Clay calls A man that Serves his country there being Almost 1300 in the district; From the Abuse you have recieved from men in this State that I am acquanted with, if you should succeed I think it would be Serving them right to to treat them As Thomas Jefferson did, dismiss them from recieving any of the public loves and fishes and I will give you their names at some future day if you should be successful, you can then do as you think right. my reasons for making these remarks, there are A number of men in Indiana that has abused you Out of all reason some of whoom are now Under pay of the Genl. goverment. I should be Glad to heare from you at all times and In concluding my remarks I remain your obedient friend

Benjamin McCarty Senr.

ALS, THi (12-0226). Published in *Nashville Tennessean,* April 25, 1909 (dated October 7). McCarty (1759–1837), who settled in Indiana about 1803, was a Methodist preacher and a member of the county court.

1. Jonathan McCarty (1795–1852), a member of the Indiana House, 1818–19, who also occupied several local offices, received appointment from AJ as superintendent of the National Road in 1829 and as receiver of public money for the Fort Wayne land office in January 1830. He served in the U.S. House, 1831–37.

2. Test (1771–1849) had served two terms in Congress before being defeated for reelection in 1826; his election to Congress in 1828 was his last.

To Richard Keith Call

Hermitage Octbr. 18th. 1828—

Dr. Genl

This will be handed you by young Mr [George K.] Walker, son of your unkle David Walker deceased, who has obtained license to practic law, & is on his way to settle himself in Florida.[1] I have given him a letter[2] to Major Clements who is about to set out for Tallahassee, & with whom I hope he may travel to Florida.

I have recd your letter inclosing your statement about the facts of the chikesaw treaty,[3] for which I thank you—I had noted the error you have pointed out—it is corrected, the fact was, the Govr. signed the treaty before we left the ground, but on our return Journey directed Col Butler to destroy the Bond given by Major Lewis to pay the last annuity if the Goverment did not ratify the treaty.[4]

Col Combs has lately visited Nashville as the *pimp* of Clay, & the Shelbys—This is an honorable station for a Col & member of the Legislature of Kentucky to fill—The Col may be a good *pimp,* but I do not believe he would make a good diplomatist—before he is done with his mission, I expect he will find himself in the same disgrace, with his colleagues Col Andrew Erwin, Dr McNairy, Wm. P. Anderson & Tanyhill, who are only thought of here, to be despised.[5]

I regret Col Butler had not sent on his statement direct to me, that it might have been embodied with yours, Eastins, [Marcus Brutus] Winchesters, Smiths, & others, which when seen, hands down, Thos Shelby & Todd with infamy & disgrace to posterity—& if they establish the sayings on the old Govr. which they have ascribed to him, his memory is damd forever.[6]

The political news from all quarters is of the most flattering kind—Newyork it is confidently believed will give against the administration 30, if not 33 votes—Ohio & Kentucky is believed to be safe for the peoples cause, but both sides are sanguine Pensylvania, & Virginia, immoveable, Newjersy & Delaware against the administration & Maryland a majority—a few days more will test the result.[7]

Present Mrs J & myself respectfully to Mary & the children & receive for yourself our best wishes—your friend

Andrew Jackson

ALS, DLC (35). Published in Bassett, 3:349 (extract).

1. George K. Walker (b. c1809) eventually received appointments from AJ as federal district attorney for middle Florida in 1833 and secretary of the territory in 1834. David Walker (d. 1820), brother of Call's mother Helen Meade Walker Call, was a revolutionary war veteran and former Kentucky congressman.

2. Not found.

3. See Call to AJ, August 25.

4. In William B. Lewis's initial statement about the Chickasaw treaty, he explained that Isaac Shelby ("the Govr.") had been reluctant to sign the Chickasaw agreement after AJ had acceded to the chiefs' demands for a fifteen-year annuity because Washington had only authorized the negotiators to offer fourteen years. To satisfy Shelby, Lewis gave a bond for $20,000 to cover the fifteenth year, and Shelby signed the treaty before leaving the treaty ground (Frankfort *Argus of Western America*, July 30). Call's memory was that Shelby had signed later, on the journey back from the treaty.

5. Jackson's latest irritation with Tannehill grew out of Tannehill's involvement with Combs and his mission to Jackson. Tannehill had delivered Combs's letter to James Jackson and reported back to Combs that James Jackson said that if requested by Jackson "he would speak willingly and *fully*," but "he did not believe that Gen. Jackson would under any circumstances make such a call" (*Chickasaw Treaty: An Attempt to Obtain the Testimony of James Jackson . . .* , pp. 7–8).

6. Robert Butler had sent a statement on the Chickasaw treaty to the *United States' Telegraph,* which printed it on October 6. The other statements that AJ mentioned—Call's letter, William Eastin to AJ, August 29, Winchester to William B. Lewis, October 1, and Benjamin F. Smith to Nathaniel P. Hart, [cJanuary 1828] (DLC-26)—were all published in the Frankfort *Argus of Western America,* October 22. Winchester (1796–1856), son of General James, was the first mayor of Memphis, Tennessee, 1827–29. Butler, Winchester, and Smith all backed up William B. Lewis's July 12 account of the Chickasaw treaty (see above, AJ to Call, August 14). Eastin wrote that Isaac Shelby had told him after the talks that he had changed his mind about AJ's management of the negotiations and considered AJ's approach wise.

7. In New York and Maryland, which chose electors by districts, AJ won 20 of 36 and 5 of 11 votes, respectively. He also carried Ohio, Kentucky, and Virginia; Adams won the three electoral votes of Delaware, whose legislature chose the state's electors.

Jackson's account below with Henry Lee Heiskell (1803–55), a physician in the Nashville area recently from Virginia, describes medical treatment afforded residents at the Hermitage in late 1828. Of particular interest is his attendance at Rachel Jackson's final illness.

Account with Henry Lee Heiskell

Genl. Andrew Jackson   Dr
                                                To Dr. Henry Lee Heiskell

1828

Octr.	21.	To visit & Cathartic powders No. 6.	$ 1:50
"	22d	" Do. & Venesection Ned[1]	1:50
"	23d.	" Do. & Do. & box pills Ned	2:00
"	24.	" Do. &c. Ned Advice for Negro Woman	1:50
"	26.	" Do. &c. Ned	1:00
"	28.	" Do. & applying bandage Ned	1:50
"	30.	" Do. & Do. Do. box Ointment	1:50
Nov	1.	" Do. ʒ. Cream Tartr. Ned	1:50
"	5.	" Do. & medicine Ned.	1:50
"	8.	" Do. & Venesection Mrs. Jackson	1:50
"	20.	" Do. & bands. leg & Medicine Ned	2:00
"	21.	" Do. & bandaging leg Ned	1:50
"	26.	" Do. & box pills Ned	1:50
"	28.	" Do. & Do. Ned	1:50
Decr.	2d.	" Do. & Venesection Alfred	1:50
"	3d.	" Do & box pills Alfred	1:50
"	4.	" Do & Diuretic powders Alfred	1:50
"	5.	" Do. Alfred box Citron Oint. for Ned	1:50
"	6.	" Do. Alfred ʒ1 Cr. Tart. box pills for Ned	2:00
"	17.	" Do. Mrs. Jackson & Venesection & attendance	2:50
"	18	" Visit Mrs. Jackson & attendance	2:00
"	19	" Do. Do. & Do. & pulv. Mer.	2:50
"	20	" Do. Do. & Attendance	2:00
"	21	" Do. Do. " Do. Cast. Oil ʒ4.	2:50
"	22	" Do. Do. & Attendance	2:00
			$43:00

Recd. from Andrew Jackson the sum of forty three dollars in full of the above account this 16th. of Janry 1829

                                                Henry Lee Heiskell

Facsimile of DS with AD in AJ's hand, Sotheby Parke Bernet Catalog 4267 (June 1979), Item 719 (12-0245).
 1. The treatment was likely for Old Ned, who died in April 1829.

From William Preston Anderson

Craggy Hope, near Winchester Ten, Oct 24, 1828.
TO GENERAL JACKSON

This hasty address needs no apology. It cannot be addressed to any of your editorial gentry. They are left to the free, undisturbed, spaniel-like wagging of their tails, and faithful employment of fawning and cringing.

In the Nashville Republican you have attacked my character.[1] This is your usual mode of warfare, when charges are preferred against you by those who do not think you ought to be made President of the U States. They must be laid prostrate. In this way you divert public attention to their case, that they may lose sight of your own. My only *crime* is, that I have been instrumental in the publication of Dr May's letters. So far as they relate to the duel between yourself and Dickinson, showing that you had killed Dickinson unfairly, is to me a source of deep regret. I believe it to be true, that you *did* kill Dickinson unfairly, and that you yourself are conscious of it. The charge has not been met and refuted to my satisfaction. I was well acquainted with all the parties concerned in this duel, and do know that Dr May was incapable of falsehood or prevarication. You impliedly admit this fact, when you resist the proof of your guilt, by alleging these letters to be forgeries, though I do not believe that you have the remotest idea they are so. The letters are deposited in Nashville open for the inspection of every body.

It will forever be a source of bitter regret to me, that these letters were published, on account of others. I mean the family of the late Col Robert Hays. It was not my wish to have disturbed the ashes of Col Hays. He was, in my opinion, a kind, good hearted man, brave, open, and generous to a fault. His widow and children are among the most respectable families in the state. No man ever heard me charge Col Hays with perjury or say any thing else derogatory to his character.[2] Some of the charges, General, which you have published in the Republican of the 3d ult, and previously, as being preferred against me by the late Capt James H Campbell, are altogether untrue, some are partly true, but none of them, when properly understood, will detract from my character.[3] Lieut Littleton Johnston now resides in Tuscumbia Alabama.[4] He is a respectable merchant and can give every information necessary on this subject. I have not even addressed him as yet, but his statement can doubtless be relied on.

At a time more propitious than the present for dispassionate and impartial reflection, I will publish a refutation of these charges and all others brought against me in the Republican of the 3d inst.[5]

1st. Your besetting sins are, ambition, and the love of money. To acquire the latter you will act *miserly* and oppress your best friends; and when in pursuit of either, you are not what you profess to be.

2d. You are naturally and constitutionally irritable, overbearing and tyrannical.

3d. You are incapable of expending any charity towards those who happen to differ with you in opinion.

4th. You cannot investigate dispassionately any interesting or important subject—and if you could, your knowledge and abilities are not equal to the task.

5th. When you become the enemy of any man you will put him down if you can, no matter by what means, fair or foul, honorable or dishonorable; and if it be consistent with your views of popularity and interest, you will turn about and support the very men you have before attempted to destroy and pull down. These examples will suffice for the present. The hon. Wm H Crawford, Gen John Adair, and Col Thos H Benton.[6]

6th. You are miserably deficient in principle, and have seldom or never had power without abusing it.

All this I propose to establish—and it will not be done by certificates—but by the tenor of your life—for forty years standing in this country. In attempting to fulfil this promise I am aware (as I have before intimated) that in this state at present, I have a fearful odds against me. It will not however be so much intended for those who are wilfully blind, as for the impartial reader. So farewell.

W P ANDERSON

Printed, *National Banner and Nashville Whig,* Oct 29 (12-0246). Published in Bassett, 3:422 (extract).

1. The October 3 issue of the *Nashville Republican* accused Anderson of forging the Francis May letters and recounted how he had been court-martialed during the War of 1812 for drunkenness, fraud, ungentlemanly and unofficerlike conduct, and other offenses. In addition, the *Republican* reprinted accusations that Anderson and May had tried to use a spurious deed in a lawsuit against the heirs of William T. Lewis (see above, AJ to Lewis, June 19 and 22).

2. The May letters had included an accusation that AJ conspired with Robert Hays to defraud Hays's creditors (see above, AJ to William B. Lewis, August 16).

3. The record of the charges, May 28, 1815, against Anderson by Campbell (d. 1815), a captain in the 24th Infantry, was among Jackson's military papers at the Hermitage.

4. Johnston (c1789–1834) was in the 24th Infantry.

5. On November 15, Anderson's son, Rufus K., addressed the charge of fraud in the *National Banner and Nashville Whig.*

6. Despite AJ's fracas with Benton in 1813, his public dispute with Adair over the performance of the Kentucky militia at the Battle of New Orleans, and his antipathy toward Crawford's candidacy in 1824, he had secured the support of all three for his presidential bid in 1828.

To John Coffee

(Private)   Hermitage Octbr. 29th. 1828
Dear Genl

From a certificate appended to Col Combs pamphlet, lately published, detailing facts that he obtained whilst acting in the honorable station of pimp to Genl Shelby, it appears that Mr James Jackson, has held out the idea that he could not unseal his lips without a written application to him for this purpose[1]—It has been stated by A. Erwin & Benton that you were concerned.[2] This you know is not the fact—Make James speak on *this* This was insidious & unmasks the rascality of James, as he intended to hold out the Idea, that he knew more than he would divulge, & that injurious to me—for this purpose I wish you to call upon James with the inclosed,[3] shew it, or read it to him;

You may rest assured I will never write James, on this subject—But I request you to apply to him, and if he refuses on reading the letter to him, to comply with my request, send me a written statement of the interview having some one present in whose respectability the world will rely—who will Join in the statement with you—James has said to Mr Ephraim H. Foster, that altho he would travel to Boston or to South america to prevent my election, that he has never knew of me a dishonest or dishonorable act—I want his statement in a tangable shape, on paper—I have in his letters in the war office,[4] a sure defence against falshood, if it should be attempted—I pray you to attend to this as early as possible, & write me upon the receipt of this[5]—with best wishes adieu

Andrew Jackson

P.S. Please send me a copy of the Alabama resolutions proposing me a candidate for the President—James Jackson was if not the mover, the warm supporter of these resolutions[6]—hence could not have thought me corrupt—If necessary, in your conversation, you can hint this to James—I do not want to entrap, but his statement to Combs is of such a rascally character, that I will expose him, if it becomes necessary. A. J.

ALS, THi (12-0250). Published in Bassett, 3:440–41.

1. AJ was referring to James Shelby's *Chickasaw Treaty: An Attempt to Obtain the Testimony of James Jackson . . .* (Lexington, 1828), which detailed Leslie Combs's activities as Shelby's emissary. In November, Combs followed with *A Reply to General Andrew Jackson's Letter of the 31st October, 1828, Published in the Nashville Republican* (Lexington, 1828). The "certificate" was James Jackson to Combs, October 11 (*Chickasaw Treaty*, p. 7).

2. On October 3 and 8, Jesse Benton had asserted that Coffee, who had initially surveyed Colbert's reserve, was connected with Jackson and others in the original purchase and subsequent sale of the salt reserve to the United States (*National Banner and Nashville*

Whig, October 11). Erwin had made a similar claim on October 21 (*National Banner and Nashville Whig,* October 25).

3. AJ's enclosure, also of October 29th to Coffee, requested Coffee to call on James Jackson, show him the letter, and "ask him to state in writing" whether, in the Chickasaw negotiations, "he knew me guilty of any dishonorable or dishonest act, or whether upon all and every occasion in my public character, I have not forgotten self to promote the public weal . . ."

4. James Jackson's letters in the war department relating to the purchase and sale of the Colbert reservation have not been found.

5. Coffee's reply has not been found.

6. The resolutions, with support from James Jackson, had been adopted by the Alabama legislature in December 1823.

From William Roberdeau Swift

On board Smboat Potomac
Chesapeake Bay 30. Oct 1828.

Dear Sir,

It is now some time since I have had the pleasure of writing you, more on account of the doubt of my letters reaching you in safety is my silence to be attributed than any other cause I assure you.

I am now on my way from NYork to pass my winter in N. Carolina principally with my friends Jno Gray & Thos H[arvey] Blount,[1] having promised that Mrs. Swift[2] and self would divide our time between them— I purpose Deo volente returning so as to arrive in Washington about the 4th. March to have the real gratiffication of congratulating you in your complete triumph over your enemies, for your election I now consider just as certain as any human event possibly can be—Some of your friends (and the *caution* may not be amiss) entertain fears that the desperation of some of your opposers may tempt them to attempt assasination, though for my own part although I know many of them who are not too good, yet I do not believe they possess the nerve—caution however, is the parent of security.

I have no allusion here to young Clay's threat, for which you must know he was knocked down *immediately* by a young Virginian.[3] I have been exceedingly amused at many occurrences on the road from NYork to the District, evidencing how well you are established in the affections of the people. At N. Brunswick (NJ) I was furnished the anecdote which probably you have seen in the papers of the old dutch farmer who called on Mr. Adams, when the latter forced an affability to which his nature is a stranger, thanking the old gentleman for this mark of respect when he replied—"I calls upon you because your President for I'm for Jackson Mr. Adams and so is all my neighbours." On entering Trenton I found they had two Hickory trees spliced together, and *120 feet high,* with a large American Ensign waving from the top! It was the day of their convention & I found them in high spirits Stockton (R[obert] F[ield])[4] who has taken a very active part with us is confident we shall yet carry the state your gain being since 1826 about 4500. & the boasted Administration 5000 majority reduced to about 500! [Joseph M.] Bispham, Chairman of the Central Jackson Committee[5] is likewise confident of success. At New Castle (Del) 3/4s of the population voted the opposition ticket—and your warm friends—Here I learned when Mr. Adams was leaving there the Boys of their own accord escorted him out of town; huzzaing "for Jackson"—and here I was furnished the particulars of the anecdote of Mr James McGrand an Irishman *[by]* birth of Wilmington[6]—Mr. Adams rode up to him made many enquiries (very honest no doubt) about his circumstances & in time came to his object of enqury how Politics went—Oh! says McGran*[d,]* "I'm for Jackson, with my six brothers and about forty cousins; all the decent men in *this* part of the state are for the General"— He carried Mr. Adams about two miles out *[of]* his way, but had not the least idea who it was until afterwards. These anecdotes may serve to amuse you, as I consider our victory *certain*—

The lengthened countenances I saw at Washington plainly indicated what their expectations were. Gales is perfectly desperate his circumstances completely so as Green told me on Tuesday, a Ca. Sa. was issued against him that day for 70$![7] His bulletins are issued by thousands— several large packages on board the Steam boat from which I write—one package directed for NCarolina to my care which I shall take the liberty of sending back—[8]

Yes, I can rejoice with and for my country and I hope disinterestedly so, as thank God I have no office to ask or wish for myself. Very respectfully

W. R. Swift

[William F.] Thornton late editor of the [Alexandria] Ph*[eni]*x Gazette has gone to Washington to take c*[ha]*rge of the Journal as [Philip Ricard] Fendall, Watkin*[s]* & Co. are preparing I presume to ba*[il]* out.[9]

Mr. Adams has at length appointed Mr [Joseph] Hopkinson Judge of the District Court Philada[10]—If you do not know it I can tell you, a written and warm application was made for this by Judges Marshall & [Joseph] Story[11] & Mr Webster and sent Mr. A at Quincy[12] he deferred it until he should discover what prospect he had in Pennsylvania, but finding the federalists getting luke warm, as consequence of his indecision of character and neglect as they conceived of Hopkinson, he caused it to be communicated to some [of] the leaders on the day preceeding the Philada election that Hopkinson should be appointed, this I have from his nephew Francis Hopkinson Smith.[13] Mr Surveyor [Peter] Stagg was making himself very busy against our cause in NYork before I left there—It will avail him but little—New York will give 26 to 30 votes in your favor—[14]

I left my old friend Sam Swartwout very busy in N Jersey, up to his eyes in ditching & Politics—[15]

ALS, DLC (35). Swift (1787–1833) was a merchant who divided his time between New York City and Washington, North Carolina. He had helped organize support for John C. Calhoun in North Carolina before the 1824 election and, with Calhoun's withdrawal from the race, shifted his allegiance to AJ.

1. The Blounts, father (1752–1833) and son (d. 1850), relatives of the Tennessee Blounts, were North Carolina businessmen and politicians.

2. Née Mary Donelson Harper (c1787–1870).

3. Thomas Hart Clay (1803–71), Henry's son, traveling in the Northeast, had reportedly said "that before Jackson should be President of the United States, he *would blow the damned old rascal's brains out*" (*Easton* [Pennsylvania] *Centinel,* October 3). The "young Virginian" has not been identified.

4. The New Jersey Jackson convention met at Trenton on October 23. Stockton (1795–1866), active in New Jersey canals and railroads, was a naval officer.

5. Bispham (1774–1832) was at this time a Trenton, New Jersey, tavernkeeper.

6. Not further identified.

7. A Ca. Sa. is a capias ad satisfaciendum, or a writ of execution. The specific action against Joseph Gales has not been identified, but at this time he was in financial straits—a condition that persisted for many years.

8. Possibly *An Examination of the Civil Administration of Governor Jackson in Florida,* by "Henry," which reprinted a series of articles assailing AJ that had first been published in the *National Intelligencer* from June through September.

9. Thornton, in addition to being an editor, was brigadier general of the Alexandria militia. Fendall (1794–1868; Princeton 1815), a cousin of Henry Lee, was a clerk in the state department until AJ dismissed him in April 1829. Swift was discussing the proposed sale of the *National Journal*. Peter Force had agreed to sell the publication to Tobias Watkins in June 1828, but Watkins had been unable to raise the necessary funds and had brought in first Thornton and then Fendall as partners. Eventually, the deal fell through, and Force managed to dispose of his paper in November 1829.

10. Washington papers announced the recess appointment of Hopkinson (1770–1845; Pennsylvania 1786) as federal district judge for eastern Pennsylvania on October 28. After he was formally nominated in December 1828, he was confirmed on the last day of the Senate session, February 23, 1829.

11. Story (1779–1845, Harvard 1798) was a justice of the U.S. Supreme Court.

12. Recommendation not found. Swift may have been reporting a garbled account of Story's letter to Adams, August 22. Story, when he received news of the imminent death of the incumbent, recommended Hopkinson and indicated that Marshall and Bushrod Washington also supported him. Webster had earlier suggested Hopkinson.

13. Smith (b. c1792) was a musician, mathematician, and philosopher in Baltimore.

14. Stagg (c1780–1842) served as surveyor and inspector of revenue for New York from January 1827 until AJ dismissed him in 1829. AJ won twenty of the thirty-six electoral votes in New York, where the electors were chosen by districts.

15. Swift may have been referring to the project, on-going since 1816 under a variety of corporate names, to reclaim a portion of the salt marsh Jersey Meadows through a system of drainage ditches. Although Samuel Swartwout was financially involved, his brother Robert was leading the effort.

To Allen A. Hall and John Fitzgerald

HERMITAGE, October 31st, 1828.

Gentlemen:

Your letter was received last evening,[1] asking me to state, whether col. Leslie Combs' statement, appended to a pamphlet of James Shelby, of October 22d, 1828, contains a correct and full account of the conversation held with me, at my house, on Saturday, the 11th instant.[2] In reply, I have to remark, that it does not: parts of our conversation are suppressed, and others, if not egregiously misrepresented, have certainly been misconceived. But extraordinary candor, ought not to be expected of any one, who could descend from the exalted station of a representative of a highminded, free people, to that of a gleaner and retailer of conversations.[3] His visit to me, it seems, was for no other purpose.

It is true, as Col. Combs has stated, that he visited my house and was politely treated. After dinner, the Colonel and myself being in the passage, he observed, that he wanted a few moments' private conversation with me. We entered the parlor and were seated on the sofa, when he presented me with an open letter from James Shelby, covering the duplicate of one which previously had been received by another special messenger, (Mr. Gott.)[4] Having read the letter which enclosed the duplicate, I observed, these were a kind of communications to which I never replied; that I considered the letter of a character highly indecorous, and believed that no person having the proper feelings of a gentleman could address another in this manner. I asked what it was Mr Shelby wanted; that if he desired me to furnish evidence to aid Thos. Shelby and Mr Todd, to blast the memory of his deceased Father, I had none to offer; but, if it was his intention and wish to exhonorate the memory of his father from the publication, by Thomas Shelby and Todd, of the declarations of their father, which I never had or could believe him to have made, and would thus write me, then, and then only, could he have access to the full explanation of the secret journal in the possession of Maj. Wm. B. Lewis for safe keeping. Recollecting at that moment, that I was alone with one who was engaged, as I conceived, in no very honorable vocation, I sent for Major Lewis, who was near at hand. When he entered, having been again asked by Colonel Combs to read the duplicate letter, I replied I should not; and a second time desired him to explain what Mr Shelby wished. The Colonel answered that he was charged by Gen. Shelby to say to me, all he wanted was to protect the memory of his deceased father from the imputations which had been cast upon it; and that he was charged to protest, in Gen. Shelby's name, against having any thing to do with the publications of Thomas Shelby and Todd. To which I replied, if Mr Shelby's real object is to defend the memory of his father from the imputations and slanders of Tho. Shelby and Todd, and had so written to me, I should cheerfully have aided him. That man while living (pointing to the portrait of Governor Shelby)[5] could not have been base enough to utter the things charged by his relations, which the secret journal, under his own proper signature, will prove; and which, by applying to Maj. Lewis he was welcome, for *his* satisfaction, to see. Col. Combs said he would like to see it, and consent was given, that Maj. Lewis should submit to him an inspection of it; but no promise was given for him to have a copy, as he alleges. Subsequently he did see it, and admitted the signature to be in Gov. Shelby's own hand writing. I told him he was at liberty to see, not only the secret journal, but also the statements of those gentlemen who were present at the Treaty. But as it appeared Mr Shelby, or his friends, had been secretly writing to Maj. B. Smith for information on this subject, without any communication or notice to me;[6] and that as Shelby and Todd had published to the world the declarations of their deceased father, which the secret journal over his signature shewed to be positively untrue—that they must now get out of the difficulty in which they had voluntarily placed themselves, the best way they could, and without assistance from me—that the journal, and every thing in relation to the Treaty, having been forwarded by the Commissioners (Gov. Shelby and myself) to the government at Washington City, General Shelby certainly had it in his power, provided it had been wanted, or deemed material, to have obtained it—that if the government chose to take the responsibility of publishing it, I had no objection to its being so done. It was only to satisfy Col Combs of the incorrectness of what Messrs Shelby & Todd had published, and to prove to him, that the secret journal had been signed in the proper hand writing of Gov. Shelby, that consent was given to see it. He must have so understood, for at the time of reading it, he was given directly to understand the reason why I had not permitted it to be published. But notwithstanding all this, he proceeded home, and lost no time in publishing garbled extracts from it, justifying himself for doing so, and for this practised breach of confidence, by no better reason than that he has been unable to perceive any substantial or sufficient reason for preserving its confidence.[7]

Col. Combs then inquired of me, if I would write to Mr James Jackson, Mr Currin and Col. Butler, who, he said, Gen. Shelby had learned were at the treaty. I asked if those gentlemen had been applied to by Mr S. and if not, why seek my consent? He answered they had not been applied to, & that *he presumed* they would not speak without *my permission.* This insinuation appeared so very impertinent, that at any other place, and under other circumstances, I might have admonished the Colonel of the impropriety of being the bearer of such insulting and ungentlemanly expressions. I replied, this insinuation, proceeding from Gen. Shelby, was highly indecorous; and that I thought no man possessing the proper feelings of a gentlemen, could so express himself. I remarked that over these gentlemen I had no control; that neither Mr James Jackson nor Mr Currin were at the treaty—that I should not write to either; but he was at perfect liberty to apply to them, and that they had my full permission to detail all and every thing they, or either of them, knew on the subject of the treaty, or any other matter respecting me; for that I had no secret keepers—that I had received a letter that morning from Col. Butler, informing me he had just seen the publication of Thomas Shelby and Todd, and was preparing a statement in reply, which would be forwarded to the U. S. Telegraph for publication[8]—that James Jackson and myself had not spoken for some years, and from his marked hostility, I had no doubt he would relate any and every thing he knew, which by any possibility might operate prejudicially to me; and he was authorized to say to Mr Jackson (then in Nashville) that he was absolved from any thing of secrecy and confidence in respect to me—repeating that I had no secret keepers; but that I would not be compelled into a correspondence with him or any body else. The Colonel enquired, if he should be at liberty to communicate this to Mr Jackson? I told him, he was perfectly at liberty, and I wished him to do so. His reply was, this will answer the same purpose as though you had written.

Col. Combs then proceeded to remark that he was politically opposed to me; but in his canvass, and in all his public speeches before the people, had studiously avoided introducing my name improperly or indecorously into them; and that if I should be elected, he would, with great pleasure, support my administration. I replied, Colonel, I have risked much that every man might possess freedom of speech, of thought, and opinion; and where they conducted themselves, in the exercise of those rights, as gentlemen always should do, it never had been, and never would be, cause of the least heart burning: but when slander was resorted to, the country ransacked for secret tales, and these promulgated to injure the feelings and character of any one, those capable of such conduct, ought to be contemned by all high minded, honest, and honorable men. With the close of this sentiment, we walked into the passage, when I observed, I was well advised, how all this matter was managed; that had not such a man as Henry Clay existed, Thomas Shelby and Todd would never have put forth such falsehoods. In making this remark, I had reference to particular information contained in a confidential letter received from Kentucky.[9] Col. Combs quotes my remark in the way "that if there never had been such a man as Henry Clay, these matters would have slept in the grave with Gov. Shelby."[10] The latter member of this sentence "these matters would have slept in the grave with Gov Shelby" is untrue. I used no such expression, and I leave with Col. C. to explain, whether his statement was made from want of memory, or thro' design, the better to fill up his diplomatic report. At the time alluded to, Gov. Shelby's name was not used by me. As to the correctness of his recollection about the secret journal, I refer you to the instrument itself, which can be seen by applying to Maj. Lewis. It will be there perceived, that either it or the statement made by Messrs Shelby and Todd, is false. Every thing done in reference to the Treaty was laid minutely before the Government. Nothing took place known to me, that was in the slightest degree objectionable, or improper; and if there did, it is equally matter of objection against Governor Shelby as myself, inasmuch as nothing was done or concluded upon, that did not receive the approbation and sanction of both of us. Between Gov. Shelby and myself there existed, so far as I have knowledge, friendship and good feeling. In his firmness and sincerity I always had confidence, nor in his life time, did he, by any course of conduct, afford any reason to infer, that his feelings and friendship were at all different from my own. So late as Dec. 1818, after the Treaty, made with the Chickasaws, the language he employs in a letter addressed to me forbids the idea, that he entertained any opinion such as has been ascribed to him by his relations. I send you the original letter, that you may perceive what was his opinion and friendly feeling directly after the conclusion of this treaty, concerning which his own family have spoken so different from himself. Another also, of more recent date is sent, by which it will be perceived, that no expression is contained, to warrant the idea of any change, either in his friendship or confidence.[11]

Col: Combs has both suppressed and perverted facts. If for this he can obtain his own forgiveness, he is quite welcome to mine. I would recommend to him however, for the future, never so far to forget, or degrade character, as to obtrude himself into a Gentleman's house, for the purpose of becoming a spy, and thereafter to retail what he learns (even should it be done accurately) without at least candidly declaring on his first appearance, the intention and object of his visit.

Make of this communication just whatever use you please. Respectfully, &c.

ANDREW JACKSON.

Printed, *Nashville Republican,* November 7 (mAJs), Washington *United States' Telegraph,* November 24 (12-0256).

1. See Hall and Fitzgerald to AJ, October 29.
2. AJ was referring to Combs to James Shelby, October 14, as printed in Shelby's *Chickasaw Treaty: An Attempt to Obtain the Testimony of James Jackson . . .* ([Lexington, Ky.], 1828), pp. 4–6. October 22 was the date of Shelby's public letter at the beginning of the pamphlet.
3. Combs represented Fayette County in the Kentucky House.
4. See Shelby to AJ, October 6, and above, September 19.
5. AJ had commissioned Ralph E.W. Earl to paint Isaac Shelby's portrait in 1818 (see *Jackson,* 4:250–51).
6. In his letter of December 10, Smith denied that Shelby had contacted him on the matter; instead, he had contacted the Shelbys of his own accord to defend AJ's handling of the Chickasaw negotiations.
7. In his October 14 letter to James Shelby, Combs abstracted parts of the secret journal, presumably from memory. AJ's stated reason for preserving confidentiality was to protect the lives of Chickasaw chiefs who had been bribed to support the treaty.
8. See Robert Butler to AJ, September 15; and Butler to Green and Jarvis, September 15 and undated (published in the Washington *United States' Telegraph,* October 6).
9. Not found.

10. The quotation is from Combs to James Shelby, October 14.
11. See Isaac Shelby to AJ, December 14, 1818, and September 1, 1824, both printed in the *Nashville Republican* on November 7.

From David Corbin Ker

New-Orleans Nov. 6. 1828

My dear General.

I am so much delighted at the result of the election for Electors in this city, that I cannot deny myself the pleasure of communicating it to you— We have Just finished counting the votes and have a majority of eighty two[1]—In July the rascally adherents of the administration obtained by bribery & corruption a majority of one hundred votes[2] & calculated to a certainty on receiving in this election a majority of from two hundred & fifty to two hundred & eighty votes—but thank God they are defeated— you cannot imagine their mortification & dissappointment—they had boasted of beating you on the very field of your Glory, in sight of the plains of Chalmette; and prematurely exulted in their imaginary triumph—

The accounts from every part of the State are most encouraging & we have every reason to believe that we shall succeed by a handsome majority, & Louisiana will wipe away from her character the foul stain of ingratitude which now attaches to it[3]—The accounts from the north are truly gratifying and leave no room to doubt of the election of the peoples Candidate by an overwhelming majority, the triumph of sound principles, and the defeat of the infamous coalition—I am almost mad with Joy— Withers[4] begs to be remember'd to you—Your letters to him were never received there has been no <failure> loss of mail from Nashville. The Post Office must therefore have made free with them—Present me most respectfully to Mrs. Jackson and have the goodness to indulge me with a few lines, that I may have the pleasure of announcing to the rascals that you are alive & well, for nothing but your death can save them from disgrace & ruin—I am most truly ys &c

David C. Ker

ALS, DLC (35). Ker (1772–1840, Edinburgh 1792), a former army physician who had attended AJ during the New Orleans campaign, was a sometime Louisiana legislator and a member of both the 1824 New Orleans Jackson committee and the committee that arranged AJ's January 1828 visit.
1. In the presidential election AJ won Louisiana's five electors with 53 percent of the vote.
2. In Louisiana's congressional elections the previous July, the administration candidate, Edward D. White (1795–1847), had unseated the Jacksonian candidate, Edward Livingston, in the district that included New Orleans.
3. Ker was referring to the 1825 election in the House of Representatives, when Gurley and Brent united behind Adams, giving him Louisiana's vote.
4. Probably William C. Withers (d. 1829), a New Orleans businessman.

To John Coffee

Hermitage Novbr 11th. 1828

Dr. Genl

I have this moment recd. yours of the 2nd. instant,[1] under cover to Major Eaton; & I find it was written before Capt A. J. Donelson reached you.

you will please to observe, that I had no information of any application being made to James Jackson by the Shelbys but that through Laslie Combs, until Shelbys Book came out with those letters appended to it, with the statement of Combs lackies, Tannyhill & Douglass [a]lso appended to it—The inuendoes contained in this, are of such a nature, that require an explanation from James, & if he has authorised it, immediate punishment—you will please to remark that the call upon James, is not for political effect, or to be used at present in that way, but to bring forth from him, whilst I am living, the truth, the whole truth, & nothing but the truth, & if he attempts to lie, that I may use all the means I have, in correcting him, & to obtain from him copies of *all letters* that he has of mine on the subject of the chikisaw treaty & Colberts reservation &c &c[2]—It appears to be the opinion of Eaton that my letter in reply to the Editors of the Nashville Republican[3] which you will have seen, is a sufficient call on James Jackson to come forth—I inclose his note to me[4] & untill Capt A. J. Donelson returns, & you hear from me, you can pospone the call

I must at a proper time, have James answer to the questions propounded in my note to Andrew J. Donelson & you,[5] my own feelings & character, is dearer to me than any other earthly thing—and if James has used inuendoes set forth by T. & D. he is one of the most base cowardly assasins of character, that ever lived—From our once friendship, if he had possessed the least magnanimity & honor, he would like all others have, come out voluntari[l]y & given the truth; which at once would have put to rest all the slang of the combination of Erwin McNairy Anderson, Benton, Tannyhill & Co—but he has on the close of the election by an inuendoe, endeavoured to give me a thrust under the 5th. rib, supposing he would be safe, as all things would be forgotten at the close of the election—but more of this hereafter—[6]

I regret to hear of your suffering, but by extracting the tooth, is the only permanant remedy—Major Lee has reached Nashville last night & brings the intelligence, that Jacksons majority in Ohio in 24 Counties heard from in cincinnati on the 5th instant was 9724, being 5800, over [John Wilson] Campbell in the same counties in the election for Governor—In Kentucky in Wycliff's—[Thomas P.] Moors, [Joseph] Lecompts,

& [Robert Lytle] McHattons Districts Jackson majority 5750. It appears Ky. & ohio are safe notwithstanding all the vile slander—[7]
With our best respects to you your lady & family—your friend

Andrew Jackson

ALS, THi (12-0261). Published in Bassett, 3:441–42.
1. Letter not found.
2. Andrew J. Donelson had gone to Alabama, ostensibly to escort home his wife, who had been visiting relatives, but his real real purpose was to extract a statement from James Jackson about the Chickasaw negotiations or, failing that, to challenge him to a duel. James Jackson, however, was not at home. Eaton was particularly concerned about Donelson's mission and so warned Coffee, but he was more alarmed about AJ's plans, perhaps to duel James Jackson. "Our friend, *the old man*," he told Coffee, "is *galled* at the assault made upon him, & will yield to no suggestion. Spite of every consideration of self, I am satisfied he has made up his mind determinately, & immovably to make J. J— personally answerable, for what he says, is a *wicked* & *unpro[vo]ked* wrong done to him" (Donelson to Coffee, October 31, John H. Eaton to Coffee, November 3, both THi). Donelson returned to Nashville on November 14, and AJ thereafter decided against pursuing the matter further (see Donelson to Coffee, November 16, Donelson Papers, DLC, and AJ to Coffee, November 24).
3. See above, AJ to Allen A. Hall and John Fitzgerald, October 31.
4. See John H. Eaton to AJ, November 9.
5. The note to Donelson and Coffee has not been found.
6. James Jackson did respond after a fashion to AJ's inquiries, stating in a letter to the public, [November 13]: "All that I intended for Col. Combs was contained in my written letter to him . . . That those gentlemen [Tannehill and Douglass] should have felt themselves at liberty, *unauthorized* by me, to make any report for publication of remarks which may then have fallen from me, has occasioned those feelings of surprise and (from the estimation in which I held them) of regret" (*National Banner and Nashville Whig*, November 22).
7. In Ohio's state elections, which closed on October 14, Allen Trimble (1783–1870), the incumbent administration candidate for governor, defeated Campbell (1782–1833), a Jacksonian whom AJ later appointed federal district judge, by a 2,967 vote margin (51.6 to 48.5 percent). But in the presidential election, for which the polls closed October 29, AJ carried Ohio by a margin of 4,143 votes (51.4 percent). Charles A. Wickliffe, Moore, Lecompte (1797–1851), and McHatton (1788–1835) were Jacksonian congressmen from Kentucky. The Frankfort *Argus of Western America*, November 12, reported that AJ carried their four districts by 5,967 votes; he won Kentucky by a margin of 7,840 votes (55.5 percent).

By late November, Jackson's overwhelming victory in the presidential election was clear to all. In the popular vote, he had won by a margin of over 135,000; in the electoral college, Jackson claimed 178 votes to 83 for Adams.

1828 ELECTORAL VOTES

	Jackson	Adams
Maine	1	8
New Hampshire		8
Massachusetts		15
Rhode Island		4
Connecticut		8
Vermont		7
New York	20	16
New Jersey		8
Pennsylvania	28	
Delaware		3
Maryland	5	6
Virginia	24	
North Carolina	15	
South Carolina	11	
Georgia	9	
Tennessee	11	
Kentucky	14	
Ohio	16	
Indiana	5	
Illinois	3	
Missouri	3	
Louisiana	5	
Mississippi	3	
Alabama	5	

From Duff Green

Washington 12th. Novr 1828

Dear Genl.

The latest accounts from the north give us 16 votes in New York & one in maine and we yet hope for Eight more in New York & Eight in New Hampshire which are yet to hear from—Four more in New York are consider'd sure—These votes with *good* old Pensylvania Va. & the South & West and the six votes in Maryland which are now *sure* make your Elevation to the Presidency certain—It will be a Triumph such as never was before achieved in this Country and permit me to unite with the millions of free men who cheer the "Hickory Tree"—

Apart from the gratification of your friends and the triumph of the great principles which involve the permanency of our Republic The change will be a sacrifice to you, but in these you will find your recompense—a rich reward for the labors & privations imposed upon you by the acclamations of a grateful people—Excuse my dear Sir the Over flowing of a heart which is almost too full to rejoice—Give to Mrs. Jackson the kiss of Joy & say to her that the slanders of Your Enemies have endeared her to a nation of intelligent people. Your Sincere friend

D Green

ALS, DLC (35).

To Thomas Cadwalader

Hermitage Novbr. 16th. 1828

My Dr. Sir

Your friendly letter of the 15th ultimo has been received,[1] and I should have done myself the pleasure of acknowledging its receipt before this, but for the desire of getting some information upon the subject of the Bank about which you express some solicitude

I assure you my Dr. Sir, that I feel myself under many obligations for the disinterested & liberal support of my friends in every section of the union, and to none am I under higher & more lasting obligations than to my Pennsylvania friends. That state is as firm in the cause of Republicanism & liberal principles as are her native mountains—she has shewn herself, by her virtue & love of liberty, worthy of the predominating influence she possesses, and from her local situation always must possess in the Union.

With regard to the Bank located in Nashville, I can say but little, altho I have made some inquiry concerning it, since the receipt of your letter. Never having been, in any manner, connected with Banks, and having very little to do with the one here, I feel myself unable to give you any satisfaction about it. The Directors[2] so far as I know, are reputed honest; but some of them, it is true, are but little known out of Nashville. Whether the President has an undue influen[c]e over the Board or not, I am unable to say; but as some of the members are young men & partly raised by him, it is quite probable that they have much confidence in his Judgment and may be influenced by his opinions. I am told the greatest objections to the present Board is, that a large proportion of the members are Europeans, and some of them residents of this place but a very few years.[3] If it is any part of the policy of the mother Bank to conciliate the states & make their Branches acceptable to the people, then I think a portion of their board at least, should have been composed of men better known, & possessing more extensive influence than the most of those in the directory of the Bank at Nashville do. I do not wish to speak as to the *competency* of the present Board in *Judiciously & Safely* managing the concerns of the Banks—for of this I am not sufficiently informed to allow myself to speak: nor am I able to say whether its management has given *General* satisfaction; but I have understood complaints have been made—whether well or ill founded I know not.[4]

Mrs Jackson requests that her kind salutations may be presented to Mrs Cadwalader to whom you will be pleased to add mine. With sincere respect and regard I am dear Sir Your Most Obt Servant

Andrew Jackson

AL copy, partly in another hand, DLC (35). Published in Bassett, 3:445.

1. See above.
2. Hereafter in a different hand, possibly that of Benjamin F. Currey.
3. At least two members of the 1828 board were fairly recent immigrants from Scotland: James Bell and Robert Farquharson.
4. The 1829 appointments to the board of the Nashville branch of the Bank of the United States addressed some of the problems identified by AJ, as James Erwin, Robert Buchanan, and the two men most closely tied to bank president Josiah Nichol, Joseph Vaulx and Harry R. W. Hill, were rotated off and replaced by Columbia merchant James Walker (1792–1864); Jonathan Curren (d. 1843), a merchant, Presbyterian elder, and sometimes alderman from Murfreesboro; former Tennessee Supreme Court Justice William Little Brown (1789–1830); and Charles J. Love.

From Amos Kendall

Frankfort Nov. 19th 1828

Dear Sir,

I have the pleasure of informing you, that the precise majority for the Ticket pledged to vote for yourself as President and Mr. Calhoun as vice president, in this state, is ascertained by a full meeting of the Sheriffs on this day, to be 7934. Permit me to congratulate you, sir, on this signal proof, that the people of Kentucky cannot be induced by management, by art, by falsehood, nor even by her attachments, to be unjust to our country's defenders or give her sanction to a corrupt administration of the general government.

Great as is my gratification at this brilliant result on your account personally, I confess that it is greater on account of our common country. The line of Secretary succession, is broken,[1] and it has now been proved by actual experiment, that the people cannot be controlled in the exercise or their elective franchise by the power and patronage of their own government.

I look forward to a new era under your administration distinguished not only by reforms in the administration of the government, but by such changes in its form as will cut off all inducements to men high in office to use the patronage or their stations for the purpose of purchasing popularity.

Our cannon is now announcing in a federal salute the triumph of principle in the state of Kentucky. Your friend & Obet Servt

Amos Kendall

ALS, ICHi (12-0277).
1. Kendall was referring to the succession of the secretary of state to the presidency as had been the case with James Madison, James Monroe, and John Quincy Adams, but Adams's loss in 1828 meant that his secretary of state, Henry Clay, would not succeed.

From Felix Grundy

Nashville, Novbr 20th 1828—

Dear Sir,

Beleiving as I do, that it is the duty of your friends to communicate to you all facts and circumstances which will enable you to Judge of the state of parties correctly—I proceed to inform you that, on this day I received a letter (not confidential) from Mr Wm H Crawford in which he says, "The State of Georgia cannot consistently with its feelings or character vote for Mr Calhoon or Mr Rush as Vice president &c["]¹

a determination to run Nathaniel Macon is then express'd and many things are said in his favor and a wish expressed, that his claims should be laid before our electoral college &c²

This is a strange step, which will fail in its object, I shall answer Mr Crawford, stating that I consider our Electors pledged to vote for Calhoon by their declarations previous to the election—This movement shews, that dissention and discord will exist among those who have supported you and that at an early day, the present dominant party will be greatly divided among themselves—and in such manner, I fear as to give you much disquietude. Should a serious disagreement rise up—nothing will be easier than for the now defeated party to assume such an attitude as will enable them to govern the affairs of the Country upon your retiring from office—not that one of them can be elected, but your successor can be made indebted to them for their support, and of course, they will possess a great degree of influence & control over him—What would most effectually prevent strife & contention and keep down a rising storm? It would be, in my opinion, a willingness on your part to continue in office a second term, or at least no avowal to the contrary—I had a strong wish to converse with you on the subject last named, but my continued absence from home will probably deprive me of seeing you before you leave this State for Washington—I wish you health & prosperity yrs respectfully

Felix Grundy

ALS, DLC (35). Published in Bassett, 3:445–46.
1. Rush was the vice presidential candidate on the Adams ticket. Only two of Georgia's nine electors voted for Calhoun for vice president. The remaining seven votes went to South Carolina Senator William Smith (c1762–1840).
2. Macon (1758–1837), a revolutionary war veteran, represented North Carolina in the House of Representatives, 1791–1815, and in the Senate, 1815–28.

To David Corbin Ker

Hermitage Novbr. [c20, 1828]

My Dr. Sir

I have Just recd. your kind letter of the 6th. instant,[1] & seize the opportunity by our mutual friend Col Livingston to answer it—[2]

I am grateful to my friends, I am grateful to Louisana, for the result of the electoral election—It is a triumph of the virtue of the people over the corrupting influence of executive patronage wielded to destroy the morals of the people, & to crush a private individual whose only crime was that the people had thought proper to select him as a proper character to fill for them the Presidential chair—The history of the world does not fur[n]ish a parallel to the late canvass—every calumny that could be invented both against my private and publick character, was trumpeted forth by the subsidised presses, supported by the patronage of the Goverment, & circulated over the whole union, by its minions & panders—The virtue of they people has prevailed—and I will, with the smiles of providence & with a hearty zeal endeavour to realise the expectations of the people.

Present me, & Mrs. J. kindly to Capt Withers & his lady, assure I sincerely regret that the espoinage in the post offices has prevented my letters from reaching him, but I hope ere long, this interruption, will cease, when friend may communicate to friend freely & without hazzard present Mrs J. & myself to your lady[3] & family affectionately, and to Mrs. [Thomas] Shields[4] & her sweet little ones, and to all my friends in orleans—I am inundated with letters from all quarters & can write but to few—I am very respectfully your friend.

A. J.

ALS draft, DLC (35).
1. See above.
2. Livingston, en route from New York to New Orleans, was a guest at the Hermitage at this time.
3. Née Margaret Benson (1781–1838) of Virginia.
4. Née Ellen Blanchard Ker (1799–1834), David Corbin's daughter.

To Amos Kendall

Hermitage Novbr. 25th. 1828—

My Dr. Sir

I have been gratified by the receipt of yours of the 19th. instant,[1] announcing the vote of Kentucky on the Presidential question—

A proof of devotedness to the principles of liberty so signal as that displayed by Kentucky on this occasion, will give her a distinguished place in the annals of our republic—The weight of gratitude imposed on me by the result, is hightened by the recollection that she had to contend against a system of intrigue and management almost impossible to detect, because it was encompassed by her pride & attachments; yet she has unravelled it, and presented to her citizens the elective franchise spotless & pure—

Could I welcome with the same confidence the part which her partiality in all probability has assigned me in the work to be done by the next administration; my happiness would be complete—But this I cannot do—Responsibility so great, I cannot anticipate without disquietude and fear, arising out of the consciousness of my inadequacy to meet its numerous, and arduous requisitions. all that I can promise is an honest disposition to execute the will of the people, and an earnest reliance on the goodness of providence, that with his aid those points in our goverment thro' which our enemies have attempted to invade our liberties may be fortified and strengthened.

Be assured, Sir, that I appreciate greatly the efforts of my friends, and take pleasure in mentioning my obligations to you as one of that number. I am very respectfully yr obt. Servt.

Andrew Jackson

ALS and Draft in Andrew J. Donelson's hand with revisions by AJ, DLC (78, 35). Published in *Cincinnati Commercial*, February 4, 1879.

1. See above.

Rachel Jackson to Louise Moreau Davezac de Lassy Livingston

Hermitage December 1st. 1828—

My dear friend

We had the pleasure of the Colos company for a day or two as he passed southward—He was in good health & fine spirits—It is at his suggestion that I now write you, and although it may be imposing upon you too much trouble I find I am compelled to avail myself of your kind offer through him "to assist in the selection of such articles of dress as might be considered necessary for the circles of the city["]—This voluntary tender on your part madam to serve me is viewed as an additional proof of that disinterested friendship which has always characterised the conduct of your family towards myself & the Genl whether surrounded by the plaudits of the virtuous & the upright or by the dark mists of slander & detraction.

I could have spent at the Hermitage the remnant of my days in peace & were it not that I should be unhappy by being so far from the General no consideration could induce me again to abandon this delightful spot; but since it has pleased a grateful people once more to call him to their service & since by the permission of Providence he will obey that call I have resolved, indeed it is a duty I owe to myself & my husband to try to forget, at least for a time all the endearments of home & prepare to live where it has pleased heaven to fix our destiny

I shall want two dresses—the measure for the waist & skirt you will find enclosed respectively marked—the colour & quality I leave entirely to your better taste & judgment—When completed have them carefully put up & consigned to my address at the city Care of Mrs Watson & should I ever meet with you & Miss *Cora* in person it will afford me great pleasure to have it in my power to shew how sensible we are of your civility & goodness

For the future health & happiness of yourself and family be pleased to accept the best wishes of the General accompanied by those of your friend & most obedient Servant

Rachel Jackson

NB You will find the measure of the length of the skirt & waist on the tape. the whole length of the tape is the measure of the skirt & to the black mark is the measure of the waist R. J

LS by proxy (Harriet Berryhill), NjP (mAJs).

Rachel Jackson to Mrs. L. A. W. Douglas

Hermitage Decmbr 3rd 18[28]

My Dear Mrs Douglas

It was with great pleasure I recieved your truly interesting letter a few weeks since,[1] & I assure you nothing has given me more heartfelt satisfaction than the perusal of it: I had hoped long ere this to had the pleasure of seeing you in Tennessee, I sincerely regret that your husband's business compels you to reside at such a distance from so many warm friends as you have in Nashville: You are frequently the subject of conversation here, particularly with Harriet Berryhill[2] and myself, who I believe loves you sincerely and regrets your removal from Nashville almost as much as she would a sisters:

You mention your expectation of seeing the General & myself on our way to Washington; I suppose from the accounts we have recieved there is no doubt of the General's being elected; I shall be much pleased to see you on my way, but believe me when I tell you my dear Mrs Douglas were it not for the many base attempts that have been made to defame the characters of my husband and myself, and the ungrateful exertions that were used to prevent his election, [I c]ould hardly be induced to leave this peaceful & delightful [spo]t; but as a grateful people have elected my husband [to] the highest office in the Union it is my duty to follow [him] without a murmur, & to rejoice at not being seperated from him who is dearer to me than all other earthly considerations; Hitherto my Saviour has been my guide & support thro' all my afflictions, (which I must confess for the last four years have been many and unprovoked) & now I have no doubt but he will still aid and instruct me in my duties which I fear will be many and arduous.

I was sorry to hear of Mr Douglas's indisposition[3] it must have been a great trial to you, I hope ere this he is entirely recovered—Miss Harriet Berryhill is here & desires to be affectionately remembered to you, & says she would have written you long since but has never recieved an answer to the letter which we wrote to you after our return from Orleans;[4] Her mother's health is not very good this winter, she expects to spend a few months in Orleans; If Mrs. Davenport[5] has not left, be so good as to present my love to her & say to her I should be happy to recieve a letter from her—

Be so kind as to present the General's & my most respectful compliments to Mr Douglas, & accept the sincere prayers for your health & happiness of your friend

Rachel Jackson

LS by proxy (Harriet Berryhill), Philip Jones (mAJs). Mrs. Douglas resided in Chillicothe, Ohio, at this time.

1. Not found.

2. Berryhill, the daughter of Nashville merchant William McLean Berryhill (1785–1836) and his wife Mary Craig (1789–1857), had been a regular companion to Rachel, going with her to New Orleans in January 1828. In July 1830 she married Edward W. B. Nowland.

3. Douglas has not been further identified.

4. Probably Berryhill to Douglas, April 15 (NN), enclosed in Rachel Jackson to Douglas, April 15.

5. Possibly Hanna Israel Davenport, the wife of William Davenport (d. 1858), an army officer.

From Samuel Smith et al.

Washington City, December 4. 1828.

Sir,

The Presidential election being now over, and the result, (although not yet officially declared), being perfectly understood and known to be in your favor, the undersigned, members of the Senate and House of Representatives of the U. States, beg leave to submit to your consideration the propriety of your repairing to the seat of government, so soon as your convenience will permit. From the commencement of this government until now, it has invariably so happened, that the President elect has occupied some public station, the duties of which required his personal attendance at the seat of government, at the period of announcing to him officially the fact of his election. No inconvenience, therefore, has ever yet been experienced in communicating this fact to the citizen selected by the people to preside over them, so as to give him ample time to prepare for the discharge of his duties on the day his term of service commenced. In your case, however, the remoteness of your habitation from this place, and the existing provisions of the statute, requiring the ballots for President and Vice President to be opened and counted on the second wednesday in February, will render it impossible for Congress, after that day, to announce to you, that you have been elected President, in time for you to assume the functions of this office on the fourth of March next, unless you approach the seat of government much nearer than your present place of abode.[1] The public duties which you are expected and have been chosen to perform must, therefore, be suspended for an uncertain period, during which possibly some public detriment may be sustained; or some plan must be adopted, by which you may be approached with more facility than can possibly exist, if you should continue where you now are until you shall have received such a communication. Several modes have been suggested by which this object might be accomplished; but that which the undersigned consider as liable to the least objection is the one they have ventured to submit to your consideration:

In taking this liberty with you, the undersigned, judging from all the past events of your life, feel well assured, that you will, with pleasure, submit yourself to the inconvenience to which their suggestion may possibly expose you, provided you shall concur with them in the opinion, that by adopting it the good of your country may in any degree be promoted, or even possible mischief prevented. Nothing but the conviction, that this will be the case, could have induced them to obtrude their suggestion on you; and such a motive, they venture to hope, will be regarded by you, as a sufficient apology for offering it at this time, even if you should not approve of the mode they have pointed out.

The undersigned will avail themselves of this opportunity to present to you their gratulations on the known result of the recent election. To be called from your chosen retirement, by the free suffrages of an immense majority of your fellow citizens, to preside over them, is the best evidence they could give of the very high estimation in which they hold that virtue, patriotism and intelligence, of which you have already furnished many signal proofs. In obeying this call, you will add one more instance of your devotion to the good of your Country. Its happiness and prosperity, the undersigned believe, will be the sole end and aim of your Administration; and they felicitate themselves in the expectation, that the attainment of these great objects will add new splendor to your character, and will render still more secure the rights of the States and the liberties of our fellow citizens.

The undersigned severally tender to you the assurance of their very great Respect.

S. Smith   A. Stevenson of Va
John Randolph of Roanoke   John Chandler

Thomas H. Benton of Misi.
Jno Branch
William R King of Alabama
Rh: M Johnson
Nathan Sanford
S[amuel] McKean
J[oel] B Sutherland
Geo: Wolf
Robert Orr Jr
Jeromus Johnson
P. P. Barbour.
J. S. Barbour
Thos. H. Hall
Robt. Allen
Jn: Macpherson Berrien of Georgia
Littn: W Tazewell of Virginia.
John Tyler of Virginia
John Rowan
I[saac] D. Barnard of Pa.
Elias K Kane
Starling Tucker
C[harles] E. Haynes.
C. A. Wickliffe
Nathl. H. Claiborne (of Va)
Joseph LeCompte of Ky
A[mbrose] H. Sevier of Arkansas
M[ichael] C. Sprigg
Wm. Drayton

Tho H. Williams of Mississippi
Oliver H. Prince of Georgia
Louis McLane, of Delaware
Robt. Y. Hayne of So. Carolina
Jas. S. Stevenson
D[aniel] H Miller
W[illiam] Ramsey
Innis Green
John I. DeGraff of New York
G[ulian] C. Verplanck
Wm. M'Coy
M[ark] Alexander.
T P. Moore
Wm Smith of So Carolina
Mahlon Dickerson of New
    Jersey.
Levi Woodbury of New
    Hampshire
J. McKinley of Alabama
C[hauncey] Forward
Gab. Holmes—
John Roane
Tho. Chilton (of Ky.)
Bob: McHatton of Ken
Chittn Lyon of Ky
Wm Stanbery
C[hurchill] C. Cambreleng
W[illiam] C Rives

DS and AD Copy in James K. Polk's hand, both DLC (36). All the signers were members of the Twentieth Congress.

1. AJ left Nashville on January 18, 1829, and arrived at Washington on February 11, the day on which Congress tallied the electoral votes.

By December 1828, the liaison between Senator John Henry Eaton and Margaret (Peggy) O'Neale Timberlake (1799–1879), daughter of Washington innkeepers William (d. 1837) and his wife Rhoda Howell O'Neale (c1771–1860), had become an issue for president-elect Jackson. Their relationship became the subject of gossip, especially after the death of Peggy's husband John Bowie Timberlake (d. April 1828), a purser in the Navy. During the campaign, anti-Jacksonians used the rumors about them to illustrate the character of some of Jackson's associates and friends. The marriage of Peggy Timberlake and Eaton on January 1, 1829, a union Jackson urged according to the letter below, would rack Jackson's first administration.

From John Henry Eaton

Washington City
7th. Dec. 1828

Your letter by Judge Isaacks has been recvd,[1] & while my sincere thanks are returned, at the solicitude manifested for my welfare, & health, I cannot but feel grateful for the kind suggestions made in referrence to another & delicate subject. Your admonition shall be regarded; because in your friendship I have every confidence, & in your judgment an equally well founded one. I assure you my dear Sir, that the *subject* brought by me to your consideration at your house and about which more recently you have written me, is on[e] that has afforded me many an anxious & distressed moment The impossibility of escaping detraction & slander, was too well evidenced to me, in the abuse heaped on those more meritorious & deserving than I could ever expect to me [be],[2] to render such ungracious assaults matter of surprise; yet in a quiet conscience, and that regular honorable course thro' life which all who know me, could not but be apprised of, I felt & hoped that a security was had by which to shield me, from the foul aspersions of a condemning and censuring world.[3] On this subject I have often wished freely to converse with you; & as often have been forced from it, because of its delicacy, & because too, that knowing you be acquainted with the honor of both myself & her whose name had been thus cruelly associated your own feelings & judgment would well suggest, all that it would be in my power to say in referrence to so unpleasant a subject. I felt assured you could not believe it, or otherwise your confidence & friendship towards me must have been withdrawn: this was my confidence and hence until lately at your own house did I forbear to speak to you on so painful a matter

But circumstances had changed—She who had in association with me, been censured by a gossipping world had been placed in a situation by the hand of Providence where it was in my power by interposing myself, to snatch her from that injustice which had been done her. Under such circumstances it was not possible to hesitate what was right & proper to be done. Her own merits, & excellence were sufficient to enlist my feelings, while all the considereartions of honor, & of justice pointed to the course which it was right for me to pursue. It was under such impulses, and such considerations that my mind labored when I stated to you, at the Hermitage, that at a *proper time* I would tender to her the offer to share my life & prospects with her. It was matter of infinite satisfaction to me, to find, that your advice & opinions accorded with my own; from that moment I was inspired with new & fresh decision as to the course to be pursued—

On reaching this place, suffcent time having elapsed as I suppose under all the circumstances, I ventured to disclose those feelings which previously had been unfolded to you. It affords me pleasure to say to you that they were met with corresponding good wishes, and a definitive arrangement consented to, that a consumation should take place after the adjournment. After that your letter reached me, suggesting the propriety of acting forthwith, or changing my residence,[4] I again brought this business before *her* and showed what were your opinions.[5] There was some difficulty, arising from that distrust, & deep rooted prejudice which ever attaches to females, in referrence to marriages *sooner* than 12 months from their widowhood. I could not tho under all the circumstances of the case, Mr T long absence & dying abroad; & more especially the whispers of those City gossippers, who attend to every bodys reputation character & business to the neglect of their own, believe that it should have any influence, & so suggested. The consequence of my course is that in the first week of January (the 6) an honorable discharge of duty to myself, & to her will be met, and more than this every thing that feeling & preference requires will be answered, & I rendered a happy & contented man. Judge Genl, you who have known me long & well if I could do such an act as this, apart from the belief, that she has a soul & above every thing of crime & dishonor. The advice & friendly remark contained in your letter, have been the great cause, why this early day has been consented to, and for it, my thanks are due, as they are to you on innumerable other considerations. If beyond the *consumation* itself, I could entertain any wish more ardent than another, it would be, that you might have been present, & honored us with your presence at the time; but the considerati*[ons]* you suggest are of a character so important as to induce us to forego this pleasure, & to close the business earlier than you can be here

For myself, & in behalf of her who soon will be identified with me in life, in prospec*[t]* and in happiness, I beg to tender to you the grateful feelings of a friendship, that with life o*[nly]* can terminate. Be health & every happiness your*[s]* is the sincere wish of both of us—With sincere regard

J. H Eaton

ALS, THi (12-0301). Published in *New York Times Magazine,* October 21, 1928.
    1. Not found.
    2. Eaton was referring to attacks on Rachel and AJ regarding their marriage. During the campaign, Eaton had been referred to as AJ's "celebrated biographer of Timberlake memory" (*Nashville Whig,* August 2).
    3. Washington society had already looked with disapproval on the Timberlake-Eaton relationship, and, more recently, the Tennessee congressional delegation had caucused and tried to dissuade Eaton from the pending marriage.
    4. Eaton was at this time residing at the O'Neale's on West Market.
    5. Many years later, Peggy wrote in her *Autobiography* (New York, 1932) that Jackson had told Eaton: "Major, if you love Margaret Timberlake, go and marry her at once, and shut their [the critics'] mouths" (p. 48).

John Henry Eaton to Rachel Jackson

Washington City 7. Dec 1828

My dear friend, for so I feel I may style you, the friends you have here, firm & numerous both male & female, have constantly enquired of me since my arrival to know if you would arrive with the genl. They regret that it can be even considered doubtful what your determination may be. There reasons are very satisfactory, & therefore have I undertaken to speak to you about it.

The past I need not repeat, for you know it well. To prejudice your husband, you well know what envenomed slander has been aimed at both of you. Not you alone, but others too, have felt its keen edge; & altho this is slender atonement to your own aggrieved feelings, it affords this consolation, that the assaults made proceeded exclusively from motives. The storm has now abated—the angry tempest has ceased to howl. A verdict by the American people has been pronounced of that high & grateful character, that for the honor of your husband, you cannot but look back on the past as an idle fading vision carrying in it nothing substantial—nothing that should produce to you one moments feeling, or a moments pain. No man has ever met such a triumph before: The voice of his Country has placed him at a sightless distance above his little tribe of little assailants; and in this high & gratifying consideration, should both of you repose, pleased & rejoiced

These remarks might have been omitted, only that they are designed merely as a prelude to what I in accord with all your friends here desire in your behalf

The attentions intended to be meeted out to the general, & to you, are such as will evince to both of you a continuance of the same high & glowing feeling which has produced his unequalled & triumphant vote from the people. The Ladies from a distance—from remote parts of the union will be here—brought essentially and altogether on your account, & to manifest to you their feelings & high regard: they will be present to welcome & to congratulate you. If you shall be absent how great will be the dissapointment. Your persecutors then may chuckle, & say that they have driven you from the field of your husbands honors. By all means then come on; & as you have had to bear with him the reproaches of foes, participate with him in the greetings of his friends

I had thought heretofore, it would be better for you to remain & come on in May. That opinion is changed, since that I have arrived here, and heard the reasonings of your friends. I am especially invited to write to you on this subject, & in the name of [those] who are your warm & sincere friends to desire that you will be here at all events by the 1st of March, ready & rested for the 4th.

Such is my confidence that you will be along with the general, under the suggestions I have made, that I shall no longer speak of it as at all doubtful; but say that you intend to proceed with the genl, & will be certainly here. A failure on your part will create disappointment [and] prove to your friends exceedingly trying with sincere regard

J. H Eaton

ALS, DLC (36). Published in Bassett, 3:449–50.

To Ezra Stiles Ely

Hermitage Decbr. 10th. 1828.

My Dr. Sir

Your friendly letter of the 21rst. ultimo[1] has just reached me—I regret that the croud of addresses & invitations from committees from various parts prevents me from fully answering it at present.

The congratulations of the friendly and patriotic citizens of Pensylvania, fill me with the highes emotions of gratitude—Republican Pensylvania has supported me thro good & bad report, and in the seventh trial has not forsaken me[2]—These acts of confidence claim, & will receive my gratitude so long as my pulsation lasts.

The kind expressions of Mrs [Margaret Means] Carswell & your amiable lady[3] towards Mrs. J. and myself as communicated by you, receives our grateful acknowledgements, and we pray you to tender to them our kind salutations—To the prayers of the pious & just may be ascribed the victory of truth over those vile slanders wielded against, & intended to destroy us, and that we did not fall victims to the powerful influence of the executive patronage of the goverment & its thousand minions, can only be ascribed to the interposition of divine providence who has so often shielded me from the snares of the fowler,[4] and realises the <truth> reality of the adage, "that truth is mighty and will prevail"—The verdict of the nation emphatically pronounced, has made the various slanders to recoil on their own head & fall harmless at our feet.

For your kind invitation & profered hospitality we sincerely thank you—If ever we pass Philadelphia we will certainly visit you & partake of your hospitality—But until the election is clearly asertained, I cannot leave home or determine on my rout—should the ohio keep open I shall pass up the ohio, and from some point on that river direct to the city of Washington, having received various invitations, & not being able to comply with all, will induce me for the present to stop at no place not in my direct way.[5]

It will afford Mrs. J. and myself much pleasure to meet you in Washington & at all times to receive any communications you may be pleased t[o] make to me—Be pleased to present to Mrs Carswel[l] your lady & family our best wishes & believe me my Dr. Sir your Mo obdt. servt.

Andrew Jackson

ALS, TNJ (12-0310); Facsimile extract, DLC (36).
1. Not found.
2. AJ's reference here may have derived from Job 5:19: "He shall deliver thee in six troubles; yea, in seven there shall no evil touch thee."
3. Carswell, widow of Samuel Carswell (c1765–1822), a Philadelphia merchant and sometime alderman with whom AJ had commercial dealings, was Ely's mother-in-law. Ely's wife was Mary Ann (c1792–1842).
4. "Snares of the fowler" comes from Psalm 91:3.
5. To reach Washington in 1829, AJ traveled by steamboat from Nashville to Pittsburgh and then overland on the National Road.

To Francis Preston

Hermitage Decbr. 18th. 1828—

Dr. Sir

I have recd. your much esteemed favour of the 9th instant.[1] The congratulations of an old friend, on the result of the recent election, are truly grateful and give rise to emotions which can better be conceived than expressed.

It is true, as you remark, that with my enemies calumny was the order of the day. There is no parallel to their conduct for the last four years— no instance is heretofore recorded of as uniform a direction of the patronage of Government against the character of a private individual. The virtue of the people became aroused by such unwarrantable procedure, and regarding it as a stain upon our national fame, have, in the majesty of their strength pro[n]ounced a verdict that, I trust, in all future time will be a solemn warning to politicians never to depart from principle, or disobay the will of their constituents, in order to gain office and power. To the people, for the confidence reposed in me, my gratitude & best services are due; and are pledged to their service.

I cannot calculate that my administration will be undisturbed by the agitations of party—but based on the constitution and devoted to the prosperity of our common country, I cherish the hope that I shall forget no cardinal principle, and that any error which I may commit, will be ascribed to the head, and not to the heart.

I sincerely thank you for the kind feelings you have expressed towards me in your letter; any information at any time, you may be pleased to communicate, will be kindly & favourably received—should I pass overland to the city, Mrs. J. & myself will avail ourselves of that occasion to pay our personal respects to you, your amiable lady, & family; & partake of your offered hospitality so far as our time, & other engagements will permit.

Mrs. J. unites with me in a tender to you, your lady, & family, of our kind salutations. believe me very respectfully your friend

Andrew Jackson

P.S. Whilst writing, Mrs. J. from good health, has been taken suddenly ill, with excrutiating pain in the left shoulder, arm, & breast, What may be the result of this violent atta*[ck]* god only knows, I hope for her recovery, & *[in]* haste close this letter, you will pardon any inacuracies · A. J.

ALS, ViU (12-0326).
   1. See Preston to AJ, December 9.

To Richard Keith Call

Hermitage Decbr. 22nd. 1828

My Dr. Call

I have been in receipt of your letter of the 14th. Octbr. last,[1] for some time. I intended answering it before this; addresses from various parts has crowded upon me, that, really, all my time has been, of late, engrossed in replying to them, and I had not a moment to spare for my friend.

Mrs. J. was a few days past, suddenly, & violently, attacked, with pains in her left shoulder & breast, & such the contraction of the heart, that suffocation was apprehended before the necessary aid could be afforded. Doctor Hogg has relieved her,[2] & altho worse today, than yesterday, I trust in a kind providence, that he will restore her to her usual health in due time to set out for washington, so that I may reach there, by the middle of February—we have been waiting to hear from you, in hopes you may reach us before we set out, which will be between the 10th. & 15th. of January—should the ohio keep open we will go by water to Wheeling, or Pittsburgh—Mrs. J. situation will make this route, necessary, as I am fearful that her strength would not be able to undergo the Journey overland, and I cannot leave her, believing as I do, that my seperating from her would destroy her, & the persecution she has suffered, has endeared her more if possible than ever to me.

The little Junto of calumniators here, have found their level; the verdict which has been pronounced against them by the people has taught them, that truth is mighty and will prevail, & calumniators will meet with the Just abhorence of a virtuous people.

I need not assure you of the pleasure it will afford me, & Mrs. J. to meet you at the city, should you not arrive at the Hermitage before we set out.

Mrs. J. is confined to her bed, unites with me in a tender of our kindest salutations & good wishes to you, Mrs. Call, & the sweet little ones, & believe me yr friend

Andrew Jackson

ALS, THer (mAJs); Extract, *The Collector* (Jan 1906), p. 28 (12-0330); Copy fragment, FHi (12-0331). Postmarked December 23.
1. Not found.
2. The two physicians attending Rachel Jackson during her illness were Samuel Hogg and Henry Lee Heiskell (see Account with Hogg, November 25, 1825, and, above, Account with Heiskell, [October 21]). Both visited on December 17, when they bled and medicated her.

Rachel Jackson died on the evening of December 22 and, on December 24, with the Reverend William Hume officiating, she was buried in the garden at the Hermitage.

To Jean Baptiste Plauché

Hermitage Debr. 27th. 1828.

Dear Sir,

I had the satisfaction to receive several weeks since, your friendly letter of the 15th ulto.;[1] but have been prevented from answering it, by that afflicting dispensation of Providence which has deprived me of the partner of my life. A loss so great, so sudden and unexpected, I need not say to you, can be compensated by no earthly gift. Could it be, it might be found in the reflection that she lived long enough to see the countless assaults of our enemies disarmed by the voice of our beloved country.

Repeating, now, my gratitude for the friendly sentiments with which you cherish the recollection of my past life, I must reserve for some other period the expression of those obligations which are due to you, and my other old companions in arms for the value assigned to my future connection with the Government. As usual Yr. sincere friend

Andrew Jackson

LS in Andrew J. Donelson's hand, THer (12-0338).
1. See Plauché to AJ, November 15.

Calendar, 1825–1828

1825

Jan 1	From Samuel Dorsey Jackson. LS, DNA-RG 94 (M688-26). Requests recommendation to the Military Academy for his son Alfred Eugene.
Jan 1	Account with Malachi Nicholson for services as overseer on Andrew Jackson Hutchings's farm. DS in John Coffee's hand, signed by Nicholson, A-Ar (10-1021). Runs to June 25.
Jan 1	Account with John Simpson & Co. for AJ and Andrew Jackson Hutchings. ADS, A-Ar (10-1023). Runs to January 1, 1826.
Jan 1	*Memorandum of Slaves and Land in Davidson County, Tennessee.* 3
Jan 3	From William Selby Harney. ALS, DLC (33). Requests endorsement for an 1826 expedition to survey the Pacific coast.
Jan 3	From James Mease. ALS, NjMoHP (10-1026). Sends a medal commemorative of George Washington.
Jan 4	To John Caldwell Calhoun (enclosure: Samuel McKee to Calhoun, Dec 12, 1824). ALS, DNA-RG 94 (M688-38); Abstract, dated Feb 7, DNA-RG 107 (M22-19). Recommends Joseph W. Walker, son of U.S. Senator George Walker (d.1819) for the Military Academy.
Jan 4	Account of Rachel Jackson with E. Abbot for dressmaking and notions. ADS, DLC (33). Runs to January 26.
Jan 5	To John Caldwell Calhoun. ALS and Copy, DNA-RG 107 (M221-99). Requests information on former army paymaster Thomas R. Broom.
Jan 5	*To John Coffee.* 5
Jan 5	From Rebecca Craine Bronaugh. ALS, TNJ (10-1029). Expresses appreciation for AJ's assistance in managing the Pensacola affairs of her late son, James C. Bronaugh.
Jan 5	From James L. Edwards. LC, DNA-RG 15 (10-1036). Discusses Andrew S. McGirk's pension claim.
Jan 5	From W[illiam] L[ee]. LC, DNA-RG 217 (10-1041). Reports forwarding to the third auditor of the treasury a letter regarding the accounts of Michael McClelland, killed in the December 23, 1814, battle at New Orleans.
Jan 5	Check for $111.54 to John Gadsby, Jr., drawn on the Bank of the

United States at Washington. Abstract, *Collector,* No. 835 (1974), p. 2 (10-1037).

Jan 5 Account with Thomas B. Griffin for shoes for Rachel Jackson. ADS, DLC (33). Runs to February 5.

Jan 5 Account of Andrew Jackson Hutchings with blacksmith John David Gaisser. DS, A-Ar (10-1038). Runs to June 3, 1826.

Jan 6 *To John Coffee.*   7

Jan 7 From [Peter Hagner]. LC, DNA-RG 217 (10-1045). Discusses Michael McClelland's accounts.

Jan 7 *From John Holmes Overton.*   8

Jan 8 *To James Mease.*   9

Jan 8 From John Nicholson Moulder et al. Printed, Washington *National Journal,* Jan 12 (mAJs, 10-1048). Citizens of First Ward of Washington express gratitude for Jackson's services at the Battle of New Orleans.

[Jan 8] To John Nicholson Moulder et al. Printed, Washington *National Journal,* Jan 12 (mAJs, 10-1050). Thanks citizens for honoring him.

Jan 8 Account of Rachel Jackson with J[ohn] Petit for clothing. ADS, DLC (33).

Jan 9 *To Chandler Price.*   10

Jan 9 *To Charles Pendleton Tutt.*   12

Jan 9 *From Charles Pendleton Tutt.*   12

Jan 10 *To John Overton.*   13

Jan 10 From John Caldwell Calhoun (enclosure: Nathan Towson to Calhoun, Jan 10). LS, DNA-RG 46 (10-1055); LC, DNA-RG 107 (M220-1). *Calhoun·Papers,* 9:485 (extract). Concurs with Towson's recommendations regarding appointment of a paymaster for the proposed military post on the Columbia River.

Jan 10 From John Caldwell Calhoun (enclosures: Thomas S. Jesup to Calhoun, Jan 8; Nathan Towson to Calhoun, Jan 8, Jan 10; William Lee to Towson, Jan 10, DNA-RG 46, mAJs). LS, DNA-RG 46 (10-1061); LC, DNA-RG 107 (M220-1). Transmits letters re settlement of Thomas R. Broom's accounts.

Jan 11 *To William Berkeley Lewis.*   15

Jan 11 From Arthur Peronneau Hayne. ALS, DLC (33). Discusses possible results of the presidential election in the House of Representatives; praises James Monroe's annual message and offers suggestions for constitutional reforms for inclusion in Monroe's farewell address.

Jan 11 *Account with the Franklin House Hotel, Washington.* 16

Jan 15 To James L. Edwards. Abstract, *American Book-Prices Current* (1974–75), p. 1106 (mAJs). Requests papers regarding revolutionary war pension for Paten Brown of Kentucky.

Jan 15 From Robert Desha. ALS, DNA-RG 94 (M688-38). Solicits recommendation for Richard Scurry of Gallatin, Tennessee, to the Military Academy and discusses upcoming presidential election in the House of Representatives.

Jan 17 To Peter Hagner (enclosures: Accounts of Erasmus Chapman, April 20, 1815, and Robert H. Boon, July 16, 1816, *HRRep* 63, 19th Cong., 1st sess., Serial 141, pp. 1–2). LC, THi (10-1074).

	Desires information on enclosed memorial (not found) of Wilkins Tannehill re unpaid claims.
Jan 17	From William Polk. ALS, DNA-RG 59 (M439-9). Recommends Gabriel Holmes for minister to Mexico.
Jan 18	From James L. Edwards. ALS, DNA-RG 15 (10-1076). Transmits papers (not found) relating to Paten Brown's pension.
Jan 18	From [Peter Hagner]. LC, DNA-RG 217 (10-1077). Discusses reasons for rejection of claims in the Tannehill memorial.
Jan 18	From Joseph Talbott and James G. Sheid (enclosure: Account of AJ with Talbott, DLC, 72). ALS, TNJ (10-1072). Transmit account for care of three horses.
Jan 18	Account with Joseph Talbott for care of three horses. AD, DLC (72).
Jan 18	Account of Andrew Jackson Donelson and Emily Tennessee Donelson with John Gadsby, Jr., at the Franklin House Hotel. AD, DLC (72). Runs to January 24.
Jan 21	*To William Berkeley Lewis.* 17
Jan 22	To James Monroe (enclosure: William Polk to AJ, Jan 17). ALS, DNA-RG 59 (M439-9). Forwards letter.
Jan 22	From Francis Preston. ALS, DLC (33). Recommends James Hagarty for consul at Liverpool; reports rumor of a coalition forming to prevent AJ's election.
Jan 23	*To John Coffee.* 18
Jan 23	From Chamberlayne Jones. LS by proxy (Fayette Jones), DNA-RG 94 (M688-24). Requests recommendation to the Military Academy for his son Fayette.
Jan 24	*To William Berkeley Lewis.* 20
Jan 25	From John McLean (1785–1861). LC, DNA-RG 28 (M601-30). Discusses claim against postal contractor James Edington, owner of stage route between Huntsville and Big Spring, Alabama.
Jan 25	Account with John Gadsby, Jr., of the Franklin House Hotel. DS signed by Peter Brady, DLC (72). Runs to January 31.
Jan 26	From John McLean (1785–1861). LC, DNA-RG 28 (M601-30). Explains his rejection of William Field's proposal for a mail stage between Louisville and Bowling Green, Kentucky.
Jan 27	*Rachel Jackson to Mary Purnell Donelson.* 20
Jan 28	From Samuel Ragland Overton. ALS, DLC (33). Details corruption among Florida territorial officials and urges reform; expounds on governments in general.
Jan 29	*To William Berkeley Lewis.* 22
Jan 31	To E. K. Ingersol. ALS, James S. Copley Library, La Jolla, Calif. (mAJs). Bassett, 6:480–81. Thanks Ingersol for naming his son after AJ; comments on value of labor and honesty.
Feb 1	Account of Andrew Jackson Donelson and Emily Tennessee Donelson with John Gadsby, Jr., at the Franklin House Hotel. AD, DLC (72). Runs to February 7.
Feb 2	Presentation to the United States Senate of a letter from the secretary of war regarding authorization to sell unserviceable ordnance, arms, and military stores. Printed abstract, *Senate Journal*, 18th Cong., 2nd sess., p. 128 (mAJs).

	Seminole campaign benefits to the forces of Thomas H. Boyles and Zachariah McGirtt. Printed abstract, *Register of Debates*, 18th Cong., 2nd sess., pp. 625, 633 (mAJs).	
Feb 18	*Account with the Franklin House Hotel, Washington.*	35
Feb 19	*To John Coffee.*	35
Feb 19	To Unknown. DS, DNA-RG 46 (10-1132). Praises George Vashon's Seminole campaign service and recommends him "to the notice of the government."	
Feb 19	Andrew Jackson Donelson to John Coffee. ALS, DLC (mAJs). Excoriates the "corrupt bargain" between John Quincy Adams and Henry Clay and discusses rumors about Adams's cabinet.	
Feb 19	Account with William Chandler for blacksmithing and for a spinning machine. DS, DLC (34). Runs to June 24, 1826.	
Feb 20	*To William Berkeley Lewis.*	36
Feb 20	*To George Wilson.*	38
Feb 22	From Eliza[beth Parke] Custis. Printed, *Niles' Register*, April 9 (10-1142). Sends a ring with George Washington's hair in celebration of Washington's birthday.	
Feb 22	To Eliza[beth Parke] Custis. Printed, *Niles' Register*, April 9 (10-1143). Thanks her for ring.	
Feb 22	*From Robert Pryor Henry et al.*	39
Feb 22	*To Robert Pryor Henry et al.*	40
Feb 22	*To Samuel Swartwout.*	40
Feb 22	From John Ragan. ALS, TNJ (10-1146). Asks AJ to act as his business agent in Nashville.	
Feb 22	Receipt of Benjamin P. Person for $400 for services as Hermitage overseer during 1824. ADS, TNJ (10-1144).	
Feb 24	Account with Thomas Smith for carriage repairs. ADS, DLC (31, 10-1154). Runs to March 8.	
Feb 25	From John Caldwell Calhoun. LC, DNA-RG 75 (M21-1). *Calhoun Papers*, 9:595–96. In response to an inquiry about the dismissal of William Walker as sub-agent to the Creeks, refers AJ to the report of the Creek commissioners, transmitted to the House of Representatives on February 5.	
Feb 25	From Peter Hagner. LC, DNA-RG 217 (10-1156). Explains rejection of Samuel Cunningham's claim.	
Feb 25	Articles of agreement between Alfred Balch, Thomas Crutcher, and AJ, executors of William Terrell Lewis, and John F. Stump, administrator of Matthew Brooks, with memorandum of compromise and other documents. AD, TFWi (10-1157). Agree to pay penalty of $2,400 if $1,200 worth of Lewis's western Tennessee lands is not conveyed in a reasonable time.	
Feb 26	From Valentine Giesey et al. ALS, DLC (33). Invite AJ to attend a public dinner at Brownsville, Pennsylvania, on his journey home.	
Feb 26	From James Monroe. ALS, DLC (33). Invites AJ to ceremony awarding medals voted by Congress to other War of 1812 generals.	
Feb 27	*To William Berkeley Lewis.*	43
Feb 28	To James Monroe (from AJ and Charles Fenton Mercer). ALS in AJ's hand, also signed by Mercer, DNA-RG 46 (10-1189). Recommend Charles P. Tutt for a federal post.	

[cFeb– Mar]   From [John] Wilie. ALS, DLC (33). Presents a complimentary six-month subscription to his newspaper, the *New Orleans Price Current, and Commercial Intelligencer.*

[cFeb– June]   *From a Creek Chief.*   44

March 1   From Paul Allen. ALS, DLC (33). Congratulates AJ on his plurality in the electoral vote and praises his conduct.

March 1   From Joseph Talbott and James G. Sheid. ALS, TNJ (10-1200). Transmit account (not found) for livery of horses during the Second Session of the Eighteenth Congress and discuss previous payments.

March 1   Account of Andrew Jackson Donelson with John Gadsby, Jr., at the Franklin House Hotel. AD, DLC (72). Runs to March 10.

March 1   Motion to discharge the Senate Committee on Military Affairs from further consideration of a memorial from assistant quartermasters general and of a resolution of December 14 regarding a fort between Missouri and Mexico. Printed abstract, *Senate Journal,* 18th Cong., 2nd sess., p. 221 (mAJs).

[cMarch 1]   To Edward J. Stiles et al. Printed, *Harrisburg Chronicle,* March 14 (mAJs). Declines invitation to visit Carlisle, Pennsylvania, on his journey to Nashville, citing Rachel Jackson's health.

March 2   *To John Coffee.*   45

March 2   From Hector Craig. ALS, PCarlD (10-1204). Washington *National Intelligencer,* March 3. Forwards gift of a suit made in the New York factory of Peter H. and Abraham H. Schenck.

March 2   *To Hector Craig.*   46

March 2   To Samuel Delucenna Ingham. Printed, *New-York Evening Post,* March 9 (mAJs). Replies to inquiry of Robert Patterson by stating that the Jacksons will be unable to visit Philadelphia because of Rachel's health.

March 2   From Ezra Stiles Ely. ALS, NjP (10-1208). Invites AJ and party to stay with him in Philadelphia on their return home; comments on the presidential election.

March 4   From Edward Patchell. ALS, DLC (33). Condemns the corruption of Adams and Clay and praises AJ's "Godlike virtue" in the presidential election; relays Stephen Simpson's report that the Philadelphia *Columbian Observer* is to cease publication.

March 4   Account with William W. Womer for $5.00 for treating Andrew Jackson Hutchings's injured slave. ADS, A-Ar (10-1213). Runs to July 24, 1826.

March 5   From Samuel Ragland Overton. ALS, DLC (33). Acknowledges two letters (not found) re his appointment as register of the land office in Florida Territory; comments on the presidential election.

[cMarch 5]   To Paul Allen. AL draft, DLC (33). Thanks him for letter of March 1.

[cMarch 5]   To Ezra Stiles Ely. AL draft, NjP (10-1215). Regrets inability to accept Ely's invitation because of Rachel Jackson's health.

March 6   To William Burke. ALS, Joseph S. Stern, Jr. (10-1216). Accepts invitation to a public dinner in Cincinnati and discusses travel plans.

March 6   *To Samuel Swartwout.*   47

March 7   From Samuel Lewis Southard. LC, DNA-RG 45 (10-1218). Regrets
               that no vacancies in the navy exist for Mary Sterett's son.
March 8   To Joseph Gardner Swift. Printed, *New-York Evening Post,* March
               23 (mAJs, 10-1223). Declines invitation to New York City dinner
               celebrating South American and Mexican independence, but
               forwards a toast honoring Simón Bolívar.
March 8   *From George Kremer.*   48
March 8   From Samuel Lewis Southard. LC, DNA-RG 45 (10-1222).
               Requests advice re letter (not found) from Midshipman Grey
               Skipwith.
March 8   Rachel Jackson to Benjamin Bakewell. Printed, *Western Pennsylva-*
               nia Historical Magazine, 6(1923):191–92 (10-1220). Thanks him
               for gift of celery glasses.
March 9   To Samuel Lewis Southard. ALS, DNA-RG 45 (M124-101).
               Suggests that [Thomas] Macdonough's charges do not show
               sufficient cause to dismiss Grey Skipwith from the navy.
March 9   Receipts for $1,296 and $48, compensation for service in the
               Senate. DS, DLC (10-1212).
[cMarch 9]   To James Barbour. Abstract, DNA-RG 107 (M22-19). Recom-
               mends Thomas L. Alexander for appointment to the Military
               Academy.
March 10   From John F. Hoss, W. K. Mitchel, and John C. Bokee. ALS in
               Bokee's hand, also signed by Hoss and Mitchel, DLC (33). Balti-
               more *American & Commercial Daily Advertiser,* March 16.
               Request AJ to present a flag to Baltimore's Forsyth Volunteers.
March 10   From Andrew Stewart (enclosure: Valentine Giesey et al. to AJ, Feb
               26). ALS, DLC (33). Forwards letter from a citizens' committee of
               his Pennsylvania district.
[cMarch 10]   Receipt of Nelson Davidson for $83.50, payment for painting and
               repairing a coach. ADS, DLC (72, 10-1192).
March 11   From John M. Scott. ALS, DLC (72). Provides distances between
               places on route from Baltimore to Wheeling and recommends inns.
March 11   Account with J. Merrill for $15.37½ for room and board for AJ's
               party. AD, DLC (72).
March 11   Account with David Barnum of Baltimore for $55.82½ for room
               and board of AJ's party of four and three servants. ADS by Andrew
               McLaughlin, DLC (72). Runs to March 13.
March 11   Receipt of Samuel Mitchell for $90 compensation for a horse lost in
               the Seminole campaign, from AJ as agent. ADS, DLC (33).
March 11   Account with James Penny for work on a wagon and gin for
               Andrew Jackson Hutchings. DS, A-Ar (10-1224). Runs to October
               4, 1827.
March 11   Itinerary listing tolls and costs of lodgings. AD in Andrew J.
               Donelson's hand, DLC (72). Runs to March 20.
[March 12]   To [John F. Hoss et al]. AL draft, DLC (33). Baltimore *American*
               & Commercial Daily Advertiser, March 16. Presents Forsyth
               Volunteers with an American flag.
[March 12]   From [John F. Hoss]. Printed, Baltimore *American &*
               Commercial Daily Advertiser, March 16 (mAJs). Thanks AJ for
               presentation.

March 13   Account with Allen Dorsey for $13.37½ for room and board at Poplar Springs, Maryland. ADS by John S. Dorsey, DLC (72).

March 14   Account with Joseph Talbott and James G. Sheid for room and board, probably in Frederick, Maryland. ADS, DLC (72, 10-1226).

March 15   Account with D[avid] Brookhart for $16.50 for room and board at Boonsboro, Maryland. ADS, DLC (72).

[March 16]   Account with [Thomas Post?] for $4.93 for breakfast at Hagerstown, Maryland. AD, DLC (72).

March 16   Account with B[enjamin] Bean of Hancock, Maryland, for $12.75 for room and board. ADS, DLC (72).

March 16   Receipt of [Andrew Jackson Donelson] for $26 from AJ for travel expenses. AD, DLC (72).

[March 17]   Account with Samuel Slicer for $9.00 for room and board. ADS, DLC (72, 10-1197).

[March 18]   Account with W[alter] Slicer for $6.62½ for room and board near Cumberland, Maryland. ADS, DLC (72, 10-1199).

March 18   Account with C[hristian] Krepps for $3.31 for room and board at Cumberland, Maryland. ADS, DLC (72).

[cMarch 18]   Account with [Pratt] for $3.00 for breakfast. AD, DLC (72).

[March 19]   Account with [James Bryant?] for $8.62½ for room and board between Cumberland, Maryland, and Brownsville, Pennsylvania. AD, DLC (72).

March 20   Account with [Cuthbert?] Wiggins of the Western Inn near Brownsville, Pennsylvania, for $6.00 for room and board. AD, DLC (72).

March 25   Account with Richard Tierney[?] for $30 for lodging at Wheeling, Virginia. ADS, DLC (72).

[March 25]   Receipt of W. C. Clarke for $133 for steamboat fares. ADS, DLC (72).

March 26   From Joseph Inslee Anderson. ALS with AJ endorsement, DLC (33). To assist in settling with the heirs of Pierce Butler (1744–1822), requests information on agreement with AJ re the David Allison Duck River lands.

[March 28]   From Robert [Todd] Lytle. Printed, *Cincinnati Advertiser,* April 2 (mAJs). Praises AJ's public services.

[cMarch 28]   From Cincinnati Boys. Printed, *Cincinnati Advertiser,* April 2 (mAJs). Welcome AJ to Cincinnati and express hope that he will become the next president.

[cMarch 28]   To Cincinnati Boys. Printed, *Cincinnati Advertiser,* April 2 (mAJs). Urges them to live virtuously and defend their country.

March 29   Account with James Edmondson for $82.27 for room and board at Union Hall in Louisville. DS by H. H. Bondurant, endorsed by Andrew J. Donelson, DLC (72).

March 29   Account of Rachel Jackson with John Mears of Cincinnati for plants. ADS, DLC (33).

	history of liberty, another Yorktown." Printed, *Nashville Republican,* April 23 (mAJs, 10-1239).	
April 20	Memorandum of AJ's endorsement of two notes as security for James Hardin at a Nashville bank. DS in AJ's hand, DLC (33).	
April 22	*From John Spencer Hitt.*	63
April 22	Account with Anderson & Knox for brass curtain pins. ADS by Robert B. Clarkson, DLC (35). With receipt November 19, 1828.	
April 23	From John Coffee. ALS, DLC (33). Regrets that he will be unable to visit Nashville during the Marquis de Lafayette's visit; discusses Alabama politics.	
April 23	Account from William Watson for $11.00 for shoes. AD with receipt in AJ's hand, signed by Levin Watson, T (10-1240). Runs to November 9.	
April 24	To James Barbour (enclosure: James G. Overton to Barbour, April 24). ALS, DNA-RG 94 (M688-38). Transmits Overton's acceptance of appointment to the Military Academy.	
April 24	*To John Coffee.*	65
April 27	From William Carroll. ALS, DLC (33). Invites AJ to review the assembled militia on April 28.	
[April 27]	To William Berkeley Lewis. ALS, NNPM (10-1248). Asks Lewis to inform Governor Carroll that, owing to illness, he will not be able to review the troops.	
April 28	To Edward George Washington Butler. Extract, LNT (10-1252). Discusses Henry Clay's *Address* (Washington, 1825).	
April 28	From Wilkins Tannehill. ALS, DLC (33). Invites AJ to dine with Lafayette and the members of the Masonic Lodge in Nashville.	
April 28	Memorandum of sale of cotton by Banks, Miller & Kincaid. AN, DLC (33).	
April 30	To Henry Baldwin. ALS, NN (10-1254). Thanks him for letter, stating that many Pennsylvanians disapprove of Clay's conduct.	
April	Memorandum by John Donelson (1755–1830) regarding the survey of a tract on Pond Lick Creek for AJ and the heirs of Samuel Donelson. ADS, THi (10-1246).	
May 4	*Account for Postage, Nashville Post Office.*	66
[May 4]	Toast at Nashville dinner honoring the Marquis de Lafayette: "The Nation's Guest—Tyrants have oppressed him, but freemen delight to do him honor." Printed, *Nashville Whig,* May 7 (mAJs, 10-1257).	
[cMay 4]	Receipt of Robert Coleman Foster for payment of $87 for tuition, room, board, etc., at Cumberland College, probably for Andrew Jackson, Jr. ADS endorsed by AJ, DLC (33).	
May 5	From Philip Lindsley (to AJ and Lafayette). Printed, *Nashville Whig,* May 14 (10-1258). Announces the naming of the Jackson and Lafayette chairs at Cumberland College.	
May 6	To Robert Ewing et al. LS copy in Andrew J. Donelson's hand, DLC (33). Regrets that he and Lafayette will be unable to accept invitation to dine at Russellville, Kentucky.	
May 6	Account with Nashville Inn for stabling a horse. ADS with receipt for payment, DLC (33).	
May 7	*To Richard Keith Call.*	67

June 11   To Andrew [Jackson] Watson. Printed, Historical Shop Catalog 9
           (1980), Item 564 (10-1311). Writes that John C. McLemore may be
           able to help him recover some of his father's land.
June 11   Account of Andrew Jackson, Jr., with Josiah Nichol for clothing,
           personal items, and other college expenses. AD, DLC (33). Runs to
           December 26.
June 18   To Joshua Haskell, Adam Rankin Alexander, and Joseph H.
           Talbot. Printed, *Jackson Gazette,* July 9 (10-1312). Accepts
           invitation.
June 18   To George Washington Martin. ALS, Mrs. William Hoffa (10-
           1314). Sends a mare for stud service of Timoleon.
June 24   *To Richard Keith Call.*   84
[June 24] *To Joseph Desha.*   86
June 25   To James Buchanan. ALS and Copy, PHi (10-1319, -1323). Bassett,
           3:386–87 (extract). Expresses gratitude for continued support in
           Pennsylvania.
June 28   Receipt from Joseph White Horton for payment of Tennessee and
           Davidson County taxes for 1825. DS, THi (10-1327).
June 29   To Andrew Jackson Donelson. ALS, DLC (10-1329). Asks him to
           meet at Nashville on June 30 to borrow money for Donelson.
June 30   *To James Jackson.*   87
[July 1]   From William H. McLaughlin et al. LS by proxy, NN (10-1331).
           Nashville Republican, July 16. On behalf of 79th Militia Regiment
           of Tennessee, invite AJ to dine at Nashville on July 4.
July 1   To William H. McLaughlin et al. ALS draft, NN (10-1333).
           Nashville Republican, July 16. Declines invitation because of
           previous engagement.
July 1   From Alexander S. Morrow. Printed, *Louisville Public Advertiser,*
           Sept 24 (mAJs). Invites AJ to public dinner at Paris, Kentucky,
           honoring the Kentucky representatives who supported AJ for
           president.
July 3   From James Monroe (enclosure: *HRRep* 79, 18th Cong., 2nd
           sess., Serial 123). ALS and AL copy, DLC (33, 10-1335).
           Stanislaus M. Hamilton, ed., *The Writings of James Monroe* (7
           vols.; New York, 1898–1903), 7:56–59. Discusses his claims
           for reimbursement by the federal government for previous
           service.
[July 3]   From Edward Breathitt. Printed, *Nashville Republican,* July 9 (10-
           1340). As mayor of Franklin, Tennessee, welcomes AJ.
[July 3]   To Edward Breathitt. Printed, *Nashville Republican,* July 9 (mAJs,
           10-1342). Thanks him for welcome.
[July 4]   From [Benjamin S.] Tappan. Printed, *Nashville Republican,* July 9
           (10-1344). On behalf of volunteer companies, welcomes AJ to the
           Franklin Independence Day celebration.
[July 4]   Toast at celebration in Franklin: "The volunteer service . . ."
           Printed, *Nashville Whig,* July 9 (10-1343).
July 5   From William Pope Duval. ALS, DLC (33). Expresses hope that
           AJ will visit Harrodsburg Springs; reports support for AJ in
           Kentucky.

July 7   To Thomas Buck Reed. Printed, TxU (mAJs). In response to a query from Reed regarding the Mississippi constitution, discusses the question of electing a member of the Mississippi legislature to the United States Senate.

July 7   From James Gadsden. ALS, ICHi (10-1345). Asks AJ whether he ordered a Creek expedition that captured slaves of Florida citizens in 1821.

July 8   From James Gadsden (enclosure: Gadsden to AJ, July 7). ALS with AJ endorsement, ICHi (10-1347). Complains of Florida officers, especially in the judiciary.

July 9   To [Josiah Nichol]. Extract, Stan. V. Henkels Catalog 1430 (1929), Item 71 (10-1355). Orders merchandise.

July 14   Account with Warren Hobbs for tuition of Andrew Jackson Hutchings. ADS, A-Ar (10-1356).

[July 17–20] From [Joseph Desha]. Printed, *Nashville Republican*, July 30 (mAJs). Discusses the July 16 gathering in Paris, Kentucky, in honor of the four representatives who voted for Jackson in the presidential election in the House of Representatives.

July 20   Account of William Schlatter with the Hutchings estate for lumber. AD with AN by AJ, A-Ar (10-1358). Runs to July 1826.

July 21   From Hardy Murfree Cryer. ALS, DLC (33). Gives Elijah Boddie's opinion of Edward Ward's deposition in Samuel K. Blythe's equity suit.

July 22   To Alexander S. Morrow. Printed, *Louisville Public Advertiser*, Sept 24 (mAJs, 10-1360). Regrets that he was unable to accept an invitation to dine with the Kentucky congressmen who supported him for president.

July 24   To Richard Keith Call. ALS, F (mAJs). James R. McGovern, ed., *Andrew Jackson and Pensacola* (Pensacola, 1974), p. 76 (10-1365), extract. Discusses rumor regarding Samuel R. Overton's disloyalty to AJ.

July 26   From Roger C. Weightman. Printed, THer (10-1377). Reports to stockholders of the Bank of the United States on charges against Richard Smith, cashier of the Washington branch.

July 30   From John Branch. ALS, DLC (33). *North Carolina Historical Review*, 14(1937):364. Introduces [Richard?] Hines.

Aug 6   To James Barbour. ALS, DNA-RG 77 (10-1403). Asks that James G. Overton be allowed to delay matriculation at the Military Academy until 1826.

Aug 6   To William Pope Duval. LS, FWpR (10-1405); ALS draft, DLC (33, 10-1408). Writes that he will not visit Harrodsburg Springs.

Aug 8   From John Catron. ALS, DLC (33). Discusses a quarrel between Samuel Houston and John H. Eaton.

Aug 8   From Samuel Houston. ALS, DLC (33). Justifies his argument with
               John H. Eaton.
Aug 11   *To Samuel Houston.*   98
Aug 13   From Wilkins Tannehill, R[oswell] P. Hayes, and Simpson Shep-
               herd. ALS, DLC (33). Request that AJ attend a meeting of the
               Davidson County Bible Society and support a resolution to solicit
               subscribers.
[Aug 14]   To Wilkins Tannehill, R[oswell] P. Hayes, and Simpson Shepherd.
               Draft in Andrew J. Donelson's hand, DLC (33, 10-1410). Declines
               invitation to attend the Bible Society meeting.
Aug 18   From Adam Dale. ALS, DLC (33). Reports growing support for AJ
               in Maryland.
Aug 21   From Gilbert du Motier, Marquis de Lafayette. ALS, DLC (33).
               Bassett, 3:290–91. Writes that he is about to leave the United
               States; requests AJ to forward letter to Frances Wright (not found),
               who wishes to consult AJ on a "delicate" subject.
Aug 25   From William Quarles. ALS, DLC (33). Discusses the court-martial
               of Alexander Cummings and politics in Arkansas Territory.
Aug 28   From Thomas Aldridge et al. Printed, *Tuscumbian,* Sept 5 (mAJs).
               Invite AJ to dine at Tuscumbia, Alabama, on September 1.
Aug 29   To Thomas Aldridge et al. Printed, *Tuscumbian,* Sept 5 (mAJs).
               Accepts invitation.
Aug 30   *To James Jackson.*   99
[Aug 30]   Toast at Florence, Alabama, public dinner: "The citizens of
               Florence and vicinity. . ." Printed, *Louisville Public Advertiser,* Sept
               21 (mAJs).
Aug 31   From Josiah Watson. Copy, DLC (33). Discusses plans to regain
               lands in Tennessee with AJ's help.
Aug 31   Memorandum of John Coffee re AJ's deposit of $3,298 to purchase
               forfeited lands for Andrew Jackson Hutchings. ADS, THi (10-
               1411).
[Sept 1]   Toast at Tuscumbia, Alabama, public dinner: "Our Revolutionary
               Fathers . . ." Printed, *Tuscumbian,* Sept 5 (mAJs, 10-1413).
[cSept 2]   From Cincinnati Presbyterians (to commissioners to locate a
               western theological seminary). Printed, *Liberty Hall and Cincinnati
               Gazette,* Sept 2 (mAJs). Offer land as a seminary site.
Sept 3   From James Barbour. LC, DNA-RG 94 (M91-1). Agrees to delay
               James G. Overton's admission to the Military Academy.
Sept 5   From Arthur Peronneau Hayne. ALS, DLC (33). Describes travels
               since leaving the Hermitage in mid-summer.
Sept 5   From William Kenan Hill. ADS, DLC (33). Welcomes AJ to
               Columbia, Tennessee.
Sept 5   Toast at Columbia, Tennessee, meeting: "*The Sovereign People;*
               they have constituted a government by their prosperity and
               happiness: palsied be the arm that shall attempt any innovation on
               its sacred guarantees." Printed, Cincinnati *National Republican and
               Ohio Political Register,* Oct 14, 1825 (mAJs).
Sept 8   To William Hambly. Copy, LNHiC (10-1414). States that, to his
               knowledge, the charges that U. S. Creek interpreter Hambly

	assisted the British at New Orleans, commanded the Negro Fort, and led Seminoles in 1818 are false.
Sept 10	To John Overton. ALS, THi (10-1417). *THQ*, 6(1947):171. Informs Overton that he has postponed his departure for West Tennessee to September 13.
Sept 11	From Henry Lee. ALS, DLC (33). Ethel Armes, *Stratford Hall: The Great House of the Lees* (Richmond, 1936), pp. 382–84 (extract). Defends himself from an intimation in the *Nashville Republican* that his acceptance of a position in the post office department involved treachery to AJ.
Sept 13	To John Overton. ALS, THi (10-1419). *THQ*, 6(1947):172. Suggests a place of rendezvous on the road to West Tennessee.
Sept 15	*From James Gadsden.* 99
Sept 15	Account with Shelby & McCall for medical treatment of Andrew Jackson Hutchings. ADS, A-Ar (10-1421). Runs to September 16.
Sept 15	Account of Rachel Jackson with H[arriett] Temple for dressmaking. AD, DLC (33).
Sept 17	From Henderson Lewis, Edward H. Tarrant, and Lucas Kennedy. ALS, DLC (33). *Nashville Republican*, Oct 7. Invite AJ to a public dinner in Paris, Tennessee.
[Sept 19]	From William R. Hess. Printed, *Jackson Gazette*, Sept 24 (10-1423). On behalf of Masonic lodge, welcomes AJ to Jackson, Tennessee.
[Sept 19]	*To William R. Hess and the Masons of Lodge 45, Jackson, Tennessee.* 102
[Sept 19]	From William Stoddert. Printed, *Jackson Gazette*, Sept 24 (10-1428). Welcomes AJ to Jackson, Tennessee.
[Sept 19]	*To William Stoddert and the Citizens of Jackson, Tennessee.* 102
[Sept 19]	Toast at Jackson, Tennessee, public dinner: "The town of Jackson—Where but lately roamed wild beasts and savages; behold now the abode of civilization, refinement and hospitality." Printed, *Jackson Gazette*, Sept 24 (mAJs, 10-1427).
Sept 20	To Henderson Lewis, Edward H. Tarrant, and Lucas Kennedy. ALS draft, DLC (33). *Nashville Republican*, Oct 7. Accepts invitation.
Sept 23	From Richard Keith Call. ALS, DLC (33). Reports the birth of a daughter, Mary Ellinore; states that he considers Samuel R. Overton an enemy.
[Sept 27]	From [John W.] Cooke. Printed, *Nashville Republican*, Oct 7 (11-0002). On behalf of Henry County militia, welcomes AJ to Paris, Tennessee.
[Sept 27]	To [John W.] Cooke and Henry County militia. Printed, *Nashville Republican*, Oct 7 (11-0004). Acknowledges hospitality.
[Sept 27]	From Lucas Kennedy. ADS, DLC (20, 11-0006). *Nashville Republican*, Oct 7. Welcomes AJ to Paris, Tennessee.
[Sept 27]	To Lucas Kennedy and the citizens of Paris, Tennessee. Printed, *Nashville Republican*, Oct 7 (11-0011). Thanks them for welcome.
Oct 7	*To Henry Lee.* 103
Oct 10	From Valentine Giesey et al. ALS, DLC (33). Invite AJ to visit Brownsville, Pennsylvania, on his return to Washington.

consideration of Allegheny College in Meadville, Pennsylvania, as site for the proposed seminary.

[cDec] To Richard Keith Call. Extract, FHi (11-0063). Compliments Mary Call.

[Dec?] From James Gadsden. ALS fragment, DLC (75, 11-0091). Advises AJ about political effects of a proposed visit to South Carolina and indicates a desire to accompany him.

[c1825] From Samuel Wilson. ALS, THer (mAJs). Presents a copy of his *Chelys hesperia . . .* (Lexington, Ky., 1825).

1826

Jan 2 From Jesse Bledsoe. ALS, DLC (33). Announces that he has switched his allegiance from Henry Clay to AJ.

Jan 2 *From John Fowler.*   129

Jan 4 Account with John & Thomas Simpson for hardware and other goods for Andrew Jackson Hutchings. ADS, A-Ar (11-0097). Runs to April 9, 1827.

Jan 5 Account with John David Gaisser for blacksmith work for Andrew Jackson Hutchings. DS, A-Ar (11-0100). Runs to August 25, 1827.

Jan 8 Account with John Shelby & Charles Pugsley for medical treatment. ADS, DLC (34). Runs to October 31.

Jan 9 Receipt from Simon Glenn for shoes for Andrew Jackson Hutchings. DS in AJ's hand, A-Ar (11-0104).

Jan 12 Account with Snow, Johnson & Moore for kitchenware. ADS, DLC (34). Runs to May 14, 1827.

Jan 12 Account of Andrew Jackson Hutchings with Josiah Nichol for clothing, school supplies, and cash advances. ADS, A-Ar (11-0106). Runs to November 20.

[cJan 12] From William Cocke. Extracts, Frankfort, Ky., *Argus of Western America*, Feb 1 (mAJs), *Port Gibson Correspondent, and Mississippi General Advertiser*, Jan 19 (mAJs). Discusses Cocke's 1812 impeachment by the Tennessee legislature for showing partiality to friends while circuit court judge.

Jan 14 *From Arthur Peronneau Hayne.*   130
Jan 15 *To George Winchester.*   132
[Jan 18] *To Jesse Bledsoe.*   133

Jan 21 Promissory note to Miles Blythe McCorkle for $80 for horse for Andrew Jackson Hutchings's farm. ADS, TIIi (11-0112). Runs to May 15.

Jan 21 Receipt from William Donelson (1795–1864) for $65 for horse for Andrew Jackson Hutchings's farm. DS in AJ's hand, A-Ar (11-0110).

Jan 22 To John Overton. ALS fragment, THi (11-0115). Refuses to pay costs of suit involving the heirs of John Rice.

Jan 24 To Edward George Washington Butler. Extract, LNT (11-0118). Gayarré, p. 13 (extract). Discusses controversies involving John Crowell and Edmund P. Gaines and the nomination of George Croghan for inspector general.

April 4	Toast at Nashville Masonic dinner: "Cumberland College: may it continue to grow in reputation and usefulness, and become, as it promises to be, a permanent and distinguished seat of science." Printed, Nashville *National Banner,* April 7 (mAJs).
April 5	Receipt from Josiah Nichol for $569.75 for a note due the estate of Charles McAlister. ADS, DLC (33).
April 5	Account with John Shelby for medical treatment at the Hermitage. AD, THer (11-0182). Runs to November 25.
April 6	From Arthur Peronneau Hayne. ALS, DLC (33). Asks for letters of introduction to AJ's friends in northeastern cities; discusses proposed constitutional amendments regarding presidential electors.
April 8	*To James Buchanan.* 162
April 8	To Samuel Delucenna Ingham. Extract and facsimile extract of ALS, Thomas Madigan catalog, n.d., Item 129 (11-0187). Discusses Panama mission and his gratitude to Pennsylvania for continued support.
April 9	To Richard Keith Call. ALS, F (mAJs). Discusses the death of Call's father-in-law, Thomas Kirkman, and efforts to secure a share of the estate for his wife Mary.
April 10	To Arthur Lee Campbell. ALS, KyLoF (11-0191). Subscribes to the *Louisville Gazette*; expresses hope that factionalism in Kentucky politics will abate.
April 10	To William Martin (1765–1846). Photocopy of ALS, TU (mAJs). Again urges settlement of Martin's dispute with William Brackin.
April 12	From Richard Chester Langdon. ALS, DLC (33). Announces his intention to start a newspaper in South America and asks for a letter of introduction to Joel R. Poinsett.
April 13	Check to Benjamin P. Person for $500 for wages as overseer for 1825. ADS, T (11-0193).
April 13	Receipt from Benjamin P. Person for $500 for overseer wages. DS in AJ's hand, DLC (33).
April 15	*To Samuel Houston.* 164
April 18	From James Barbour. ALS, DLC (33). Encloses warrant for James G. Overton's admission to the Military Academy.
April 19	From William Martin (1765–1846). ALS endorsed by AJ, "not to be answered," DLC (33). Continues to argue his views on the disputed deed question.
April 19	From Thomas Gleaves. ANS with Watson's ANS receipt, May 13, DLC (33). Requests AJ to pay $3.00 to William Watson.
April 22	Account with William Watson for shoes and shoe repairs. ADS, DLC (34). Runs to July 15, 1827.
April 22	Receipt from David Hubbard for $15, legal fees for his defense of Samuel Bell's suit against AJ as guardian of Andrew Jackson Hutchings. ADS, A-Ar (11-0199).
April 26	From Willis Alston. ALS, DLC (33). Assesses criticism of the Adams administration and AJ's growing strength as a presidential candidate.
April 27	From Hamilton Lochart. ALS, DLC (33). Discusses national politics and AJ's defeat in the previous presidential election.

May 2 To John Coffee. ALS, THi (11-0201). Discusses arrangements to locate land claims of the heirs of John Donelson (c1718–86).

May 3 *To William Gibbes Hunt.* 165

May 3 *To James Knox Polk.* 166

[cMay 3] From [John Henry Eaton]. AL fragment, DLC (75, 11-0203). Discusses deliberations of Congress, especially regarding the judiciary bill, and administration efforts to promote a third presidential candidate.

May 5 *From John Henry Eaton.* 168

May 5 From Henry Ewing. ALS, DLC (33). Requests payment of balance of AJ's pledge of $150 to Cumberland College.

May 6 To James Barbour. ALS, DNA-RG 94 (M688-38). Acknowledges receipt of the warrant for James G. Overton's admission to West Point.

May 6 From Daniel Hughes. ALS, DLC (33). Introduces Baker Johnson.

May 6 From William Tyler. ALS, DLC (33). Introduces Baker Johnson.

May 7 From Francis Wells Armstrong. ALS, DLC (33). Discusses the Washington political scene and strongly criticizes the Adams administration.

May 9 From Robert Minns Burton. ALS, DLC (33). Discusses efforts to settle estate of William Donelson (1758–1820).

May 10 From John Hamlin Camp et al. Printed, *United States' Telegraph,* Aug 19 (11-0211). Invite AJ to Fourth of July celebration in Pulaski, Tennessee.

May 12 From Eliakim Littell. ALS, DLC (33). Sends a subscription to the new series of his *Museum of Foreign Literature and Science* as a token of his appreciation for AJ's views.

May 12 Receipt from Henry Ewing for $32.25 for summer session tuition for Andrew Jackson Hutchings at Cumberland College. ADS, THi (11-0212).

May 13 Check to Anderson Cheatham for $100. DS, Annette Tennin (mAJs).

May 13 Receipts from Anderson Cheatham for board and laundry charges for Andrew Jackson, Jr., and Andrew Jackson Hutchings. ADS, A-Ar (11-0214).

May 13 Receipt from William Watson for shoes for Andrew Jackson Hutchings. DS in AJ's hand, THi (11-0216).

May 14 To John Hamlin Camp et al. Draft in Andrew J. Donelson's hand, DLC (33); Printed, *United States' Telegraph,* Aug 19 (11-0211). Accepts invitation to Fourth of July celebration at Pulaski.

May 18 To Willis Alston. ALS copy, DLC (33). Bassett, 3:301. Criticizes the Adams administration and particularly its policy on the Panama mission.

May 18 Account with Anthony Latapie for china. ADS by H. Beekman, DLC (33).

May 23 From James Lloyd. ALS, DLC (33). Invites AJ to visit Boston during the summer for the fiftieth celebration of American independence.

May 26 From Josiah Watson (enclosure: Watson to AJ, Aug 31, 1825). LS, DLC (33). Seeks further assistance in claiming Tennessee lands.

May 26   Check to Ephraim Hubbard Foster for $368. DS, T (11-0218).
May 27   William Douglass (d. 1831) to Rachel Jackson. ALS, DLC (33).
          Thanks her for fabric from the Hermitage, which he plans to have
          made into a suit.
May 27   Motions to Cumberland College Board of Trustees: that contracts
          relating to college property be reduced to writing and signed and
          that AJ and others form a committee to draft an address to the
          Tennessee legislature to "procure a modification of the memorial to
          Congress on the subject of unappropriated lands" in Tennessee for
          the support of education. Copy, T (mAJs).
May 28   To Edward George Washington Butler. Extract, LNT (11-0222).
          Gayarré, p. 14 (extract). Disclaims any charges for expenses against
          the Edward Butler estate.
May 28   *From Henry Banks.*   172
May 29   From Henry Banks. ALS, DLC (34). Sends opinions on politics and
          the political campaign.
May 30   *To Felix Grundy, with Enclosure.*   174
June 4   To Eliakim Littell. ALS copy, DLC (34). Thanks him for subscrip-
          tion to the *Museum of Foreign Literature and Science.*
June 4   *From John Caldwell Calhoun.*   177
June 8   Prosecution bond for Elizabeth Anderson, with John Wright and AJ
          as sureties in the case, *Elizabeth Anderson* v. *Richard G.
          Waterhouse.* DS, TFWi (11-0226).
June 9   Account with Stout & Pope for bagging and rope for Andrew
          Jackson Hutchings's farm. ADS by Richard Cochran, A-Ar (11-
          0240). Runs to September 23.
June 10   From John Coffee. ALS, THi (11-0242). Reports sale of Andrew J.
          Hutchings's cotton; discusses land claims of the heirs of John
          Donelson (c1718–86); requests information about the reported
          conveyance of claim to Allison lands in Robertson and Montgom-
          ery counties from AJ to Coffee and James Jackson.
June 10   From William Moore, William Edmiston, and James Bright. ALS
          in Moore's hand, also signed by Edmiston and Bright, DLC (34).
          Invite AJ to a public celebration in Fayetteville, Tennessee, on
          July 6.
June 10   Attestation to the May 26 deposition of George Fields regarding his
          service in the Creek War. ADS, DNA-RG 15 (mAJs).
June 10   Account with William Winborne for expenses in recovering a stray
          horse for Andrew Jackson Hutchings. ADS, A-Ar (11-0246). Runs
          to December 6.
June 12   *To Arthur Lee Campbell.*   178
June 13   Receipt from Joseph White Horton for $80.50 for Tennessee and
          Davidson County taxes for 1826. DS, DLC (34).
June 15   To William Moore, William Edmiston, and James Bright. ALS
          copy, DLC (34). Accepts invitation to public celebration in
          Fayetteville.
June 18   From William C. Emmit. Printed, *National Banner and Nashville
          Whig,* June 28 (11 0252). On behalf of a committee, invites AJ to
          Fourth of July celebration and dinner in Nashville.
June 19   *To John Coffee.*   180

June 19   From Thomas Patrick Moore. ALS, DLC (34). Asks AJ when he intends to visit Harrodsburg and admonishes him to ignore charges that such a visit would be political.

June 21   To John Coffee. ALS, THi (11-0257). Asks Coffee to loan $1,000 to John C. McLemore from the proceeds of Andrew J. Hutchings's cotton.

June 22   To Edward George Washington Butler and Frances Parke Lewis Butler. Extract, LNT (11-0261). Gayarré, pp. 14–15 (extract). Relates political considerations for his declining to visit with the Butlers at Harrodsburg Springs.

June 26   To William C. Emmit. Printed, *National Banner and Nashville Whig,* June 28 (11-0262). Declines invitation to Fourth of July celebration in Nashville.

June 26   From Thomas Brandon et al. ALS, DLC (34). Invite AJ to a public dinner in his honor at Huntsville, Alabama.

June 28   To Thomas Patrick Moore. ALS draft, DLC (34). Declines invitation to visit the Harrodsburg Springs until after Kentucky elections; thanks Moore and Robert P. Henry for defending him against David Trimble's attack during the April 1 congressional debate.

June 30   To Thomas Brandon et al. ALS draft, DLC (34). Declines invitation to Huntsville.

June 30   To John Haywood Lewis. Photocopy of ALS, TU (mAJs); Extract, Anderson Auction Company Catalog 800 (1910), Item 139 (11-0263). Declines invitation to Huntsville.

June 30   From Robert Butler. ALS, DLC (34). Comments on Panama mission; discusses family, friends, and his farm in Florida.

[cJune]   *To Eleanor Parke Custis Lewis.*   181

July 1   From Henry Lee. ALS, DLC (34). Bassett, 3:305–306. Describes a meeting with Thomas Jefferson, confined to his bed at Monticello.

[July 3]   From [William C. Flournoy]. Copy, DLC (20, 11-0266). *United States' Telegraph,* Aug 19. Welcomes AJ to Pulaski, Tennessee.

[July 3]   To William C. Flournoy and the Citizens of Pulaski, Tennessee. Printed, *United States' Telegraph,* Aug 19 (mAJs). Thanks them for welcome.

[July 3]   From John Rivers. Printed, *United States' Telegraph,* Aug 19 (mAJs). Welcomes AJ to Giles County.

July 4   From James Coffey. ALS, DLC (34). Seeks assistance in securing a revolutionary pension.

[July 4]   From Aaron Venable Brown. Printed, *United States' Telegraph,* Aug 20 (11-0264). Welcomes AJ to Pulaski.

[July 4]   To Aaron Venable Brown and the Citizens of Pulaski, Tennessee. Printed, *United States' Telegraph,* Aug 20 (mAJs, 11-0265). Thanks Brown for his address; honors revolutionary heroes.

[July 4]   Toast at public dinner in Pulaski: "The policy of Washington: Peace, commerce and friendship with all nations, entangling alliances with none . . ." Printed, *United States' Telegraph,* Aug 20 (11-0270).

July 5   From Samuel Ragland Overton. ALS, DLC (34). Suggests that recent severe attacks on the Adams administration have harmed the cause of Adams's opponents.

[July 5]   From William Pitt Martin. AD, DLC (33, 11-0271); Printed, Fayetteville *Village Messenger*, July 12 (11-0275). Welcomes AJ to Fayetteville, Tennessee.

[July 5]   *To William Pitt Martin and the Citizens of Fayetteville, Tennessee.*   182

July 6   From George Walker Call. ALS, DLC (34). Reports that friends wish AJ to visit Kentucky.

July 6   From William Patten (enclosure: Deposition of George Fields, May 26, with AJ's attestation, June 10). ALS, DLC (34). Returns Fields's deposition for forwarding to Washington.

[July 6]   From John H. Morgan. AD, DLC (58, 11-0279); Printed, Fayetteville *Village Messenger*, July 12 (11-0283). Praises AJ's services to country.

[July 6]   To John H. Morgan and the Citizens of Fayetteville, Tennessee. AD draft in Andrew J. Donelson's hand, DLC (18, 11-0285); Printed, Fayetteville *Village Messenger*, July 12 (11-0289). Thanks them for reception and honors.

[July 6]   Toast at Fayetteville public dinner: "The general and state governments: May all their functionaries feel a just responsibility to the people and not overleap the pale of their respective constitutions." Printed, Fayetteville *Village Messenger*, July 12 (mAJs, 11-0278).

July 7   To [Thomas Buck Reed]. Printed (Mississippi?, 1826), TxU (mAJs). In reply to an inquiry of June 17 (not found), offers opinion that the Mississippi constitution would allow a state legislator to be elected to the U.S. Senate.

[July 7]   From James McKissick. AD, DLC (59, 11-0291). *Nashville Republican*, July 29. Welcomes AJ to Bedford County and praises his course in the recent presidential election.

[July 7]   To James McKissick and the Citizens of Bedford County, Tennessee. AD copy, DLC (33, 11-0296); AD draft, DLC (59, 11-0300); Draft in Andrew J. Donelson's hand, DLC (59, 11-0301). *Nashville Republican*, July 29. Thanks them for their "friendship and regard."

July 8   From Charles Anderson Wickliffe. ALS, DLC (34). Invites AJ to Bardstown, Kentucky.

[July 8]   From Archibald Yell. ADS, DLC (33, 11-0305). *Nashville Republican*, July 29. Welcomes AJ to the Shelbyville Masonic Lodge and praises his services to the country.

[July 8]   To [Archibald Yell] and the Masons and Citizens of Shelbyville, Tennessee. Copy in Andrew J. Donelson's hand, DLC (22, 11-0308). *Nashville Republican*, July 29. Thanks them for their reception.

[July 8]   Toast at Shelbyville public dinner: "*Our Fellow Citizen Gen. Lafayette*—The compatriot and friend of Washington." Printed, *Nashville Republican*, July 29 (mAJs, 11-0304).

July 10–11   From Henry Banks. ALS, DLC (34). Urges AJ to visit Kentucky after the election and reports on efforts to promote the Jackson cause in the state.

July 11   Receipt from James and Mary McCully for payment of $400 as cosigner on a promissory note from Robert Butler. DS in AJ's hand, DLC (33).

July 13   From Henry Cotten. ALS, TNJ (11-0311). Discusses pedigrees of two mares that he will send to AJ.

July 14   To James Lloyd. ALS, MH-H (11-0317); LS copy in Andrew J. Donelson's hand, DLC (34). Declines invitation to visit Massachusetts.

July 14   *From Edward George Washington Butler.*   184

[July 14] To William Berkeley Lewis and Andrew Jackson Donelson. Abstract, American Art Association Sale, April 8, 1926, Item 257 (7-1153). Instructs them about invitations to dinner at the Hermitage, July 20, to honor John H. Eaton.

July 15   *To William Berkeley Lewis.*   185

July 16   From Samuel Houston. Printed, Tallahassee *Floridian and Advocate,* March 24, 1831 (mAJs, 11-0322). Introduces Joseph M. White.

July 16   Receipt from Robert Armstrong for $117.80, paid on Robert Butler's promissory note of November 19, 1825, to Armstrong. DS in AJ's hand, DLC (34).

July 18   *To John Haywood Lewis.*   186

[July 18] *To John Caldwell Calhoun.*   187

July 19   From John McNairy. ALS, DLC (34). Declines invitation to Hermitage dinner because of pressing court business.

July 19   Account with Decker & Dyer for a decorated pound cake and three dozen sponge cakes. DS, DLC (34).

July 20   *From Arthur Peronneau Hayne.*   188

July 21   From Thomas Patrick Moore. ALS, DLC (34). Bassett, 3:309. Again urges AJ to visit Kentucky.

July 22   To James Barbour (enclosures: Depositions of Gilbert D. Taylor, Thomas Fearn, and George Fields, all May 26, DNA-RG 15, mAJs). ALS, DNA-RG 15 (mAJs); ALS draft, DLC (34). Forwards depositions to support the claim of Fields for a War of 1812 pension.

July 22   To James Barbour. LS in Andrew J. Donelson's hand and Copy, DNA-RG 107 (M221-103); ALS draft, DLC (34). Requests settlement of George Wilson's claim against the war department.

July 25   Proceedings of Committee in Nashville to memorialize Thomas Jefferson and John Adams, AJ chairman. Printed, *Nashville Republican,* July 29 (mAJs).

[July 25] Address to Nashville meeting on the deaths of Thomas Jefferson and John Adams. Printed abstract, *Nashville Republican,* July 29 (mAJs).

July [26] *To Richard Keith Call.*   190

July 29   *To John Dabney Terrell.*   192

July 29   Account of Andrew Jackson Hutchings with Julian Neal for wagon repairs. DS, A-Ar (11-0329).

July 31   *To John Coffee.*   193

July 31   *To [Thomas Patrick Moore].*   194

[July]   From Edward George Washington Butler. AN fragment, DLC (75). Forwards copy of Edmund P. Gaines's official notices on the deaths of Jefferson and Adams.

Oct 11   From James Barbour. LC, DNA-RG 107 (M6-12). Refuses to reconsider the claim of George Wilson.

Oct 11   From John Coffee. ALS, DLC (34). Reports that he has decided to retain Jesse Winborne as overseer on Andrew J. Hutchings's farm and that he will soon depart for the Indian treaty negotiations.

[Oct 11]   Report by AJ et al., trustees, on the condition of Cumberland College. Printed, *National Banner and Nashville Whig,* Oct 11 (11-0379).

Oct 12   From Alfred Balch. ALS, DLC (34). Discusses AJ's draft for memorial regarding Cumberland College; relays information that AJ's candidacy stands well in Maryland.

Oct 15   To James Buchanan. ALS, PHi (11-0381). Moore, *Works of James Buchanan,* 1:218. Expresses gratitude for political support in Pennsylvania.

Oct 15   To Andrew Wills et al. Facsimile of ALS, Joseph Abram Jackson, *Masonry in Alabama: A Sesquicentennial History, 1821–1971* (Montgomery, Ala., 1970), p. 36 (11-0383). States that he will visit Helion Lodge in Huntsville when he goes to Florence later in the year.

Oct 17   Account with Anthony Latapie for cards, cigars, and violins purchased by Andrew Jackson, Jr. AD, DLC (35). Runs to March 19, 1827.

[cOct 18]   Memorial to the legislature of Tennessee (AJ, chairman of committee for drafting on behalf of the Trustees of Cumberland College) for instructions to Tennessee's congressional delegation to support Cumberland College and other schools in the state from the proceeds of the sale of public lands and for changing the name of Cumberland College to University of the State of Tennessee. Draft in Andrew J. Donelson's hand with revisions by AJ, TNJ (10-0882); Printed, *National Banner and Nashville Whig,* Oct 28 (mAJs).

Oct 22   Check to self for $65.85. DS, THer (11-0384).

Oct 23   To John Rust Eaton. ALS draft, Gallery of History, Inc. (mAJs). Thanks him for a pipe and comments on the horse Roanoke.

Oct 23   *To Samuel Houston.*   228

Oct 23   *To Samuel Houston.*   229

Oct 24   From Thomas Dickens Arnold. Printed, Lexington *Kentucky Reporter,* April 11, 1827 (11-0387). Asks for clarification of AJ's stand on internal improvements.

Oct 24   *From Samuel Swartwout.*   231

Oct 26   From Arthur Peronneau Hayne. ALS, DLC (34). Reports on elections in Pennsylvania and AJ's popularity there.

Oct 27   From Richard Mentor Johnson. ALS, DLC (34). *RegKyHi,* 39(1941):265–66. Thanks AJ for his attention to the Creaths, discusses politics, and urges him to visit Kentucky during the next year.

[cOct]   From John Henry Eaton (enclosure: Eaton to Charles A. Wickliffe, [cOct]). ALS, DLC (72). Sends copy of a letter re Kentucky militia at the Battle of New Orleans and warns AJ not to be drawn out on the issue.

Nov 4   Account with John Shelby & [Charles] Pugsley for medical
             treatment for Andrew Jackson Hutchings. ALS, A-Ar (11-0388).
             Runs to November 25.
Nov 5   Receipt from Benjamin P. Person (agent for AJ) to Joshua Starkey
             for 1,502 pounds of seed cotton. DS, DLC (34).
Nov 6   To [John?] Buchanan. AN in unknown hand, THi (11-0390).
             Invites him to dinner at the Hermitage on November 11.
Nov 7   From Samuel Ragland Overton. ALS, DLC (34). Defends himself
             against accusations of disloyalty and opposition to AJ, stemming
             from his attendance at the July 4th celebration in Pensacola.
Nov 7   Receipt to William Chappell from Benjamin P. Person (agent for
             AJ) for 547 pounds of seed cotton. ADS by Person also signed by
             Chappell, DLC (34).
Nov 8   *From Richard Keith Call.*   232
Nov 9   Account with Thomas Wells for ammunition, medicines, and
             sundries. ADS, DLC (34). Runs to July 10, 1827.
Nov 15   Account with Decker & Dyer for cakes, raisins, and almonds. ADS,
             DLC (34).
Nov 15   Account with Ward & Lippincott for a seal cap purchased by
             Andrew Jackson, Jr. ADS, DLC (34). With receipt for payment,
             October 1, [1827?].
Nov 17   To Thomas Gassaway Watkins. Printed, *Richmond Enquirer*, Dec
             27, 1827 (mAJs, 11-0391). Thanks him for the gift of a breastpin
             with a lock of Thomas Jefferson's hair.
Nov 18   From Henry Lee. ALS, DLC (72). Bassett, 3:318 (extract). Reports
             his resignation from the post office department; announces inten-
             tion to write a biography of AJ and requests information.
Nov 21   *To Richard Keith Call.*   233
Nov 21   Agreement with John W. Phillips for management of Andrew
             Jackson Hutchings's plantation. ADS in AJ's hand, also signed by
             Phillips, THi (11-0401).
Nov 21   Account of Andrew Jackson Hutchings with Josiah Nichol for
             clothing and sundries. ADS, A-Ar (11-0398). Runs to October 20,
             1827.
Nov 22   *To Samuel Houston.*   235
Nov 23   To Edward Livingston (enclosure: Deposition re troop positions at
             New Orleans, Nov 25). LS in Andrew J. Donelson's hand, NjP
             (mAJs). Sends affidavit supporting John Rodriguez's claim for
             damages.
Nov 24   Receipt from Anderson Cheatham for $45 for board and laundry
             for Andrew Jackson Hutchings. DS in AJ's hand, A-Ar (11-0405).
Nov 25   Deposition re troop positions at New Orleans. ADS, DNA-RG 217
             (mAJs). *HRRep* 27, 19th Cong., 2nd sess., Serial 159, p. 2 (ex-
             tract).
Nov 25   Receipt from Henry Ewing for $37, Andrew Jackson Hutchings's
             tuition at Cumberland College. ADS, A-Ar (11-0407).
Nov 26   From John Overton. ALS, THi (11-0409). Invites AJ and Rachel
             Jackson to spend the night at Travellers' Rest en route to Florence,
             Alabama.
Nov 30   John H. Wallace to Samuel Houston. ALS, DLC (72). Reports

Samuel Southard's comments at dinner in Fredericksburg re Battle of New Orleans.

[Nov]   *From "An Enquirer."*   236

Dec 2   Deposition of Elizabeth Brown Craighead re the Rachel Jackson–Lewis Robards marriage. DS, DLC (34); Copies in Andrew J. Donelson's hand, T (11-0628, -0415); Copy in William B. Lewis's hand, NN (11-0411). Bassett, 3:319–21.

Dec 4   *From James Knox Polk.*   238

Dec 4   From John G. Vought. AN, THer (11-0419). Presents AJ with a copy of his *Treatise on Bowel Complaints* . . . (Rochester, N.Y., 1823).

Dec 6   From Thomas J. Garrett. ALS, DLC (34). Inquires about the character of [Addison W.] Lane, AJ's neighbor and a veteran of the War of 1812.

Dec 6   Receipt from Thomas Darby for $5 for horse breeding for Andrew Jackson Hutchings's farm. DS by proxy (John Coffee), A-Ar (11-0421).

Dec 7   To John Overton. ALS, THi (11-0423). Reports his return home from Alabama and his attention to the request regarding the Joseph Coleman estate.

Dec 7   Receipt from Winslow W. Wade for $131 for forty-two hogs and a shoat. DS in AJ's hand, DLC (34).

Dec 10   Deposition of Sarah Michie Smith re the Rachel Jackson–Lewis Robards marriage. DS in hand of Daniel S. Donelson, signed by Smith, DLC (34); Copy, T (11-0632). Bassett, 3:322–23.

Dec 11   Promissory note to Anthony Winston (1750–1827) for $92.25. DS, THi (11- 0426).

[Dec 11]   From Edward George Washington Butler. ALS fragment, DLC (75). Announces the birth of a son.

Dec 12   *To William Berkeley Lewis.*   240

Dec 13   *From Samuel Houston.*   241

Dec 14   From John Coffee. ALS, DLC (34). Announces that he is en route to Washington; reports state of Andrew J. Hutchings's farm; informs AJ of George A. Dawson's application for a Cumberland College professorship.

Dec 15   *To Samuel Houston.*   243

Dec 17   Deed of relinquishment of a quarter section of land in Lauderdale County, Alabama, from John H. Smith to Andrew Jackson, guardian of Andrew Jackson Hutchings. DS, THi (11-0430).

Dec 18   *From Samuel Houston.*   244

Dec 20   To John Coffee. ALS, THi (11-0432). Reports that Coffee's daughter Mary has matriculated at Nashville Female Academy; approves Coffee's arrangements in regard to Andrew J. Hutchings's farm.

Dec 20   To Thomas J. Garrett. ANS abstract, DLC (34). Discusses the character of Addison W. Lane.

Dec 20   Check to Hardy Murfree Cryer for $200. Facsimile of ADS, THer (11-0435).

Dec 21   Deposition of Mary Henley Bowen re the Rachel Jackson–Lewis Robards marriage. DS by proxy in Andrew J. Donelson's hand with

	ANS by William B. Lewis, DLC (34); Copy in Lewis's hand, T (11-0636). Bassett, 3:325–26.
Dec 22	To Edward George Washington Butler. Extract, LNT (11-0436). Gayarré, p. 15 (extract). Congratulates him on the birth of his son; asks him to send copies of Cincinnati newspapers relating to Charles Hammond's conversations slandering Rachel Jackson.
Dec 2[2]	To Richard Keith Call. ALS, F (mAJs). Discusses the Kirkman will and Call's dispute with Joseph M. White.
Dec 22	*From John Henry Eaton.* 245
Dec 23	Account with Robert Lusk & Co. for a coat for Andrew Jackson, Jr. ADS, DLC (34). Paid June 2, 1827.
Dec [2]4	*To James Knox Polk.* 246
Dec 25	*To Henry Lee.* 247
[cDec 29]	From "Justice." Printed, *United States' Telegraph*, Dec 29 (mAJs). Praises AJ's actions in defending New Orleans in 1814–15.
Dec 30	From Vincent Gray (enclosure: Gray to Baring Brothers, Nov 20, 1814, DLC-71). ALS duplicate, DLC (34). Reveals that he was AJ's anonymous informant about British plans in 1814.
Dec 30	Cargo manifest for forty-five bales of cotton shipped from Florence to New Orleans for Andrew Jackson Hutchings. DS, A-Ar (11-0448).
[cDec]	To Henry Clay (letter probably not sent). Printed, *New York Times Magazine*, Oct 28, 1929 (11-0996). Excoriates Clay for allegedly snubbing Rachel and for his connections to Charles Hammond's attacks on her.
[1826]	To Hugh Lawson White. Abstract, William Evarts Benjamin's Sales Catalogue No. 51 (May 1893), p. 6 (mAJs). Comments on Panama mission and reciprocity.
[1826]	List of town lots subject to taxation in Florence, Alabama, belonging to AJ and to Andrew Jackson Hutchings. ADS by John Coffee as agent, THi (11-0088).
[1826]	Receipts from Henry Garrard for payment of taxes on Andrew Jackson Hutchings's land and slaves and AJ's town property in Lauderdale County, Alabama. DS, A-Ar (11-0093).
[c1826]	To Fidelio C. Sharp. Extract, *Louisville Focus*, April 1, 1828 (mAJs). Comments on the murder of Fidelio's brother Solomon P. Sharp.
[c1826]	Rachel Jackson to George Washington Martin. Typed copy, T (11-0095). Thanks him for letter and for articles he brought her; urges him to come with his mother to visit the Hermitage.
[1826]	"Genl. Jacksons Letters, &c." (Enclosed in Houston to AJ, Jan 5, 1827). AD, DLC (75). Lists letters AJ had sent to the war department.

1827

Jan 2	Account of Andrew Jackson Hutchings with John David Gaisser for blacksmithing. ADS by AJ, also signed by John W. Phillips and Finch Scruggs, A-Ar (11-0456). Runs to April 15, 1828.
Jan 2	Charles Hammond to John Henry Eaton. ALS draft, OHi (mAJs).

Denies that Henry Clay furnished him any information on the irregularities of the Jacksons' marriage; reports that he received copies of documents from Edward Day.

Jan 4   From Anthony Butler. ALS, DLC (34). Reports on the election of Powhatan Ellis to the United States Senate from Mississippi and on his recent trip to Texas.

Jan 4   Account with G. & C. Carvill for subscription to the *United States Review and Literary Gazette.* Printed form with ms insertions, DLC (34).

Jan 9   Account with John H. Woodcock for medical service for a slave at Andrew Jackson Hutchings's farm. ADS, A-Ar (11-0464). Runs to December 1828.

Jan 10   Receipt from D. L. Thompson for $10 for screw and screw bolts for cotton press. ADS, DLC (34).

Jan 15   To James Gettys McGready Ramsey. LS in Andrew J. Donelson's hand, TU (11-0466). Heiskell (2nd Edition), 2:120. Thanks him for the print of the Mecklenburg Declaration of Independence.

Jan 16   To Robert Johnstone Chester. ALS, THi (11-0467). Asks Chester to secure a statement from Obadiah Gordon, a former Nashville blacksmith, about the settlement of AJ's accounts with Benjamin P. Person.

Jan 16   Receipt from John H. Clopton for $15 for a cotton press screw. DS in AJ's hand, DLC (34).

Jan 18   To Richard Keith Call. Extract, *Collector* (March 1904):51–52 (11-0471). Comments on recent Indian attacks in Florida, the settlement of Call's dispute with Joseph M. White, and political prospects.

Jan 18   To the Medical Faculty of Transylvania University. LS in Andrew J. Donelson's hand, THer (mAJs). Introduces Dr. M. D. L. F. Sharpe and recommends him for an honorary medical degree.

Jan 20   Account with John Coffee for lumber for Andrew Jackson Hutchings's farm. ADS, A-Ar (11-0473). Runs to November 20.

Jan 20   Account with John & Thomas Simpson for general merchandise for Andrew Jackson Hutchings's farm. ADS by John Simpson, A-Ar (11-0476). Runs to February 27, 1828.

Jan 23   Account with Robertson & Elliot for Andrew Jackson Hutchings's school supplies. ADS by Alexander McIntosh, THi (11-0478). Runs to January 21, 1829.

endorsement to file so that historians can see the justification of his attack on Pensacola, DLC (34). Sends extracts of private letters detailing projected British attack on Mobile.

Feb 15 *To Samuel Houston.*   291
Feb 15 To Samuel Lewis Southard. LS in Andrew J. Donelson's hand, DLC (72). Repeats the demand of January 5 that Southard explain his alleged statement belittling AJ's role in the New Orleans campaign.
Feb 15 From Samuel Houston. ALS, DLC (72). Bassett, 6:494. Reports that Samuel L. Southard offered a sealed letter for AJ explaining the Fredericksburg remarks, which Houston refused to accept.
Feb 15 Receipt to John Coffee for $500, payment to the estate of John Hutchings. ADS, THi (11-0488).
Feb 16 *To Hugh Lawson White.*   293
Feb 16 From James Hamilton, Jr. ALS, DLC (34). Bassett 3:344 (extract). Sends copy of his speech in the House of Representatives, February 5, 1827, on the abuses of a government press; reports AJ's growing strength among New York Republicans.
Feb 16 From Samuel Lewis Southard (enclosures: Southard to AJ, Feb 9; Southard to Samuel Houston, Feb 12). ALS and Copy, DLC (72); Presscopy of ALS, T (mAJs). Forwards his letter of February 9 by mail since Houston refused to receive it sealed.
Feb 20 From William Brackin. ALS, DLC (34). Notifies AJ to attend Sumner County Circuit Court to defend land title in suit brought by William Martin (1765–1846).
Feb 22 Deed to Andrew Jackson Donelson for 840 acres of land in Haywood County. DS in Andrew J. Donelson's hand, witnessed by Andrew Jackson, Jr., Samuel J. Hays, and Daniel S. Donelson, DLC (34).
Feb 22 Deed from Andrew Jackson Donelson for 107 acres of land in Davidson County adjoining the Hermitage and altering the land division of October 11, 1824. ADS signed by AJ, Andrew J. Donelson, and witnessed by Daniel S. Donelson and Samuel J. Hays, DLC (34).
[Feb 24] From Edward George Washington Butler. ALS fragment, DLC (75). Discusses dispute between the federal government and Georgia over the Treaty of Indian Springs with the Creek nation, proceedings in Congress, and news of family and friends.
Feb 25 From John Caldwell Calhoun. ALS, DLC (34). *Calhoun Papers,* 10:267–68. Discusses Joseph G. Swift's impending move to Tennessee and the investigation of the Rip Raps Shoal charges.
Feb 26 *From John Donelson (1787–1840).*   294
Feb [2]8 *To William Berkeley Lewis.*   295
March 1 *To Hardy Murfree Cryer.*   295
March 1 To Jacques Philippe Villeré. ALS, THi (11-0490). *THQ,* 6(June 1947):172. Introduces John Overton.
March 1 Rebecca Motte Alston Hayne to Rachel Jackson. ALS, THer (mAJs). Renews friendship and presents her with card racks and a watch case.
March 6 *To Samuel Lewis Southard.*   296
March 7 *To John McLean (1785–1861).*   300

March 8   From Daniel Steenrod and John Good. ALS, DLC (34). Express
               support for AJ's presidential candidacy.
March 12   *From Henry Lee.*   301
March 13   Toast at public dinner in Gallatin, Tennessee: "*The citizens of
               Gallatin and of the county of Sumner:* My early acquaintances,
               supporters and friends—may their prosperity and happiness be
               commensurate with their hospitality." Printed, *National Banner
               and Nashville Whig,* March 17 (11-0503).
March 13   Account with Bradford & Stacker for flour, raisins, salt, salmon,
               shad, whiskey, and other general merchandise. AD, DLC (34).
               Runs to July 10.
March 13   Account with David Lowe for leather for Andrew Jackson
               Hutchings's farm. DS in John Coffee's hand, also signed by Charles
               Baker, A-Ar (11-0501). Runs to August 14, 1828.
March 16   To John Coffee. ALS, THi (11-0504). Bassett, 3:348–49 (extract).
               Reports that he has not yet met with Mary K. Call; discusses his
               quarrel with Samuel L. Southard and Hugh L. White's dispute with
               James Monroe.
March 17   Account with Maunsel White for freight, storage, weighing, and
               sale of AJ's cotton. ADS, DLC (34). Runs to June 14.
March 19   To Benjamin P. Person. ALS draft, DLC (33). Offers to settle out of
               court the dispute over compensation as overseer.
[cMarch 19]   Memorandum regarding settlement of account with Benjamin P.
               Person. AD, DLC (58).
March 20   Account with John G. Wilson, endorsed to Duncan Robertson, for
               a frame for John Henry Eaton's portrait. DS, DLC (34).
March 21   Bill of complaint in *William Brackin* v. *AJ and William Martin*
               (1765–1846). Copy with AJ endorsement noting his scheduled
               appearance to answer in September, DLC (34).
March 21   Case file of *William Brackin* v. *AJ and William Martin* (1765–
               1846). DSs and Copies, T (mAJs). Runs to March 26, 1829.
March 22   From James Allen. ALS, DLC (72). Reports allegations by AJ's
               enemies in Kentucky.
March 22   From DeWitt Clinton. LC, NNC (11-0508). Introduces Basil Hall,
               a British naval officer traveling in the United States.
March 22   Account with Western Territory Rucker for medical services for
               Andrew Jackson Hutchings's slaves. DS with AN by AJ, A-Ar (11-
               0509). Runs to March 13, 1828.
March 23   To John M. Davis. Photocopy of ALS, T (mAJs). Thanks Davis for
               naming his son for AJ; expresses pleasure at continued support in
               Pennsylvania; and complains about a widespread "system of
               espoinage" in the post offices, which precludes his letters reaching
               their destination.
March 24   From Richard Gilliam Dunlap. ALS, DNA-RG 77 (11-0511). Asks
               AJ to help secure renewal of appointment to the Military Academy
               for William K. Morgan; reports death of Hugh L. White's daughter
               Lucinda.
March 24   John Hooe Wallace to Samuel Houston. ALS, DLC (72). Notes that
               John S. Wellford has obtained statements from those present at the

dinner at Fredericksburg regarding Samuel L. Southard's
comments; requests copies of AJ's correspondence with Southard.

March 25   To George Washington Martin. Copy of ALS, Don Lake (11-0514). Regrets that poor health prevents his visit to Martin's home in Courtland, Alabama.

March 28   From Arthur Peronneau Hayne (enclosures: AJ to Hayne, Jan 25, 1815; Statement re services of Wade Hampton (1791–1858) at the Battle of New Orleans, n.d., DLC–34). ALS, DLC (34). Relates family news; requests that AJ return copies in his own hand of enclosed documents.

March 29   To Daniel Steenrod and John Good. LS copy and Drafts in Andrew J. Donelson's hand, DLC (34). States his agreement with George Washington's warning against entangling alliances and affirms that he will serve if elected president.

March 30   Receipt from Florence, Alabama, jailer John Dickey for $8.55 for confining George, Andrew Jackson Hutchings's runaway slave. ADS, A-Ar (11-0517).

April 2   Account with Percifor F. Pearson & Co. for general merchandise for Andrew Jackson Hutchings's farm. ADS, A-Ar (11-0550). Runs to January 1, 1828.

April 3   To Willie Blount. ALS, NSyU (mAJs). Forwards a copy of William Johnson's *Sketches of the Life and Correspondence of Nathanael Greene* (Charleston, 1822).

April 7   From Maunsel White. ALS, DLC (34). Reports purchase of cotton bagging on favorable terms because of great respect for AJ in New Orleans; discusses sale of AJ's cotton.

April 8   To John Coffee (enclosures: Agreement with John W. Phillips, Nov 21, 1826; Deed of relinquishment from John H. Smith, Dec 17, 1826) ALS, THi (11-0559). Bassett, 3:353–54 (extract). Discusses attacks by his political enemies, the attempted murder of John Donelson (1787–1840), and Andrew J. Hutchings's farm.

April 9   William Berkeley Lewis to [John Christmas McLemore] (enclosure: Statement of Elizabeth Brown Craighead, Dec 2, 1826). ALS, NN (11-0563). Sends statement and asks McLemore to secure a corroboration of her comments from Samuel Brown, her brother.

April 15   Attestation by AJ to land transfer from Elizabeth and William Donelson as guardians of the heirs of Severn Donelson. DS, DLC (34).

April 15   Account with Lewis Ezell for building gin house on Andrew Jackson Hutchings's farm. DS in John Coffee's hand, A-Ar (11-0567). Runs to April 20.

April 17   Receipt from M. C. Hoover for payment for shoes. ADS, DLC (34).

April 21   From Isaac Lewis Baker. ALS, DLC (34). Assures AJ of Louisiana's support in the forthcoming presidential election and urges him to attend the January 8 celebration in New Orleans.

April 23   To Richard Keith Call. ALS fragment, F (mAJs). Reports on the visit of Mary K. Call and the decision not to contest the Thomas Kirkman will if the executors will award Mary a share from her father's estate.

April 26   Receipt from Duff Green for $10 for two-year subscription to the tri-weekly Washington *United States' Telegraph.* Printed form with ms insertions, signed by John C. Rives, DLC (34).

April 27   From Edward George Washington Butler.   312

April 27   Receipt from Peter Force for $13 (paid by John H. Eaton) for subscription to the Washington *Daily National Journal,* August 7, 1824, to April 27, 1827. Printed form with ms insertions, signed by Singleton S. Walker, DLC (34).

April 28   To James Barbour (enclosure: Richard G. Dunlap to AJ, March 24). LS in Andrew J. Donelson's hand, DNA-RG 77 (11-0569). Urges reappointment of William K. Morgan to the Military Academy.

May 3   To Richard Keith Call.   315

May 3   To Arthur Peronneau Hayne. ALS draft partly in Andrew J. Donelson's hand, DLC (34). Testifies to the services rendered by Wade Hampton (1791–1858) at the Battle of New Orleans.

May 5   To William Berkeley Lewis.   317

May 8   From Auguste G. V. Davezac. ALS, DLC (34). Expresses pleasure that AJ will attend the January 8 celebration in New Orleans; requests letters of introduction for his brother and Sebastian Hiriart.

May 10   Henry Banks to John Overton. LS, DLC (72). Asks for information on AJ's marriage; recounts story from Peyton Short, the man who allegedly first aroused Lewis Robards's jealousy; and relates William Steele's high opinion of Rachel Jackson and contempt for Robards.

May 10   Receipt from Elijah Reaves for $13.25 for hewing lumber for Andrew Jackson Hutchings's farm. DS in John Coffee's hand, A-Ar (11-0580).

May 11   Receipt from Kirkman & Livingston for $17.37½ for a silk dress, other clothing, and shoes for Rachel Jackson. ADS by Talbot Martin, DLC (34).

May 12   From Richard Gilliam Dunlap.   317

May 12   From James Gadsden. ALS, DLC (34). Requests AJ's aid in securing employment for Joseph G. Swift, who plans to establish a military academy in the West.

May 12   Receipt from John Coffee for $78.76 for Scotch bagging for Andrew Jackson Hutchings's farm. ADS, A-Ar (11-0582).

May 12   Promissory note to Ira Walton for $400. ADS, DLC (32).

May 14   From John Overton.   319

May 14   Receipt from Anderson Cheatham for $45 for Andrew Jackson Hutchings's board and washing at summer session, University of Nashville. AD signed by Cheatham, THi (11-0584).

carpenter's work at Andrew Jackson Hutchings's farm and for ferriage. DSs in John Coffee's hand, A-Ar (11-0699, -0701).

June 16	*To William B. Keene.*	343
June 16	To Henry Lee. Extract, Stan. V. Henkels Catalog 988 (Jan 29, 1909), Item 389 (mAJs). Invites Lee and his wife to visit the Hermitage.	
June 16	To Thomas Patrick Moore. ALS copy, DLC (34). Bassett, 3:364. Agrees that a trip to Kentucky during the summer would be seen as electioneering and expresses regret that the death of several horses renders a trip to Harrodsburg Springs after the election impossible.	
June 16	*To John Overton.*	345
June 16	From John Loving. ALS, DLC (34). Introduces George Work.	
June 17	To Richard Riker. LS, Max Rambod, Inc. (mAJs). Thanks Riker for a copy of Cadwallader David Colden's book, *Memoir . . . Presented . . . at the Celebration of the Completion of the New York Canals* (New York, 1825).	
June 18	From Thomas Stratton. ALS, DLC (34). Acknowledges receipt of $5 for season of AJ's mare to Powhatan.	
June 19	From Hugh Lawson White (enclosures: William H. Crawford to White, May 27; White to Crawford, June 19). ALS, DLC (34). Bassett, 3:365. Discusses campaign against John Williams; sends correspondence expressing fear that AJ's election will elevate John C. Calhoun.	
June 20	From Oliver B. Ross. ALS, DLC (34). Requests that AJ give a deposition re the good character of Susan W. J. Watkins in the pending divorce case brought by her husband Thomas G. Watkins.	
June 20	From Hugh Lawson White (enclosure: Robert Y. Hayne to AJ, June 5). ALS, DLC (34). Reports on John Williams's campaign for the Tennessee Senate and on East Tennessee politics.	
June 21	From John Coffee. ALS, DLC (34). Reports on crops and discusses political attacks on AJ.	
June 23	From John Overton. ALS, T (11-0709). Forwards material on the Dickinson duel and states that he composed, over AJ's signature, the letter to Thomas Eastin of June 28, 1806, published in the Nashville *Impartial Review.*	
June 23	From John Overton. LS in John H. Eaton's hand, THi (11-0706). Asks, on behalf of the Nashville Committee, if AJ's views on the tariff have changed since 1824.	
June 24	*To John Overton.*	346
June 25	*To Henry Daniel.*	346
June 25	From Alfred Balch. ALS, TNJ (11-0713). Sends a letter from Thomas H. Benton (not found) relaying news from Indiana.	
June 27	*From Carter Beverley.*	347
June 29	From John M. A. Hamblen. ALS, THer (11-0716). Announces that he is about to fight a duel with John Hughes and asks AJ to look after his wife and daughter should he be killed.	
June 30	To Edmund Pendleton Kennedy. Copy, ViW (11-0718); Draft in Andrew J. Donelson's hand, DLC (34). Agrees to serve as godfather to Andrew Jackson Kennedy, with James Barron as proxy at the christening; lauds the navy.	

	(published in the *United States' Telegraph,* July 16); relates that he encouraged Henry Lee to write a biography of AJ because John H. Eaton had shown little interest in revising his.	
July 18	From Thomas Paine Taul. ALS, DLC (34). States that Jacob C. Isacks can corroborate AJ's statement re the "corrupt bargain."	
July 18	*Rachel Jackson to Elizabeth Courts Love Watson.*	367
July 20	To George Walker Call (enclosures: AJ to the Public, July 18; Statement of Philip Pipkin, April 16; General Order of Jan 22, 1815; Robert Butler's order for court-martial, Nov 21, 1814, DLC-64). ALS draft, DLC (34). Sends documents on the "corrupt bargain" and the execution of the six militiamen; refers Call to his April 26, 1824, letter to Littleton H. Coleman and his Senate votes for his views on the tariff and internal improvements.	
July 20	From Samuel Swartwout. ALS, DLC (34). Praises AJ's response to opposition attacks and denounces the administration.	
July 21	From John Hartwell Marable. ALS, DLC (34). Introduces John Hanna.	
July 22	From William Owens. ALS, DLC (34). Requests information on the 1815 execution of John Harris and other militiamen for use in his Kentucky congressional campaign.	
July 23	To William Berkeley Lewis. ALS, NNPM (11-0766). Requests that he meet the Jacksons at Robertson Springs and that he deliver a message to Thomas Sewell King, who has loaned AJ a carriage for the trip.	
July 24	Account with Rucker & Powell for medicines for Andrew Jackson Hutchings's slaves. DS in John Coffee's hand, A-Ar (11-0768). Runs to March 13, 1828.	
July 26	*To William Owens.*	369
July 27	To John Henry Eaton. ALS with endorsement by William B. Lewis noting that he wrote the essay on the execution of the six militia men for the Nashville Committee, and Copy, NN (11-0772, -0776). Sends material for use in discussing the mutiny of Philip Pipkin's regiment in the Creek War.	
[July 27]	To William Berkeley Lewis (enclosure: AJ to John H. Eaton, July 27). ALS and Copy, NN (11-0774). Transmits letter.	
July 28	From Thomas Henderson. ALS, DLC (34). Discusses Ohio politics and the reaction to AJ's July 18 letter on the "corrupt bargain"; reports that Henry Clay and Charles Hammond have had a private four-hour meeting.	
July 29	From Peter Bertrand. ALS, DLC (34). Sends bill for subscription to the *Florence Gazette* (Alabama), 1824–26.	
July 30	*To John Coffee.*	372
[July?]	From "Fellow Citizen" (pseudonym). Printed, Lexington *Kentucky Reporter,* Aug 4 (mAJs). Critiques AJ's letter of July 18, To the Public.	
[cJuly 1827 –June 1828]	Rachel Jackson to Henry Lee. Copy, DLC (11-1155). Thanks Lee for his letter to AJ (not found) and sends lock of AJ's hair.	
Aug 4	From Maunsel White. ALS, DLC (34). Reports on the reaction in Louisiana to Henry Clay's denial of the "corrupt bargain" charge and AJ's July 18 rejoinder.	

(34). Regrets inability to attend dinner in Frankfort, Kentucky, and discusses Jacksonian success in recent Kentucky elections.

Donelson to answer the letter, DLC (34). Reports on AJ's candidacy in Kentucky and relays political news from Virginia and North Carolina.

Oct 12   From Isaac McKeever. ALS, DLC (34). Details his patrol of the northeastern fisheries aboard the schooner *Shark*.

Oct 15   From Arthur Peronneau Hayne. ALS, DLC (34). States that he will attend the January 8, 1828, celebration in New Orleans.

Oct 24   Account with Buchanan & Sproule for rope for Andrew Jackson Hutchings's farm. ADS, A-Ar (11-0893). Runs to April 17, 1828.

Oct 25   Receipt from Josiah Nichol for $242.58 for Andrew Jackson Hutchings's November 21, 1826, account. ADS, A-Ar (11-0895).

Oct 26   Account of Josiah Nichol with Andrew Jackson Hutchings for general merchandise and cash advances. ADS, THi (11-0897). Paid by AJ, December 29, 1828.

[Oct 28]   From John Blount. LS by proxy (Stephen Richards), DLC (58, 11-0903). Requests AJ's aid in securing silver medal due from the government but withheld by Florida Governor William P. Duval.

Nov 1   From Carter Beverley. ALS with AJ endorsement: "not answered," DLC (34). Reports on development of the "corrupt bargain" charge and on politics, particularly in Pennsylvania, Maryland, New York, and Virginia.

Nov 3   From John Randolph Grymes. ALS, DLC (35). Introduces Martin Gordon.

Nov 5   From Carter Beverley (enclosure: Beverley to AJ, Nov 1). ALS, DLC (34). Explains the publication regarding his conversations with AJ and relays political news of Ohio and Virginia.

Nov 5   From Richard Chester Langdon. ALS, DLC (34). Requests information on the execution of the six militiamen so that he can, under the pseudonym of "Mississippi," defend AJ from attacks in the *Natchez Ariel*.

Nov 6   From Thomas M. W. Young. ALS, DLC (34). Albany *Argus,* May 23, 1828. Presents a hat produced in his factory in New York.

Nov 7   To Samuel Houston. Photocopy of AD in Andrew J. Donelson's hand, Tx (11-0914). Invites Houston to dinner on November 10.

Nov 7   To John Overton. ALS, THi (11-0916). *THQ,* 6(1947):174. Announces his return from Alabama; invites Overton to dinner on November 10 (along with members of the Tennessee legislature) to discuss details of the upcoming trip to New Orleans.

Nov 8   Act appointing AJ et al. trustees of the University of Nashville. Printed, *Acts Passed at the Stated Session of the Seventeenth General Assembly of the State of Tennessee,* 1827 (Nashville, 1827), p. 42 (11-0918).

Nov 9   To Reuben McCarty. Photocopy of LS, TU (mAJs). Sends letter of recommendation for McCarty for surveyor general's office in Mississippi.

Nov 11   From Edward Livingston. ALS, DLC (72). Announces the success of the friends of "true republicanism" in New York state elections;

Sedgwick Springs, Nov 29). ALS, DLC (35). Forwards copies of letters and discusses sales of lands for Springs in West Tennessee.

Dec 1   To Henry Lee. ALS, TNJ (11-0941). Transmits letterbooks from July 21, 1812, to March 1813, and from July 11 to September 22, 1814.

Dec 1   To Sedgwick Springs. ALS copy, DLC (35). Encloses letter from John C. McLemore to AJ, November 27 (not found); commends McLemore's character and reports that McLemore has forwarded a check to settle an old debt.

Dec 3   From Jean Baptiste Labatut et al. LS and Copy fragment, DLC (35, 75, and 11-0944). As local committee of arrangements for January 8, 1828, celebration, request the time and manner of AJ's arrival in New Orleans.

Dec 3   Resolution by the Common Council of New York City, presented by Campbell P. White, giving AJ a gold medal commemorating the opening of the Erie Canal. ADS, NNMu (mAJs).

Dec 4   Resolutions of New York City citizens requesting that the city's Common Council secure a painting of the Battle of New Orleans and that the United States Congress do the same. Printed form with AJ endorsement, DLC (35).

Dec 5   To John Coffee. ALS, THi (11-0946). Bassett, 3:384 (extract). Discusses financial dealings of John W. Phillips, the recently discharged overseer at Andrew J. Hutchings's farm.

Dec 5   Account with Josiah Nichol for general merchandise. DS, Stanley F. Horn (11-0950). Runs to December 30, 1828.

Dec 6   To Jeremiah Goodwin. ALS copy, DLC (35). Declines offer of galoshes, since they will not arrive in time for New Orleans celebration.

Dec 6   To Edward Livingston. ALS, NjP (mAJs). Thanks him for news of New York state elections and claims that "espoionage" of the mail restrains him from discussing politics.

Dec 10   From Jean Baptiste Labatut et al. LS duplicate, DLC (35). Announce that the steamboat *Pocahontas* has been engaged to convey AJ's entourage from Nashville to New Orleans and that a committee will meet him in Natchez.

Dec 11   *From John Branch.*   403

Dec 13   Receipt from John W. Phillips for $22.50 for farm implements and the capture of the slave George for Andrew Jackson Hutchings. DS in James H. Weakley's hand, A-Ar (11-0958).

Dec 13   Receipt from John W. Phillips for $250 for wages as overseer at Andrew Jackson Hutchings's farm. DS in James H. Weakley's hand, THi (11-0403).

[cDec 14] Endorsement by Andrew Jackson et al. Printed, *National Banner and Nashville Whig*, Jan 5, 1828 (mAJs). Attest to the competence of George W. McGehee to conduct a school in Pulaski, Tennessee.

Dec 17   To John Coffee. ALS, THi (11-0960). Introduces Lucien J. Feemster.

Dec 17   To Henry Lee. ALS, DLC (35). Bassett, 3:385. Sends another of his letterbooks for Lee's biographical research.

Dec 17   To Maunsel White. ALS, NcGM (11-0963). States that he will soon ship his cotton crop.

Dec 18   To Jean Baptiste Labatut et al. AL draft, DLC (35). Outlines plans for his New Orleans trip.

Dec 18   To William Berkeley Lewis (enclosures: Caleb Atwater to AJ, Nov 30; Atwater to Lewis, Nov 30, NN). ALS, NN (11-0964). Forwards letters and details travel plans to New Orleans.

Dec 18   To James Ronaldson. LS in Andrew J. Donelson's hand, DLC (75). Reaffirms his support of the 1824 tariff; thanks Ronaldson for gifts sent to New Orleans.

Dec 19   *To William Berkeley Lewis.*   404

Dec 21   Account of John David Gaisser with Andrew Jackson Hutchings for blacksmithing. DS certified by Finch Scruggs, Dec 29, 1828, A-Ar (11-0969). Runs to May 21, 1829.

Dec 22   *To John Coffee.*   405

Dec 24   From Richard Keith Call (enclosure: Call to AJ, Dec 24). ALS, DLC (35). States that he has written Duff Green denying the Stephen Decatur-John W. Eppes incident; regrets inability to meet AJ in New Orleans.

Dec 24   From Richard Keith Call. ALS, DLC (35). Encloses invitation (not found) to the Jacksons for a ball in Tallahassee on January 8, 1828.

Dec 24   From William Berkeley Lewis. ALS with undated AJ endorsement: "I salute you fellow citizens, with my prayers for your prosperity & happiness & that our union & liberties may be perpetual," DLC (35). Reports that he has engaged the *Carroll* to depart for New Orleans on December 27 in case the *Pocahontas* does not arrive on schedule.

Dec 25   To William Berkeley Lewis. ALS, NNPM (11-0978). Discusses final arrangements for his departure for New Orleans.

Dec 26   Check to self for $400. Printed form with ms insertions signed by AJ, TxHSJM (11-0982).

[Dec 26]   To William Berkeley Lewis. ALS, NNPM (11-0984). Discusses final preparations for the trip to New Orleans.

Dec 27   To Stephen Simpson from "A Subscriber" (pseudonym for AJ). Printed, *Louisville Journal and Focus,* March 21, 1832 (11-0988). Attacks the reputation of Edward Coles, who had alleged that Thomas Jefferson questioned AJ's fitness for the presidency.

Dec 27   From Arthur Peronneau Hayne. ALS, DLC (35). Bassett, 3:386. Offers suggestions for AJ's speeches in New Orleans.

Dec 27   Receipt from Jesse Winborne for expenses incurred in recovery of Andrew Jackson Hutchings's runaway slave John (enclosures: Receipts from Chamberlain Townsend for $5 and Nathan McClendon for $.50, both December 27). DS in John Coffee's hand, A-Ar (11-0990).

Dec 28   From Absalom Morris (enclosure: John J. Steele to AJ, Dec 28). ALS, DLC (35). Transmits letter and other papers (not found) regarding internal improvements and domestic manufactures.

Dec 28   From John J. Steele. ALS, DLC (35). Warns that doubt about AJ's support for the tariff is costing him support in Pennsylvania and asks for a statement favoring protection.

1827   From Henry Garrard. DS, A-Ar (11-0451). Sends tax receipts for
               AJ's and Andrew J. Hutchings's property in Lauderdale County,
               Alabama.
[1827]   From Unknown. AL, DLC (35). Expresses support of AJ for the
               presidency; complains about the tariff system and warns that it
               could break up the union.
[1827]   Draft of response to charges by Charles Hammond that AJ padded
               his expense accounts while in the army. AD fragment, DLC (59).
[c1827]   To Andrew Jackson, Jr. Extract, American Art Association catalog,
               April 8, 1926, Item 271 (11-0453). Informs him that a horse is
               being sent for him to ride to the Hermitage for dinner with Philip
               Lindsley.
[c1827]   From John W. James et al. AD, DLC (35). Send resolutions of a
               Boston citizens' committee, adopted on November 26, endorsing AJ
               for president.
[c1827   Memorandum by "A Farmer" (AJ pseudonym). AD, DLC (36).
   –1828]   Article for publication, berating Henry Clay as a "poltroon," the
               architect of the "H." letter, the Southard affair, and the attacks on
               Rachel Jackson.

1828

Jan 1   Account with John & Thomas Simpson for Andrew Jackson
               Hutchings's overseer John W. Phillips. ADS by John Spalding, A-Ar
               (11-1004). Runs to February 27.
Jan 3   From Thomas Buck Reed (enclosure: Reed to AJ, Jan 4). LS, DLC
               (35). Reports arrangements for AJ's reception in Natchez.
Jan 4   From Thomas Buck Reed. Printed, Natchez *Statesman & Gazette,*
               Jan 10 (mAJs, 11-1006). Welcomes AJ to Natchez.
Jan 4   To Thomas Buck Reed. AD draft, DLC (35). Natchez *Statesman &
               Gazette,* Jan 10. Acknowledges welcome.
Jan 4   From Eleazar Wheelock Ripley. AD, DLC (35). Natchez *Statesman
               & Gazette,* Jan 24. On behalf of New Orleans arrangements
               committee, welcomes AJ.
Jan 4   To Eleazar Wheelock Ripley. Printed, Natchez *Statesman &
               Gazette,* Jan 24 (mAJs, 11-1010). Acknowledges welcome.
Jan 4   From George McCook. ALS, DLC (35). Requests for Ohio voters a
               clarification of AJ's views on the tariff and internal improvements.
Jan 4   From Charles Pendleton Tutt. ALS, DLC (35). Reports on Loudoun
               County, Virginia, political meetings and states that AJ's supporters
               there oppose the tariff but favor internal improvements.
Jan 4   Toast at public dinner in Natchez: "David Holmes, late Governor
               of Mississippi. His fearless energy did much for the defence of this
               country, during the late War." Printed, Natchez *Statesman &
               Gazette,* Jan 10 (mAJs, 11-1005).
[cJan 4]   Memorandum of meeting at Natchez with New Orleans committee.
               AD, DLC (58).
Jan 5   From John Henry Eaton. ALS, DLC (72). Expresses concern for
               AJ's safety and urges that he not reply to Henry Clay's recent
               address to the public on the "corrupt bargain."

Jan 5   From Philip Hicky et al. ALS, DLC (35). Welcome AJ to Baton
             Rouge and invite him to a dinner on his return from New Orleans.
[Jan 5]   To [Philip Hicky et al.]. Draft in AJ Donelson's hand, DLC (35).
             Declines dinner invitation.
[Jan 8]   From Auguste G. V. Davezac. Printed, Natchez *Statesman &*
             Gazette, Jan 24 (mAJs, 11-1011). Praises AJ's services to the country.
[Jan 8]   To Auguste G. V. Davezac. Printed, Natchez *Statesman & Gazette,*
             Jan 24 (mAJs, 11-1014). Expresses appreciation for reception.
Jan 8   From Lucius C. Duncan (enclosure: Duncan to AJ, Jan 9). ALS,
             DLC (35). Relays greetings of the Philadelphia Jackson Club.
[Jan 8]   From John Randolph Grymes. Printed, Natchez *Statesman &*
             Gazette, Jan 24 (mAJs, 11-1020). Welcomes AJ to New Orleans.
[Jan 8]   To John Randolph Grymes. AD drafts, DLC (36). Natchez
             Statesman & Gazette, Jan 24. Thanks him for welcome and
             reminisces about the War of 1812.
Jan 8   From James Alexander Hamilton, Saul Alley, and Thaddeus Phelps.
             AN in AJ Donelson's hand, DLC (33, 11-1042). Natchez *Statesman*
             & Gazette, Jan 24. Convey congratulations from New York and
             advocate AJ's election as president.
[Jan 8]   *To James Alexander Hamilton, Saul Alley, and Thaddeus*
             Phelps.   407
[Jan 8]   From Henry Johnson (1783–1864). Printed, Natchez *Statesman &*
             Gazette, Jan 24 (mAJs, 11-1045). Welcomes AJ to Louisiana.
[Jan 8]   To Henry Johnson (1783–1864). Printed, Natchez *Statesman &*
             Gazette, Jan 24 (mAJs, 11-1046). Expresses appreciation for the
             governor's welcome.
[Jan 8]   From John Harris Johnston. AD, DLC (59, 11-1048). Natchez
             Statesman & Gazette, Jan 24. Welcomes AJ to New Orleans and
             invites him to meet with the legislature and the governor.
[Jan 8]   From Jean Baptiste Plauché. Printed, *Mobile Daily Register,* Jan 31
             (mAJs). On behalf of veterans, welcomes AJ to New Orleans.
[Jan 8]   To Jean Baptiste Plauché. Printed, *Mobile Daily Register,* Jan 31
             (mAJs). Acknowledges welcome.
[Jan 8]   To Antonio de Sedilla. AD draft and draft in Henry Lee's hand,
             DLC (36, 20, 11-1017). Natchez *Statesman & Gazette,* Jan 24.
             Thanks him for welcome (not found) and blessing.
[Jan 8]   Toast at public dinner in New Orleans: "*Mr. Bernard Marigny,* the
             president of the day." Printed, *Mobile Daily Register,* Jan 24
             (mAJs).
[Jan 8]   Toast at public dinner in New Orleans: "*The State of Louisiana,*
             distinguished alike for valor, patriotism, and fidelity." Printed,
             Mobile Daily Register, Jan 24 (mAJs).
[Jan 9]   From Lucius C. Duncan. Printed, Natchez *Statesman & Gazette,*
             Feb 7 (mAJs). On behalf of Jackson Club of Philadelphia, praises
             AJ's services to country.
[Jan 9]   To Lucius C. Duncan. Printed, Natchez *Statesman & Gazette,* Feb
             7 (mAJs). Expresses appreciation for address.
[Jan 9]   From Robert John Walker. Printed, Natchez *Statesman & Gazette,*
             Feb 7 (mAJs). Welcomes Jackson on behalf of Natchez, Mississippi,
             delegation.

[Jan 9]   To Robert John Walker. AD draft in Henry Lee's hand, DLC (36).
            Natchez *Statesman & Gazette,* Feb 7. Thanks him for his greetings.
Jan 10   To Dominique [You]. Printed, New Orleans *Bee,* Jan 14 (11-1054).
            Expresses regret that he could not meet with You's company during
            the celebration.
Jan 10   From Charles Laveaux. ALS, DLC (35). Requests aid in recovering
            his position as assistant engineer in the army.
Jan 10   Invoice for jewelry purchased for Rachel Jackson in New Orleans
            from Henry Harland, receipted by John Bliss. Abstracts, American
            Art Association Catalog (April 8, 1926), Item 350 (11-1051),
            Forest H. Sweet Catalog, (c1930), (11-1052).
[Jan 11]   Toast at public dinner in New Orleans: *"The Governor and
            legislature of Louisiana*—To their liberality and courtesy I am
            indebted for the happiness of my visit to this state." Printed,
            Natchez *Statesman & Gazette,* Feb 7 (mAJs).
Jan 12   *To Edward Livingston.*   409
[Jan 12]   Toast at public dinner in New Orleans: *"The ladies of this fair and
            flourishing city*—that arm must be palsied which would not rise in
            defense of so much grace and loveliness." Printed, Natchez
            Statesman & Gazette, Feb 7 (mAJs).
[Jan 12]   Toast at public dinner in New Orleans: *"Louisiana*—her sons are
            brave and faithful." Printed, Natchez *Statesman & Gazette,* Feb 7
            (mAJs).
Jan 13   Henry Johnson (1783–1864) to Rachel Jackson. Printed, *Knoxville
            Register,* March 26 (11-1057). Offers her the furniture used by AJ
            during his recent visit to New Orleans.
Jan 13   Rachel Jackson to Henry Johnson (1783–1864). Printed, *Knoxville
            Register,* March 26 (11-1058). Accepts gift.
Jan 14   Receipt from Jesse Winborne for $159 for three mules for Andrew
            Jackson Hutchings's farm. DS in John Coffee's hand also signed by
            James H. Weakley, A-Ar (11-1059).
Jan 15   Receipt from John W. Byrn for $60 for a mule for Andrew Jackson
            Hutchings's farm. DS in John Coffee's hand, A-Ar (11-1061).
Jan 15   Memorandum of Enoch P. Connell and Allen Mathis re the
            proportion of slaves received by Robert Minns Burton and John
            McGregor in the division of the estate of William Donelson (1758–
            1820). ADS in Connell's hand, also signed by Mathis with AN by
            AJ, DLC (35).
Jan 16   From Edward Livingston. ALS, DLC (72). Reports on January 8
            celebrations in the northeast and states that some of his correspon-
            dence with AJ has been intercepted.
Jan 19   Account with John Coffee for lumber for Andrew Jackson
            Hutchings's farm. ADS, A-Ar (11-1063). Runs to December 16.
Jan 20   From the Mississippi General Assembly. ADS, DLC (mAJs). *Journal
            of the Senate of Mississippi . . . ,* 11th sess. (1828), pp. 59–60.
            Welcomes AJ to Mississippi.
Jan 20   To the Mississippi General Assembly. Printed, *Journal of the Senate
            of Mississippi . . . ,* 11th sess. (1828), p. 60 (11-1065). Expresses
            appreciation.
Jan 20   From Carter Beverley. ALS, DLC (35). Complains that Henry Lee's

pamphlet, *A Vindication of the Character and Public Services of Andrew Jackson,* first published under the pseudonym "Jefferson" in the *Nashville Republican,* contains attacks upon his character.

Jan 21   To Citizens of Memphis. Printed, *Memphis Advocate and Western-District Intelligencer,* Jan 26 (mAJs). Declines invitation since it would delay the *Pocahontas,* conveying his party to Nashville from New Orleans.

Jan 21   *From Robert Desha.*   411

Jan 21   From John Henry Eaton. ALS, DLC (35). Bassett, 3:389–90. Urges AJ to let friends respond to Henry Clay's publication on the "corrupt bargain"; asks for a copy of James Monroe's letter to John C. Calhoun, September 9, 1818, on the Seminole invasion.

Jan 22   From Susan Wheeler Decatur. Printed, Frankfort *Argus of Western America,* Aug 27 (mAJs, 11-1068). Denies that Stephen Decatur, her late husband, harbored ill feeling for AJ.

Jan 26   From Maunsel White (enclosure: Receipt for Andrew J. Hutchings's cotton, Jan 23). ALS, THi (11-1075). Reports sale of Hutchings's cotton.

Jan 27   From John Lyde Wilson. ALS, DLC (72). Sends a newspaper copy of AJ to William C. C. Claiborne, November 12, 1806, warning of activities possibly associated with Aaron Burr, and asks AJ to confirm that he wrote the letter.

Jan 29   From Robert Elliott. ALS, DLC (35). Sends prospectus of *The Independent Whig,* reminiscences about army career, and assures AJ of Pennsylvania's political support.

Jan 29   From William Emmons (enclosure: Bill, Jan 29). ALS, DLC (35). Transmits two sets of Richard Emmons, *The Fredoniad, or Independence Preserved: An Epick Poem on the Late War of 1812* (4 vols.; Boston, 1827), to which AJ subscribed.

Jan 29   Invoice from William C. Emmit for $21.00 subscription for dinner at Nashville Inn for the officers and owners of the *Pocahontas.* ADS, DLC (35). With receipt for payment, April 21.

Jan 29   Bill from William Emmons for $10 for two sets of *The Fredoniad, or Independence Preserved.* Printed form with ms insertions, DLC (35).

Jan 29   Promissory note to Elijah Williams for $50. ADS, DLC (35). With receipt of James T. Carruth for payment, May 26.

Jan 30   From James Brown Ray. Printed, Dorothy Riker and Gayle Thornbrough, eds., *Messages and Papers Relating to the Administration of James Brown Ray, Governor of Indiana, 1825–1831,* in *Indiana Historical Collections,* 34(1954):319–28 (11-1078). Transmits resolutions of the Indiana legislature asking for a statement of AJ's position on the American system, particularly internal improvements.

Jan   From "Truth's Advocate" (pseudonym). Printed, *Truth's Advocate,* Jan. (mAJs). Inquires about AJ's views on the tariff and internal improvements, since there is much uncertainty about his position.

Feb 1   To William Paulding. Printed, Albany *Argus,* May 23 (mAJs, 11-1088). Thanks Paulding, the mayor of New York, for the Erie

[cFeb 20–24] To John Coffee.   418

Feb 20   From "Fellow Citizen" (pseudonym). Printed, Lexington *Kentucky*
              Reporter, Feb 20 (mAJs). Contends that AJ was put forward as a
              presidential candidate in 1824 to injure William H. Crawford and
              to elect John Quincy Adams.

Feb 21   To Edward Livingston. ALS, NjP (mAJs). Thanks him for the
              proceedings of the January 8 celebration in Washington.

Feb 21   From Robert Butler. ALS matched fragments, DLC (75). Discusses
              business of James R. Donelson and sends money to clear up
              Donelson's debt to Jackson.

Feb 22   From John Milton Goodenow. ALS, THer (11-1128). Presents copy
              of his *Historical Sketches of the Principles and Maxims of Ameri-*
              can Jurisprudence [Steubenville, Ohio, 1819].

Feb 22   *From Hugh Lawson White.*   420
Feb 23   *To Nathaniel W. Williams.*   421

Feb 24   From Robert Cravens. LS, DLC (35). Asks for rebuttal of a report
              that AJ, when in Congress, voted against a resolution approving of
              George Washington's administration.

Feb 25   From Henry Post, Jr. (enclosure: Stephen Simpson to AJ, Feb 18).
              ALS, DLC (35). Discusses politics and the death of DeWitt Clinton.

Feb 25   Rachel Jackson to Hannah Israel Davenport. LS by proxy, PHi (11-
              1141). Discusses trip to New Orleans.

Feb 25   Receipt from Thomas Ivey for $31.25 for labor at the Hermitage.
              DS in AJ's hand, DLC (35).

Feb 25   Receipt from Peter Moseley to Thomas Ivey for $10.12 for bricks
              for chimney. ADS, DLC (35).

Feb 26   To John Coffee. ALS, THi (11-1145). Bassett, 3:392 (extract).
              Discusses settlement of his accounts with the Hutchings estate,
              donation of a lot in Florence to the Freemasons, and business and
              family matters.

Feb 26   To John Ellis Wool. LS by proxy, N (11-1149). Thanks him for
              pamphlet (not identified).

Feb 27   *From Nathaniel W. Williams.*   423

Feb 27   From "Fellow Citizen" (pseudonym). Printed, Lexington *Kentucky*
              Reporter, Feb 27 (mAJs). Continues discussion of AJ's "numerous
              crimes," with focus on the execution of the six militiamen.

Feb [28]   To James Brown Ray. Copy, TNJ (11-1130). Dorothy Riker and
              Gayle Thornbrough, eds., *Messages and Papers Relating to the*
              Administration of James Brown Ray, Governor of Indiana, 1825–
              1831, in *Indiana Historical Collections,* 34(1954):338–41. States
              that his views on internal improvements and the tariff are the same
              as they were in 1824.

Feb 28   Receipts from Joseph White Horton for $69.02 for Tennessee and
              Davidson County taxes for 1827 for AJ and Benjamin Clements.
              Printed forms with ms insertions, DLC (35).

Feb 29   From Caleb Atwater. ALS, DLC (35). Bassett, 3:394 (extract).
              Discusses death of DeWitt Clinton and urges AJ to find government
              jobs for Clinton's sons.

Feb 29   Certification of the pedigree of the horse Orelio. Printed, *National*
              Banner and Nashville Whig, March 8 (mAJs).

Feb 29   Check to Josiah Nichol for $850. Abstract, Robert F. Batchelder
            Catalog 87 ([Nov 1992]), Item 201 (mAJs).
[Feb]   From Edward George Washington Butler. ALS fragment, DLC (75).
            Reports the death of his two infant daughters; discusses his plan to
            buy an interest in a Louisiana plantation; describes attempts to pay
            a judgment against his sister Caroline S. (Butler) Bell.
Feb   From *"Truth's Advocate"* (pseudonym). Printed, *Truth's Advocate,*
            Feb. (mAJs). Critiques AJ's treatment of Henry Clay in the presi-
            dential campaign and especially in his letters to Samuel Swartwout
            and Carter Beverley.
March 1   *From Thomas Stuart.*   424
[cMarch 1] Nathan Cross (to the Trustees of the University of Nashville).
            Copy, T (mAJs). As the only faculty member living on campus,
            complains that he has a disproportionate share of the work at the
            university.
March 2   From Hugh Lawson White. ALS, DLC (72). Bassett, 6:496 97.
            Discusses James Monroe's neutrality in the presidential contest and
            AJ's correspondence with Monroe during and immediately after the
            Seminole campaign.
March 3   *To William Berkeley Lewis.*   426
March 3   Check to self for $150. Photocopy of ADS, T (mAJs).
March 4   *From John Henry Eaton.*   427
March 4   From James Hamilton, Jr. ALS, DLC (35). Discusses the February
            11 congressional report on the six militiamen incident.
March 4   From William Mitchell et al. Printed, *Nashville Republican,* March
            25 (mAJs). Invite AJ to dinner honoring him in Murfreesboro,
            Tennessee.
March 5   To William Mitchell et al. Printed, *Nashville Republican,* March 25
            (mAJs). Accepts invitation.
March 6   To Hardy Murfree Cryer. ALS, THi (11-1160). Bassett, 3:395–96.
            Instructs Cryer on breeding AJ's mares.
March 6   From Wilson Lumpkin. ALS, DLC (35). Discusses the national
            political scene.
March 7   To John McLean (1785–1861). ALS, University of Leipzig (mAJs).
            Encloses letter for delivery to Senator Hugh Lawson White because
            of the unreliability of the postal service.
March 7   From Edward Livingston. ALS, DLC (72). Warns that a pamphlet,
            View of General Jackson's Domestic Relations in Reference to
            His Fitness for the Presidency, has been printed in Washington
            and is being franked around the country; urges restraint in respond-
            ing to it.
March 8   *To William Berkeley Lewis.*   432
March 10   From William Emmons. ALS, DLC (35). Acknowledges payment
            for *The Fredoniad, or Independence Preserved*; complains about
            the employment of foreigners and blacks as messengers in federal
            offices in Washington and about the treatment accorded those with
            claims against the federal government.
March 10   From Richard Mentor Johnson. ALS, DLC (35). *RegKyHi,*
            39(1941):269. Acknowledges receipt of letter for William Emmons
            (not found) and expresses confidence in AJ's election.

March 11   From Richard Keith Call. ALS, DLC (72). Praises Jackson's
            reception in Louisiana; discusses Clay's reply to the "corrupt
            bargain" charge, his hope to write on the subject, and other issues
            of the campaign; notes his dissatisfaction with a portrait of AJ
            by Ralph E. W. Earl.

March 12   From Arthur Peronneau Hayne. ALS, DLC (35). Reminisces on the
            recent New Orleans celebration, discusses the political effects of
            DeWitt Clinton's death, and transmits a copy of the first issue of
            the *Southern Review.*

March 12   From Richard C. Tunstall. ALS, DLC (35). Informs AJ of his
            election to membership in the Franklinian Debating Society of the
            College of William and Mary.

March 12   From "Fellow Citizen" (pseudonym). Printed, Lexington *Kentucky
            Reporter,* March 12 (mAJs). Discusses AJ's lack of respect for the
            laws of the country.

March 15   From Samuel Hervey Laughlin. Printed, *National Banner and
            Nashville Whig,* March 29 (11-1169). Welcomes AJ to public
            dinner in Murfreesboro.

March 15   To Samuel Hervey Laughlin. Printed, *National Banner and
            Nashville Whig,* March 29 (11-1171). Expresses appreciation for
            honor.

March 15   Toast at Murfreesboro public dinner: "The memory of De Wit
            Clinton, the patriot, the philanthropist, and the distinguished
            statesman: In his death New-York has lost one of her most useful
            sons, and the nation one of its brightest ornaments." Printed,
            Jackson Gazette (Tenn.), March 29 (11-1167).

[cMarch 15] To John Henry Eaton. ALS, DLC (11-1151). Asks him to ascertain
            who—Edmund P. Gaines or Winfield Scott—will succeed Jacob J.
            Brown as commanding general of the U.S. Army.

March 17   To Benjamin Clements. ALS, THi (11-1173). Discusses payment of
            taxes on Davidson County lands.

March 17   Memorandum of Samuel Houston and Andrew Jackson Donelson
            on Duff Green's statements regarding support of the Jacksonians
            for John C. Calhoun as opposed to DeWitt Clinton for vice-
            president. ADS in Donelson's and Houston's hands, DLC (35).

March 20   Carter Beverley to Samuel Houston. ALS, DLC (72). Acknowledges
            return of enclosures transmitted to AJ on January 20; protests AJ's
            interpretation of his motives and declares his good faith in all
            dealings with AJ.

March 22   To Hardy Murfree Cryer. ALS, THi (11-1184). Bassett, 3:396
            (extract). Discusses horse breeding; sends letter (not found) to be
            forwarded to Robert Desha through Jesse Haynie.

March 22   From John Donelson (1787–1840; enclosure: Nelson P. Jones to
            Donelson, Feb 15). ALS, DLC (35). Discusses personal business and
            family news.

March 26   From "Fellow Citizen" (pseudonym). Printed, Lexington *Kentucky*

Reporter, March 26 (mAJs). Defends his critiques of the career of the military chieftain.

[March]   To James Alexander Hamilton. Extract, Hamilton, *Reminiscences of James A. Hamilton* (New York, 1869), p. 75 (11–1153). Laments death of DeWitt Clinton.

[March]   From Jesse Miller. Printed, *Nashville Republican,* March 25 (mAJs). Denies remarking that AJ reacted violently to Henry Clay's December 1827 publication rebutting the corrupt bargain.

[cMarch–   Draft of speech. AD, DLC (36). Expresses thanks for welcome and
July]   hopes that the public will ignore attacks on his character.

April 1   To [William] Brand. Extract, Carnegie Book Shop Catalog 249 (1960), Item 125 (11-1199). Introduces Major McCorry.

April 1   To John Randolph. Abstract, Anderson Galleries Catalog 2096 (1926), Item 391 (11-1200). Introduces William B. Lewis.

April 1   From Henry Baldwin. ALS, DLC (35). Introduces his son Henry, Jr., who considers settling in Nashville.

April 2   Samuel Hervey Laughlin to Samuel Houston (forwarded to AJ). ALS, DLC (72). Describes an administration meeting in Rutherford County and urges that Joel Parrish, Jr., not challenge James L. Armstrong to a duel.

April 3   Deposition of [George Washington Campbell] stating that Thomas Jefferson saw Jackson's letter to Campbell of January 15, 1807 (*Jackson,* 2:147–50), and copied the portions relating to Aaron Burr. AD, NjMoHP (11-1202).

April 8   From William Roberdeau Swift. ALS matched fragments, DLC (35, 36). Bassett, 3:397–98 (extract). Sends a barrel of wine and discusses the election campaign in New York, New Jersey, and North Carolina.

April 9   To Gilbert du Motier, Marquis de Lafayette. LS in Andrew J. Donelson's hand, THer (11-1208). Introduces John F. Schermerhorn.

April 11   John Coffee's statement of account with AJ as guardian of Andrew J. Hutchings. ADS, A-Ar (11-1210).

April 13   From John Coffee. ALS, THi (11-1211). Discusses Andrew J. Hutchings's accounts; gives family news and crop reports.

[cApril 13] Statement of AJ's account with the John Hutchings estate. AD in William Eastin's hand, endorsed by John Coffee, A-Ar (11-1197).

[April 14] To Stephen Simpson. ALS draft, DLC (35). Asks Simpson to relay thanks to Henry Post, Jr., for letter and to inform Post that AJ does not write on politics.

April 15   From James Knox Polk. ALS, DLC (35). Bassett, 6:499. Suggests that the reply to James B. Ray not emanate from AJ.

April 15   Rachel Jackson to Mrs. L. A. W. Douglas (enclosure: Harriet C. Berryhill to Douglas, April 15, NN). LS by proxy, NN (10-1235). Thanks her for a letter and seeds.

	April (mAJs). Discusses AJ's treatment of William Rabun in 1818, but one "link in a long chain of flagrant abuses."
May 1	From John Coffee. ALS, THi (11-1226). Discusses payment from Anthony Winston (1782–1839) to AJ for the Big Spring farm in Franklin County, Alabama, and AJ's account with the Hutchings estate.
May 1	From Eleazar Wheelock Ripley. ALS, DLC (35). Introduces A. D. Weld, Jr., and discusses New Orleans city elections.
May 3	*To James Knox Polk.* 451
May 4	To Auguste G. V. Davezac. ALS, NjP (mAJs). Acknowledges Davezac's April 7 letter (not found); discusses Louisiana politics and opposition to Edward Livingston's reelection to Congress; complains about abuse of the franking privilege.
May 5	*To Hardy Murfree Cryer.* 452
May 5	From David Byrne. ALS, DLC (35). Sends two versions of an acrostic poem that he has written.
May 6	*To John Henry Eaton.* 453
May 6	To Abner Greenleaf. ALS, DLC (75). Thanks him for *Address Delivered at Jefferson Hall, Portsmouth, N.H., Jan. 8, 1828, Being the Thirteenth Anniversary, of Jackson's Victory at New Orleans* (Portsmouth, 1828); complains about the attacks on the Jacksons' marriage and the franking of slanderous pamphlets by members of Congress.
May 6	To Jonathan Harvey. ALS, NNPM (mAJs); Extract, Charles Hamilton Catalog (October 17, 1963), Item 138 (11–1240). Thanks him for copy of Abner Greenleaf's January 8 address.
May 7	From "Fellow Citizen" (pseudonym). Printed, Lexington *Kentucky Reporter,* May 7 (mAJs). Discusses the shortcomings of AJ's military career.
May 8	From Henry Lee (enclosure: Roll of the Grenadier Company, 79th Regiment, accounting for the killed and wounded for June 16 and 18, 1815, at Waterloo). ANS, DLC (35). Sends document.
May 11	To Hardy Murfree Cryer. ALS, THi (11-1241). Bassett, 3:401–402 (extract). Announces death of his mare, just returned from Cryer's.
May 12	*To Richard Keith Call.* 455
May 12	*To John Coffee.* 457
May 12	From Robert Allen et al. Printed, *Nashville Republican,* June 10 (mAJs, 11-1244). Invite him to July 4 celebration at Carthage, Tennessee.
May 12	From James Hervey Witherspoon et al. ALS, DLC (35). *Congressional Record,* 67th Cong., 2nd sess. (1922), p. 2. Invite AJ to a public dinner on July 4 at Lancaster, South Carolina.
[cMay 12]	Receipt from Anderson Cheatham for $45 for board and washing for Andrew Jackson Hutchings at summer session of the University of Nashville. ADS, A-Ar (12-0008).
[cMay 14]	From John Harris. Printed, *Kentucky Reporter,* May 21 (mAJs). Attacks AJ for the execution of his father, one of the six militiamen.
May 14	From "A Tennesseean" (James Loudon Armstrong). Printed, Lexington *Kentucky Reporter,* May 14 (mAJs). Reexamines the John Wood case.

with dateline in AJ's hand, DLC (35). Washington *United States' Telegraph,* Aug 2. Declines invitation to Salem, Indiana.

June 2   To William Roberdeau Swift. LS copy in Andrew J. Donelson's hand, DLC (35). Bassett, 3:408 (extract). Reports arrival of the barrel of wine and thanks him for his report of New York politics; laments the prominence of the William Morgan affair in politics.

June 2   To James Hervey Witherspoon et al. Photocopy of ALS, Lancaster Public Library, Lancaster, S.C. (12-0016); ALS draft, DLC (35); Copy, WHi (12-0018). Bassett, 3:409. Declines invitation to July 4 celebration in the Lancaster District, the site of his birth.

June 4   From William Alexander and William Lauderdale. LS by proxy, DLC (35). *Nashville Republican,* July 18. Invite AJ to a public dinner and ball on July 5 in Hartsville, Tennessee.

June 4   To William Alexander and William Lauderdale. ALS draft, DLC (35). *Nashville Republican,* July 18. Accepts invitation.

June 10   From Richard Gilliam Dunlap. ALS, DLC (35). Reports that the Knoxville *Enquirer* has accused AJ of misappropriating rations during the Creek War; details efforts to get testimony on the matter.

June 19   To John Andrew Graham. ALS draft, DLC (35). Thanks him for his *Memoirs of John Horne Tooke* and comments on death of DeWitt Clinton.

June 20   From Martin Gordon. ALS, DLC (35). Offers AJ a painting by a New Orleans artist of the steamboat procession at the recent January 8 celebration.

June 20   From Edward Livingston. ALS, DLC (72). Describes his reply to a query concerning his and AJ's votes against the 1796 resolution endorsing the sentiments of George Washington's address to Congress; states that he is working on a proposal for penal reform.

June 20   From Samuel McCutchon. ALS, DLC (35). Thanks AJ for offer to help his son Richard B. gain admission to the University of Nashville but reports that he has decided to keep him in Louisiana; sends fruit.

June 20   Account of Rachel Jackson with John Williams & Co. for fabric and apparel. ADS by L. D. Baker, DLC (36). Runs to January 1, 1829.

June 21   From Thomas Cadwalader. ALS, DLC (35). Bassett, 3:410–11. States that he is so accustomed to Philadelphia that he cannot relocate to an area near the Hermitage; invites the Jacksons to visit him after the election.

June 21   To Richard Gilliam Dunlap. ALS copy, DLC (35). Details the shortcomings of Barclay McGhee as Creek War contractor and asks for details on how John Williams obtained Francis May's letters discussing the Dickinson duel.

June 22   To Henry Lee (enclosures: AJ to Martin Van Buren and to Levi Woodbury, June 23). Copy in Andrew J. Donelson's hand, DLC (35). Regrets that Lee's health requires him to leave Nashville and sends him letters of introduction.

Aug 28   To James Knox Polk. Facsimile of ALS, Superior Galleries Catalog (Nov 7, 1992), Item 465 (mAJs); Extract, Phillips Catalog (Jan 27, 1983), Item 57 (12-0176). Acknowledges Polk's letter of August 26 (not found).

Aug 28   To James P. Stabler. ALS, DLC (12-0177). Acknowledges August 8 letter (not found) and agrees to subscribe to an unidentified work.

Aug 28   From Leonard Cassell McPhail. ALS, DLC (35). Sends a copy of his *Oration Delivered . . . in the City-Council Chamber, before the Jefferson and Franklin Associations of Young Men . . . July the 4th, 1828* (Baltimore, 1828).

Aug 28   Statement of John Coffee re AJ's relations with Aaron Burr. Printed, *United States' Telegraph, Extra,* Oct 11 (mAJs); Bassett, 3:429-31.

Aug 29   To Unknown. AL copy, DLC (35). Introduces James Somers.

Aug 29   From William Eastin. ALS and Copy, DLC (72). Frankfort *Argus of Western America,* Oct 22 (extract). Testifies that Isaac Shelby regretted his dispute with AJ at the 1818 Chickasaw Treaty.

Aug 29   From Robert J. Ward. ALS, DLC (35). Urges AJ to visit Kentucky to rally support in the wake of William T. Barry's defeat for the governorship.

Aug 30   From William L. Newton. ALS, DLC (35). Invites AJ to a dinner in Green County, Kentucky; requests a sword for his infant son, AJ's namesake.

[Sept 1]   *To Richard Mentor Johnson.*   501

Sept 2   Statement of Edward Ward re AJ's asking Aaron Burr about his "views and designs." Printed, *United States Telegraph, Extra,* October 11 (mAJs); Bassett, 3:432.

Sept 2   Check to self or bearer for $50. ADS, NjMoHP (12-0181).

Sept 3   *From Alfred Balch.*   503

Sept 3   From Robert Young Hayne. ALS, DLC (35). Bassett, 3:432-36. Discusses opposition to the tariff in South Carolina and denounces the administration's effort to gain political advantage from the issue.

Sept 4   From O[liver] Williams. ALS, DLC (35). Reports that Isaac Sebastian, who was living at AJ's house during Aaron Burr's visits, can give useful testimony regarding AJ's dealings with Burr and that William P. Anderson has gathered Burr letters with a view to destroy AJ.

Sept 4   Check to Jordan Uzzell for $33. Facsimile of ADS, Manuscript Society Sale Catalog (Feb 13, 1991), Item 33 (mAJs).

Sept 4   Receipt from Jordan Uzzell for $33. DS in AJ's hand, DLC (35).

Sept 5   From [George Poindexter]. Copy, Ms-Ar (12-0182). Discusses his health and election news from the East.

Sept 6   From Henry Bantz, Jr. ALS, DLC (35). Asks about the market for leather in Tennessee and discusses AJ's political support in and around Frederick County, Maryland.

Sept 6   Interrogatories to and deposition of AJ in the case, *William Brackin* v. *William Martin (1765–1846).* DS, T (mAJs); DS (interrogatories only) by Hadley & Craighead, DLC (35); AD draft (deposition), DLC (31).

Sept 6   Solomon Weathersbee Downs to Andrew Jackson Donelson. Copy in Benjamin F. Currey's hand, DLC (72). Testifies to Isaac Shelby's regard for AJ, including his behavior at the Chickasaw negotiations; discusses AJ's political prospects in Louisiana.

Sept 8   From James Knox Polk. ALS, Robert M. McBride (12-0190). *Polk Correspondence,* 1:196–98. Urges AJ not to reply publicly to his critics; states that he forwarded to John H. Eaton statements useful for the Nashville Committee's reply on AJ's alleged complicity in the Burr conspiracy.

Sept 8   Sampson Williams to [William Berkeley Lewis?]. Extract in Lewis's hand, DLC (35). Reports meeting with Isaac Shelby in 1818 at which Shelby praised AJ's actions at the Chickasaw treaty negotiations.

Sept 9   To William L. Newton. ALS copy, DLC (35). Declines invitation to visit Kentucky since it would likely be misconstrued as electioneering.

Sept 9   To Robert J. Ward. LS draft, DLC (35). Declines invitation to visit Kentucky.

Sept [10?]   From Henry Banks (enclosure: William B. Banks to Henry Banks, Aug 8). ALS, DLC (35). Transmits letter from his brother about the presidential campaign in Virginia; discusses his reply to charges that he has supported AJ chiefly to elect a person who would rule favorably on his claims against the government.

[cSept 11]   Draft of the Nashville Committee's response to accusations of Jackson's involvement in the Burr affair, with supporting documents. AD, TNJ (12–0063).

Sept 12   To Leonard Cassell McPhail. ALS copy, DLC (35). Thanks McPhail for sending a copy of his *Oration.*

Sept 13   To Ralph Eleazar Whitesides Earl. ALS, NjP (12-0194). Instructs Earl on distribution in Louisiana of copies of the September 12 *Nashville Republican,* which contains the Nashville Committee's reply to the Burr charges.

Sept 13   From William Berkeley Lewis. ALS, DLC (35). Sends letters (not found) from Martin Van Buren and Samuel D. Ingham advising against Jackson responding publicly to charges leveled against him by the opposition; forwards a copy of the September 12 *Nashville Republican.*

[Sept 13]   To William Berkeley Lewis.   504

Sept 14   From James Morgan Bradford. ALS, DLC (35). States that he has organized an association of Louisianians to settle near the mouth of the Columbia River and asks that AJ support the association after he becomes president.

Sept 14   From James Roane. ALS, DLC (35). Describes how Boyd McNairy and Wilkins Tannehill showed him AJ's bank book with the memorandum on slave trading.

Sept [14]   To William Berkeley Lewis.   504

Sept 15   From Robert Butler. ALS, NN (12-0198). Reports that he will send Duff Green a statement on the 1818 Chickasaw treaty negotiations; laments attacks on AJ's character but adds that the challenge of the presidency will compensate AJ for them.

Sept 15   William Berkeley Lewis to John Lyde Wilson. ALS, DLC (35).

	Sends copy of the Nashville Committee's publication on the Aaron Burr affair; suggests that the publication will not offend Burr's friends.
Sept 15	Inventory of the personal effects of Joseph Hughes. ADS in AJ's hand, also signed by Thomas Ivey, DLC (35).
Sept 16	To James Knox Polk. ALS, DLC (12-0202). *Polk Correspondence,* 1:200. Acknowledges Polk's endorsement of AJ's policy of silence towards his critics.
Sept 16	From John Speed Smith. ALS, DLC (35). Urges AJ to visit Kentucky before the election.
Sept 17	From Henry Lee. ALS, DLC (mAJs). Discusses AJ's prospects in New England.
Sept 17	From "Fellow Citizen" (pseudonym). Printed, Lexington *Kentucky Reporter,* Sept 17 (mAJs). Discusses AJ's tyrannical actions in New Orleans.
Sept 18	From Isaac Oliver. ALS, DLC (35). Reports on AJ's political support in Dinwiddie County, Virginia.
Sept 19	To Peter Moseley. Printed, Forest H. Sweet Catalog 49 (Nov 1937), Item 22 (12-0208). Announces that he must turn down Mr. Hill, whom Moseley had recommended as an overseer, because he has already employed Graves W. Steele; thanks Moseley for intelligence on Virginia politics.
Sept 19	From John P. Helfenstein. ALS, TNJ (12-0204). Reports on AJ's popularity in Ohio; discusses plan to manufacture Turkey stones.

Sept 20	From William James MacNeven. Printed form with ms insertions, DLC (35). Appeals for funds for the "Friends of Ireland in New-York."
Sept 20	Account of David Lowe with AJ, guardian of Andrew J. Hutchings, for leather and tar. DS in John Coffee's hand, also signed by James H. Weakley, A-Ar (12-0209). Runs to June 2, 1829.
Sept 21	From William Douglass (d. 1831). ALS, TNJ (12-0211). Reports on a public dinner in Louisville honoring William T. Barry.
Sept 22	From Jesse Bledsoe. ALS, DLC (35). Praises AJ and reports on political support in Kentucky.
Sept 23	From John Breathitt. ALS, TNJ (12-0214). Predicts that AJ will carry Kentucky, Indiana, Illinois, and Missouri.

Sept 24	From "Fellow Citizen" (pseudonym). Printed, Lexington *Kentucky Reporter.* Sept 24 (mAJs). Again criticizes AJ's violence.

Sept 25	From Harmon A. Hays (enclosure: Statement of Robert Smith and A. H. Wynne, n.d., DLC-59). ALS matched fragments, DLC (35, 72). Discusses the development of the Anderson controversy and his role in securing Francis Woodward's statement regarding William P. Anderson.
Sept 26	To William Berkeley Lewis (enclosure: James Shelby to AJ, Sept 19). ALS, NNPM (12-0217). Transmits letter for information of Lewis and John H. Eaton.

Sept 26   To John Speed Smith. ALS draft, DLC (35). Restates his
            determination not to campaign for the presidency.
Sept 26   From Hector Craig. ALS, DLC (35). Reports on Martin Van
            Buren's nomination for governor of New York and on state
            politics.
Sept 26   From L. J. M. ALS, DLC (35). Sends William Jenkins et al.,
            Address to the Catholic Voters of Baltimore (Baltimore, 1828), and
            assures AJ of the support of Baltimore Catholics.
Sept 26   Promissory note to Albert G. Ward for $130 due March 1, 1829.
            ADS, T (12-0219).
Sept 26   Statement of Benjamin Franklin Currey regarding the behavior of
            Thomas Gott during a visit to the Hermitage. ADS, DLC (72).
Sept 29   From David McMurtree. ALS, DLC (35). Reports that Huntingdon
            County, Pennsylvania, will vote for AJ; requests some Nashville
            newspapers.
Sept 30   From Henry Banks. ALS, DLC (35). Complains that Kentucky
            newspaper editors are refusing to publish his writings.
Sept 30   From Edward Patchell. ALS, DLC (35). Warns AJ of possible
            assassination attempt.
[cSept]   To William Berkeley Lewis. ALS, NNPM (12-0257). Bassett,
            3:407–408 (dated June 1828). Discusses collection of statements to
            counter charges of William P. Anderson and the Shelbys.
[cSept]   From Edmund Pendleton Gaines. ALS, DLC (12-0221). Discusses
            AJ's political strength in Ohio, New York, Kentucky, and
            Pennsylvania; describes the political contest as one between
            "aristocracy and *democracy."*
Oct 2   From Donelson Caffery. ALS, DLC (mAJs). Discusses Louisiana
            politics and the Burr affair and denounces AJ's enemies, particu-
            larly Boyd McNairy.
[Oct 2]   Motion by AJ at University of Nashville trustees meeting: "Re-
            solved that the President cause a plate for Batchelors of Arts to be
            engraved, for the use of this University." Copy, T (mAJs).
Oct 3   From James Alexander Hamilton. ALS, DLC (35). Announces that
            his brother William, of Illinois, will visit AJ, and that Edward
            Livingston is the legatee of Janet Livingston Montgomery; promises
            to send items to Edward Ward.
Oct 3   Account with Nichol & Co. for Rachel Jackson's clothing.
            Abstract, Forest H. Sweet Catalog, n.d. (12-0225).
Oct 4   From John Strode Barbour. ALS, DLC (35). States that he is
            sending a Virginia newspaper containing a piece he wrote refuting
            allegations on the Burr conspiracy.
Oct 4   From Finis Ewing. ALS, DLC (35). Reports on Jacksonian victories
            in Missouri state elections.
Oct 4   *From Hugh Lawson White.*   510
Oct 6   From John M. Davis. ALS, DLC (35). Predicts AJ's victory in
            Pennsylvania and invites him to stop in Washington and Fayette
            counties en route to Washington.
Oct 6   From James Shelby. ALS with AJ endorsement calling Leslie Combs
            a "pimp" and indicating a desire to "cowhide" him, DLC (72).
            Lexington *Kentucky Reporter,* Oct 29. Sends by Leslie Combs a

duplicate of his September 19 letter discussing Isaac Shelby and the Chickasaw Treaty.

Oct 8   From Spencer Darwin Pettis. ALS, DLC (35). Discusses AJ's certain victory in Missouri and his prospects in other states.

Oct 8   From "Fellow Citizen" (pseudonym). Printed, Lexington *Kentucky Reporter,* Oct 8 (mAJs). Discusses the John Harris case.

Oct 9   From John W. Thompson. ALS, DLC (35). Asks for appointment as postmaster of New York City upon AJ's election.

Oct 10   From John Fleming. ALS, DLC (35). Denounces the Adams administration's attitude towards immigrants, especially the navy's plan to exclude foreigners and naturalized citizens from service; suggests that the post office is thoroughly corrupt.

Oct 11   William Berkeley Lewis to Amos Kendall. ALS copy, DLC (72); ALS draft, NN (mAJs). Gives account of interview between Leslie Combs and AJ.

Oct 15   To William Berkeley Lewis. ALS, NN (12-0230). Bassett, 3:438 (extract). Furnishes more information on the undated letter regarding the Burr affair published by Boyd McNairy; asks Lewis to secure a sword for William L. Newton's son, Andrew Jackson's namesake.

Oct 17   To Hugh Lawson White. Extract, Heiskell (2nd edition), 1:655 (12-0235). Thanks him for advice and friendship.

Oct 18   From James Ewell. ALS, DLC (35). Asks for a $600 loan to repay money borrowed to publish his *Medical Companion, or Family Physician,* 7th ed. (Washington, 1827), dedicated to AJ in August 1827.

Oct 19   To James Ewell. ALS, ICN (12-0236); LS copy, DLC (35). Bassett, 3:439–40. Regrets that his financial situation precludes a loan.

Oct 19   To William Berkeley Lewis (enclosure: James A. Hamilton to Lewis, Oct 3). ALS, NN (12-0237). Reports election victory in Philadelphia and orders Lewis to deny in the *Nashville Republican* William P. Anderson's claim that in 1808 Patton Anderson paid over to AJ money he had received from Aaron Burr.

Oct 20   From Henry Hipple. ALS, DLC (35). Gives Ohio election news and claims that during the past two years he has written over 500 letters on AJ's behalf.

Oct 20   From L. P. ALS, DLC (35). Credits AJ's Philadelphia majority to efforts of Charles Stewart and James Ronaldson.

Oct 20   From Thomas Jefferson Randolph. ALS, DLC (35). Introduces Mr. Wills, who seeks subscribers for Randolph's edition of the *Writings of Thomas Jefferson* (Charlottesville, 1829).

Oct 20   From Caleb Stark. ALS, DLC (35). Praises AJ and reminisces about his father, John Stark, who, like AJ, faced constant attacks from his political enemies.

Nov 12   To George T. Lindley. ALS copy, DLC (35). Sends him $5 in response to a request for assistance, and returns Lindley's certificate of good character by John Quincy Adams.

Nov 12   *From Duff Green.*   531

Nov 12   From Benjamin Chew Howard. ALS, DLC (36). Reports on the presidential election in the Baltimore area.

[cNov 12]   From William Preston Anderson. Printed, Lexington *Kentucky Reporter*, Nov 12 (mAJs). Writes, in an open letter, that AJ is ruled by ambition and love of money, that he is totally deficient of principle.

Nov 13   To Robert Johnstone Chester. ALS, THi (12-0265). Introduces Mr. Fleming of Virginia.

Nov 13   From Robert Coleman Foster & Son. ALS, also signed by Thomas Foster, Nov 24, DLC (35). Transmits account for rope, linen, and twine.

Nov 14   To James Barron. ALS, ViW (12-0267). Introduces Thomas Petway, a navy midshipman.

Nov 14   From Thomas Chilton. ALS, DLC (35). Reports on AJ's victory in Kentucky.

Nov 14   From Thomas D. Davis. ALS, DLC (35). *North Carolina Historical Review*, 14(1937):364–65. Restates his offer to drive AJ to Washington in a "Stage Coach with six elegant greys."

Nov 14   From William Field. ALS, DLC (35). Reports election returns from Kentucky, Ohio, Indiana, and Pennsylvania; invites AJ to a public celebration in Louisville en route to Washington.

[cNov 14]   To William Berkeley Lewis. ALS, NNPM (12-0270). Discusses funds for Benjamin F. Currey and James Jackson's statements regarding the Chickasaw treaty.

Nov 15   From Leslie Combs. Printed, *A Reply to General Jackson's Letter of 31st Oct., 1828* (Nashville, 1828, 12-0269). Expresses, in an open letter, resentment at AJ's personal attack upon him in the letter of October 31 to Allen A. Hall and John Fitzgerald.

Nov 15   From James Hamilton, Jr. ALS, DLC (35). Sends copy of his *Speech on the Operation of the Tariff on the Interests of the South. . .* (Charleston, 1828), stating his opposition to the tariff and outlining the doctrine of nullification.

Nov 15   From Arthur Peronneau Hayne. ALS, DLC (35). Bassett, 3:442–44 (extract). Reports the death of Joseph Woodruff and describes that of Thomas Pinckney; informs AJ that Pinckney was the first to recommend AJ's commission in the regular army; announces AJ's victory in South Carolina and his own election to the state legislature.

Nov 15   From David Corbin Ker. ALS, DLC (35). Rejoices in AJ's victory and suggests the purge of Jackson's opponents, particularly Beverly Chew, from federal posts in Louisiana.

Nov 15   From Jean Baptiste Plauché. ALS (in French), DLC (35). Congratulates AJ on his victory in Louisiana and particularly commends the efforts of Bernard Marigny in the campaign.

Nov 15   From James Shannon. ALS, DLC (35). Corrects information previously sent concerning Henry Clay's 1824 visit to Isaac Shelby;

reports on the exchange in print between himself and Charles S. Todd and on the public contempt Leslie Combs has earned by his campaign against AJ.

Nov 15   From James Workman et al. LS, DLC (35). Announce victory in New Orleans and congratulate AJ on his election.

Nov 16   *To Thomas Cadwalader.*   532

Nov 16   From Henry Baldwin. ALS, DLC (35). Announces AJ's victory in Pennsylvania and Ohio; proposes to send the steamboat *Pennsylvania* to bring AJ up the Ohio River on his way to Washington.

Nov 16   From Martin Van Buren. ALS, DLC (12-0272). Reports on AJ's victory in New York.

Nov 17   To Finis Ewing. ALS draft, DLC (35); Facsimile of ALS (extract), Charles Hamilton Catalog 29 (Sept 1968), Item 146 (12-0276); Typed copy, The Forbes Magazine Collection (12-0275). Declares that the election has vindicated him and thanks Ewing for his support.

Nov 17   From William Taylor Barry et al. (enclosure: Resolutions of citizens of Fayette County, Kentucky, Nov 18). ALS, DLC (35). Congratulate AJ on his election and invite him to visit Lexington on his way to Washington.

[Nov 18]   From Patrick G. C. Nagle. ALS, DLC (72). Offers to make AJ a pair of waterproof boots.

Nov 19   From David Coons. ALS, DLC (72). *Cincinnati Commercial,* Jan 8, 1881. Warns AJ of possible assassination attempt should he pass through Harpers Ferry, Virginia, on his way to Washington.

Nov 19   *From Amos Kendall.*   533

Nov 20   From Leslie Combs. Printed, *A Reply to General Andrew Jackson's Letter of the 31st Oct., 1828* (Nashville, 1828, 12-0279). Defends his behavior during his visit to the Hermitage to discuss the 1818 Chickasaw treaty.

Nov 20   *From Felix Grundy.*   534

Nov 20   From George Newell. ALS, DLC (72). Asks for commission to construct a public building.

[cNov 20]   *To David Corbin Ker.*   535

Nov 21   From George Gibson. ALS, DLC (36). Conveys invitation for AJ and party to stay with Gibson's brother John Bannister Gibson at Carlisle, Pennsylvania, on the trip to Washington.

Nov 22   From John Jordan Cabell et al. Printed, *Richmond Enquirer,* Dec 30 (mAJs). Congratulate AJ on his victory and invite him to visit Lynchburg, Virginia, on his way to Washington.

Nov 22   From Edmund Pendleton Gaines (enclosure: Isaac Hill to Henry Lee, Sept 16). ALS, DLC (35). Congratulates AJ on his victory, particularly his unexpected vote in New England, and offers the hospitality of his family should AJ pass through Kingsport, Tennessee, on his way to Washington.

Nov 23   To Thomas Butler (1785–1847). ALS, Gilder Lehrman Collection, NNPM (mAJs); Typed copy, LU (12-0285). Describes his election as a triumph over corruption.

Nov 23   From Nathan Jackson. ALS, DLC (35). Reports victory of

	Jacksonians at all levels in Ohio except the governorship and urges the removal of Adams proponents from office in that state.
Nov 24	To John Coffee. ALS, THi (12-0288). Bassett, 3:447 (extract). Discusses settlement of the debt of Anthony Winston (1782–1839); complains about the actions of James Jackson regarding the 1818 Chickasaw Treaty negotiations.
Nov 24	To John Coffee. AL (signature removed), THi (12-0286). Further discusses settlement of the debt of Anthony Winston (1782–1839).
Nov 24	From Henry Baldwin et al. (enclosure: Resolutions of Pittsburgh, Pennsylvania, meeting, Nov 22). LS, DLC (35). Congratulate AJ on his victory and invite him to stop in Pittsburgh en route to Washington.
Nov 24	From James Alexander Hamilton. ALS, DLC (35). Discusses plans for AJ's trip to Washington and the inauguration.
Nov 24	From John R. Peters. ALS, DLC (35). Offers suggestions for cabinet appointments.
Nov 24	Moses Dawson to Rachel Jackson. ALS, DLC (35). Thanks her for letter (not found) and the gift of a suit made at the Hermitage; congratulates her on AJ's election.
Nov 25	*To Amos Kendall.* 535
Nov 25	From Stephen Burrows. ALS, DLC (35). Congratulates AJ on the election and urges suspension of Sunday mail delivery.
Nov 27	To William Berkeley Lewis. ALS, NNPM (12-0291). Asks Lewis to inquire about a pair of matched gray carriage horses.
Nov 28	To Robert Armstrong. Photostat of ALS, TU (mAJs). Invites him to the Hermitage with Samuel Houston to see their "mutual friend," Gideon Morgan.
Nov 28	To William Taylor Barry et al. ALS copy, DLC (35). Agrees if possible to visit Lexington, Kentucky, on his way to Washington.
[cNov 28]	From Henry Lee (enclosure: James Hamilton, Jr., to Lee, Nov 15, DLC-35). ALS, DLC (59). Transmits Hamilton's letter warning AJ of South Carolina's attitude on the tariff.
Nov 29	From Jonathan Cushman et al. ALS, DLC (35). Congratulate AJ on the election and invite him to visit Martinsburg, Virginia, on way to Washington.
Nov 29	From Eveline Anderson Porter. ALS, DLC (35). Congratulates AJ on his victory, discusses her husband, Commodore David Porter, and denounces rumors of her infidelity.
Nov 29	From John Peter Van Ness (enclosure: Extract of proceedings of Jackson Central Committee of the District of Columbia, Nov 26). ALS, DLC (35). Congratulates AJ on the election.
Nov 30	From Richard Gilliam Dunlap. ALS, DNA-RG 59 (M639-14). Recommends William Lyon for marshal of East Tennessee and reports the death of Hugh L. White's son James.
[cNov]	From Samuel McCutchon. AL fragment, DLC (mAJs). Discusses sending a colt to McCutchon's plantation.
Dec 1	From David Campbell (1779–1859). ALS, DLC (35). Invites AJ to visit Abingdon, Virginia, en route to Washington.
Dec 1	From James Knox Polk. ALS, DLC (35). Bassett, 3:447–48

White, Dec 8). ALS, DLC (36). Discusses the need for united and coordinated action among Jacksonians in West Tennessee.

Dec 8   From John Henry Eaton. ALS, DLC (29). Bassett, 3:450–51. Suggests route to Washington and advises AJ to decline invitations for formal appearances along the way.

Dec 8   From William Elliott et al. LS, DNA-RG 59 (M639-25). As members of the Indiana legislature, recommend John Vawter for reappointment as federal marshal.

Dec 8   From Henry Augustus Philip Muhlenberg et al. LS, DNA-RG 59 (M639-12). Recommend Charles J. Jack as marshal for the Eastern District of Pennsylvania.

Dec 8   From Andrew Stevenson (enclosure: Thomas Miller to AJ, Dec 3). ALS, DLC (36). Congratulates AJ and forwards letter.

Dec 8   From Daniel Sturgeon et al. (enclosure: Resolution, [Dec 8], *Harrisburg Chronicle,* Dec 11). Printed, Harrisburg *Pennsylvania Reporter and Democratic Herald,* Jan 20, 1829 (mAJs). Invite AJ to visit Harrisburg, Pennsylvania, on his way to Washington.

Dec 9   To John Jordan Cabell. LS in Andrew J. Donelson's hand, ScCleU (12-0305). Declines the invitation of Lynchburg, Virginia, citizens.

Dec 9   To John Jordan Cabell et al. Printed, *Richmond Enquirer,* Dec 30 (mAJs, 12-0308). Declines invitation.

Dec 9   From Calvin Blythe et al. ALS in Blythe's hand, DLC (36). Invite AJ to visit Harrisburg, Pennsylvania, on his trip to Washington.

Dec 9   From Lyle Fulton. ALS, DLC (36). Invites AJ to visit Fultonham, near Zanesville, Ohio, en route to Washington and to review the "Jackson Guards" while there.

Dec 9   From Francis Preston. ALS endorsed: "answered in haste 18th. Decbr 1828 whilst writing Mrs J. taken violently ill," DLC (36). Congratulates AJ, offers advice on government policy and organization, and invites AJ to stop in Abingdon, Virginia, on the way to Washington.

Dec 10   To Ezra Stiles Ely.   544

Dec 10   From Benjamin Fort Smith. ALS, DLC (36). Regrets controversy regarding the 1818 Chickasaw Treaty negotiations and denies that the Shelbys contacted him on the matter.

Dec 10   From [James Thomas]. AN, THer (12-0312). Presents copy of *The Question of Retrocession, Stated and Discussed* (Georgetown, D.C., 1826).

Dec 11   To John Coffee. ALS, THi (12-0313). Bassett, 3:452–53. Relates plans for the trip to Washington, noting that he will not leave until he has heard from John H. Eaton whether a congressional committee has been appointed to inform him of election; authorizes Coffee to buy additional land for Andrew J. Hutchings.

Dec 12   To David Campbell (1779–1859). LS in Andrew J. Donelson's hand, NcD (12-0317). Expresses pleasure at forthcoming edition of Thomas Jefferson's papers; declines invitation to visit Abingdon en route to Washington, since he plans to go up the Ohio.

Dec 12   To Maunsel White. LS fragment, City of Mobile Museum (12-0321). Introduces Mr. Wills, who is seeking subscriptions for an edition of Thomas Jefferson's writings.

Dec 12   To Maunsel White. LS in Andrew J. Donelson's hand, NjP (mAJs). Introduces William Robinson of Virginia.

Dec 12   From John Crozier et al. Printed, *Knoxville Register,* Jan 7, 1829 (12-0320). Congratulate AJ on victory and invite him to visit Knoxville en route to Washington.

Dec 13   To Sterling M. Barner. ALS, OHi (12-0323). Sends Dunwoody with a colt for Samuel McCutchon, which Barner will transport to Louisiana.

Dec 13   To Nicholas Fain, Peter Parsons, and Dicks Alexander. LS in Andrew J. Donelson's hand, DLC (12-0324). *Knoxville Register,* Jan 7, 1829. Declines invitation to visit Rogersville en route to Washington.

Dec 18   *To Francis Preston.*   545

Dec 18   From Theophilus E. Beekman. Printed form with ANS, DLC (36). Invites AJ to Eighth of January ball in Hudson, New York.

Dec 18   From Robert Fenner. ALS, DLC (36). Congratulates AJ on his victory and welcomes government reform.

Dec 18   From Robert Young Hayne. ALS, DLC (36). Bassett, 3:453–54. Congratulates AJ and encloses note from his wife, Rebecca M. A. Hayne (not found), offering her aid to Rachel Jackson.

Dec 18   From Morgan Neville (enclosure: Resolutions of congratulations from the Jackson Executive Committee of Cincinnati, Ohio, Dec 18). ALS, DLC (36). Sends resolutions and introduces John S. Lytle, who will give AJ a confidential summary of Ohio politics.

Dec 19   From Robert Breckinridge et al. LS, DLC (36); LS duplicate, TNJ (mAJs). *Louisville Public Advertiser,* Jan 14, 1829. Congratulate AJ on election and invite him to visit Louisville en route to Washington.

Dec 20   To John Crozier et al. Printed, *Knoxville Register,* Jan 7, 1829 (12-0329). Declines invitation to visit Knoxville.

Dec 20   From Leven Browning. ALS, DLC (36). Invites the Jacksons to stay at his home in Nashville before their trip to Washington.

Dec 20   From Alexander M. Muir et al. LS, DLC (72). Invite AJ to public dinner at Tammany Hall in New York City on the Eighth of January.

Dec 22   *To Richard Keith Call.*   546

Dec 22   From Richard Gilliam Dunlap. ALS with AJ endorsement commending Dunlap's idea of drawing cabinet members from outside the Congress, DLC (36). Denounces the party system and suggests candidates for cabinet appointments.

Dec 23   From Edward George Washington Butler. ALS, DLC (72). Recommends a Dr. Knox as professor of chemistry at the University of Nashville; blames John Quincy Adams's leniency toward the killer of Maj. Sanders Donoho for the recent murder of Lt. John Mackenzie.

Dec 23   Account with McCombs & Robinson for Rachel Jackson's coffin. Photocopy of DS, THer (12-0332). With receipt, December 26.

[cDec 23]   Address (undelivered) welcoming AJ to the December 23 celebration at Nashville and congratulating him on his election to the presidency. AL, DLC (36).

[cDec 23]   Speech (undelivered) for December 23 celebration in Nashville. Draft in Andrew J. Donelson's hand, DLC (36).

Dec 24   From Philip Lindsley. ALS, DLC (36). Offers consolation upon Rachel Jackson's death.

Dec 24   From Jesse Wharton. ALS, DLC (36). Offers condolences upon Rachel Jackson's death.

Dec 25   From Elizabeth Parke Custis. ALS, ViMtvL (12–0344). Burke, *Emily Donelson of Tennessee,* 1:167. Congratulates AJ on election and inquires if he has received a brooch she sent weeks earlier.

Dec 25   Andrew Jackson Donelson to the Jackson Central Committee of Baltimore, Maryland. Washington *National Intelligencer,* Jan 14, 1829 (mAJs, 12-0333). On AJ's behalf, declines invitation to visit Baltimore en route to Washington.

Dec 26   From William Alexander. ALS, DLC (36). Sympathizes on Rachel's death.

Dec 27   *To Jean Baptiste Plauché.*   547

Dec 27   From Jesse Bledsoe. ALS, DLC (36). Congratulates AJ on his victory and reports on the defection of some of AJ's supporters in the Kentucky legislature, the defeat of Richard M. Johnson in the contest for the U.S. Senate, and the eventual victory of George M. Bibb, a Jacksonian, for the Senate.

Dec 27   From James H. Bowman. ALS, DLC (36). Sympathizes upon Rachel Jackson's death; complains about parsimony of Wilson County residents who will not support his church.

Dec 27   From James S. Hay. ALS, DLC (36). Offers to make Rachel Jackson's gravestone.

Dec 27   From George Washington Martin. ALS, DLC (36). Sympathizes upon Rachel Jackson's death; informs AJ of dissolution of partnership with Willoughby Williams.

Dec 27   From James Brown Ray (to the President of the United States). ALS endorsed: "Rec. 7 March 1829." DNA-RG 59 (M639-15). Recommends Abner McCarty for federal marshal of Indiana.

Dec 27   Samuel Granville Smith to Samuel Houston. ALS, DLC (36). Mourns Rachel Jackson's death.

Dec 29   To Morgan Neville. LS in Andrew J. Donelson's hand, NN (12-0341). Regrets that Rachel Jackson's death has prevented a lengthy conversation with the Cincinnati committee's emissary, John S. Lytle, and expresses gratitude to his supporters in Ohio.

Dec 29   From Thomas Givens et al. LS, DNA-RG 59 (M639-12). Recommend Samuel Judah for federal district attorney of Indiana.

Dec 29   From Worden Pope et al. (enclosure: Resolutions of condolence from Louisville citizens, Dec 27). LS, DLC (36). *Louisville Public Advertiser,* Jan 21, 1829. Transmit resolutions on death of Rachel Jackson.

Dec 30   To Daniel Sturgeon et al. ALS, PHi (12-0351); Draft in unidentified hand, DLC (36). Harrisburg *Pennsylvania Reporter and Democratic Herald,* Jan 20, 1829. Declines invitation to visit the Pennsylvania legislature.

Dec 30   Power of attorney to John Coffee to superintend all business re AJ's

	guardianship of Andrew Jackson Hutchings. DS in Coffee's hand, also signed by John Overton and Ralph E. W. Earl, THi (12-0345).
Dec 30	Power of attorney to John Coffee to sell AJ's lots in Florence, Alabama. DS in Coffee's hand, also signed by John Overton and Ralph E. W. Earl, THi (12-0347).
Dec 30	Receipt from Henry Ewing for Andrew Jackson Hutchings's winter term tuition at the University of Nashville. ADS, THi (12-0349).
[Dec]	To Richard Keith Call. Extracts, *Collector* (Dec 1905), p. 17 (12-0293), FHi (12-0294). Announces his electoral victory.
[1828]	Memorandum of blacksmith accounts with [James T.] Carruth. AD, DLC (36).
[1828]	From Unknown. AL fragment, DLC (75). Expresses admiration for AJ.
[1828]	Receipts from Henry Garrard for 1828 Lauderdale County, Alabama, taxes of AJ and Andrew Jackson Hutchings. Printed forms with manuscript insertions, signed by Garrard, THi (mAJs).

Index

Page-entry numbers between 549 and 630 refer to the Calendar. Numbers set in boldface indicate identification of persons. The symbol * indicates biographical information in the *Dictionary of American Biography;* the symbol †, in the *Biographical Directory of the United States Congress, 1774–1989.*

miscalculates national debt, 155–56;
Second Auditor, 15
United States Department of War, 454,
461; and presidential campaign of
1828, 336, 396; and documents re six
militiamen, 434, 437, 442; contract for
boats, 497; Jackson correspondence in,
242; papers of, 465
United States House of Representatives;
and call for investigation into mail
espionage, 339; and corrupt bargain,
24–26, 36, 338, 359–60, 364–65, 376;
and election of president in 1825, 3, 6,
14, 27–28, 30, 39, 63, 166, 461, 550;
and Isaac Phillips case, 132–33; and
issue of execution of six militiamen,
398, 412, 433–34, 439; and Panama
Congress, 142–43, 145, 151, 165; and
presidential campaign of 1828, 414;
and proposed constitutional amendment re presidential elections, 144,
146–48, 161; and Rip Raps Shoal
scandal, 265–66, 281–83, 287; bill for
sale of relinquished lands in Alabama,
158–59; Committee on Indian Affairs,
418; Committee on Military Affairs,
135, 410–11, 418, 439; Committee on
Military Affairs Report on Execution
of Six Militiamen, 436–37, 612;
Committee on Retrenchment, 446–47;
Committee on Ways and Means, 155–
56; debate on administration's use of
newspaper patronage for electioneer
ing, 284, 419; debate on McDuffie's
constitutional amendment, 161;
election of printer in 1825, 43; Indian
removal discussed, 418; Naval Affairs
committee, 133; reaction in to
Harrisburg resolutions re Jackson, 147;
Report of the Committee on Expenditures in the State Department, 452;
Report . . . Correspondence and
Documents from the War Department,
411, 433, 436, 438, 446; separation of
powers question, 142–43
United States Marines, 567–68
United States Military Academy, 8, 10, 51,
165, 561, 562; appointments, 144,
164, 549, 551–52, 555, 558, 564–65,
569–70; recommendations for, 146
United States Navy, 132–33, 565;
appointments, 555; dismissals, 168;
plan to exclude foreigners from, 621;
support for AJ in, 588
United States Post Office, 354, 390, 551,

605; alleged espionage of the mails,
172, 203, 256–57, 267, 269–70, 274,
277, 283–84, 286, 291, 300, 312, 324,
338, 410, 506, 528, 535, 597; and
Henry Lee, 563; Jackson's letters in,
244–45; problems with mail delivery,
144, 219, 269; alleged corruption in,
379, 601, 621; Sunday delivery, 625
*United States' Review and Literary
Gazette,* 581
United States Senate, 62, 161, 187–88,
199–200, 212, 216, 226, 551–52, 555,
573; action on Panama mission, 141–
43, 145, 147–48, 151, 153–55, 158–
59, 163–64, 204; and AJ memorial re
Seminole campaign, 202, 248; and
Creek Indian treaty, 184; and grant to
John Donelson (c1718–86) heirs, 180–
81; and Henry Clay appointment, 30,
36, 38; and Henry Lee nomination,
105; and land laws, 503; and public
land sales, 158; and Seminole
campaign, 202, 212, 253; and
separation of powers, 151; and Treaty
of Indian Springs, 44, 94; Committee
on Military Affairs, 549, 552, 554;
Foreign Relations Committee, 141;
removal of injunction of secrecy on
Panama question, 164; Select
Committee on Executive Patronage,
168, 171
United States State Department, 418, 451
United States' Telegraph (Washington,
D.C.), 92, 151, 155, 165, 204, 250,
321, 330, 339, 348, 361, 381, 389,
431, 465, 468, 477, 516, 526; AJ's
subscription to, 586; and corrupt
bargain, 332, 339, 349, 376, 382; and
Nashville post office controversy, 157;
and Southard affair, 228, 356;
commences publication, 156; defense of
AJ in campaign of 1828, 355; execution
of six militiamen, 399; publishes AJ's
letter to Carter Beverley, 366
United States' Telegraph—Extra, 432
United States War Department, 202, 229,
355, 397, 504; AJ's letters in, 271,
284; and AJ correspondence with, 230,
242; and documents re the Battle of
New Orleans, 270; and AJ's accounts
with, 336; and presidential campaign
of 1828, 411–12; and six militiamen
controversy, 398, 411; and William
King court-martial, 198
University of Nashville, 9, 327, 395, 397,